cop.1

29.50

DATE			

**WOODSON REGIONAL CENTER
9525 SOUTH HALSTED ST.**

© THE BAKER & TAYLOR CO.

THEATRES
and AUDITORIUMS

To **Anita Burris-Meyer and Alice Cole**

THEATRES and AUDITORIUMS

**SECOND EDITION
WITH NEW SUPPLEMENT**

by Harold Burris-Meyer *and* Edward C. Cole

ROBERT E. KRIEGER PUBLISHING CO., INC.
HUNTINGTON, NEW YORK

Selections from ARCHITECTURE FOR
THE ARTS: THE STATE UNIVERSITY
OF NEW YORK COLLEGE AT PURCHASE
edited by Arthur Drexler. Copyright 1971
The Museum of Modern Art, New York.
All rights reserved. Reprinted by permission.

Original edition 1964
Reprint 1975 With Supplement

Printed and Published by
ROBERT E. KRIEGER PUBLISHING CO., INC.
645 NEW YORK AVENUE
HUNTINGTON, NEW YORK 11743

© Copyright 1964 by
LITTON EDUCATIONAL PUB. INC.
Assigned to Robert E. Krieger Publishing Co., Inc., May 1974
© Copyright 1975 New Material by
ROBERT E. KRIEGER PUBLISHING CO., INC

All rights reserved. No reproduction in any form of this book, in whole or in part (except for brief quotation in critical articles or reviews). may be made without written authorization from the publisher.

Printed in the United States of America.

Library of Congress Cataloging in Publication Data

Burris-Meyer, Harold, 1902–
   Theatres and Auditoriums
   Reprint of the 1964 Ed., published by Reinhold, N.Y.

   1. THEATRES––CONSTRUCTION. 2. AUDITORIUMS

   I. Title
   (NA 6821. B8 1975) 725: 822 75–17792

   ISBN 0-8825-170-0

PREFACE

TO 1975 AUGMENTED EDITION

This edition is perhaps best explained by borrowing from a review of the 1964 Second Edition.

"Sixteen years ago (1949——Ed.) a book entitled THEATRES AND AUDITORIUMS quietly appeared and proceeded to revolutionize the building and planning of theatres throughout the country — — — —

"It gathered together all the best current planning and design in the field of theatre architecture and made it readily available — — — —

"Perhaps the finest accolade for this book is the sure fact that it stimulated and provided the germ for newer and even more experimental designs for the theatre ever since — — — —

"The Second Edition of Theatres and Auditoriums (1964——Ed.), like the First, is a must for every architect's office if his firm is concerned with the building of public auditoriums of any sort— — — —

"If anyone is thinking of planning a theatre or assembly hall, large or small, here is the book for him. In fact, he avoids it at his peril."

— Professor Henry B. Williams in the Dartmouth Alumni Magazine (1964).

The 1964 edition came out in time to report the completion of some outstanding new theatres, but it could do no more than forecast several major projects still in the planning stages. Actually the decade following the appearance of the Second Edition became one of the most prolific periods of theatre building in the twentieth century.

The prospect of reprinting the Second Edition which arose in 1973 offered the authors and their new publisher the opportunity to include a report on trends and developments and include drawings, photographs and textual appraisal of many 1964–74 theatres in a supplement, which becomes Chapter 16 with its own index, acknowledgements, and photo credits list. In preparing it we have had, and are grateful for, consideration and expert assistance from Robert E. Krieger, publisher; Ms. Beverly Beyer, editor; Ms. Gail Mau, typist; and David Kiphuth, draftsman. We especially appreciate the cooperation of those listed in the Acknowledgements and Photo Credits for supplying the visual material and written information without which the supplement would be ineffective.

Our wives, Alice Cole and Anita Burris-Meyer continue to have our highest affection, particularly in their roles of authors' caretakers.

HAROLD BURRIS-MEYER
EDWARD C. COLE

June, 1975

PREFACE SECOND EDITION

Theatres & Auditoriums (first edition, 1949) set forth for the first time a procedure by which theatre plan could be derived from an analysis of function. Oriented toward the showman, it undertook to help him to define, the architect to interpret, and the engineer and builder to achieve a structure in which performer and audience could participate in the experience which is theatre. The deadly similarity of theatres of that era and their almost identical shortcomings imposed unwarranted limitations on the showman's presentation, the impresario's chance of profit, the artist's imagination, the poet's fancy.

That situation is now past. New theatres illustrate, in form, flexibility, and suitability to the needs of people, the principles set forth in this book, but there are still, alas, too many theatres, old, new, and even projected, which attest the need for restatement, re-emphasis, illustration, and further exposition of the basic necessities of theatre and the means of their achievement.

This edition undertakes to fill that need, to illustrate what could only be defined in the first edition, to show the application of new scientific developments to the solution of theatre problems, to exploit the growing and progressively refined expertise in theatre, to assess new forms of theatre, their scope, limitations, and capability of achieving the total cumulative impact which is the showman's goal.

As in the first edition, this book treats auditoriums almost exclusively as parts of theatres. This treatment is warranted on the ground that an auditorium almost never succeeds in remaining only an auditorium. Sooner or later, somebody uses it for a theatre and its effectiveness as a theatre is the ultimate measure of its usefulness.

We cite with gratitude the kindness and generosity of our professional associates and our fellow showmen. Our wives, Alice Cole and Anita Burris-Meyer, have supplied constant encouragement. Eugene Gurlitz made the line drawings and our editors, Gessner Hawley and Dorothy Upjohn Lewis, put the book together. We record here our thanks to them and to all those who have supplied information and illustrative material, as tabulated at the back of the book.

HAROLD BURRIS-MEYER
EDWARD C. COLE

October, 1964

CONTENTS

1:	Existing conditions	1
2:	Audience traffic	37
3:	The audience sees	63
4:	The audience hears	75
5:	Comfort and safety of the audience; front service rooms	89
6:	Power, heat, air-conditioning, plumbing	111
7:	Acting area, proscenium, orchestra	125
8:	Backstage operation	153
9:	Scenery	171
10:	Stage machinery: on the stage floor	197
11:	Stage machinery: in the flies	227
12:	Light	259
13:	Sound and intercommunication	287
14:	Production services	307
15:	Over-all considerations	327
16:	THEATRES 1964-1975	368
	Reference materials and credits	449
	Index	456

1: Existing conditions

Definition

The desire of people to witness performances by other people appears to be so deeply rooted in the human spirit as to be instinctive. Theatre is the gathering together of a group of people to witness a planned performance. It is one of the major modes of diversion of modern civilization. It is materially nonproductive, its values being entirely spiritual and cultural.

The building of theatres, from the fifth century B.C. to the present, has been the provision of the essential physical equipment for the gratification of the playgoing urge. The planning and building of modern theatres and the modernization of old ones involve the use of current materials, methods, and practices to maintain that equipment.

Types of theatrical entertainment have varied in the last twenty-five centuries from Dionysian revel to big screen television. Some productions of almost every epoch have the timeless and universal significance necessary to draw audiences today. Audiences have varied no less widely than productions. They have supported the court masque and the productions of the brothers Minsky. Their demands vary as do the material equipment, economic aspects, modes, manners, customs, and spiritual concepts of human living.

Basic Requirements

The audience comes to see the show and to hear the show. It wants a maximum of comfort, a minimum of distraction, and complete safety.

The producer wants a plant which will attract an audience. He wants facilities for preparing the show, good conditions of performance, efficient production organization and machinery; in short, a fair showing at low cost. (Cost to a producer must be taken as all-inclusive; noncommercial producers must think of labor as part of their costs, even when it is low-cost apprentice labor or free volunteer labor which does not show on the books.)

Theatre artists (playwrights, composers, directors, actors, dancers, musicians and designers) want adequate facilities for the achievement of their theatrical projects.

This chapter undertakes to list types of production, describe existing theatre structures, and indicate wherein and why structures impose unwarranted limitations on production.

	Subject Matter	**Visual Components**	**Auditory Components**
Pageant	Incidents from history or local folklore having historical or religious appeal assembled into a plow boy's epic. Story oversimplified, direct, romanticized, salutes a glorious past, promises paradise as a just reward for something or other. No controversial matter included.	Realistic dramatic episodes acted or mimed. Period costumes. Mass movement. Ballet, folk dances. Marches. Permanent decorative backgrounds with movable scenic pieces. Scenery simple, suggestive rather than closely representational. Local geographic features included. Stage machinery in operation. Elaborate lighting. Steam and water curtains. Pyrotechnics. Display of technical virtuosity. Individual performer counts for little.	Music: symphonic, organ, choral. Synthesized descriptive score. Speech: narrator's, principals'. Speech dubbed on pantomime scenes. Incidental sounds, descriptive effects. All sound amplified. Level often too high for comfort. Reproduction often less natural than in motion pictures.
Grand Opera	Classic tragedy, folklore, sagas, mythological tales, superheated passion, men vs gods. As currently produced, subject and story are of little importance.	Elaborate conventionalized pantomime by principals. Elaborate costumes, symbolic color. Occasional mass movement by chorus and ballet. Monumental settings (Valhalla, the bottom of the Rhine). Elaborate lighting. Technical tricks: appearances, magic fire, etc.	The world's best music sung by the most accomplished artists, accompanied by thoroughly competent orchestra and chorus. Soloists sing everything at relatively high intensity to achieve audibility and dominate orchestra.
Vaudeville Revue	Vaudeville: Assorted songs, dances, dramatic episodes, blackouts, trained animals, acrobats, bell ringers, jugglers, magicians, ventriloquists, mindreaders, musicians, clowns; in fact any feat or phenomenon of man or beast (not excluding elephants) which can be gotten onto a stage and which is calculated to have sufficient audience appeal through uniqueness, novelty, skill, virtuosity, renown or notoriety. Revue: same material assembled about a central theme, produced for a run, trouped as a unit.	Performers principal visual element. Costumes bright. Scenic background unimportant except as it contributes necessary paraphernalia or adds flash to act. Lighting conventional; follow spots on principals; no illusion of time or place. All scenic elements combine to center attention on performer. Revue: Design unity sometimes runs through whole production. Much more elaborate and effective setting than in vaudeville.	Speech and music. Not subtle, high in intensity, aimed at the gallery. Popular and classical songs, instrumental and orchestral numbers. Revue has musical unity and balance.
Musical Folk Opera Operetta Musical Comedy	Line of demarcation between types not clear. Often the best in musical theatre. Reasonably simple story. Framework garnished with music and dancing. Book generally satirizes some current situation of general interest. Boy meets girl in fanciful rather than realistic surroundings.	Actor's business realistic or appropriate to script: conventionalized for musical numbers and dancing. Elaborate costumes harmoniously keyed to color scheme of the production. Scenery usually functional, decorative, stylized rather than realistic. Machinery for quick change and for effect. Lighting arbitrary and for novelty and visibility rather than for conformity with dramatic necessities. New production forms and techniques readily adopted. Pleasant eye entertainment.	Auditory component given appropriate importance relative to visual as dictated by necessity for achieving maximum total effect. Semiclassical and popular music (sweet, hot, and blue), sung by principals, occasionally with chorus and usually with pit orchestra accompaniment. Subject matter and personality of singer often more important than musical excellence. Noisy entr'acte, overture, and covering pieces played by pit orchestra (about 20 pieces). Spoken dialogue between songs. Ear entertainment.

Routine	Audience	Comment	Theatre Required
One or two a day, generally long. Sunday shows where permitted. Realistic episodes connected by spoken narrative. Dance, march, choral, orchestral interludes. Single intermission. Closely integrated, carefully timed performance. High production costs.	Same as country fair. Pageant is the only type of live show many ever see. Best mannered audience in the show business. Subject matter principal attraction: production next. Ball-park system of seating. Considerable advance sale. Admission low.	Always good for a season when there is an event or institution which can generate enough interest to draw an audience. More truly the people's theatre than any other dramatic form.	Large open-air amphitheatre, stadium or ball park.
8 a week in repertory. Show, 2 to 5 acts or two short operas on one bill. Long performance. Long intermissions to shift scenes usually set full stage. Despite repertory organization, rehearsals slighted to save costs which are excessive. Performance often slipshod in all save rendition of songs. Names in cast count.	Gallery and standing room: Music lovers. Boxes: The guests of patrons. Sometimes patrons. Orchestra: Average theatre goers with a special liking for music, averaging about 62 years of age. Large potential audiences alienated by shabby productions and high prices. Boxholders' manners worst in show business. Admission high.	Democratization of opera under way in America. Dramatization of plot started by Herbert Graf. Mass attendance at conventional repertoire questionable, since the subject matter of most operas is so far removed from American cultural heritage. Present efforts to revitalize opera are handicapped by stuffy tradition and record of dullness.	In cities: A large theatre needed to pay high production and operating costs. Comfortable seats and lounges—the performance is often long. Opera houses being built into municipal arts centers. Summer opera can often do with a tent or shed.
Vaudeville: Two-a-day to five-a-day (continuous cycle: noon to midnight). 8 to 15 acts per performance. Each act 10 to 15 minutes long. Acts arranged in ascending entertainment value with preferred spot next to closing. Acts alternate full stage and shallow to facilitate changes. Changes fast, covered by music from pit orchestra, and patter by a master of ceremonies. Revue: Eight a week, otherwise similar to vaudeville. Production costs vary widely from peanuts up.	Vaudeville: The late George V, Judy O'Grady and a large coterie of people who prefer vaudeville to any other type of theatrical performance. Vaudeville addicts had attendance habits more thoroughly ingrained than any other audience. Admission prices moderate. Revue: Audience and admission same as for musical comedy.	Vaudeville is too ancient a form and has survived too many vicissitudes to justify fear that its present eclipse is permanent. Simple motion picture routine and low film costs have induced managers to abandon it. Ominously falling motion picture attendance now apparent, may bring it back. Revue: Similar in genre to vaudeville. Overworking of the principals constitutes a severe handicap and makes for a dull final half-hour.	Large enough to pay operating costs with ticket price below opera. Small enough so facial expression counts. Equipped for fast changes of simple scenes.
Eight-a-week. Six evenings. Matinees Wednesday or Thursday and Saturday. Combination production. Running time about two and a half hours. Conventionally two, at most three, acts. Few but elaborate sets. Stage machinery used in view of audience for novelty. All changes except act change covered by music or singles in one. Star often more important than show. Production costs high.	Operetta: The whole family, particularly in the case of Gilbert and Sullivan. Musical comedy: downstairs, the tired business man, the hostess and her party, the deb and her boy friend. Upstairs: The clerk and his date, the suburbanite and his wife, Tilly and the girls (with chocolates at matinees). The holiday spirit is to be found in the audience at the musical show more than in any other audience except at circuses. Admission high: only slightly below opera.	Folk opera (*Porgy and Bess, Oklahoma*) and Operetta: Operetta very durable, good for revival as long as grand opera. Popularity of chamber opera with components similar to those of operetta, increasing. Musical comedy perishable but source of songs with lasting popularity. Both forms good all-season entertainment.	High production costs necessitate a large theatre, though the importance of the individual performer and the required subtlety of effect rule out the grand opera house. Equipment similar to, but more than in, a good legitimate house. Large orchestra pit.

3

	Subject Matter	**Visual Components**	**Auditory Components**
Legitimate Drama	Plays. Live shows employing all dramaturgical, artistic, and technical devices to persuade the audience to suspend disbelief and credit the characters and the story as presented.	The actor. Human scale used for all elements of production. Business realistic or in conformity with any other stylistic idiom. Costume appropriate to the character, situation, and production style. Visual elements of the production coordinated to achieve maximum dramatic impact. Lighting in conformity with style of production; provides visibility sometimes greater than that in nature.	Human voice in speech. Incidental sound to indicate locale, advance plot, create and sustain atmosphere and mood. Overture and entr'acte music from orchestra (by no means universal). Vocal, instrumental or reproduced music as required within the play.
Concert	Music. From Beethoven to boogie woogie, from a solo (with piano accompaniment) to an augmented symphony orchestra with cannon for the *1812 Overture*.	White tie and tails or any other costume that seems appropriate.	Music, requiring optimum acoustics, varying with the music, if possible, but not with the size of the audience.
Night Club Cabaret	Personalities with topical or sentimental songs and patter (Sophie Tucker, Edith Piaf, Judy Garland) alternating with dance, tableau, slapstick, juggling.	Bright lights, spangles, bare skin, some effects—waterfall, the suspended glass runway. Period or national decor.	High-intensity amplified song. Orchestra appropriate to atmosphere. Soloists, choruses.
Motion Pictures	Original screenplays. Adaptations from plays, musicals, short stories, novels, comic strips, and television plays to the celluloid medium, changed in conformity with intellectual and artistic limitations of the producers to what they think is palatable to an audience. Boy meets girl, etc., ad infinitum. Current events and animated cartoons.	Rectangular screen on which are projected moving images in black and white or in color of anything which can be photographed. The 18 x 24 face that launched (or sank) a thousand ships. Infinite variety (giants to dwarfs, planets to microorganisms, moving glacier to humming-bird's wing). The wide screen and the A-O optical system make film the most flexible medium in the theatre.	Reproduced sound of anything that can be got onto a sound track and off through a loudspeaker. Multi-channel systems with wide-screen picture make possible superb exploitation of the auditory element of the show.
Dance	Dance, for many years confined to playing in any available hall, has now demonstrated enough popular appeal to warrant building theatres especially for it. A dance theatre should provide flexibility in stage levels and backgrounds, sufficient rise for audience seats so that the routine may exploit its three-dimensional character, and an orchestra location.		
Burlesque	Burlesque can use almost any theatre which can accommodate legitimate dramas. Routine like musical with emphasis on individual performer. New theatres are not built for burlesque—old ones are adapted if necessary.		

Routine	Audience	Comment	Theatre Required
Same as operetta and musical comedy. Considerable variation in structure from no intermission (HOTEL UNIVERSE) to 52 scenes (GÖTZ VON BERLICHINGEN). Performance length varies from one hour (THE EMPEROR JONES), usually played with a curtain raiser, to three evenings (MOURNING BECOMES ELECTRA). Production combines generally most skillful planning and direction and most painstaking rehearsals of any popular entertain-	People with sufficient culture to appreciate a conventionalized and aesthetic form of entertainment. As the general cultural level rises, audiences for legitimate drama increase. Small house and high production costs keep admission scale above that of motion pictures. ment form—resulting generally in most finished performance and best obtainable interpretation of playwright's script.	Legitimate drama is best dramatic medium for revealing character or constructing plot. It is the freest and most flexible form in the theatre, and therefore the tryout ground for new ideas, concepts and techniques. The legitimate theatre is always reported to be on the verge of total and final collapse, and probably will be for another twenty-five centuries or so.	Most varied requirements of any theatrical type. Small enough so facial expression is significant, equipped for fast changes and effects. Specialized theatres (Shakespearian, Arena) limited in usefulness.
Soloist or orchestra seldom repeats the same program at successive performances or performs more than 6 times per week.	More people attend concerts than major-league baseball games.	Concert popularity is growing rapidly. Concert halls appear in plans for most new art centers. The visual aspects of concert are too often neglected.	Acoustics are the prime consideration. Given good acoustics, a forestage or a wide proscenium and a concert set will make any house a concert hall.
Twice nightly for large shows, oftener for singles. Last show ends by 2 A.M. Acts arranged as in (and may be the same as) vaudeville. Show changed as often as necessary to keep the customers coming. Elaborate shows once a season.	Out-of-towners who like to dine, drink and dance. Expense account patrons. Some regulars.	This symbol of the affluent society has absorbed the best of the talent which once graced the vaudeville and presentation stages. Found where money flows freely: Las Vegas, Paris, New York, Miami Beach.	Audiences at tables in tiers around 3 sides of the stage. No stage depth required.
As many shows per day as can be run profitably. Picture Palace: Feature, shorts (travel, cartoon, one-reel dramatic sketch, etc.), news, trailers. Total show time two hours. Ten A.M. to midnight seven days a week. Five-minute intermission between shows covered by recorded music or the mighty organ. Neighborhood: 1:30 to midnight or three a day. Show changed twice or three times weekly. Second feature takes place of news and shorts. Intimate: Single feature plus news. Newsreel: One-hour show, news, shorts, and cartoons.	The American people. Frequency of individual attendance ranges from habitual addiction to occasional patronage of selected programs. Little attention given to announced starting times; hence, continuous flow of audience with some concentration in early afternoon, late afternoon, early evening and late evening. Admission low.	Once the most popular type of theatrical production; television has superseded it as purveyor of horse opera and the machine-made plot. Quality improves with declining quantity. Potentially the most significant form of theatre.	Neighborhood: Comfortable seats and popcorn. Metropolitan: The old presentation house or motion picture palace (no more of these will be built). Drive-in: Pictures in the parking lot. Easy access, roads from many directions requisite. Intimate: Small luxurious, in a metropolitan location.
Presentation		A form once very popular, now limited to a few metropolitan locations. Prime example: Radio City Music Hall. New theatres will not be built for this form. The ground in the appropriate location can earn more money with another type of structure.	
Puppets		Puppet shows have played successfully in everything from Radio City Music Hall to the living room at home, to the trailer in the park. Whatever will accommodate an audience is suitable for puppets.	

Multiple Uses of the Theatre

Theatres can also be used for church services, town meetings, and assemblages of all sorts. Yesterday's presentation house is today's motion picture palace, doubles as opera house and may well be the vaudeville house of tomorrow.

The theatre which houses opera, concert, and ballet is economically sounder than a theatre limited to any single type of show. The legitimate theatre will have to show motion pictures if only as a part of a legitimate production. It is proverbial that the new owner of a building tries to make money with it in a way different from that of the previous owner who lost money. To limit architecturally the uses of the theatre is to reduce its potential income and shorten its useful life. To provide for multiple uses of the theatre, planning must be based on an analysis of attendance and performance requirements of each type of production to be housed.

Changing Demands on Theatre Buildings

The last decade has seen a large increase in the number and variety of production types, patterns and techniques, and many theatres have been built to provide for them. Notable among the trends for which architectural provision has been made are:

1. Liberation of the performance from the proscenium arch. Exponents call attention to the distracting influence of ornate, badly lighted proscenium arches and the separation of audience and performance.

2. Contact between playing and audience areas. Steps, ramps, and aprons which provide such contact must be made *flexible*. Otherwise they limit the use of the theatre.

3. Arena performance in which the audience surrounds a central acting area.

4. Simultaneous settings and *a vista* changes (set changes in view of audience and integrated with the performance).

5. Abstractionism in scenery. In the belief that each member of the audience can supply for himself imaginatively the best surroundings of the dramatic action, attempts have been made either to eliminate scenery altogether, to strip it of limiting detail, or to reduce scenery to the elements of pure design.

6. Multiplication of scenery. Episodic plays mirror the increasingly peripatetic nature of human living which demands frequent change of locale. Unlike the foregoing trends, this one demands not less but more scenery, and with it greater stage facilities for changing scenes.

7. Reactionary trends. Currently noticeable are two separate and allied tendencies, both revolting from the strong realism of drama and theatre. The one calls for a return of poetry and romance to the theatre. The other demands a recognition of the fact that theatre is theatre, that it is not real, cannot be real, and to be most effective must be frankly artificial, and theatrically conventional, calling a stage a stage. These

tendencies are opposed to the foregoing because they demand stage and theatrical facilities of an established kind: painted scenery, wings, borders and backdrops, in fact such scenery as can most easily be handled on many somewhat archaic, present-day stages.

8. Technological developments. The application of electromechanical techniques to theatrical production in the control of lighting, the generation and control of sound, the movement of scenery and the control thereof, the variation of the size, shape and arrangement of the acting area and even of the building itself has increased and bids fair to solve some of the problems inherent in the infinite variety which constitutes theatre.

9. Resident companies. Professional companies have recently been organized in a few cities. Whether or not they succeed in reorienting the professional theatre away from the Broadway Mecca, they will at least supply a step in the career progress of young professionals which has been missing since the demise of local stock companies in the twenties. And they will need theatres suited to the particular needs of self-sufficient, resident producing companies.

10. Centers for the Performing Arts, Arts Centers (sometimes labeled Cultural Centers). In recognition of the burgeoning interest in cultural pursuits and sometimes in connection with urban renewal, several municipalities have built or plan to build centers to house the creative and performing arts—these buildings to accommodate various forms of theatrical performance according to the predilections of the planners and the limitations of local situations.

Theatres have been built in which several of these trends may be followed. However, to satisfy all is seldom artistically requisite or economically sound, and to satisfy several requires painstaking analysis of function prior to design, great ingenuity in planning, and astute engineering.

Few efficient or even practical multiform theatres have been built. In fact, even the basic demands set forth in the foregoing table have seldom been adequately, efficiently, or economically met, as the analysis of existing theatre types which follows will indicate.

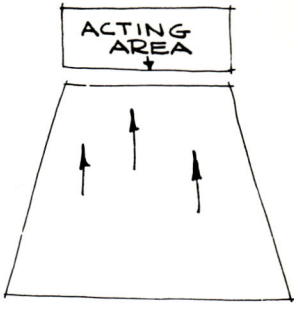

PROSCENIUM

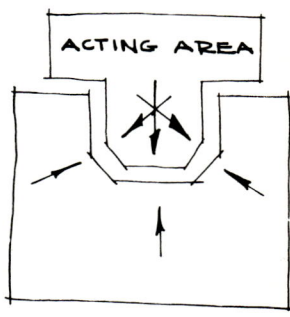

OPEN STAGE

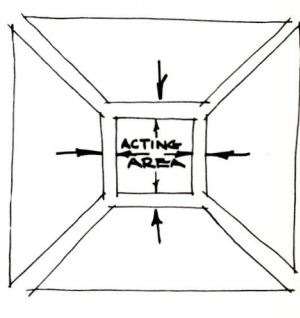

ARENA

Opera House

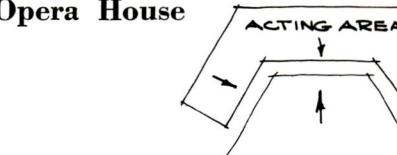

EXTENDED STAGE

The opera house is the oldest, and was, until the advent of the motion picture palace, the largest theatre in the community. Its shortcomings are primarily due to antiquity. The traditional horseshoe plan and many balconies entail bad sight lines. Public rooms are adequate, but ventilation is an afterthought, acoustics accidental, gallery seats crowded. The stage is large enough to accommodate more than one production in repertory. Stage equipment is antique and inefficient.

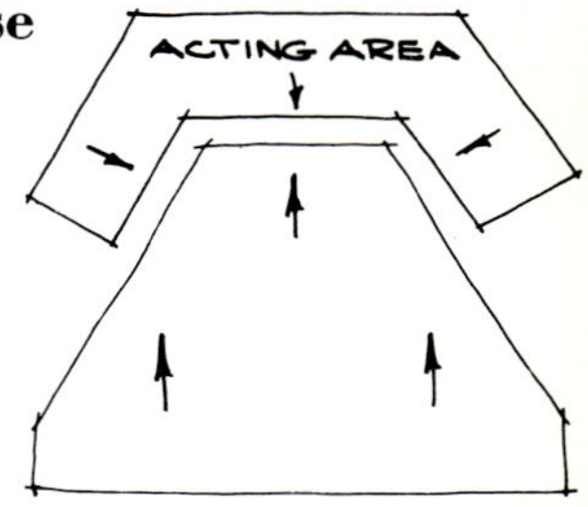

The term "opera house" has been used colloquially in America to designate the only theatre in town. Such theatres were, of course, multipurpose in a time when theatre and theatregoing were unsophisticated in comparison with present standards, and housed all attractions from MAZEPPA, through DOCKSTADER'S MINSTRELS, to UNCLE TOM'S CABIN. The term thus used has no relation to *opera,* per se.

The opera house was a good theatre in the era of gaslights and wing-and-border sets. Changed standards of audience comfort, and changed production techniques have outmoded both house and stage. Modern opera houses (the new municipal and civic auditoriums are usually advertised as having been built for opera) are, in many cases, patterned so closely on their antique equivalents that despite improved chairs and machinery, they are ill-suited to the demands of modern operatic production and are highly inefficient.

Inefficient structures resulting in high operating costs have been a contributing factor to the disappearance of resident opera companies in America. Conversely, productions whose budgets are burdened with

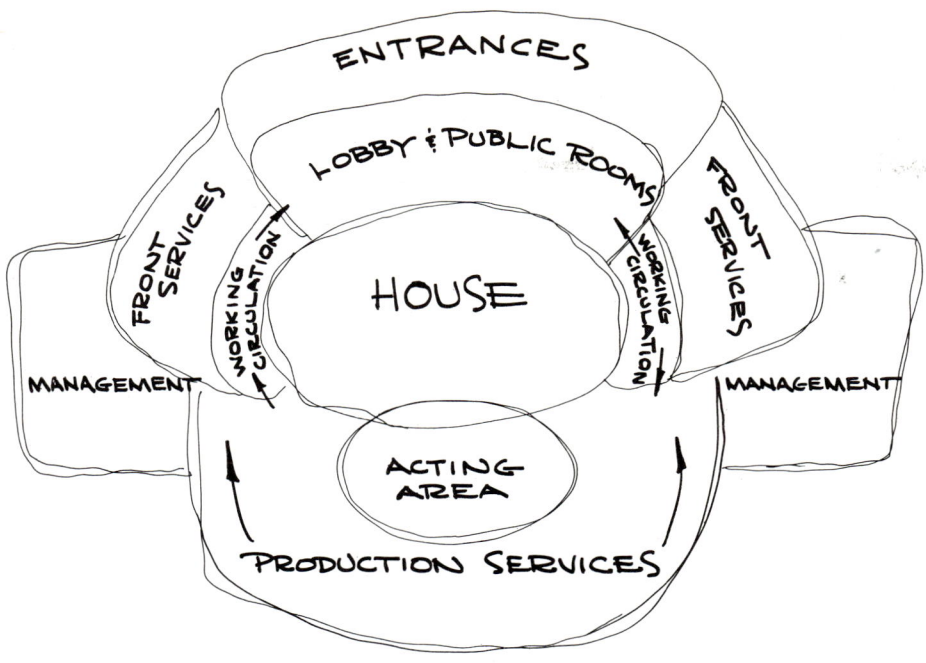

Ideagraph of functional relationships.

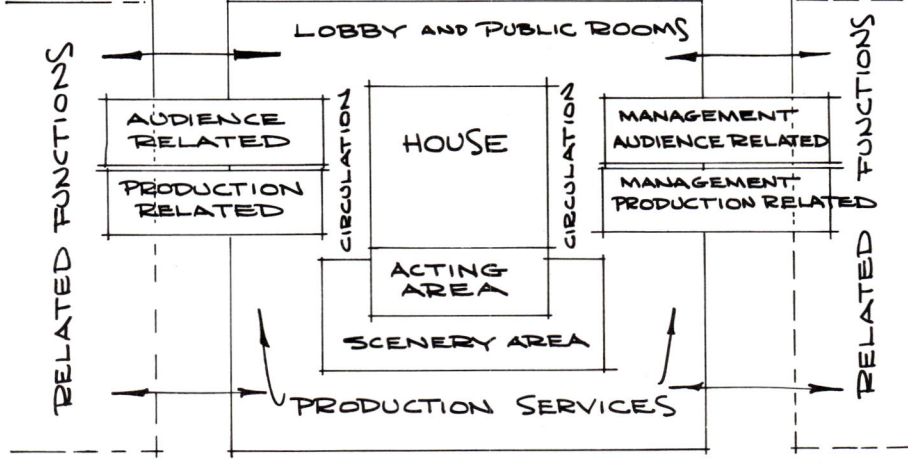

Schematic ground plan of proscenium form. Related functions may include restaurants, studios, galleries, reception rooms, classrooms, laboratories, workshops, etc.

◄ *The Queen Elizabeth Theatre, Vancouver, designed to modern standards of audience comfort provides ample lobbies, lounges, underground parking, exterior plaza, adjoining restaurants and an adequate stage house. Affleck, Desbarats, Dimakopoulos, Lebensold, Michaud, Sise, architects.*

Proscenium theatre.

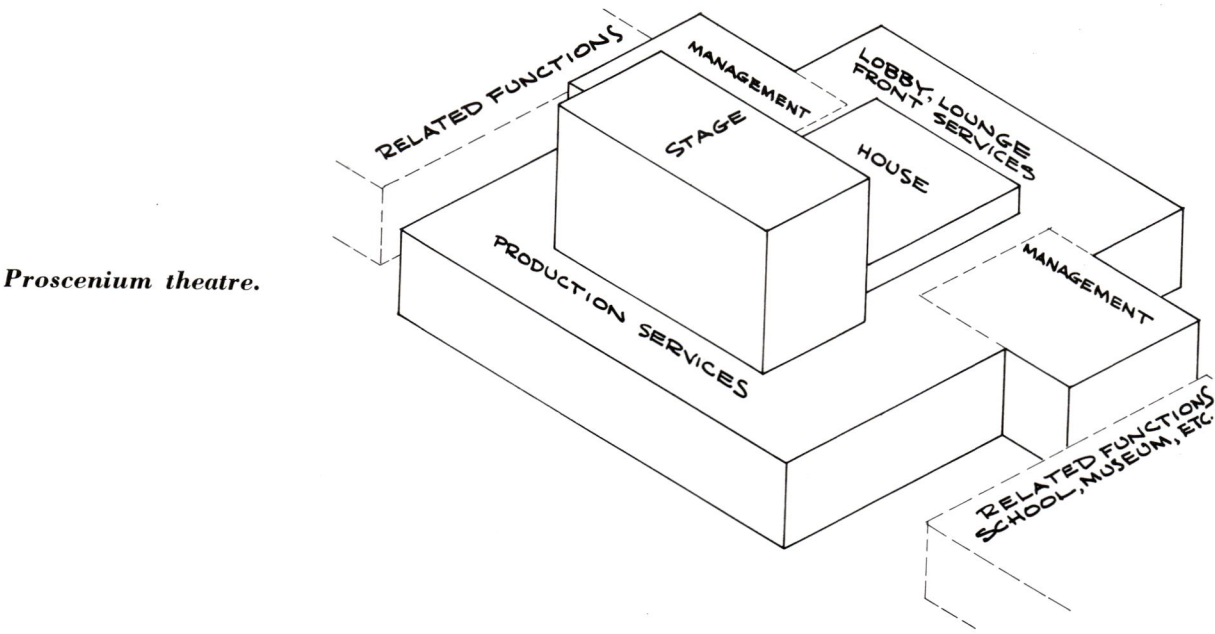

Open-stage theatre.

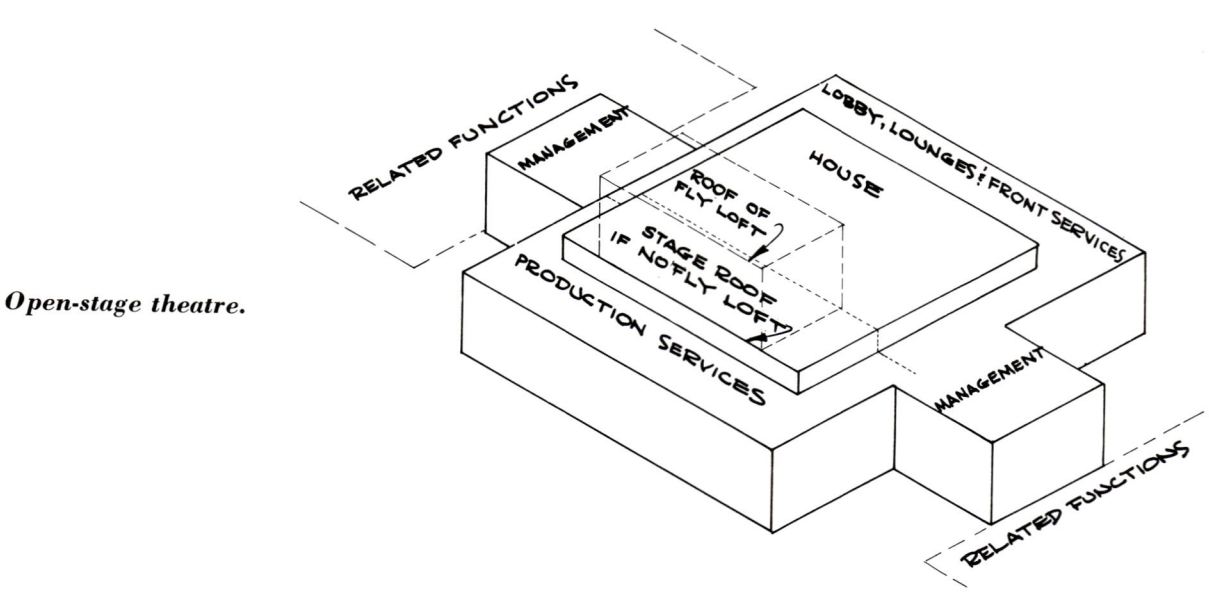

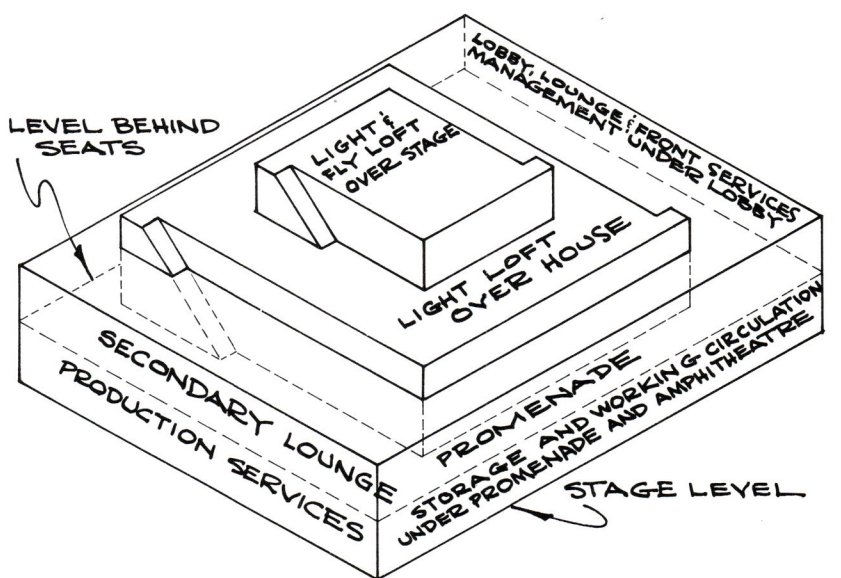

Arena theatre.

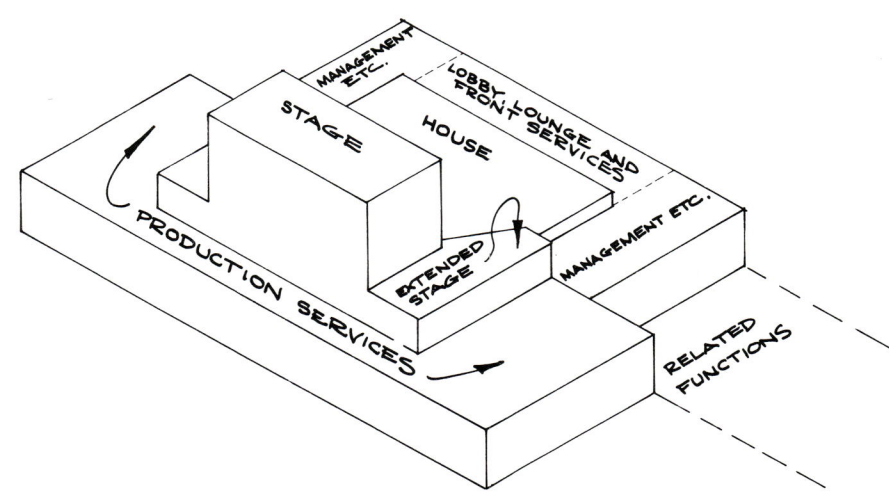

Extended-stage theatre.

excessive technical charges suffer from lack of rehearsals and substandard visual production (scenery, costumes, lighting, stage direction) to the point that the music alone must carry the show and attract the audiences. The serious opera audience is almost entirely limited to music lovers. Theatre lovers stay away by the thousands.

The ironical result is that the Metropolitan Opera Company runs a very short season and loses money, traveling opera companies play in antiquated opera houses or in motion picture presentation houses, and old opera houses now serve for motion pictures or touring legitimate productions.

The scenic investiture and production routine of grand opera exerts the maximum demands upon the equipment, machinery and personnel of production. It therefore is conducive to inefficiency and high cost and can benefit most from the introduction of modern machines and techniques.

Several new municipal and civic auditoriums and large theatres in art centers are being planned with the purpose either of showing the annual tour of a renowned opera company like the Metropolitan or the San Francisco Opera or of housing a locally developed opera company.

The opportunity exists to design greatly improved facilities for the production of opera, but the road opera house must always be capable of receiving the traveling company with production designed to fit the poorest house in the circuit. Often the most modern of equipment such as electronic lighting control in a road house will not be used by the traveling show which must, perforce, carry its own old-fashioned resistance-type dimmer boards.

Hence in general, the condition of resident repertory for opera is more conducive to modernization of equipment and techniques than is the touring situation.

Commercial Legitimate Theatre

The commercial legitimate theatre offers more discomfort per dollar of admission than any other theatre. From about 30 per cent of the seats, it is impossible to see the whole show. Seats are cramped, the atmosphere is stifling in the house, foul in the jammed public rooms. Acoustical conditions are generally bad, varying with the size of the audience.

The stage is as small and ill-equipped as it can be and still find a play willing to use it. It is unsuited to economical handling of more than single set shows. Multi-set shows often call for extreme ingenuity to get them into the stage house and shift them when they are there. Lighting equipment and all stage machinery except simple rigging must be brought in with the show. Dressing rooms are stacked about with no thought of the actors' comfort.

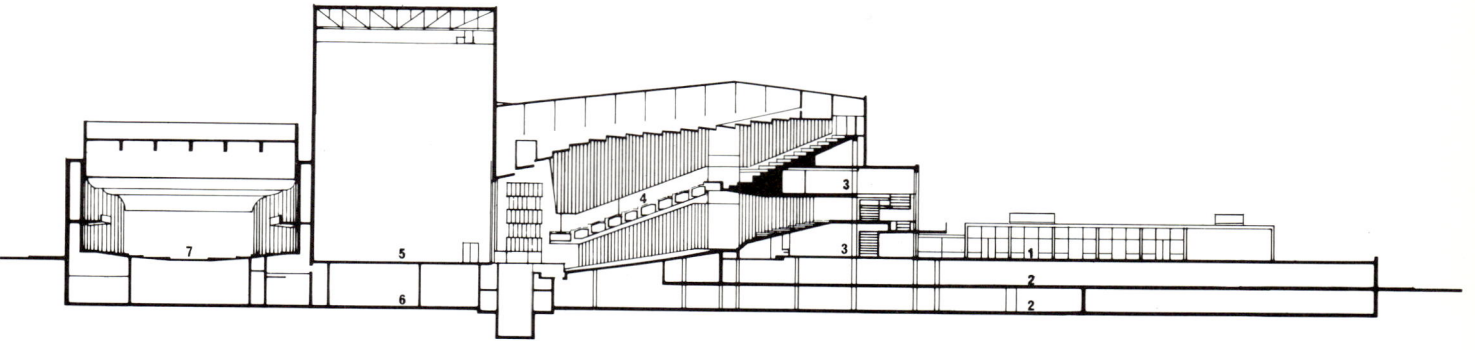

The Queen Elizabeth Theatre, Vancouver. Section ABOVE, *plan* BELOW. *Underground parking, coat check rooms, extended stages, sound isolation of the two houses, spacious public rooms and relative proportioning of spaces to functions are notable.*

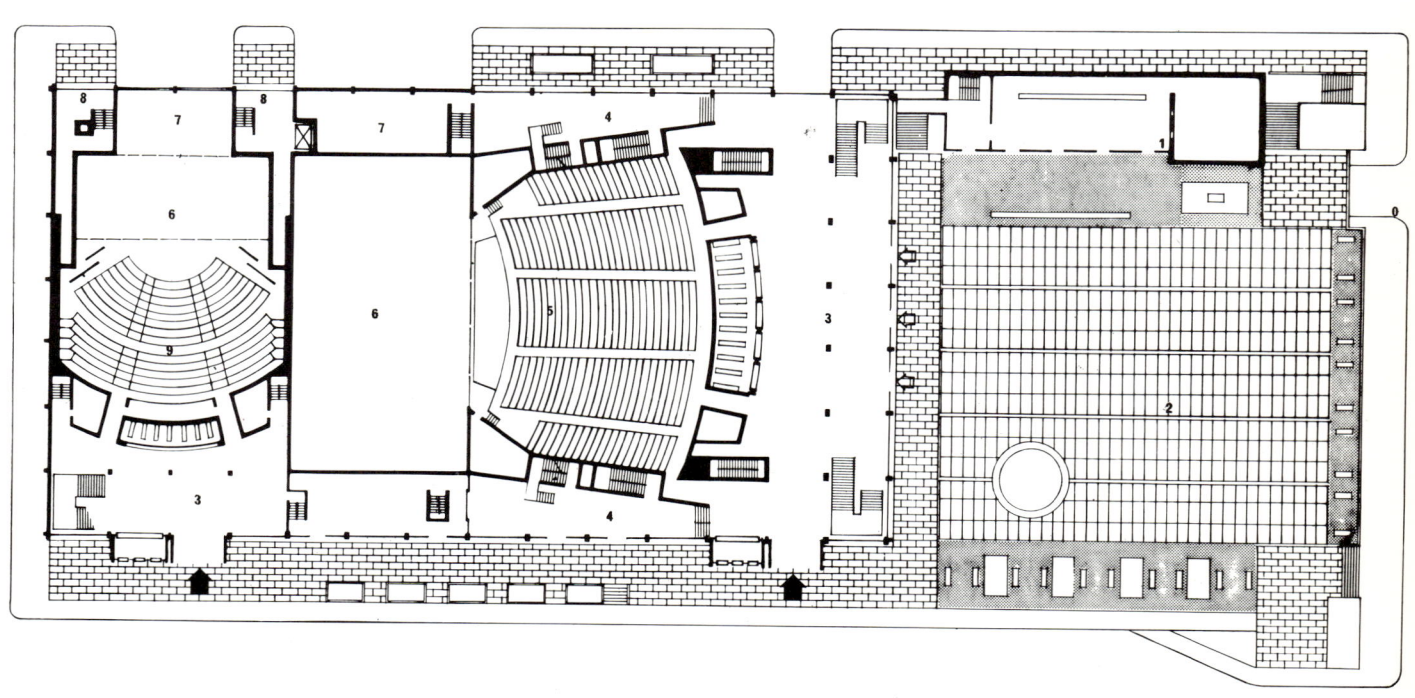

13

Within limits imposed by site and structure some New York theatres have recently been renovated, improved and redecorated. In the Helen Hayes Theatre, ABOVE, *permanent provisions have been made for balcony-front and side-wall spotlights to replace unsightly improvised devices. In the Lunt-Fontanne Theatre,* OPPOSITE, *a side-wall panel opens to make a slot for spotlights.*

The commercial theatre was built as a speculative real estate enterprise during boom times. It was planned to squeeze the maximum number of income-producing seats into the minimum ground space. The builder was not a showman. Audience comfort and production efficiency were not major concerns to him as long as there were more shows seeking theatres than there were theatres to house them. Furthermore, he got his return from the box office gross, not the net.

Theatre inefficiency breeds high production cost which necessitates high ticket prices. This keeps people at home beside the television. More than half of the legitimate theatres have disappeared in the last thirty years. Many theatres on the road have been torn down; the touring show often has to play the Masonic Temple, the high school auditorium, the municipal arena or the motion picture palace, all less suitable than the old theatres. Where no theatre remains, thousands of customers do without playgoing and the theatre loses considerable potential income.

The marquee extends the full width of the theatre and contains radiant heating devices to warm the audience during intermission.

Sincere efforts have been made by New York theatre owners to improve some of the existing theatres. Air conditioning has been added to make summer theatregoing more comfortable, ventilation has been improved, and redecoration has been undertaken. Despite these improvements, the difficulties inherent in the original structures still remain. The audience still has to crowd into the street at intermission. It is doubtful if private venture capital will support the building of new commercial theatres; theatres now being built are, for the most part, financed by municipalities, colleges or nonprofit organizations, which do not seek a profit return on the initial costs of land and building.

High School

There are more performances of plays in high school auditoriums in a year than there are in any other single type of theatre. Such auditoriums vary widely in size and equipment. Their faults are so widespread and varied, irrespective of construction date, as to make one realize that their designers have not understood the requirements of the performing arts. Audience comfort is less than in the standard commercial theatre. Seats are hard and cramped, floors are often flat. Sight lines are usually very bad. Acoustical conditions are usually accidental. The school ventilation system is often shut off at night when the play takes place. Corridors are neither designed nor furnished to serve as substitute for nonexistent public rooms.

The stage, called the platform, merits the title. It lacks wing space, depth, flying facilities, and has a hardwood floor. If there are shops, access to them is difficult. A single box set with no upstage windows is all that can be gotten on the stage.

Many designers of high school auditoriums have apparently worked under the illusions that (1) professional (commercial) theatres are good theatres; (2) amateurs can do with poorer facilities than professionals need.

Where budget limitations prevent building a theatre, the attempt has sometimes been made to add a stage and the associated backstage facilities to the gymnasium or the cafeteria. Such a combination is never a good theatre. Nor is it possible to slice a theatre into classrooms with movable partitions and have either classroom or theatre as good as it should be. The cost of a sliced-up theatre may well be as much as a good theatre and good classrooms built separately.

The poorly designed high school theatre usually costs as much to build as does a good theatre of the same seating capacity—often more. But this is not the only respect in which a badly planned theatre proves costly to the community. The educational program is vitiated; half a theatre is as bad pedagogically as half a play. Plays produced under limitations are shabby, invite a patronizing attitude on the part of the audience, do not draw enough paying customers. The local community

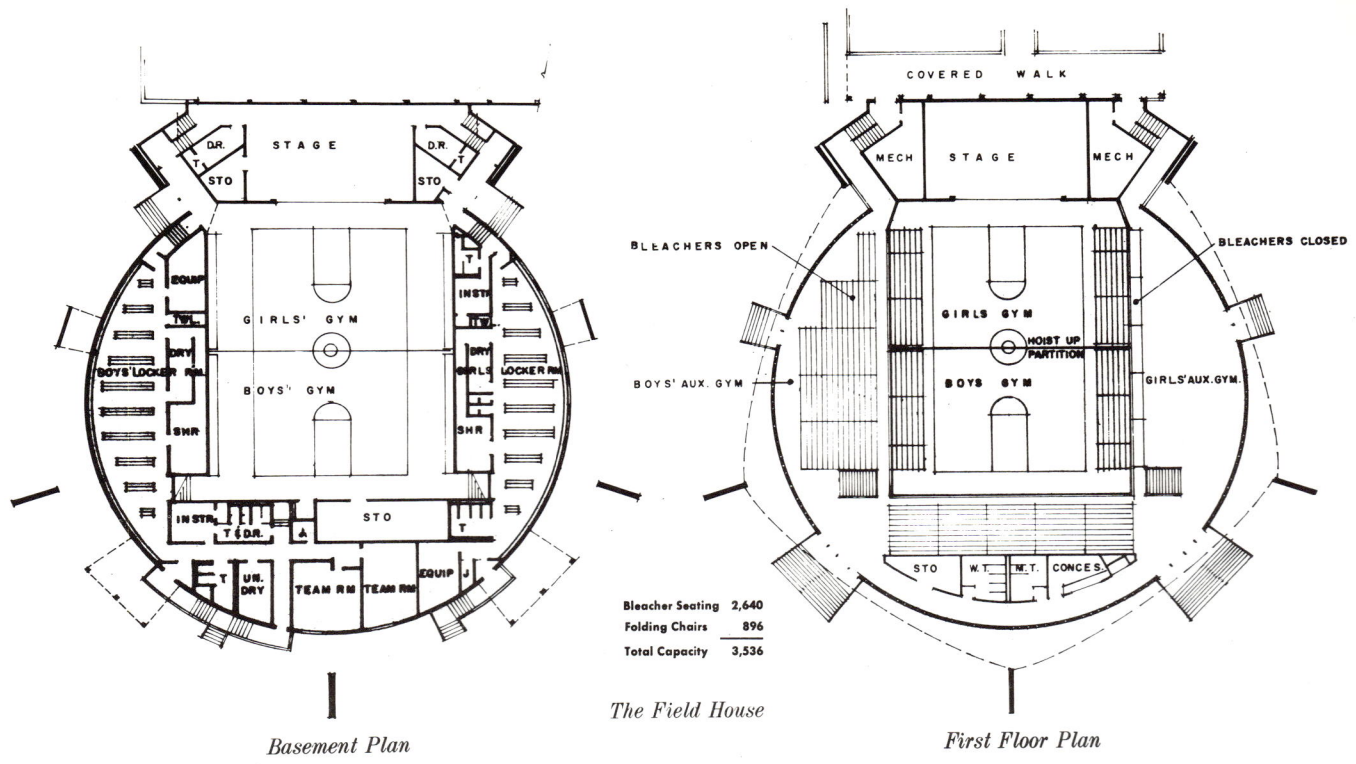

Gymnasium with a stage. Walt Whitman High School, Bethesda, Maryland. McLeod and Ferrara, architects.

amateur producing group cannot use the theatre. Traveling professional companies cannot rent the theatre and often, therefore, cannot play the town.

Many of the faults here inveighed against have been removed with the razing of archaic schools, but not all faults have been eliminated. Inexpensive and uncomfortable bent plywood seats, the absence of acoustical study and design for the auditorium, uninformed and unskilled use of electronic sound reinforcement, wide stages and low stage houses are frequent faults, and inadequate production service facilities are the rule.

The architect cannot bear all the blame for wasting public money and sabotaging the school and community theatre and educational programs. The school board which sanctions such procedures plainly does not value the performing arts as being educational.

Many conflicting considerations, to be sure, enter into the design of the high school auditorium. Its intended use may include various school activities, community plays and concerts, and visiting companies. The capacity considerations include school assembly, now outdated because of the school public address system, single performances by visiting artists or companies, graduations. Concert and ballet require large capacity; drama, small. The performing arts educational program— teaching, performance, criticism—is best assured with a small audience.

Where the dramatic arts have been recognized as curricular or non-curricular activity and given serious consideration as contributing

The Hopkins Center Theatre is the core of a complex of related educational, social and artistic functions. Harrison and Abramovitz, architects.

components of education, secondary school theatres have often been well planned. In too few instances, however, has the full potential of the dramatic arts been realized and accommodated in the building program. To try to reconcile all these considerations is folly. A good, well-equipped theatre will serve many educational purposes; an assembly hall is good for little else.

College Theatre

Within the last decade there has been a building boom in college theatres, many of them excellent. The best theatre in the community is now often the college theatre. As part of a university art center, the theatre profits from the proximity of ballet and music, specialized rehearsal facilities and may use its large public rooms as exhibition halls. However, too many college theatre plants are still designed and, unfortunately, built primarily for nontheatrical purposes: the student assembly, concerts, lectures, commencement exercises. When theatrical productions have been envisioned as a primary purpose, specifications have often been drawn by persons either unfamiliar with the processes of production or, worse, obsessed with a single style of production, as a result of which, productions in that style can be adequately mounted, but all others suffer. Donors of buildings often impose limitations on theatre plans by insisting on the incorporation of some pet features. Persons responsible for campus layout may prescribe limiting dimensions or architectural style to assure consistency in campus appearance. Imposition of limitations in response to nontheatrical considerations violates the principle of designing an educational institution for educational purposes.

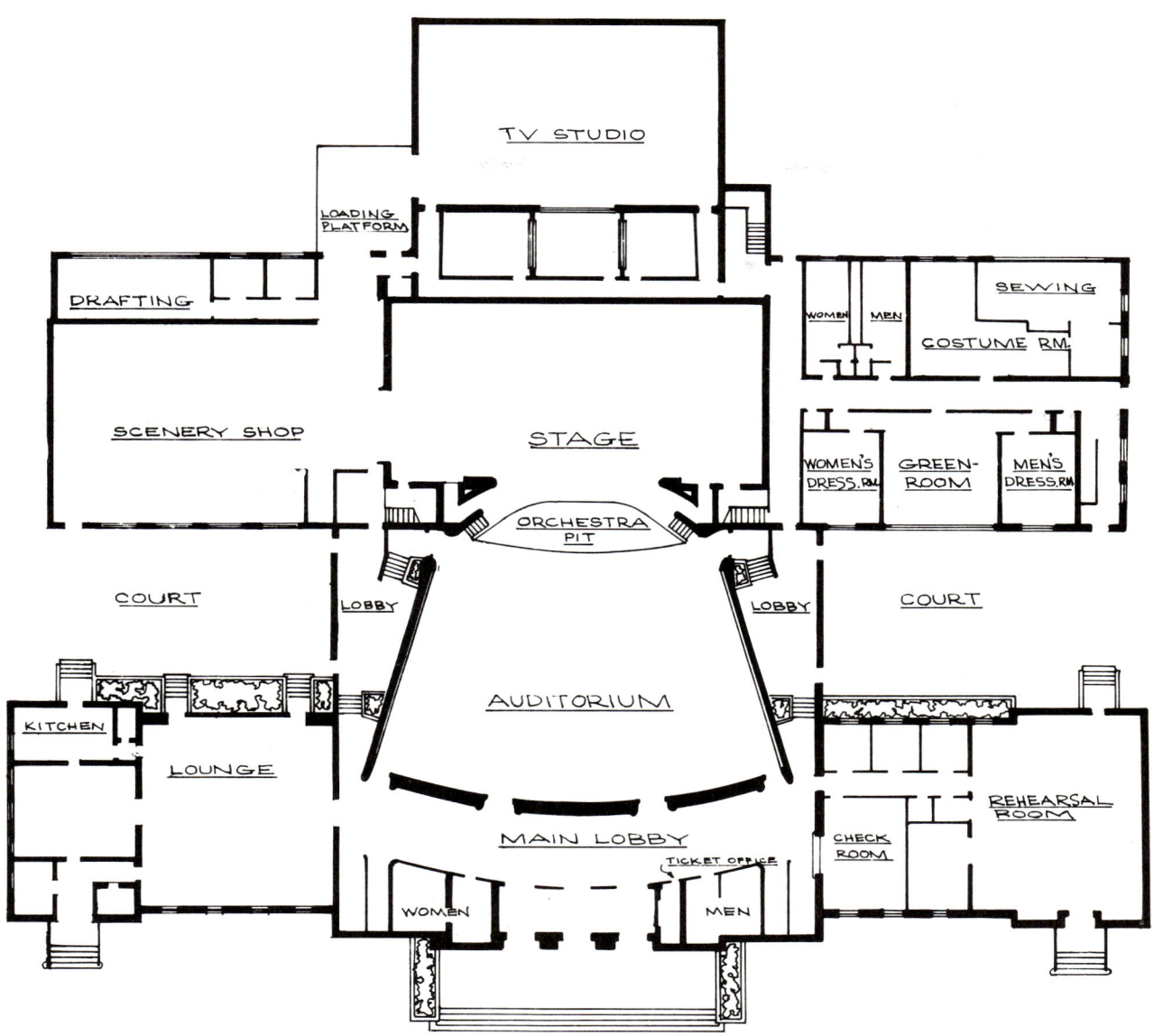

Phi Beta Kappa Hall, ground plan.

◀ Phi Beta Kappa Hall, College of William and Mary, Williamsburg, Virginia. One wing houses the Alpha Chapter of Phi Beta Kappa. Walford and Wright, architects.

Community Theatre

During the past decade many community theatres have largely outgrown the converted fire houses, churches, morgues and barns they originally occupied.

One community theatre is subsidized by its city government. One community theatre was built by its city government particularly to house the community players. Federal agencies assisted in the construction of a number of theatres. One community theatre produces plays in the local high school auditorium, which was designed to specifications drawn by the community theatre. Private philanthropies have helped several organizations to build their theatres, and the community theatre is the heart of many a new community art center.

Insofar as the community theatre has control over the planning of its plant, there is an effort to provide for maximum audience comfort and production efficiency within the limits of the building budget. Conditions are, however, often primitive, due partly to limited funds and partly to the fact that amateurs, being familiar only with restricted producing conditions, don't know how to plan a theatre when they have the funds available.

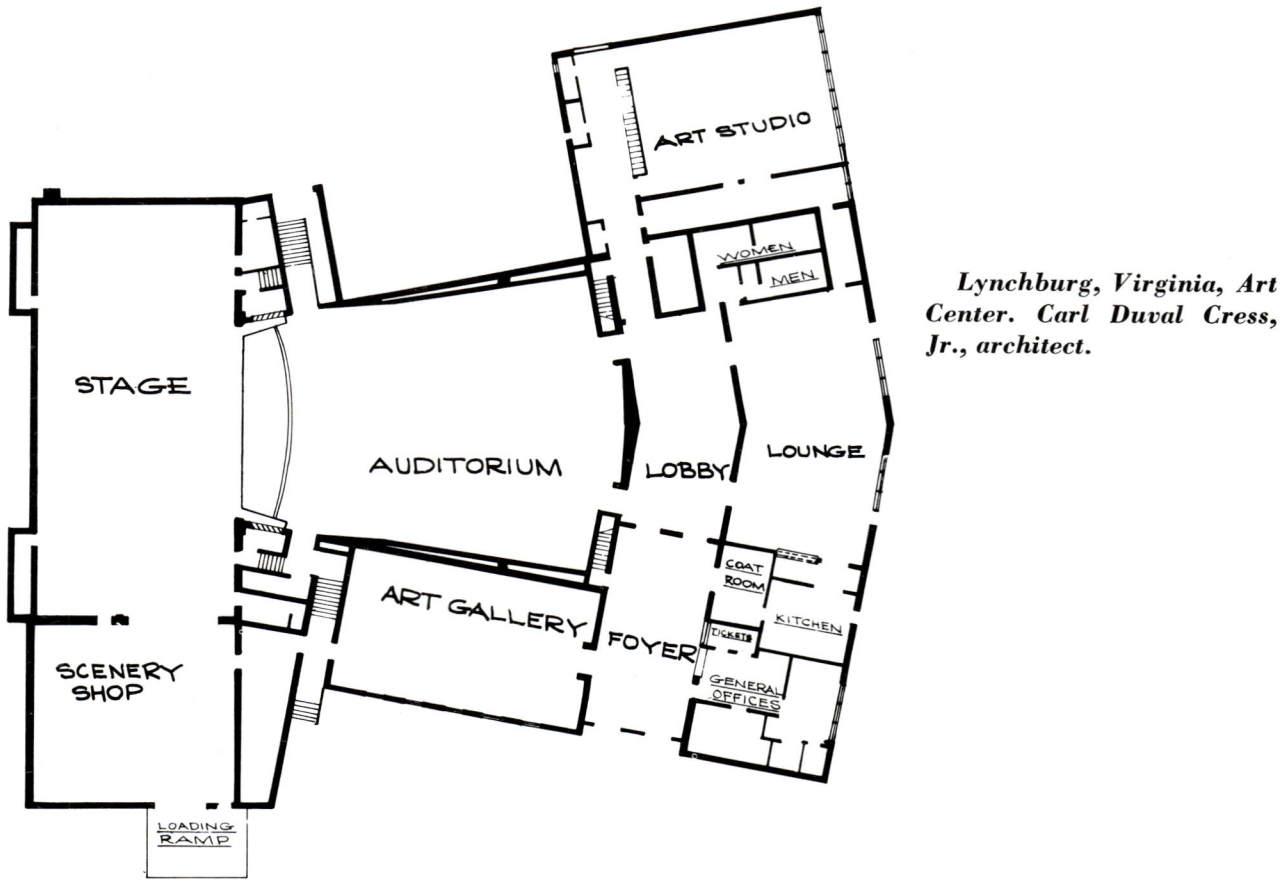

Lynchburg, Virginia, Art Center. Carl Duval Cress, Jr., architect.

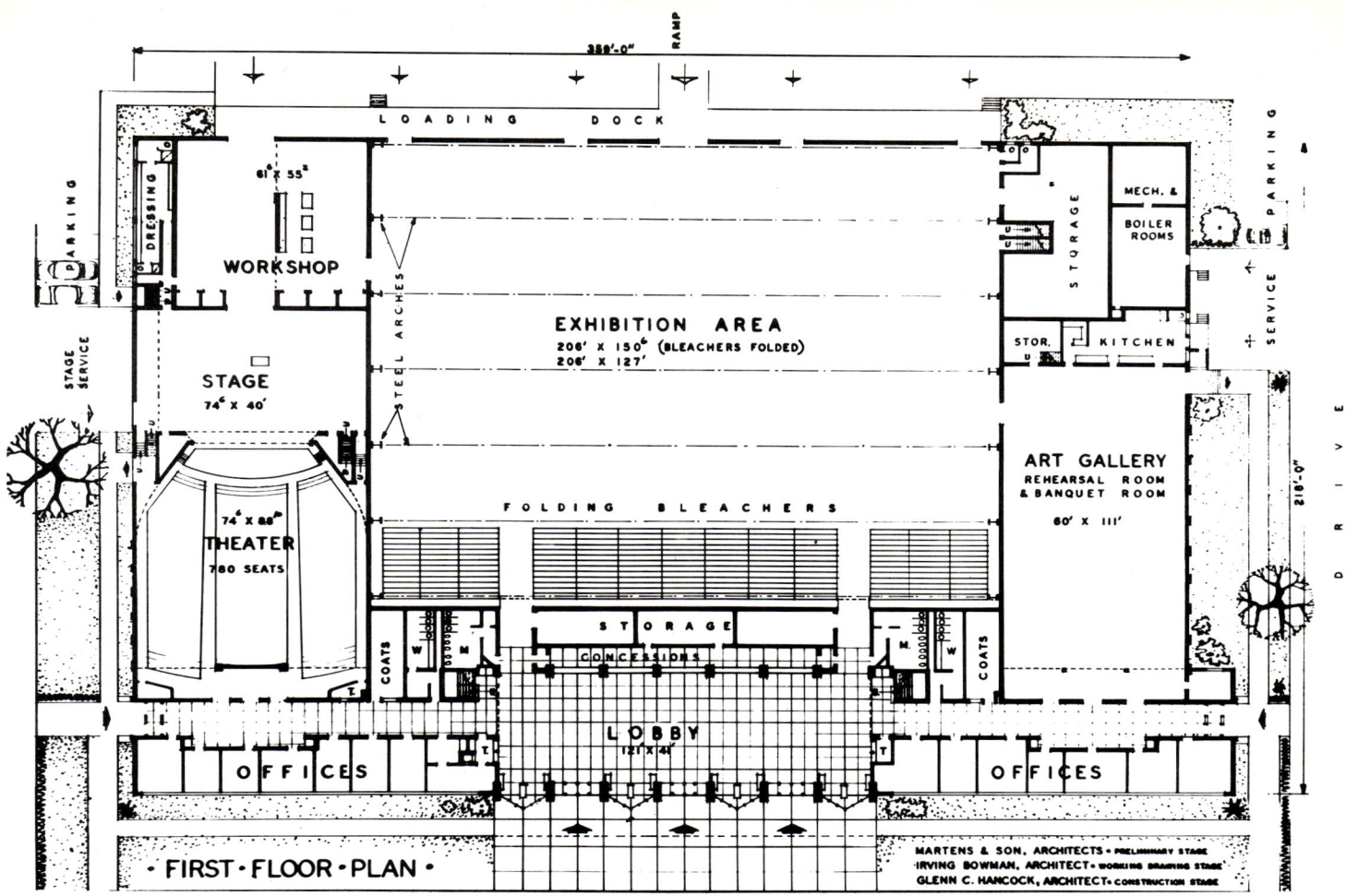

Charleston, West Virginia, Civic Center. Irving Bowman and Associates, architects.

Arts Center

Related to the community theatre and symptomatic of the growing concern of citizens for the affairs of the mind and spirit are community arts councils and community arts or cultural centers. Theatre, including drama, ballet, opera, and performed music, usually bulks large in such organizations, and arts centers built to house such councils and their activities usually contain two or more theatres or auditoriums. The Hopkins Center for the Arts at Dartmouth College contains a concert hall, a theatre for drama, and an experimental studio theatre. The new complex of buildings for the School of Fine Arts at the University of New Mexico will contain, when complete, an opera house-concert hall, a chamber music auditorium, a theatre for drama and a free-form experimental theatre. The Lincoln Center in New York City has planned five separate facilities for the performing arts, four specialized to specific art forms—symphony, dramatic repertory, opera, operetta—and one all-purpose facility for a school of the performing arts. The three examples cited are but a few of many that are either in existence or projected.

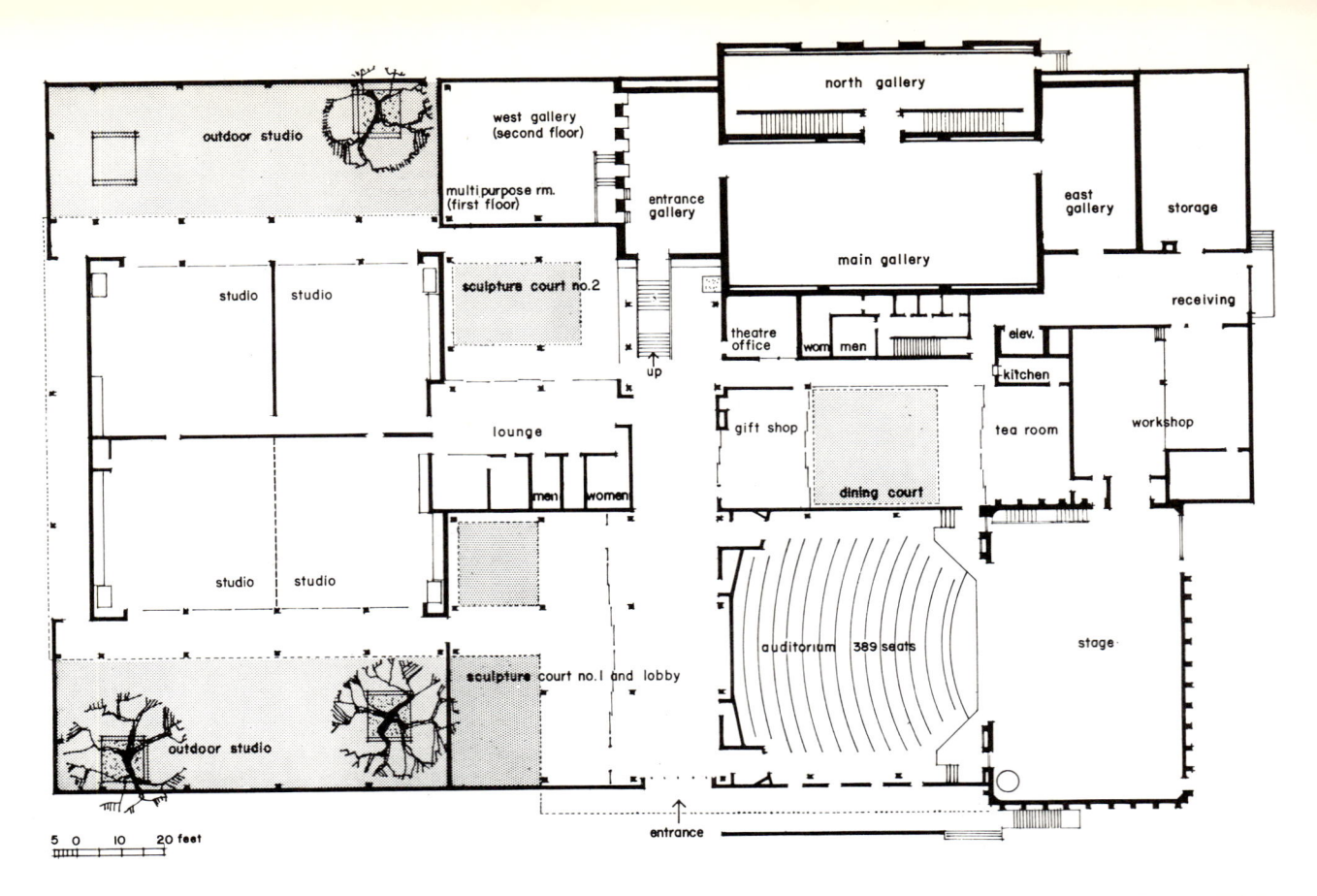

outdoor studio		west gallery (second floor)		north gallery		
		multipurpose rm. (first floor)	entrance gallery		east gallery	storage
studio	studio	sculpture court no. 2		main gallery		receiving
			up			
		lounge	theatre office	wom men	elev. kitchen	workshop
		men women	gift shop	tea room		
studio	studio			dining court		
outdoor studio		sculpture court no. 1 and lobby	auditorium 389 seats		stage	
			entrance			

5 0 10 20 feet

Arkansas Art Center, Little Rock. Ground floor plan.

◀

The stagehouse, Arkansas Art Center, exemplifies effective exploitation of this vertical element.

◀

Interior of theatre, Arkansas Art Center. Ginocchio, Cromwell, Carter, Dees and Heyland, architects.

Motion Picture Palace and Presentation Theatre

The difference between the motion picture palace and the presentation house is that the latter puts on a stage show while the former does not. The palace usually has at least a rudimentary stage and changes categories on occasion. The last structures to be built in these categories set the standard for audience comfort in all respects save horizontal sight lines. Though acoustics be bad, intelligibility is assured through sound reinforcement. Stages are usually too shallow for effective use of projected scenery and too narrow for live storage of large rolling units. Stage equipment and permanently installed lighting equipment are usually adequate for the demands of presentation programs.

Luxury is one of the principal commodities on sale at the box office. Production facilities have been consciously somewhat limited in favor of high seating capacity.

High operating costs make the life of the motion picture palace or presentation house precarious. Luxurious, easily accessible neighborhood houses can take away its business. The Center, the best theatre originally designed for presentation, and the Roxy, the largest, have been torn down.

Radio City Music Hall. Reinhard and Hofmeister, architects.

Intimate Motion Picture Theatre

And while the palace or presentation house can, and occasionally does, mount productions for which it was not designed (road shows, opera) it does so only inefficiently. The type is obsolete.

The intimate motion picture house is a small theatre generally devoted to the running of exceptional pictures with intelligentsia appeal or newsreels and shorts. The most recent newsreel theatres are the best of the type. They offer unsurpassed facilities for audience comfort even to coffee and cigarettes. They are efficient. Many use entrance turnstiles to simplify audience handling. A number have very good sight lines.

Neighborhood Motion Picture Theatre

The neighborhood motion picture theatre, pleasant and popular twenty years ago, has lost out to television. Where it survives, the admission price is high and popcorn bolsters the income. Many of the structures are being converted into bowling alleys, super markets and even theatres for the local community theatre organizations.

Outdoor theatre for Shakespeare in the Park. The New York Shakespeare Festival, Joseph Papp, producer.

Summer Theatre

The summer theatre is now an accepted element of show business. It grows in importance. While many summer theatres still occupy accommodations adapted from other uses, the number with plants designed expressly for them grows each season.

The summer theatre at Cain Park, Cleveland Heights, Ohio, which uses a large and well-equipped outdoor theatre especially designed for summer theatre productions; the Roanoke Pageant; THE COMMON GLORY and THE FOUNDERS at Williamsburg; Jones Beach; Robin Hood Dell and the St. Lous Municipal Opera are all housed in reasonably adequate outdoor plants. Aquacades and other similar summer spectacles generally use plants designed for those productions only. Some summer theatres such as the Ogunquit Playhouse, the Berkshire Musical Festival Theatre, and the Deertrees Theatre use plants designed specifically as summer theatres. Stratford, Ontario, and Stratford, Connecticut, have good theatres, but where one summer theatre gets a good plant, two more spring up, working in barns or tents, as did their predecessors.

In most cases the summer theatre has to make money if it is to continue in operation. It keeps down expenses by severely limiting production costs other than stars' salaries. The average provision for audience comfort in the summer theatre is inadequate. The parking lot is usually present but notable for poison ivy, dust or mud. The stage and its equipment are usually makeshift and inadequate.

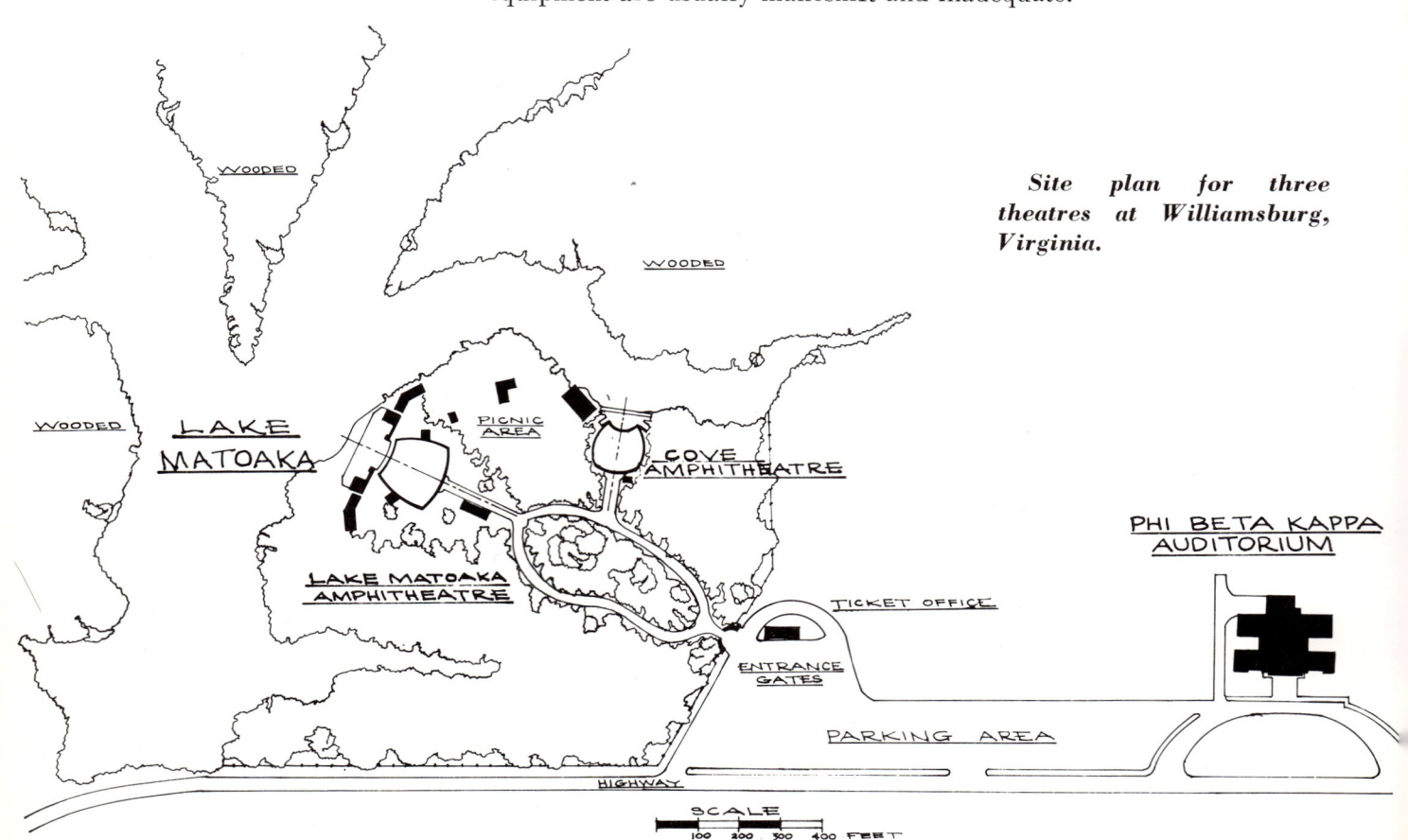

Site plan for three theatres at Williamsburg, Virginia.

The Black Hills Playhouse, Black Hills, South Dakota. A summer theatre in a resort area has a small capacity, good side-stage space, but no fly loft.

Ground plan, Black Hills Playhouse.

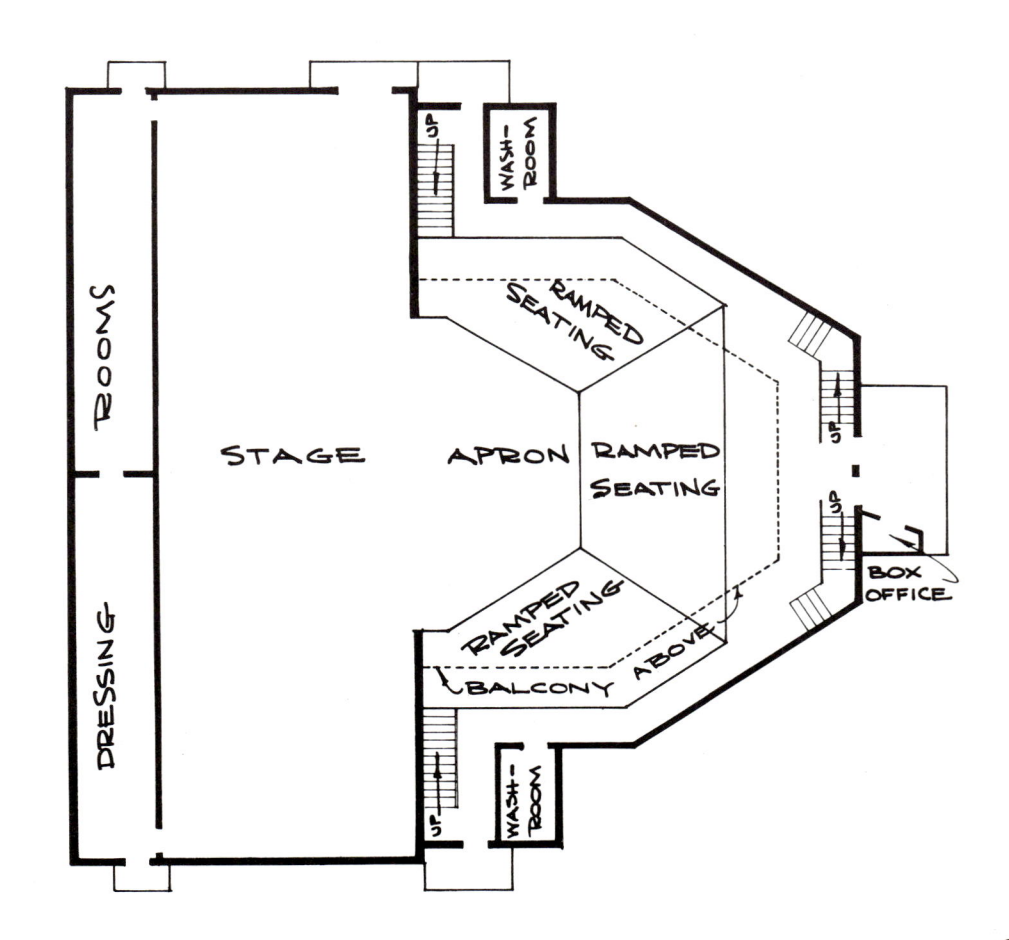

Theatres in Shopping Centers

Lately, retail merchants have evolved a twentieth-century version of country fairs in the form of the suburban shopping center where a covey of shops and consumer services are grouped around a large parking area in a location which has been considered to be reasonably accessible to a sufficiently large number of citizens to make for profitable business.

It is logical that theatres should spring up in these suburban centers. For the theatre entrepreneur, much work has already been done. The merchants have already studied the area and determined the probable efficacy of the venture. The shops have already created a popular pattern of movement toward the center. The parking areas created for the daytime customers are available for the evening's theatre patrons. Now motion picture theatres are being included in shopping centers, and the first dramatic theatre in a shopping center was opened in 1961.

Festival Theatres

The great increase in vacation travel has given rise to festival theatres which depend for audiences upon the disposition of many people to travel great distances for pleasure. The Shakespeare Festival Theatre at Stratford, Ontario, draws large audiences from Detroit, Toronto, Hamilton, Buffalo, New York City, Chicago, and from all parts of the world. Salzburg and Oberammergau have long been renowned festival cities. Lately the festival idea has proliferated.

The festival theatre is a particular problem. Dependent on a short season, it must have large capacity and, consequently, large operating costs. A balanced financial statement is generally made possible only by an income other than box office, usually either purely philanthropic gifts or quasi-philanthropic contributions from persons and businessmen who hope to profit from the presence of many theatre patrons in the vicinity of the theatre. Ultimate solvency divorced from subsidy is unlikely in most cases and is only possible if the season can be long and the audience maintained at near capacity without a proportionate increase in operating and production costs.

Theatre Facilities in Buildings Primarily for Other Uses

Amateur theatricals are ubiquitous, and because they are the incubators of future performing and producing talent, as well as a popular social activity, they deserve adequate facilities. A large percentage of amateur productions is presented in buildings which are intended for all kinds of social and recreational activity, in situations whose economic and social nature precludes the possibility or even the necessity of a theatre. If an organization or community can afford only a rudimentary building as a general social and recreational center, then that building must be designed to serve all purposes for which it is intended. If the hall must be used for dancing, basketball, Girl Scouts, bingo, bridge and the harvest supper, it is unreasonable to expect that it should have a sloping floor and fixed theatre seats. But too frequently in planning such a building, those provisions for theatrical production which might be incorporated in it for the general benefit of its theatrical users are either omitted, slighted, or wrongly planned. Inclusion of well-planned minimal provisions for good seeing and hearing, for backstage preparation and installation, for dressing and make-up, and for lighting increases the usefulness of a social hall or community center enough to justify the cost of the facilities thus provided.

Summary

The foregoing survey has shown that theatres built prior to 1940 generally failed to provide for audience comfort or operating efficiency, were seldom suited to more than one type of production and in too many cases could not earn their upkeep. It has also indicated that there have been some theatres built since World War II which have corrected the faults that characterized earlier buildings.

Portents

There is increasing interest in the improvement of theatres as is evidenced by the following:

1. At least three national associations and one New York City organization have active committees on theatre architecture: The American Educational Theatre Association's Theatre Architecture Project, the Theatre Architecture Committee of the United States Institute for Theatre Technology, the American Institute of Architects Theatre Architecture Committee, and the Board of Standards and Planning of the Greater New York Chapter of American National Theatre and Academy.

2. Two international organizations, the Association Internationale des Techniciens de Théâtre and the International Union of Architects, have theatre architecture under active study.

3. Philanthropic foundations, notably the Ford Foundation, have underwritten the development of plans for new types of theatres.

4. The American Association of School Administrators has included in its convention programs sessions devoted to school theatres.

5. The theatre consultant has been accepted into the planning organization for an increasing number of theatres.

6. The governments of several nations have increased their sponsorship of new buildings for the performing arts by direct subsidy, as with the Montreal Place des Arts, and through indirect subsidy, as with the gift of land by the U. S. Congress for the National Cultural Center in Washington, the Urban Redevelopment Agency's aid to the Lincoln Center in New York City, the State Department's sending of theatre advisors to African and Asiatic nations, and the French government's sponsorship of arts centers throughout France.

7. Leading institutions of higher learning are increasingly admitting the performing arts to the status of academic respectability by creating

faculties and facilities adequate to their proper study and practice. In fact, the lead in the improvement of the buildings and equipment for these arts has been with the universities and colleges.

8. Architectural schools frequently undertake problems in the design of theatres.

9. The amount of published material on theatre achitecture in periodicals and books has increased substantially in the last ten years.*

Arena Stage, Washington, D.C. The front of the house is essentially a separate building from the theatre. An addition to accommodate production services is projected. The ground floor under the lobby contains dressing rooms. Harry Weese, architect.

---

* A continuing inclusive bibliography of theatre architecture is maintained at the University of Pittsburgh.

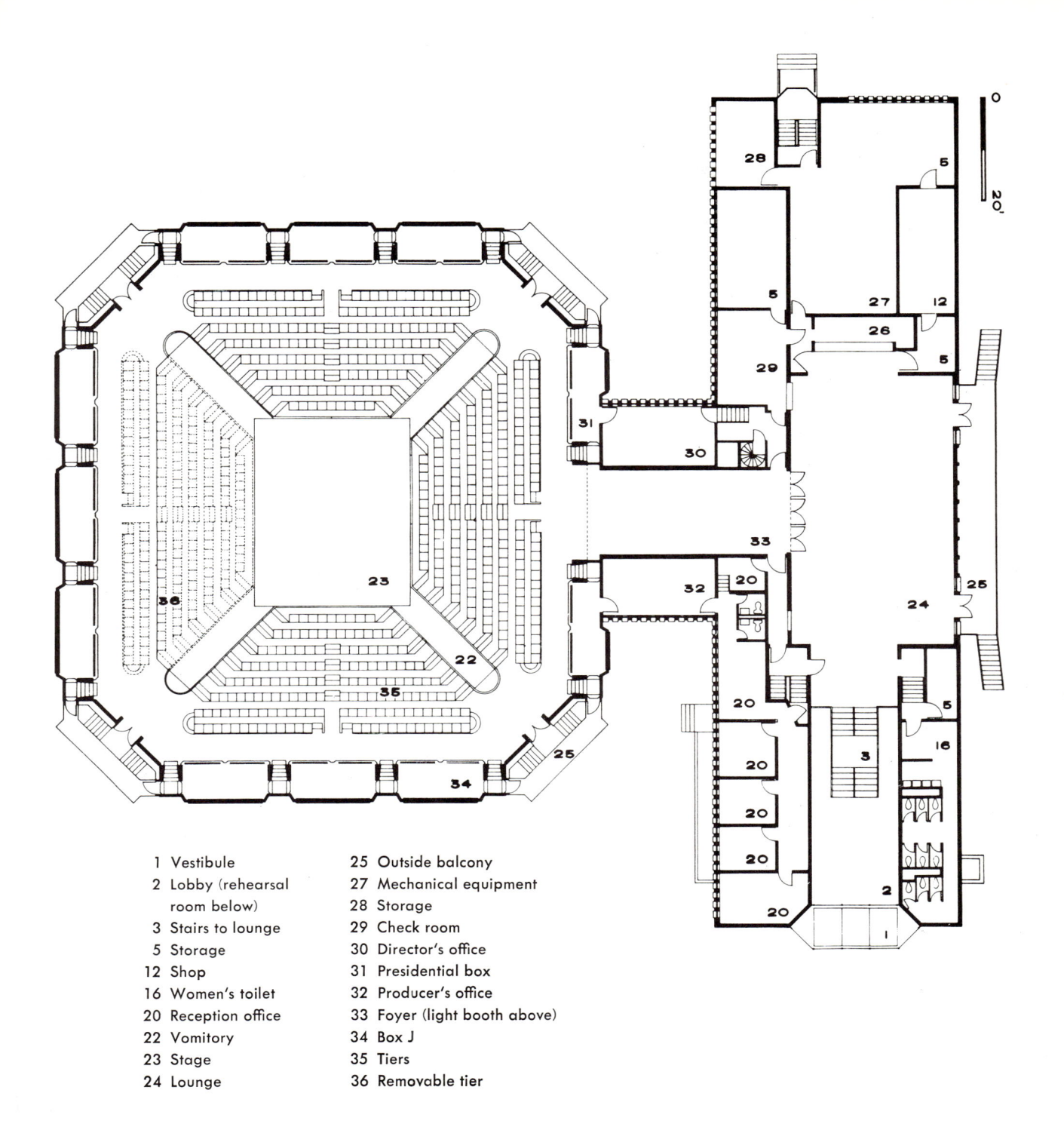

1 Vestibule
2 Lobby (rehearsal room below)
3 Stairs to lounge
5 Storage
12 Shop
16 Women's toilet
20 Reception office
22 Vomitory
23 Stage
24 Lounge
25 Outside balcony
27 Mechanical equipment
28 Storage
29 Check room
30 Director's office
31 Presidential box
32 Producer's office
33 Foyer (light booth above)
34 Box J
35 Tiers
36 Removable tier

Building Codes

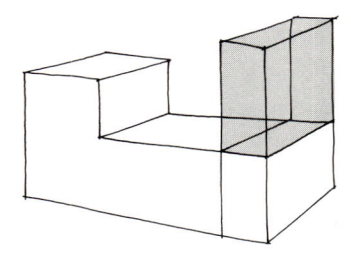

10. The New York City Building Code, modified a generation ago to permit including a theatre in a building primarily designed for other purposes, is currently under study. It is anticipated that the theatre section of the revised code will take advantage of new materials and devices, and lose some of the obsolete restrictions which have severely limited theatre building since 1929.

In several instances variances from existing local building codes have been granted when the petitioners have proven that the proposed buildings included provisions for public safety equal to or better than those required by the codes.

So far it is apparent then that (1) there is a need for good theatres; (2) there is a demand for them; (3) legal restrictions to their erection have been removed; (4) new theatres are being designed and (5) built. It would seem then that all is well and that time and financial backing will give this country what it needs in the theatre. Unfortunately this is not the case, for a new theatre is not necessarily a good theatre; in fact it can easily be, and often is, a very bad theatre.

The Architect's Problem

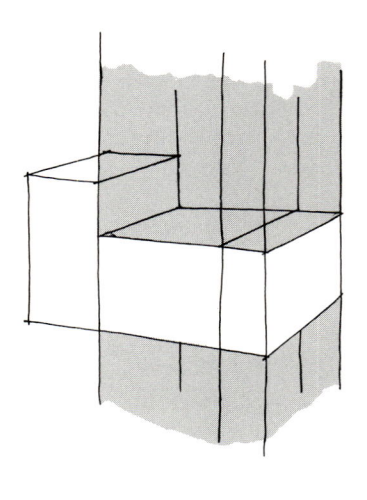

This deplorable circumstance arises out of the highly specialized nature of the theatre plant. The plant is, in fact, to a large extent, a machine, and those who do not actually operate it cannot be expected to know its structural requisites. In any case the architect is, to use the vernacular, on the spot.

The plan of any modern building depends on a knowledge of the purposes for which it is to be built. An architect designs a factory only after consulting freely with his client regarding the processes of manufacture to be housed; he does not design a residence without first studying at length the composition, personalities, habits, and circumstances of the family; nor does he design a church without knowing thoroughly the services, rites, and ceremonies to be celebrated therein. He cannot succeed in designing a theatre unless he obtains, from some source, information regarding the uses of the building.

In the case of the factory, residence, and church, the architect can get the necessary particular information directly from his client. In the case of the theatre this is not often possible. In many instances of theatre planning, the people who are in the position of client to the theatre architect do not know.

The Client's Problem

As has been pointed out, the commercial theatre owner is not a showman. Operating efficiency does not concern him since his income is based on gross receipts rather than on net profit. He runs a boarding house for shows, not a theatre.

The aegis of theatre building in the field of education is variously located depending upon the type of institution. A board of trustees, a generous alumnus, president, general faculty, committee on policy, building committee, drama faculty, municipal school board, the state board of education, the legislature's committee on education, the legislature as a whole and the governor may each exercise some degree of authority over the architect. To these may be added, if a federal contribution is received, officials and bureaus of the federal government up to and even including the latest equivalent of the administrator of public works. In this line-up there is a great scarcity of comprehension about what goes on beyond the footlights of a theatre. This is fitting, proper, and condonable if those uncomprehending people refrain from making decisions which should be based solely and essentially upon knowledge of the theatre's arts, crafts, and methods.

The fact that the client often does not know enough about the theatre to be of any help to the architect does not prevent him from insisting on certain features toward which he has a predisposition: a fly loft only 30 feet high to keep the outside appearance of the building consistent with something or other; a greenroom where wing space ought to be; an organ console fixed in position on stage; organ pipes in the fly loft. He may be a faddist or insist on specialized forms with limited usefulness or income potential.

The architect, unable to get information from his client or, worse, saddled with requirements which are patently wrong, is flung on his own resources. Architects who have had a chance to familiarize themselves with the particular group of conditions and specified requirements which govern the planning of a theatre are very few. Compared with the planning of residential, commercial, or industrial buildings, the planning of a theatre or even of a building containing auditorium and stage is a rare commission to the average practicing architect. The architect must live by work other than the designing of theatres; it is little wonder that he gives his attention to residential, commercial, and industrial building problems, and leaves a study of theatres until he is actually commissioned to plan one.

A decade ago there was little organized reliable information on theatre building available to the architect, but this situation is improving. The American Educational Theatre Association keeps a roster of theatre consultants. A large number and variety of useful technical papers on theatre architecture and equipment are published by the professional associations cited and by theatre equipment manufacturers.

This book and more specialized recent works on light and acoustics have found their way into the architects' drafting rooms. There are able consultants in all phases of theatre planning, capable of reconciling many planning considerations to achieve the best theatre the budget will justify. But this situation does not completely solve the architect's problem. He must match every element of the structure against a wide variety of considerations. One good element may vitiate others. And in the last analysis, the architect is responsible for the *design objectives*.

The *derivation* of these objectives and the *presentation of the means and devices by which a design may be tested* to see if the objectives have been accomplished are the subject of the rest of this book.

Ultra realism in scenery lingers on at the Stardust Inn in Las Vegas. The flood of real water from the broken dam wreaks vast destruction as members of the affluent society look on, safe and externally dry.

2: Audience traffic

The showman's first direct contact with any member of his audience occurs when that individual comes in sight of the theatre. From that moment until the patron is on the highway or the subway headed for home, his every movement is the showman's concern. The easier and pleasanter the patron's progress from home to theatre seat and back again, the better are the showman's chances of making and holding a repeat customer.

TABLE 1. The Audience Goes to the Theatre

Type of Production	Theatre	Audience Transit Time	Audience Assembly Time
Pageant Spectacle	Considerable latitude in type. Large seating capacity only requisite. Stadium or sports arena.	Weeks (Oberammergau) Days (Lost Colony) Hours (Aquacade)	1 hour. Audience is on time.
Concert	Any auditorium with a platform.		40 min. from advertised curtain time until half hour after show begins.
Opera	Opera house when available.	Average 30 min.	
Dance	Demands vary from as simple as concert to as complex as opera.		
Legitimate and Musical	Commercial, school, college, university, professional school, community. Lacking these: barn, opera house or tent.	Less than an hour except for summer theatre. Average 30 min.	20 min. beginning approximately 13 min. before advertised curtain time.
Vaudeville	Presentation house Commercial	Slightly shorter than legitimate.	Continuous show. Now alternates with pictures.
Motion Pictures	Motion picture palace	15 min.	Continuous
	Intimate	10 min. maximum	"
Burlesque	Old commercial	15 min.	Same as legitimate.

Spacious site for a theatre in an urban center. O'Keefe Centre, Toronto. Earle C. Morgan and Page and Steele, architects.

This chapter deals with audience traffic to, through, and away from the theatre, together with the architectural implications thereof. Architectural planning for clear, straight paths of movement must be preceded by a study of the phenomenon of theatregoing. The figures in the tables which follow are obtained by analyses made in New York and in various other communities on the eastern seaboard. Whoever plans a theatre will do well to make similar analyses for his own community rather than to trust implicitly these figures which are averages, and cannot encompass special cases. The planner is warned, however, that the figures here stated are a much better guide than a guess, an estimate, or an unsupported prediction in any locality.

Motor Transportation

The average car (owner-driven, taxi, chauffeured) carries three theatre patrons. To the theatre patronized by owner-drivers, patrons come irrespective of weather if there is a convenient parking space. Chivalry dictates getting into the congestion close to the theatre and parking after discharging passengers; expediency dictates getting the

Spacious suburban site for a theatre. American Shakespeare Festival Theatre. Howard and Thorn, architects.

TABLE 2. Transportation Methods according to the Location of the Theatre

	Metropolitan Urban	Metropolitan Suburban	General Urban	General Suburban	Rural	Institutional (School and College)
Public Transit System and/or Pedestrian	Majority	Large Minority	Large Minority	Small Minority	Small Minority	Large Minority
Owner-driven Motor	Small Minority	Large Minority	Large Minority	Large Majority	Majority	Majority
Taxi or Chauffeured	Large Minority	Small Minority	Small Minority	Small Minority	Small Minority	Small Minority

first convenient parking space and the whole party walking to the theatre. Most theatregoers would drive to the theatre in preference to using public transportation at additional expense and inconvenience if they could park. Many of them prefer the neighborhood movie or home television over the metropolitan theatre for, though access to the metropolitan area is usually easy on parkways and super highways, traffic congestion and the absence of parking facilities in the immediate vicinity of the theatre make the trip an ordeal. From the foregoing tables it is apparent that facilities for easy handling of motor-borne traffic are of increasing importance to the theatre owner. There are two principal problems: loading facilities and parking.

Loading Facilities

The amount of curb space which is available for discharging passengers at the theatre is limited by the length of the theatre wall facing the street or through driveway. Simple calculation based on the foregoing figures and tables will show that only the metropolitan urban motion picture presentation houses can have adequate curb-loading facilities. Other theatres will have congestion even if the curb extends around all four sides of the theatre. Under fortunate circumstances such congestion might be only momentary, but the showman is interested in the

Extended loading for two lines of cars under cover. Washington National Airport.

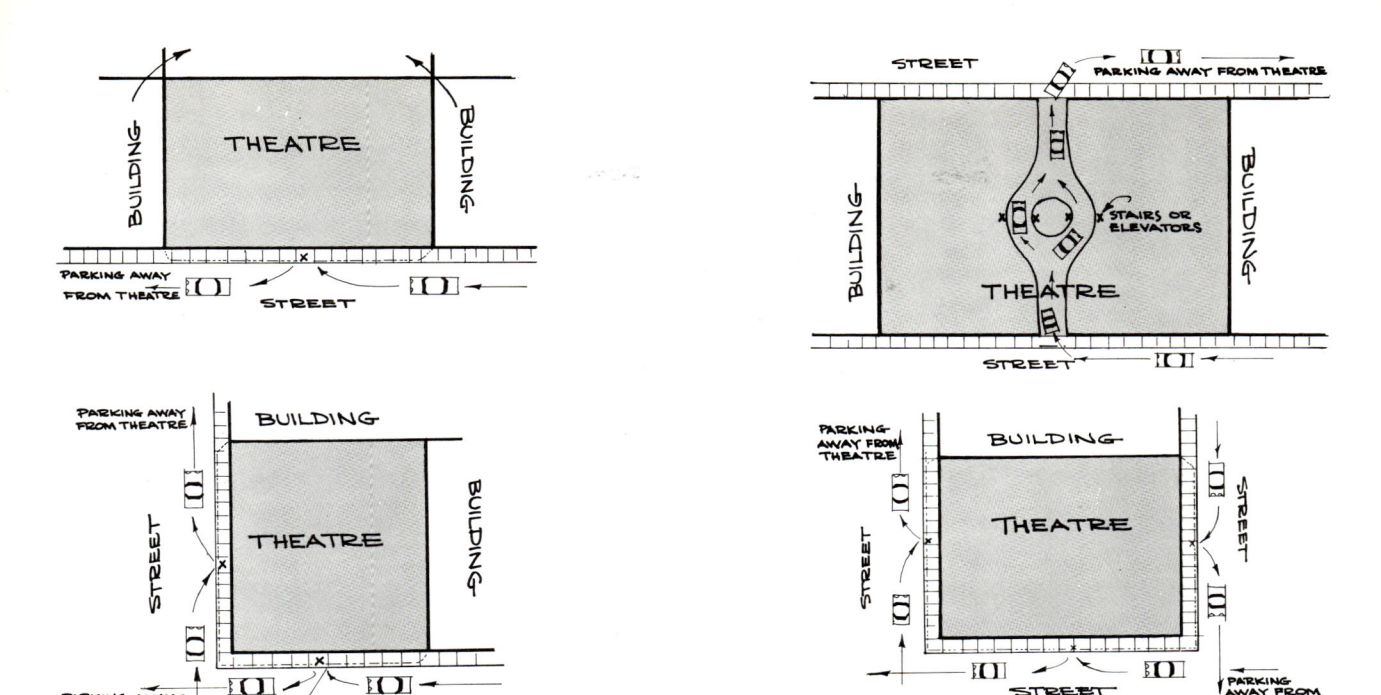

The longer the street frontage, the more ample the loading facility. Driveway through the building affords shelter and reduces congestion on the street.

patron who is trying to discharge passengers at that moment. It follows, then, that no plan to facilitate the approach of traffic to the theatre is likely to be overelaborate; that no length of curb at front, side, or even back, of the theatre is too long. It is also axiomatic that driveways around the theatre be one-way, and at least two lanes wide; that the sidewalk be at least 10 feet wide and that the marquee cover all the curb-loading area. Where snow is a problem, walks not covered should be heated.

The problem of curb-loading for metropolitan urban theatres cannot usually be solved by private driveways extending around the house because of high land costs. Therefore there is considerable advantage in having a theatre which occupies an entire block, as is the case with the old Metropolitan Opera House where marquees cover substantial portions of three sides of the theatre. Where as many as two sides face the street, it is possible to provide for discharge of passengers and loading underneath the theatre, as is the case with Severance Hall in Cleveland. Several new theatres provide for loading and parking under the theatre and under adjacent plazas.

Cars may be guided into proper approach lanes by signs in the highways and by curbs in the pavement. Multilevel ramps may further divide motor traffic and direct it toward the parking garage and toward loading curbs at various levels of the house.

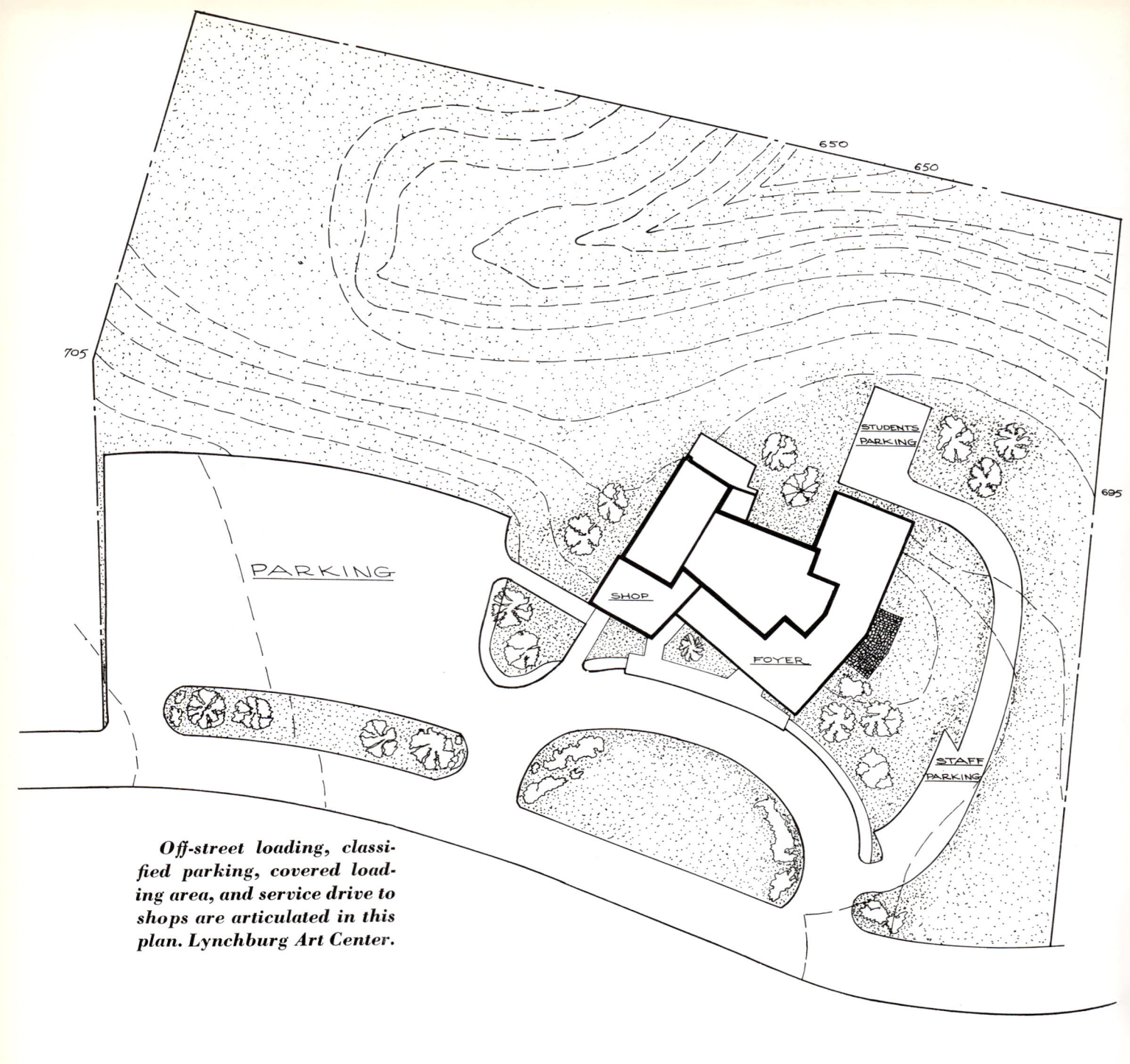

Off-street loading, classified parking, covered loading area, and service drive to shops are articulated in this plan. Lynchburg Art Center.

Parking   Suburban theatres with their own parking lots large enough to handle one-third as many cars as there are seats in the house often find that the capacity of the parking lot is taxed. It is probable that legitimate theatres and urban motion picture theatres would attract larger and more dependable audiences if easily accessible parking facilities existed. Since land costs, except in suburban and rural areas, are usually too high to make it feasible for the showman to plan parking facilities for the theatre alone, he must look upon his parking problem as one which is part of the whole community problem, particularly that of enterprises near the theatre. Before 1940, parking for the Radio City theatres was no problem except at matinees and occasional times of congestion such as New Year's Eve. The Rockefeller Center Garage, taxed to capacity in the daytime, could handle cars coming to Radio City theatres in the evening. If parking space is provided near the theatre, it may well earn its keep from daytime, nontheatrical patronage. When a theatre is built as part of a shopping center, the parking problem is well solved, even for matinees, in most cases.

Motor transportation and its components, loading and parking, are problems common to many urban and suburban enterprises and as such have been taken under study by traffic specialists and urban planners. The theatre planner will do well to consult these experts to see that their plans and ideas are in accord with the needs of the theatre in these respects. Solutions of these problems in recent urban-renewal projects have simultaneously overcome the problem of audience access to theatres in urban centers.

The Encino Theatre, Los Angeles. A convenient arrangement for parking around a theatre, but only a partial solution to the problem because the fifty-one cars accommodated will transport only about one quarter the orchestra seating capacity. W. L. Pereira, architect.

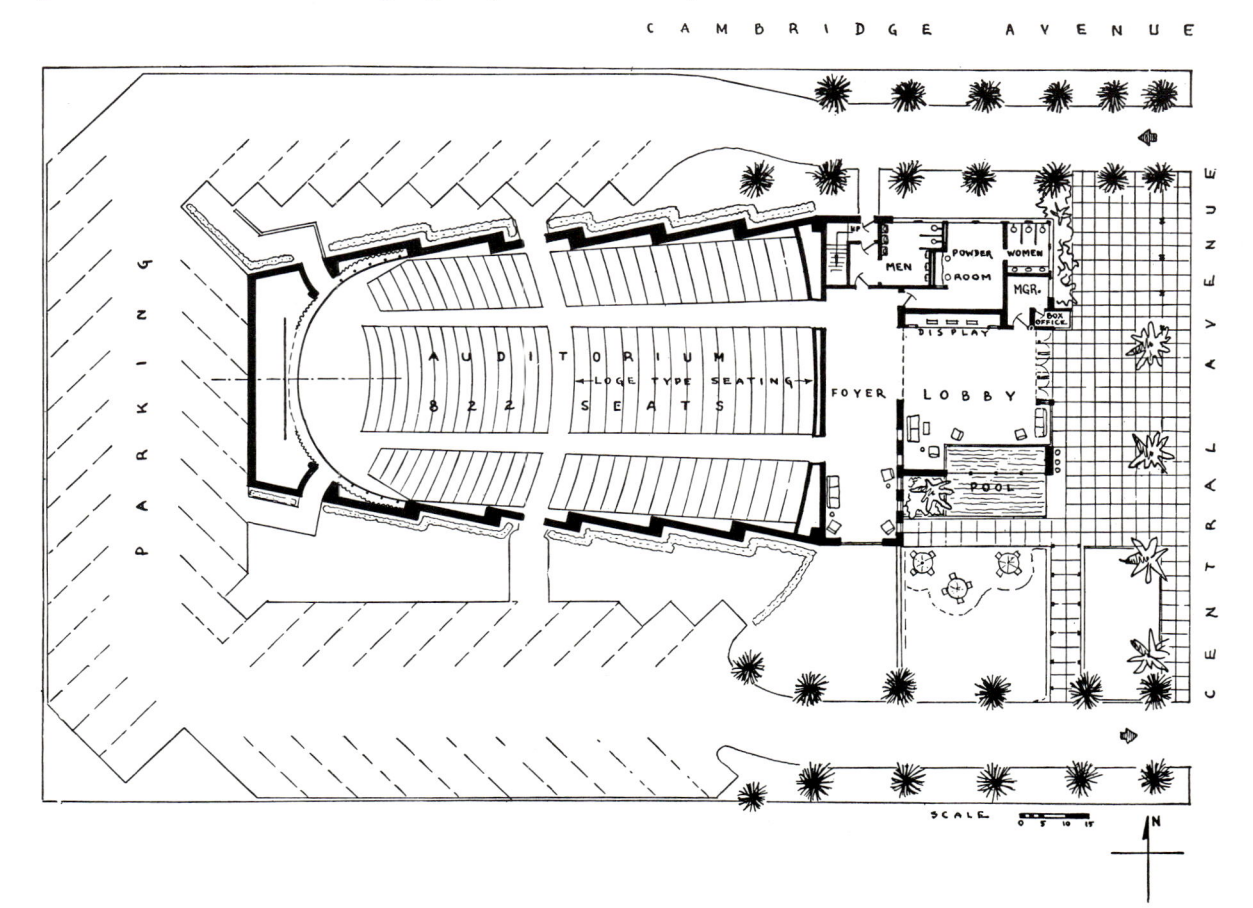

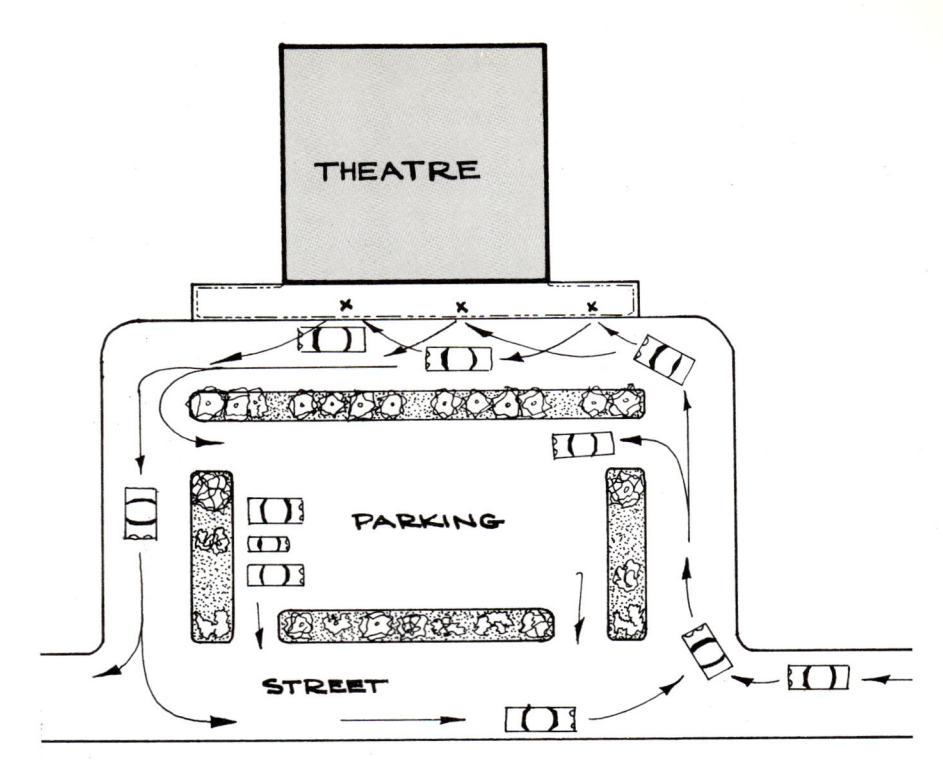

Rotary traffic to theatre and parking lot. Theatre is removed from highway noise. Late arrivals are sent directly to parking lot to reduce noise near theatre.

Parking under plaza of the Queen Elizabeth Theatre, Vancouver.

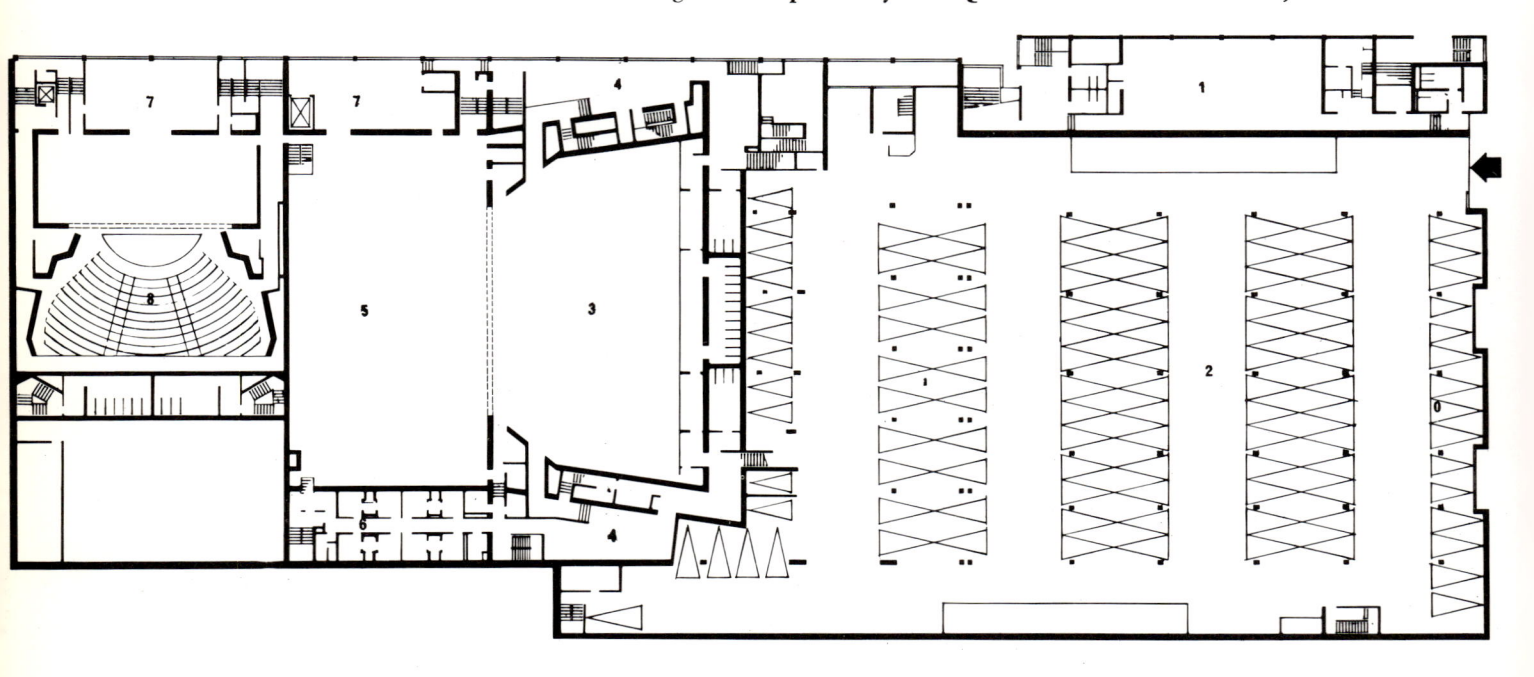

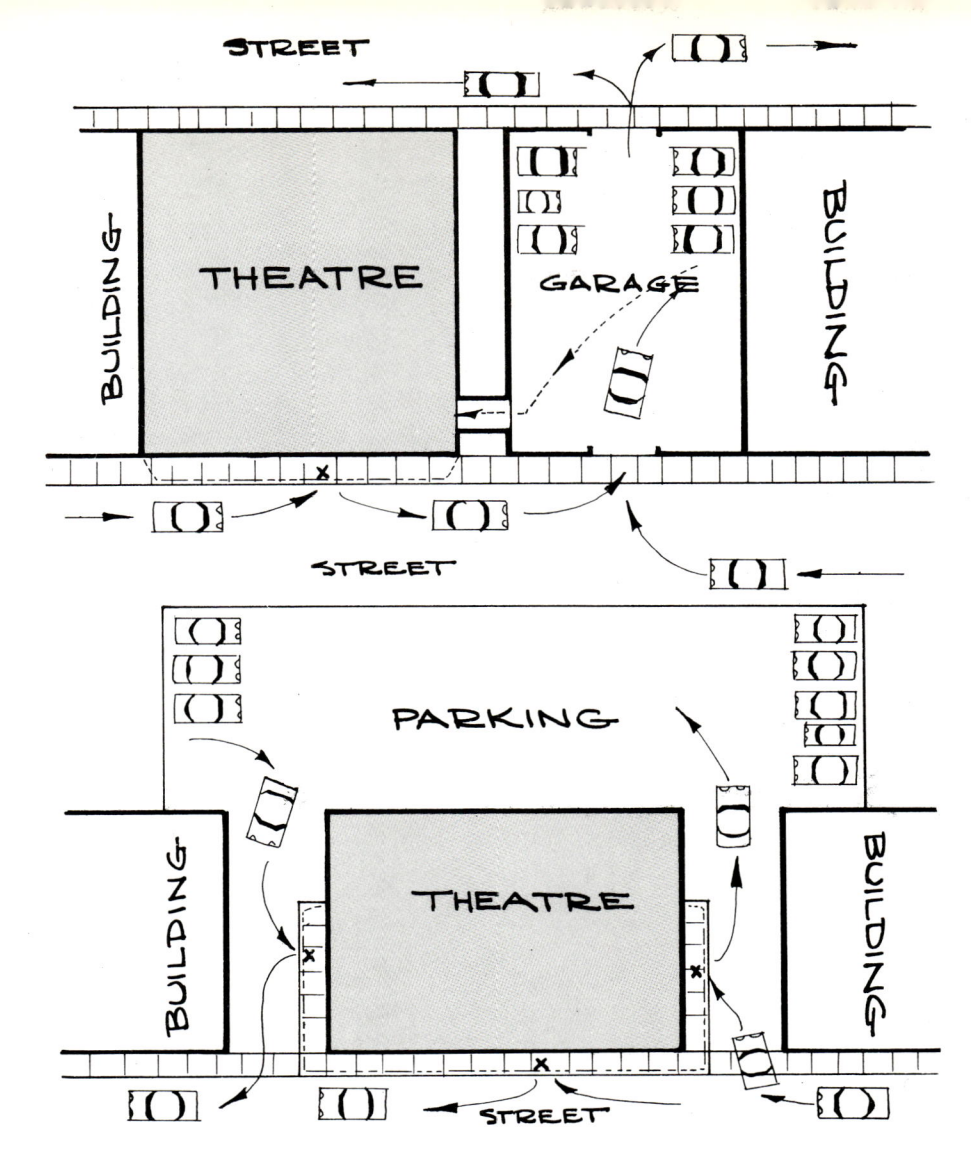

Two solutions to the parking problem: urban ABOVE *and suburban* BELOW. *One-way circulation is essential.*

Underground parking on four levels serves three performance facilities. Los Angeles Music Center. Walton Becket and Associates, architects.

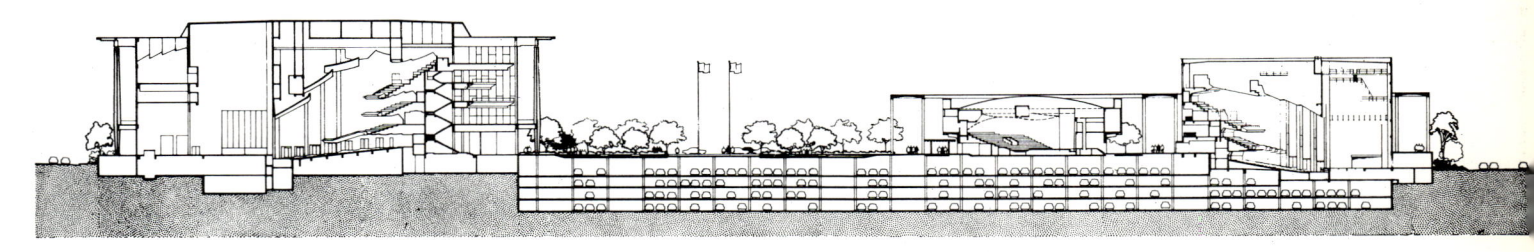

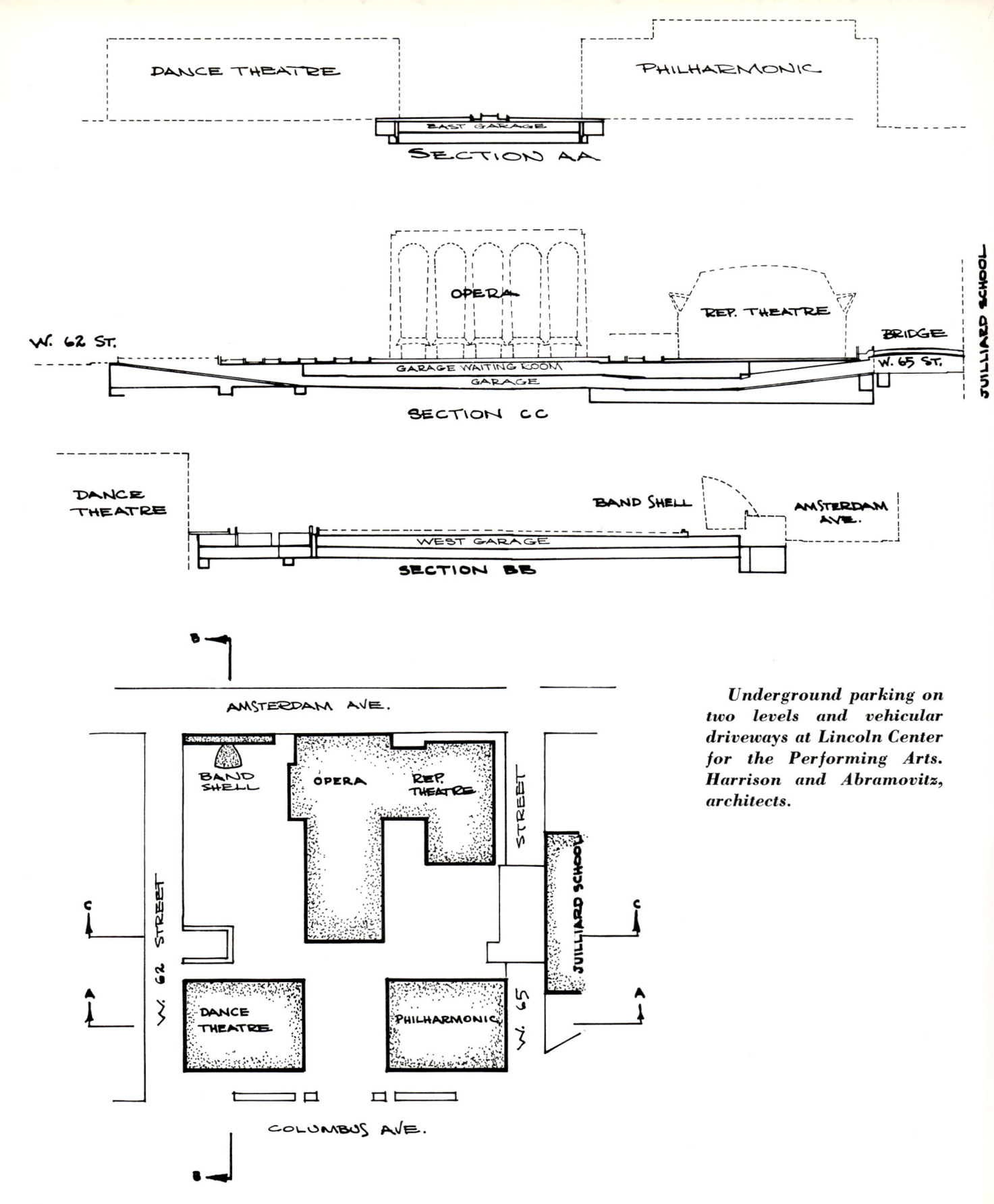

Underground parking on two levels and vehicular driveways at Lincoln Center for the Performing Arts. Harrison and Abramovitz, architects.

46

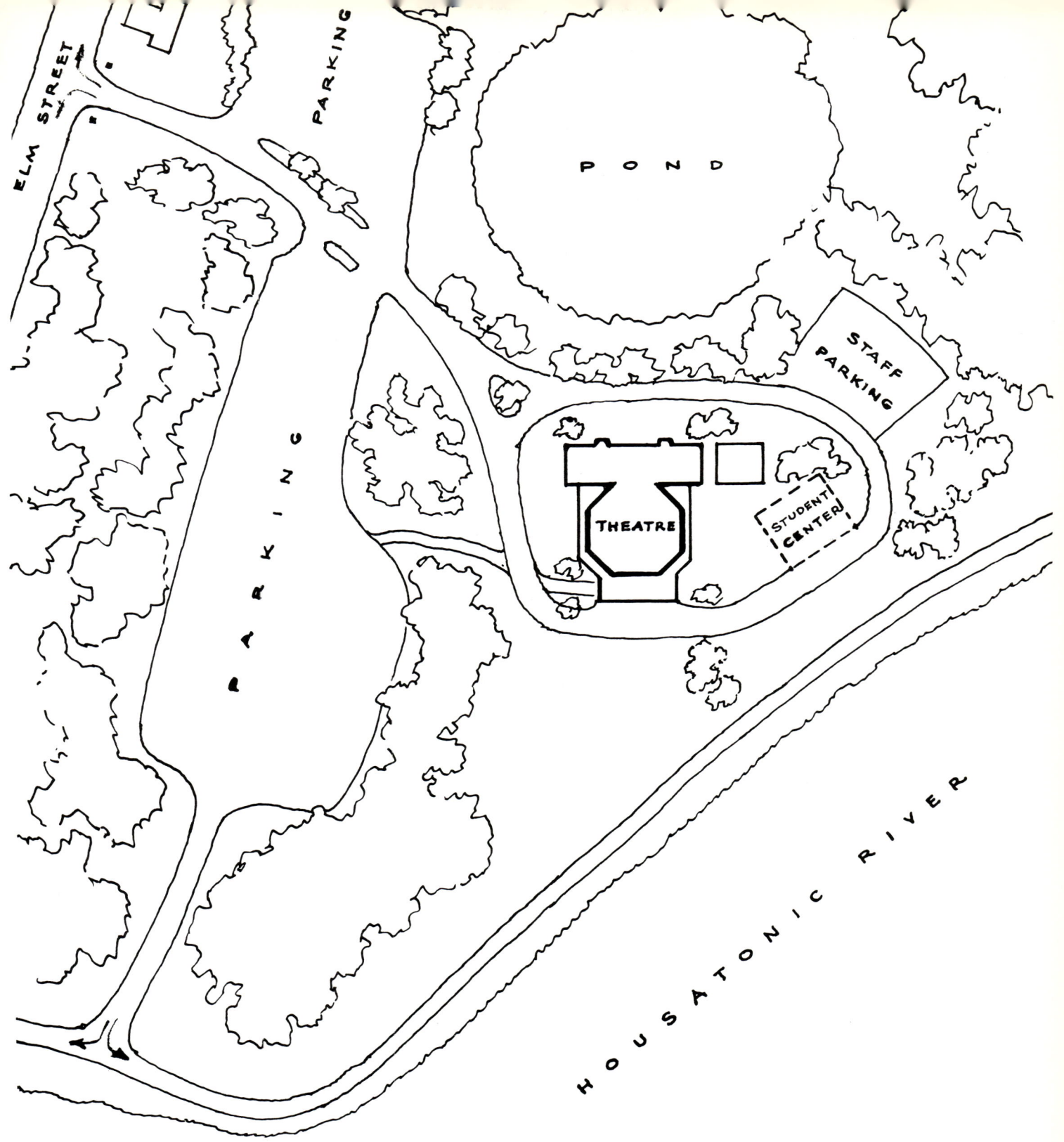

The site of the American Shakespeare Festival Theatre contains ample parking lots with one-way circulation. There are moorings nearby for water-borne patrons.

Site Curb-loading and parking facilities constitute an extremely important consideration in the original siting of the theatre, in planning architectural revision of the plant, in policy concerning acquisition of abutting property and in collaboration with enterprises in the neighborhood and the municipality. In Garden City, Long Island, many parking lots are situated behind the buildings which face the street in the business zone. Such an arrangement has obvious advantages for the showman. He may find it to his advantage to build a theatre near a municipal parking lot; in fact it is now generally agreed among suburban motion picture exhibitors that they have more to gain by locating their theatres where access and parking are easy rather than on a congested main street.

The theatre in the college is often surrounded by spacious grounds which are a liability to theatre operation because patrons have to wade long distances through the heavy dew to get to the theatre, or shake the snow out of their shoes once they are there. A theatre can look just as well if a marquee surrounds a substantial portion of it, a wide paved driveway encircles it, and a parking lot is adjacent, as if it is handicapped by the want of such facilities. Parking facilities associated with athletic stadia may serve theatre patrons.

TABLE 3. Marquee to Seat

Statistically the playgoers' progress averages as follows:	Opera and Concert	Legitimate and Musical	Pictures and Presentation
% of audience which waits to meet friends in the foyer	6	10	Negligible
% of audience which buys tickets within 20 minutes of curtain time	8	20	100
Time spent in line for tickets purchased or reserved	2 to 15 min.	2 to 5 min.	Negligible
Time spent in line to ticket taker	1 min.	1 min.	0
Over-all time, curb to seat	4-12 min. depending upon location. 4 min. to box	6 min. to orch. 8 min. to mezz. 9 min. to balcony	2-5 min. depending upon location.
% of audience which checks its wraps	18	10	Negligible

Vestibule In places where weather requires, whether because of extremes of cold or extremes of heat and humidity, a vestibule serves as the first architectural barrier against the elements. Substantially a passageway, it may be equipped with special circulation of warm air and may be pressurized to keep either cold or hot, humid air from entering the foyer.

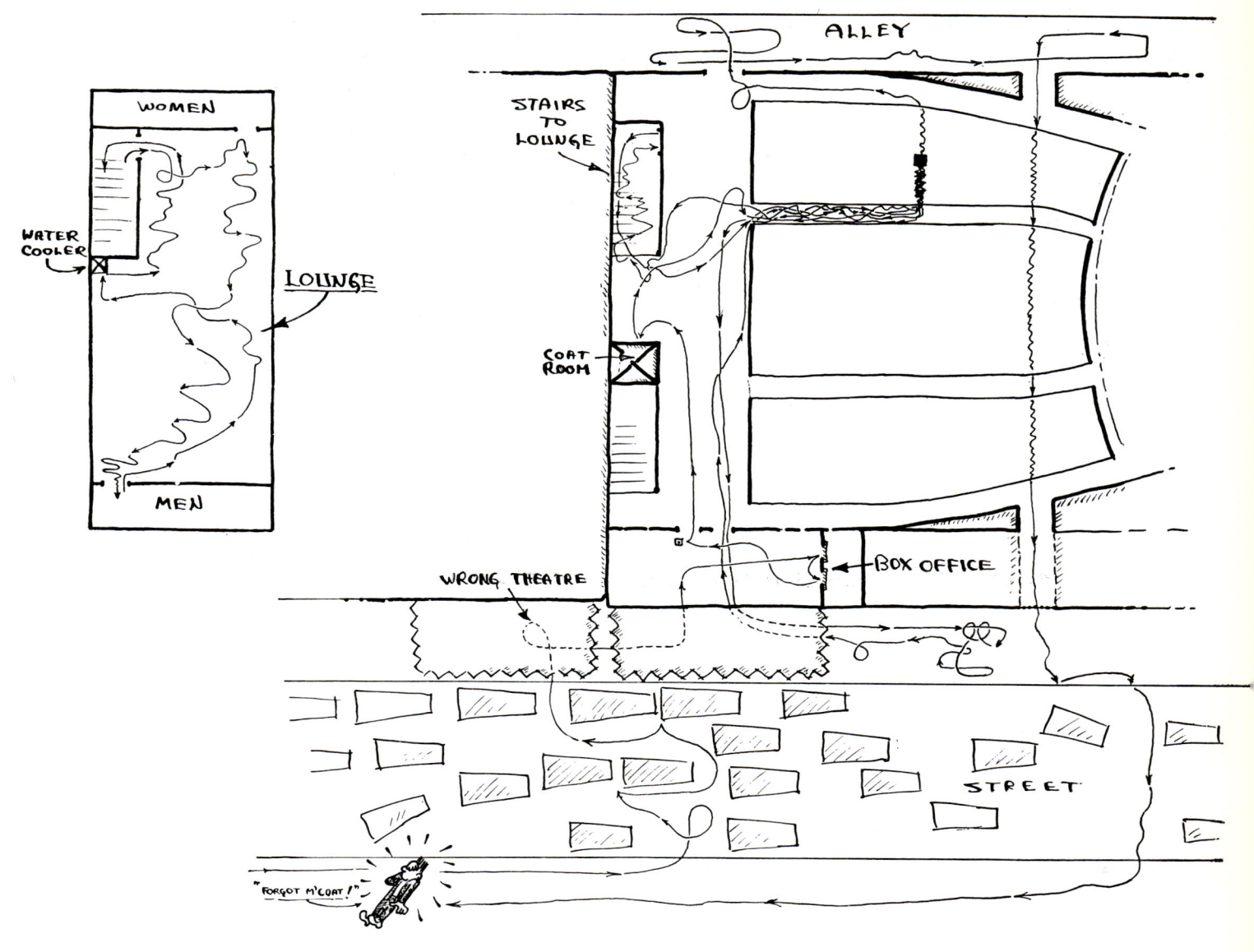

Playgoer's progress, New York, 1964. Retained from first edition, 1949; the conditions have not changed.

The first hiatus in the smooth flow of audience traffic is the waiting line for tickets. There is no occasion for this at a newsreel theatre with a turnstile entrance. The line waiting at the advance sale window for a popular production is often long, and patrons may stand for hours. For the average legitimate house (capacity approximately 1200), one ticket window can usually handle seat purchases by that portion of the audience which buys immediately preceding curtain time. The architect's concern with these hiatuses is in providing a comfortable foyer and enough ticket windows so located and arranged as to make possible as speedy a sale of tickets as the management may find efficient.

Foyer

In addition to accommodating ticket queues, the foyer must provide space for members of the audience waiting to meet friends. While fulfilling these functions, the foyer must be so arranged that the patron who has his ticket can pass through without getting tangled in the queues or being obstructed by the waiting patrons.

Foyer Area per Seat

A reasonable minimum allowance in anticipation of periods of congestion is one square foot per theatre seat.

No less important than the foyer capacity is its arrangement. Patrons waiting for friends habitually stand just inside the doors. Therefore doors are best placed on the long dimension of the foyer. Patrons having seats bought in advance must cross the foyer, therefore the direction of queues at ticket windows must be so arranged as not to interfere with the straight path from foyer door to lobby door. These two requirements are sometimes well met by having the foyer doors to the street on two sides and establishing queues to ticket windows along the third side, or by building the foyer around the corner of the lobby and keeping the queue line and ticket windows on the side where lobby entrances are not located. It is obvious that there should be direct access to the foyer on all sides of the theatre where there is a marquee.

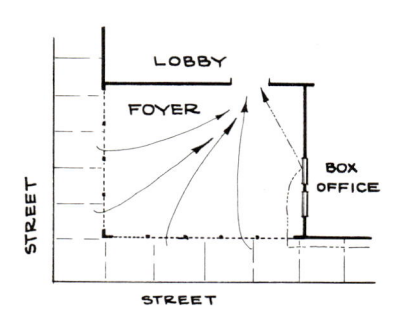

Inadequate space for a box-office queue.

Exhibition foyer serves as intermission space for concert hall, recital hall, gallery, and theatre and as a thoroughfare during class hours. Fine Arts Center, University of New Mexico. Holien and Buckley, architects.

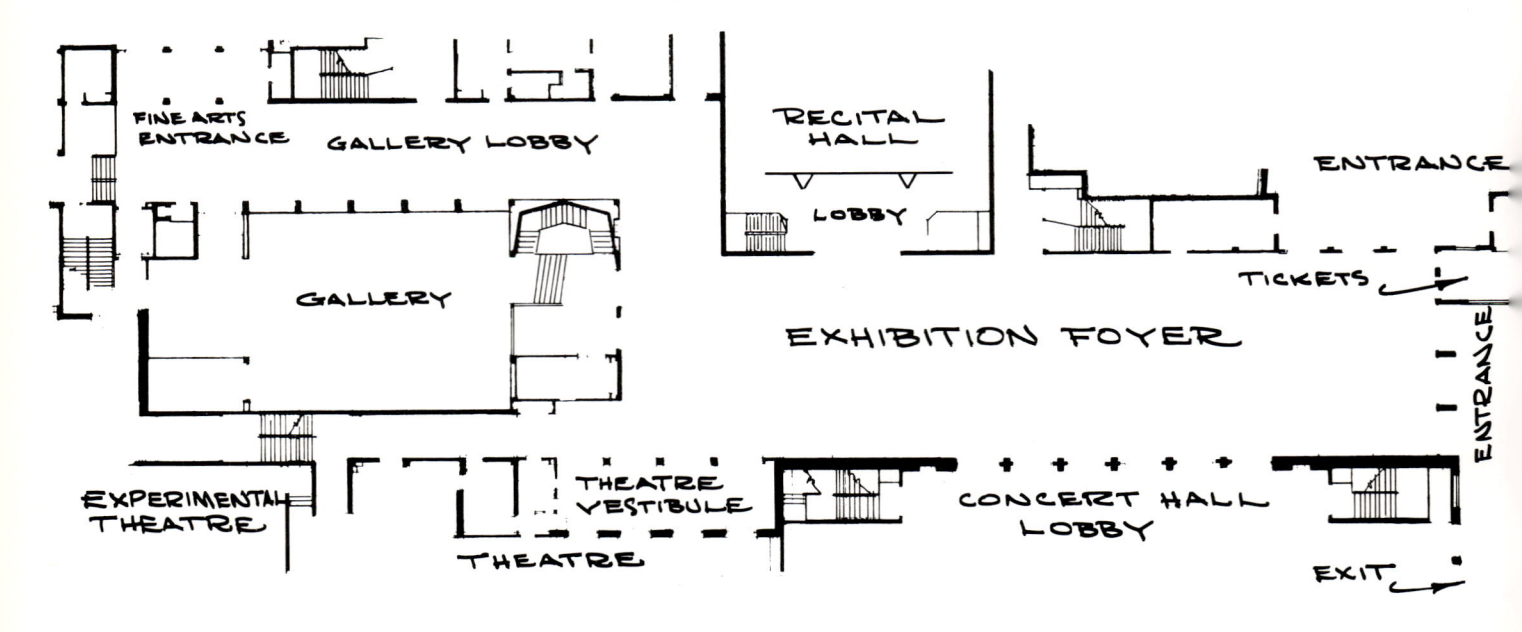

The ticket taker presides over the next traffic bottleneck. His entrance can easily be planned to facilitate through traffic but it must also be opposite a portion of the lobby affording short, straight paths to aisles, staircases, and elevators. No position has been discovered to date better than on the center line of the house. For legitimate production, a single entrance door can usually handle 1000 to 1500 persons. Since building codes require entrance-exit doors on the street at the rate of approximately one five-foot door to every 300 persons of audience, the bottleneck is not in the amount of entrance space but rather in the number of ticket takers. Auxiliary entrance doors, if used, should be adjacent to the first since the path of movement from street, through foyer, to lobby, will not thereby be forced to deviate. The lobby is principally a distribution area. Like the foyer its efficiency is measured not only by its size but by its arrangement. If the head usher standing inside the lobby door can direct each patron to his aisle or staircase by a route which will not involve the crossing of the route of any other patron, or even having tangential contact therewith, the lobby may be small but adequate.

Lobby

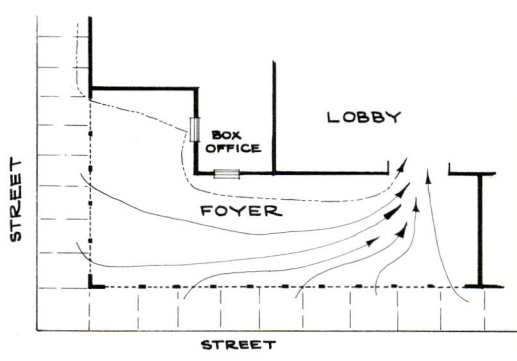

Space for box office queue separate from through traffic.

The complicating factors in lobby design are access to the coatrooms and to the lounge. Obviously, the coatroom is most efficiently located where the entering line will pass it before dividing. Where adequate checkroom facilities exist almost every member of the audience checks something. Theatre is one of a few forms of indoor entertainment at which patrons carry their outer garments with them. There is little logic in this and certainly neither comfort nor pleasure.

As far as lobby design is concerned, there must be enough length of coatroom counter and sufficient floor area to make it possible to check wraps as rapidly as the audience moves. This requirement is seldom met in America. Many European opera houses may serve as models.

Checking Facilities

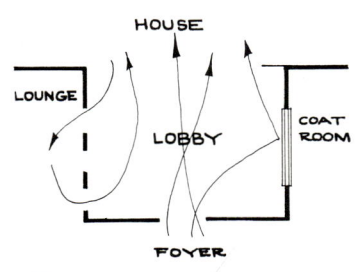

Pattern of traffic in lobby.

TABLE 4. Lobby Area Per Seat

Opera House	2 sq. ft.
Commercial Theatre	1.8 sq. ft.
Noncommercial Theatre	
School	1.2 sq. ft.
College and University	1.4 sq. ft.
Community	1.4 sq. ft.
Intimate Motion Picture	1 sq. ft.
Summer Theatre	1 sq. ft.

Composite audience flow chart.

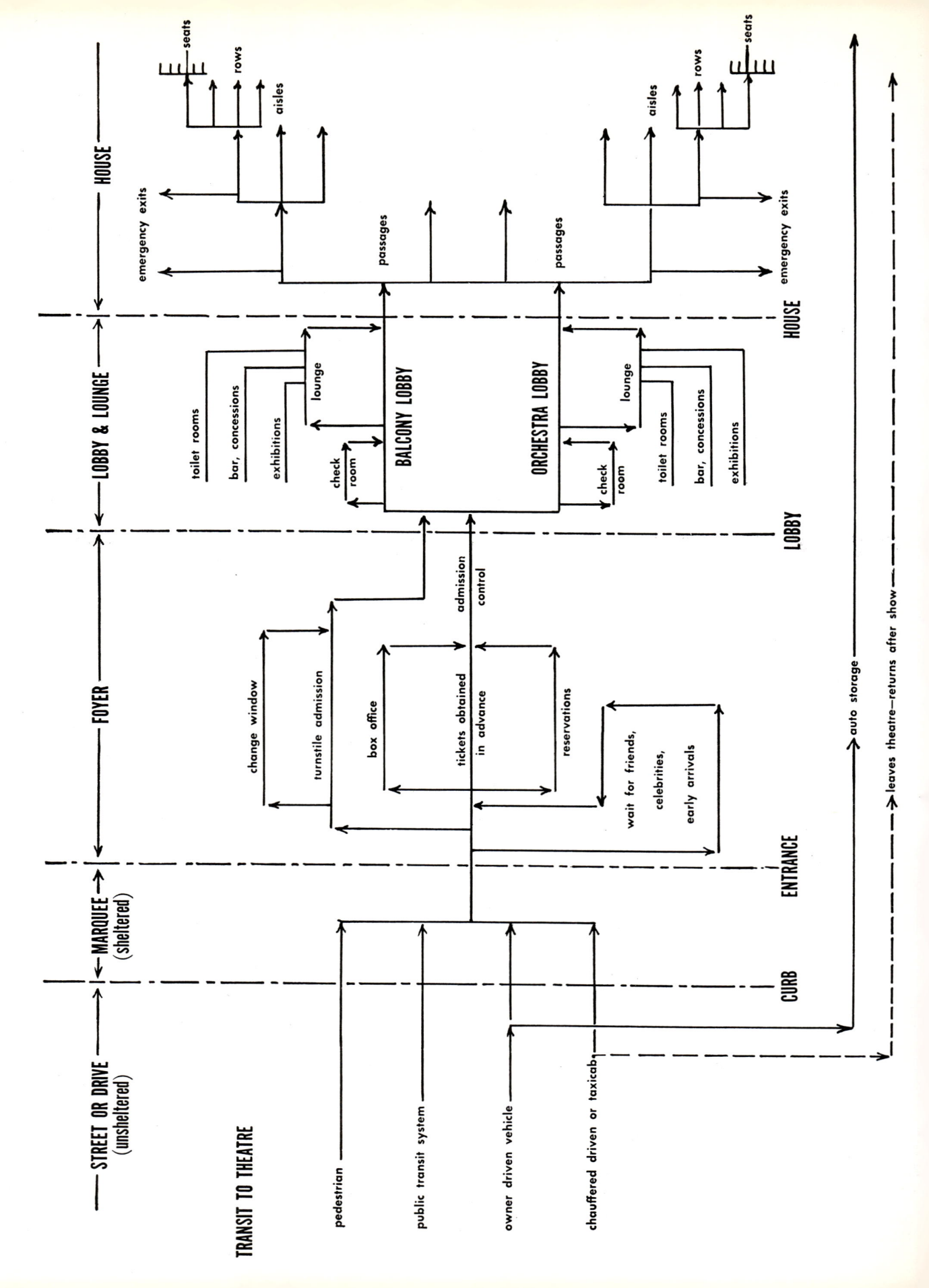

Access to the lounge is from the lobby. Lobby planning involves locating lounge doors so that traffic to and from the lounge will logically follow a one-way path. The same rules which govern orchestra lobby planning apply to balcony lobbies. As in the case of the foyer, lobby area is, relatively, not as important as *lobby arrangement*. The theatre with a fixed-hour performance must provide for peak lobby loads which never occur in continuous run houses. However, as has been pointed out, it is generally unwise to plan for one type of production only. Lobby areas which have been found to be adequate where arrangement is average to good are stated in Table 4.

For house capacities above 1500, incoming audience congestion may be relieved by the provision of separate foyers, box offices, ticket takers, lobbies, and passages for subdivisions of the house, viz., orchestra, dress circle, mezzanine, balcony, or left, center, and right. Very little congestion occurred in the seating of 8400 people for four performances daily of Billy Rose's New York World's Fair (1939) Aquacade, thanks to the multiplicity of entrances and clear paths of movement inside the gates.

In calculating floor area per theatre seat to satisfy building ordinances, the areas of foyer and lobby are added.

Though, as shown in the audience flow chart, the functions of foyer and lobby are different and the admissions control is located between them, it is possible for both to be in one architectural enclosure, provided that there is other adequate sound isolation of the house from outside noises and there is a portable barrier—panels, screens or velvet-covered rope—guiding the audience through the admissions control. Removal of the portable barrier makes the two areas into one large area for intermissions or for social functions.

Foyer-Lobby Combinations

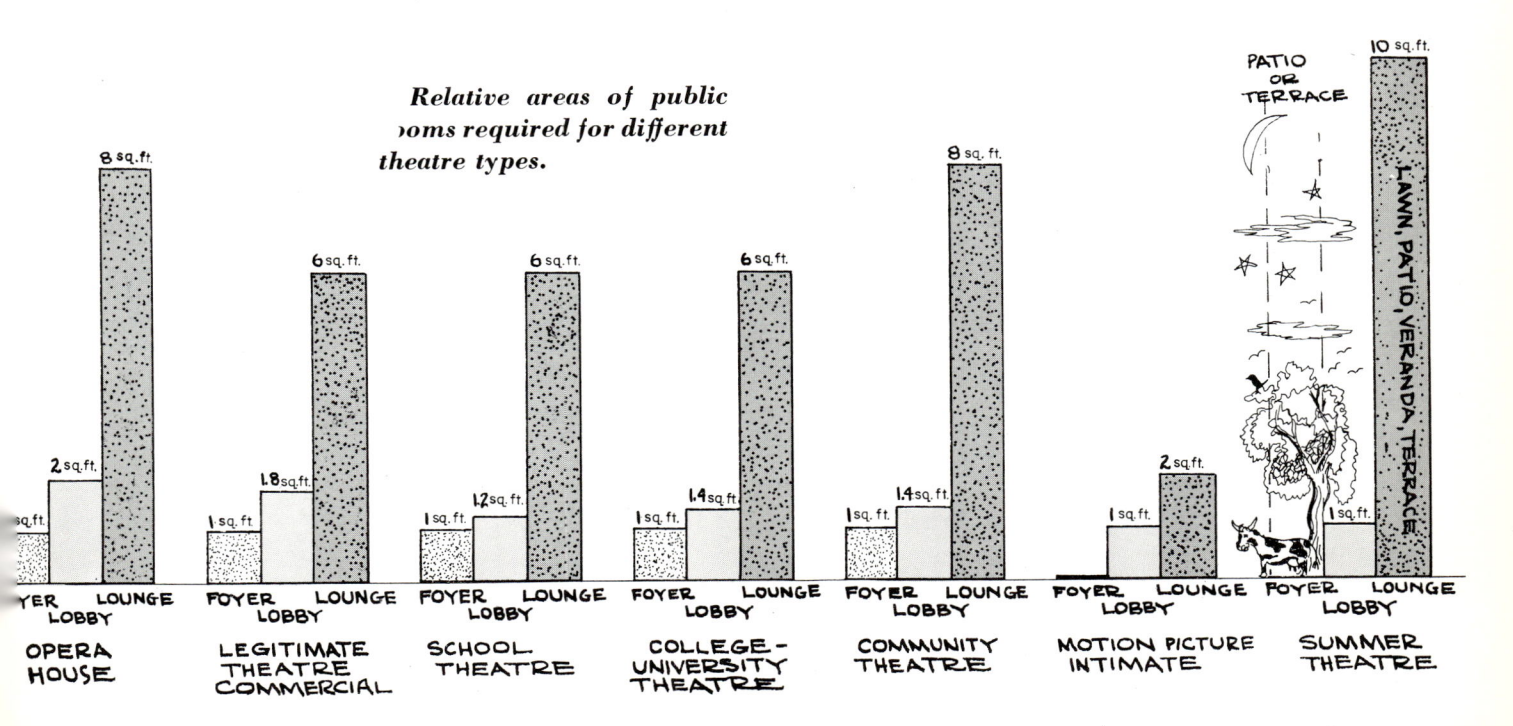

Relative areas of public rooms required for different theatre types.

Theatre Type	Foyer	Lobby	Lounge
OPERA HOUSE	1 sq. ft.	2 sq. ft.	8 sq. ft.
LEGITIMATE THEATRE COMMERCIAL	1 sq. ft.	1.8 sq. ft.	6 sq. ft.
SCHOOL THEATRE	1 sq. ft.	1.2 sq. ft.	6 sq. ft.
COLLEGE-UNIVERSITY THEATRE	1 sq. ft.	1.4 sq. ft.	6 sq. ft.
COMMUNITY THEATRE	1 sq. ft.	1.4 sq. ft.	8 sq. ft.
MOTION PICTURE INTIMATE	1 sq. ft.	2 sq. ft.	—
SUMMER THEATRE	1 sq. ft.	—	10 sq. ft. (PATIO OR TERRACE / LAWN, PATIO, VERANDA, TERRACE)

54

▲ *Outdoor lobby in a benign climate. The John Fitzgerald Kennedy Theatre, University of Hawaii. McAuliffe, Young and Associates, I. M. Pei and Associates, architects.*

◀ **The lobby, Philharmonic Hall, Lincoln Center.**

Crossovers

The best condition of traffic exists when there are passages from lobby to house directly in line with every aisle. When the plan renders this impossible, the crossover behind the seating area is part of the path followed by the audience between lobby and aisle. Since the crossover may have to carry at peak load the combined traffic of several aisles, its minimum width must be the combined width of the aisles it serves. In addition it furnishes standing room for those waiting to be shown to seats and for those who buy standing room. Ample crossover width is essential in motion picture houses where the crossover is generally used to accommodate four ranks of standing patrons. The motion picture house

Admission control by portable barriers which are removed after the audience has been seated. American Shakespeare Festival Theatre.

Lobby and box offices, Arena Stage, Washington. Stairs lead up to lounge and theatre, under stairs to working areas at stage level.

finds its peak crossover load at change of program. For this reason the normally planned crossover width must be increased to accommodate people waiting for seats. In legitimate houses, fire regulations usually forbid more than a single rank standing in the crossover. Since these people are close to the lobby, they are not in the way at the time of peak traffic. Arena and open stage theatres in which the audience surrounds all or a large part of the stage are not exempt from these considerations.

Crossover congestion in many theatres arises from assigning the lobby function to the crossover and from terminating balcony stairs in the orchestra crossover. Such practices produce discomfort and increase panic hazards.

Aisles

The load for which building codes require the width of aisles to be planned occurs when a capacity audience leaves the theatre at one time in an emergency. From this safety requirement is also derived minimum seat spacing. The location of aisles in American theatres is governed by a code requirement, generally prevalent, which limits the number of seats between aisles to fourteen and the number of seats between an aisle and a wall to seven. Minimum seat spacing provided in the codes is too close for comfort and, therefore, too close to be considered by the theatre planner. If seats are spaced farther apart than the code provides, the number of people served by a code-width aisle is thereby

Lobby, Hopkins Center Theatre, Dartmouth College, a student thoroughfare to art galleries, studios, post office, lecture-concert hall, workshops, music departments and snack bar. Stairs up to a student lounge and balcony of theatre.

reduced and congestion is minimized. Nevertheless, the safety-minimum-width aisle is seldom adequate for peak loads of audience entering or leaving through the lobby, but not using the emergency exits. To eliminate congestion when a capacity audience leaves the theatre by this means, aisles must be wider than code minimum. The width may be calculated on a rate of flow basis, as developed by the National Board of Fire Underwriters.

Continental Seating

Some codes allow as an alternate plan the so-called continental seating in which there may be any number of seats between aisles, provided seat spacing, aisles, and exits satisfy concomitant special requirements. For continental seating, it is necessary to make the side aisles wide enough to

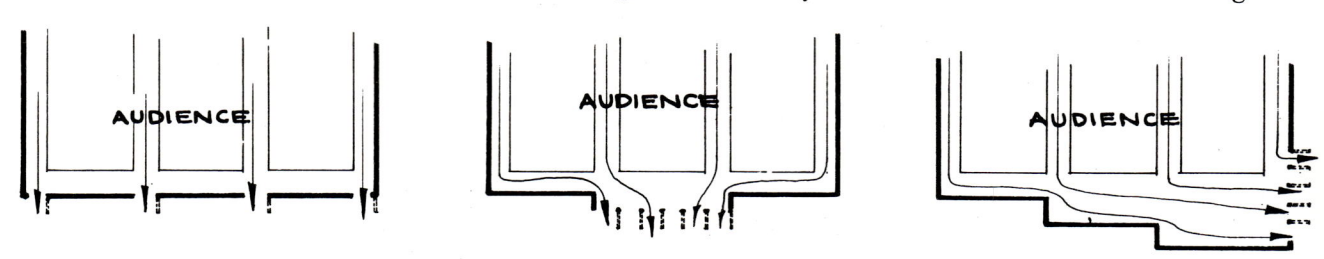

The width of the cross aisle equals the sum of the widths of the aisles.

permit emptying the house within the time allowed under local fire ordinances or to plan numerous side wall exits into corridors.

Minimum code requirements for safety, generally prevalent, do not produce comfort. Traffic and comfort must determine seat spacing. Under minimum code spacing, patrons cannot pass other seated patrons. This condition is barely remedied with a seat spacing of 36 inches and is adequately overcome by a spacing of 42 inches. Since the depth of seat-back upholstery is a factor, the type of seat must be specified before spacing can be accurately planned.

A type of seat has been developed which can be slid back by the person seated in it and which also folds up when not occupied to afford adequate clear passage whether seats are empty or occupied. With one version of this type, the back-to-back spacing can be held to 36 inches in continental seating.

The theatre patron is often annoyed by the fact that the curtain is 7 to 15 minutes late. It is common practice to attempt to get it up 7 minutes after the advertised time. This delay theoretically provides the necessary time to seat patrons who are in the theatre at the advertised curtain time. In most commercial, legitimate and musical houses the time is insufficient, the curtain is further delayed, and people are standing in the aisles when the curtain goes up. Bad weather brings an increased number of cabs, further taxes the curb-loading area and coatroom, and further delays the curtain. Bad audience manners, to some extent stimulated by the knowledge of congestion at curtain time, tend to delay the curtain further. The architect is concerned with facilities for getting people to their seats expeditiously. The theatre management cannot train the audience in punctuality if conditions conducive to congestion are built into the theatre.

Seating

The chamber music auditorium, an intimate theatre of the Malmö Municipal Theatre. Seats are wide and generously spaced consistent with continental seating.

TABLE 5. Intermission Routine

	Opera and Concert	Legitimate and Musical	Optimum
% of audience which leaves seats during intermissions	75	60	100
Walking time: seat to lounge	4 min.	4 min.	2 min.
Time in lavatory line	1 min.	6 min.	0
Time spent in line at check room after show	3 min.	5 min.	0
Seat to curb time (without check room stop)	5 min.	6 min.	2 min.
Waiting time for cab or car	0 to 15 min.	0 to 15 min.	0 min.

Intermission and Exit Traffic

Gregariousness, a desire for a smoke or refreshment, and uncomfortable seats drive many of the audience to lounge, lobby and foyer during intermissions. Those who remain seated often do so because the public rooms are too congested. For those who leave their seats the difficulties of returning to them often exceed those of getting seated at the start of the show.

Inadequate lobby and lounge facilities in a New York theatre force the audience onto the sidewalk during the intermission. A recent improvement has been the installation of radiant heating units in the marquees.

These facts viewed in conjunction with the foregoing tables establish conditions which militate against theatregoing. They are to be contrasted with facilities for audience handling and comfort provided in presentation and news motion picture houses. There is this additional fact to consider: adequate, even luxurious, facilities for audience comfort in a presentation or news movie may be inadequate for a fixed performance where all facilities are used at the same time by the whole audience. A number of theatres, built during the last decade, particularly civic opera houses and civic and academic art centers, have adequate public rooms and easy access to them. To make it possible for the audience to keep its attention on the show, instead of fretting at bodily discomfort, unimpeded traffic to and from the lounge, and adequate lounge area must be provided.

In theatres so designed, particularly in Europe, the whole audience usually leaves its seats during intermission. As the audience proceeds from seat to aisle, to crossover, to lobby, to lounge, and back again, paths of movement must not cross; therefore, lounge entrance from lobby must be close to the crossover and easily distinguishable. If the exit from the lounge to the lobby is less plainly visible, and located farther away from the seat area than is the entrance, a natural circulatory traffic movement will develop, and persons entering and leaving the lounge will not collide in the lobby.

Lounge

Traffic in the lounge itself is to bar, refreshment stand, and lavatories. Lavatories located left and right of, and close to the lounge entrance, split the traffic. A bar directly in front of the entrance and across the room, and telephone near the exit, help to spread out the traffic. Traffic eddies tend to form in corners, for which reason they can best be used for chairs, ashstands, etc. Large tables and groups of chairs in the center of the lounge help to keep traffic circulating to the left. Few theatres have adequate lounge space. The figures in Table 6 may be taken as adequate but not luxurious.

Foyer, lobby, and lounge have separate functions. Astute planning may in numerous instances make it possible for the same area to serve, in part, more than one purpose, but the space requirement for each function must be observed. Lobby and lounge can be structurally combined where paths of movement are so routed that both functions can be fulfilled simultaneously without crossing. Some lounge and lobby functions may be filled in school or college buildings by facilities having uses (*e. g., exhibition hall*) other than those demanded by the theatre. The theatre which because of season or climate can use a garden, lawn, or patio for lobby, lounge or both, need have no public room congestion. In any case, almost everybody wants to leave his seat during intermission. The total public area must therefore be adequate to accommodate the whole audience.

TABLE 6. Lounge Area Per Seat

Opera House	8 sq. ft.
Commercial Theatre	6 sq. ft.
Noncommercial Theatre	
School	6 sq. ft.
College and University	6 sq. ft.
Community	8 sq. ft.
Motion Picture	
Palace and Presentation	1 sq. ft.
Intimate	2 sq. ft.
Neighborhood	1 sq. ft.
Summer Theatre	10 sq. ft. out of doors (veranda, lawn, garden, patio)

Final Curtain

Aisles, passageways, lobby, foyers, marquee, and curb have peak loads at the end of the show. The theatre patron's return home is surrounded by conditions identical with those that obtained when he came to the theatre save that they are met in reverse order, and (1) buses, street cars, and subway trains do not run as often, and (2) in inclement weather there may be a taxi shortage. Different also is the fact that arrival was spread over 20 to 30 minutes and departure is simultaneous for the whole audience. The use of auxiliary exits, ample marquees for shelter against weather, maximum loading curbs, and efficient parking lot management are essential, if the theatregoer's final impression is to be favorable.

The theatre planner must be diligent in separating those elements of theatregoing routine which are engendered by structural inadequacies (shivering under the marquee during intermission) from those which are germane to the process (waiting for friends in the foyer). If he is to build a useful theatre he must eliminate the former by providing facilities for the latter and thereby establish an effortless, comfortable, and pleasant routine of theatre attendance.

Elegance and glamour restored to two New York theatres by exterior and interior refurbishing and new names.

3: The audience sees

This chapter treats of the principles by which a theatre must be planned if the audience is to see the show, and the showman is to be able best to exploit the visual component of the show. The interest in and development of open stage, extended stage and arena forms have drawn attention anew to the question of what, how and how well does the audience see.

The audience comes to the theatre to see the show. This is the primary consideration governing all planning on the audience side of the proscenium. The audience generally thinks of the show as that which takes place on the stage or the screen. The competent showman, however, sees to it that the audience feels itself part of the show from the moment it comes within sight of the theatre until it has turned the corner after leaving. He endeavors to make the impact of his showmanship felt every minute the audience is present. He must then provide, by means which the audience appreciates visually, for convenience, comfort, safety, and for the audience's desire to see and be seen, the control of attention, the elimination of distraction, the creation and maintenance of mood.

As each member of the audience enters the auditorium he wants to see the usher, the steps, the aisles, row and seat (including the hat rack), his wife's gloves (on the floor), the program, the show (at an angle and distance consistent with visual fidelity and credibility), the emergency exit, the regular exit. Many members of the audience will want to see and be seen by other playgoers. No member of the audience wants to see a silhouette of the occupant of the seat in front, the show distorted by angle to the side, above, or below, or insignificant because of distance, or an illuminated exit sign, or a twinkling galaxy of orchestra-stand lights when he is trying to pay attention to the show.

The showman wants the audience to see: walls and ceiling only as they contribute to the atmosphere of the theatre, objects of decoration which are significant as focal points in the decorative scheme and contribute to the feeling of luxury, the organ console and orchestra when they are part of the show. The showman wants to conceal from view all elements in structure or equipment which will detract from the desired atmosphere of the house or fatigue the audience, such as backstage areas sometimes visible through the wings, loud-speakers about the proscenium, stage

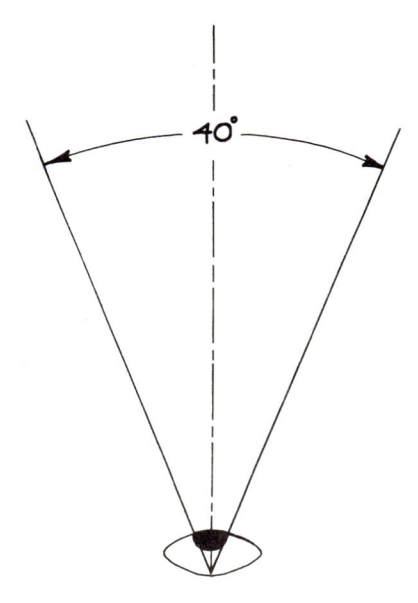

The horizontal angle of polychromatic vision (no eye movement) is approximately 40°.

lighting units (balcony pans, insufficiently masked booms at the sides of the proscenium), orchestra and organ console when their visual aspects are not essential to the show, or bright open light sources.

It is the job of the architect to satisfy completely the demands of audience and showman. To ignore or neglect any of the items listed or to fall short of a satisfactory solution of the problems implicit in them will inevitably increase hazards and impair the theatre's function and earning power.

The horizontal angle to the center line at which objects onstage, upstage of the curtain line, cease to bear the intended relationship to other objects onstage and to the background is approximately 60°. The horizontal angle to the projection screen at which distortion on the screen becomes substantially intolerable is 60°.

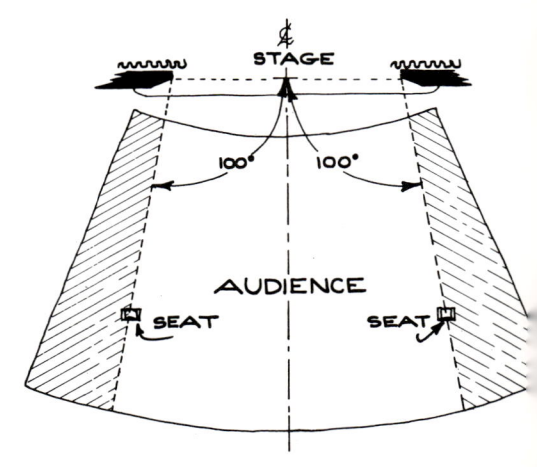

Audiences will not choose locations beyond a line approximately 100° to the curtain at the proscenium. The shaded areas contain undesirable seats.

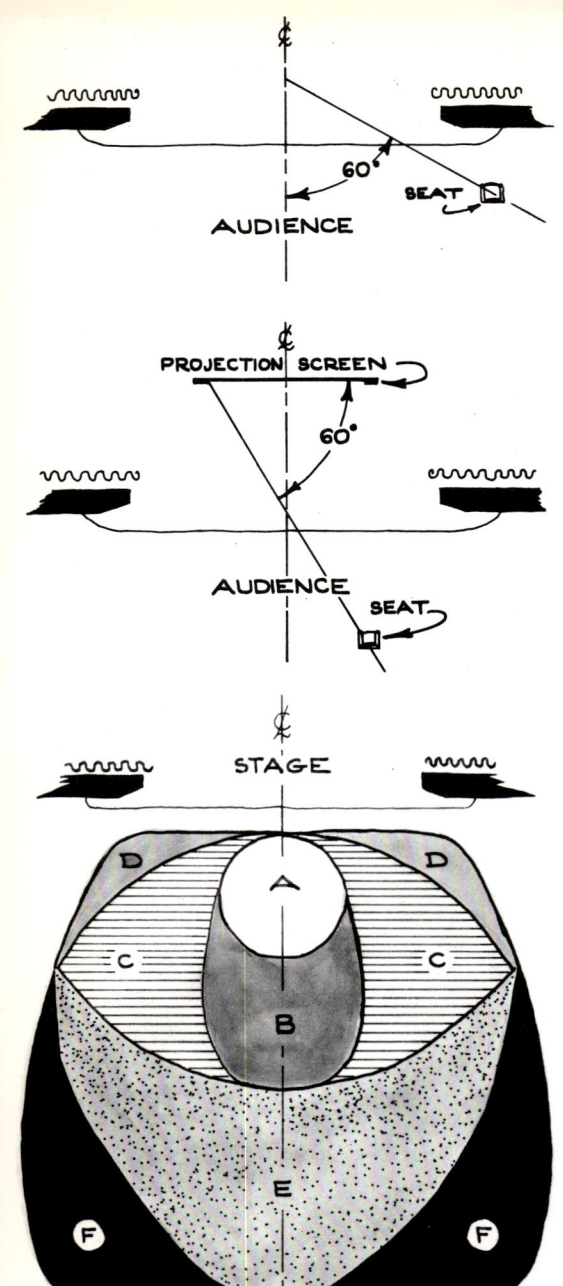

Based on the ability to recognize shapes and confirmed by sequential seat selection of unreserved seats, the order of desirability of locations is: A. front center, except when the picture screen is close to the front row; B. middle center; C. middle side; D. front side; E. rear center; F. rear side.

Sight Lines

If the patron is to see satisfactorily, plan and section must conform to a number of limitations which are set forth in the following list. To design an auditorium is to determine a seating area within these limitations and to establish position (not shape) of walls and shape of floors therefrom.

1. The horizontal angle of polychromatic vision (no eye movement) is approximately 40 degrees.
2. The horizontal angle to the center line at which objects onstage, upstage of the curtain line, cease to bear the intended relationship to other objects onstage and to the background is approximately 60 degrees.
3. The horizontal angle to a flat projection sheet at which distortion on the screen becomes substantially intolerable is 60 degrees measured to the far side of the projected image. Curvature introduced into the screen may render the distortion less from the extreme seats on the opposite side of the center line of the house but will increase distortion from the seats on the same side of the center line.

4. Judged by the audience's ability to recognize shapes, and confirmed by free audience choice of seats, the following is the order of desirability of locations:
   a. front center (except when the screen is close to the front row);
   b. middle center
   c. middle side
   d. front side
   e. rear center
   f. rear side.

5. Audiences will not choose locations beyond a line approximately 100 degrees to the curtain at the side of the proscenium.

6. The vertical angle beyond which ability to recognize standard shapes falls off very rapidly is approximately 30 degrees.

7. The recommended maximum angle of motion picture projection to the horizontal is 12 degrees.

If the foregoing limitations are applied in the horizontal plane for any given proscenium opening, they will limit an area of maximum value as seating space which is approximately elliptical. It is interesting to note that this shape for an auditorium plan was pioneered by the late Joseph Urban who had little of the present data to work with and may safely be assumed to have chosen the shape largely on esthetic grounds. A fan shape provides additional seating space at minimum sacrifice of sight lines, but nobody wants the seats in the extreme rear corners.

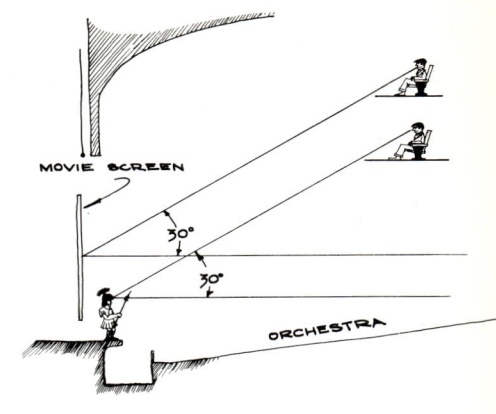

The vertical angle above which ability to recognize familiar shapes falls off very rapidly is 30°.

PLAN

A scene of direct conflict loses its visual significance to spectators outside the angles D_1-D-D_1, etc. One performer covers the other for spectators inside the angles D_1-D-D_2.

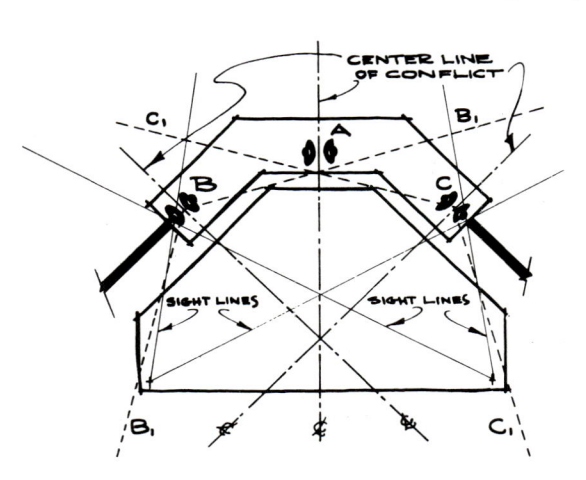

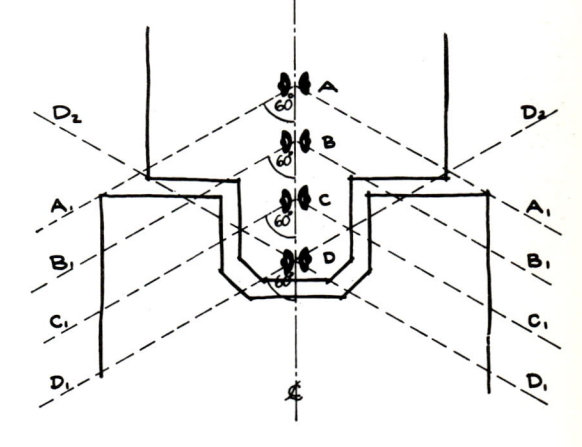

Scenes of direct conflict staged anywhere between B and C on an extended stage retain visual significance for all spectators between lines BB_1 and CC_1.

65

Seating

Occupants of all seats are visually related to the performance when the seats are oriented toward the stage. This necessitates curving the rows of seats. The center of curvature is located on the center line of the auditorium approximately the depth of the house behind the proscenium. Budgetary limitations may dictate that seats be in straight rows to simplify construction; these rows can at least be related to the center of attention on stage by being placed on chords of the optimum row curvature.

Stagger

To provide best visibility from any seat, no patron should sit exactly in front of any other patron unless more than one row distant. This requirement makes it necessary to stagger seats. Staggering is accomplished by the nonuniform placement of seats of varying widths in succeeding rows. Unless the walls of the theatre are parallel (which is acoustically hazardous), it is extremely unlikely that more than a very few rows can be made up of seats of uniform width. The lack of uniformity thereby introduced provides the means by which staggering can be accomplished. Seats are made with uniform standards and interchangeable backs and seats so that a wide variation of seat width is possible and a variation from seat to seat of an inch or two, cumulative enough to accomplish satisfactory stagger and make rows even, is not noticed by the patron.

Various seating companies have their own schemes and formulas for seat stagger, some of them patented. The client may ask a seating company for a seating plan and should examine it critically for (1) insufficient stagger in occasional areas of the house and (2) the introduction of seats narrower than the acceptable minimum.

Seating in the Park Theatre, Stockholm, is staggered to allow unobstructed vision. Seats are fully upholstered and have nearly flat backs. Continental seating. Björn Hedvall, architect.

Aisles

Aisles are of questionable desirability except in the largest houses. They must, however, be employed in many localities because of building laws which make no provision for continuous-row or so-called continental seating in which all rows are widely spaced and serve as transverse aisles. Many a bad sight line has resulted from putting the maximum legal number of seats, usually 14, into each row in every section. Obviously, for purposes of seeing, radial aisles are best, with curved aisles only slightly less efficient. Aisles perpendicular to the curtain line often have the accidental result of making side section seats undesirable because people using the aisles interrupt the view toward the stage. The box office would like a theatre with all seats in the center section. A center

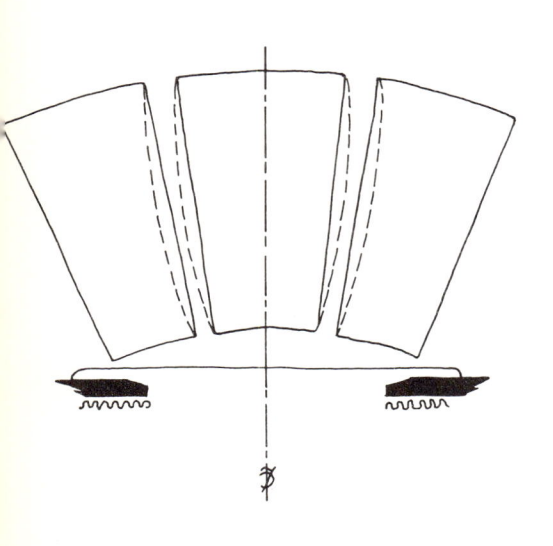

Straight radial aisles are better than aisles which curve or bend.

aisle wastes the most desirable seating area in the theatre and inevitably causes the objectionable condition of seats near the aisle being directly in front of each other.

There are many formulas used to determine the depth of the house, or more accurately, to determine the relationship between depth of house, width of house, and width of screen or proscenium. They vary considerably and are all empirically derived on the basis of existing theatres, with too little reference to whether such theatres are good or not. Typical are the following: Optimum depth equals 4 times screen width. Maximum depth equals 6 times screen width. Depth equals 1.25 to 2.35 times house width when house width is 2.5 to 3.5 times screen width. Practically, there are only two significant considerations in planning the depth of the house:

1. Visual acuity. Normal human vision can perceive a minimum dimension or separation equal to 1 minute of visual arc. Translated into space measurement this means that at 10 feet a normal eye can perceive a dimension of .035 inch, at 50 feet, .175 inch, and at 100 feet, .35 inch. Details of actors' make-up and facial expression are not plainly recognizable at distances of more than 50 feet from the stage.

2. Capacity. The larger the house, the lower can be the price per seat or the greater the gross. If the box office is not to be considered, capacity may be limited by optimum seeing requirements, and the last rows kept within 50 feet of the stage. As various requirements operate to increase capacity, the distance of the rear seats from the stage must be increased and seeing conditions impaired in proportion. The theatre operator may compensate the occupants of these seats by charging less for them. For shows involving live human actors, 75 feet is generally accepted on grounds of visibility as maximum house depth.

In theatrical entertainment which has as its chief visual component human actors (live shows) the degree to which these performers must be seen to satisfy the audience and put the show across varies.

A. Details of facial expression and small gesture are important in legitimate drama, vaudeville and burlesque, intimate revue and cabaret.

B. Broad gesture by single individuals is important in grand opera, presentation, musical comedy, and the dance.

C. Gesture by individuals is unimportant and movement of individuals from place to place is the smallest significant movement in pageant.

It follows then that theatres planned for the types of entertainment listed under A must be limited in depth of auditorium so that visibility from the remotest seat still allows the occupant to perceive facial expressions (not over 75 feet).

Theatres planned for the types listed under B may have greater distance from the stage to the remotest seat, but this distance is set at a

Depth of House

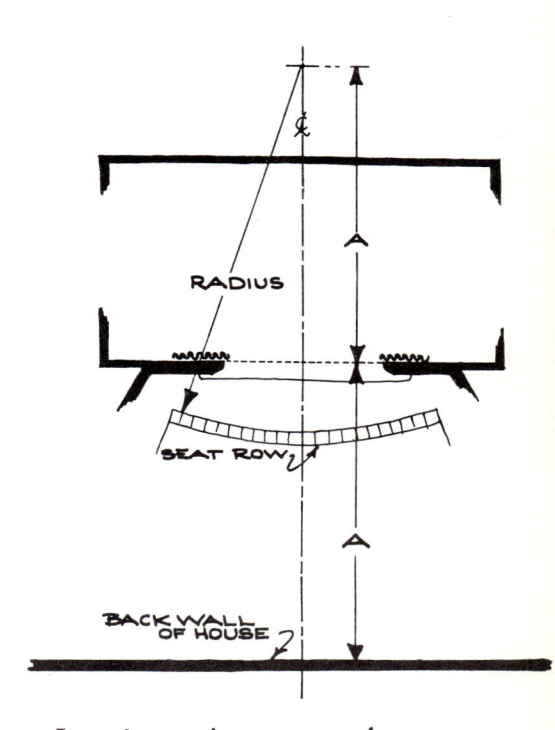

Location of center of curvature for rows of seats.

maximum beyond which the individual actor is diminished to insignificance (approximately 125 feet).

Spectators in the last rows at the Radio City Music Hall in New York, looking through a distance ranging from 160 feet to over 200 feet, depending on the location of the performers onstage, see a ballet reduced to the size of midgets, and an individual performer, even with the dramatic enhancement of a follow spot, is a very insignificant figure indeed.

Summary

Given the proscenium opening and capacity, laying out the orchestra and balcony or balconies in plan becomes a simple and straightforward process. Sight lines determine proscenium splay and house width. Visibility limits and capacity determine depth. Minimum distance from stage or screen to first row is determined in the section.

As can be realized from the foregoing requirements for seeing, any scheme which attempts to provide flexible audience-performance relationships sacrifices something, usually in every form attempted. The multiform theatre cannot be justified except as a laboratory, where certain limitations are an acceptable price for flexibility and the box office does not need to support the enterprise.

SECTION

The vertical angle of 30 degrees at the spectator's position establishes the distance from the closest seat to the screen or to the highest significant object on the stage. The lowest seat in the orchestra must be located where the patron can just see the stage floor (except in the case of theatres built for motion pictures only). The highest seat in the balcony must be on a line which is not more than 30 degrees to the horizontal at the front curtain at the stage floor if it is not to be above the limit of reasonable distortion. The standing patron at the back of the orchestra must be able to see the top of the screen, which is usually as high as any significant portion of a stage setting. Each spectator must see the whole stage or screen over the heads of those in front of him. Within these limits the floor slope of orchestra and balcony can be laid out: the first step in determining auditorium section.

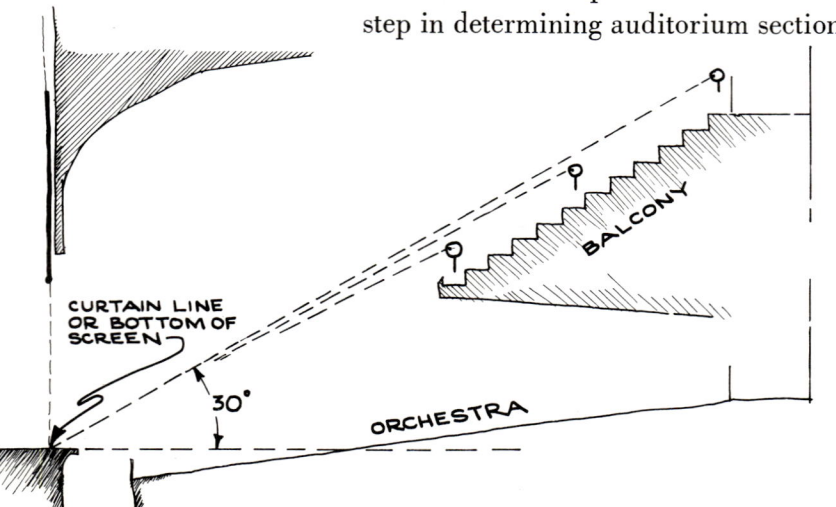

Maximum tolerable downward sight line angle from balcony.

Several methods have been offered heretofore for developing the floor slope. Doubtless others will be offered in the future. The authors present the following method as one which assures unobstructed vision from all seats. It may be noted that this system produces a floor slope considerably steeper than that in many existing theatres. It also produces better seeing conditions.

To determine floor slope, establish eye position of spectator in first row on center line by approximately 30 degree vertical angle above. For live shows, stage floor will be approximately 2 inches below this level. For theatres designed solely for motion pictures, the location of the stage floor is not critical; the position of the bottom of the screen is.

A point 3 feet 8 inches below, and 18 inches in front of the eye position will be the floor level for the front row. (1) Draw a sight line from the eye position to downstage edge of stage, and extend it back of the eye position for the front row, step off horizontal seat spacing (back to back), and draw vertical lines at the points thus established. (2) Establish a point 5 inches above the intersection of the extended sight line and the next vertical line. (3) This is the eye position for the second row and the floor level at the front edge of the second row seat is 3 feet 8 inches below and 18 inches in front of the eye position. Repeat steps (1), (2) and (3) to the back of the house and draw in the floor slope. Where the slope exceeds 1½ inches per foot, platforms are required under the seats, and steps in the aisles. A cross-aisle which divides the orchestra into front and back sections entails the elevation of the first row of seats behind it to make up for horizontal width of the aisle.

The standing spectator's eye level behind the rear row of seats is assumed to be 5 feet 6 inches above the floor level of the last row. The sight line from this position to the top of the screen or highest probable curtain trim establishes the minimum height for ceiling under balcony.

Raising the stage will make it possible to reduce the floor slope but at the penalty of producing upward sight lines in the first two or three rows which are uncomfortable and unnatural for viewing stage setting and action. If the stage floor is above the elevation of the first row eye position, the upstage portion of the floor will be invisible from the first row. Leaving the upstage floor out of sight by perhaps as much as 6 inches from the first row is generally preferable to having an excessive floor slope, especially if more than one balcony is used.

When planning for motion pictures only, the lower sight line from the first row will come to the bottom of the projected picture, approximately 24 inches above the stage floor, or still higher if a reverse floor slope is planned.

In laying out the balcony, sight lines are laid out from rear to front because it is unsafe to change balcony slope. The focal point onstage is the point farthest downstage at which visibility is requisite, or, in

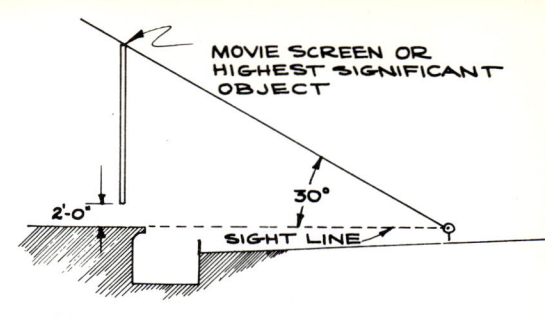

Maximum tolerable upward sight line angle for motion pictures.

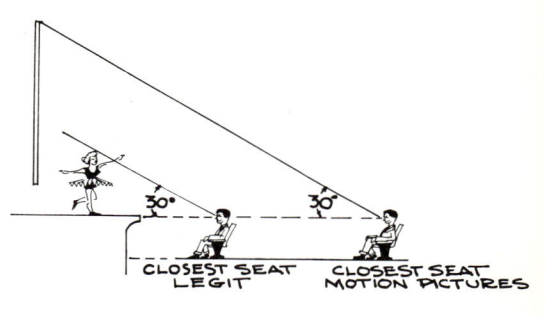

Maximum angle determines location of closest seats.

Basic dimensions for plotting floor slope.

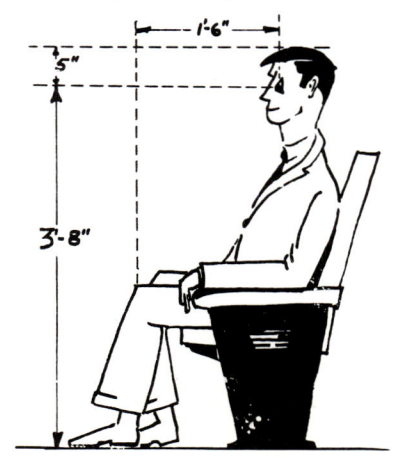

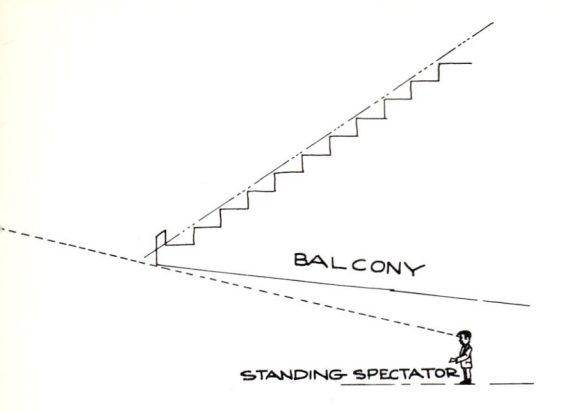

The sight line of the standing patron limits the balcony overhang.

the case of motion pictures only, the bottom of the screen. The maximum forward extensity of the balcony is then determined when the location of the spectator's eye position has been moved forward to a point beyond which the floor and supporting structure would intersect the upper sight line of the spectator standing at the rear of the orchestra.

The pitch of balcony floors should not change since that would entail a change of riser height for aisle stairs and introduce attendant hazards. If vision from the rear row in the balcony is adequate, the rest of the balcony is satisfactory.

In theatres designed only to show motion pictures, the first row need not be located so that the patron can see the stage floor. It is satisfactory if he sees without obstruction the bottom of the screen which is seldom placed less than 2 feet above the stage floor. Raising the screen makes it possible to flatten the contour of the orchestra floor. The reversed floor slope developed by Ben Schlanger makes use of this relationship to get the maximum number of seats into the zone of least visual distortion, and to hold the height of motion picture theatres to a minimum. A result of the reversed floor slope is to place balcony seats in the zone of optimum seeing.

It is apparent that a theatre designed for maximum efficiency for motion pictures (reverse floor slope) is almost completely useless for any other sort of production except large screen television. The principle survives in the angle of the car stands in the drive-in motion picture theatres.

Floor Dish

The planning of the floor slope is not completed when pitch of orchestra and balcony has been laid out on the center line. It depends also on the curve of the rows of seats. The whole row must be at the same elevation if the seats are to be level. The floor therefore is not a sloped plane, but a dished surface in which horizontal contours follow the seat row curve. The floor section at the center line, rotated horizontally about the center of curvature of the rows of seats, will determine the orchestra floor shape. The balcony is planned the same way save that the floor is terraced to take the seats.

Comment

It has been established that conditions of seeing limit the depth of the house. Since capacity is a function of depth and width, increasing the width increases the capacity. However, since sight lines from the side

Developed floor slope for unobstructed vision.

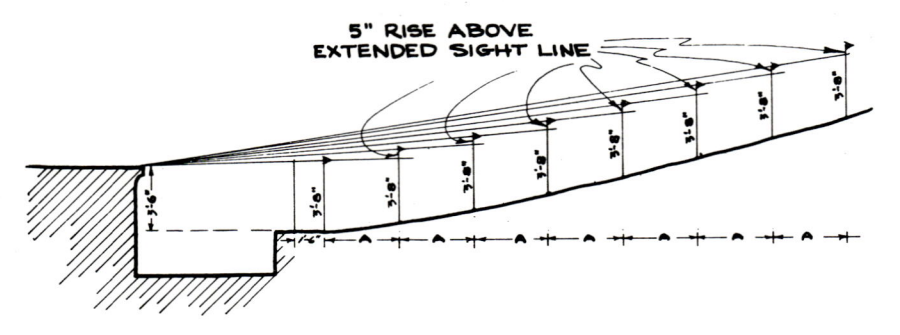

seats limit the angular spread of the side walls, the width can only be increased by increasing the proscenium opening. The width of the proscenium opening is a function of the kind of production contemplated for the theatre. The dimensions given in the following table are derived from the requirements of the types of production noted when the performances are so staged as to assure maximum effectiveness.

TABLE 7. Proscenium Widths for Kinds of Theatrical Production in Feet

	Minimum	Usual	Reasonable Maximum
Drama	26	30 to 35	40
Vaudeville, Revue	30	35	45
Musical Comedy Operetta	30	40	50
Presentation Opera	40	60	80

Where budget permits building to have better than minimum visibility standards, wall angles may be narrowed, floor angles increased, and balcony omitted, and visibility from the worst seats thereby improved to a point considerably better than what is just salable. A very real problem, however, is to prevent precedent or personal prejudice from so influencing auditorium design as to cause the inclusion of large numbers of unsalable seats. One manager insisted, after floor slope and stage height had been determined and the auditorium floor laid, that the stage floor be lowered some 10 inches below the height called for in the plan, in the interests of, as he put it, "intimacy." From the middle of the orchestra in that theatre it is hard to see below the level of the actor's navel.

Greek theatres were semicircular (horizontal sight-line angle 90 degrees to center line). This was all right in Greece where there was no proscenium. It is obviously not all right where a proscenium is used. Yet, a misguided reverence for ancient practice still gives us some theatres with impossible sight lines.

Opera houses of the Renaissance had side boxes for the very good reason that the people in the boxes competed (often successfully) with the stage show for audience attention. This condition persists, but it is worth noting that the best example of such a theatre in America has not made a nickel for a generation. Nevertheless, theatres with at least vestigial side boxes are still built.

It is perhaps unnecessary to add that theatres planned in conformity with the principles here set forth may adhere in spirit to almost any architectural style by the discreet planning of service and decorative

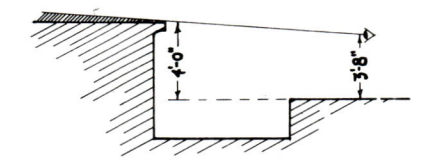

Zone of invisibility. Causes: stage too high, front seats too low.

elements which do not affect the basic shape of the theatre. In theatres which are being rebuilt, it is often possible to retain the desirable features and still provide a good theatre.

Open Stage and Extended Stage

The open stage form in which sight lines must be directed to the edge of the acting area necessitates steep balconies. The balcony of a theatre which is convertible from proscenium to open stage form must follow the requirements for open stage. Any theatre in which performance extends beyond the proscenium onto either forestage, open stage or extended stage, requires very careful planning to provide good seeing from all balcony seats to all parts of the acting area.

Arena Stage

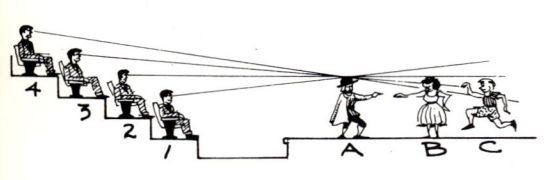

Few, if any, arena-form theatres have balconies, nor are they likely to have since the all-around seating of the arena form seems to satisfy seating capacity demands without balconies. Moreover, to satisfy the requirements of good seeing in arena, it is necessary to elevate successive rows of seats more than in proscenium form as a partial solution of the insoluble problem of actors covering other actors from some spectator's direction.

If seat rows are successively and sufficiently elevated, the audience may see over the heads of near actors to the heads, and partially the bodies, of actors farther away.

The sight line problem inherent in the arena form: A hides B and C from first two rows.

LIGHT

Seeing requisites determine the shape of the house and to some extent its size. They also determine the provisions for house illumination.

Requisites for lighting are mentioned earlier. There are three basic functions involved: 1. Visibility 2. Decoration 3. Mood

To fulfill these functions it is necessary to plan the lighting for each separately, combining instruments only if and when the requirements of each function are satisfied. It is axiomatic in stage lighting that a different light is assigned to do each individual job. The McCandless method is the most economical of any which can accomplish a creditable result, and it does not duplicate functions of any instrument or group of instruments. This basic approach is as applicable to the house as to the stage, as examination of houses thus lighted will show.

It is as important to keep light away from areas where it is not needed as to get it where it is wanted, and a great deal harder. To the application of this principle we may trace much of the improvement in appearance and comfort that has come to interiors in the last two decades.

The best light by which to read the program will not produce a pleasing effect if it strikes the walls. The light which gives the house warmth and intimacy will require programs in Braille if that's all the light there is. The bunch light, chandelier, sconce, or other open light source may be a desirable decorative device, but if it is bright enough to see by, the audience won't see anything else, and will be seeing spots instead of the show when the curtain goes up.

Visibility

Light for visibility in the auditorium by which the patrons may find their seats, read their programs, and recognize their friends must be generally distributed with a minimum of shadows and preferably from concealed or low-brightness sources installed in the ceiling, the light passing through small holes or louvered openings. Even distribution at moderate intensity (15 foot-candles) is desirable. White light is best. Light thus controlled will not upset the balance of the house; in fact, the house may seem dim, though the patron sees and is seen. And the light source will not be seen unless the patron looks directly upward, and not many theatregoers do that often or gracefully.

Special visibility lights are requisite for safety. Building codes in many localities provide that in the interests of safety, aisle lights be provided near the floor on each or on alternate aisle seats. This number is clearly in excess of what is needed to give the requisite visibility, but a minimum safe number and arrangement of such lights is one for every three rows on alternate sides of the aisle, plus lights on both sides wherever there is a step or change in pitch of the floor and at intersections and ends of aisles and crossovers. Luminous guide lines and tread edges in the carpet, activated from ultraviolet sources, promote safety with minimum distraction.

All doors must have exit lights over them. Most fire regulations require that the lights be red. It is unfortunately true that red lights attract attention even when there isn't any fire. When they are close to the arc of vision of the spectator, they often constitute a source of visual distraction. Blue exit lights are perfectly visible when the spectator wants to see them, but do not intrude upon his consciousness when he is looking at something else. Therefore, blue exit lights are desirable.

Decorative Lighting

Decorative lighting is a part of the decorative scheme. In itself and by means of that which it illuminates, it establishes the character of the house. It does this by:

1. Illumination of walls, ceilings, and proscenium: balanced background lighting, intensity less than for audience area, color chosen to give desired quality to wall and ceiling color.
2. Highlighting of focal points in decorative scheme: niches containing objets d'art, wall hangings, etc.
3. Decorative lights: chandeliers, sconces.

The instruments for decorative lighting may be concealed direct sources, or indirect cove lights, to illuminate the walls and ceilings. Transverse ceiling louvers reduce the apparent depth of the house.

Highlights, of course, require special instruments. Open light sources serve a decorative purpose (chandeliers sometimes serve an acoustic purpose) only when they can be seen by a considerable portion of the audience. If they are bright enough to supply illumination they are more annoying than attractive and are therefore to be thought of as decorative objects rather than as lighting sources. They may contain concealed lighting sources for visibility, decoration, or mood.

Mood It has never been absolutely established that the use of an appropriate color in house lights can do much to set the mood called for by the play in advance of the curtain, though theory inclines in that direction and almost every director will try to accomplish something by means of color if given the opportunity. Color control on house lights is always useful for spectacle, as is amply demonstrated in New York's Radio City Music Hall, and it is probable that that fact alone justifies provision therefor. To achieve it, two things are necessary: concealed lights in primary colors controlled as are the footlights, and a neutral tinted wall and ceiling surface to be illuminated by those lights.

Distractions The music stand lights are often a source of a good deal of distraction and consequent annoyance to the audience, except perhaps at some performances of opera where the enjoyment is in inverse ratio to the visibility of what transpires on the stage. While it is easy to mask the music stand lights, it is impossible to stop reflection from scores and thus a relatively bright area will be in the audience line of vision whenever the musicians are visible. Several ways to overcome this are: (1) An orchestra lift, (2) A deep pit, (3) A louvered orchestra pit cover, (4) Scores with white notes on black paper.

Comment There are two elements which tend to prevent the lighting of auditoriums from being good as it should be:

1. The unwillingness of architects to plan lighting before wall and sultant is called in more often to correct what has been incorrectly built than to insure the correct design of a theatre. The design, construction, installation, and consultant's fee for one of the most elaborate theatre lighting projects in America cost less than just the installation costs in many smaller theatres lighted without expert counsel, and badly done.

2. There is an inexplicable illusion among some architects and builders that light must come from "fixtures," despite the obvious fact that if you hang a light out where you can see it, when it is turned on you can't see much else.

While seeing is the first consideration in planning the position of proscenium, walls, floors, seating, and house lighting, all of these elements must also be planned with relation to the acoustics.

4: The audience hears

The audience and the showman find it to their mutual advantage and satisfaction for the audience to hear only what it wants to hear, or the showman wants it to hear, and that, clearly. This chapter will concern itself with those parts of the theatre building which have a direct bearing on the audibility of the show.

Requirements

The audience wants to hear the actor, the singer, the orchestra, the instrumental soloist, the organ, the audible component of the sound motion picture, and any other sound which is part of the show. It does *not* want to hear the elevated, auto horns, fire sirens, wind or rain outside the theatre while the show is in progress, or scraping feet in the aisles and rows, rattling foot rests, squeaking seats, banging lobby doors, or whistling fans, roaring blowers, knocking radiators, or telephone bells, buzzers, snap switches, the noisy shifting of scenery, or any unplanned distortion of any sound which is a part of the show.

It is up to the architect to insure perfect audibility of the show, and by the same token to protect the audience against distracting sounds such as those listed above. He must (1) eliminate from the audience area all unwanted sound (noise, that which is not part of the show); (2) assure audibility for all sound which is part of the show.

Noise Level

Unwanted sound is noise. Noise in the theatre masks portions of the show and limits subtlety. It is therefore desirable to keep the theatre as free as possible from outside noise, and noise originating inside the theatre.

The average noise level in existing metropolitan theatres with audience present is about 50 db.* In the same location 40 db is an entirely feasible level involving little, if any, additional construction expense. The best theatres often have a level of about 30 db or less at midfrequencies. The level of ordinary conversation (at 3 feet in open air) is about 65 db.

Sound Transmission

Noise is either air-borne or solid-borne. Steel structural members

---

* db = decibel, the handy unit of sound intensity; the log of the ratio of the sound power to a standard reference: 10^{-16} watts per square centimeter.

75

transmit sound with considerable efficiency. Sound thus transmitted becomes air-borne when wall, floor, or ceiling areas or fixtures are vibrated by the structural members and act much as the sounding board of a musical instrument. Vibration from sump pumps, blowers, etc., hardly noticeable as noise in the air, becomes noise when structurally transmitted to the house. A brick wall is usually a more efficient sound barrier than a concrete slab.

Procedure

1. List the sources of noise (this will include a noise survey of the site).
2. List the means of transmission by which such noise might be conveyed to the house.
3. Provide in specifications for elimination of noise at the source wherever possible, e.g., maximum allowable noise from machinery, vibration insulating mounts, etc.
4. Provide in design for minimum transmission of sound to the house: doors opening on alleys, roof insulation, no single door having direct access from outside to house or stage which must be used during performance, etc.
5. Provide in specifications for minimum sound transmission by materials in all places where sound exclusion is a factor: adequate sound attenuation by emergency exit doors, interior walls.

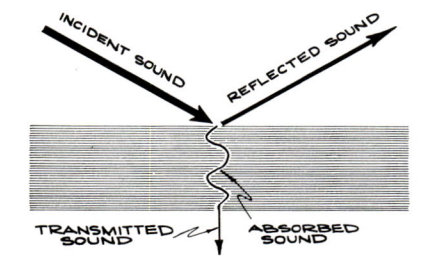

The specification (5) is arrived at by subtracting the desired house sound level from the level of the maximum outside noise. (30 db inside level, 90 db outside level—minimum allowable attenuation by door in frame 60 db.) Acoustical characteristics of most buildings materials are known and widely published. Most suppliers of building materials will have sound transmission tests made of their products if they have not been made. Most contractors who install machinery will, if required to, plan their installation with reference to a maximum noise specification and guarantee to meet such a specification.

Note: All specifications dealing with sound should include a statement of the frequency range to be covered. Acoustical measurements are conventionally made at octave intervals from 128 to 4096 cycles per second. A 60-cycle hum can be most annoying, as can a 10,000-cycle squeal. The ear responds to frequencies from 16 to 16,000 cycles per second, and a subway rumble is felt at even lower frequencies. For building material specifications and noise level calculations then, materials must sometimes be tested for transmission of higher and lower frequencies than has been conventional practice.

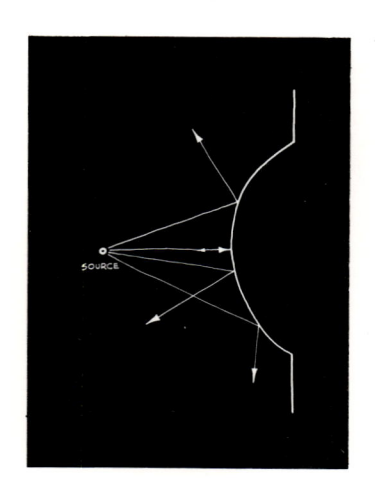

Action of sound on encountering a solid medium. In addition to being partially reflected, absorbed or transmitted, sound is also refracted (changed in direction) by the more dense medium.

A convex surface diffuses sound which strikes it from any angle.

TABLE 8. Air-borne Noises Originating Outside the House and Methods of Exclusion

Ingress	Method of Exclusion
Doors	Airtight fit. A hairline crack will raise the transmitted sound level 6 db. Tight fit is also necessary for efficient operation of ventilation system. Elaborate and usually double-door systems are necessary to isolate the scene shop from the stage if the shop is to be used while the play is on. Doors opening on alleys or halls are often less of a problem than if they open on the street. Preferably open only into spaces which can be kept reasonably quiet.
Windows	Do not belong in a theatre. Double where used and not capable of being opened.
Ceiling Slots	Exclude sound from loft by roof insulation, solid catwalks, tight doors.
Projection Booth	Quiet machines. Sound absorbent walls and ceiling in booth. Glass in viewing ports.
Ventilation Ducts	(1) No metal connection between blower and steel structural members, or blower and duct. (2) Ducts and diffusers large enough not to rattle or whistle when blower operates at full speed (above normal operating speed). (3) Sound-insulated ducts.
Roof	A massive slab with a tight ceiling below it, if necessary. Hang ceiling on flexible mounts.
Alternator, for Motorized Rigging	Locate in soundproof vault outside the theatre.

TABLE 9. Air-borne Noise Originating in the Theatre and Methods of Prevention

Source	Method of Prevention
Radiators	Heat the house entirely by circulated air, or wall or floor radiation. On stage (1) Radiator return line graded to avoid condensate and resultant banging. *No valves to hiss.* (2) Circulate hot water rather than steam.
Stage Wagons Discs (Noise magnified because of reverberant stage floor)	(1) Well-made ball or roller bearing casters running on level tracks installed over stage floor. (2) Revolving stage on its own support structure (quieter than disc on stage floor). (3) Elevators are quiet unless they are of the screw-jack type and run too fast.
Audience (Talk, Shuffling)	(1) Make rear crossover as sound absorbent as possible. (2) Lobby doors opposite aisles used for exit, *not* during show. (3) Divide rear crossover from house by a wall—a glass wall for motion picture houses. (This eliminates the rail for the waiting line.) (4) Carpets. (5) Silent seats.
Orchestra Pit	Rubber feet on chair legs and stands.
Telephones	Locate only where one open door will not permit sound to reach house or stage. Light instead of bell on stage.
Snoring	Put on a good show.

TABLE 10. Solid-borne Noises and Methods of Prevention

Source	Method of Prevention
Train Rumble (Subway, Elevated, Surface)	Vibrant-isolating mounts under columns, vibration-isolating joints in walls. Compliant substance between grade walls and back fill. In case of excessive vibration, float interior walls, as in radio broadcast or recording studio design.
Air-handling Units	Locate below foyer. Isolation mounting and a soundproof room.
Vibration from Non-theatre Functions of Building (Gymnasium, Bowling Alley)	See above, or float the floor of the facility at which the vibration originates.
Motors, Machinery	Vibration-isolating mounts.
Switches	Mercury switches.
Plumbing	More than one wall between house and facility. Isolate from structural members.

To Hear the Show

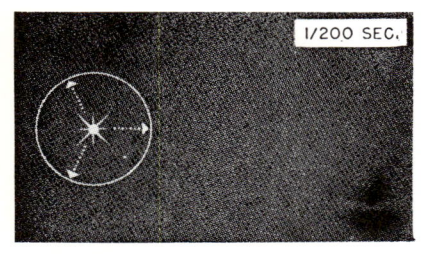

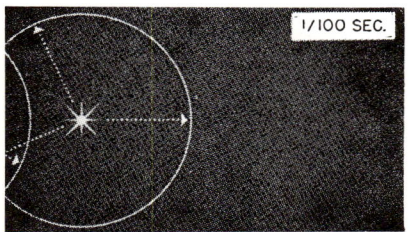

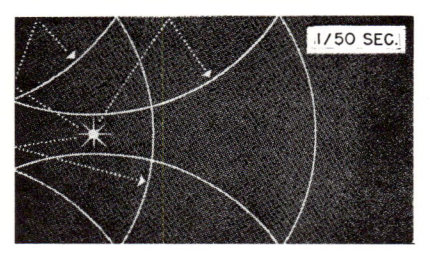

Action of Sound

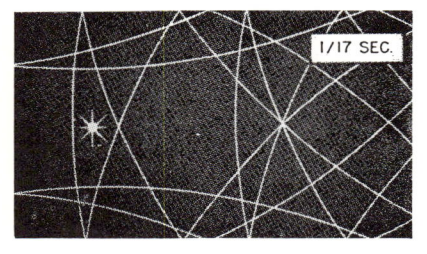

Progressive reflection of a single sound wave in an enclosed space.

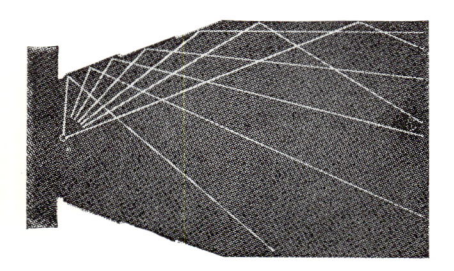

Sight lines are apparent on blueprints. Anyone can take a ruler and see from the architect's designs whether or not it will be possible for the audience to see the show, and presumably anyone who builds a theatre will make a reasonably thorough sight-line analysis of the designs before approving them. No matter how much faith he has in his architect, he seldom cares to overlook any chances of error when he has a large investment to protect. Blueprints per se will not, on the other hand, show whether or not the audience will be able to hear. Structural and surface materials and their positions relative to each other, types, location and operating conditions of machinery and the routine of the performance itself all have a bearing on how and what the audience hears.

Obviously acoustical planning must proceed as an integral part of the architectural design. And this practice has become, *Deo gratias*, increasingly common during the past decade. The worst of the faults of many of the pre-depression structures are missing in most new theatres.

The architect who knows show business well enough to design a theatre will often feel competent to prepare plans and specifications which will result in adequate exclusion and elimination of noise. The more specialized task of getting the sound of the show to the audience usually calls for the services of an acoustical consultant or engineer trained in acoustics to undertake the requisite calculations and tests.

In the theatre useful sound emanates from actors, orchestral instruments, organ, and loud-speakers, located on the stage, in the pit, and above and at the sides of the proscenium. The architect's job is to get it to the paying customers no matter where they sit without distortion or appreciable loss of intensity. Getting the sound to *all* the customers is a problem of *distribution*. Getting it there at almost equal intensity everywhere and having it die away rapidly at a predetermined interval after it has ceased to emanate from the source, so as not to interfere with the next sound as it comes along, is a problem to be solved by achieving a certain *reverberation time*.

Part of the sound pressure wave goes straight from the source to the auditor. Part of it is reflected from ceiling and walls. Part of it gets to the auditor after it has been reflected back and forth about the house many times. Part of it has been for a trip around the stage, or has been reflected from the scenery or cyclorama.

Section and plan of an auditorium. Ceiling and side walls are designed to provide maximum reinforcement especially in the audience area farthest from the sound source.

Ceilings are the principal distribution surfaces. When ceilings are laid out, they must be planned to reflect the sound back to the audience, either directly or via walls, but in such a manner that it will neither be concentrated in certain spots, nor reflect back and forth between parallel surfaces, nor get to the audience out of phase with the direct wave. Moreover, since sound travels only about 1150 feet per second in air, the length of the path of the first reflected wave must not exceed that of the direct wave by more than 50 feet (preferably less) or the audience will hear everything twice.

Distribution

Diagram showing multiple reflections of a succession of waves in a horizontal plane as they appear in a ripple tank.

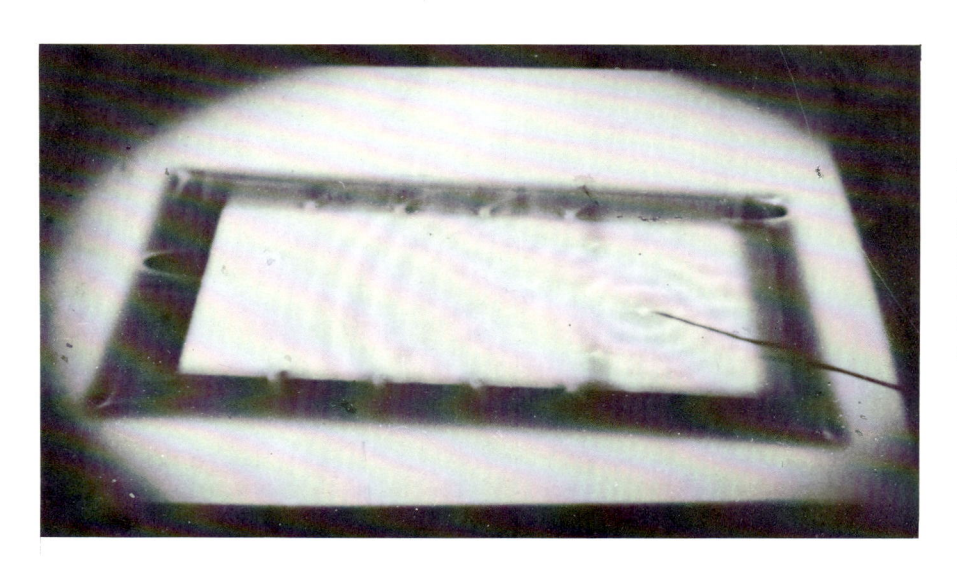

Ripple tank test of a stage-auditorium model. Simple tests of this type will sometimes reveal standing waves or dead spots. Much more elaborate types of model tests are currently under development.

The position of the side walls is determined by sight lines. The depth of the house (curtain to back wall) is governed by visibility requisites. Sound distribution requirements govern the shapes of the side walls, ceiling, ceiling under the balcony, and rear wall. The fact that the angle of reflection of a sound wave is equal to the angle of incidence (neglecting diffraction phenomena at low frequencies) makes it possible to lay out tentative shapes on paper. But since even the most unorthodox appearing shapes sometimes result in good theatres and vice versa, tests are necessary to establish the workability of any design. Plan and section of the theatre may be tested for distribution in ripple tanks, three-dimensional models by spark photographs and by tracing reflections of a small beam of light. The technique of testing is fairly complex. It can only be pointed out here that rough approximations are possible with single gravity waves in water and mercury tanks and that, within some limitations, varying frequencies may be studied stroboscopically with capillary waves. Photographs and visual observation reveal (1) desirable distribution; (2) undesirable standing waves (repeated reflections between two surfaces); (3) echoes (a number of reflected waves whose path of travel is long coming to the audience, or part of it, in phase); (4) dead spots, into which very little sound penetrates (as is sometimes the case under balconies or where direct and reflected waves arrive out of phase and cancel out); (5) focal points (such as the concentration of reflected waves on a small area of seats from a ceiling vault). When the wave pattern is rapidly broken up, and waves from all directions, of approximately equal size, cover the audience area, the distribution is probably satisfactory.

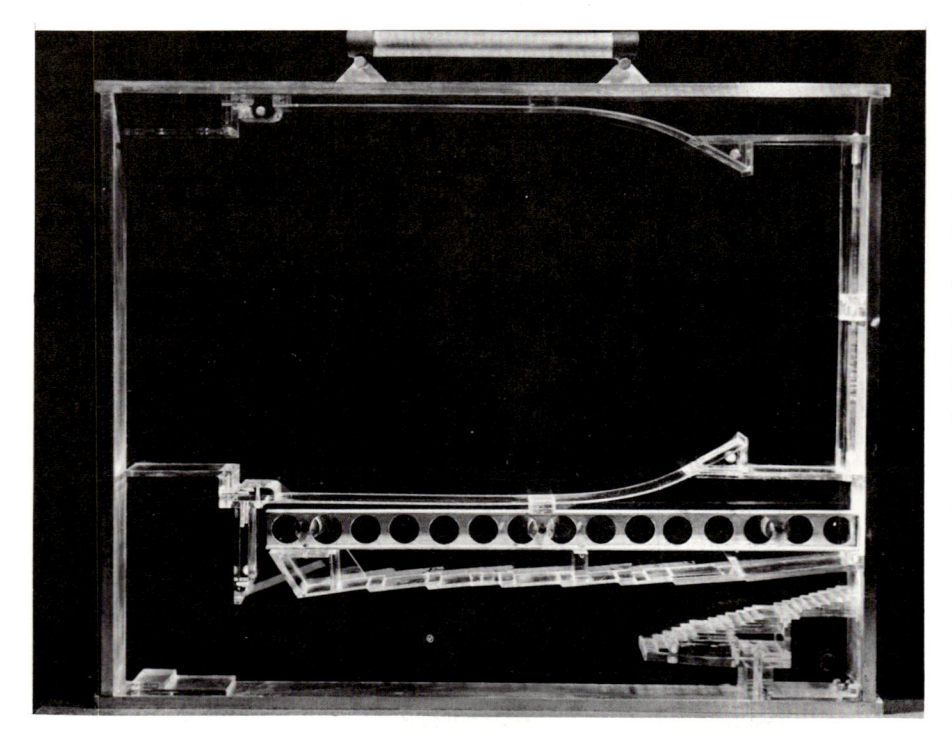

Plastic plan and section of model of final design of the Jorgensen Auditorium, University of Connecticut. The concert set (not shown) was developed in this model. Perforated beam only provides rigidity to side and ceiling of model.

Spark photographs (actual pictures of the sound waves in air) have the advantage of greater clarity than most ripple tank pictures and are useful in the study of diffraction phenomena and precise location of sources of trouble.

A small beam of light, reflected from surface to surface in a model, makes it possible to trace with reasonable exactness the path of the center of a sound wave.

There are pitfalls to be avoided when sound distribution tests of architectural shapes are made:

1. Sound sources are at numerous locations and tests must be repeated for from 6 to 12 locations on the stage with various teaser * trims as well as for all sound sources other than the stage.

2. Absorbent surfaces must be made nonreflecting (open or beached) in the model.

3. Stage and house must be tested together. They constitute a pair of coupled rooms. Plaster cycloramas *must* be designed as part of the acoustical planning of the *house* and tested with the house model. (A cyclorama can be tipped toward the back of the stage far enough to put its focal point out of harm's way. Thus built it is also easier to light than if it is vertical.)

4. Chandeliers, ceiling slots for lights and ventilation diffusers *must* be included.

5. If reverberation calculations show any absorbent wall material to be desirable, its location must be determined by test so as not to interfere with sound distribution.

Finally, a ceiling under a balcony sloped up toward the back of the house, or a back wall which follows the curve of the seats, will almost invariably render good hearing impossible in at least part of the theatre.

Prefabricated plaster or metal reflecting panels are cheaper to erect than continuous ceilings. They furnish flexible lighting and sound-projection positions and can in some cases be adjusted in height and angle to compensate for some acoustical shortcomings. Their theoretical virtues have, at this writing, not always appeared in practice.

A concert set or orchestra shell is necessary when a stage is used for concerts. In a concert hall it is permanent. In a theatre with a stage it must be so constructed that it can be flown or otherwise cleared. Its function is to direct the sound to the audience and keep it from getting lost or generating unwanted reverberation in the stage house. It is designed to continue the reflecting pattern of house walls and ceiling. A portable set may require special rigging because of its weight, for it must have mass to be any good.

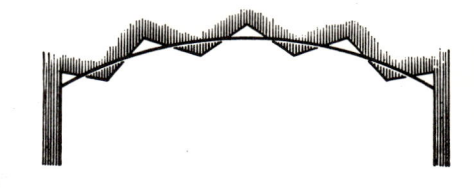

Methods of treating a curved rear wall of an auditorium to prevent focusing of the reflected sound.

---

* Masking piece of drapery which establishes effective height of proscenium opening.

Reverberation

Reverberation is easy to calculate. But *what reverberation is desired* is another thing. The scale of desirable reverberation times runs from long for Bach to short for speech which requires a high percentage of definition. In legitimate production, reverberation will vary from scene to scene depending upon the settings. The ideal theatre will have provision for controlling reverberation. At least one attempt to do this has been made, using wall panels which can be changed, but an analysis of the results is not at hand. Unless some means of controlling reverberation is provided, the best that can be achieved is a compromise between the optimum times for the various types of productions.

Reverberation optima have been the subject of much investigation. Recent studies directed toward the determination of optimum reverberation time for various house volumes show slightly longer times than

Jorgensen Auditorium, University of Connecticut, showing permanent concert set made of heavy corrugated Transite. Pivoted side panels are for entrances and are closed during performance. Frederick Teich, architect.

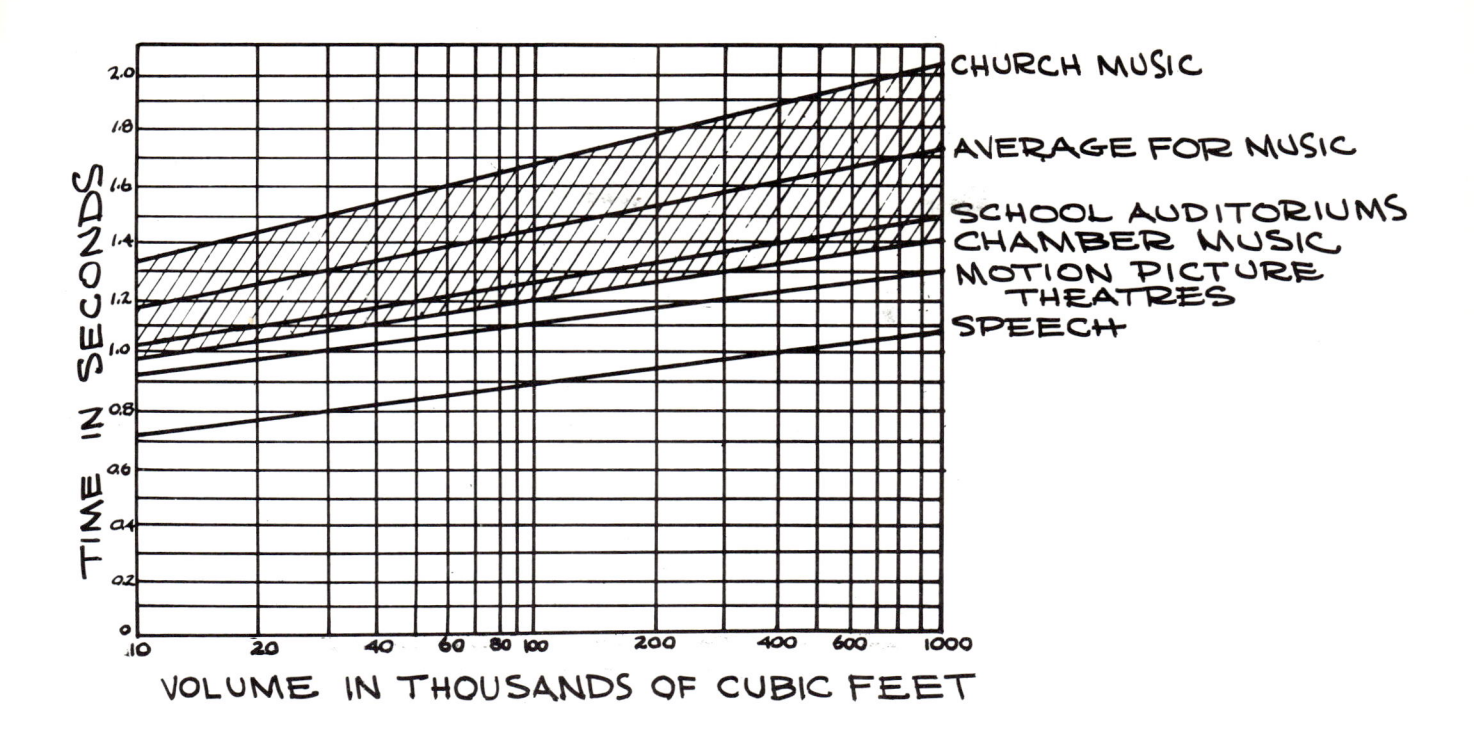

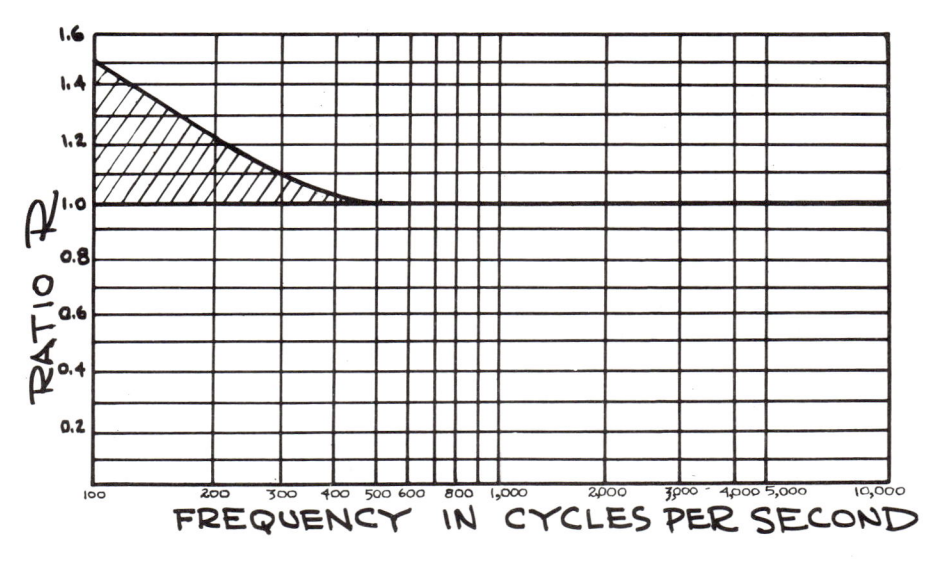

Optimum reverberation times for different auditorium uses defined by Knudsen and Harris and generally used to establish acoustical design objectives. The values in the upper figure are for 512 cycles. When calculating reverberation for lower frequencies, it is necessary to apply the ratio R from the lower chart. Example: $t_f = t_{512} R$.

Ceiling under balcony sloped to reflect sound to the rear section of the orchestra. O'Keefe Centre.

those considered optimum five years ago. Moreover, as clients demand more and more precise acoustical conditions, optimum reverberation times tend to increase slightly. In a theatre planned for more than one type of production, if means are not provided for reverberation control, it is well to choose a reverberation time which is an average between optima for speech and orchestral music. The better the first reflections are controlled, the closer orchestral optima should be approached.

For the calculations, the house and the part of the stage enclosed in a box set are considered. Tolerances, if any, are best taken on the long side. This is done for two reasons. (1) Tolerance involves a margin of error. If the house is too dead, its correction is costly; if it is too live, correction is usually simple and cheap. (2) In calculation of reverberation time no account is taken of the stage house outside the set. The stage house has, however, some effect on the reverberation: when plein-air sets are used, the effective volume is greater than with a box set. In hung shows in which the flies are full, there is more absorption than with a box set. Both these conditions in practice call for slightly longer reverberation than would be requisite in the house with the proscenium closed.

Optimum reverberation time, it must be noted, varies with frequency. In large houses (over 200,000 cubic feet), a slightly longer reverberation in the low frequencies than in the highs is generally considered requisite. If the reverberation time is made equal throughout the audible frequency range, the sound absorption characteristics of the audience will slightly unbalance it in favor of the lows.

Unfortunately, the theatre does not play to the same-sized audience at every performance. And the most neglected feature of acoustical planning is the provision of means of compensation for audiences of varying size. Yet it is possible to have the reverberation time the same with no one present as with a capacity house.

Each person in the audience absorbs a certain amount of sound. The unit of absorption is the *sabine*. If the acoustical specifications for the seats are so drawn that each seat empty absorbs as many sabines at the same frequencies as the seat plus a person sitting in it, the total absorption (and therefore the reverberation time) will be unchanged whatever the size of the audience. Seats and audience are therefore used to keep the reverberation time the same though the audience may vary in size. Before drawing seat specifications it is necessary to look into the question of what kind of people will constitute the audience and how they will dress. An audience of children will have fewer sabines than a matinee audience of women shoppers. Stiff shirts and bare shoulders are reflective as compared to soft shirts and afternoon dresses, a phenomenon which makes the traditional first night audience, at least acoustically, live.

Massive steel concert set in Northrop Auditorium, University of Minnesota. George C. Izenour, designer.

Special rigging to clear and set concert set. Northrup Auditorium.

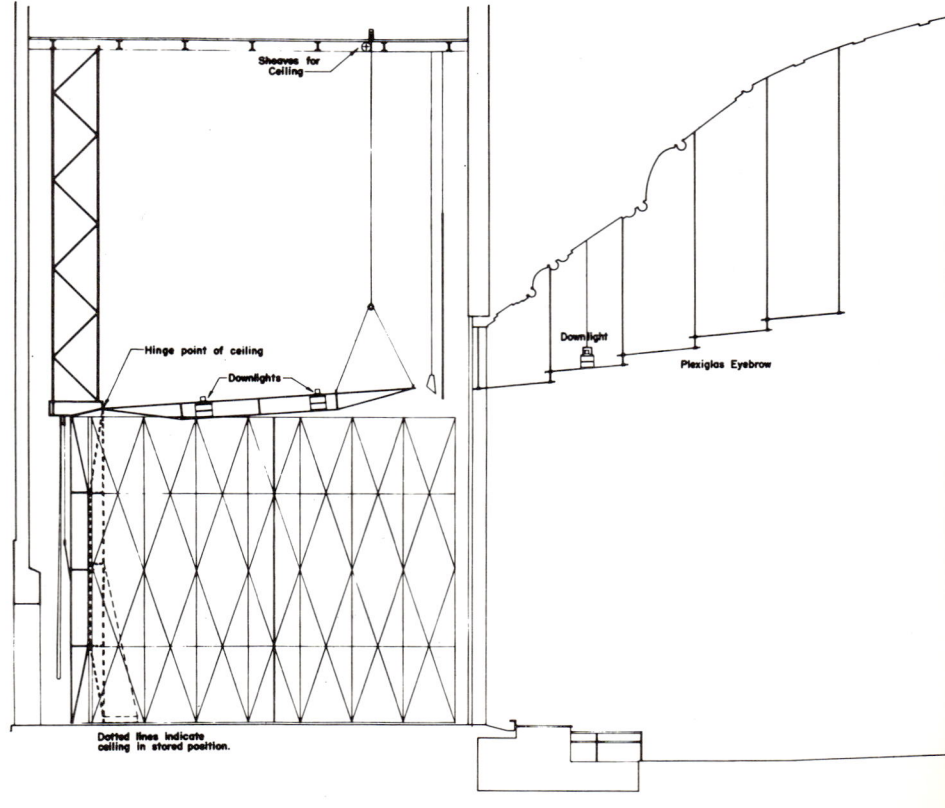

When more absorption than that furnished by the seats or audience is necessary, it is well to get it next from carpet (which serves to eliminate the distraction of noise emanating from the audience), next from decorative hangings or draperies concealed behind grilles which can be changed in position and size, and last from permanent absorbent wall-surface materials located so as not to interfere with sound distribution.

Caveats

With the growth of acoustical knowledge it has become possible to get almost any desired acoustical result. However, since acoustical quality is subjectively measured, standards and design objectives vary with individuals and groups. The musician and the conductor listen analytically to music and require a much more precise (dry) acoustical environment than the lay audience for whom the showman, the composer or playwright attempts to achieve a total cumulative impact. The unquestioning surrender of design objectives to acoustical planners guided only by the most sophisticated professional musicians has resulted in some bizarre structures which suffer in appearance, which are too small to earn their keep or which leave the lay listener unsatisfied. The architect must not let oversophistication in acoustics distort his plan and damage other elements of his structure. Most of the theatres and auditoriums which are acclaimed by performers and audiences are designed and built simply.

The architect must not assume that the word acoustical applied to a material or device guarantees good acoustics if it is used. Acoustical materials on the ceiling have ruined many theatres. Such materials belong, but how much and where is part of the detailed design problem.

The electronic control of sound is not an architectural crutch. It can do much to help the audience hear the performance in the desired manner, but it should not be depended upon until all architectural measures have been taken, and then must be planned as part of the architectural design.

Finally, poor workmanship can negate the best acoustical planning. A brickbat between the two halves of a double-wall makes it no better than a single wall. An uncaulked hole through the slab for a radiator pipe will acoustically join the rooms the floor should separate.

Procedure *

The architect determines his house size from the necessary number of seats; its wall splay and depth from the requirements of good seeing; ceiling shapes from sound distribution and front stage lighting requirements; back wall and plaster cyclorama shapes by the necessity of preventing echoes and focal points. When model tests confirm the correctness of this much of the design, he may proceed.

* For detailed list of elements of the theatre structure which require acoustical planning, see Burris-Meyer, H., and Goodfriend, L. S., *Acoustics for the Architect*, New York, Reinhold Publishing Corp., 1957.

His structure is conditioned by the necessity of avoiding resonance (it is generally believed that the organ caused the collapse of the roof in one theatre). His wall surface and heat-insulating materials are specified to give him (1) the correct total reverberation time, (2) absorption where and to the extent he needs it. His ceiling is generally kept as highly reflective as possible to insure undiminished sound distribution. He specifies seats which provide the same amount of absorption empty as do seat and occupant together when they are occupied. He insulates the theatre against outside noise and prevents inside noise. In very few theatres have all these requirements been scrupulously met. No theatre in which an honest attempt is not made to meet them is worth building.

Crampton Auditorium, Howard University. Rear wall shaped to avoid focusing sound. Ceiling panels sloped to achieve even sound distribution throughout the theatre. Hilyard Robinson, architect.

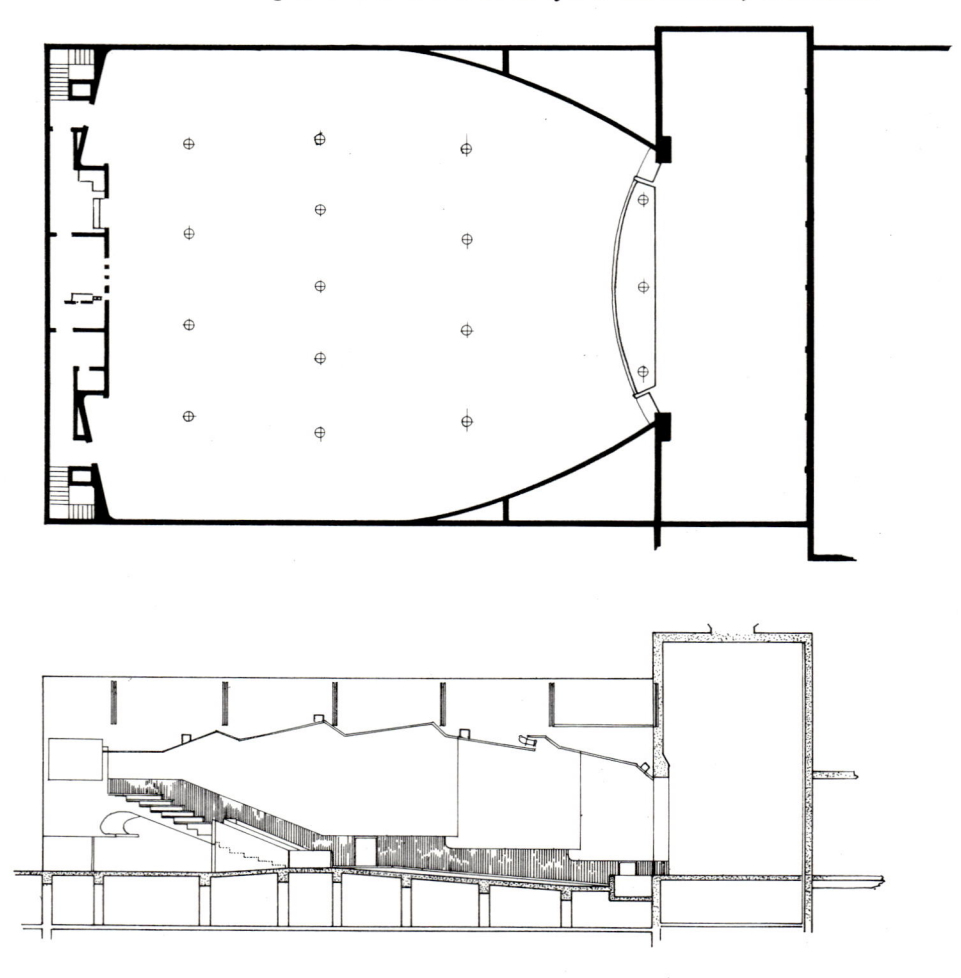

5: Comfort and safety of the audience; front service rooms

The playgoer arrives under the marquee and proceeds to foyer, box office, lobby, house, lounge, and back to marquee again usually via lobby and foyer. It is good showmanship to conceive of the playgoer's progress through the theatre as a parade in which the playgoer will enjoy participating. Comfort and safety are primary considerations in planning those parts of the theatre through which the patron moves.

When the annual visit of the circus constituted the only show business in a community, the audience stood for crowding, hard seats, soiled clothes, dust, and perhaps a long trip home, and could spend the next day recuperating from the fatigue, excitement, and condiments. The audience could, would, and did take it. The fact that people now buy seats in second balconies of theatres and in the bleacher sections of ball parks shows that hardy souls are still among us. However, there aren't enough people willing to look upon theatregoing as a challenge to their fortitude to pay the bills for any but a very few exceptional theatres.

In the preceding chapters, causes of discomfort have been cited, and provision for comfort as it applies to traffic, sight, and hearing have been considered. This chapter considers provisions for comfort and safety from traffic, sight and hearing requisites, and the functional design of the front service rooms not elsewhere considered.

Exterior

Comfort and safety become the concern of the showman when the patron first approaches the theatre. Architecturally, plenty of light on the street in front of the theatre, on driveways about it (5 fc * minimum), clearly marked crosswalks, a lighted parking area (5 fc minimum) and lights under the marquee (10 fc minimum) and illuminated automobile traffic markers are requisite. An illuminated automobile call is indispensable where any substantial number of patrons use chauffeur-driven cars.

If illumination in front is not provided by the marquee, it may be

---

* 1 fc = the illumination from 1 standard candle on a surface 1 foot square at a distance of 1 foot. The unit measure of illumination.

Federal legislation and public and private subsidy produce spacious monumental buildings for the performing arts. The Philharmonic Hall, Lincoln Center, New York City. Harrison and Abramovitz, architects.

obtained from floodlights which illuminate the building, decorative lampposts, bracket lights, or portico lights. Illumination under the marquee of minimum safety standard is poor showmanship. The higher the illumination, the more the audience makes its own show. Illumination of more than 25 fc may be in order.

The marquee must be drained so that a curtain of water is not interposed between the automobile and the sidewalk.

A high degree of illumination is especially necessary wherever there are steps outside the marquee or between marquee and foyer. Outside illumination is no less important if the theatre is hidden away in a school building. It is not enough to make it possible for the audience to see after it has got into the building, the school building plant which contains the theatre must include theatre requisites in the planning of the whole building.

Changes of level from sidewalk through the vestibule, foyer and lobby into the house are best made by ramps. Stairs are forbidden by some building codes and permitted under careful restrictions by others. Isolated steps and steps at doors are to be avoided as hazardous. When steps occur they must be adequately lighted. White painted strips on the outer edges of steps are helpful.

Interior illumination of lobbies below and a student lounge make the façade of the Hopkins Center Theatre, Dartmouth College, a clear and attractive statement of purpose.

Doors into Foyer

Fire regulations provide that all theatre doors must open out. Traditionally the doors to the foyer are hung in pairs, and in new theatres are often glass or clear Lucite. For the sake of fulfilling their function, there must be enough doors to handle the whole audience without congestion in a few minutes. For the purpose of making foyer doors architecturally impressive, they are often much wider than is efficient. Thirty-two inches should be considered a maximum width for the single unit of a pair of double doors. The glass lights are principally for the purpose of giving daylight illumination to the foyer, one of the few places in the theatre where there is any use for it. If glass or Lucite doors are used there must be a positive light lock between the foyer and the house.

Where the theatre building is used for other purposes and access is via corridors, the entrance to the building itself must be so planned as to conform to minimum foyer standards.

The vestibule of the Crampton Auditorium, Howard University, Washington, D.C.

◄ *Fixtures in the marquee light the exterior doors of the O'Keefe Centre, Toronto.*

Vestibule and Foyer

Foyer area and arrangement are determined by a study of the traffic loads (Chapter 2). In addition to traffic, the architect is concerned with doors and other entrances, floor, wall and ceiling materials, heat, ventilation, and light.

There is more traffic through the foyer than through any other part of the theatre. It is a room outside the theatre proper. The floor surfaces, therefore, must stand a lot of traffic, must not be stained or rendered hazardous by standing water, must be easily cleaned, must not be uncomfortable to stand on. Stone and tile are popular and good but are best covered by perforated rubber matting in wet weather as they tend to become slippery. The patron waiting for friends or in the ticket queue often has a dripping umbrella. Wall surfaces must resist defacing to at least shoulder height and must be easy to clean, and the junction between wall and floor must be watertight. These requisites rule out plaster walls and, except where foyer is so large as never to be crowded, wood paneling. Doors must all be silent and self-closing. If there is access from foyer to offices or other parts of the building, the doors are made as inconspicuous as possible to keep theatre patrons from trying to use them.

Hard-surfaced rooms tend to be excessively noisy; it is therefore desirable to surface the ceiling and, where appropriate from a decorative point of view, upper sections of the walls, with sound absorbent material. Such materials must be easy to clean. The higher the absorption coefficient, the more appropriate is the material.

Since occupants of the foyer are dressed for the weather outside, provision for heating or cooling need not provide the difference between outside and inside conditions demanded by the interior of the theatre. There is no need for heating to achieve temperatures above 60° F, or cooling to more than 5° lower than the outside temperature. Humidity control is welcome to the same degree as that provided for the house. If air is blown into the foyer to accomplish any or all of the tasks of air conditioning (heating, cooling, ventilation, humidity control), it must *not* be recirculated. Warm air may be forced into the foyer in winter as a buffer against outside cold air and cool air in summer as an attraction to passers-by.

The purposes and requisites for lighting in the foyer are the same as those which apply under the marquee. If any variation in illumination is undertaken, the bright spots must be at steps, areas in front of ticket windows, and area about the ticket taker's stand at the entrance to the lobby. Bright light sources within the normal visual angle are a source of annoyance and fatigue, which rules out sconces, standlights and usually chandeliers.

Standard equipment for foyers includes the ticket taker's box (portable) which is only in place when it is in use, and rails to prevent the forming of double lines at ticket windows. If the foyer is so planned that lines of traffic do not intersect, the rails are dispensable. It goes without saying that the decorative treatment of the foyer must be such as to make it a pleasant place to be. A cold, dark, forbidding foyer discourages theatregoing.

Box Office

The most efficient box office is the change booth at the turnstile employed in some motion picture houses. Next in order of efficiency is the ticket cage at the entrance to the foyer which dispenses tickets automatically for unreserved seats. In both these types of box offices, the speed with which change can be made is the factor which determines the number of persons who can be handled. Automatic change dispensers are now practically universal in such box offices.

The problem of the theatre which has reserved seats is much more complex. Ticket purchasers often request specific locations. There is often considerable discussion, and change-making is not restricted to silver. The size, arrangement, and equipment of the booth constitute the most complex problem in booth design when reserved seats are to be handled. For all except the smallest or most specialized houses, the reserved seat policy must be envisioned.

Lobbies, Hopkins Center.

Ticket counter, Hopkins Center. Pulldown locking grille connects with business office. Ticket racks set into sockets in the counter.

The box office needs at least one window for current sale per approximately 1250 seats, and one window for reservations. The farther apart these windows are, the easier the traffic problem will be. If the box office is at a corner, one window can be on one side and one on the other. The island box office can have lines on either side. The ticket bar as used in Europe has the advantage of handling more simultaneous transactions than any other type since the staff is not restricted to the number of windows. It has a further advantage in that it eliminates the elements of remoteness, formality, and regimentation which the window box office so often fosters. In large houses ticket sale may be divided between windows or sections of the ticket bar as follows: current show sale; reservations for current show; advance sale; each category further subdivided by price or location, or both.

Size and shape of box office are determined by (1) number of windows with their attendant equipment, change drawer, automatic change machine and (2) wall space for the ticket racks which include the day board for the current performance, the rack containing tickets for the rest of the current week, and racks containing tickets for subsequent weeks. Two day boards help to minimize ticket purchase time if one is used for the current and one for the next performance, especially on matinee days. Rack sizes vary with the size of the house but are seldom less than 20 inches × 30 inches. For large houses, orchestra and balcony tickets are sometimes efficiently handled at separate windows. If the day board is on the wall containing the ticket window, the ticket seller does not need to turn around during the transaction. Telephones, a desk, and a safe complete the useful box office equipment. The safe must be large enough to contain all the racks without removing tickets from them, in addition to the usual cash box and ledger. Access to the box office is by a single door inside the theatre, often from an adjacent business office. Where the ticket bar is used, racks are on the wall behind the bar and the door in that wall leads into an office which serves all

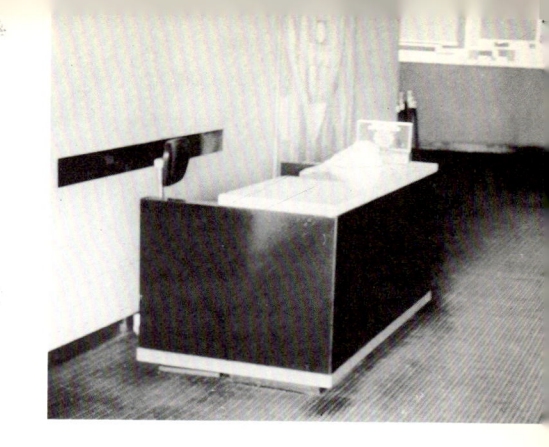

Ticket desk, Cinema 2, New York City. Geller and Schlanger, architects.

Ticket counter, ANTA Theatre, New York City.

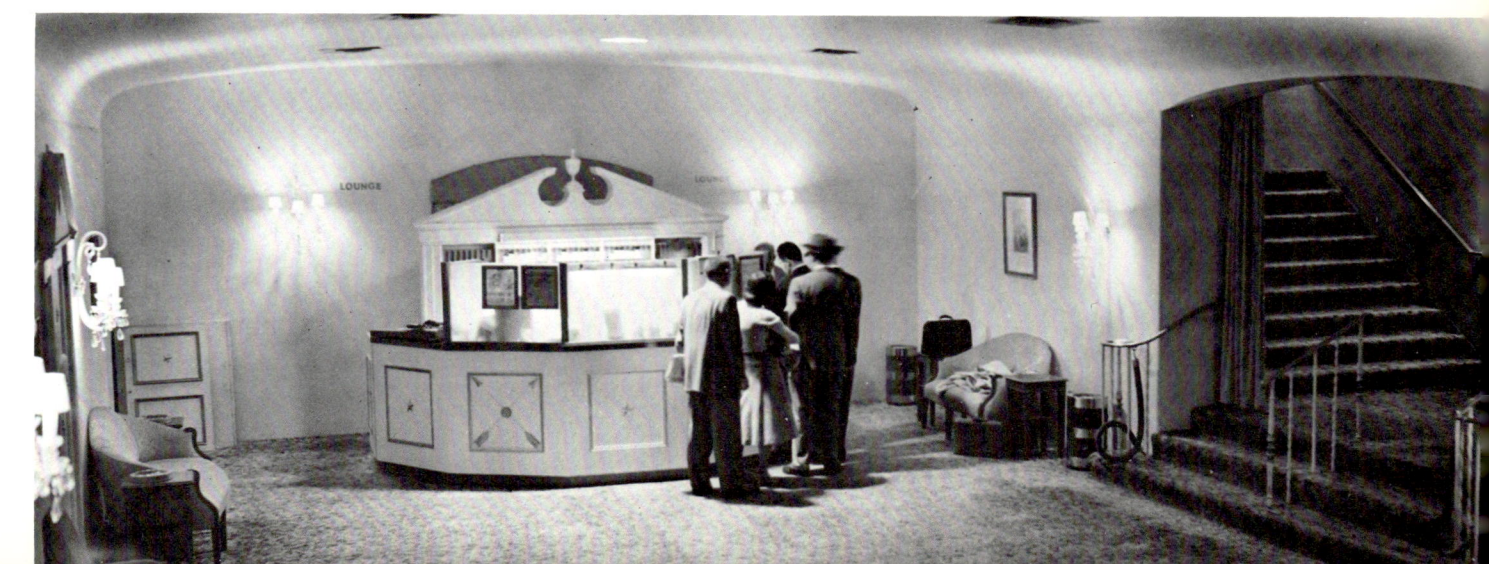

Lobby, O'Keefe Centre. Escalators supplement the stairs.

other box office purposes except ticket dispensing. The light in the box office is best concentrated on working areas with additional general illumination. School and college theatres are often handicapped because they were designed without box offices.

Confusion, inefficiency, and ill will engendered from lack of adequate architectural provision for the one point at which the theatre staff has business dealings with its customers can do much to discourage patronage. A typical condition is one in which the curtain is held while ticket sellers fumble through the box of tickets to try to accommodate the last-minute box office rush. The box office takes up very little space and cannot be neglected in any type of theatre.

For turnstile box office and the automatic dispensing motion picture theatre box office, specifications drawn by the manufacturers of the box office equipment may be followed.

Lest it be forgotten, the box office needs ventilation as much as any other part of the theatre and heating to counteract blasts of frigid air from the foyer.

Lounge, Lunt-Fontanne Theatre, New York City.

The requirements for lobby size and shape are derived from traffic studies. In the interests of safety, doors must usually occupy the whole wall between foyer and lobby. Their equipment and swing must fill specifications for foyer doors save that there is never any reason for glass lights in them. Doors between lobby and house may not be necessary unless the show is continuous. Between lobby and lounge no doors are necessary. Whether or not there are doors to the house, the lobby must be quiet, for which reason the floor must be completely carpeted; the walls, sound-absorbent or containing sound-absorbent panels or covered with draperies; and the ceiling, sound-absorbent. Sound from the lobby must not leak into the house.

Lobby

Lobby, Crampton Auditorium.

Outdoor balcony is lounge of John Fitzgerald Kennedy Theatre, University of Hawaii.

99

Lighting in the lobby must be warm enough to be flattering, bright enough to highlight jewels, so directed that it will not spill into the house. If lobby lights are dimmed during performance, there must still be enough illumination to read the ticket stub, see the stairs, find the coatroom or the lounge. For continuous-run motion picture houses, it is desirable to have the general illumination of the lobby of lower intensity than the foyer, to facilitate dark adaptation for the entering audience. These requirements can only be met by carefully planned combination of direct and indirect illumination, i.e., coves and louvered reflectors recessed in the ceiling, chandelier and ceiling containing a large indirect source of light or many small, flush, ceiling lights with frosted covers, lenses, or louvres. Illuminated signs indicating coat room, lounge entrance, and balcony stairs or elevator are desirable. Exit signs are requisite over all doors leading to the foyer.

Ceiling height may well depend upon other elements in the theatre structure, and a high ceiling contributes to a feeling of luxury. If the stairs have a complete run along lobby walls, the ceiling may well be as high as that of the house. The aim of all decorative treatment must obviously be the promotion of the feeling of luxury.

The furnishings of the lobby are fairly obvious. They include mirrors. In them the theatregoer can be sure he is seen if only by himself. Mirrors have no value unless they are tall and obviously a part of the decorative scheme. A tinted mirror is to be preferred to the standard silver mirror; it is not so harsh and may be flattering to the modern Narcissus.

Wall tables for flowers and to hold the hat while the coat is being put on, benches to facilitate putting on rubbers, complete the necessary lobby furnishings save where lounge limitations and local law and custom demand ash receivers.

Furniture in the lobby must be located in space over and above the clear width required as passageways by building codes. Care must be taken that furniture does not impede audience traffic.

The best carpet is the cheapest in the long run. The original chenille carpet in the lobby of the Roxy Theatre in New York lasted more than a decade. No carpet could be subjected to heavier wear. Wilton is a good carpet but will not last as long as a good chenille. The design of the carpet may well be planned to lead the audience in the direction conducive to minimum traffic congestion, i.e., from foyer to checkroom, to stairs and crossover, from audience area to lounge entrance by circular path to the left, back to the house. When low-intensity lighting is employed to accommodate the audience in a dark house, fluorescent lines in the carpet, energized by overhead UV lamps, have proved useful.

Stairs leading to balconies require carpeting for the same reason that the rest of the lobby is carpeted. Maximum comfortable riser height is 7½ inches, and minimum tread width 10½ inches. For added wear, for quiet and for comfort, carpets must be laid on padding.

Balcony lobby provisions for comfort and safety are derived by observing the same rules which apply in orchestra lobby planning.

Checkroom

The checkroom counter should be wide enough for five attendants per 1000 seats in the house. With adequate checkroom facilities, the efficiency of checking is governed by the size of the staff, not by architectural limitations. Checkrooms in balcony lobbies reduce orchestra lobby congestion. Racks built to accommodate coats, hats, sticks, umbrellas and parcels, used in some of the new dining rooms and checkrooms of some modern hotels, may well serve as models for theatre checkroom equipment. Self-service checking apparatus, using locking clothing holders, may be considered.

In conformity with the principle of keeping traffic moving to the right, the checkroom is best located at the right side of the lobby as the patron enters from the foyer. The fact that it is on the patron's left as he leaves the theatre is of little consequence because he faces no opposing traffic and he has already found out where the checkroom is.

Coat checking counters, the Waldorf-Astoria. Colored checks guide patrons to the proper counters. Guests proceed from elevators to counters to ballroom.

Lounge

As the audience comes out of the house at intermission time, it finds the lounge most easily if it is located at the right, i.e., at the opposite side of the lobby from the checkroom. The lounge, as its name implies, is the place where the audience stretches, talks, and refreshes itself during intermissions. Its hallmarks are the deeply upholstered chair and the sand-filled receptacle for butts. In it are bar, telephones, water coolers, and entrances to lavatories.

Floor, walls, and ceiling of the lounge merit the same treatment as their counterparts in the lobby and for the same reasons. Lavatories

Lobby-lounge, Arena Stage. Refreshment counter in background, displays at right.

may be located either at the right or left of the lounge entrance provided they are both visible without turning halfway around as the patron enters the lounge; or they may be located one after the other as he starts a circuit of the room, keeping to the right.

The lounge needs overstuffed chairs arranged as though in a living room, save that their normal groupings for conversational purposes need seldom provide for more than four. The occasional straight chair will serve to make the normal groupings flexible. Small but rugged tables to hold lamps, ash trays and drinks, and many ash receivers complete the requisite equipment. A piano is decorative and useful if the lounge serves as a room for gatherings other than the intermission audience. A fireplace is useful only if it can contain a real fire and does when the weather makes one appropriate.

Light

Light intensity at lounge entrance, exit, lavatory entrances, and bar will naturally be higher than at other areas. For maximum effectiveness, it may well be planned so that as the patron walks through the lounge he passes through alternating areas of medium (10 fc) and high (25 fc) intensity. If direct light from ceiling to floor is a part of the scheme for the high-intensity areas, sequins and jewelry will sparkle in them and a dramatic effect will be gained from the movement of groups of people.

White light is harsh and not very dramatic. Pale magenta is good for general illumination but must be supplemented by white or steel blue to highlight the audience as mentioned previously. Color is best achieved in shades and roundels or fluorescent tubes. Amber lights in public rooms make the audience look like cadavers, eight days drowned. The exposed bulb has no decorative value in most schemes.

Stairs connect upper and lower lounges, O'Keefe Centre.

Bar

A bar in the lounge is a source of income not lightly to be dismissed. In London, a play may run at no profit to the box office or even at a very slight loss, and the theatre may still operate on the profit from the bar. Aside from this, however, a bar undeniably adds to the spirit of carnival and helps to make theatregoing an event. The bar belongs in or near the lounge. Congestion, discomfort, and hazards introduced by soft-drink vendors in the lobby or crossover are familiar to everyone.

The proportion of the audience which uses the lounge is, with little exception, limited only by the capacity of the lounge. Lounge area is inadequate in most theatres. It may well occupy all the space under the

The bar and restaurant, Philharmonic Hall.

seating area of the house and the lobby and be supplemented by balcony lounges. In theatres located in warm, dry climates, the lounge may well be outdoors, in which case a large lobby is needed and the lavatories are located adjacent to it. The large indoor lounge constitutes, when properly planned, useful rental space for exhibitions, parties, lectures, and meetings at times when the audience is not in the theatre. For these ancillary uses a kitchen, kitchenette or serving pantry may be added. The lounge is traditionally used for rehearsal.

Most building codes require, and wisdom dictates, exits from the lounge sufficient to evacuate its capacity crowd at the same rate at which the house may be emptied.

Spacious hospitable lounges characterize recently built theatres.

Hopkins Center

O'Keefe Centre

Crampton Auditorium

Lavatories

It goes without saying that lavatories must have anterooms: a smoking room for men, and a powder room, equipped with at least one dressing table per 600 seats or fraction thereof in the house, for women. Five urinals, three wash basins and two toilets per 1000 seats are minima for the men's lavatory; five toilets and five wash basins per 1000 for the women's lavatory are minima. Where performances run over three hours, the lavatory traffic is increased fourfold, for which reason it is wise to exceed the lavatory equipment minima by a considerable margin. The roaring, hot-air, hand driers have no place in a theatre. Lavatories must be sound-isolated from the house and stage. In multi-tiered theatres, lounges and related facilities should be equally commodious on each tier.

Multiple Uses

Restricted building budgets sometimes lead clients and architects to slight or limit the public rooms, or attempt to combine their functions. People still have to get from here to there and still take up the same amount of room whether the builder likes it or not. A theatre wrongly designed in the first instance is seldom susceptible to much improvement. In planning front service rooms in the face of a restricted budget, the same precept applies as has been recommended for other parts of the theatre, i.e., plan a complete and adequate plant, build or finish only as much as the budget provides for, leaving provision for completion when funds are again available. Temporary expedients necessary to

Fully-upholstered, well-spaced seats with adequate armrests. Hopkins Center.

the operation of the uncompleted plant are seldom any more annoying than restrictions resulting from compromises and have the virtue of being remediable.

Compromises

When the theatre plant includes, or is a part of, an architectural unit which contains shops, restaurant, a broadcast station, or of a school or college, the public rooms of the theatre may well be planned to serve other than theatrical purposes at hours when no audience is present. Conversely, public rooms planned to serve nontheatrical purposes in hours when the theatre is dark may be made to serve the theatre. This condition is a critical one for the theatre in the school, located in a building which is used in part for nontheatrical purposes. If special front service rooms are not provided for the theatre in such a building, the lounge, lavatories, and hallways of the building must be arranged to satisfy the requirements of theatre.

House

If doors between lobby and crossover are used, they will normally stand open except while the play is in progress. The glass partition behind the last row of seats (found in some motion picture theatres) is no substitute for a wall and doors. A 4½ foot high wall behind the seats is desirable, to prevent draft and to accommodate standing patrons.

Comfort in the house depends upon (1) shape and upholstery of seats and the distance between rows; (2) position and width of aisles; (3) temperature, humidity and freshness of air; (4) house lighting; (5) decoration; (6) floor slope; (7) absence of distraction. Theatrical requirements other than audience comfort and safety prescribe adequate comfort specifications for some of these items.

The seat which is acoustically correct will be comfortably upholstered. No less important than the upholstery is the shape of the seat. For some unknown reason the curved-back, bucket seat has been popular in America and is installed in many theatres. Sitting with the shoulders pinched forward becomes extremely uncomfortable by intermission time. Flat-backed chairs are therefore the only proper equipment for the theatre. A chair of this sort developed for the Chicago Civic Opera House became a widely used type, but is no longer produced.

Adequate, but seated patron must stand to permit another to pass, unless seat slides back.

Despite the past record of the Provincetown Theatre and the present success of the Hedgerow Theatre, hard seats won't encourage repeated patronage. The comfortable seat is no less important in the school or college theatre. Assemblies and commencements held in the theatre will benefit from comfortable seats.

Seats need to be spaced sufficiently far apart to permit passage of people without the occupant's rising. Cramming them close together for the purpose of slightly increased capacity is a very shortsighted policy. Closely spaced seats cause extreme discomfort, especially to

Allows one patron to pass another patron who remains seated.

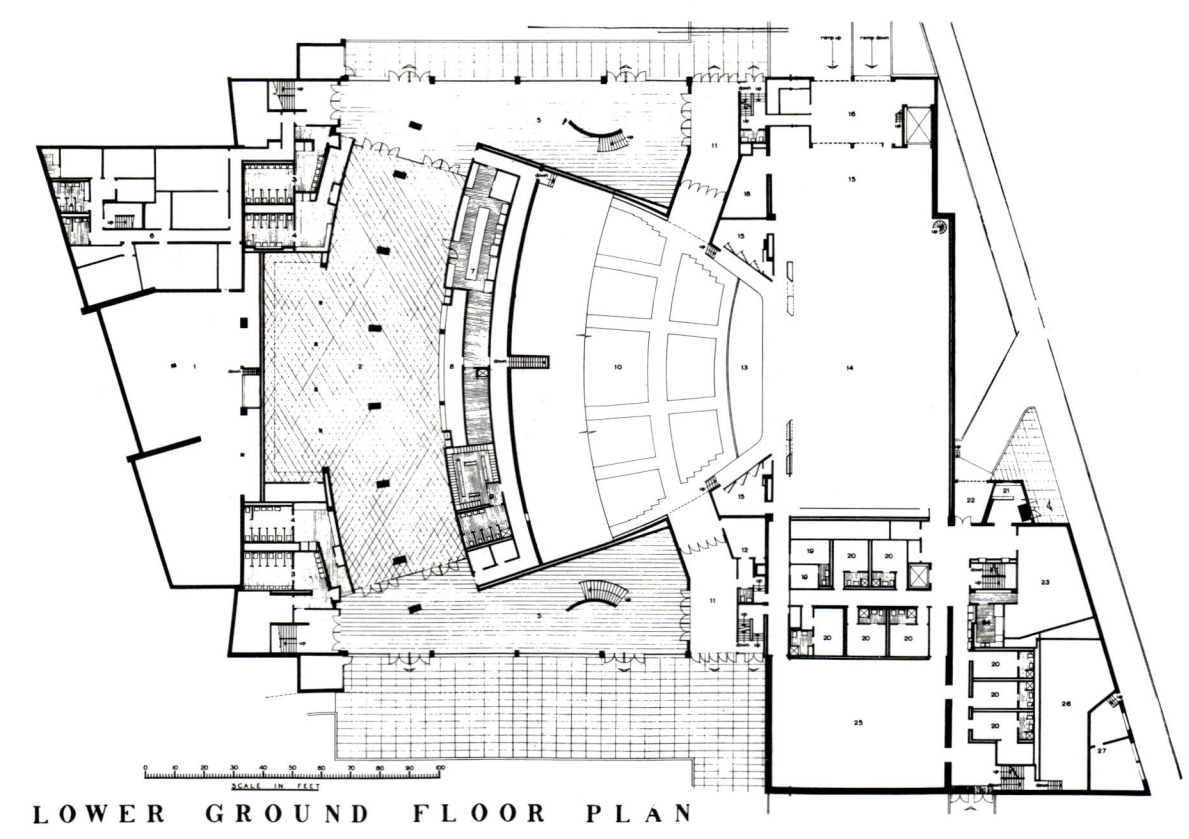

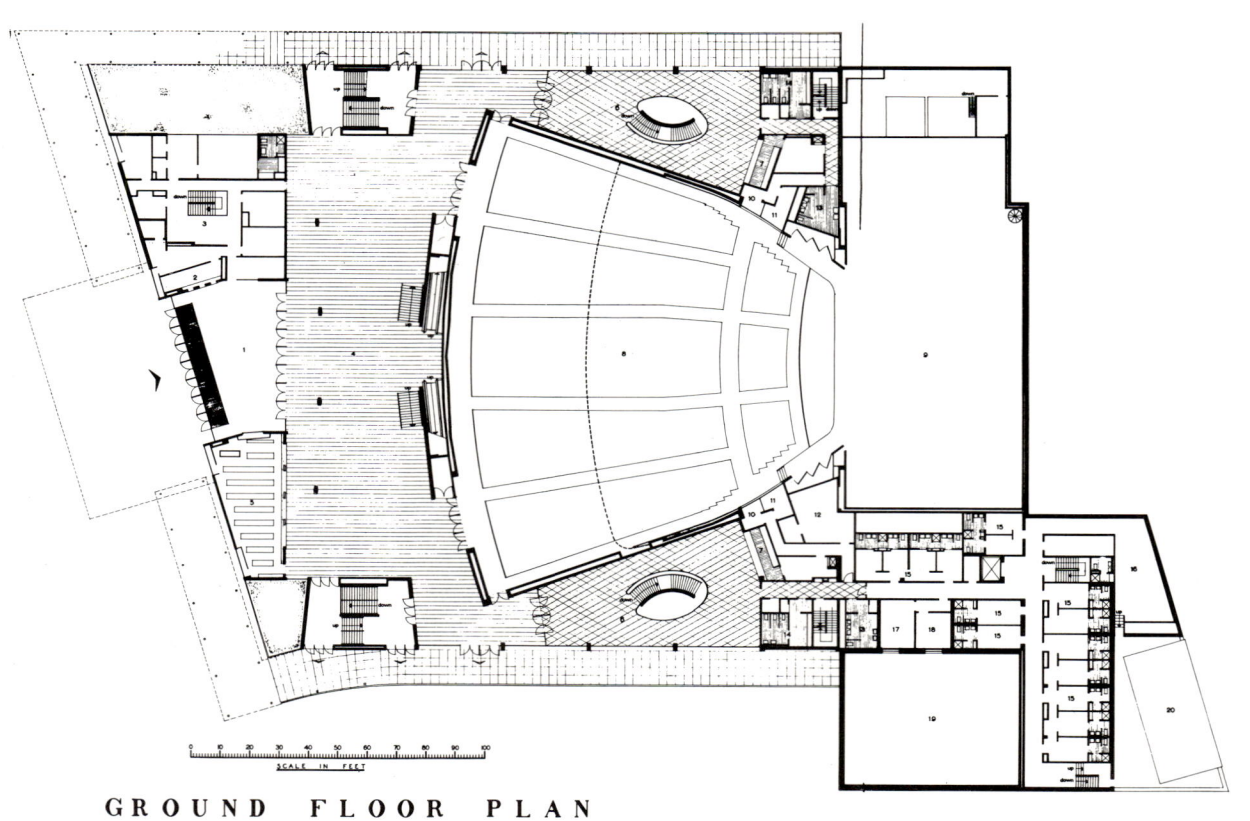

LOWER GROUND FLOOR PLAN

GROUND FLOOR PLAN

108

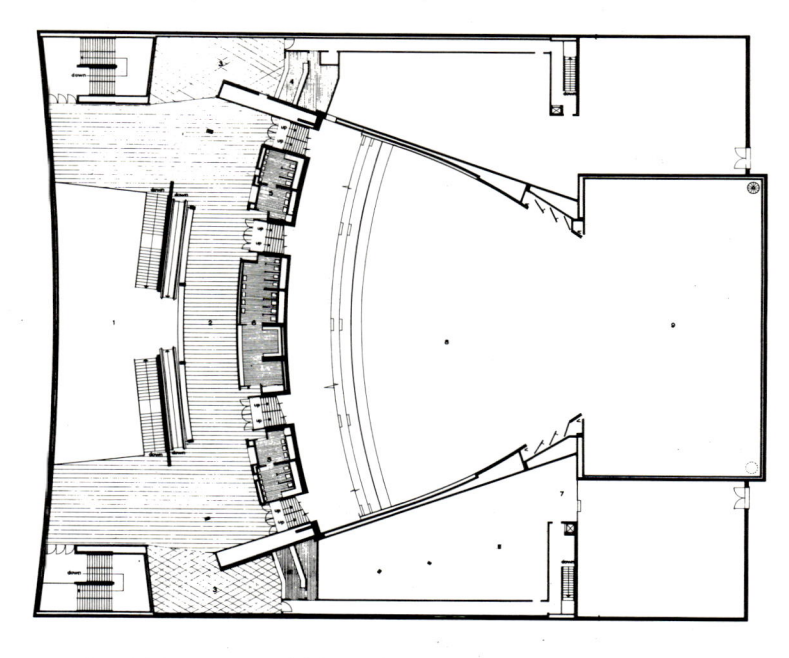

BALCONY FOYER PLAN

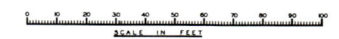

OPPOSITE: *Lower ground floor plan*
1. mechanical room
2. refreshment lounge
3. men's washroom
4. powder room and washroom
5. foyers
6. administration
7. kitchen
8. refreshment bar
9. staff lockers

OPPOSITE: *Ground floor plan*
1. vestibule
2. ticket office
3. administration
4. entrance foyer
5. coat room
6. refreshment lounges
7. refreshment bars
10. announcer
11. control room
12. master control

ABOVE: *Balcony foyer plan*
1. upper part of entrance foyer
2. balcony foyer
3. refreshment lounge
4. refreshment bar
5. men's rooms
6. powder room and washroom
7. mechanical rooms

The O'Keefe Centre in Toronto exemplifies the modern concern for audience comfort with three refreshment lounges and foyers enveloping the house, exits onto garden terraces, ample coat rooms and public rooms and escalators paralleling stairways. Performing and working personnel are equally well accommodated.

tall people, and some inveterate theatregoers will not go into certain New York theatres no matter what the show. The marginal comfortable spacing, back to back, is 34 inches. Spacing to permit easy passage past seated patrons is 45 inches, back to back. Continental seating with slide-back seating requires only 39 inches between rows.

Seats with springs which raise them automatically simplify cleaning and save many barked shins. If employed they must be considered in the acoustical planning.

The building codes in most localities set minimum limits for aisle width and number of seats in a row. For economic reasons it is generally wise to use the maximum number of seats per row. Under no circumstances is a center aisle tolerable. Actors abhor center aisles for the very good reason that they split the audience and make the achieving of mass reaction difficult.

Exits Local and state ordinances governing buildings for public assembly prescribe the number, size and, to some extent, the location of exits. In the absence of specific requirements in the laws, the planner may refer to the recommendations of the National Board of Fire Underwriters.

Satisfaction of the code requirements for emergency exits, plus provision for the comfort and safety of the audience, as set forth in this chapter, will result in a house in which the audience will be psychologically and physically conditioned to enjoy the performance to the maximum.

Philharmonic Hall, Lincoln Center for the Performing Arts.

6: Power, heat, air-conditioning, plumbing

The architectural and engineering practices and building code requirements which govern the installation of power, light, heat, ventilation, and plumbing in buildings are well standardized. This chapter will concern itself only with variations from standard practice made necessary by the peculiar demands of the theatre.

Power

The theatre differs from almost any other type of building in that its power requirement is 85 per cent of outlet capacity, considerably more than the code requirement for residences, hotels, and office buildings. The reasons for this are obvious: it is not uncommon for every lamp and every motor in the theatre to be in use simultaneously. Failure, through overloading, must not occur during performance. It is wise at the outset to bring in enough power to handle the maximum load based on final installed requirements. Facilities for stage lighting must be included in the original building plans. Because of the increasing efficiency of light sources, it is improbable that future additions to lighting equipment will require more power than does the completely equipped theatre for which the power load is calculated.

Power Plant

Because of the intermittent use of the theatre, it is seldom economical for the theatre to generate its own power. If the theatre is part of a school which has its own power plant, the school plant must usually have capacity considerably in excess of that which is normal for an academic plant. A theatre imposes peak loads not only in the evening but often during the day, for which reason planning to divert power from darkened departments in the evening places undue restrictions on the daytime use of the theatre.

Auxiliary Power Supply

An emergency power supply from a source entirely separate from the regular one is required by law in most cities. This supply must be adequate to illuminate the house, all exit passages, and all exit lights. An auxiliary power supply capable of meeting the total load requirements of the theatre is desirable, though not required by law.

Schematic diagram of power distribution.

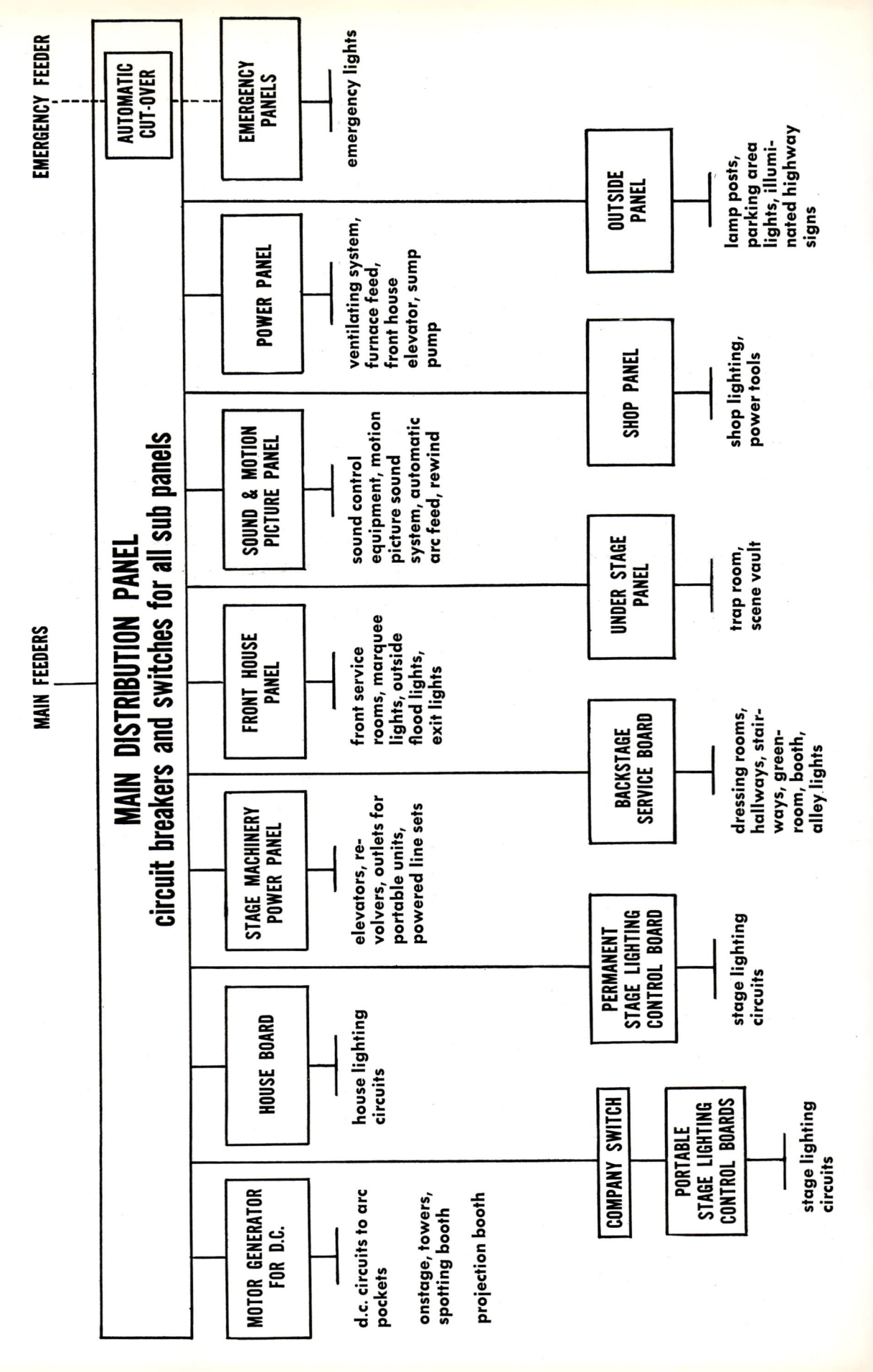

MAIN DISTRIBUTION PANEL
circuit breakers and switches for all sub panels

EMERGENCY FEEDER → **AUTOMATIC CUT-OVER** → **EMERGENCY PANELS** — emergency lights

MAIN FEEDERS → MAIN DISTRIBUTION PANEL

- **POWER PANEL** — ventilating system, furnace feed, front house elevator, sump pump
  - **OUTSIDE PANEL** — lamp posts, parking area lights, illuminated highway signs
- **SOUND & MOTION PICTURE PANEL** — sound control equipment, motion picture sound system, automatic arc feed, rewind
  - **SHOP PANEL** — shop lighting, power tools
- **FRONT HOUSE PANEL** — front service rooms, marquee lights, outside flood lights, exit lights
  - **UNDER STAGE PANEL** — trap room, scene vault
- **STAGE MACHINERY POWER PANEL** — elevators, revolvers, outlets for portable units, powered line sets
  - **BACKSTAGE SERVICE BOARD** — dressing rooms, hallways, stairways, greenroom, booth, alley lights
- **HOUSE BOARD** — house lighting circuits
  - **PERMANENT STAGE LIGHTING CONTROL BOARD** — stage lighting circuits
- **COMPANY SWITCH** → **PORTABLE STAGE LIGHTING CONTROL BOARDS** — stage lighting circuits
- **MOTOR GENERATOR FOR D.C.** — d.c. circuits to arc pockets onstage, towers, spotting booth, projection booth

112

Current

For stage use, both AC and DC are required. Either AC or DC may be employed where resistance plates are used as dimmers. AC is required where dimming is done by autotransformers or by electronic means. DC is required for arc spotlights (on stage and out front). Motors for blowers, furnace feed, marquee moving sign, power tools in the shop, and other similar equipment are most efficient if they operate on AC. For elevators, motorized flying equipment and revolving stages AC is required because of electronic control devices. The amount of each kind of current is easily determined by totaling the requirements of each type of equipment. Standard voltage is 110 and single-phase, except where the demands of specific motors or lighting control equipment require three-phase.

Location

It is wise to keep generating equipment—transformers, rectifiers, and motor generators—away from the operating areas in the theatre, in a separate building back of the stage house or in the corner of the basement under the stage farthest away from the proscenium. Such equipment is automatic, needs little attention, and needs to be kept out of the way. Some items cause interference or distortion in electronic equipment.

Alternators

The synchronous winch flying system requires alternators which howl like jet aircraft engines. They must be housed in a vault outside the theatre.

Main Distribution Panel

If current enters the theatre in the form in which it is to be used, entry normally should be at the point which will require the shortest run of conduit from the main distribution and breaker panel to the stage loads.

This panel is located at the point of entry or origin of the current. It includes circuit breakers on all incoming feeders, except the solid ground on 4-wire AC installations, and provision for distributing each type of current to sub-panels at the next point of control. The sub-panels are:

1. House board located onstage from which all house lighting circuits branch.
2. Company switch.
3. Permanent stage lighting control.
4. Power panel for stage machinery.
5. Backstage service board from which are distributed circuits to dressing rooms, hallways, stairways, greenroom, stage doorman's booth, alley lights.

6. Under-stage panel for distribution to trap room, basement scene vault, and other understage areas.

7. Front house panel carrying circuits for all front service rooms, marquee sign, and outside floodlight equipment.

8. Motion picture projection panel for all circuits feeding motion picture, sound, and other electronic equipment (not including stage lighting control).

9. Power panel from which come the individual circuits for ventilation equipment and furnace feed.

10. Shop panel from which are distributed circuits for shop lighting and power tools.

11. Outside panel feeding lampposts, parking area lights, and illuminated highway signs.

12. Exit light panel which supplies all exit lights which burn while the audience is in the theatre.

The main distribution panel is equipped with switches, circuit breakers and, in the case of small circuits, fuses. These are grouped according to sub-distribution points, and each group contains distribution facilities for every type of current to go to the sub-panels. In other words, each type of current is distributed to sub-panels from the same main panel.

Variations within this distribution scheme will be treated after consideration of the individual sub-distribution points.

Company Switch

The company switch is traditionally located on the operating side of the stage. From it are tapped the main feeders for portable switchboards. When a portable switchboard is used, stage lights and lights in ceiling and side-wall slots, in boxes and on balcony fascia are fed directly from the portable board.

House Board

Dimmers for house lights are standard equipment in all theatres. From the main panel the lines go to a sub-panel and thence to the house light switches and dimmers. Electrical or mechanical mastering facilitates even dimming of all or selected house lighting circuits.

In addition to the main switch and circuit breakers, small individual switches control orchestra pit lights, pinrail and scene dock work light, rehearsal lights and convenience outlets. *All these switches must be silent.*

Permanent Stage Lighting Control Boards

All theatres except commercial theatres have permanent stage lighting control boards. Feeders from the main distribution panel run to the point where control is applied to the load voltages. The location of this point varies with the control system used (see Control Systems in Chapter 12).

A guiding principle is to make the runs of large-sized conductors as direct as possible, consistent with other factors governing the location of the control point.

Sub-Panels

Three conditions govern the location of all sub-panels: (1) they must be easily accessible to the persons responsible for their operation; (2) in the interest of efficient construction, they must be located in as direct a line as possible between the main distribution panel and the instruments served by their branch circuits; (3) no panels must be located at any point to which the audience has access.

The power panel for stage machinery is located beside or in the house board if the motors controlled are onstage or above it; in the trap room, if the motors are belowstage; or, if motors are located in both places, two panels individually fed from the main distribution panel are employed. In any case *control* is at the stage manager's position.

The backstage service board is located in the stage entrance corridor in or near the stage doorman's booth.

The understage panel is located at the foot of the backstage stairs leading to the basement.

The motion picture projection panel is located in the rear wall of the projection booth or the projectionists' office.

The power panel for ventilation and heating is located on a wall of the room which contains ventilation equipment or furnace feed.

The shop panel is located in the shop near the entrance at a point where there is no occasion for stacking scenery.

The outside panel is located in an office at the front of the theatre.

Sub-panel assembly follows standard practice except that (1) more than one kind of current may be controlled through switches in the same panel; (2) all switches in all panels, in all walls, which surround the stage or any portion of the theatre occupied by the audience, must be silent. This restriction applies also to wall switches in individual circuits.

Variations

It is obvious that the arrangement here outlined is too elaborate for the small theatre, and inadequate for the opera house. The routine of theatre operation, plus sound engineering practice, prescribe that the minimum power distribution facilities be a combination main distribution panel, a house board, a company switch, and a front house panel. The expansion of this system for very large houses can be developed from an analysis of the organization of such a theatre. When there is a permanent engineering or electrical maintenance staff attached to the theatre, sub-panel locations, with the exception of company board and motion picture distribution panel, are susceptible of considerable variation. In any case, however, the principle of grouping loads on sub-panels as here outlined must be adhered to if operation and maintenance are to be easy and effective.

Only by keeping branch circuits independent of each other can the varying load conditions in a theatre be successfully met. Typical results of variations from this practice are: In one theatre, the electronic organ would not play when the moving marquee sign was turned on, because the marquee sign caused the voltage in the AC line to drop to 92. In another theatre, the characters on the motion picture screen spoke something which sounded like monkey chatter because a transformer was too near. In another theatre, the grounded sump pump blew the fuses in the line which fed the motion picture projection arcs.

Outside Lights

The only aspect of outside theatre lighting for which specifications do not naturally arise from the foregoing principles is the marquee billing and the theatre name sign. Whether or not these are used depends upon the location of the theatre. The urban theatre will want to dominate the block, and the rural theatre transfers its identification and billing from the marquee to the side of the highway. In either case, light is needed. Fluorescent tubes have considerable visibility per unit of power consumption. To determine the power for house identification and marquee billing, it is necessary to make a light survey of the locality and calculate therefrom the number of foot candles which will achieve the desired degree of visibility over the area to be illuminated. Theatre identification, marquee billing, under-marquee illumination and driveway lights—the last two discussed in previous chapters—constitute a large load.

Air-Conditioning

Air conditioning is now belatedly recognized as a necessary feature without an approximation of which not even the meagerly equipped New York legitimate house can draw customers in hot weather. There are many systems and devices which allegedly provide air conditioning and do, in the sense that they do something to the air, but whether the processed air is thereby rendered any more conducive to comfort is, alas, another story. Briefly, the function of air conditioning is to provide comfort for the audience by providing the requisite amount of fresh sterile air (about 10 cfm per person), at the proper temperature (about 70° F) and humidity (50 per cent or less). Important subsidiary functions include protecting seat coverings, drops, and hangings from mildew. Metal surfaces and duct linings will rust through excess moisture in the air. Fabrics will be discolored and ultimately destroyed by dust if the air is not kept reasonably dust free.

Air Intake

The air-conditioning cycle is as follows:
The air is drawn out of the house through grilles at the front or back

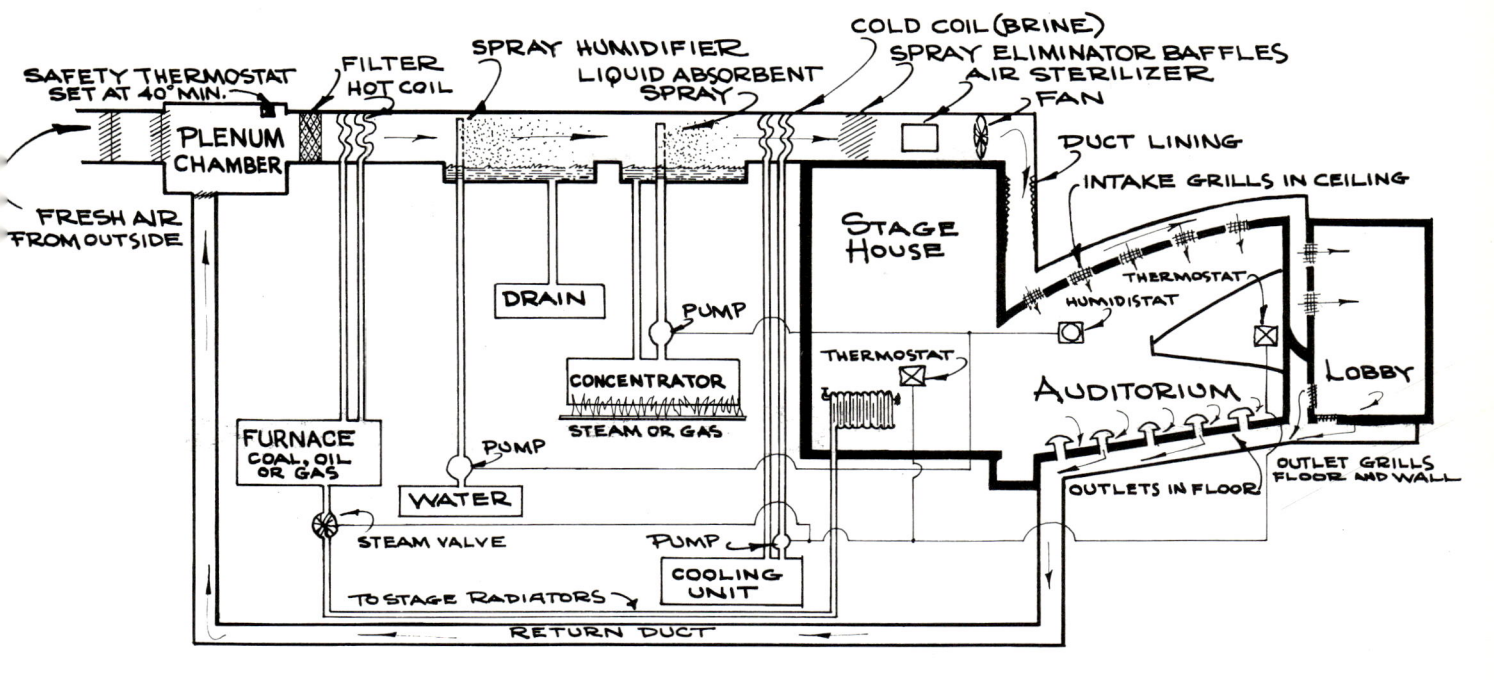

Schematic diagram of a complete air-conditioning system. The auditorium is carried at slightly higher pressure than stage or public rooms so that a stage fire will not spread toward the audience and tobacco smoke will not drift into the house when lobby doors are opened.

of the house or mushrooms under the seats, preferably built into the seat legs to conserve foot room, through ducts to a plenum chamber. There it is mixed with fresh air drawn from outside the building. Dampers on fresh and return air ducts control the proportion of the mixture. The highest proportion of recirculated air is used in the winter when it is uneconomical to throw away heated air after going to the expense of heating it. When the air is well-conditioned, as little as 20 per cent fresh outside air will suffice to re-establish an adequate oxygen content. The wide range of heating requirements makes it necessary to induce varying amounts of outside air from the minimum to 100 per cent, and to alter the proportion rapidly and easily during performance.

From the plenum chamber the air is drawn through the filter to have odors and dust particles filtered out. Dust, but not odors, can be removed by spray or electrostatic precipitation. For large motion picture houses which run 12 to 14 hours a day, electrostatic precipitation may be the most economical system.

Dust and Odor Removal

Since a system of forced ventilation is necessary in any case and since heat is needed only when the ventilation system is also required, it is

Heating

cheaper to heat the house by a radiator in the main air duct than by any other system. Therefore, the next unit in the air-conditioning circuit is the heating coil, a steam coil fed from the boiler as in any other steam heating system.

An audience coming into a theatre will raise the house temperature approximately 1° F per minute for the 15 minutes before curtain. This rate of change is too rapid for some control instruments to follow or for most systems to compensate. It is therefore necessary especially in cold weather to start with an empty house below ordinary operating temperature and thereafter concentrate on keeping the house cool (usually by feeding cold outside air only into the ventilating system) until the standard working temperature is reached. With an outside temperature below freezing in a well-insulated house where about 60 per cent of the air is recirculated, no heat may be needed until the third act. A theatre system must be capable of rapid adaptation to changed conditions in the house and large excess capacity to minimize the change.

Humidifying

Heating the air reduces its relative humidity not infrequently to a point below 40 per cent which is generally considered minimum for comfort. Moisture can be added by bleeding steam from the heating system into the air stream after it passes the hot coil. A humidistat supplies satisfactory control. Heating and humidifying are fairly simple processes and may be all that are needed where the weather is never excessively hot and damp. Most of the theatres in the United States, however, need apparatus for cooling and dehumidifying the air if they are to operate from June to September.

Cooling

Cooling is accomplished in most installations by piping a liquid refrigerant, often water at about 45° F, through a coil in the air duct. The refrigerant may be cooled by a cycle similar to that used in an ice plant, or home refrigerator. Such a system has the advantage of being self-contained and capable of a wide range of temperature control.

In a primitive method of cooling once popular in many legitimate houses in New York, water that had been sprayed over and melted from ice was run through the cold coil. This system is uneconomical if used for more than a few hours a day.

Similarly, city water or well water may be run through the cold coil if it is cheap enough and does not get warmer than 55° F. City and well water should be quite popular as cooling agents since they require no complex and expensive equipment, sometimes only a little piping which the local plumber can install at small expense. Ironically, several theatres use water to cool their expensive mechanical cooling plants which, if run directly through the cold coil, would cool the theatres adequately without the mechanical plants. Then operation would be simplified and made less expensive if they threw their mechanical coolers away and just used the water.

Dehumidifying

Cooling the air causes it to precipitate moisture. This is fortunate, for the drier the air, the warmer it may be without causing discomfort. However, for most theatres, dehumidifying thus achieved is not sufficient. In fact, fashion designers have developed jackets to be worn with evening gowns to protect the wearers against the dank chill of allegedly air-conditioned theatres.

It is sometimes unpleasantly difficult for the body to adjust itself to a wide difference between the temperature inside and outside of the theatre, particularly in hot weather. In fact, it is now accepted as axiomatic that a 15° F difference in hot weather is all that can be maintained without subjecting the audience to the danger of shock, particularly on leaving the theatre. However, comfort can be maintained in temperatures of 90° F or even greater, by reducing the relative humidity to a point where perspiration is immediately evaporated, lowering the temperature of the skin. The dry heat of the desert is not uncomfortable —in the shade.

The most flexible system for achieving a desirable balance between temperature and humidity in hot weather is to employ chemical means of humidity control. Several substances, notably triethylene glycol (also used for air sterilization), absorb moisture from the air readily and are easily reconcentrated to keep the drying process constant. Any desired relative humidity may be maintained with systems using chemical dehumidifiers.

Glycol vaporizer installed in a plenum. Vaporization is by heat and a glass wick.

Sterilization

Air sterilization removes the threat of airborne infection in the theatre. It belongs in any modern theatre and can easily be provided in old ones. The principle is the maintenance of a germicidal vapor (triethylene or propylene glycol about 50 per cent concentrated) in the air. The quantity of glycol necessary is only one ounce per hour per 3000 cfm of air. Since glycol decomposes at temperatures below its boiling point, vaporizing must be accomplished at a temperature held within a very few degrees. Glycol vapor is introduced into the airstream by a small pressure drop. About 20 cfm pass through the vaporizer which is located in a plenum before the fan or outside the duct ahead of the fan. Vaporizing equipment is electrically interlocked with the fan motor since it need only operate when the ventilating system is in use.

Fan

The fan or blower which keeps the air moving through the theatre and the conditioning apparatus must be silent as pointed out in Chapter 4, even when operating at maximum speed. It must be so placed that it is not supported on any of the steel which supports the walls of the house or from which the ceiling is hung, or some of the sounds incident to its operation will be transmitted to the audience. A popular but poor location for air-handling units is over the house. A good location is under the foyer. Of the fans now on the market, those which are most efficient are the noisiest; thus efficiency must be sacrificed to silence in all but certain highly specialized instances.

Ducts

It is easy to lay out ducts which will take the air where you want it, but the requirements of the theatre are much greater than that. There must first be absolute silence, which almost always means sound insulation in the ducts, at least near the fan, and an air speed considerably less than that which is satisfactory in homes or office buildings. House input grilles must be artistically appropriate, quiet, must assure appropriate distribution (no drafts), and must not direct currents of air along walls or ceiling where dust streaks will show. The sound entering the house through the ventilation system must be below the ambient when the system is shut down and the house is empty.

Circulation

Hot air rises. Dust settles. If the air is used as the means of heating and the path of the air in the house is from floor to ceiling, the balcony will become overheated while the orchestra shivers, because body-heated air rises and the temperature throughout the house cannot be kept constant. Furthermore, even warm air brought in through floor vents feels cool to the ankles, especially to those clad in sheer nylon. Therefore the best cycle of air in the house is from ceiling to floor. Such a cycle will minimize dust, ensure uniform efficient heating, and eliminate drafts.

The generally accepted amount of air needed in any room is 10 cubic feet per minute (cfm) per person. Experience shows this to be adequate for theatres if the air is fresh or well-conditioned. The figure is a minimum, however, for American audiences, and a smaller amount of air or improperly conditioned air will bring complaints of stuffiness.

Public Rooms

For all theatres except those in which motion pictures are run continuously, it is not wise to recirculate air from the public rooms because of the difficulty of eliminating the great quantity of smoke which rises from the audience at intermission. Such rooms can be adequately conditioned under most circumstances by exhaust air from the house, where not much is needed during intermission.

There will be no air return from the foyer unless it is designed to serve more purposes than those assigned to it in Chapter 5. The air conditioning of theatre offices is desirable, as in all offices, but may depend on their use and whether or not the building budget is limited. When public rooms and offices are in continuous use and the house is not, they may best be served by a separate air-conditioning system.

Production Shops

Dehumidification is desirable to dry paint in the paint shop, and to dry fabrics in the dye room. For high-capacity paint and dye shops, a separate system with exhaust to outside air may be desired.

The Stage

The stage heating installation (radiation) will usually take care of the house between performances when the asbestos is up. The stage is cooled and ventilated from, and as part of, the house during performance. The house and stage may be integrated in a single system of circulation by the installation of exhaust ducts on the stage, but the blowing of air into the scenery from supply ducts onstage is likely to cause motion of the scenery, annoying the audience and possibly fouling flown scenery. *There must be no drafts on a stage.*

Dressing Rooms

Cooling and humidity control are quite desirable in the dressing rooms if the theatre operates in the summer. It is difficult to make up a perspiring face. Not all theatrical costumes are designed to be worn or to stay fresh at 90° F in the shade. Conditioned air, blown into the dressing room corridor, entering the rooms through door grilles and exhausted to atmosphere, will keep the cast comfortable and help the show.

Control

The control devices for the air-conditioning system are the conventional thermostat and humidistat. They must be located in the house at the average audience elevation. If placed on the wall, they must be well insulated from it so that they will not be affected by the wall temperature or by a particular local humidity condition induced by the proximity of the wall. There must also be numerous automatic control devices in the air-conditioning unit to control amount of steam injected into the air, steam valve leading to hot coil and flow of cooling liquid in the cold coil. Of particular importance is the thermostat placed just ahead of the heating coil, which controls the dampers on the fresh air intake and allows them to close when the steam is off and the air gets down to 32° F to prevent the freezing of any condensate.

Outside Sources

It is sometimes possible to have excellent air conditioning in a theatre without the installation of anything but ducts, by the simple expedient of buying the conditioned air from an adjacent hotel whose system has a greater capacity than is immediately necessary, or from a store which would otherwise shut down its system during the hours when the theatre needs conditioned air. The buying of conditioned air is perhaps most feasible where a number of theatres closely grouped can buy the surplus capacity of a department store installation.

A single air cooling system supplies the Shubert, Broadhurst, Majestic, Golden, Royal, Plymouth and Booth theatres, all grouped about

Shubert Alley. Lincoln Center is served by a single air-conditioning system. And in Hartford, conditioned air can be purchased from the local gas company.

Heating the Stage

The most efficient system for heating the stage house is by the conventional wall-type radiator. The following restrictions limit the manner of its installation:

1. Radiators must be on the wall and at least six feet off the floor so that they do not use up floor space and so that rubbish will not accumulate on the floor behind them.

2. To avoid using scenery stacking space, radiators must be set in wall bays. Where the stage wall is not divided into bays, radiators must be as close to the wall as possible.

3. Feed and return pipes must not project into the stage space and may sometimes be partially countersunk into the masonry.

4. Battens must be placed in front of all radiators so that scenery stacked against the walls will not come into direct contact with the radiator.

Since lights, resistance dimmers, and leakage from the house heating system through the proscenium all contribute some heat to the stage, the capacity of the stage heating system need not be calculated to provide a stage temperature level of more than 65° F in the coldest weather. The stage heating system, like that of the rest of the theatre, must be so planned as to eliminate the possibility of hissing valves or pounding pipes. The theatre with a noisy heating system has to shut off the heat at show time in order to get the show on.

In below-freezing weather, a downdraft develops at the walls of the stage house caused by the cooling of the air at the walls with a resultant updraft near the center of the stage. This also produces a draft of cold air into the auditorium. When the act curtain is raised, it causes discomfort to actors and stage hands, and sometimes produces disturbing movement of hanging scenery and curtains. The heating and ventilating system must be designed to break up this phenomenon.

Wall radiators on stage.

Plumbing

The uses of the theatre impose special limitations on plumbing installations no less than on provision for power, heating, and ventilation. The admirable practice of putting pipes where they do not clutter up the stage and where they are not visible to the audience, often results in a trap room or scene dock so filled with piping as to render useless large sections of those two areas. If exposed piping must run through the scene dock, it must be on the wall or ceiling and the position of the wall and ceiling must be determined with respect to the plumbing installation so that the clear interior dimensions of the finished theatre will be those originally contemplated. This same principle applies, of course, to the planning of understage corridors, dressing room halls and other places where exposed piping runs. The trap area below stage must be kept clear of piping. Steam, water and drain pipe locations must be determined in advance of the final decision about the building arrangement if the systems they serve are to be efficient in installation and not interfere with the operation of the theatre.

Sprinkler System

The stage, scene docks, shop, sometimes the trap room and various other areas must be provided with a sprinkler systems as prescribed in building codes. A sprinkler installation, in addition to fulfilling its safety function, must be out of the way. Therefore, sprinkler heads must be protected by beams, or other structural members from accidental impact of moving scenery or machinery which might set them off. This feature is particularly critical on the stage; sprinkler pipes are best run parallel to and above the bottom level of the roof beams. The pipes will then not be hit when work is being done on the gridiron. Some codes prescribe stage sprinkler systems below the gridiron. In such cases, pipes must run parallel to the battens and between them so that an up-running batten will not strike a row of sprinkler pipes and cause all the heads in the group to discharge. In the trap room, sprinkler pipes located directly under the permanent supporting beams have some measure of protection and do not prevent the use of traps. As in the case of all other piping, clear heights must be calculated on the basis of the installed sprinkler system.

Fire Hose, Standpipes, Water Tank, Water Curtain

Building codes, underwriters' requirements, and local fire-fighting facilities govern the inclusion of hose lines in a theatre. A common regulation is that there must be two hose lines of specified length and diameter connected to pipes having equal diameter and specified pressure on each floor level backstage and on each floor in the house or lobby. A water tank atop the stage house is likewise commonly required.

A perforated water pipe across the proscenium opening with a hand-operated valve near the stage floor adds fire resistivity to an asbestos curtain.

Lavatories, Showers, and Wash Basins

The well-equipped theatre will have wash basins in all dressing rooms; lavatories containing wash basins, showers and toilets for actors and crews; lavatories with wash basins and toilets for front house organization, and lavatories for maintenance and janitorial staffs.

Miscellaneous

Slop sinks will be installed conveniently accessible to all locations where floors are to be mopped.

For water effects, rain, and the like in performance, water connections

123

and drains must be available onstage, and there must be a drain in the trap room.

Sump pump and cooling coil and vacuum cleaning piping must be planned as part of the complete plumbing layout. Pumps and blowers must be silent.

For easy maintenance, it is often wise to plan to have all the piping in the theatre follow, so far as is feasible, the same path. All piping of the front of the house and all piping to the dressing room wing or shops may well be hung in basement corridors on the same hangers. Color-coding of pipes is distinctly advantageous. But wherever they are located, pipes, ducts, conduits and mechanical devices must not reduce the clear space required for the theatrical function of that space as set forth in the specification.

7: Acting area, proscenium, orchestra

Foregoing chapters have treated the means of making the front of the house and the house itself suitable to their function, the accommodation of an audience. It is now in order to consider those factors which determine the suitability of the stage to its function, the accommodation of the performance.

The stage is easily defined: it is that part of the theatre where the performance takes place. Its size, shape, arrangement, and equipment, therefore, must logically develop from the nature of the performance. The table of production types in Chapter 1 lists the visual and auditory components of all types of productions. Inasmuch as architectural acoustics and the electronic control of sound can provide for optimum audience perception of the auditory components, regardless of the form of the stage, development of the requirements for the stage may proceed from a consideration of the visual components and the routine of performance.

Stage Space

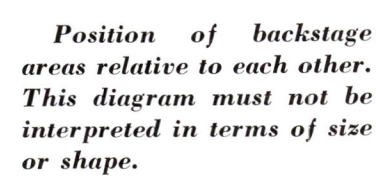

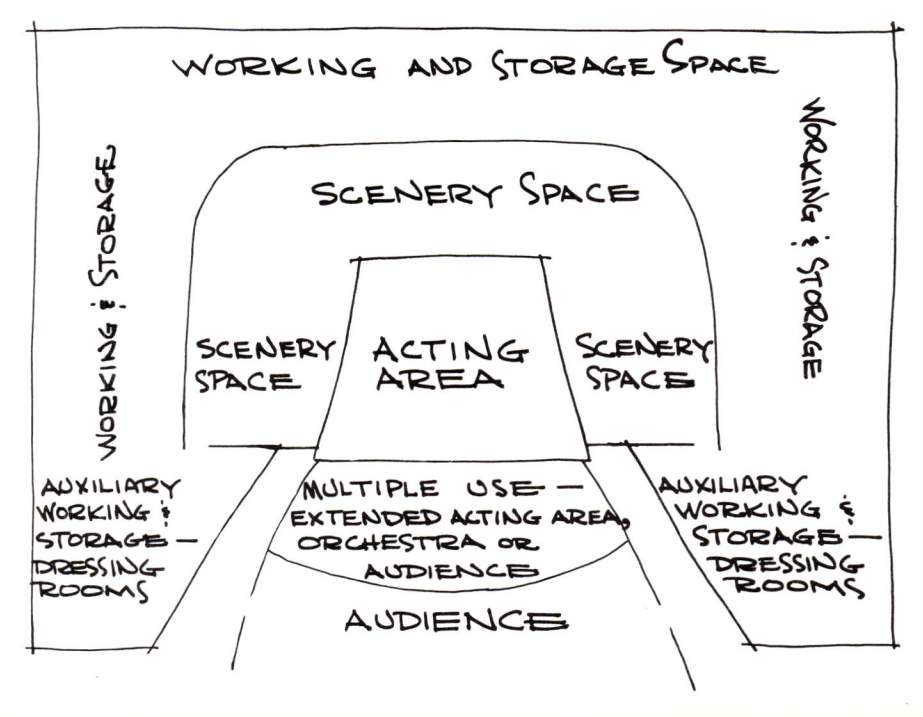

For all production types, the visual components divide into two categories: performers and scenic investiture. These indicate the functional divisions of the stage: (1) the space in which the performers

Position of backstage areas relative to each other. This diagram must not be interpreted in terms of size or shape.

work, which, though actually three-dimensional, is usually referred to as the acting *area*, and (2) the space wherein the scenic investiture is arranged, which will be called hereafter the scenery *space*. A corollary of the presence of scenic investiture is the need for its operation and storage. This indicates a third functional division of the stage: working and storage space.

There is a functional relationship between acting area, scenery space and working and storage space. The size, shape and arrangement of the acting area must be determined before the other spaces can be logically developed. This chapter will develop the form and equipment of the acting area. Development of the form and equipment of the scenery space and of the working and storage space will follow in subsequent chapters.

Position of backstage spaces.

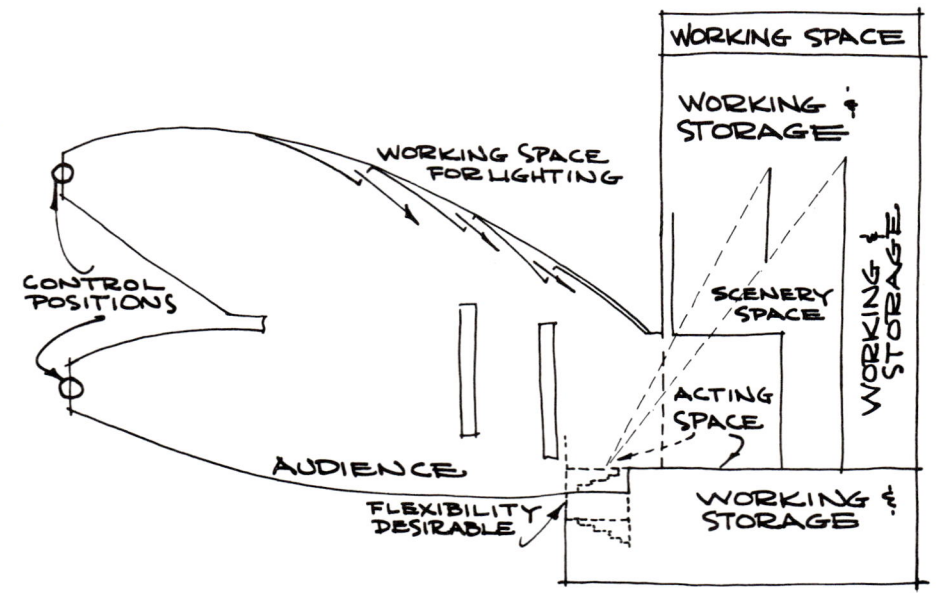

Performance-Audience Relationship

The theatre situation is fundamentally one of the relationship between the performers and the audience. The audience wants to hear and see the show without distraction and in comfort and safety, as stated, but its ultimate objective in attending the show is to receive the utmost sensory stimulation toward the maximum emotional and intellectual experience. Maximum appreciation and enjoyment of, and in a very real sense participation in, the theatre experience by each individual member of the audience depend upon the maximum enjoyment of it by the entire audience. Group reaction to a single performance stimulus is something less than total unless that stimulus be perceived *at the same time, in the same measure, and with the same significance by the entire group.*

Total Uniform Effect

If the theatre does not permit total uniform stimulus and reaction, the performance can never reach its peak of effectiveness. The best efforts of theatre artists stand the best chance of appreciative reception by audiences if the audience-performance relationship fosters total uniform stimulus and reaction, hereinafter called *total uniform effect*.

The producer and the theatre artists have requirements consistent with these: they want the physical facilities which will allow their show to stimulate the audience to the maximum of intellectual and emotional appreciation. The skilled theatre artist applies knowledge of audience reaction to the preparation of every part of the performance. If, because of inadequacies of the theatre building the audience cannot perceive the performance as the artist has planned it, the artist fails through no fault of his own, and the audience is disappointed.

Not only is it the height of theatrical artistry for the showman to achieve this condition of total uniform effect, but it is good business. The spectator who does not see or does not hear or does not comprehend a speech or action because of inadequate physical orientation toward the performance feels to some degree cheated of his admission fee, and less inclined to return to the theatre than does the spectator who perceives all the components of the performance fully and who feels that the performance is projected toward him and those close to him.

Expert showmen and artists use their productional knowledge and skills to the fullest within the limits of the physical plants at their disposal. It is the duty of the theatre planner to provide them with facilities which neither limit nor hinder their efforts.

Performance-Audience Arrangements

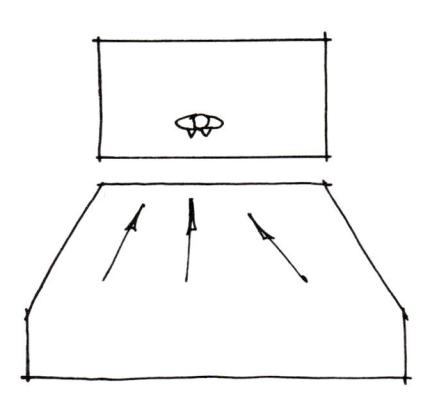

The performance and the audience can be related to each other in a limited number of combinations with some degree of variation possible in each arrangement.

Audience Looking in One Direction toward the Performance: *Proscenium*

This has been the conventional arrangement of the twentieth-century theatre in the United States. It has the following attributes:

It affords the maximum confrontation of performers and audience and is best for lecturers, concert singers, recitation and dramatic presentation. It establishes a limited orientation of performers to audience. The audience being in one compact group within a narrow horizontal angle, the performers can relate their actions to the whole audience simultaneously.

It creates a limited, unified, fixed frame for the pictorial composition of the performance. Scenery can approach the quality of fine art in the refinement of its design elements.

127

It permits the director and designer to relate performers to scenery, secure in the knowledge that the whole audience will perceive the relationships in the same way.

It is the best arrangement for presenting to an audience a dramatic action of conflict or opposition of forces because the line of action of the opposition or conflict is across the line of vision of the audience and hence is maximally perceptible.

It is the form most conducive to the production of total uniform effect.

Being the established conventional form, it stands vulnerable to attack by avant-gardists who often seek change for the sake of change.

It is limited in seating capacity because the principal direction of expansion is away from the performance; the limit of good seeing becomes the limit of expansion. Expansion laterally tends to destroy total uniform effect by making occupants of the side seats view the performance from widely divergent angles and thus see the actors, action and scenery in nonsignificant relationship.

Theatrical production refuses to be contained within a strictly limited space behind a rectangular opening. The existing proscenium form has been called the picture frame stage, and the peep show stage, and even during its incidence and rise to prevalence there were objections to its restrictive character. The theory of theatre admits, and numerous modern plays contain, instances where the contact between performance and audience must be more intimate than the formal frame permits. History of theatre shows twenty-four centuries in which the picture frame was either nonexistent or modified by the use of acting areas in front of it, against the last century and a quarter during which the proscenium developed in prominence. Modern theatrical practice contains frequent instances of the performance's attempting to come through the frame, into, about, and around the audience.

Audience Partially Surrounding the Performance: *Open Stage*

In several variations this arrangement has gained in popularity during the mid-century. Essentially an old arrangement descended from Greek, Roman, Renaissance and Elizabethan theatres, it has been readopted for several reasons:

It places the performers in the same space envelope as the audience. This is said to produce a unity of experience between performers and audience, though the authors believe that the essential dichotomy of function between performers and audience persists regardless of spatial relationship and that attempts to resolve this dichotomy are futile, fallacious and irrelevant.

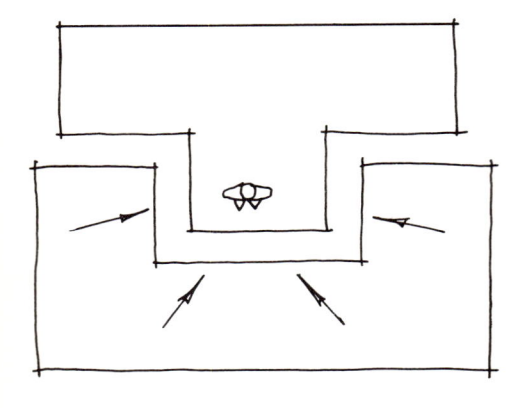

It places more spectators closer to the performance than does the proscenium arrangement and in this way contributes to good seeing, but it places a burden of diffused orientation upon directors and performers and makes impossible the achievement of total uniform effect.

It contains inherent difficulties in the entrance and exit of actors which are usually solved by providing entrances beneath the seating area.

Difficulties pertaining to the scenic investiture which are common to both this arrangement and the arena arrangement will be considered together.

Audience Surrounding Performance: *Arena or Central Staging*

Variously called *bandbox, arena, theatre-in-the-round, circle theatre* and deriving certainly from circus, ancient amphitheatre (*double theatre*), and primitive ritual sites, the arrangement of the acting area in the center of a surrounding ring of audience has gained in popularity in the twentieth century for a number of reasons:

Expediency. At a time when formal theatres have been decreasingly available and increasingly expensive to build, while simultaneously the number of play production groups has been increasing rapidly, the arena arrangement, achievable in any large room, makes a rudimentary theatre possible.

Economy. As well as seating maximum audience in the minimum enclosure, this arrangement seats the largest audience within the shortest distance from the acting area. It is therefore attractive to the showman and also to the spectator who attaches value to proximity to the stage.

The claims of intimacy which are voiced for the open stage arrangement are repeated for the central stage and the same demurrers apply with the additional statement of positions *pro* and *contra* the feature of seeing the audience across the acting area.

pro: seeing other members of the audience enjoying the show stimulates one's own enjoyment.
contra: the opposite audience seen beyond the actors is no part of the performance and is therefore a negative factor to the degree that it is distracting. It is surely a negative factor in that it is not a part of the design and plan of the performance; it is not scenic investiture.

Economy is also affected by the effective limitation of scenery: There can be no scenery or properties that the audience cannot see over, under or through. This restricts scenic investiture to paint or other coverings on the stage floor, very low platforms, devices suspended above the acting area, outline representations of such objects as must be set on the stage for use by the actors (doors, windows, and similar architectural details) and low pieces of furniture.

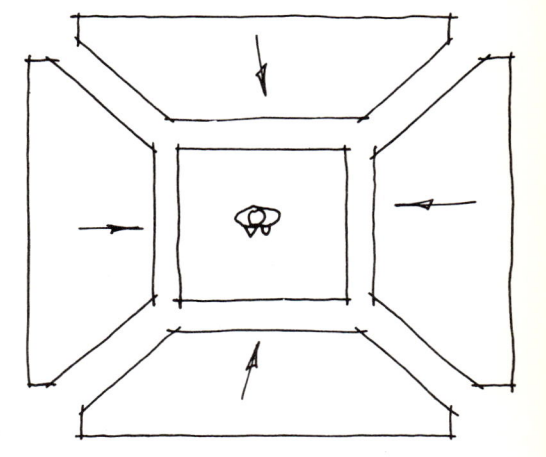

Disadvantages. Because the audience is seated all around the acting area, it is unavoidable that viewpoints will be maximally different and it becomes impossible for director and actors to compose the performance so as to produce a total uniform effect. Furthermore because the conditions of *covering* (one actor blocking audience vision of another actor) are also maximized, it is necessary to prevent covering by increasing the pitch of the seating area.

An unavoidable disadvantage of this form lies in the anterior-posterior aspect of every actor and the fact that the most dramatically expressive side is oriented in only one direction. The summary comment on this aspect was made by the late David Itkin: "I have seen one-half of the show; now I will buy a ticket on the other side of the house and see the other half of the show." Unfortunately, because the performance must (at times) be oriented toward the sides where he has not yet sat with his two tickets, he would have had to buy two more tickets, four in all.

Performance Extending around Audience: *Extended Stage*

Variously called *side stages, multi-proscenium, theatre-all-around* and even *theatrama*, this arrangement has gained some acceptance in the mid-century decades.

This form begins as an extension of the conventional acting area to left and right, usually as *parodoi* entrances on the audience side of the proscenium, or as doors in the side wall splays which may be used when desired as frontal entrances onto the stage. Its fullest development is in the four-stage form which requires that the audience sit in swivel chairs.

Its uses in production are various:
1. Small scenes played on side stages while scenery is being changed on the main stage;
2. Processions entering from the side stages and moving into the main stage;
3. Expansion of acting area for simultaneous showing of several settings or locales;
4. Elimination of changes of scenery by having all scenery set up on the various stages and moving the action and even rotating the audience. (This form relates directly to the television studio method of having several settings set up and moving actors and cameras from one set to another.)

Performance Interpenetrating the Audience

Various kinds of theatrical performance and certain styles of dramatic production embody and justify interpenetration of audience by performance. Examples are the display of pulchritude in a Parisian night club, the asides to the audience of a Kabuki actor, comedians

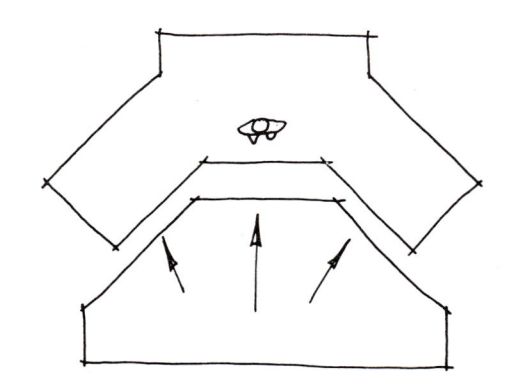

LE PONT D'ARGENT, *one of a pair of thrust stage extensions set and struck during blackout. Floor is glass. The Lido, Paris.*

running about the aisles, and *in character* entrances and exits via the aisles in central staging. The first act ending of Thornton Wilder's THE SKIN OF OUR TEETH with ushers carrying theatre chairs down the center aisle to feed the fire to save the human race may have influenced other playwrights and many subsequent productions, but note must also be taken of a performance of Leopold Atlas's L in the Yale University Theatre in 1928 when the play opened with newsboys running about the aisles shouting "Extra!"

There are obvious limitations to this kind of performing, even when aesthetic distance is maintained by means of lighting differences, acting method, or protocol. *Total uniform effect* is lost because of the widely varying viewpoint of the audience; discomfort and resulting disgruntlement may affect those who are in unfavorable viewing positions.

Any one performance-audience relationship is, of course, limiting, and each different relationship has its intrinsic attractiveness, if only of difference from the others. The proscenium arrangement affords maximum facilities for scenic investiture, visual composition and aesthetic distance. The open stage recalls production styles of Elizabethan England and seems to accommodate Shakespeare best. The arena

Combinations:
Multiform

arrangement minimizes scenery, minimizes last row distance, and maximizes performer-audience intimacy. The wrap-around arrangement fills audience vision.

There are cogent reasons which may be offered in support of any of the arrangements as sufficient reasons why the showman should want to offer performances in every arrangement. To do this he has several choices: to build four different theatres, to select certain of the arrangements for inclusion in one theatre, to build one theatre capable of all four arrangements.

The Ace Morgan Theatre, Denison University. An experimental theatre for a production seminar, capable of many arrangements: proscenium, extended-stage, open-stage, arena, or three-proscenium form. The flat floor, for dances, was a condition of the program. Arrangements are changed manually. William Gehron, architect.

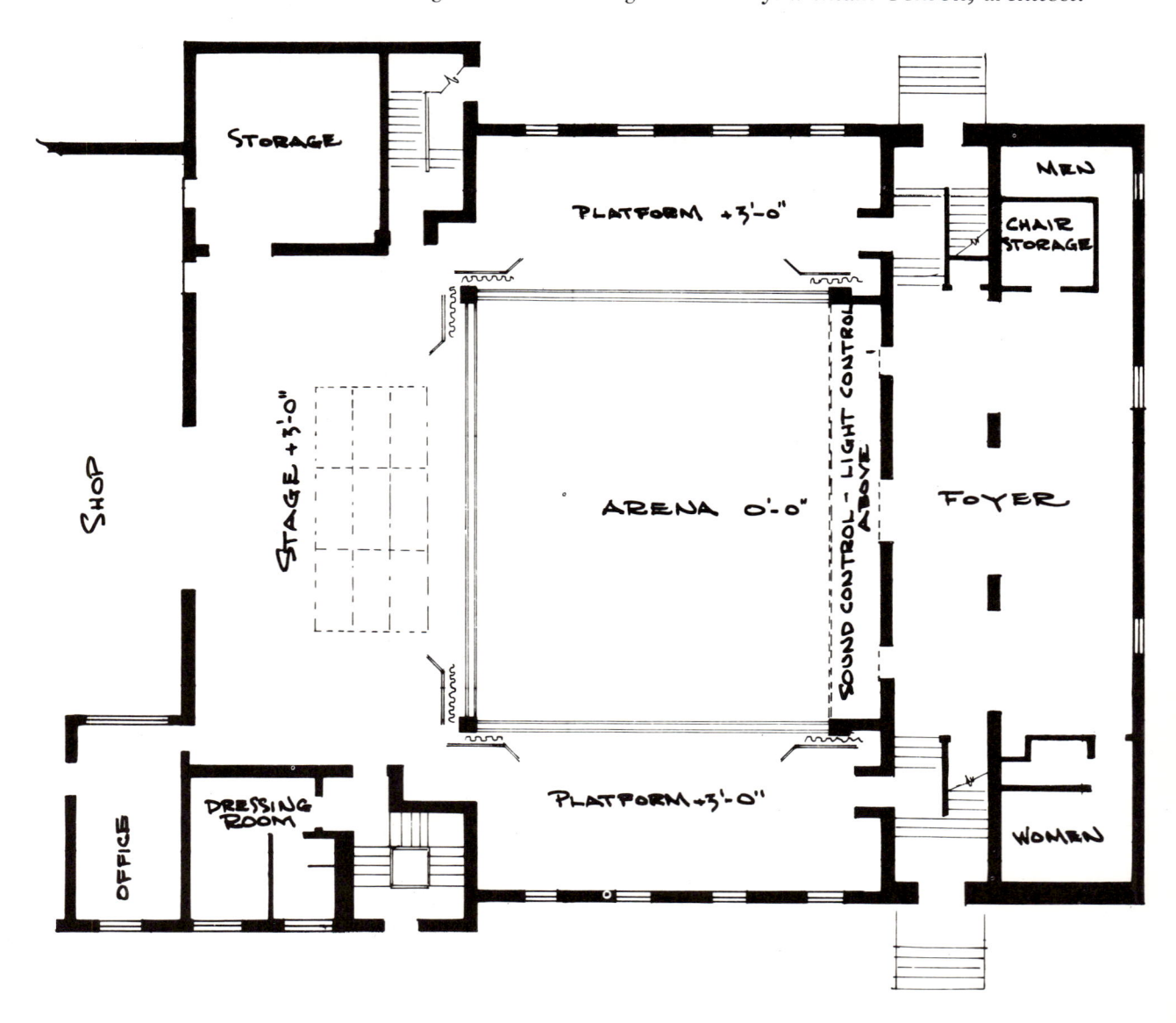

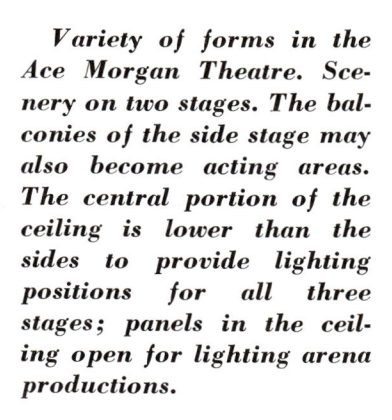

Variety of forms in the Ace Morgan Theatre. Scenery on two stages. The balconies of the side stage may also become acting areas. The central portion of the ceiling is lower than the sides to provide lighting positions for all three stages; panels in the ceiling open for lighting arena productions.

The scenery is set against the back wall of the house; the audience is seated on the floor and on all three stages.

The stages used for seating audience.

Free Form: *Flexible, Experimental*

The application of electromechanical techniques to the movement of parts of the theatre makes possible the alteration of the form of the theatre. This intriguing notion has led to exploration of the possibilities of creating a theatre in which the size, shape, arrangement and interrelationship of the performance and audience areas (or spaces) might be changed at will and without limit.

Reasonably, certain limits have appeared and require recognition. The theatrical event is always concerned with human beings as members of the audience; hence the parts of the theatre in which the audience is to go are limited in their divisibility to a module based upon the area or space which a human being occupies. The performance, though not always, is usually likewise concerned with human beings and is therefore subject to the same module.

The movement of parts is usually mechanically restricted in direction and rate, and critical decisions are required of persons planning such a facility regarding the degree of flexibility desired, the speed of change desired, the amount of power and control (automation or cybernation) desired, all within the limits of the available funds.

The free-form theatre is essentially an architectural enclosure within which all parts, except the foundation, exterior walls and roof, front-of-house and production service facilities, are movable, so that the whole space in which the performance is presented may be designed and arranged to become the space most congenial or suitable to the production to be presented.

This form of theatre depends for its aegis upon essentially adventurous theatrical entrepreneurs, sufficiently sophisticated and theatre-

A scheme for converting from proscenium form to open stage designed for the University of New Mexico. Elevators raise the two seating banks which pivot and roll to side positions. The elevators become the open stage. George C. Izenour, designer, Holien and Buckley, architects.

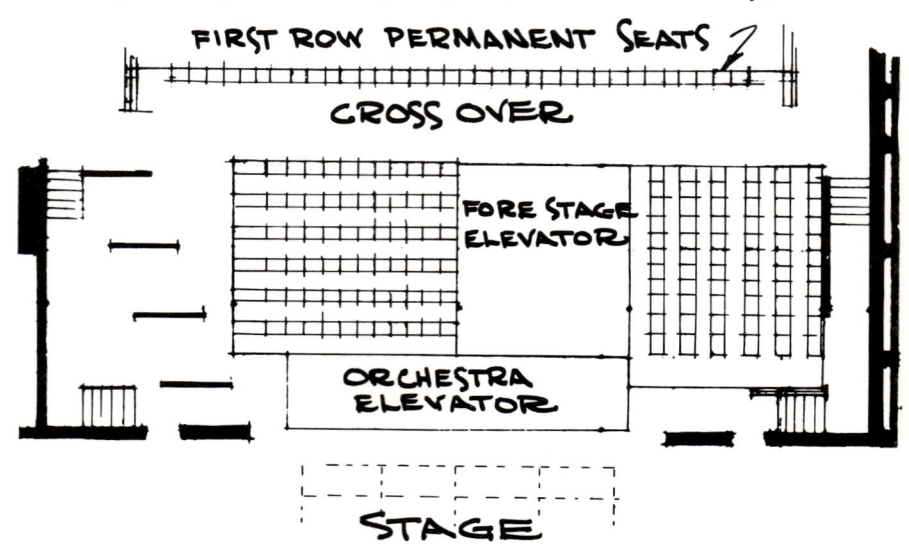

wise audience members, and an essentially experimental situation in which the experiment in variable theatre form is its own justification.

The adventurous producer-director, in quest of variety and novelty as legitimate concomitants of entertainment, may be intrigued by still other, perhaps as yet unthought-of, performance-audience relationships. Some, which have been employed in the past, are upper proscenium stages (Steele Mackay's Madison Square Theatre), upper side stages (Middlebury College), tripartite balconies over side proscenium stages (Denison University), and continuous side balconies (Studio Theatre in Hopkins Center, Dartmouth College). On at least one occasion in the Yale University Theatre, an actor has stuck his head through a lighting slot in the ceiling and uttered lines. *Variety*, the magazine of show business, is not misnamed.

Other Relationships

A design by George C. Izenour for a flexible theatre space capable of many arrangements achieved by programmed electromechanical devices.

Acting Area

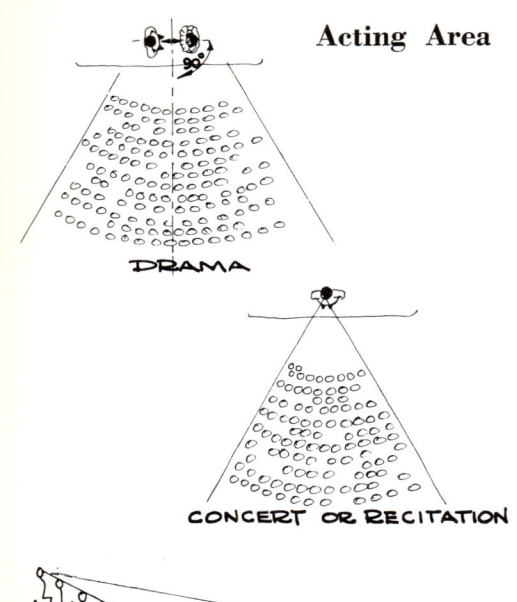

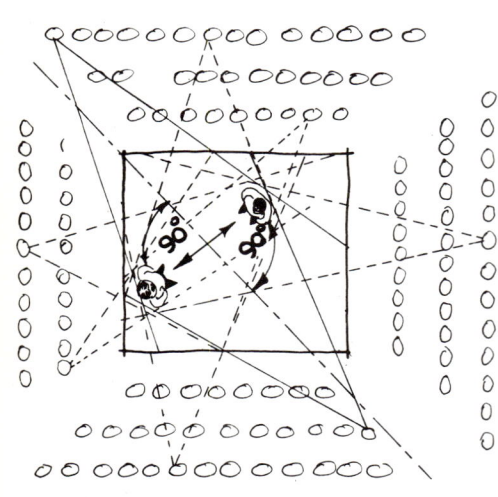

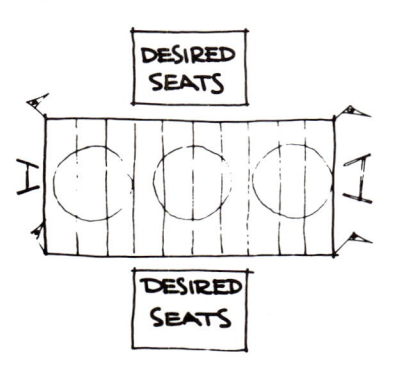

The *size* of the acting area is a direct function of the number of performers who use it, their costumes, and the nature of their performance. A single performer, engaged in a static recitation, lecture, or soliloquy, without gestures and in plain modern dress, requires about 4 square feet. Elaborate period costume and sweeping arm gestures may enlarge the requirement to 25 square feet. Solo dancers of the more energetic sort require a minimum floor area of about 300 square feet.

The shape and arrangement of the acting area are functions of the kind of action and amount of movement inherent in the production type, and of the audience-performance relationship which provides total uniform effect for the particular kind of action. (1) If the action is of the concert or recitational kind, face-to-face relationship between audience and performer is necessary. If any part of the action, whether by individual performers or groups, requires the optimum condition for expressive communication between the performers and the audience, the shape and arrangement must permit the entire audience to see the performers face to face. Most of the expressive parts of the human anatomy are in front. (2) If the performance involves communication, interaction or opposition between performers, the shape and arrangement of the acting area must permit that action to take place on a line perpendicular to the general audience sight line to be uniformly perceived by the audience.

(3) If the movement is to any considerable degree two-dimensional, as in ballet, optimum perception requires that the audience be elevated so that it may have a good view of the entire acting area, and thus become aware of the dimensionality of the movement. (4) And if the entire action is truly two-dimensional, with no necessity for frontal expression by any of the performers, with no situations involving linear opposition between performers or groups of performers, and with no purely linear movement of performers, the acting area may be centrally located within a closed circle of audience. It should be noted, however, that because of the complete diversity of audience viewpoint in this situation, it is impossible for any but truly two-dimensional action, divorced from frontal expression, to produce a total uniform effect on the audience. (5) In most of the group entertainment media employing this form at present (circus, athletic arena, stadium), the audience has expressed the truth of the perceptual relationship by placing a premium on the seats which are at right angles to the line of competitive movement, and by preferring the seats facing the band and the center ring of the circus.

Before considering the construction of a theatre for central staging, planners must measure the certain loss of total uniform effect against other possible advantages of the form.

The acting area is used by actors. To use it they must get to it. In the proscenium form, actors can enter the acting area from the offstage space freely from all directions if there is no enclosing scenery or through openings located at a great variety of positions if there is scenery; they may also enter the acting area from below the stage through traps, from above the stage by flying devices or from in front of the stage by way of the orchestra pit or through the aisles. They can leave the stage by the same routes.

In the extended stage form all these entrance routes are available with the addition that stage extensions themselves constitute additional entrances to the main acting area.

In the open stage form, actors' entrances must be supplied not only from the backstage area (that side of the theatre not occupied by audience) but also from the direction of the audience if the entrances and exits are to be as dramatically effective as they are in the proscenium form.

In the arena form there is no backstage side of the acting area; all entrances must perforce be from the directions of the audience. These entrances must either use the aisles which serve the audience or tunnels below the seating banks. Such aisles or tunnels seldom permit as much variety or as great a dramatic effect (total and uniform) as do entrances in the proscenium and extended stage forms.

The audience looks at the performance through the proscenium opening. Sometimes the action of the performance extends through it, toward, into, and around the audience.

The design of the proscenium is of twofold importance: visually the design controls the attention of the audience and directs it toward the stage; physically, the proscenium conceals and discloses the stage and the acting area. Proscenium equipment is described in Chapter 11.

The typical proscenium in existing theatres is formed by a narrowing (splay) of the side walls of the auditorium toward a rectangular or round-topped opening in the wall between the auditorium and the stage, through which the audience sees the show. In older theatres the side walls contained audience boxes with very bad sight lines and various kinds of architectural ornament, most of it distracting. In presentation houses the space formed by the splay often contains organ pipes behind wall grilles. The acoustic function of these splayed walls is discussed in Chapter 4.

The typical form of proscenium is the early twentieth-century terminus of an historically long development of the proscenium through many forms. Its functional foundation lies in the supposition that the entire performance is to take place in the space behind the curtain line

Actors' Entrances and Exits

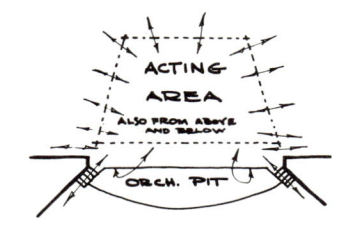

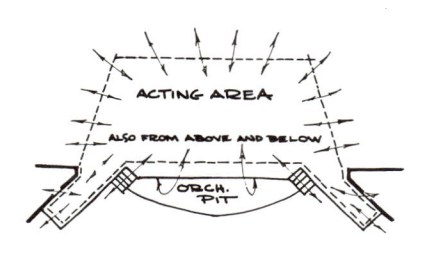

Proscenium

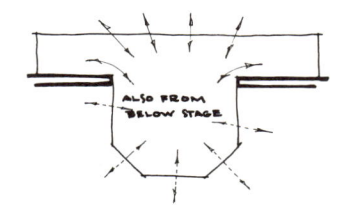

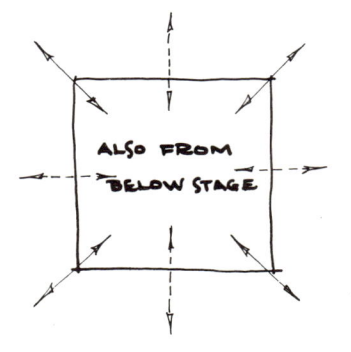

137

Arena Stage, Washington, D.C. Actors enter at the corners of the stage. Scenery is confined to the space above the highest sight lines. Access to the light slots in the sloping ceilings is difficult. Flying rigging is rudimentary.

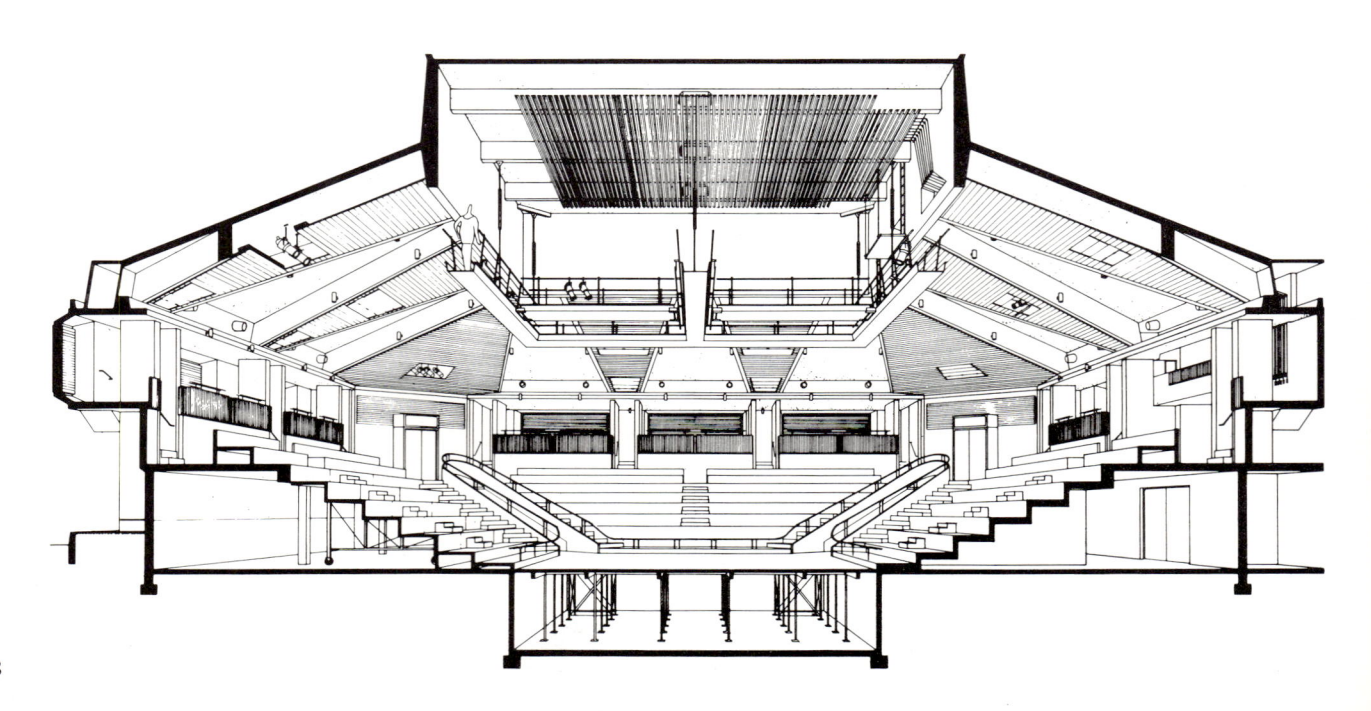

or directly before the curtain line on the so-called apron. It sets rigid limits to the acting area and consequently limits the performance-audience relationship available to the showman.

Notable about recently constructed theatres are attempts to modify the fixed and inflexible proscenium. Part of this experimentation is due to a justified recognition that theatrical production demands more freedom of audience-performance relationship than the typical proscenium allows, and part is due to a penchant for novelty, amounting even to a grim determination to be original. Critical appraisal of these efforts must be based upon sound understanding of the demands which theatrical production makes. A proscenium which is variable according to requirements of several production types renders the theatre more useful to the showman.

Radio City Music Hall.

The Tyrone Guthrie Theatre, Minneapolis. Ralph Rapson, architect.

Extended stage and side stage. Hopkins Center.

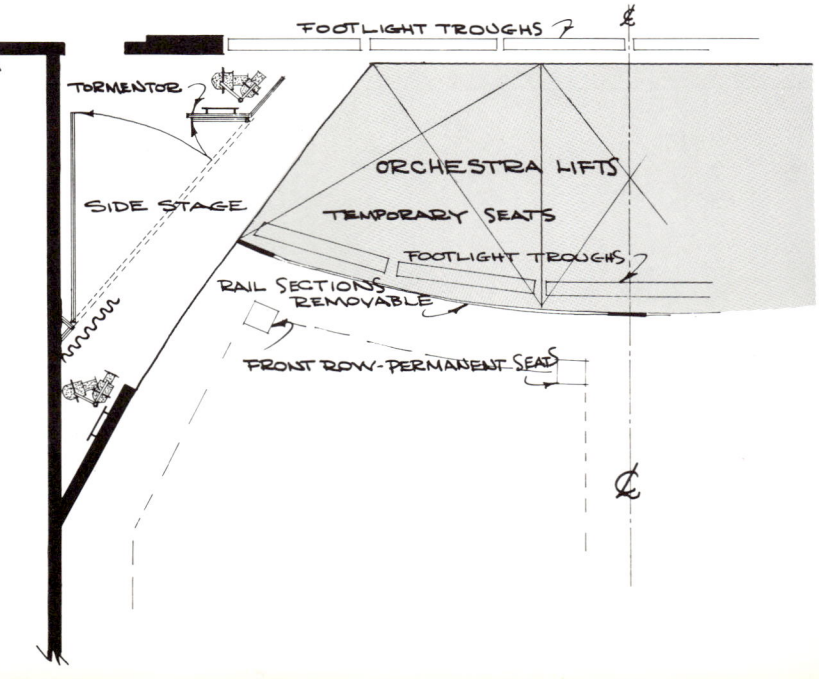

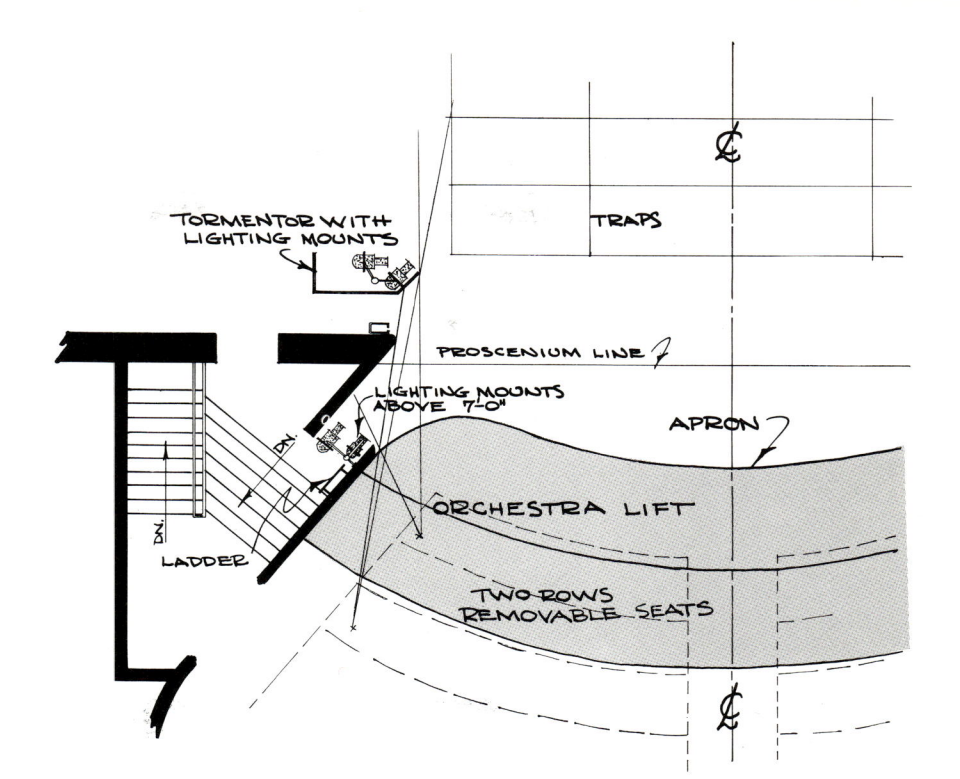

Proscenium entrance and light slot. Virginia Museum of Fine Arts Theatre.

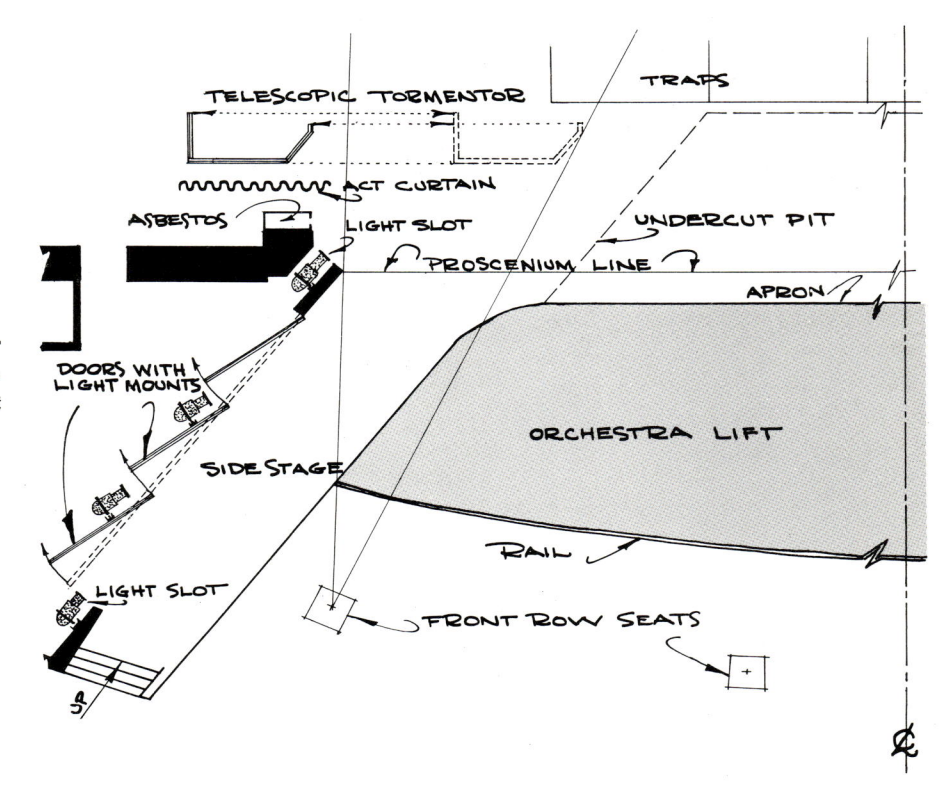

Extended stage, University of Oregon Theatre. Doors swing to make light slots or entrances.

141

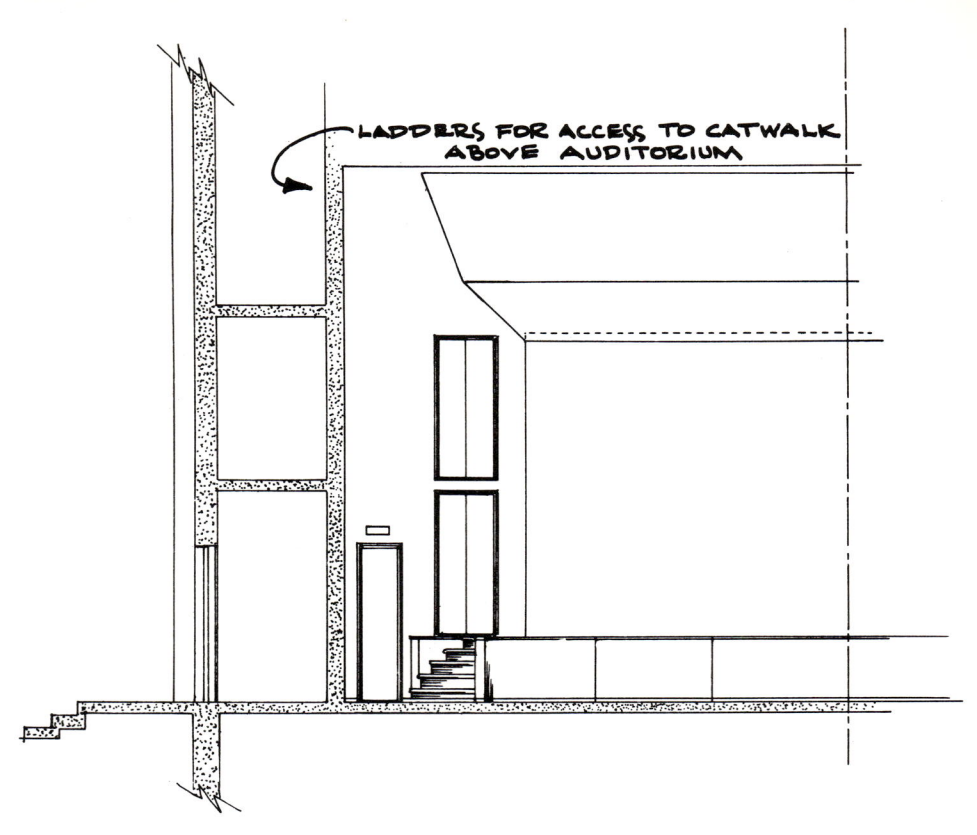

Elevation of proscenium. Wright Memorial Theatre, Middlebury College. Upper and lower side stages make acting areas for small scenes. McKim, Mead and White, architects.

Side stages, Wright Memorial Theatre.

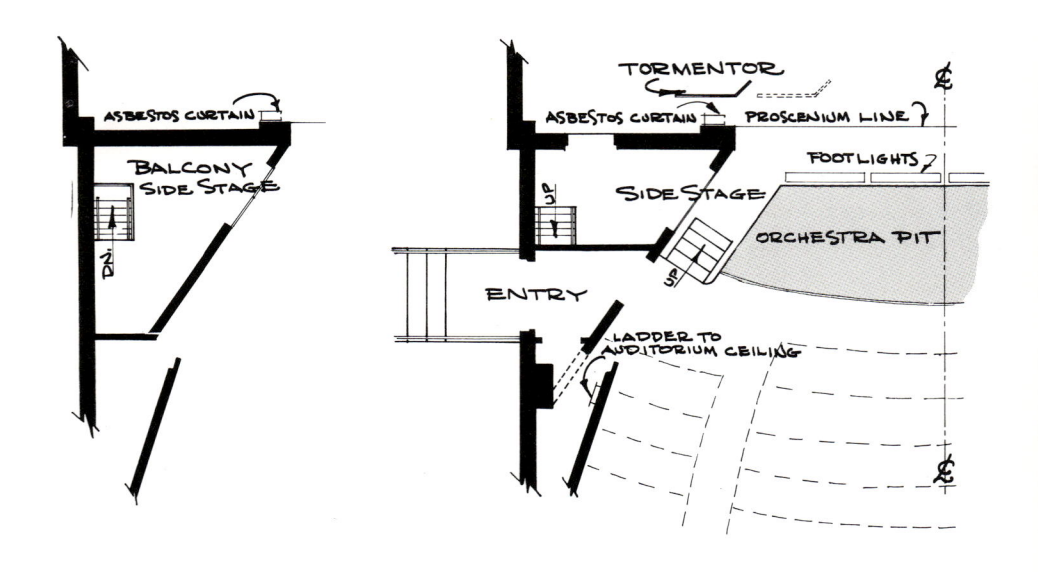

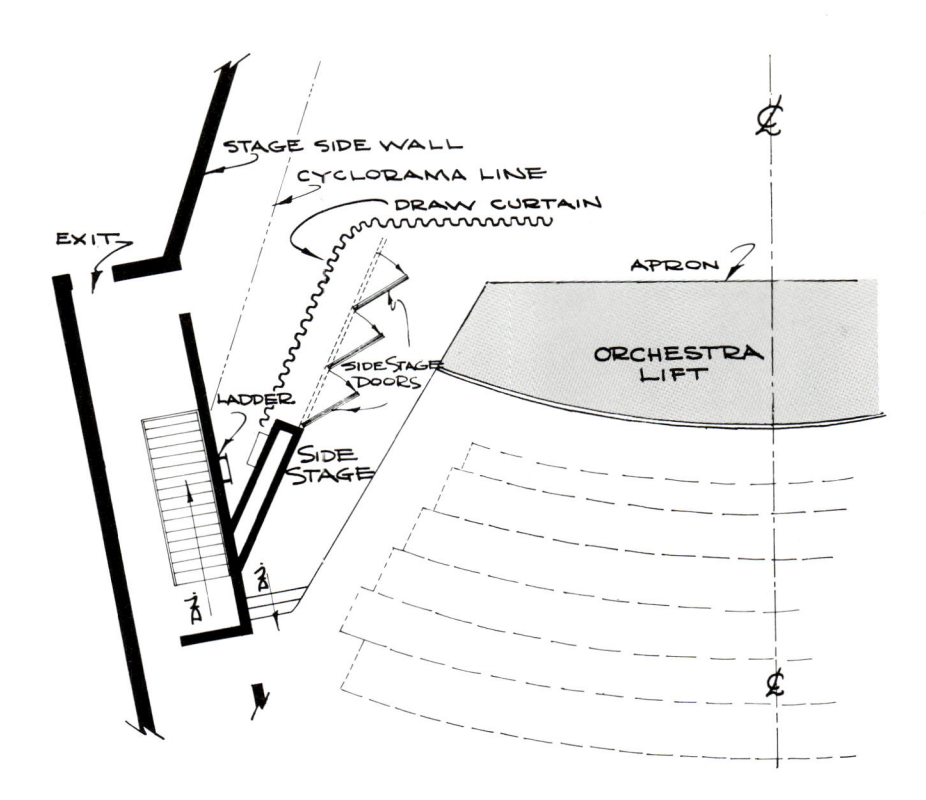

Extended stage, Colorado State College. James M. Hunter, architect.

Fire Wall

The wall between the house and the stage in which the proscenium is both an opening and a feature is prescribed by law in most states and nations to be a fire-resistive wall with restrictions, varying with local laws, on the number and size of openings which it may contain and the nature of the doors or curtains which must fill such openings. The laws derive from a time when theatres were of combustible construction and before modern methods of retarding combustion were developed. Strict adherence to these laws has tended to perpetuate the conventional picture frame theatre and to prevent the introduction of more flexible performance-audience relationships. In instances where clients, architects and consultants have been able to obtain either changes in the laws or variances by proving that the intended theatres contained adequate provisions for the safety of the audience, the fire wall has been either eliminated or modified to permit more flexible relationships. Primary among provisions for the ultimate in audience safety has been the inclusion of more than ample exits from the house, assuring the speedy escape of the audience.

Orchestra Pit

Music is an important auditory component of most production types, and an integral visual component in some. The developed location of the orchestra is in a pit between the acting area and the audience. If the production type requires exact cueing and close interrelation as in opera where the musical conductor directs not only the orchestra but the singers, the orchestra pit is essential. It is usually desirable, however, to conceal the orchestra while providing for the conductor a complete view of the acting area. The open stage theatre form precludes an orchestra pit unless the open stage is itself wholly or partially adjustable to produce a pit. The theory of arena theatre—equally good seeing and hearing from all directions—opposes fixing the location of the pit, but its very pit nature makes such fixing necessary. The position of the conductor imposes an orientation of the performance in his direction and thus favors the seats in a certain sector of the house.

Sight lines relating to the orchestra pit: patrons' vision must not be obstructed by orchestra or conductor; performers must see conductor; conductor must see singers.

Modern techniques for the electronic control of sound facilitate the location of the orchestra remote from the stage for situations in which the immediate interrelation of orchestra, performers, and conductor is not essential. Electronic techniques also include the transcription of music and other sound onto tape in advance of performance and playback during performance under precisely controlled conditions. Closed-circuit television provides the means whereby the conductor of an orchestra in a remote location can both see and be seen by the performers.

Space planning for the orchestra should allow 10 square feet per person, except 20 square feet for a harp, 50 square feet for a standard grand piano, 100 square feet for a concert grand piano, and 50 square feet for the tympani. And the pit must be at least as deep as the trap room, with a floor adjustable in height according to the demands of the performance.

Proscenium and orchestra lift, John Fitzgerald Kennedy Theatre, University of Hawaii. Rigid panels drawn out of slots in the proscenium vary the opening or form a reflecting background for presentations on the forestage.

Apron, forestage, orchestra pit must be considered as elements affecting the audience-performance relationship. A sinking forestage may produce several arrangements suitable to different production types: forestage, continuation of the house floor, or sunken orchestra pit. Sectional elevators increase the number of possible arrangements.

If budget limitations preclude the installation of a sinking forestage, a cheaper though cumbersome substitute is a set of platforms designed to fit into the orchestra pit to produce (1) a continuation of the floor of the house to the apron, (2) a forestage, (3) steps leading from house floor to stage, (4) a variable arrangement of levels.

A system of posts and beams, broadly adjustable between the limits of the stage floor and the bottom of the pit, which affords an inexpensive, flexible forestage, may be made using such standardized structural parts as Unistrut, Mult-A-Frame, or portable steel scaffolding.

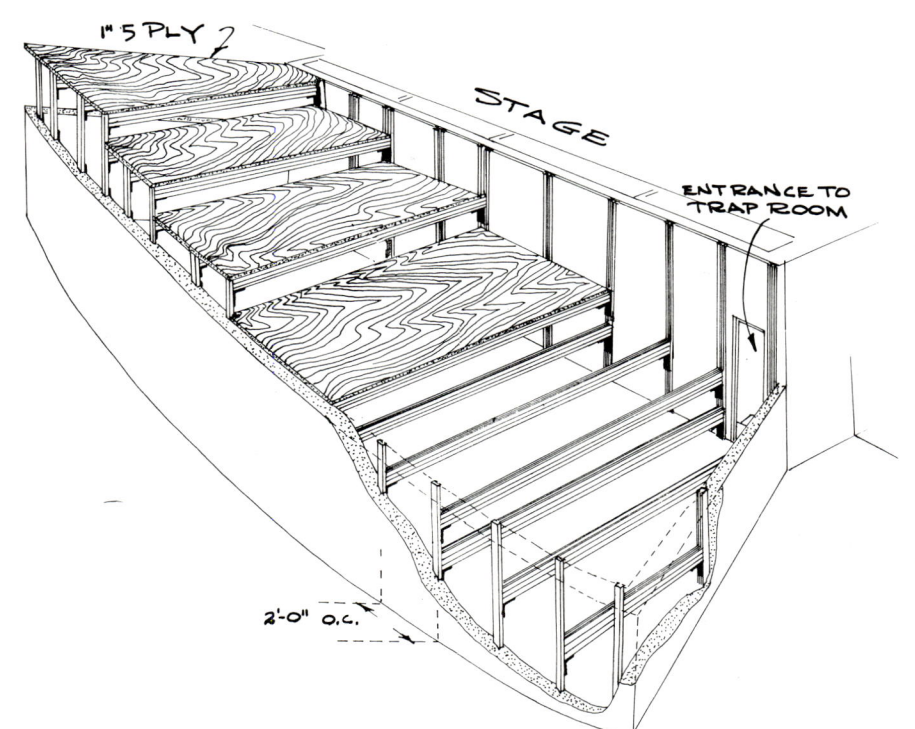

Sinking Forestage

Variable, manually adjusted orchestra pit-forestage. Unistrut channels are set into the concrete wall of the pit with extensions above floor level; others set beneath the stage apron. Beams are adjustable to any level between pit floor and stage floor. The plywood sections are removable. Additional unistrut members may be used to obtain a great variety of steps, ramps and levels.

The spaces behind the splayed proscenium walls and above the ceiling of the house are the best locations for organ pipes. The blower for the organ must be located in the basement. There is no space for either of these items within a well-designed stage. When solo performance on the organ is envisioned as a production feature, the console must be seen by the entire audience, either on an organ lift adjoining the orchestra pit, on a side stage in the proscenium splay, or on the stage itself, in which case there must be means for lowering it into the orchestra pit.

Organ Pipes, Blower, and Console

	General Characteristics	Acting Area Size	Shape
Pageant and Symphonic Drama	Dramatic episodes, processions, marches, dances and crowd scenes. Masses of performers engaged in simple but expansive movements before very large audiences.	From 2000 to 5000 sq. ft., depending on the scale of the pageant.	Rectangular with aspect ratio between 1 to 3 and 2 to 3.
Grand Opera	Large numbers of performers on the acting area at one time; often more than one hundred in big scenes and finales. Movement is martial processions and group dances and the costumes are elaborate. Soloists perform downstage center, close to the footlights but within the bounds of the conventional proscenium, principals play twosome and group scenes in the area near the audience, and choruses and supernumeraries require space upstage. The ballet and the chorus of soldiers, pilgrims, peasants, or what not, sometimes fill the entire acting area. The performance is viewed objectively by the audience and does not benefit by intimate contact between performance and audience.	Minimum: 1000 sq. ft. Usual: about 2500 sq. ft. Reasonable maximum: 4000 sq. ft.	Quadrilateral with an aspect ratio between 1 to 2 and 2 to 3. Sides converge toward the back of the stage, following the sight lines from the extreme lateral positions.
Vaudeville, Revue	Vaudeville and revue emphasize the human scale. Although the vaudevillian keys his performance for the last row in the gallery, the form is characterized by intimate direct relationship between performer and audience: monologues straight to the front, confidential asides to the front row, and audience participation in illusions. Other acts (acrobatics, etc.) are played across the line of audience vision for maximum effect.	Minimum: 350 sq. ft. Usual: About 450 sq. ft. Reasonable maximum: 700 sq. ft.	Rhomboid with aspect ratio about 1 to 3. Sides converge toward back of stage following the sight lines from the extreme lateral seats.
Dance	Graceful and expressive movements of human figures in designed patterns, chiefly in two dimensions but with the third dimension introduced by leaps and carries. Occasional elevation of parts of the stage floor. Singles, duets, trios, quartets, groups. The movement demands maximal clear stage space.	Anything under 700 sq. ft. is constricting. Reasonable maximum: 1200 sq. ft.	Rhomboid with aspect ratio about 3 to 4. May project into and be surrounded by audience (open stage or arena) since frontal aspect of performers has minimal, and space-filling quality has maximal, significance.

Arrangement	Proscenium	Orchestra	Comment
Long dimension of acting area perpendicular to general sight line. Audience entirely on one side, elevated to perceive two-dimensional movement. Large openings at ends and in side opposite audience for processions, group entrances, and exits. Some elevation of portion of acting area opposite audience, purely for compositional reasons.	Either no proscenium with performers entering the "pageant field" from beyond the lateral sight lines, or structural or natural barriers to delineate the side limits of the acting area and conceal backstage apparatus and activity. "Curtains" of sliding panels, lights or fountains for concealing the acting area; often the concealment is by blackout only.	Space for 100 musicians between audience and acting area. Conductor must see performance.	Primarily an outdoor form, it is often staged in makeshift or adapted theatres, utilizing athletic fields and stands or natural amphitheatres. A few permanent pageant theatres have been built.
Long dimension perpendicular to the general sight line. Audience elevated to perceive two-dimensional movement.	Width equal to the long dimension of the acting area.	Pit for 60 to 80 musicans. Conductor must have good view of action.	Movement in two dimensions in acting area is a significant visual component, predicating elevation of the seating area to make this movement visible.
Long axis of the acting area perpendicular to the optimum sight line. Audience grouped as close as possible to the optimum sight line. The forestage is an essential part of the acting area; steps, ramps, and runways into the house are useful.	Width equal to the long dimension of the acting area. Flexibility is to some advantage in revue but of little value in vaudeville.	Music and music cues closely integrated with both vaudeville and revue performances. Pit space for from 15 to 30 musicians. Conductor and percussionist must have good view of the action.	Most of the visual components of vaudeville and revue are such that they are perceived best in the conventional audience-performance relationship. The comic monologist who must confront his audience is defeated by the open stage and arena arrangements.
Nearly square acting area so that dance patterns may be arranged in depth, and movement may be in many directions including along the diagonals. Many dance figures require circular movement. Many entrances desirable, especially from the sides of the acting area.	Proscenium not really necessary; though useful as concealment for lighting instruments and dancers awaiting entrances, other devices such as pylons, movable panels and curtains may be substituted.	Music almost always accompanies dancers. For dance as part of opera or musical show, orchestra is in pit. For dance as specific performance, as in ballet, orchestra may be in remote location and music piped in. Maximum orchestra for dance: 60 musicians in pit for classical ballet. Minimum: one drummer.	Dance in its various manifestations is the performance form best suited to the open stage or arena since it possessed the least amount of facial-expression significance and the greatest amount of movement and pattern in two or three dimensions. Elevation of the audience to perceive best the patterns of dance is desirable.

	General Characteristics	Acting Area Size	Shape
Musical: Folk Opera, Operetta, Musical Comedy, Musical Drama	These forms embody on a smaller scale the production elements of grand opera, plus a certain freedom and a quest for novelty which encourage the development of new performance devices. Close audience contact of soloists and specialists is borrowed from vaudeville and revue. Big scenes involve many dancers, singers, and showgirls, often with space-filling costume and movement. Fifty people on stage at one time is not unusual.	Minimum: 600 sq. ft. Usual: About 1200 sq. ft. Reasonable maximum: 1800 sq. ft.	Proscenium: Rhomboid with aspect ratio between 1 to 2 and 2 to 3. Sides converge toward the back of the stage following the sight lines from the extreme lateral seats. Arena: Circle, square, or rectangle (3 x 4 aspect ratio) or ellipse (3 x 4 aspect ratio).
Legitimate Drama	Of all production types, legitimate drama places the greatest emphasis upon the scale of the human actor. The importance of the individual actor requires that stage space and scenery do not dwarf him. Dominance of plot, locale, and characterization requires verisimilitude in the size and relationship of scenic objects. Too small an acting area crowds actors and furniture, hampers stage action, and detracts from the dramatic effect which is the sole aim of the performance. Too large an acting area diminishes the actor in scale and renders his performance ineffective by weakening the effect of his gestures and movement.	Minimum: 240 sq. ft. (12' x 20') Usual: about 525 sq. ft. (15' x 35') Reasonable maximum: 1000 sq. ft. (25' x 40')	Proscenium: Quadrilateral with an aspect ratio about 1 to 2. Sides converge toward the back of the stage following the sight line from the extreme lateral seats. Open Stage: Semicircle, quadrilateral or polygon projecting from a proscenium or from an architectural facade. Arena: Circle, square, rectangle, polygon or ellipse with about 3 x 4 aspect ratio. Entrances from diagonal corners and in middle of one or both long sides.

Arrangement	Proscenium	Orchestra	Comment
Proscenium: Long axis of acting area perpendicular to the optimum sight line. Mechanized mobility of structural parts to produce changes in acting area arrangement are desirable. Forestages, sidestages, acting area elevators. **Arena:** Numerous wide entrances for actors and stage hands via the aisles or through tunnels under the seating banks. Ramps preferable to stairs or steps. Experimentation possible in rendering stage flexible by lifts, and in development of flying systems over the acting area.	Usually as wide as the acting area, but should be adaptable to changes in the arrangement of the acting area described in the preceding column. **Arena:** None	Music an integral auditory component, sometimes integral visually. Elevating orchestra pit to accommodate from 20 to 40 musicians. **Arena:** Orchestra pit beside the acting area parallel to long axis and opposite principal entrance. This unavoidably imparts a performer orientation toward the orchestra and favors the seats in that general direction.	The assumption by ballet of a greater share in the performance of musical comedy indicates the need for a high general sight line from the audience. A phenomenon of the last twenty summers has been the growth of the musical theatre arena under canvas by which huge audiences have been enabled to see revivals of standard and Broadway musicals at popular prices though with general reduction of scenic investiture to that which is possible in the arena form. The movement has been economically feasible and generally profitable.
The realistic style of dramatic production confines the performance to an acting area entirely inside the proscenium. The apron is not used. Most historic styles and much modern dramatic theory demand more freedom of audience-performance relationship than the realistic style and call for the projection of the performance toward, into, and around the audience. For this projecting aprons, forestages, sidestages, runways, steps and ramps into the aisles are all to some degree useful. To meet the demands of different styles and stylists the acting area for drama must be capable of assuming many shapes. To confine it within the proscenium opening is adequate for the realistic style but inadequate for the others; to project it toward, into, or around the audience in any rigidly unalterable form is likewise adequate for one style but inadequate for others.	Width equal to long dimension of the acting area. Moving panels to vary width, openings in proscenium splay to form side-stages, movable pylons or columns by which opening may be subdivided are all desirable. Flexibility and mobility are increasingly desirable. The application of motive power under remote control to the movement of structural parts, to produce different arrangements appears desirable but is costly. Manually alterable parts, particularly forestage proscenium panels and sections of the stage floor, if not unwieldy, are reasonable substitutes.	Orchestral music is sometimes an integral visual part of the performance, but most generally it is a purely auditory component. It is not generally necessary for the orchestra to be seen by the audience, but because cueing of music is so exacting, the conductor must see the action. It is reasonable to provide a pit for from 15 to 30 musicians, but the flexibility cited at the left must be provided, either by portable pit covers, steps, and platforms, or by mechanized orchestra lifts. There is opportunity for originality of arrangement.	The various forms of theatre used by legitimate drama are discussed fully earlier in this chapter.

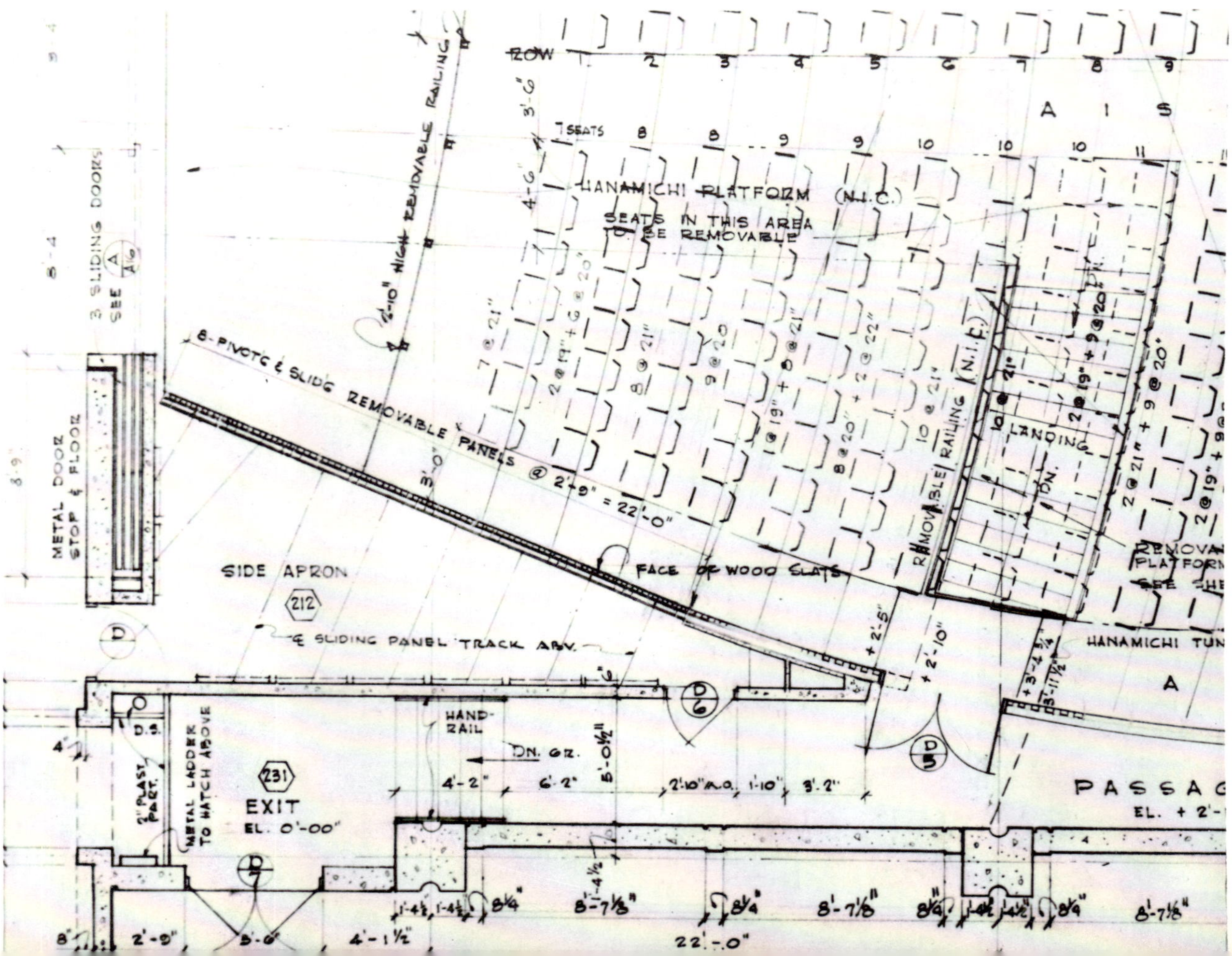
ROW
7 SEATS
HANAMICHI PLATFORM (N.I.C.)
SEATS IN THIS AREA TO BE REMOVABLE
3 SLIDING DOORS SEE A/A6
8-PIVOTS & SLIDE REMOVABLE PANELS @ 2'-9" = 22'-0"
METAL DOOR STOP & FLOOR
SIDE APRON
212
FACE OF WOOD SLATS
℄ SLIDING PANEL TRACK ABV.
REMOVABLE RAILING
LANDING
DN.
HANAMICHI TUN
D.S.
2" PLAST. PART.
METAL LADDER TO HATCH ABOVE
HAND-RAIL
DN. 6R.
231
EXIT
EL. 0'-00"
PASSAG
EL. + 2'-
22'-0"

ABOVE: *To make possible the* hanamichi, *the characteristic entrance way of Kabuki Theatre, seats are removed and a stairway from the basement opened. The John Fitzgerald Kennedy Theatre, University of Hawaii.* OPPOSITE: *Panels of the wall may be moved back to produce upper and lower side stages in a variety of arrangements.*

Radio City Music Hall Orchestra in place on pit elevator. Organ console extended from recessed position. This pit elevator can also carry a band car on which the whole orchestra may be moved across the apron and upstage.

8: Backstage operation

The process of preparing a theatrical production culminates in an operation called loading-in the show, which means assembling all the elements of the show within the theatre and making them ready for the performance. The process takes place whether the component parts of the production are prepared at other locations and brought to the theatre or are prepared in production service areas in the theatre building and brought to the stage.

An involved sequence of operations must be analyzed and the elements examined to determine how they best may be accommodated backstage in the working portions of the theatre building. This chapter proposes to state first the sequence of operations and then to consider how each of the elements of the show fits into the sequence, in order to derive the architectural requirements of each operation and element. The outline form is used as being more concise and more indicative than continuous description.

Operations Involved in Loading-in the Show

1. *Architectural alteration of the theatre.* Necessitated by
   a. archaism of the theatre,
   b. production requirements: production very large; theatre too small, more often the case; production designs require it, as for JUMBO, THE ETERNAL ROAD, THE GREAT WALTZ. The theatre planner must anticipate a variety of demands and provide a theatre which is large enough to meet reasonable maxima.

2. *Adjustment of permanent equipment.* The varying demands of theatrical productions require that all equipment of the stage including even the stage floor and the act curtain (fire curtain excepted by law) be either movable or removable.

3. *Installation of new equipment.* Special flying equipment, cycloramas, tormentors, light bridges, stage elevators, and even stage floors come under this heading. Original installation in a theatre of durable, dependable, and flexible stage equipment in sufficient quantity to meet carefully studied probable demand facilitates the "take-in" of every production which uses the theatre. Mechanization under electrical controls is indicated when frequent change and variation of major items of stage equipment are anticipated.

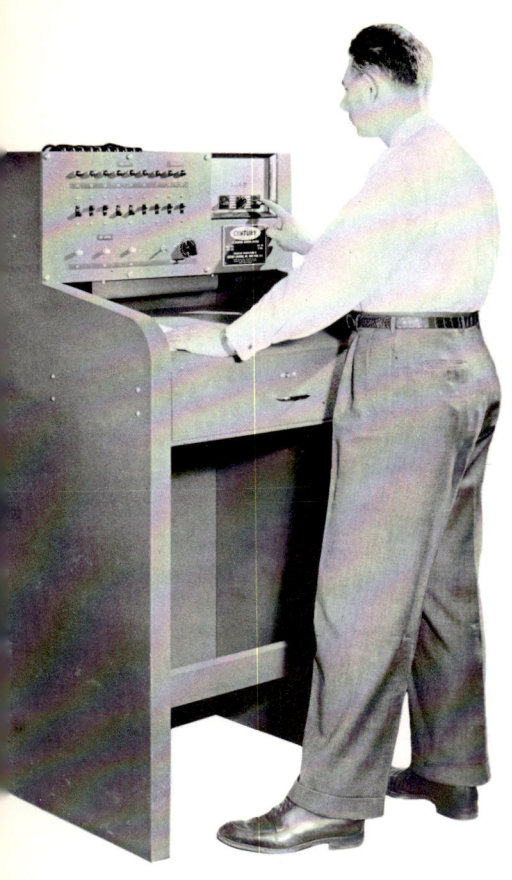

A stage manager's console.

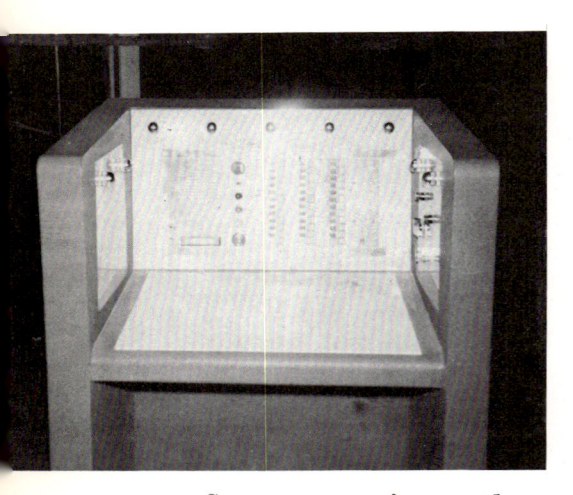

Stage manager's console, Hopkins Center.

4. *Installation and adjustment of lighting and sound equipment.* In present-day commercial theatre practice, no such equipment is in the theatre. The producer of each production must furnish all equipment required. In theatres which house resident companies, most lighting and sound equipment is owned either by the theatre owner or by the company and may be kept in place, though subject to movement to satisfy the productional requirements particular to each show. Stage lighting technique and electronic sound control are the newest of the elements of theatrical production. Their recent rapid development postdates most existing theatres, and advancement in instruments and techniques is still rapid. Few theatres, therefore, have adequate mounting and operating positions, branch circuits, outlets and control boards for stage lighting or speaker positions, conduits, mike lines, control apparatus or control booth for sound. Recently built college theatres approach a condition of adequacy in this regard, although even in this case it is to be suspected that provisions for stage lighting and sound control are the last items included in, and the first items cut from, building budgets. The theatre planner must make certain that the structural provisions for stage lighting and sound are provided in the building regardless of whether or not the portable items are included.

5. *Installation of scenery.* Scenery is brought to the stage in many pieces. These are fitted together, attached to stage equipment, assembled into sets, separated and stored in planned positions on the stage. The handling of scenery is routined and rehearsed by stagehands before the performance. When stage and scene shop are contiguous and the production schedule permits, it may be possible to build scenery in place on stage with resulting simplification of construction techniques, fastenings and handling, and savings in materials and effort.

6. *Properties fitted to sets.* Properties are all objects which ornament the scenery and stand in the acting area: furniture, draperies, art objects, pictures, rugs, shrubs, flowers, etc., as well as all objects which are manipulated by the actors. Props are brought to the stage in trunks and crates, are unpacked, fitted to each set of scenery, and placed in planned storage positions. The handling of props is routined and rehearsed by property men.

7. *Rehearsal of lighting, sound, and scenic effects* by stage manager and stagehands.

8. *Rehearsal of parts of the production* in which actors are closely involved with lights, sound, or mechanical parts.

9. *Costumes* received, unpacked, inspected, fitted, altered, repaired, pressed, distributed to dressing rooms.

10. *Dress parade.* Actors wear costumes in sets and under lights. Move about to test costumes under performance conditions.

11. *Dress rehearsals*. Actors wear make-up and costumes and rehearse entire production. All conditions are as much like a performance as they can be.

12. *Performances*.

13. *Put-out*. When a show moves from one theatre to another or from one town to another, time is of the essence. Therefore, the plan and equipment of the theatre must be conducive to speed and efficiency. In resident theatres when a show is not followed immediately by another, the process of *striking* the show involves returning the stage to its pre-show condition and disposing of all the productional components by returning to sources, salvaging and storing re-usable parts, and reducing the balance to removable trash. In repertory the whole production may be stored intact. If another show follows immediately, the put-out of the one and the take-in of the other are overlapped in a process called a "change-over"—a weekly event in stock company production.

Stage manager's console, South Florida University.

Production Elements

The elements of a theatrical production may be divided categorically into animate and inanimate, or people and things.

People: talent (actors, performers, singers, dancers, musicians); stagehands; stage managers; directors; designers.

Things: scenery, properties, lights, sound apparatus, costumes, musical instruments. Performing animals may best be considered in this category.

All these elements exert specific demands upon the size, shape, arrangement, and equipment of the backstage portion of a theatre. The outlines below will take each important element into the theatre and through the process of a dress rehearsal or performance and out again, indicating at each point of each tour the significant requirements.

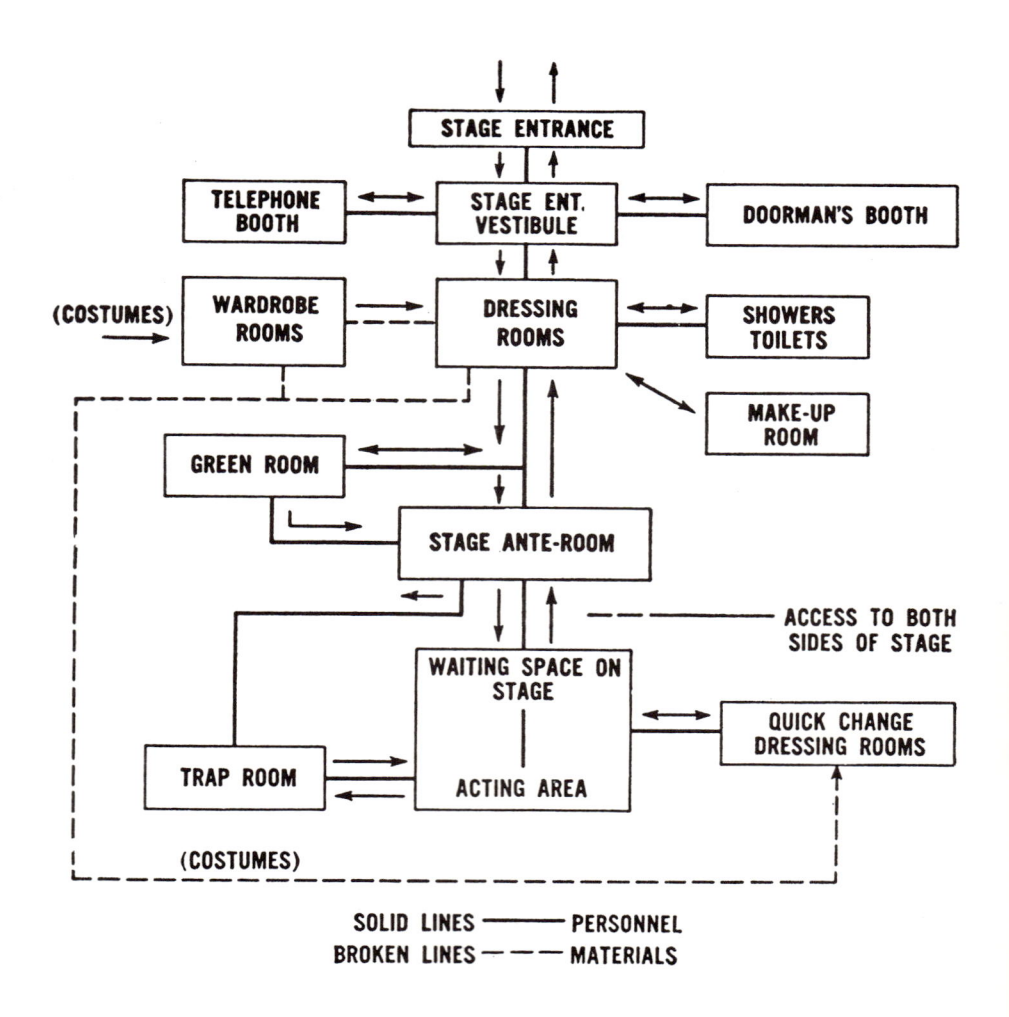

Flow chart for actors in the theatre.

Actors, performers, dancers, singers, and musicians on stage.

PEOPLE

Talent

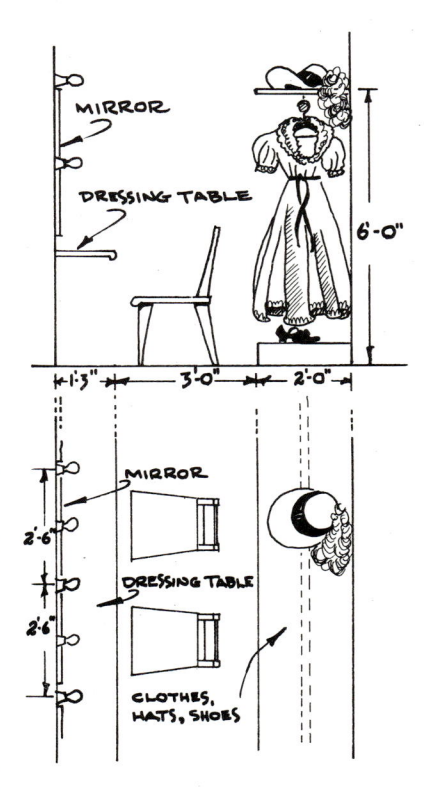

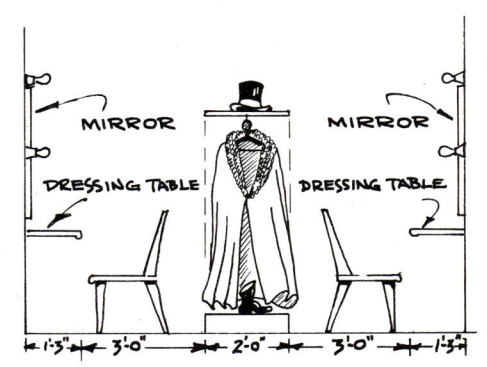

Enter the theatre

Check in, get mail and messages, read calls and notices.

Stage entrance

Vestibule: minimum 50 sq ft, shape variable. Equipment: time clock or other in-out indicator, bulletin board, telephone booth with muffled bell.

Location: central to all backstage departments.

Doorman's booth: 30 sq ft, shape variable.

Equipment: counter, mail box, small desk, key rack.

Location: adjacent stage vestibule to control all traffic to backstage part of building.

Dress for performance: take off street clothes, put on make-up, put on costume, inspection of costume.

Dressing room: minimum 16 sq ft per person. (See table.) School, college, community: group dressing rooms.

Professional: stars, individuals, choruses.

Opera: principal singers, choruses, ballets, supernumeraries.

Equipment: clothes and costume hangers, 2 linear feet of rod per person, 2 linear feet of shoe rack per person, no doors on cabinets, curtains if anything, make-up table 30″ wide per person, 15″ deep, mirror 18″ wide per person, well diffused light, no shadows, 25 fc minimum on face before mirror, one wall outlet per two persons. Full-length mirrors: one in each star's dressing room, one per eight persons in each chorus room, one in corridor on way to stage. Call system, phone outlet, monitor loud-speaker. One lavatory in each small dressing room, one per four people in large dressing rooms.

Stars, guest artists and principal performers merit more space and more congenial accommodations than the minima stated above. Lounge chair, sofa or day bed, dressing table with three-part mirror, reception room, toilet, stall shower or tub shower and drying room, all in pleasing décor, should be considered if the budget allows.

Location: near stage but not necessarily adjoining stage. (See Greenroom and Stage anteroom below.)

157

	Make-up room: minimum 100 sq ft. Desirable in schools, colleges, and community theatres where actors are unskilled at make-up.
	Equipment: make-up tables or benches, chairs on two sides. 25 fc general light on faces.
	Location: adjoining dressing rooms.
	Toilets: use concentrated into short periods of time before show, and during intermissions. Peak load inevitable. Minimum one per six persons.
Wait for call to stage	**Greenroom:** minimum 300 sq ft. Stage manager checks cast, assembles choruses. Directors talk to cast. Actors' social room.
	Equipment: lounge furniture, tables, smoking accessories, card table set, full length mirror. Call system outlet, telephone outlet, monitor system loud-speaker.
	Location: near stage, same level.
	Stage anteroom: alternate to greenroom, minimum 150 sq ft.
	Equipment: chairs or benches.
	Location: adjoining stage near proscenium. Same use as greenroom but stripped of lounge aspects. Strictly business. May be merely an enlarged passage between dressing rooms and stage.
Go to stage	**Passage:** minimum width 5 ft. Short and direct, *no stairs,* use ramps to change level.
Enter set and perform	
Leave set	
(The next four actions are alternates)	
(1) **Wait for next entrance**	**Waiting space on stage:** minimum 50 sq ft, chairs.
	or

Plan of minimal dressing rooms for a small theatre. The program prescribed accommodations for a guest artist. ▶

Chorus dressing room, Radio City Music Hall.

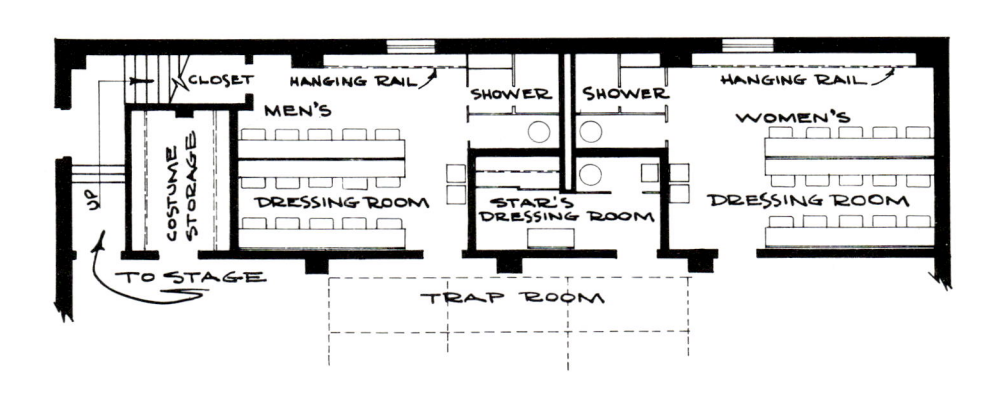

Greenroom, Crampton Auditorium, Howard University. Located at the stage entrance, it serves as a retiring room, reception room and robing room for dignitaries.

Stage anteroom.

Actors are responsible for re-entrances. Must stay where they can hear show. Monitor loudspeaker.

(2) **Quick change** of costume and/or makeup before next entrance

Quick change dressing room: minimum 50 sq ft per actor. Space for dresser to help actor.

Equipment: same as other dressing rooms.

Location: immediately adjoining stage.

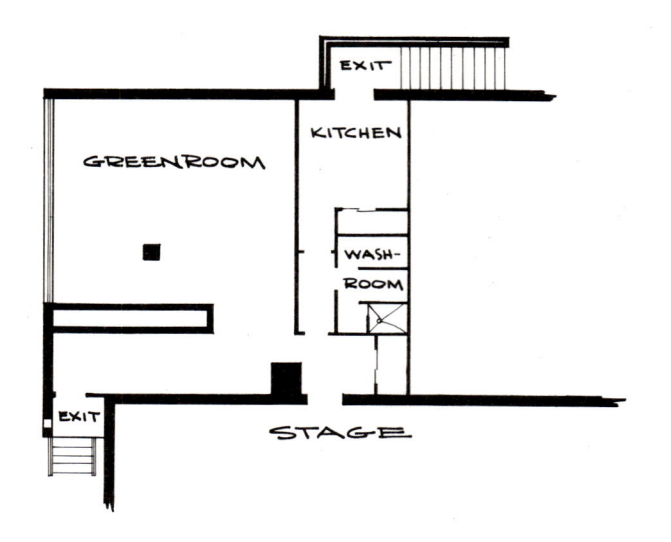

Plan of Crampton Auditorium Greenroom.

160

(3) **Slow change** of costume and/or make-up	**Regular dressing room** (See above)
(4) **Wait for curtain calls**	**Greenroom or stage anteroom.**
Remove costume, clean up, and dress for street	**Showers:** one adjoining each star's dressing room, one for six actors otherwise. Peak load immediately following performance; body make-up may necessitate baths by entire company.
Confer with stage manager or director	
Entertain friends after show	**Greenroom:** kitchenette adjoining. **Reception room:** adjoining stars' dressing rooms for private entertainment of guests apart from the general bustle of the greenroom. Comfortable furniture and pleasing décor.
Check out and leave theatre	**Vestibule and stage entrance** (See above)

Flow chart for stage hands.

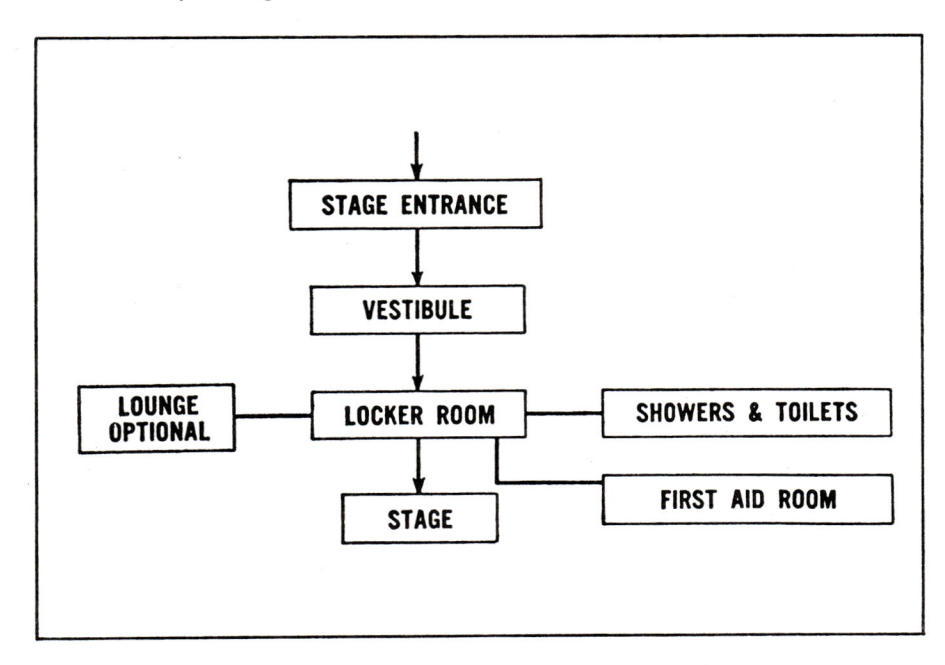

```
            STAGE ENTRANCE
                  ↓
              VESTIBULE
                  ↓
LOUNGE  ──  LOCKER ROOM  ──  SHOWERS & TOILETS
OPTIONAL          ↓
                            FIRST AID ROOM
               STAGE
```

Musicians in the Pit Musicians who perform on stage follow substantially the same route as other talent. The following applies to musicians who play in the pit.

Enter theatre, check in, get mail, messages, calls.

Stage entrance, vestibule, doorman's booth, as above.

Prepare for performance: remove wraps, tune instruments, get out music, practice.

Musicians' room: minimum 300 sq ft.

Equipment: lockers or clothes racks, chairs, music cabinets, telephone and call system outlets.

Location: basement level near pit and stage.

Large instruments usually kept in pit.

Visiting orchestra's instruments, stands, and music trunks may be received through prop-loading door (see properties below), and large cases stored on stage.

Go to pit

Passage: direct.

Large doors to allow carrying instruments.

Orchestra pit: 10 sq ft per musician plus 100 sq ft for grand piano and 50 sq ft for tympani. Width from stage figured on a per man basis. Depth should keep musicians below audience sight line to stage. Conductor must see stage. Singers and orchestra must see conductor. Podium.

Elevating orchestra pit floor (1) features orchestra as part of performance, (2) adds floor for chairs if brought to auditorium level, (3) makes forestage when desired.

Portable steps or platforms may be set over orchestra pit.

Leave pit and leave theatre

Lavatories and toilets same as for actors. Dressing room with lavatory and shower for conductor.

Stage Hands **Enter theatre,** check in

Stage entrance and vestibule.

Change from street clothes to work clothes

Locker room: according to number of men.

Equipment: individual lockers, chairs, benches. Call system outlet; phone outlet.

	Location: may be in basement, near stage, serves as stage hands' lounge.	
Go to stage	**Passage:** direct to either side of stage.	
Work the show	**Passages:** easy access from stage to fly galleries, gridiron, light bridges, trap room, and auditorium ceiling. Clear passage across stage at back.	
Wait between scene shifts	**Locker room** may serve as stagehands' lounge. Equipment: lounge furniture, card table set, smoking facilities, if allowed, adjoining toilets. There is little provision for comfort of stagehands in existing theatres. Traditionally they play pinochle in the trap room between shifts.	
Treatment of accidents	**First-aid room:** minimum 50 sq ft. Equipment: surgical table, stools, chair, first aid cabinet, sink, hot water. Seldom proper provision for first-aid backstage. Stage work is hazardous on occasion. For co-educational organizations (amateur, school, college) dual locker rooms, showers, toilets, for crews. Common lounge.	
Clean up and dress for street	**Locker room** Showers: one to every four men. Peak load after performance inevitable. Stage work is dirty work.	
Enter theatre, check in	Use stagehands' locker room.	**Stage Managers**
Manage the show	**Stage manager's desk:** on stage near proscenium on working side. Equipment: nerve center of backstage signal system: calls, phones, monitors, moving stage controls, etc.	
Care of scripts, cue sheets, etc.	**Office:** minimum 50 sq ft. Necessary only in permanent theatre organization: repertory or stock.	

163

Directors and Designers

No specific routine, but they need backstage offices in permanent organization. Conference room near all offices is desirable. Empty dressing rooms may serve as pro tem offices.

THINGS
Scenery

Brought to theatre

Loading door: 8′ wide, 12′ high at side or rear of stage.

Loading platform: height above grade equal height of average van floor. Width to accommodate two vans. Avoid change of level inside. Use ramps outside to adjust to grade. Roof over. Clear and direct approach for vans.

Stored pending setup

Receiving space: minimum 200 sq ft, 20′ high.

Equipment: pipe frames at right angles optional for stacking scenery, otherwise clear wall and floor space.

Receiving space is lacking or scanty in existing theatres. Result: when delivered, scenery is stacked on stage, necessitating much rehandling during setup. Scenery left outside theatre, sometimes damaged by weather.

Setup

Stage equipment for flying, rolling, sinking scenery.

Rehearsed and operated during show

Note: the considerations determining the size, shape, arrangement, and equipment of the stage are treated in detail in three chapters.

Repaired

Repair shop: minimum 100 sq ft.

Equipment: work bench, tools for working wood, tin, iron (cold), sewing, painting, electrical work. This shop will also serve property and electrical departments. This is in no sense to be considered a shop for the production of scenery, properties, or electrical equipment; it is merely the necessary repair shop in the event that scenery, properties, and lights are produced elsewhere.

Dismantled

Receiving space.

Shipped out

Loading door.

			Properties
Brought to theatre	**Loading door:** 6' wide, 8' high, separate from scenery door. Adjacent on loading platform.		
Unpacked	**Receiving space:** 100 sq ft minimum. Separate from scenery receiving space. Property crates stored in this space when empty.		
Fitted to sets of scenery			
Stored on stage	Floor space, racks, shelves.		
Operated during show			
Repaired	See under scenery (above).		

PERSONNEL REQUIREMENTS FOR MAIN TYPES OF THEATRICAL ENTERTAINMENT

TYPE OF SHOW	ACTORS PRINCIPALS	EXTRAS	PLAN DRESSING ROOMS PRINCIPALS	EXTRAS	STAGE HANDS	MUSICIANS	STAGE MANAGERS	DIRECTORS	DESIGNERS
PAGEANT	10 TO 50	100 TO 2000	40	500	50	100	4 TO 10	3	3
GRAND OPERA	4 TO 10	20 TO 100	10	100	50	80	2 TO 4	3	3
PRESENTATION	4 TO 10	20 TO 100	10	50	30	30 TO 200	2 TO 4	3	3
VAUDEVILLE OR REVUE	4 TO 10	20 TO 50	10	50	20	10 TO 30	2	0 TO 3	0 TO 3
OPERETTA OR MUSICAL COMEDY	4 TO 10	20 TO 50	10	50	30	10 TO 30	2 TO 4	3	3
PLAYS ("LEGIT")	2 TO 20	0 TO 50	20	30	3 TO 30	0 TO 20	1 TO 4	1	3
MOTION PICTURE PALACE	NONE EXCEPT WHEN, AS, AND IF ONE OF THE ABOVE TYPES OF SHOW MOVES IN				2	0 TO 50	0	0	0
MOTION PICTURE NEIGHBORHOOD					0	0	0	0	0

165

	Struck, packed, and shipped out	Receiving space (above).
Lighting Equipment	Brought to theatre	**Loading door** (may use property loading door).
	Unpacked	**Receiving space:** minimum 100 sq ft additional to space for scenery and properties. Crates are stored here when empty. May be in alley or on loading platform.
	Installed	**Lighting equipment** may be placed in any position on the stage floor, in the space at the sides of the stage, above the stage, in slots or ports in the auditorium ceiling, in wall slots or box, or on the fronts of balconies or boxes. See Chapter 12.
		Portable switchboards are set in areas up to 200 sq ft on the working side. Power supply through company switches up to 500 kw.

Flow chart for scenery. Sequence A-B-C-D-E for commercial theatre and touring show. Series E-F-G-H-D-E for self-contained theatres (repertory, community, college, school): Omit D-1 in this sequence. J. (scenery storage) completes the cycle for scenery which is salvaged.

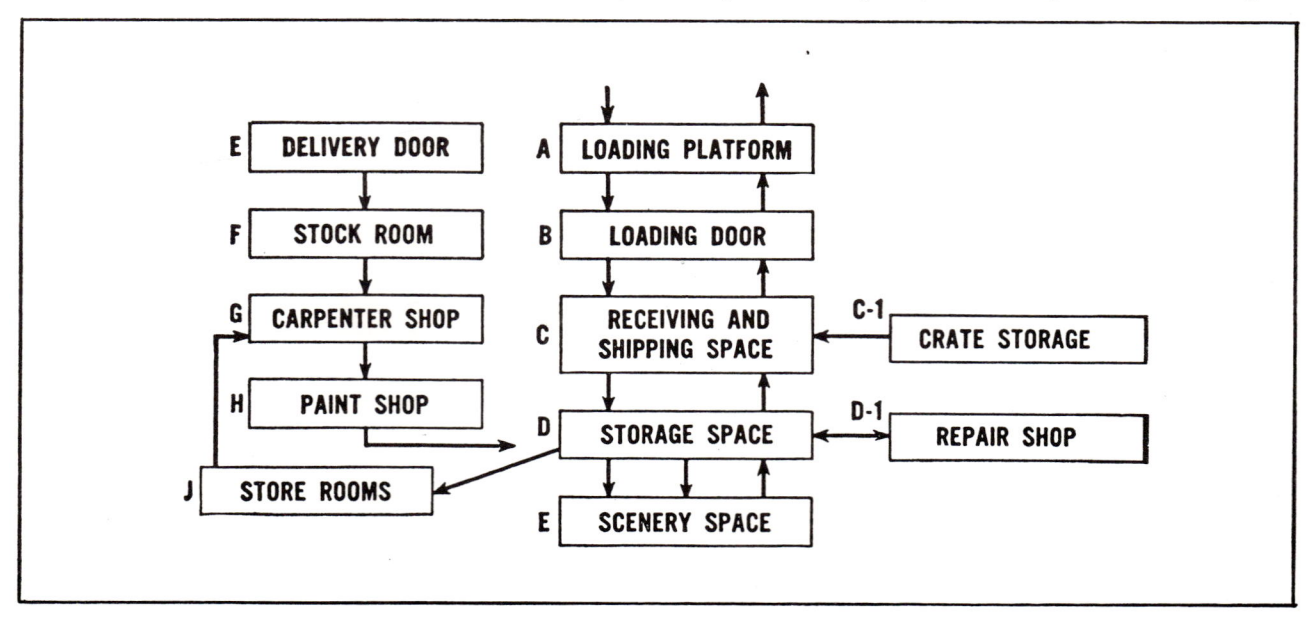

Operated

Dismantled and
   shipped out

With less bulk by 75% essentially the same as lighting equipment.   **Sound Apparatus**

Brought to theatre	**Loading door:** property door above.	**Costumes**
Taken for inspection	**via Passage:** 5′ clear width, no stairs, ramps where needed.	
	or Lift: minimum 6′ x 8′.	
	to Wardrobe room: minimum 120 sq ft.	
	Equipment: costume hangers 12 linear feet, ironing board and iron, electric ironer, outlets, sewing machine, and table.	
Hung in dressing rooms	castered garment trucks à la 34th Street.	
To actors' persons **To stage and return**	**Passages:** 6′ clear width for widest costumes, no protuberances on which costumes may catch.	
Cleaning, pressing, repairs to trunks and shipped out.	**Wardrobe room.**	

A common requirement in theatres planned for vaudeville was the animal room. The Hippodrome in New York contained provisions for housing a menagerie. An occasional performing animal or troupe must be accommodated today. Hence a completely equipped theatre must have an animal room, adjacent to the stage but separated from it by masonry walls, with separate outside door, ventilation, drainage, and water.   **Animals**

The movement and storage of pianos, used either in concert performance or in the orchestra pit, require adequate clear paths from outside the building to the points of use and storage, protective storage clear of other activity, and motorized lifts if pianos are to be moved vertically.   **Pianos**

Working Circulation   Essential to the effective operation of a theatre is a system of passageways which connects all working and operating positions by the most direct and easiest routes, both horizontal and vertical. Electricians must be able to get from control room to equipment rooms in the basement, to light mounting positions and operating positions in the overhouse space, in side-wall slots, on stage galleries, on light bridges and below the stage. Stagehands must be able to get from one side of the stage to the other at stage level, at gallery level and below stage, from stage floor to galleries, gridiron, and basement. Actors must have easy travel from dressing rooms to stage, to trap room, and to side stage entrances and entrances from the orchestra pit and house. Despite the increased use of electrical communicating devices there is ultimate need for the house manager to get backstage and for the stage manager to get out front, quickly.

In principle, this working circulation should be kept separate from audience circulation. It is doubtful if the sight of actors in costume and make-up outside their working milieu, the stage, or of stagehands in working clothes threading their way among a gala-dressed audience at intermission contributes much to the total effect which the showman wishes to achieve. In practice, the separation of circulation can be achieved almost completely in the proscenium, open stage and extended stage forms because the audience can be oriented to the stage through 180 horizontal degrees and the performance through the other 180 degrees, and audience circulation can be segregated on certain levels while working circulation can be placed at other levels. For example, audience passageways at the sides of the house can be at the main floor level while working passageways to side-wall light slots can be directly above.

The arena form presents a difficult problem because orientation of both audience and production personnel to the stage must extend through the entire 360 degrees surrounding the stage, and whereas audience circulation may be contained in one, or at most two levels, working circulation must be horizontal at levels both above and below the audience levels with vertical connections which cut through the audience circulation.

In general, insufficient attention is paid to this need for efficient working circulation. Passageways are often circuitous, steep, narrow, or absent entirely, and headroom in overhouse spaces and gridirons is inadequate or missing. In amateur production, time is inefficiently used; in commercial production, money is paid out for time spent rigging ladders and bosun's chairs, hauling up bosun's chairs, moving bosun's chairs, crawling over grids under too low roof structure and recovering from concussions incurred by bumping roof beams.

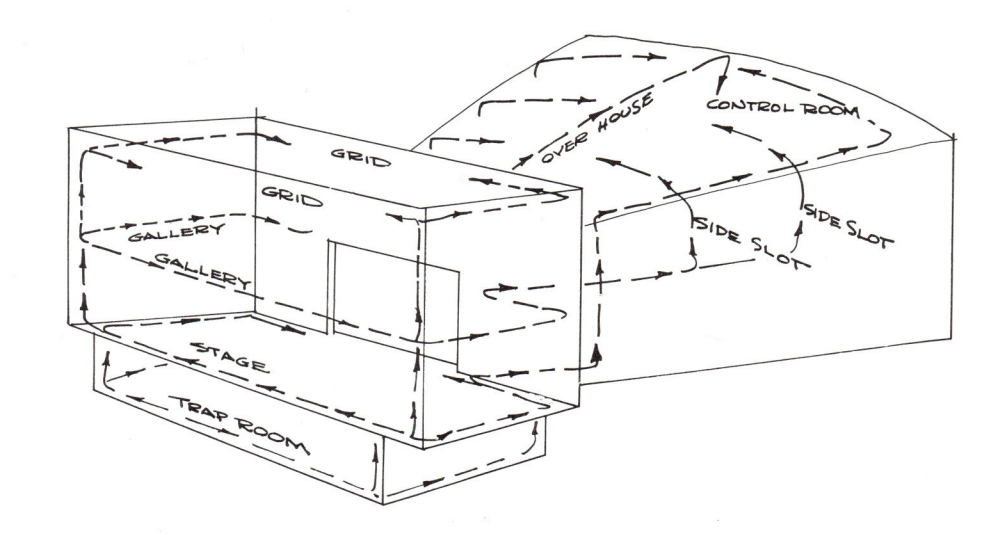

Working circulation for a proscenium theatre.

Theatre at South Florida University, Tampa. Stagehouse and side-stage wings.

Motor-driven traverse wagons in motion during a scene change. John Fitzgerald Kennedy Theatre, University of Hawaii.

9: Scenery

Most of the types of production listed in Chapter 1 require scenery. By the same token, most theatres, except perhaps drive-in motion picture theatres, are likely to try to employ scenery at some time. Using scenery where only concert or motion pictures were originally contemplated results in waste of labor, time and money, and in artistic compromises. Inferior productions often come about because people will not be deterred by such drawbacks. Since the theatre planner cannot cure this insistence on using scenery, it behooves him to learn its nature and make its effective use possible.

History

The development of scenery has paralleled that of theatres. The most generously designed and ingeniously mechanized theatres provide the greatest scope in the use of scenery and maximum latitude in the production of plays. Good plays are extremely durable, and while many plays are susceptible of being set in a number of ways, it is unlikely that there will be more than one way, often the original one, as in the case of Shakespeare, in which the total emotional value of the play is most effectively projected.

As is the case in most arts, the passing generations have introduced new materials and new ways of using them, but almost nothing has been discarded. HIGH TOR by Maxwell Anderson, A.D. 1937, includes the suspension of two actors high above the stage in a steam shovel. THE CLOUDS, by Aristophanes, 423 B.C., contains the stage direction: "The machine swings in Socrates in a basket." Three-dimensional structural scenic units were used in ancient Greece, and the wing and border set was developed in the Renaissance.

Elaborate mechanization of the basic wing and border set by ropes, pulleys, drums, windlasses and counterweights and the development of scene painting through four centuries produced stagecraft based on the parallelism of flat scenery which has lasted into the twentieth century to be shocked out of its complacency by a series of developments. Appia theorized that three-dimensional actors were inconsistent with two-dimensional scenery and that three-dimensional scenery was aesthetically more significant. Realism and naturalism as artistic styles opposed the box set and irregular forms to the flat symmetry of the wings and

171

borders. Finally, in this century, factors deriving from the plastic and graphic arts (abstraction), from motion pictures and radio (frequent and rapid locale changes) and theatre economics (the costs of producing, taking-in, operating, putting-out and touring elaborate realistic productions) have influenced scenery form and style away from the realistic and representative toward the suggestive, the abstract, the symbolic and especially toward the easily built, easily painted, easily handled kinds of scenery.

Today, play production may and does embrace all historical forms of scenery, including both the elaborate and the simple forms, and all historical techniques of changing it, while at the same time including forms and techniques unique to this century (projected scenery and electromechanical techniques for changing scenes).

Functions

Scenery contributes an essential element to the total effect of a theatrical production. It is used to establish locale, atmosphere, mood, to assist in the revelation of character and the advancement of the plot. The functions of scenery are admirably stated by a designer in *Scene Design and Stage Lighting*, Parker and Smith.

Because playwrights set their plays in all conceivable and imaginable times and places, scenery must be capable of representing any time or place, real or imagined. Since playwrights find it necessary to change the locale of their action from place to place, scenery must be capable of quick and easy changes.

In addition to its function of projecting the playwright's concept, scenery has the following purely technical functions:

1. It encloses and delineates the acting area.
2. It supplies openings of proper form and in sufficient number and location so that the actors may enter and leave the acting area as required.
3. It masks the stage walls, machinery, crews, and actors awaiting entrance cues.

Structure

Scenery is essentially fake, temporary, light in weight, and portable. The structural elements conventionally consist of lightweight soft-wood frames. Surfaces visible to the audience are lightweight, durable fabrics, board materials, or wire and plastic substances, mounted on the frames, and painted to resemble whatever the scene designer requires.

Structural types of scenery are based upon the necessity of demounting and transporting it, and upon the available sizes of materials. A general rule is that all scenery must be capable of division, folding, or rolling into units, each with one dimension not greater than 5 feet 9 inches.

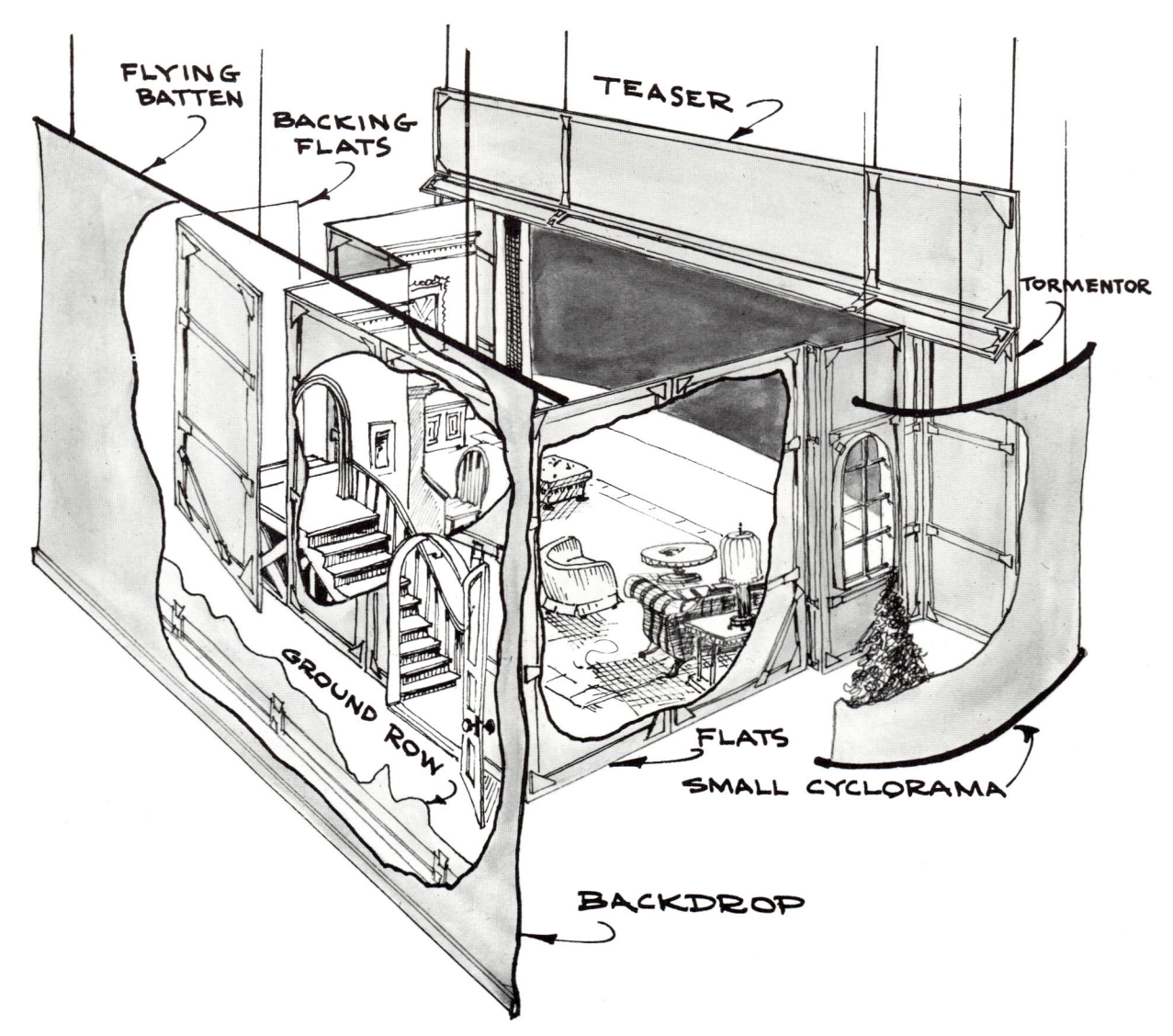

A set of scenery in place on stage showing several types of scenery.

In self-contained theatres with scene shops adjoining or near the stage, this rule may be violated and scenery built to the maximum sizes allowed by the doors and passageways. Sometimes sets are assembled on wagons and rolled to the stage, sometimes the materials are taken to the stage for first and only assembly, and sometimes when space is needed the stage is used as an auxiliary shop.

A drop, the simplest structural unit of scenery, is composed of widths of cloth sewn together and suspended from a wooden batten. Another batten is attached to the bottom edge to impart a stretch to the cloth.

Types of Scenery

173

The drop and its variations, such as leg drops, scrim drops, translucent drops, cycloramas, borders, and teasers, provide large expanses of scenery, in great variety, by the easiest possible means. Since one dimension of the drop can be made very small by rolling it, the other dimension is limited only by the stage requirements. Storage space for drops must accept the long dimension. The projection sheet for motion pictures or television is a drop, usually laced into a four-sided frame. The theatre planner must provide facilities for rigging, handling, and storing drops which are one-third wider than, and twice as high as, the proscenium.

Curtains or draperies are much used as stage decorations, occasionally as representational scenery, but more frequently as frank masking devices. Musical productions, which require little representational scenery and much stage decoration, make free and effective use of draperies and achieve brilliant effects by clever operation and the use of novelty fabrics, dye, paint, and light. Draperies are rigged as curtains or drops, either hung from tracks above the stage to draw sidewise, hung from battens to be flown into the space above the stage, or rigged with lines, to be lifted vertically (contour) or diagonally (tableau).

Flat Framed Scenery

Scenery of architectural derivation, such as interiors and exteriors of houses, is usually composed of frames, covered with cloth or board material hinged or lashed together, the joints concealed, and the surfaces painted. These framed pieces, called flats or wings, are generally rectangular, though they may be of any shape, seldom more than 16 feet high and 5 feet 9 inches wide. Any number of flats may be joined to form an expanse of wall. Details of architecture, such as windows, doors,

Plan of the simplest interior setting.

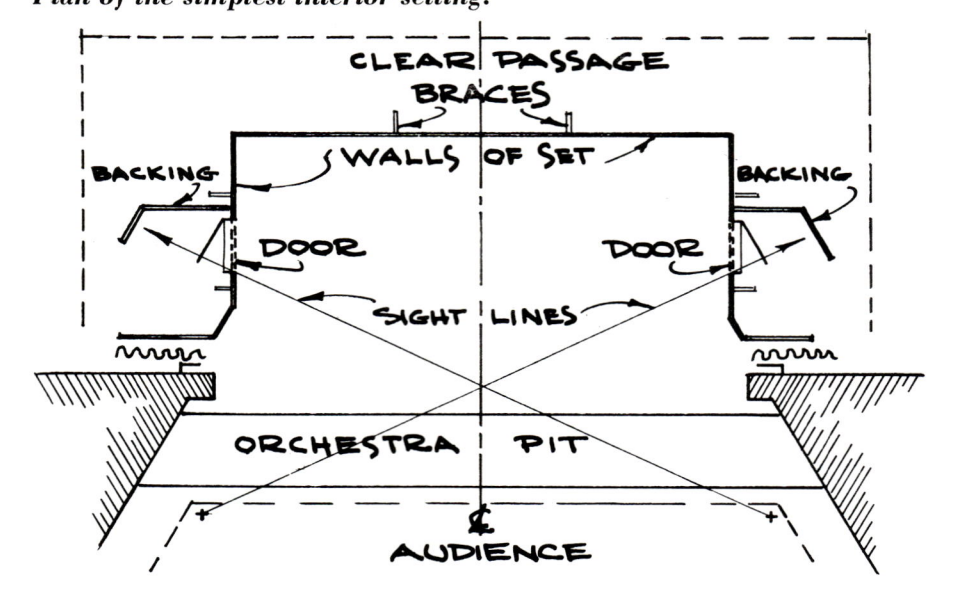

Plan and section of an interior setting showing space requirements of a window in the back wall. Lights illuminate (a) the interior, (b) the backdrop, (c) the interior through the window and (e) actors passing the window along the path D-D. Clear crossover space behind the backdrop is F. Broken line denotes the limit of space required.

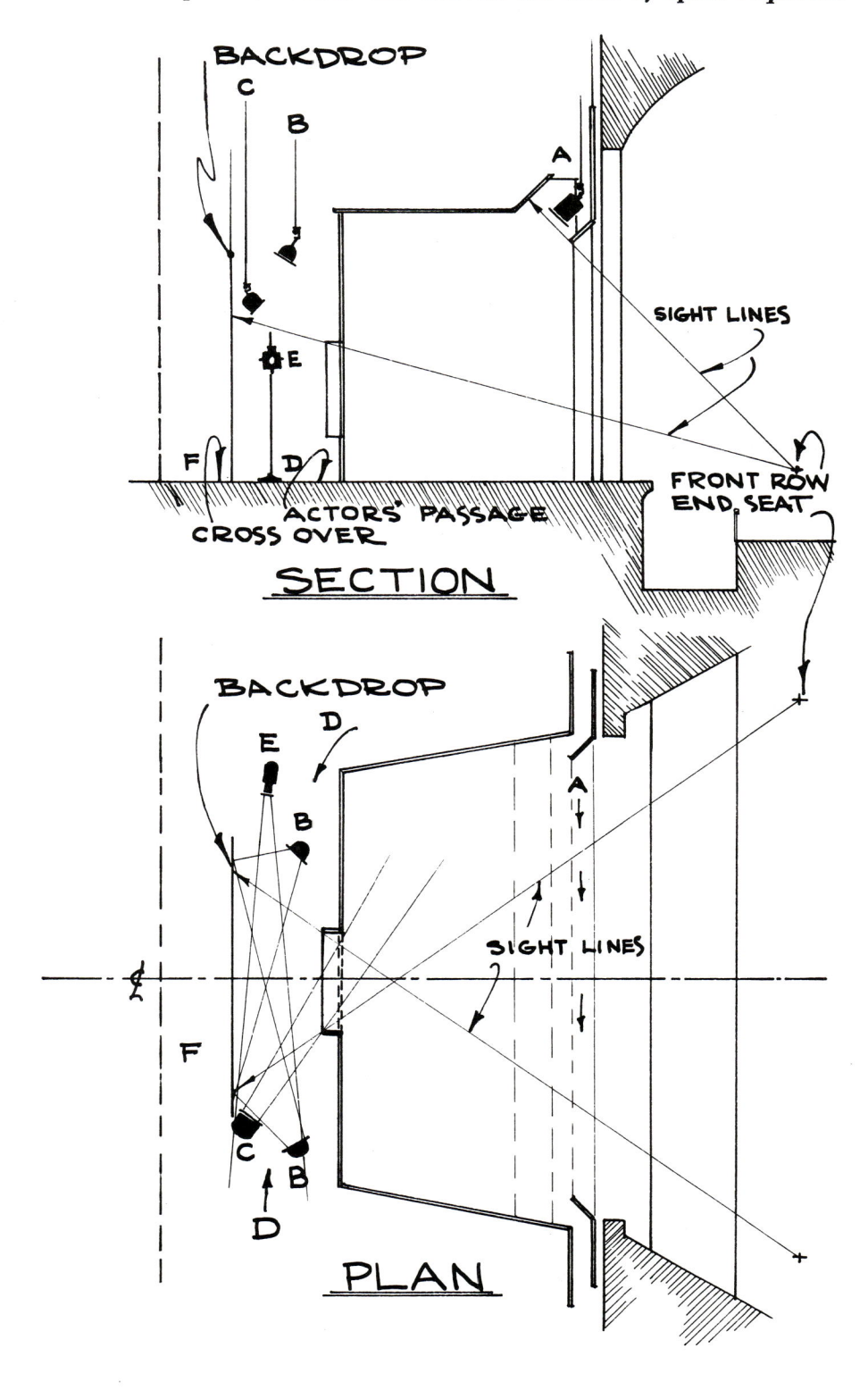

mantels, wall thicknesses, and cornices, are attached to, or inserted into openings in, the flats. Small detail is painted. Ceilings are of cloth stretched on demountable frames. Ground rows for exteriors (which represent garden walls, parapets, distant buildings, land contours, mountains and the like) are flat framed pieces.

Scenery to represent nature is similarly built on frames. Surfaces simulating earth, bark, or stone are achieved by covering the frames with wire mesh and modelling thereon a plastic material, such as papier-mâché. Foliage is artificial with wire stems woven into wire mesh. Standard limitations of size are observed as with flat scenery.

Three-dimensional scenery is an assemblage of demountable or collapsible frames, designed as structural members and calculated to carry specified loads.

Since it is rarely possible for scenery structures to be erected permanently on the stage where the performance is to be given, even bulky and relatively heavy weight-bearing platforms must be made up of numerous frames, assembled in the scene construction shop with semipermanent fastenings, taken apart, and reassembled on the stage before dress rehearsals begin.*

Space Requirements

The audience must see:
1. Significant contributive portions of the stage setting;
2. Scenery (backings, cycloramas, etc.), extending to limits of vision.

The theatre planner must make it possible for the entire audience to see all or a large part of the stage setting (see Chapter 3 and Chapter 7, Proscenium), and must allow space offstage, at the sides and back, for scenery used solely for masking purposes.

Scenery occupies space, both when set in playing position and when stored, either on the stage or in the scene dock (Chapter 8). A series of examples will develop the size and shape of the space in which scenery is set, which will hereafter be called the *scenery space*.

Interiors

The simplest kind of interior set, with the minimum number of doors and no windows, requires more space than is occupied by the portion of the set seen by the audience. Braces behind the walls support them and make them rigid. There must be entrance space outside each of the doors sufficient to allow actors to approach and prepare to enter the set. The entrance space, furthermore, must have a backing, that is, a unit of flat scenery to intercept extreme horizontal sight lines. Finally, because it is often necessary for actors, stagehands, and stage manager to get quickly from one side of the stage to the other, there must be a *crossover* passage behind the scenery. Thus this simple box set, the admitted minimum,

---

* For a detailed presentation of kinds and types of scenery, materials, methods of construction, assembly, and handling, see Burris-Meyer, H., and Cole, E. C., *Scenery for the Theatre*, Boston, Little, Brown & Co., 1938.

176

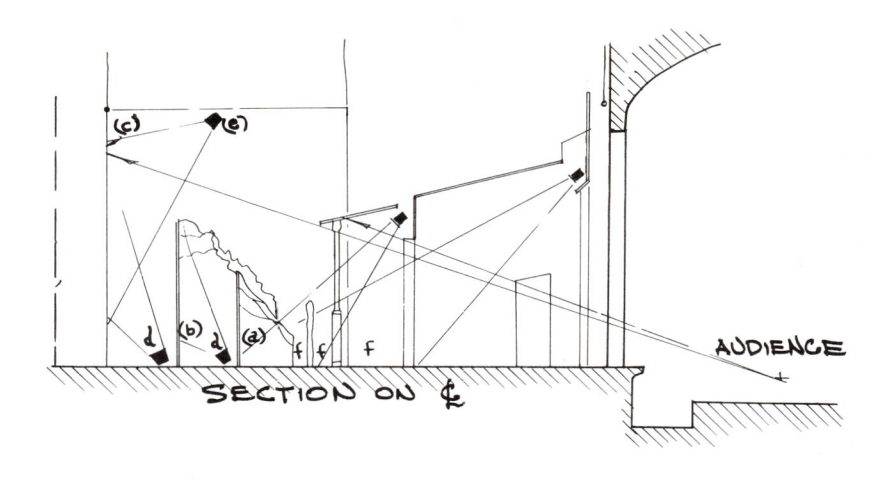

Plan and section of interior setting having large openings in the back wall through which exterior landscape is seen. The text explains the space requirements.

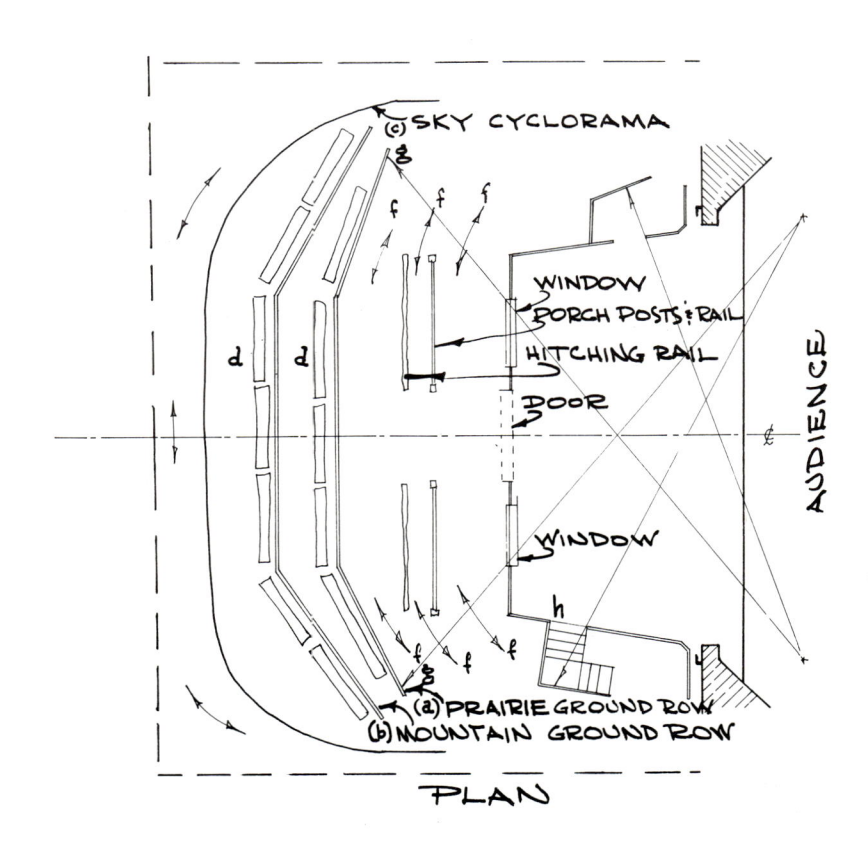

A balcony cantilevered over the acting area requires offstage space for landing and steps.

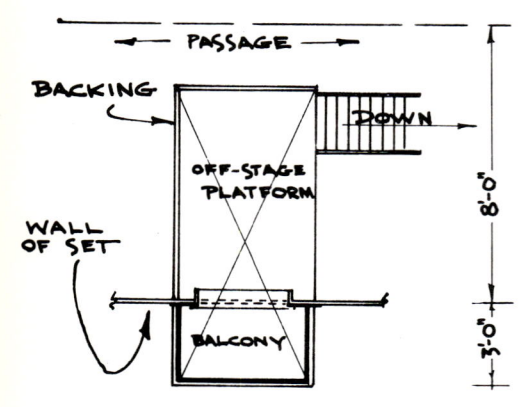

with no openings of any kind in the rear wall, requires a zone of space at least 5 feet wide behind scenery where there are no openings, and at least 6 feet wide at the openings. *Very few plays can be performed in sets as meager as this example.*

As additional and more elaborate openings are made in the walls of a box set, to meet the requirements of action, locale, or pictorial design, additional demands are made for scenery space. A window in the back wall of the set is an example. The window reveals a world outside the set which must be plausibly represented if the locale represented within the set is to be believed. A simple backdrop, possibly painted with distant hill, skyline, and sky, may suffice. Space between the set and the drop is required:

1. To prevent light inside the set from casting shadows of the window on the painted landscape;
2. To allow sufficient spread of light on the drop from instruments outside the set;
3. To allow lights outside the set to be directed through the window into the set;
4. To allow passage for actors whom the audience must see passing the window, and
5. To allow spread of light for illuminating such actors.

This space may have to be as much as 10 feet. Furthermore, ample crossover must be provided if people are to pass behind the drop without causing it to move or ripple.

A complex, though quite common problem of masking openings in the back wall of a set is illustrated by the preceding plan and section of a country store. The entire back wall is a series of openings through which the audience looks at rolling prairie (a), distant mountains (b), and sky (c). Diurnal light changes during the play require that the ground rows and cyclorama be elaborately lighted from instruments on the floor (d) and overhead (e). The action of the play demands passage for actors both on and beyond the porch of the store (f). Thus scenery space outside the set must aggregate more than the acting area inside the set. Dimensions given are normal, rather than maximum or minimum. The sight lines (g-g) indicate the great expanse of space outside the set which is visible to some members of the audience, and therefore the expanse of sky backing which must be provided.

Scenery and side space are conserved and adequate masking achieved by angling the scenery, which represents mountains and prairie, and by curving the cyclorama.

The staircase in the side wall of this same set (h) illustrates another way in which scenery occupies space. This simple representation of a staircase requires an offstage platform and stairs down to the floor if actors are to use it. Similarly Juliet's balcony requires an offstage platform and stairs.

Combining the possible requirements of masking and auxiliary structure, *a single interior set of scenery in playing position will often require a space twice as deep as the acting area and one and a half times as wide.*

Exterior Sets

Exteriors, with the exception of the conventional, implausible sets of another era, require more stage space than do interiors both in playing position and stored.

Realism demands that a scenery tree have as thick a trunk as one in a forest, that rocks and mountains on stage be rough and apparently solid, and that the sky be open and spacious rather than closed and floppy. In contrast to the old-fashioned exterior set with its arbitrarily smooth floor and rows of profiled wings and borders, the modern exterior scene consists chiefly of dummy or weight-bearing three-dimensional structures, ramps and levels to represent terrain, built-up or flat scenery to represent trees and shrubs, profiled ground rows to represent the horizon, and a great expanse of cloth, plaster, or plywood to represent sky. Sky borders and cloud borders are used sparingly above the stage,

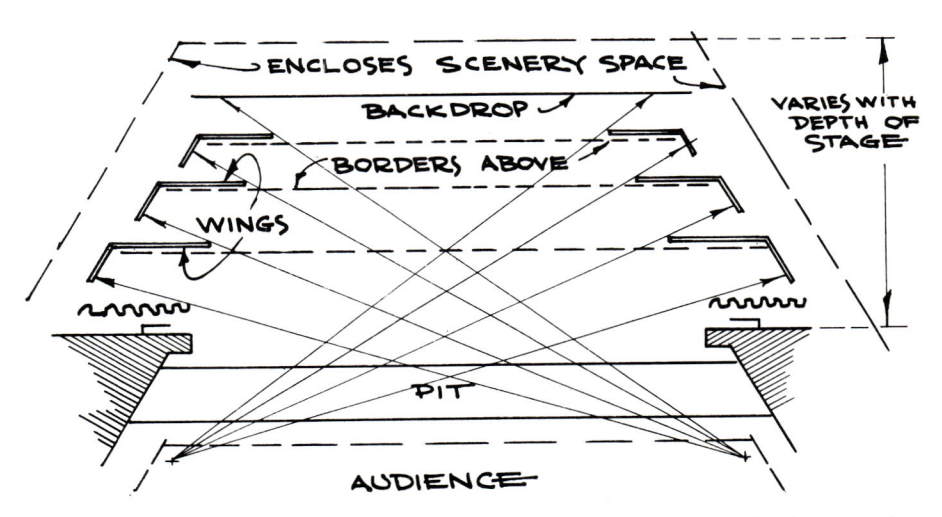

The traditional wing and drop setting was economical of space but was lacking in illusion.

but foliage borders are used when the presence of tree trunks on the stage requires them. Convincing illusion in exterior settings is achieved chiefly by an emphasis on openness, a *plein-air* quality, which demands the elimination of all elements of scenery which tend to close in the set and places great importance on the ultimate background, the cyclorama.

Different from scenery which attempts to make a complete representation of locale is that which supplies instead only those elements of scenery which are necessary and appropriate to the action, the backstage being arbitrarily concealed by nonrepresentational draperies or panels. A high degree of artistic discrimination is implicit in this mode

The setting for HE WHO MUST DIE *by Michael Antonakes, produced at the Yale University Theatre. The ground plan shows the elaboration of levels and the extension of the scenery beyond the proscenium, utilizing the side wall doors. Rolf Beyer, designer.*

of scenery, since the elements which are shown take on great significance; at the same time the backgrounds may be either contributary or neutral, but must not detract or distract.

Multi-scene Schemes The prevalence of multi-scene plays, much like motion pictures in which scenes change instantaneously at the whim of the scenarist, has imposed a demand for rapid changes of scenery. This demand has been answered in four ways by theatre artists. The first, and perhaps the least meritorious, reduces scenery to its least possible components or to nothing, as in arena or open stage. The second abstracts scenery into barely recognizable, and sometimes meaningless, symbols. The third attempts to set many scenes simultaneously within the sight lines, which usually constricts the acting space in each scene and inhibits the actors. The fourth increases the mobility of scenery in both horizontal and vertical directions.

In this scheme, locales are represented by significant fragments either flown in from the flies or rolled in on wagons, the size, shape and direction of the wagons being designed to fit the particular play. This re-

FASHION, by Anna Cora Mowatt, produced in period style at the Yale University Theatre. Robert Darling, designer.

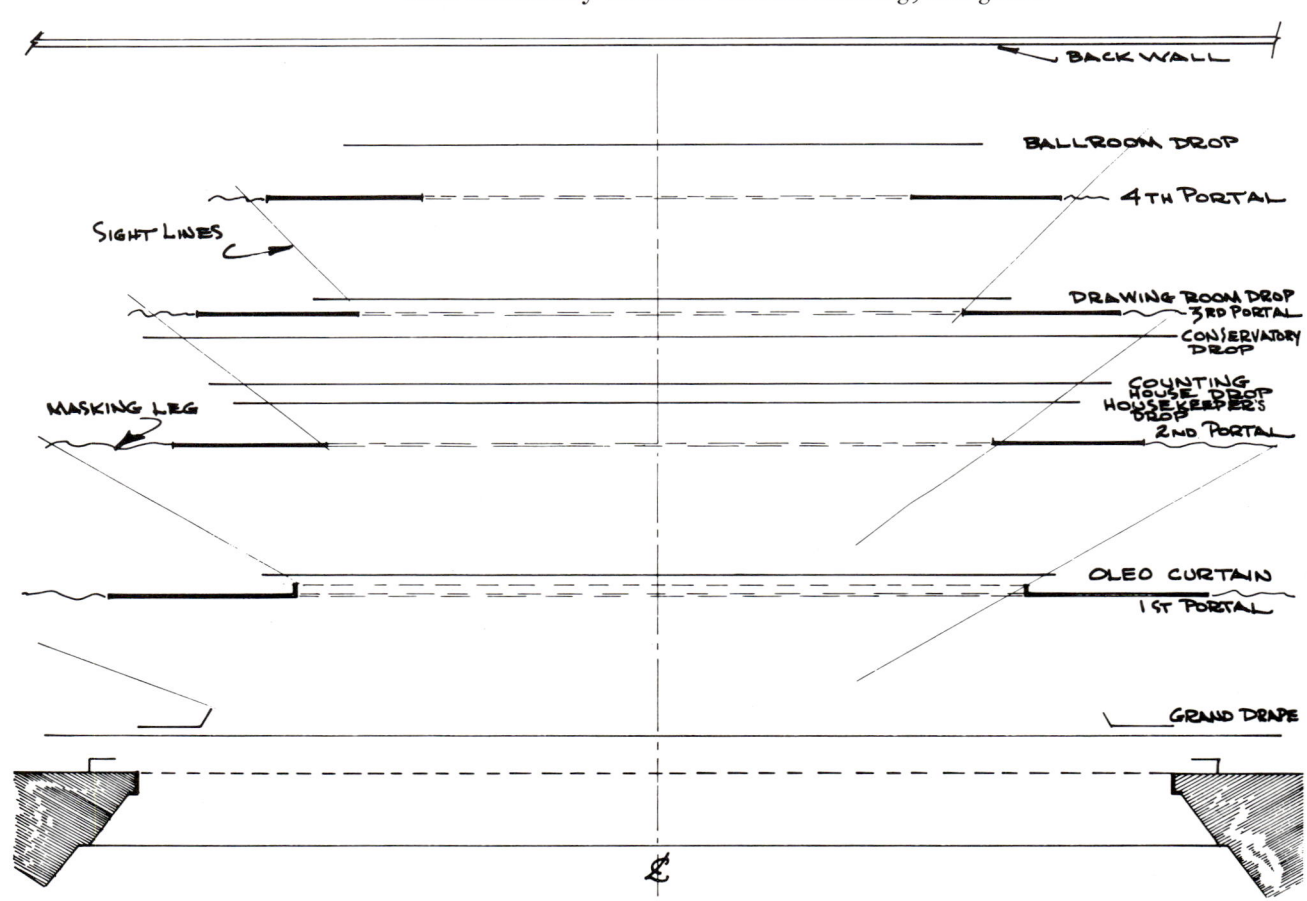

quires, in general, that there be space all around the scenery area sufficient to accommodate both the wagons in their offstage positions and the stored scenery which may be struck off the wagons or waiting to be set on them. In this kind of scenic scheme the masking is placed as required to conceal the wagons in off position. Panels may guillotine out and in, during blackouts, to allow the scenery to be changed, or the panels and wagons may be operated candidly under lights, in view of the audience.

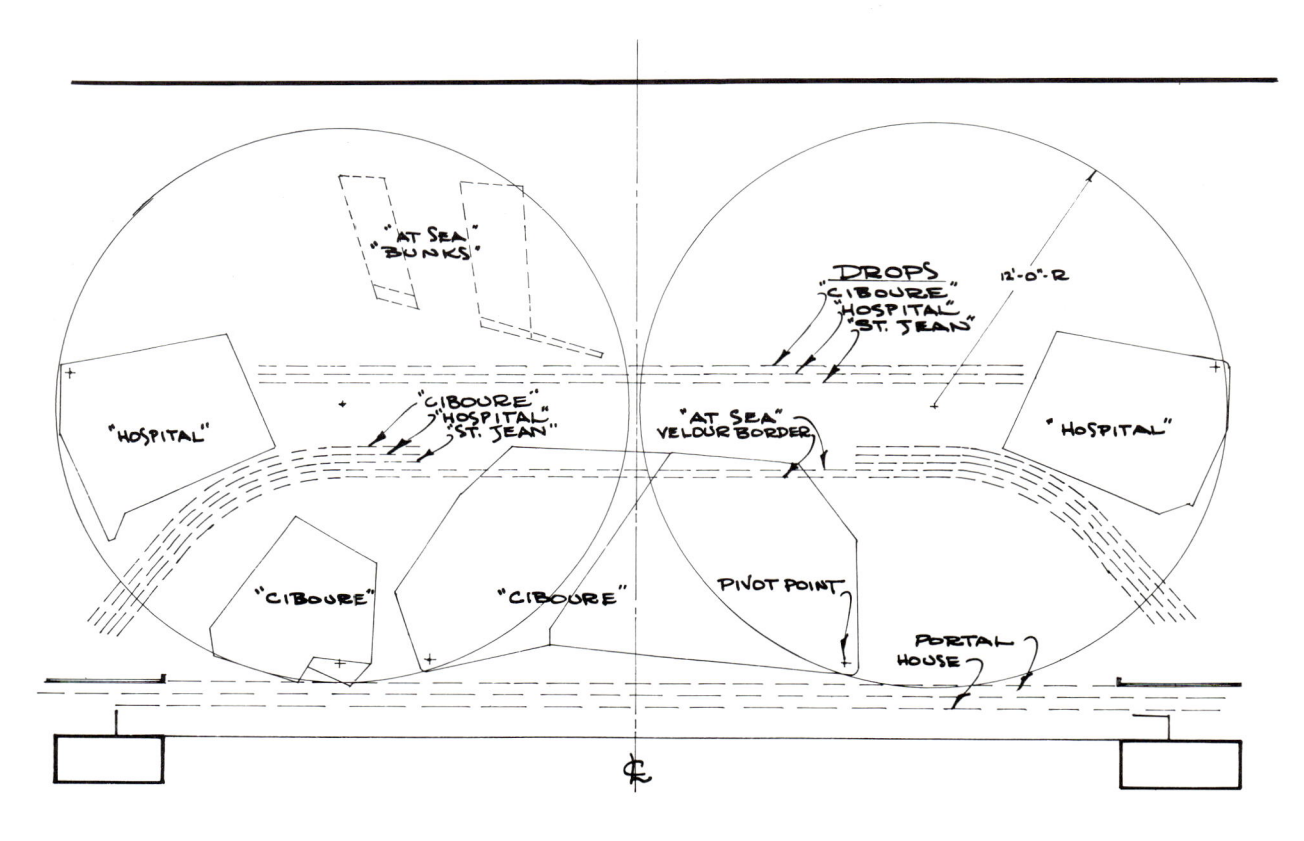

Ground plan for GIFT OF TIME, Boris Aronson, designer. Pivoting pallets on revolving discs with curved drops.

The Cyclorama

The functions of a cyclorama are:

1. To supply the ultimate scenic background. With representational scenery, the cyclorama has some recognizable scenic aspects: commonly sky, less commonly landscape, forest, seascape. With abstract scenery the cyclorama may be a decorative curtain hung to enclose the scenery space, a black velour curtain hung flat or in folds to absorb all light and give a background effect of total darkness, or various other fabrics or combinations of fabrics, variously lighted to make the background an

THE VISIT by Friedrich Duerrenmatt, designed by W. Oren Parker at the Yale University Theatre, used shuttle wagons to carry fragmented scenery into the acting area during a vista changes synchronized with the action. A raked floor filled the acting area and the scenery space.

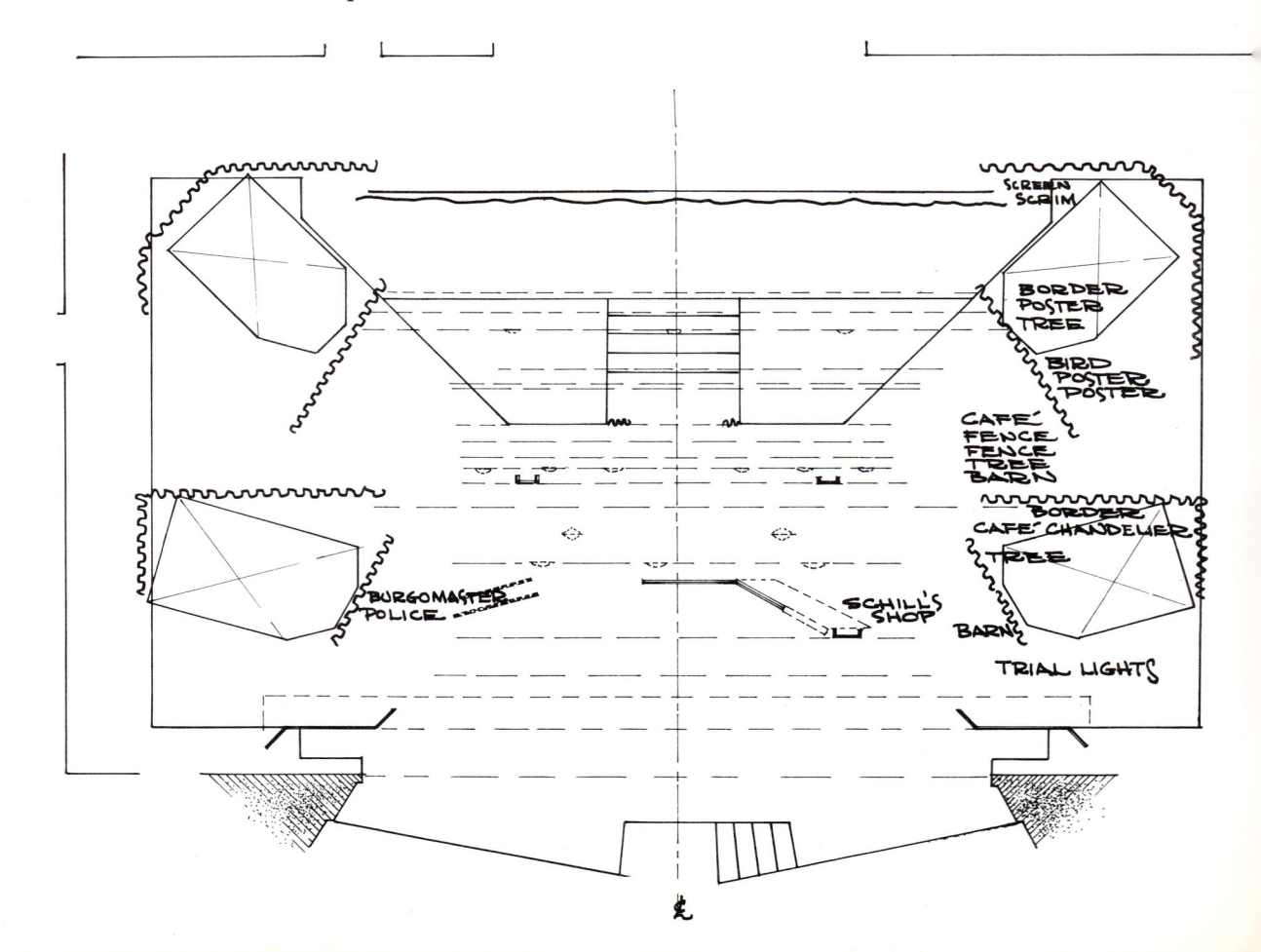

integral part of the stage design. The cyclorama may be used as a screen upon which light patterns are projected, from either front or rear, as a part of the scenic scheme. These light patterns may be abstract or representational, static or mobile, even motion pictures.

2. To supply the ultimate masking. For open scenes the cyclorama may mask the entire stage space as delineated by the extreme horizontal and vertical sight lines through the maximum proscenium opening. Whether or not a cyclorama is part of the original equipment of a theatre, the stage must be planned so that one may be used. In 116 sets of scenery at the Yale University Theatre, a cyclorama was used 42 times.

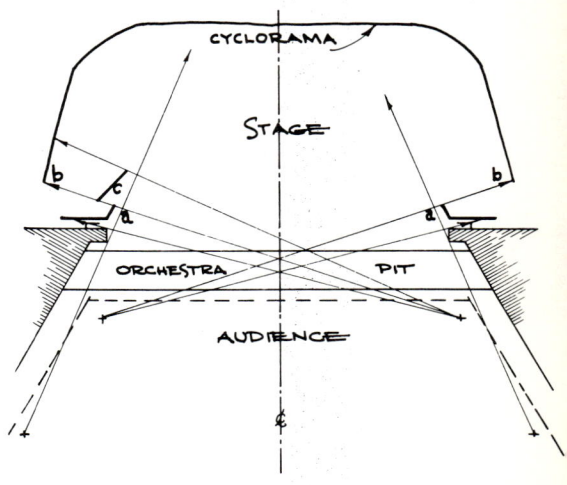

The basic sight lines.

Types of cycloramas are:
1. Cloth, sewn in horizontal strips, and dyed or painted.
  a. Laced at top and bottom to shaped battens of pipe or wood and rigged to fly with guide wires at front edges.
  b. Laced to shaped rigid frame of pipe or steel, rigged to fly.
  c. Back section laced to rigid frame, side panels laced to separate frames, and all three frames rigged to fly independently or together. When flying height is limited the lower part of the side panel may be framed and the upper part "soft" to fold when the lower part is flown.
  d. Rigged to travel horizontally on a curved overhead track and to roll into a vertical cylinder at one side. Bottom edge weighted with chain to impart stretch. The cylindrical or conical drum on which the cyclorama rolls may be located at any convenient position on the stage by extending the cyclorama track toward the proscenium wall or the side wall or by returning the track toward the back wall. The choice of storage drum position is critical because the rolled-up cyclorama becomes an obstacle to movement about the stage.

Cycloramas for special uses may be installed on the permanent equipment (battens, frames, or tracks) of any of these types.

2. Plaster on metal lath, on a shaped steel frame, painted.
  a. Back section built permanently in place and side sections, cloth stretched on frames, rigged to fly or to roll backward.
  b. Back section built permanently in place, and side sections rigged to travel downstage on horizontal tracks from vertical storage roll behind curved ends of the back section.
  c. Rigged to travel backward, rolling on overhead tracks.

The cyclorama may be designed with widely spreading sides which intercept the extreme horizontal sight lines without extending downstage, thus providing free access to the scenery space without the necessity of clearing the cyclorama. This is a very space-consuming arrangement. A rigid cyclorama, whether fixed or movable, may have its top edge follow the highest sight line.

Types of cycloramas described in the text.

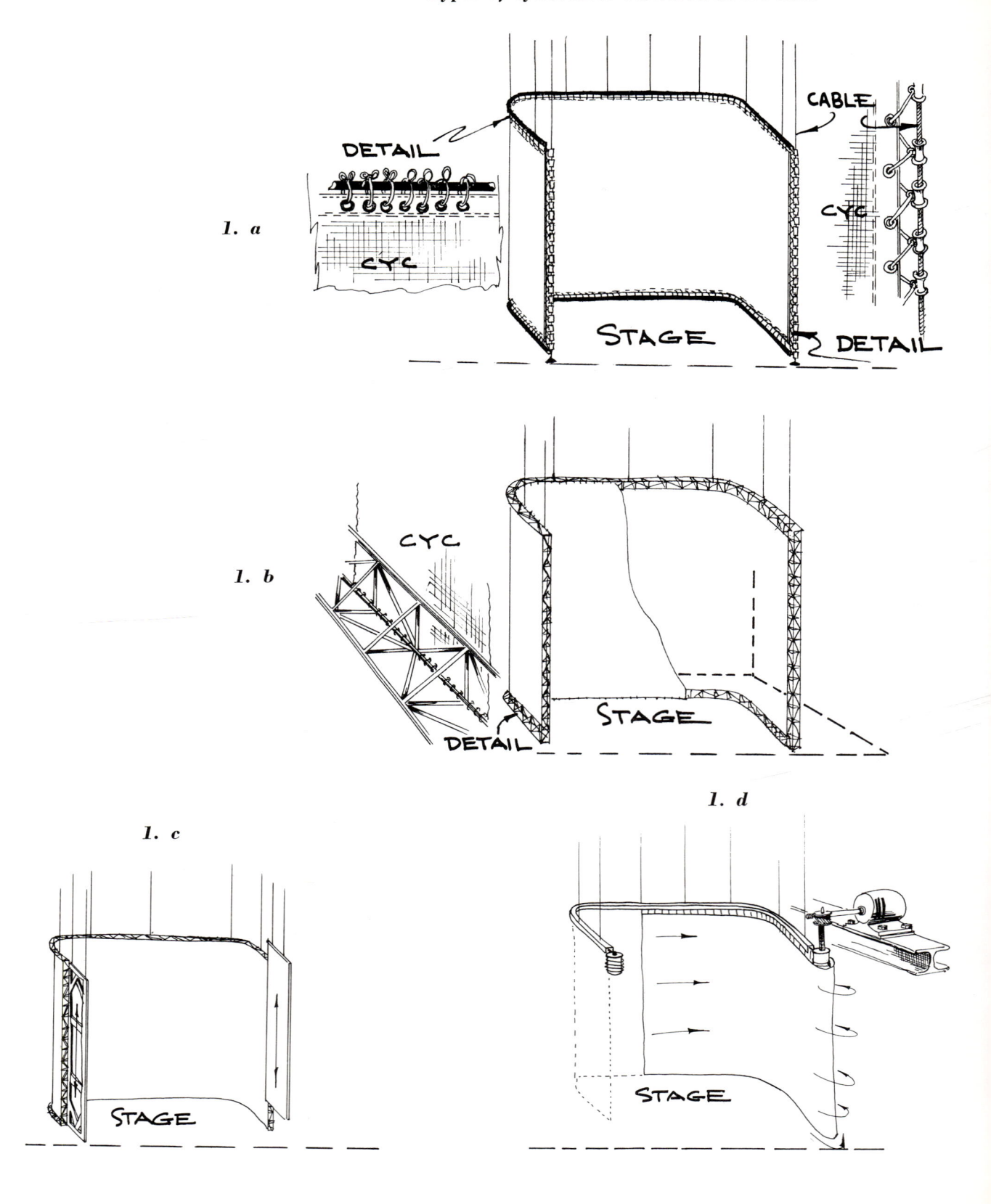

1. a

1. b

1. c

1. d

Plaster cycloramas may be part of the permanent structure of the stage house. In these cases, crossover passage at stage level must be provided behind the cyclorama.

The advantages and disadvantages of cloth and plaster cycloramas are compared below. The theatre planner and his client must weigh them in determining the kind of cyclorama most suitable to the particular situation.

Plaster Cyclorama	*Cloth Cyclorama*
Built as part of the building under the general contract.	Installed as stage equipment under a subcontract.
First cost relatively high.	First cost relatively low.
Replacement cost: nil.	Replacement cost of rigging nil, of cloth moderate.
Replacement frequency: never.	Must be replaced about every ten years.
Maintenance consists of occasional washing and infrequent repainting.	Tears must be sewn. Impossible to clean. Must be kept flame-retardant.
Light reflectance up to 80%; totally opaque.	Light reflectance seldom over 50%. Light translucence seldom over 50%.
Surface excellent for front projection.	Surface fair for front projection. Fair for rear projection.
Smooth, hard, matte surface.	Soft, subject to wrinkles, stretching, shrinking and tearing. Matte surface.
Shape and position are critical because cyc is highly sound-reflective.	Sound-absorbent.
Scenery may be shifted to sides only when side panels are raised or rolled back.	Scenery may be shifted to sides and back if cyclorama is rigged to fly.

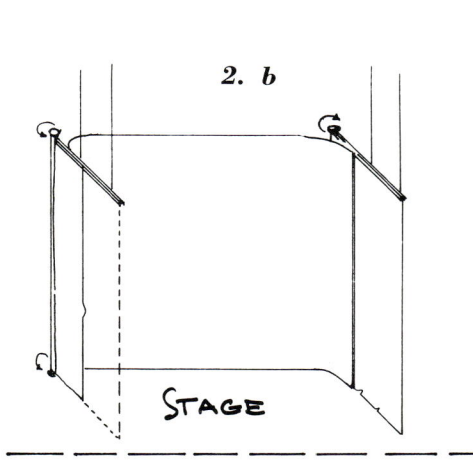

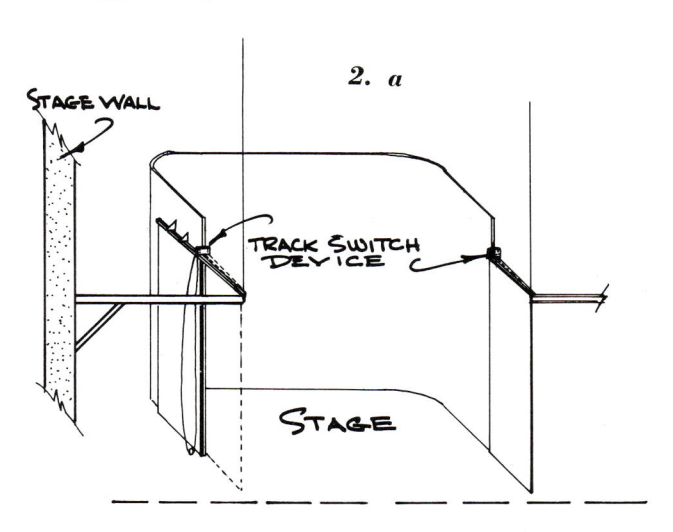

2. b

2. a

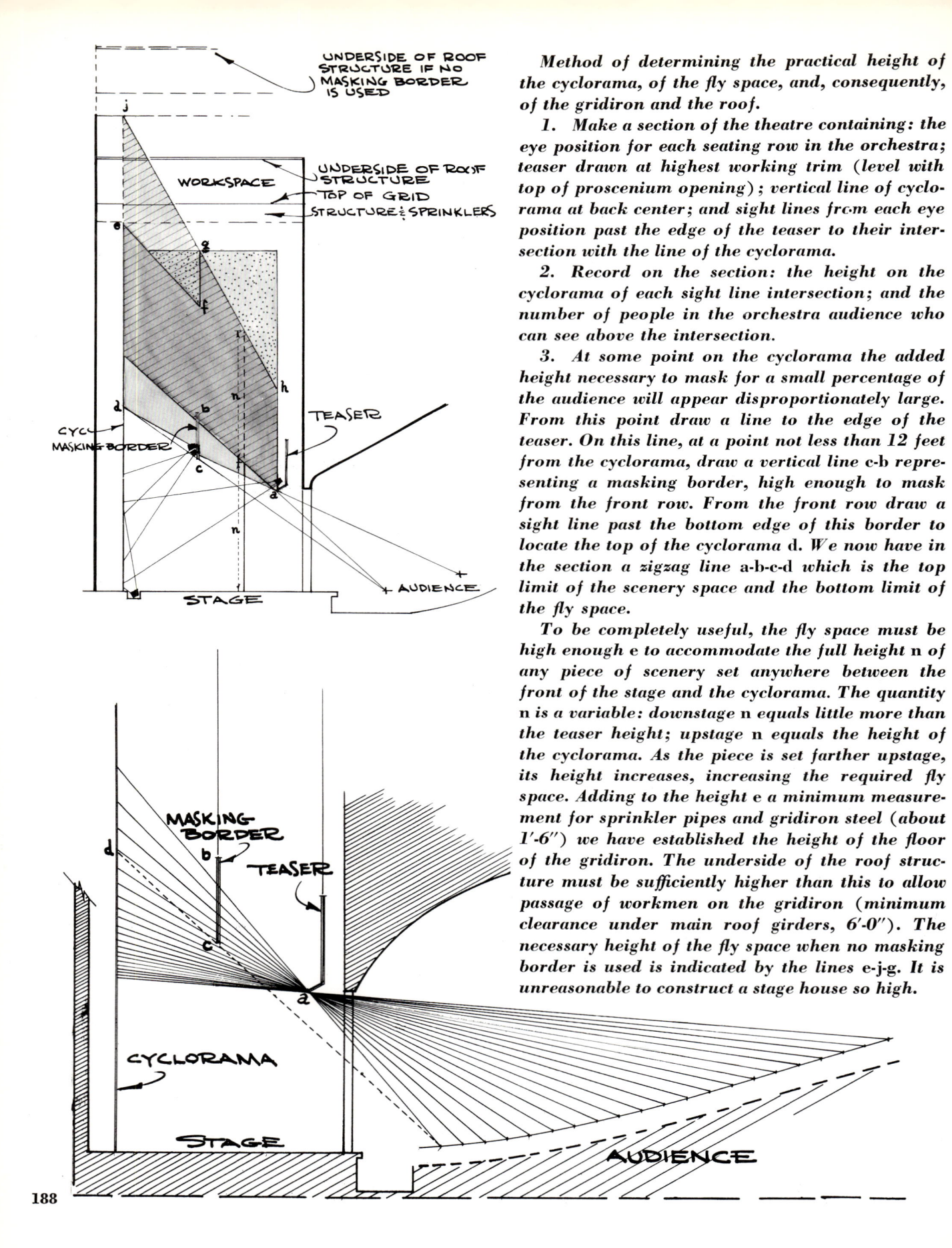

Method of determining the practical height of the cyclorama, of the fly space, and, consequently, of the gridiron and the roof.

1. Make a section of the theatre containing: the eye position for each seating row in the orchestra; teaser drawn at highest working trim (level with top of proscenium opening); vertical line of cyclorama at back center; and sight lines from each eye position past the edge of the teaser to their intersection with the line of the cyclorama.

2. Record on the section: the height on the cyclorama of each sight line intersection; and the number of people in the orchestra audience who can see above the intersection.

3. At some point on the cyclorama the added height necessary to mask for a small percentage of the audience will appear disproportionately large. From this point draw a line to the edge of the teaser. On this line, at a point not less than 12 feet from the cyclorama, draw a vertical line c-b representing a masking border, high enough to mask from the front row. From the front row draw a sight line past the bottom edge of this border to locate the top of the cyclorama d. We now have in the section a zigzag line a-b-c-d which is the top limit of the scenery space and the bottom limit of the fly space.

To be completely useful, the fly space must be high enough e to accommodate the full height n of any piece of scenery set anywhere between the front of the stage and the cyclorama. The quantity n is a variable: downstage n equals little more than the teaser height; upstage n equals the height of the cyclorama. As the piece is set farther upstage, its height increases, increasing the required fly space. Adding to the height e a minimum measurement for sprinkler pipes and gridiron steel (about 1'-6") we have established the height of the floor of the gridiron. The underside of the roof structure must be sufficiently higher than this to allow passage of workmen on the gridiron (minimum clearance under main roof girders, 6'-0"). The necessary height of the fly space when no masking border is used is indicated by the lines e-j-g. It is unreasonable to construct a stage house so high.

188

Size and Shape

The theatre planner is concerned with the following aspects of the cyclorama as they determine the size, shape, arrangement, and equipment of the stage:

1. The size and position of the cyclorama is established by two requirements: It must not encroach upon the scenery space as developed above, and it must provide complete masking. Complete horizontal masking is essential. Complete vertical masking is desirable but is possible only in the case of a cyclorama which is not flown. In the case of a flown cyclorama, the height to which the cyclorama must be flown to allow the passage of scenery under it added to the height of the cyclorama itself results in a disproportionately high and costly stage house. It is reasonable to plan to use a masking border which is visible to a small percentage of the audience, allows a considerable reduction in the height of the cyclorama and the stage house, and serves as concealment for the lights which illuminate the cyclorama from above.

2. The shape is established by four factors.

a. The cyclorama must surround the scenery space.

b. The cyclorama must, by its shape, and distance from the proscenium, permit uniform and adequate distribution and color mixing of light over its entire surface from lighting instruments located within the scenery space and flyspace, and possibly from instruments outside the cyclorama. This requirement dictates that there must be no sharp curves in the surface of the cyclorama in plan or section; all radii must be at least 12 feet; the surface of the cyclorama must be smooth. Wrinkles in a cloth cyclorama cause accidental streaks of light and shade, often in different colors. Unevenness in a plaster cyclorama causes patches of light and shade. Lighting the cyclorama from outside requires that there be no seams in the area to be lighted and that the cloth be treated to produce uniform translucency.

c. The shape of a plaster cyclorama must be acoustically designed to prevent the convergence of reflected sound, with time delay, in the seating areas. Tipping the cyclorama backward prevents this and also has other benefits: good orientation of the cyclorama as a projection surface to the light bridge, which is a good projection position, and passageways behind the cyclorama but inside the stage house at floor and fly gallery levels. In cold climates the plaster cyclorama must be held away from the exterior wall of the stage house to prevent the development of a dew point and subsequent condensation on its inside surface.

Movements

The cyclorama must perform its functions and, at the same time, not interfere with the normal operation of other stage equipment. Surrounding the scenery space as it does, it must be capable of rapid removal, entirely or in part, so that scenery, properties, and lighting equipment

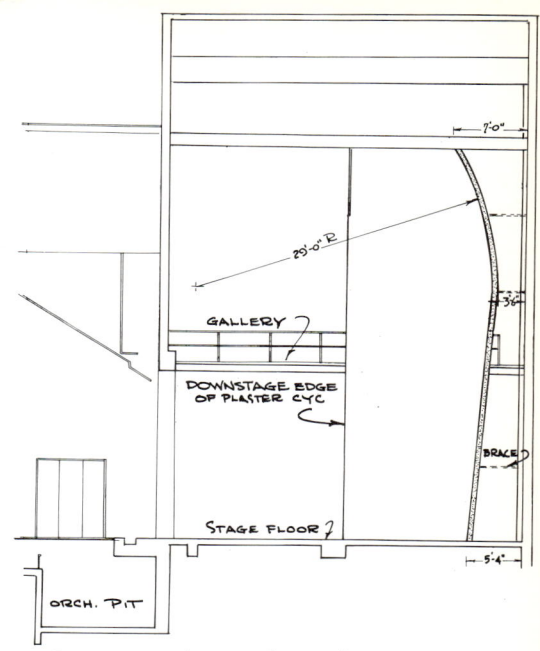

Section of rigid cyclorama, leaning back and curved overhead.

Construction of plastered cyclorama.

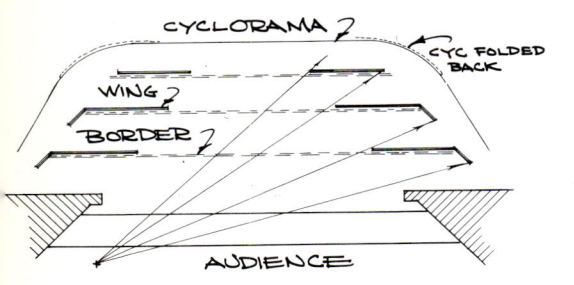

may be taken into and out of that space. If the plan for handling scenery involves movement to sides and back, the entire cyclorama must either fly to a height which will allow movement of the highest scenery under it, or travel sidewise on a horizontal track and roll at one edge. The flying operation is the more rapid. If the plan for handling scenery involves only movement to the sides, the following methods of moving the cyclorama are possible:

1. The whole cyclorama to fly.
2. The side panels to fly or roll back.
3. The whole cyclorama to roll back.
4. The whole cyclorama to travel on a horizontal track and roll up at one edge.

Wing and Drop Settings

The cyclorama is not the sole answer to the problem of enclosing the maximum area. Many productions are best set in scenery which permits the entrance of many actors, or dancers from side entrances. Ballet especially makes this requirement, which is best resolved by the drop and wing set. Ballet likewise requires a wide and deep acting area. Musicals which include ballet numbers have a similar requirement.

The plaster cyclorama should be wide enough to enclose a wide and deep drop and border set, and its permanent sides should not extend downstage to block entrances. A cloth cyclorama can be unrigged or furled and flown to the grid to clear the flies for changing such a set and to allow clear entrances from the sides.

Storage and Working Space

It is obvious that multi-set shows will need space to store sets and properties, while other sets are playing. The cyclorama usually establishes the largest single fly loft requirement. A loft which accommodates an adequate cyclorama can hold all other scenery which it is feasible to fly in or near its playing position.

While the fly loft can contain much scenery, considerations of speed, or simplicity of shift make it necessary to move settings intact, horizontally on wagons or discs between playing and storing positions. If such a shift is to be accomplished, space outside the scenery space, equal to one or more acting areas, must be available. Less space makes it necessary to dismantle scenery at least partly before moving it.

The theatre planner will easily realize that with fewer operations needed to bring in scenery, handle it on stage and take it out again (see Chapter 8), shows can be handled more efficiently and fewer people will be needed to handle them. This last item is often a critical and determining one in theatre operation (see Chapter 15). In the theatre in which the process of production is complete, the set can sometimes be built on a wagon, rolled intact with complete props into the acting area, and struck the same way. The ultimate inefficiency occurs when the sets must be pulled apart and elements moved individually. Stage area alone is no guarantee of efficiency in scenery handling. The area must be so planned that it can store large scenic units without thereby interfering with any other function of the stage. The principles here involved will be further developed in Chapter 10, Stage Machinery.

The creation of scenic backgrounds by projecting images in light upon large surfaces is of sufficient use to require consideration in the planning of the stage. Projection supplies scenic background but cannot supply solid scenery or properties required by the action of a play. Highly effective in some instances, projection cannot be substituted for built scenery.

Projection is of two kinds: (1) *shadow projection,* in which the light from a concentrated source (arc or concentrated filament) illuminating the projection surface is modified by a large slide or profile placed in the path of the beam; and (2) *lens projection,* which employs condensing lenses, slides, and objective lenses. The second kind of projection, by the concentration of light and the use of an optical system, produces images of greater intensity and higher definition than the first.

Projected Scenery

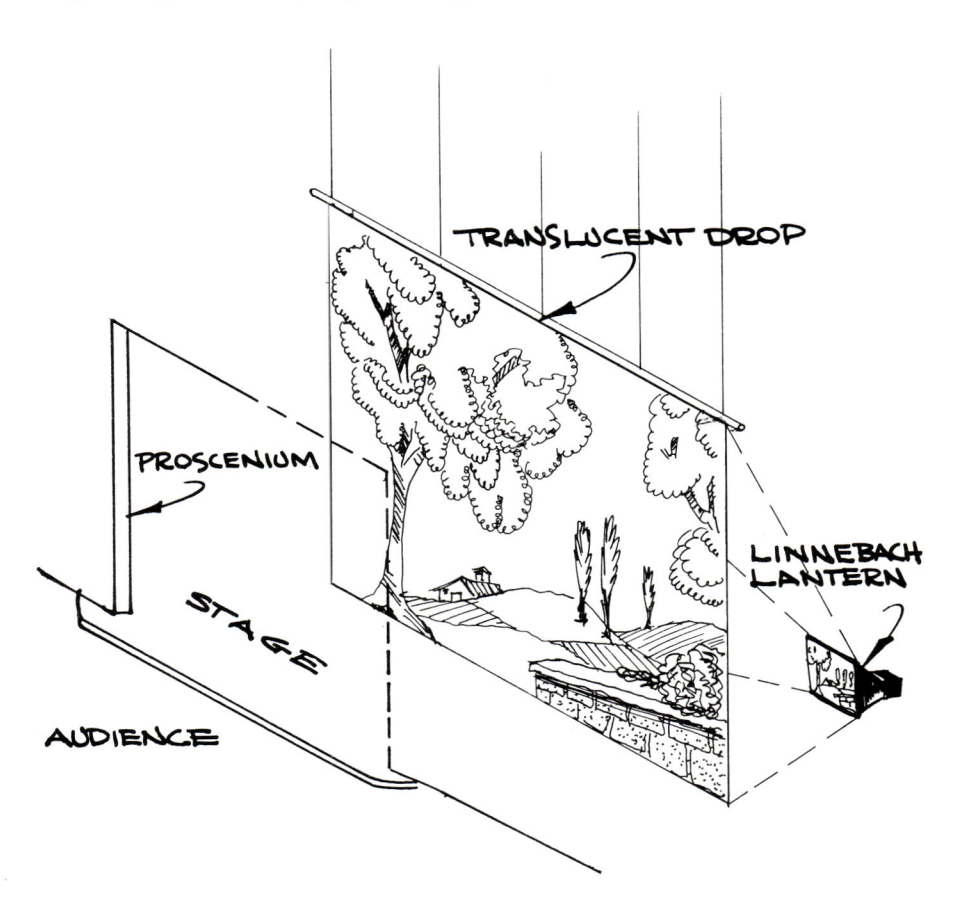

Projection may be in either of two directions: from the front, onto a near-white opaque surface, or from the rear, onto a translucent surface.

Front projection makes no special demand upon the stage space or equipment, but it is limited in scope. Surfaces suitable for front projection are easily made; drops and cycloramas are frequently used. Obviously the intensity of the image is affected by the efficiency of the reflecting surface, and matte surfaces of relatively high reflecting power, such as silver sheets and flat-white drops, are most useful. To cover the entire projection surface and neither light the actor nor cast his shadow on the surface, the projector must be either above the proscenium, or on the stage floor behind the acting area.

Rear projection makes exacting demands on both stage space and equipment. The distance of the projector from the projection surface must be at least equal to the largest dimension of the image desired. Thus to project images 30 feet high on a cyclorama from the rear requires a band of clear space outside the cyclorama at least 30 feet wide. Limited rear projection may be obtained by the provision of large openings through the stage walls into adjoining rooms. The opening between the stage and shop at the Yale University Theatre affords opportunities for rear projection of large images. Rear projection, to be most effective, must be on a specially constructed translucent screen which renders the light source invisible to the audience and equalizes the intensity of the image over its entire area. The screen must be seamless over the projection area. The best material for rear projection is an homogenous acetate sheet having a graded opacity to correct intensity variation. Such sheets are at present prohibitively expensive and too flammable for stage use, although they are much used in motion picture process shots and may be useful for open-air productions. Development of a cheap, fireproof product with similar properties for stage use is anticipated.

The multi-projector system of rear projection developed by Elemer Nagy makes less demand for space behind the projection screens, employs fiber glass as the projection surface and dual projectors with concentrated filament low-voltage lamps for each of several panels, so that changes of scene may have the effect of "dissolves." This system reduces the work of designing, building and painting scenery to that of making a series of slides for the projectors, but it imposes a geometric rigidity upon the floor plans of the settings. Within the stylistic limits set by the system, Dr. Nagy has achieved some striking effects very efficiently.

Projected scenery is limited to certain styles of production.

When acting areas are brightly lighted the spill and floor reflection of the acting area spots illuminates the projection surface and reduces the contrast and the clarity of the projection.

Complete reliance upon projections for backgrounds forces a sameness on the mode of production which tends toward monotony.

Solid cycloramas are useful for front projection and are, obviously, of no use for rear projection. At least one solid cyclorama has been constructed with a flat translucent cloth panel in the center of the back for rear projection. The faults of this were: visible joints between the solid part and the translucent panel, and limitation of the projection area. Cloth cycloramas are suitable for both front and rear projection with the following reservations: a painted cyclorama has greater reflection and less transmission than a dyed one and is therefore better for front projection. On the same basis, a dyed cyclorama is better for rear projection than a painted one.

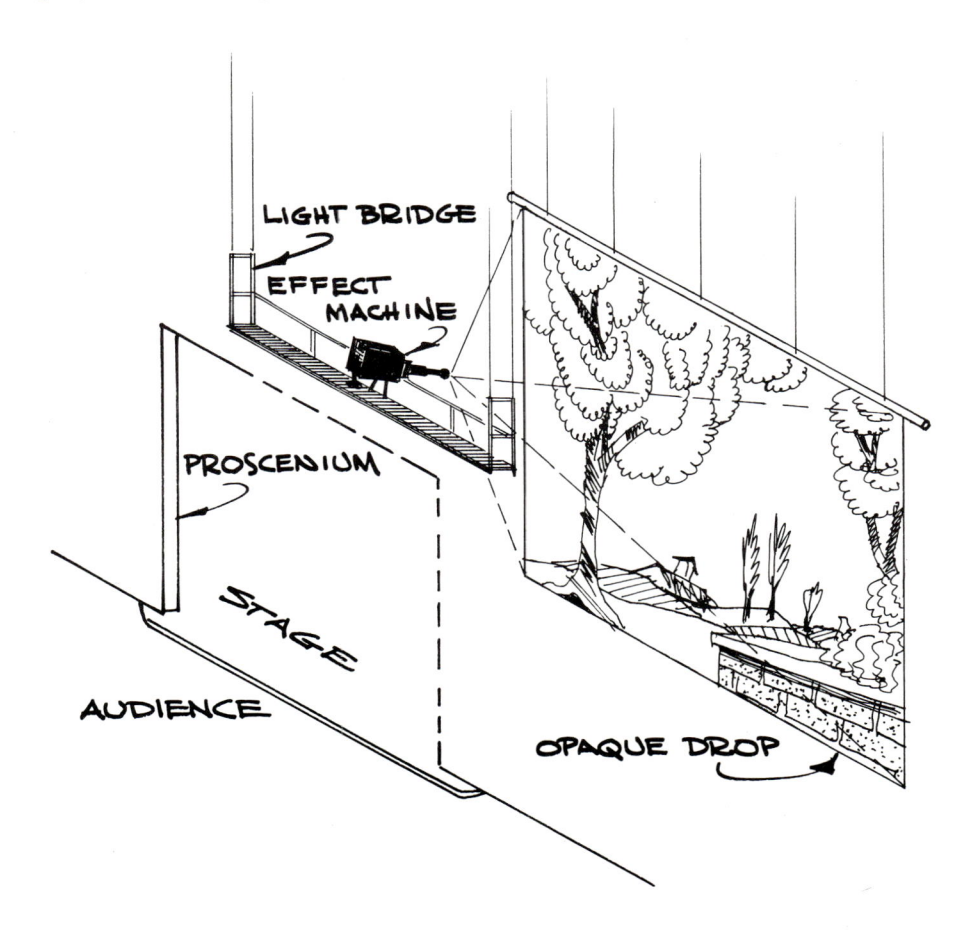

Curves in the projection surface for either front or rear projection cause distortion in the image and variation in light intensity over the area of the image. Although correction can be made in the slide to eliminate distortion, it is difficult to correct for intensity variation. It is therefore desirable that the projection surface be flat or curved on a large radius (12 feet or more).

Requisites for front projection of scenery determine the minimum downstage position of the cyclorama, and rear projection, the minimum clear space outside the cyclorama.

Infinite Variety

While an effort is made to keep scenery light, some sets cannot be so constructed. ROAR CHINA used a tank of water which covered the whole acting area. The water was only two feet deep but even so it imposed a load on understage structure which required special columns placed in the trap room. Such a requirement has a bearing on the kind of footing used in the trap room. TOBACCO ROAD with its many tons of genuine earth on the stage required similar special support. A tank of water for a diving act was flown in one of the Winter Garden shows.

There are a few occasions when it is reasonable to plan a theatre to extreme requirements. These usually occur in connection with world's fairs when a nation or corporation feels justified in declaring the wide blue to be the limit and designers respond with vigor and imagination. The usual case in theatre planning calls for careful consideration of *reasonable* maxima in the factors which limit the planning. It is always possible for a playwright, director, and designer to imagine a production that requires altering a theatre; it is rarely that they get the opportunity to realize one.

Scenery for Open Stage and Arena Stage

As has been stated in Chapter 7, the historical development of the proscenium form of the theatre has been toward the goal of *total uniform effect*. The size, shape, arrangement and equipment of the stage is a part of this development and has the same purpose. These attributes of the stage must be considered as aids to the performance of the actor, to the artistry of the director and designer, and to the creative imagination of the playwright.

Effectiveness (total uniform effect) of performance in any form of theatre depends on these productional aids, and to the extent that they cannot be supplied, the production tends to be to that degree less effective.

Scenery for the open stage and the arena is subject to the same requirements as scenery for the proscenium theatre and to the limitations inherent in the open and arena forms.

Requirements

1. It must be changeable as the play requires.
2. To be artistically effective, it must compose well when seen from all audience viewpoints.
3. It must have the same visual significance to all members of the audience.

Limitations

1. It must not conceal the action from the audience, which is arranged

in from 180 to 360 degrees of horizontal angle and in from 10 to 35 degrees of vertical angle around the acting area.

2. It is deprived of the means of shifting (flying systems and wagons —see Chapters 10 and 11) and of the means of rapid change and rapid concealment and disclosure that the proscenium stage has.

Scenery for open stage and arena must therefore:

1. If opaque, be outside, above or below the extreme audience sight lines.

2. Be transparent if within any of the sight lines. This requires in effect that scenic elements within sight lines be either of Plexiglas, scrim, or similar materials, or that they be the outline structures of very thin materials such as 1 inch x 1 inch wooden stock, metal bars, rods, wire or pipe.

3. Platforms in the acting area must not elevate actors so that they cover action beyond them from any audience viewpoint.

4. Devices for shifting scenery, both vertically and horizontally, which are as efficient and effective as those available in the proscenium theatre, must be developed and installed.

The requirements from which stage size and shape are derived are many. The basic shape and maximum size are determined by the nature of scenery and provisions for handling it. Before shapes and sizes are frozen, however, they must be checked against requisites for lighting (Chapter 12), and the operation of the show (Chapter 8) and economics (Chapter 15).

Fiberglas panel in place, center beyond piano, has side panels of plywood which can be hinged back, left, or closed over the Fiberglas to form an orchestra shell. Ceiling panels of plywood may be flown out. Projecting forestage covers a pit for a full orchestra for opera. Millard Auditorium, Fuller Music Center, University of Hartford. Moore and Salsbury, architects.

Multiscreen system invented by Dr. Elemer Nagy in which paired projectors cover relatively small projection surfaces from the rear. A pair of master dimmers is used to dissolve one projected scene into another. In this picture the Fiberglas screen has been removed to show the projectors.

Performance photograph at Arena Stage, Washington, D.C. The floor and the furniture become the most important scenic elements. Spectators, with greater visual acuity than a camera film, see other spectators as background of the action on the stage. Compare this picture with that of FASHION on page 182.

10: Stage machinery: on the stage floor

Plays require all possible variations in kind and amount of scenery. The production which requires varied and quickly changed sets represents the peak load on the stage space.

Existing theatres impose space restrictions upon scene designers. The designer's creative energies are often devoted to the problem of contriving scenery which will fit the stage rather than scenery which is suitable for the play. In some theatres it is even necessary to reduce the acting area in order to provide scenery space and working and storage space.

The theatre planner must be aware of the capabilities of the stage which he is planning. This chapter presents, schematically, the capabilities of various sizes and shapes of stages.

Scenery must be set and struck quickly. Scene plots (the sequence of scenes and the time allowed for changes) vary from a single unchanging set to as many as 20 scenes in a one-act play lasting 45 minutes. Efficient setting and striking of the one-set show results in economies in take-in, rehearsal and put-out expenses, but is in no way germane to the audience's appreciation of the play. Changes of scene during an intermission between acts (ten minutes or so) make no exacting demands on the scenery, stage equipment or crew, provided established and tested stagecraft procedures are followed. The multi-scene play with many changes within an act exerts the greatest demands on the designer, equipment and organization of the stage. Any gap in the sequences of stimuli which are holding the attention of the audience and exciting its emotional response is intolerable in that it weakens total uniform effect. As theatre artists say, "It drops the performance," or "It loses the audience." Hence changes must be effected so that this loss will not occur.

Three methods of changing scenes meet this strict requirement:

1. A cross-fade of lighting from one stage area containing one setting to another stage area containing another setting.

2. A lap dissolve of front or rear projected backgrounds having different scenic connotations.

3. An *a vista* change of scene in which scenic elements are moved

Basic Requirements

from set position to storage position in view of the audience in a rehearsed sequence which is stylistically compatible with the play.

Five facts regarding the scene shift are important to the theatre planner. (1) The scenery space must be cleared of one set before the other can be brought into it. (2) There must be storage space to accommodate all the sets. (3) Paths of movement of scenery must be direct and clear of obstacles. (4) The fewer the pieces into which a set must be divided to strike it, and the fewer parts which must be fitted and joined to assemble it, the more rapid may be the scene shift and the better may be the scenery. (5) Scenery occupies space when stored.

A concept borrowed from Friedrich Kranich * is useful in appraising stages. Methods of handling scenery are divided into two categories:

The Old Stagecraft embodies those methods by which a set of scenery is assembled piecemeal within the scenery space and is struck by a reversal of the process. It is suitable to plays which allow ample intermission time for shifts. It is obligatory on stages where storage space for scenery is limited. If a skilled stagehand is assigned to each move of the shift and performs only one operation, and that perfectly, there is still a sequence of operations which consumes time.

The Modern Stagecraft includes those methods by which whole sets or large parts of sets already assembled are brought into and taken out of the scenery space. This stagecraft recognizes the necessity of making scene changes in ten seconds, of changing scenery in a blackout without lowering the act curtain, or of changing scenery concurrently with the action of the play. The methods involve assembly of the set outside the scenery space in advance of its use; they predicate ample storage and working space outside the scenery space but within the stage walls. Present-day American commercial theatres were not planned for this Modern Stagecraft, although, because of the continued production of multi-scened plays, some of its features have been laboriously and expensively adopted and used. A few educational theatres and non-commercial theatres have been so planned and several exist in project form.

It is not possible to qualify scenery-handling methods according to the type of production, because any type of production, except motion pictures, may call for any kind of scenery. A well-planned stage must have facilities for handling all kinds of scenery according to the five facts stated above. Proceeding from the proscenium and acting area to the scenery space, and next to the working and storage space, the planner must incorporate one or more of the methods of handling scenery set forth hereafter. He can then proceed sensibly to develop the size, shape, arrangement, and equipment of the entire stage space. There follows a

---

* Kranich, Friedrich: *Bühnentechnik der Gegenwart*, Munich and Berlin, R. Oldenburg, 1929.

table of the most common methods of shifting scenery, accompanied by illustrations. Types of stages which arise from the use of these methods are subsequently shown in plan.

In this chapter a system for rating the items of stage equipment will be used to denote the authors' experience as to the utility of the various items, and as an aid to architects and clients in selecting equipment. Each item will be given a code index consisting of a letter and a number. The key to this code follows:

A equals essential. Necessary to equip a stage adequately for performance.

B, generally useful, but not essential. Recommended to be included if money permits.

C, occasionally useful, but by no means essential. To be included in all-purpose theatres if the budget is very liberal. Some of the items in this letter classification are downright luxuries.

1, must be installed during construction if at all. Later installation would require major structural alterations to the building.

2, may be installed after construction, but only at disproportionate expense and with great inconvenience to the occupant. Might even mean suspending use of the building during the work.

3, may be installed after construction with ease, and at not much more cost than if installed during construction. Items in this number category might be purchased and installed piecemeal if budgets require.

RUNNING
Description

Stagehands divide a set into pieces of size and weight to permit portability, and manually slide or carry the pieces to the storage space. Scenery is as far as possible reduced to two dimensions: thicknesses are removed or folded, and platforms are collapsed. Movement is in the horizontal plane on the stage floor or, in connection with stage elevators, on the floor below the stage. The direction of movement is governed by the location of the storage space, which preferably should be at the sides.

Minimum allowance of stage space for setting and handling scenery by the Old Stagecraft. Space allowances below those indicated hamper the designer and the technician.

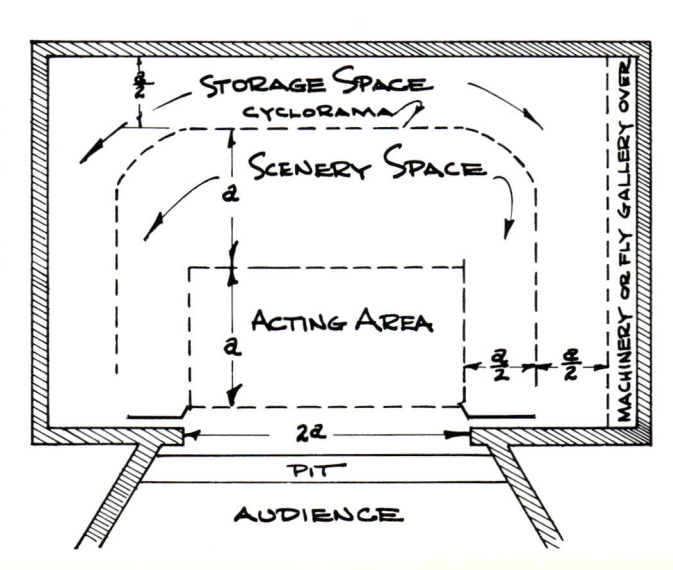

199

Speed of Shifts   The minimum shift time from one full stage set to another cannot be less than two minutes even with an adequate number of expert stagehands.

Power   Manpower. Skill is necessary to the handling of large, cumbersome, often top-heavy, pieces.

Kinds of Scenery   All kinds of framed scenery which are supported by the stage floor. The size of individual pieces is limited.

Storage Space (A, 1)   1. Stacking space for flat scenery with about 15 feet of clear wall space on each side of the stage, and floor space for three-dimensional scenery and properties aggregating minimum of 150 square feet on each side.
2. Clear height to accommodate highest flat scenery that will be used.

Equipment   Walls must be clear of openings and apparatus, or guard rails (A, 3) must be bracketed out from the walls to allow stacking over such apparatus. These are called *outriggers*, and are regularly placed over the side-wall elements of a counterweight system between 10 and 20 feet from the floor.

Pipe frames (B, 3) may be set either permanently or temporarily on the stage floor. If a stage contains a plaster cyclorama against which no scenery can be stacked, temporary pipe frames are essential for the stacking of flat scenery.

Comment   This is the only method possible on the ill-planned and ill-equipped stages of many schools, town halls, social halls, and commercial theatres. It is wasteful of time and labor, prevents any attempt at a rapid sequence of scenes, and requires that the scenery be built in small pieces for *individual handling* and storage. Some scenery will be handled by this method no matter what other methods are also employed. Restriction to this method imposes high labor and scene-building costs on producers, indirectly inclines the producer to select plays which require no shifts of scene, and thereby indirectly influences playwrights to constrict the locales of their plays to one setting.

ROLLING: INDIVIDUAL CASTERED PIECES

Description   Parts of sets which are too heavy to run or too intricate to be divided for running are equipped with casters and propelled from the scenery space to the storage space. Movement is horizontal on the stage floor. Universal casters permit movement in any direction, and fixed casters establish straight line movement if it is desired.

This is the first and simplest addition of machinery (wheels) to the task of handling scenery. By increasing the size of the individual scenery units it reduces the number of joints which have to be fastened and unfastened, reduces the complexity of the shift routine and reduces the amount of physical effort. Current practice on inadequate stages is to limit the size of the castered piece by the size of the space into which it can be shifted.

Minimum shift time is faster than in running, but seldom less than 1½ minutes for changing from one full-stage set to another.

Speed of Shifts

Manpower, sometimes aided by hand levers to overcome starting inertia. No lifting, consequently less physical effort and less danger of injury to scenery and stagehands than in running.

Power

All kinds which are supported by the stage floor. Generally complex or heavy assemblies, essentially three-dimensional.

Kinds of Scenery

Variable. The larger the space, the larger the piece which can be stored. Any increase over the minimum storage space indicated for running is advantageous. Clear height to accommodate highest flat scenery which will be used. Located preferably at the sides of the stage, but space at the back is better than none.

Storage Space (A, 1)

None. Casters are considered as scenery and are supplied with it as required. Stage floor must be firm and level (A, 1).

Equipment

When combined with running, advantages of this method are greater possible variety in settings, more three-dimensional assemblies, freer use of platforms, some reduction in the time required to change scenes, and a slight reduction in the number of stagehands required to make a scene change. Because settings need not be divided into so many units, the appearance of scenery is generally better than in running.

An ultimate development of individual-castered pieces is the design of a scenic scheme for a multi-scene play in which a number of castered pieces are rolled into and out of the scenery space in reciprocating motion along determined paths from established storage positions. An elaboration of this is the change of scenery on small reciprocating wagons to make multiple use of each path of motion.

Comment

Two wagons, each containing half a set, split in the center and rolled to the sides of the stage. Movement is horizontal in a straight line parallel to the proscenium.

ROLLING: DIVIDED WAGONS
Description

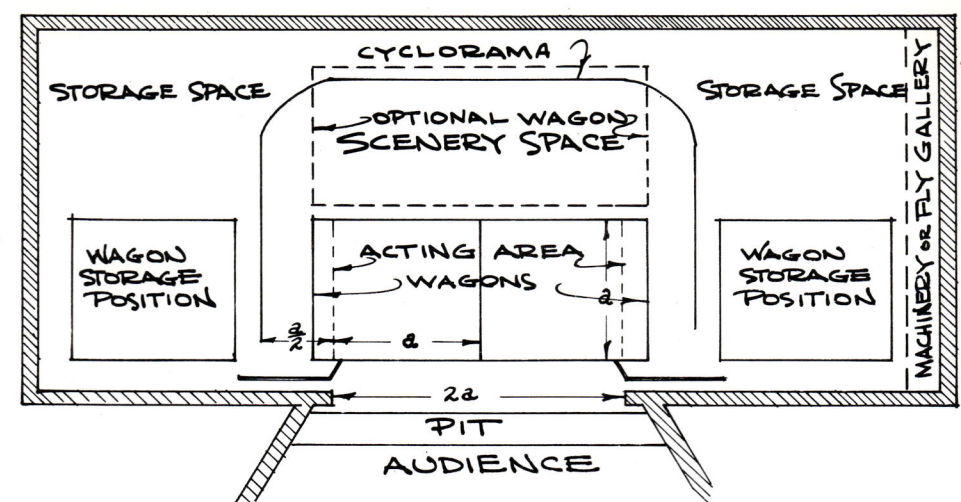

Stage space required for divided wagons.

Speed of Shifts	The stage can be cleared in five seconds. The total shift time depends on the method of setting the next set.
Power	Manpower, applied by pull-ropes and pushing. May be applied through windlass. Electric power possible, using windlass and cables.
Storage Space (A, 1)	Floor area equal to the area of the wagon at each side, plus space around this for storage of scenery and properties taken off and put on wagon, plus passageways. Clear height to accommodate the highest scenery used plus height of wagon.
Equipment	Two wagons (B, 3) each slightly larger than one-half the acting area. Stage floor tracks (B, 2) to guide the wagons, countersunk into stage floor if this method is contemplated when the theatre is planned, superimposed on the floor if not. Portable raised apron (B, 3) set in place and used when wagons are used, extending full width of the proscenium and from front edge of wagon to the footlights, height equal to height of wagons.
Comment	This method regularly requires the designing of settings to conceal a necessary break-line in the back wall. It is occasionally used in New York theatres where offstage space is barely sufficient to accommodate the wagons. Sometimes used in combination with a full-width wagon moving directly up- and downstage. This method permits changing scenes on the wagons, offstage, while action is in another set. This advantage is common to all methods employing wagons which move to storage positions, if sufficient scene storage space is allowed between the wagons and the stage walls.

202

Costs and assembly time are lower than in the previous methods if the wagons and their tracks are part of the equipment of the theatre, greater if wagons and tracks must be brought into the theatre with a production.

ROLLING: UPSTAGE WAGON

A complete setting is preassembled on a full-stage wagon which is propelled from the scenery space directly upstage to storage space. Movement is horizontal at stage level, and in a straight path.

Description

The wagon can be brought into or taken out of the scenery space in approximately 5 seconds. The total shift time depends upon what must be cleared before the wagon can be moved, and the method used to set the next scene. Range: 20 seconds to 2 minutes.

Speed of Shifts

Direct manpower; manpower with mechanical advantage through a windlass; electric power through windlass (B, 3).

Power

All standing scenery. Hung scenery and background scenery must be cleared before wagon can be moved.

Kinds of Scenery

Floor space equal to the wagon area upstage of the acting area and preferably upstage of the cyclorama, plus storage space for scenery off the wagon. Minimum clear height to accommodate highest standing scenery (A, 1). Fly space over wagon storage is useful (B, 1).

Storage Space (A, 1)

One full-stage wagon (B, 3) slightly larger than the acting area, portable tracks (B, 3) to be laid only when wagon is to be used. Permanent tracks cannot be installed without interfering with the stage floor traps.

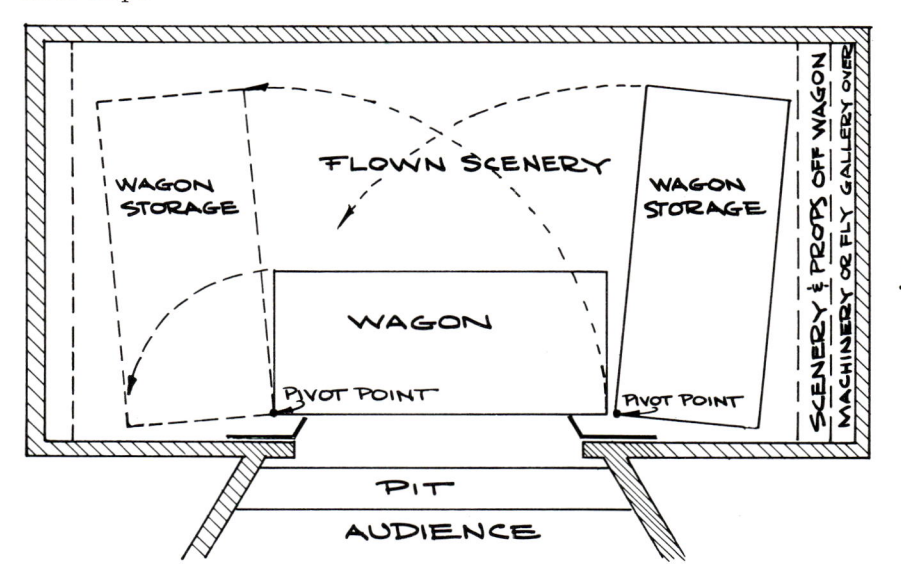

Equipment

Jackknife wagons.

203

Comment	The depth of stage required for an upstage wagon will, if supplied, provide sufficient stage depth for all other purposes, including rear projection of light images upon translucent drops. Because so many settings contain elaborate background effects in scenery and light, which must be dismantled before an upstage wagon may be moved, this method is less useful than traverse wagons.
ROLLING: JACKKNIFE WAGONS **Description**	Complete settings are preassembled on two full-stage wagons, each wagon pivoting around its downstage corner through 90 degrees to a storage position at the side of the stage. Movement is horizontal on the stage floor, and circular about centers near the proscenium.
Speed of Shifts	Approaches that of one-movement shift, but slightly slower because the arcs of the two wagons overlap. The first wagon must move through about 80 degrees before the second can move into position. Time: about 15 seconds. Fastest so far.
Power	Manpower applied directly by pushing and pulling; electric power applied through motor windlasses and cables (B, 3).
Storage Space (A, 1)	Wagons are stored in what is normally part of the scenery space, extending sideways into the storage space. Space equal to full-stage wagon extending offstage from the acting area plus stacking space and storage space off the wagons, plus passageways. Clear height equal to the highest standing scenery plus wagon (A, 1).
Equipment	Two full-stage wagons, slightly larger than the entire acting area (C, 3). Pivot mountings for each wagon near proscenium, portable

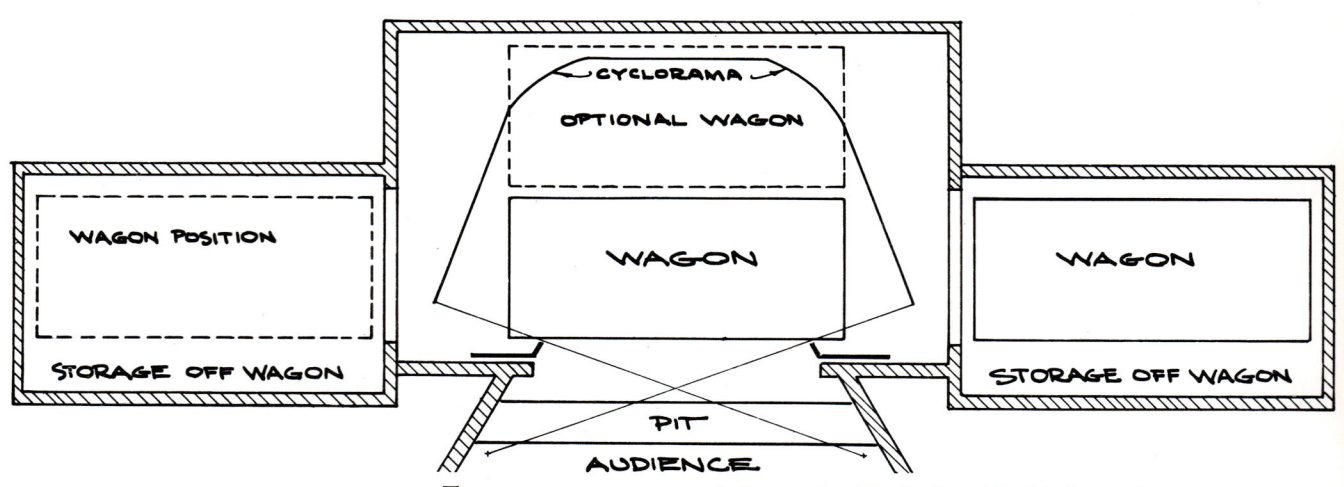

Traverse wagons, straight path. Fly loft with high roof over center block only. Wagon rooms may be used as shop, rehearsal rooms, dance practice, or classrooms.

forestage as for divided wagons. Wagons, pivoted and forestage, must be removable because many shows will not require their use. Tracks to provide smooth surface for wheels of wagons must be portable (C, 3).

This method works best when a production requires two interior sets which alternate in a series of scenes. Side entrances are congested. Scenery may be shifted on one wagon while action takes place on the other. Flown pieces must be raised before the wagons can move. Because wagons swing through a large arc, it is not feasible to have elaborate background effects. This method is better as a solution of a scenic problem in existing theatres than as a basis for the plan of a new theatre.

Comment

ROLLING: STRAIGHT-PATH TRAVERSE WAGON

Full-stage settings are assembled on full-stage wagons and propelled from scenery space to storage spaces at each side of the stage. Scenery may be shifted on one wagon while a scene is being played on the other. This process may be aided by the installation of flying equipment over the storage spaces, so that pieces of scenery may be flown off the wagons.

Description

The fastest possible change from one full-stage setting to another. Both wagons move simultaneously. If cyclorama is used it must be cleared before wagons can move. Time: 10 seconds.

Speed of Shifts

Manpower applied directly by pushing or pulling, about three men to each wagon; manpower applied indirectly through hand windlasses and cables; electric motor windlasses with remote control, automatic speed control and limit switches.

Power

All standing scenery. Elaborate background setups behind the wagons are not disturbed by the movement of the wagons. Complete built-up exteriors may be mounted on the wagons.

Kinds of Scenery

Floor area equal to the area of a full-stage wagon at each side of the stage, plus scenery storage around this for scenery and properties off the wagon, plus passageways. Clear height to accommodate highest scenery on wagon, plus 1 foot 6 inches for trusses above ceiling of set. Flying height over storage space useful but optional.

Storage Space (A, 1)

Two wagons (C, 3) each slightly larger than the entire acting area; tracks in the stage floor to guide the wagons; portable raised forestage (B, 3) optional, electric windlasses and controls (B, 3) optional; auxiliary flying equipment over storage spaces (B, 1).

Equipment

205

Comment Because of the advantages cited, this method is strongly recommended. It requires generous allowance of space backstage, but the returns in efficient handling, variety of scenery, and speed of changes warrant it.

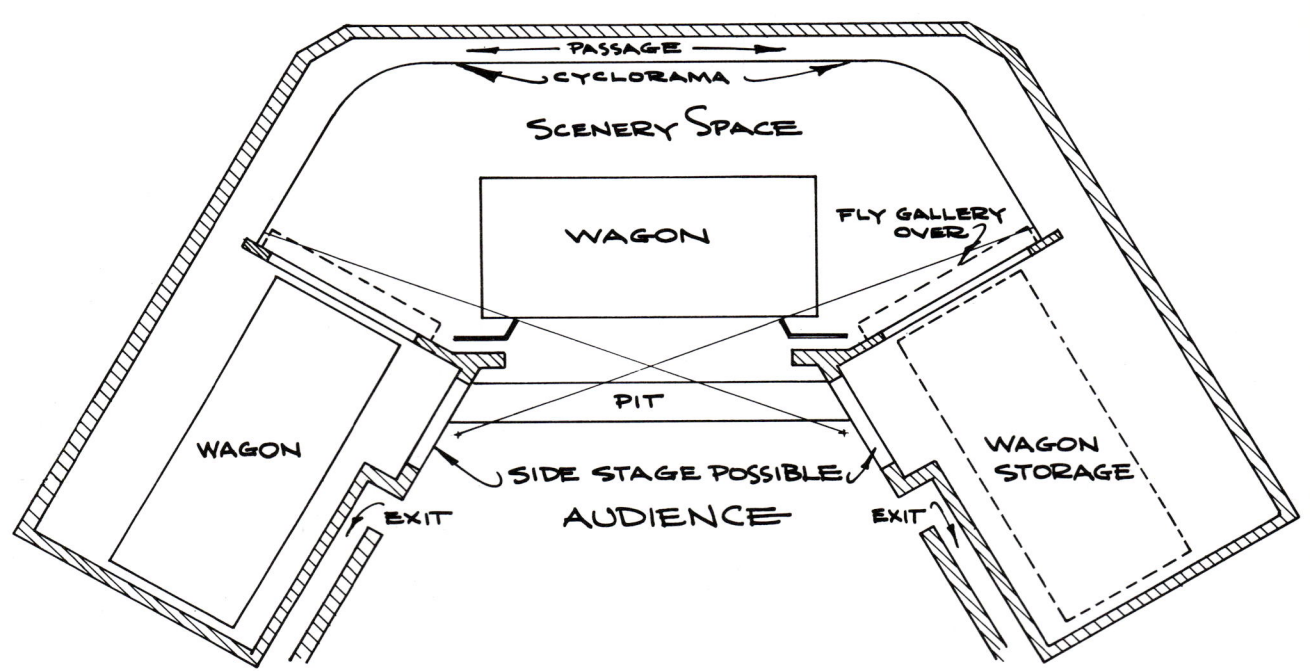

Traverse wagons, curved path. Fixed cyclorama is out of the way of wagons. Auxiliary uses for the wagon rooms. Impressive open-air effects possible.

ROLLING: CURVED-PATH TRAVERSE WAGONS
Description

Full-stage settings are assembled on full-stage wagons which are propelled from the scenery space to storage space flanking the auditorium at the sides. Architecturally, certain walls of the storage space become party walls with the auditorium, rather than exterior walls. Permits shifting full-stage wagons without disturbing the cyclorama or background scenery. The cyclorama may be integrated with the back wall of the stage.

Speed of Shifts Full-stage change in about 10 seconds.

Power Same as for straight path traverse wagons.

Kinds of Scenery All standing scenery. Ceilings may be placed on sets and move with them.

Storage Space (A, 1) Same as for straight path traverse wagons. In both these methods, the storage space may be planned for auxiliary uses and partitioned from the stage by rolling doors or overhead doors.

Tracks to guide wagons (A, 2), either countersunk permanently into the stage floor, or portable (A, 3) to be laid when wagons are used. Permanent tracks should not conflict with stage floor traps.

Two full-stage wagons (A, 2).

Auxiliary flying equipment over the storage spaces (B, 1).

Equipment

Sectional, portable revolving disc.

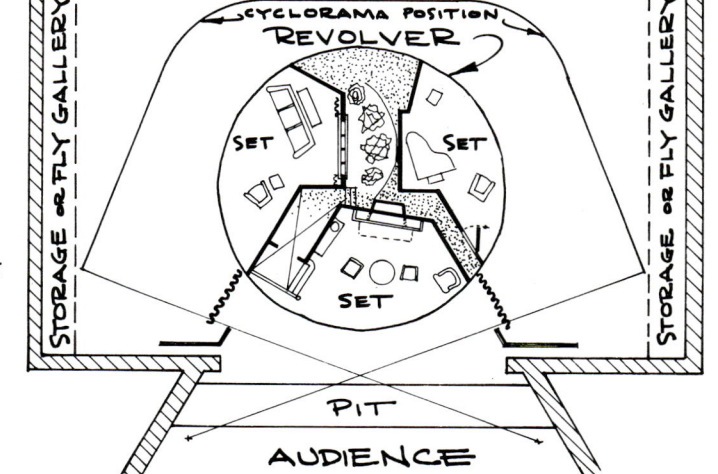

Scenery on revolving stage or disc.

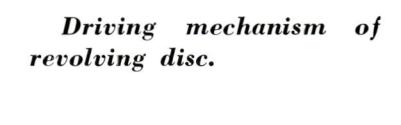

Driving mechanism of revolving disc.

ROLLING: REVOLVING STAGE OR REVOLVING DISC

Description

A revolving *stage* (C, 1) is built in, the stage floor structure being designed so that the floor of the revolver is level with the surrounding floor. In some elaborate examples, the structure of the revolver extends below stage sufficiently to contain elevators. A revolving *disc* (C, 3) is essentially portable and is placed on the permanent stage floor. The surrounding floor must be built up to the level of the disc when it is used.

Speed of Shifts

Change of scenes which are preset on the revolver can be truly instantaneous. Scenes can be changed while action goes on in other scenes.

Power

Manpower applied directly at edge of disc by pull-ropes or push-bars (A, 3); electric power applied through either drum or endless cable around revolver, or pinion and rack gears, or motor drive contained in revolver (C, 1).

Kinds of Scenery

Sets of scenery are designed to fit onto sectors of the revolver, which is rotated to bring successive sets into position. Sets are changed during stage action on other sets. It is difficult to use exterior and interior settings in combination. All interiors tend to have triangular floor plans. Background effects are limited to what can be achieved above the scenery. Hung scenery must be flown before stage can revolve. Some scenery must be run and set to fit between the revolver and the proscenium.

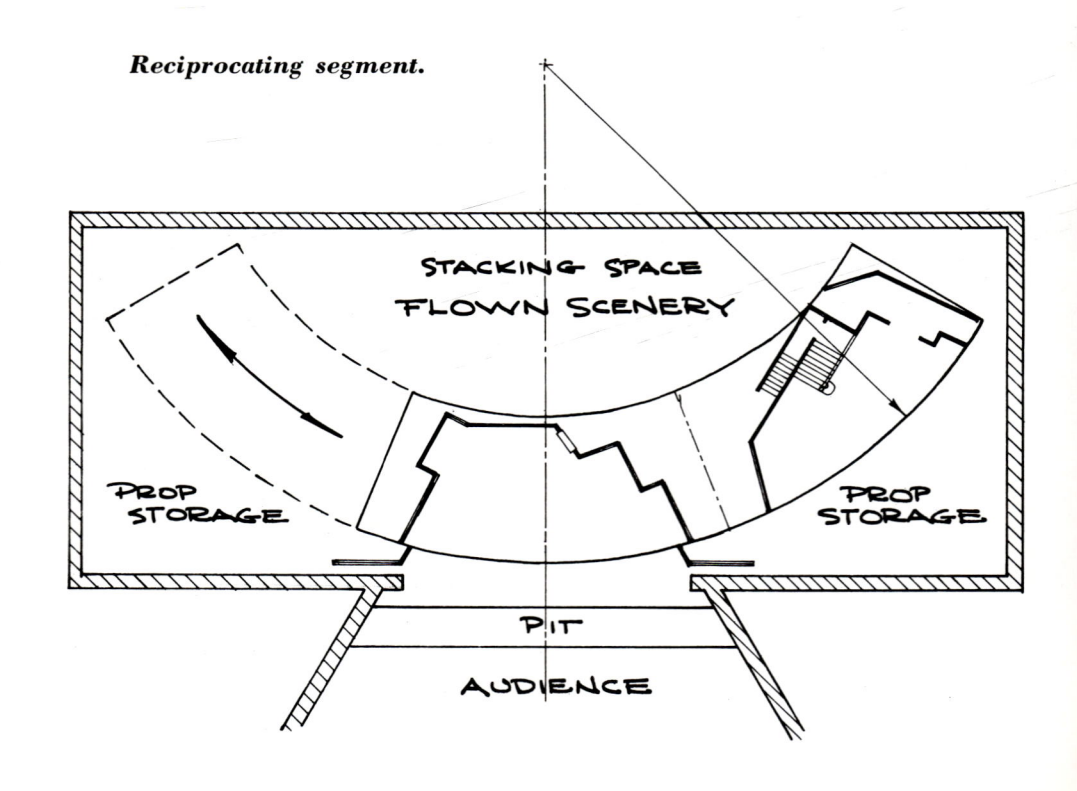

Reciprocating segment.

Storage space off the revolver must equal and resemble that required for running. As any of the rolling methods may be combined with this method, the storage space must follow the requirements of any method selected.

Storage Space

Revolving stage (C, 1): stage floor with built-in circular track in which the wheels of the revolver run. Revolving portion, being unsupported from below, must have heavy beams of deep trusses to support the long spans. A deep revolving stage may be built up from tracks far below stage and contain elevators.

Revolving disc (C, 3): portable tracks laid on the stage floor; central pivot; driving mechanism. The disc may be built in portable sections for transportation and storage.

Equipment

A wagon, large enough to hold at least two full-stage settings, in the shape of either a sector of a circle or a segment of a ring stage is pivoted about an upstage center so that the scenery assembled on it is propelled from the scenery space into the rear corners of the stage. This method has been adapted to the shallow stages of American commercial theatres in preference to revolving stages, because the large radius permits sets which are nearly rectangular. It is more a method to be used on existing stages than one to be recommended for new stages.

ROLLING: RECIPROCATING SEGMENT
Description

Full-stage change in ten seconds, of limited kinds of settings (see below).

Speed of Shifts

Manual or electric through motors, drums, and cables.

Power

All standing scenery. Because the wagon moves through space which background scenery and the cyclorama occupy, full-stage exteriors are difficult. Hung scenery must be flown before wagon can be moved.

Kinds of Scenery

Space equal to acting area at each side for wagon.

Floor space at least equal to that required by running, for storage off the wagon, on each side. Clear height to accommodate the highest standing scenery, on the wagon.

Storage Space

Wagon, tracks, and motor mechanism.

Equipment

Two or more circular discs are used to revolve scenery into and out of the scenery space: (1) small discs rotated to change side walls and

ROLLING: MULTIPLE DISCS

209

Description

properties; (2) two large discs tangent at the center of the stage, each disc carrying side wall, half the back wall, and half the properties; (3) one large disc and two small discs to change the entire set. The first type permits the use of hung scenery, the second and third limit the use of hung scenery. These methods are not versatile, and are not recommended as permanent installations.

Variations and combinations of the foregoing methods of handling scenery on the stage floor are numerous in project though rare in actual existence. To attempt a detailed listing, description, and criticism of them all would require more space than their importance warrants. An exhaustive listing with description and illustration may be found in Friedrich Kranich's *Bühnentechnik der Gegenwart*, Vol. I, pp. 281-346.

Wagon Stage Frequency

Since the sets for which wagons are impossible or unnecessary will outnumber those for which wagons are used, it is wrong to plan the stage solely for the use of wagons. Twenty-eight sets out of about 120 analyzed could have been handled best on full-stage wagons. In the Kirby Theatre at Amherst College where there is storage space offstage on one side for a full-stage wagon, in almost every production all or part of at least one set is mounted on casters or a wagon and rolled into that space.

Tracks and Guides

Tracks are necessary for all types of rolling stages whose direction of movement is established. Temporary tracks (B, 3) may be superimposed on the stage floor to provide truly level surfaces on floors which are uneven, and to provide directional guides.

When the use of rolling stages is contemplated in the planning of a theatre, it is sensible to include built-in tracks in the plan.

Tracks

Tracks may have two functions: to provide a level, smooth surface for the casters or wheels and to control the direction of movement. Stages with rotary movement have their direction of movement governed by fixed pivots and require tracks only as surfaces under the wheels: jackknife stages, revolving discs, revolving stages, multiple discs. For stages the direction of which cannot be controlled by a pivot (divided wagons, traverse wagons, ring stage, reciprocating segment), direction must be controlled by the engagement of the casters or wheels and the track.

Tracks to provide surface only may be flat steel countersunk into the stage floor. Tracks to control direction may be: (1) two pieces of flat steel spaced about ½ to ¾ inch apart on a third piece, the whole countersunk into the stage floor; (2) steel angles 1½ inches x 1½ inches back to back set into the stage floor and spaced ½ to ¾ inch apart.

If the stage floor under the rolling stage is firm and level, only a few of the casters need engage the tracks, or all of the casters may be clear of the tracks, and steel rods or sheets may be rigidly attached to the rolling stage and inserted into the tracks as guides only.

Storage for Portable Wagons and Discs

Wagon stages and revolving discs are not used frequently enough to warrant their being left permanently in place on the stage floor. Methods of storing them are:

1. Reduction to units small enough to permit easy transportation to storage rooms outside the stage.

2. Subdivision into sections small enough to permit vertical storage against a side wall or a back wall of the stage house. Suspension from the gridiron is bad practice and should not be planned.

3. Up-ended and sunk through a slot, to be stored vertically, whole or in parts, in the space below stage.

4. A wagon stage may be stored by rolling it, whole or in sections, onto an elevator and sinking the elevator so that the floor of the wagon is level with the stage floor.

Inertia and momentum are involved in the operation of rolling stages. The greatest motive power is required to start the stages in motion; speed must be reduced as they approach the end of their motion; the stop must be precise but not abrupt. For electrical motive power there must be four adjustments of speed or power: (1) starting power, which after starting immediately reduces to (2) running power which continues until near the end of the run and where (3) a slowdown takes effect until (4) the stop is reached. For some rolling stages, mechanical stops can be placed at the ends of the run. In manual operation, either by direct application (pushing and pulling) or indirectly through a windlass, the operators may apply the correct amount of power.

Propulsion of Rolling Stages

Except for differences in the details of the installation all rolling stages, whether with straight-line movement or curved movement, may be propelled by similar methods:

1. Manpower, directly applied. Wagon stages may be pushed or pulled, generally with the aid of short pull-ropes; revolving discs, jack-knife stages, and reciprocating segments by pull-ropes and push-bars, the latter inserted into sockets.

2. Manpower indirectly applied through hand-operated windlasses and cables: either two winches and two cables, each to pull the stage in one direction, or one winch and endless cable reversed over pulleys to control movement in both directions.

3. Motor windlasses. Wherever hand windlasses can be used, electric motors may replace manpower and provide the added feature of remote control. Automatic stop switches may reduce the operator's job to the

starting operation only. For *a vista* changes, silent operation is mandatory.

4. Electric motive power may be contained in all rolling stages. A unit, consisting of motor, gears, and drive shaft may be mounted in the stage, to move it by one of the following drives: (a) friction of a rubber-tired wheel on a track fixed to the floor; (b) pinion on the drive shaft and rack fixed to the stage floor; (c) drum on the drive shaft and cable attached to the floor.

5. Revolving stages and ring stages may be propelled electrically by motors mounted outside the stages as follows: pinion on motor shaft engaging a curved rack on the edge of the stage. Motor bevel-geared to a shaft on which is a pulley, which in turn drives the stage by an endless belt or cable wrapped around the stage.

6. Developments in the electromechanical techniques and equipment for remote control, principally by and under George C. Izenour in the Yale Drama School's Electro-Mechanical Laboratory, have made possible the control of the movement of motor-propelled rolling stages with precision to the least required differential unit. (See Control at end of Chapter 8.)

Integration with Stage Floor Traps

Although not dimensioned, the illustrations show the size of stage wagons relative to acting area and proscenium. Certain direct benefits derive from integrating the design of wagon stages and other types of rolling stages with the trapping arrangement for the stage floor to permit entrances through the stage floor and the use of stage elevators when the rolling stage is in position. To meet this requirement, the framing structure of the rolling stage must coincide with framing of the stage floor when the rolling stage is in position.

Location of the Wheels on Wagon Stages

For greatest stability wheels on rolling stages must be placed to run on the main beams of the stage floor, rather than on the floor between the beams. This design regulates the layout of the frame of the rolling stage to coincide with the frame of the stage floor, and facilitates the registering of openings in both.

The Stage Floor

The stage floor must be considered as an important part of the stage equipment, to be designed expressly for its particular uses, which are: a suitable level upon which the actors may perform, adaptable to the requirements of several or all types of performance, and a level upon which scenery may be set, and shifted.

Excerpt from the Building Code, City of New York, 1938:

"Section C26-722 Paragraph a. That portion of the stage floor extending from each side of the proscenium opening to the enclosure walls and from the stage side of the proscenium wall to the front edge of the apron shall be of construction having a fire-resistive rating of at least four hours. Regardless of the height of the structure, untreated wood flooring may be used on the stage floor. For a width of six feet more than the proscenium opening the stage may be constructed of wood."

"Section C26-344 Paragraph e. Live loads for public spaces and congested areas.—The minimum live load shall be taken as one hundred pounds per square foot, uniformly distributed, for . . . theatre stages . . ."

The stage floor is the level upon which the show is performed. As such it must meet all the requirements imposed upon it by performances. These include (1) stability, (2) entrances for actors from below, and (3) alteration of the size and shape of the acting area by the provision of raised or sunken acting levels.

Stability: Floor Loads

The New York City Building Code, 1938, sets 100 pounds per square foot as the minimum allowable, evenly distributed live load for stage floors, but the National Building Code (1949 edition) recommended by the National Board of Fire Underwriters contains the recommendation of 150 pounds per square foot for the same load. Stages may be subject to a particularly violent form of live load in the form of vigorous ensemble dancing. The deflection of a stage floor, particularly if it is produced by a live load applied rhythmically, may cause perceptible disturbance of the scenery which is set upon the floor. Therefore stage floors must be designed not only strong enough but stiff enough to withstand serious deflection under maximum loading. Deflection of more than 1/360 of the span must be considered serious.

Where two or more beams of different cross section have the same strength, the one with the greatest stiffness is to be preferred.

Scenery, properties, and lighting equipment are set up on the stage floor in and around the acting area by any of the various methods previously described. Salient features of this function are the following:

1. The stage floor must be firm and truly level. The stage floor which sloped upward as it receded from the footlights has been obsolete for at least half a century. An occasional sloping stage floor, as a required part of the scenic scheme of a single production, should be treated as scenery and built *ad hoc*.

2. Movable beams and floor traps must be closely fitted and fastened.

Soft Wood Floor (A, 1)

3. The stage must be floored with a tough wear-resisting wood which is at the same time receptive to nails and hand-driven stage screws. Edge-grained yellow pine or similar wood (nominal 2 x 3 or 2 x 4, matched) is satisfactory. It is absurd to use maple, birch, oak, or other hardwood flooring on a stage.

4. Every precaution must be taken to counteract expansion and contraction of the flooring, especially in the trap area.

5. Thoroughly seasoned wood is essential for the floor beams, so that

shrinkage or warping after construction will not throw the floor out of true level.

It has been the custom in America to floor the stage from the front of the trap area to the footlight trough with hardwood, such as maple. This appears to be almost as pointless as covering the whole stage with hardwood, since it is frequently necessary to drive carpet tacks, nails, screws, and even stage screws into this portion of the floor. Again yellow pine or a similar wood is recommended. An exception is the stage intended primarily for musical comedy, revue, or vaudeville, where a hardwood apron is a necessity for the tap dancers. Even in this case a portable *tap strip,* of matched hardwood cemented to a canvas back, may be used instead.

Stage Floor Traps (B, 1)

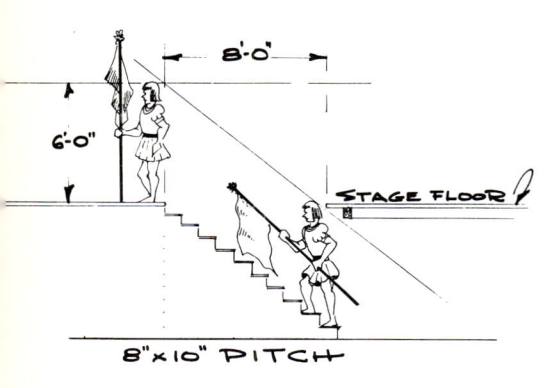

In approximately 20 per cent of the major productions in one theatre over a twenty-year period, traps in the floor have been opened to provide entrances and exits of actors. Once a heavy stage property which could be set in no other way was elevated into position during a blackout. Once a mine-shaft lift was operated through a trap in the stage floor. Twice, instantaneous disappearance of actors was achieved by the use of sinking traps. Thus in about one production in every five, desired dramatic effects have been made possible by the presence of traps in the stage floor.

The smallest, generally useful, single trap must be rectangular, wide enough to allow two people to ascend side by side (3 feet, 3 inches minimum) and long enough to produce headroom under the floor framing using stairs or ladders. This is achieved in 8 feet of length.

The unit size of a trap may be established at 4 feet x 8 feet. A few smaller traps based on even subdivision of these dimensions make possible small adjustments in position.

Flexibility of location requires that the floor framing and posting, if any, under the trapped area be demountable.

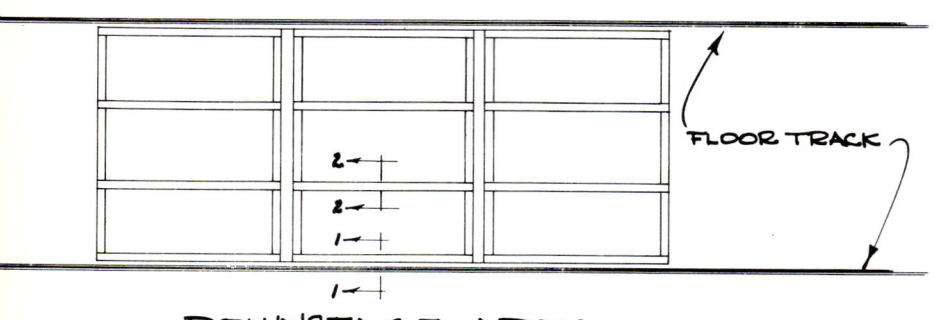

Removable beams for stage floor traps. Sections are detailed on page 216.

214

Four Systems of Stage Floor Traps

I Entire trap area free of permanent beams.
  Transverse beams movable up- and downstage.
   Advantages: Great flexibility in lateral position of traps.
                  Beams at front and back of opening carry little load.
   Disadvantages: Span makes necessary very deep transverse beams.
                  Load makes necessary very heavy beams at sides of opening.
                  Up- and downstage location of traps limited to four positions. Flexibility beyond this requires considerable reconstruction.

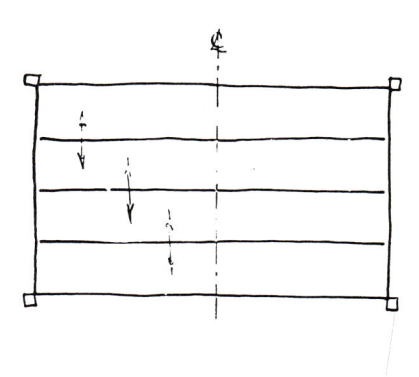

II One fixed beam on center line of stage in middle of trap area.
   Movable transverse beams.
   Advantages: Shortened spans and reduced loads permit smaller beams than in System I.
                  Within limits set by the fixed beam variety of location is obtained with less reconstruction than in System I.
   Disadvantages: Fixed beam is in most important stage space where trapping is likely to be wanted.

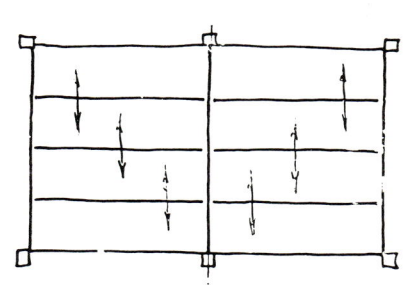

III Two fixed beams ¼ from each side of trap area.
    Movable transverse beams.
    Advantages: Flexibility of location and size within center area, with only moderate amount of reconstruction. Shortened spans and reduced loads require smaller beams than Systems I or II.
    Disadvantages: Fixed beams prevent trapping in two fairly important zones of the acting area.
   To be preferred over System II.

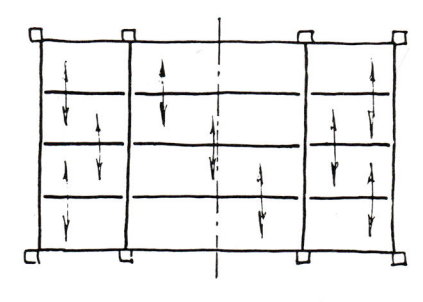

IV No fixed beams in trap area. All beams movable and removable.
   Full-length movable beams running up- and downstage. Short purlin beams across stage.
   Advantages: Complete flexibility of location and size with only moderate amount of reconstruction. Possible to standardize on spare parts to allow considerable flexibility.
   Disadvantages: Very limited flexibility without at least some reconstruction.
   Columns in center of long spans at front and back of trap area may be used to reduce size of beams. To be omitted if possible.

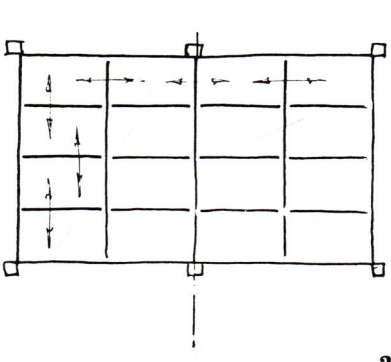

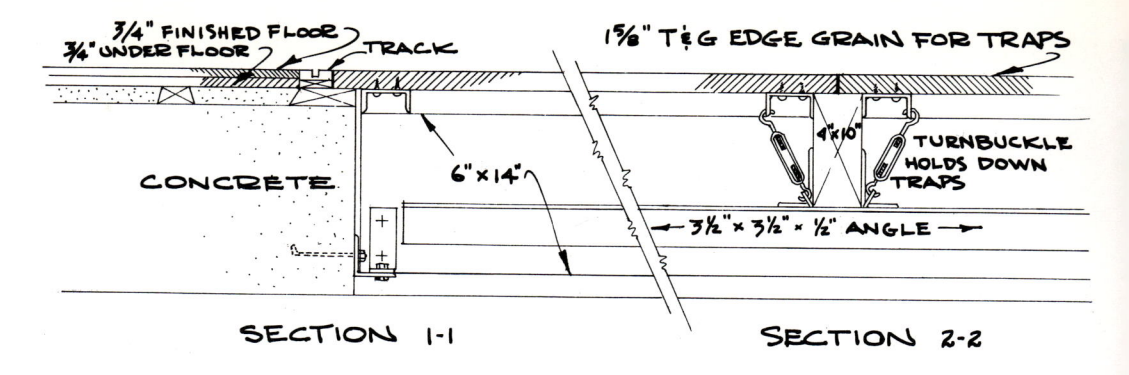

Sections from plan on page 214.

It is sounder practice to plan and install a complete system of traps than to lay a solid floor. Traps built and fitted during construction can be carefully made and tested by skilled workmen. A system, once established, will be followed by the users of the theatre, provided it does not impose too much limitation. Traps cut at random in a solid floor to fit the demands of individual productions by the person who happens to be the stage carpenter at the time produce a mutilated stage floor which is soon in need of major repairs, for which the cost of a complete trap installation is easily spent.

Size and Location of the Trap Area

Study of 60 varied productions in one theatre has shown that traps have occurred in all parts of the normal acting area, and also beyond the sides and back of the acting area. The most extreme side traps have extended about half their length outside the acting area, and the upstage traps have been in a narrow zone across stage behind the acting area. From these facts, it may be deduced that the trap area should be slightly wider and deeper than the acting area.

TABLE 11. Proscenium Widths, Recommended Trap Areas, and Unit Trap Sizes

Proscenium Width	Trap Area Width	Depth *	Unit Trap Width	Depth *
26′	31′-6″	17′-6″	7′	3′-6″
28′	35′	21′-0″	"	"
30′	38′-6″	21′-0″	"	"
32′	42′	24′-6″	"	"
34′	42′	24′-6″	"	"
36′	45′-6″	24′-6″	"	"
38′	48′	28′	8′	4′
40′	48′	28′	8′	4′

* Horizontal distance perpendicular to proscenium.

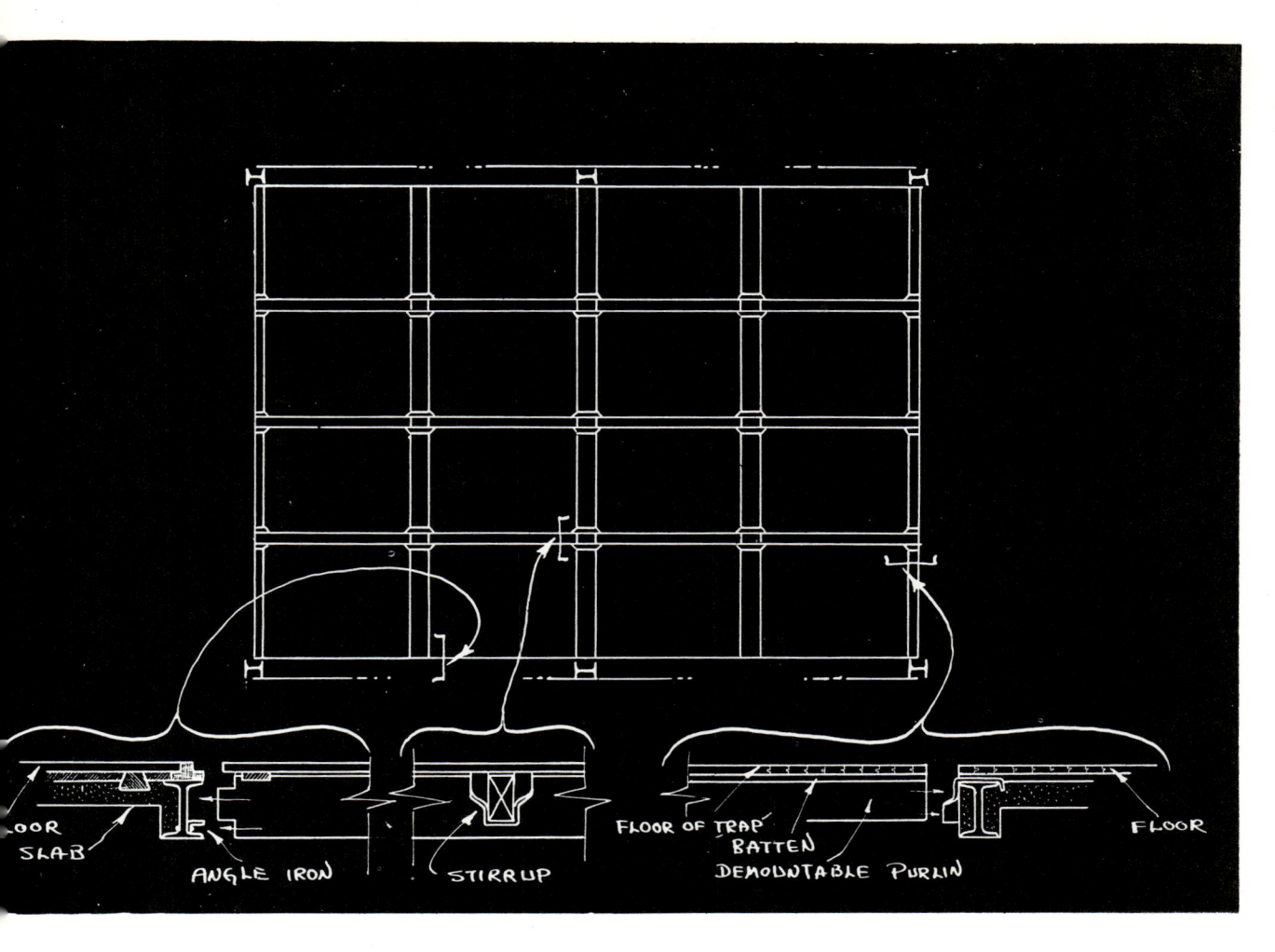

Removable framing for trapped area.

Frequency of use of traps from a study of sixty typical legitimate productions.

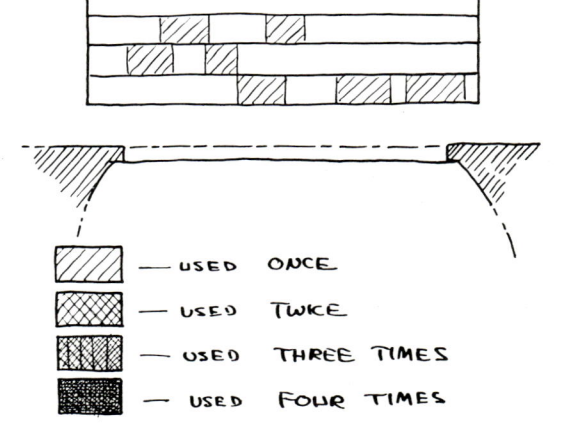

— USED ONCE
— USED TWICE
— USED THREE TIMES
— USED FOUR TIMES

217

Inasmuch as traps may be called for by playwrights, designers, or directors in any part of the acting area, the front edge of the trap area must coincide with the front edge of the normal acting area. When permanent side stages are provided, it is advisable to provide at least one trap in each of these.

The design of the trapped area must permit the planned use of rolling stages.

Mentioned here and discussed fully in Chapter 12 are two other openings in the stage floor, the footlight pit (A, 1) and the cyclorama base light pit (B, 1).

Size of Trap Room

An actor ascending or descending stairs through a stage trap must have a landing at the bottom of the stairs which is beyond the edge of the trap. Therefore the walls of the trap room (the room below stage) must be located at least 4 feet beyond the perimeter of the trapped area of the stage.

Stage Floor Coverings

It is customary to cover the unfinished stage floor for most performances. Temporary coverings (B, 3) of duck or carpet are chosen and laid at the option of the theatre user. Permanent floor coverings (B, 1) which obviate the necessity for temporary coverings are the concern of the theatre planner. Materials for permanent coverings must be hard-wearing but resilient. It must be possible to penetrate them with nails, screws, and stage screws. They must reduce somewhat the sound of footfalls and other impacts and attenuate any sounds originating in the trap room below the stage. Battleship linoleum and certain other modern composition floor coverings satisfy these requirements.

It is inadvisable to lay a permanent floor covering on a stage floor in which traps may be cut at random. Such a covering is desirable only on a stage floor in which no traps may be cut or on a floor which has been designed and constructed as a trapped floor. In the latter case, all the traps are covered separately with the material and all edges are permanently finished with durable edging strips.

UNDERSTAGE MACHINERY

Raised and Sunken Acting Levels

The acting area is not always a single level of stage floor. Since the beginning of the century in Europe and since the early nineteen twenties in this country, there has been a steady increase in the use of *plastic form* in stage settings, with a resulting increase in the use of levels, steps, and ramps, in the acting area. The use of raised levels for emphasis is a stage director's axiom. Of 60 consecutive productions in one legitimate theatre, raised levels were used in 49.

Trap elevators.

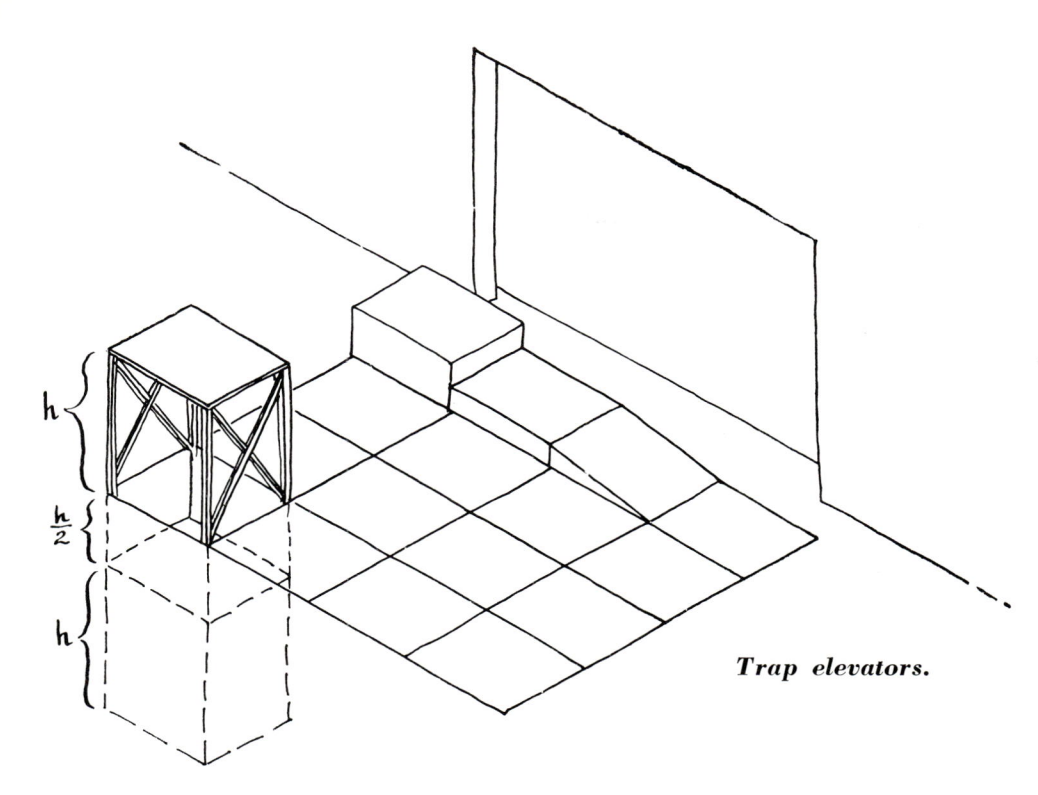

Raised levels within the acting area may be produced by two methods: by building platforms as scenery and setting them in the acting area; by elevating sections of the stage floor on understage machinery. The former method must be used on stages which have a solid floor and no elevating devices. It involves the maximum of effort in building and handling, the maximum of time and materials, and the maximum of storage space if platforms are to be kept for re-use. The second method reduces effort, time, and materials, and storage space. The desideratum is the greatest variety of size, shape, position, height, and slope.

There are similar reasons, though they occur less frequently, for sinking portions or all of the stage floor below stage level: the creation of a scenic effect of a high place surrounded by open space, as a mountain top, a tower, or a plane; the creation of aquatic scenic effects by the use of a water tank; the creation of the grave in HAMLET or of trenches on a battlefield. Similarly, unless carefully designed equipment is provided for creating these effects, great effort, much material, time and labor, and considerable jerry-building go into constructing them for particular productions.

Elevators

Vertical movement of the stage floor is produced by elevators, which may be considered under three main divisions: trap elevators, table elevators, and plateau elevators. Trap elevators and table elevators may be either fixed, that is, capable of operation in only one position, or portable, capable of being moved about horizontally, below stage to be brought into action at various trap positions. Plateau elevators are entirely fixed in one position.

All elevators are operated by one or the other of two methods: hoists, which comprise cables running through pulleys fastened to the permanent understage structure; plungers, which by hydraulic force or screw-jack action push the elevators up from below. The important difference to be noted between these two methods is that the hoist method requires the existence of understage structure extending upward to just below stage level, whereas the plunger method requires no such structure.

Trap Elevators

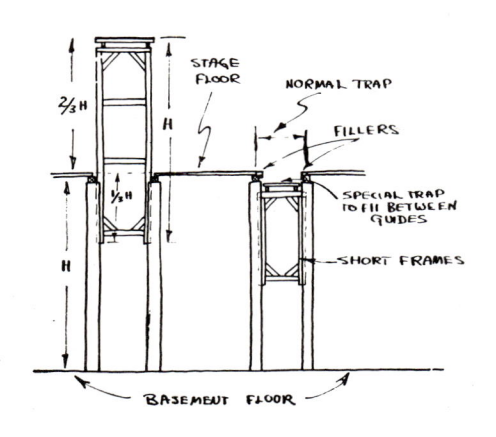

Trap elevators provide means for moving a section of stage floor the size of a single trap or smaller. They make possible the raising and lowering of individual actors, single properties, and small pieces of scenery, and the creation of small raised levels above, or small sunken levels below, the stage floor. An entire trap area, equipped with trap elevators, would provide the stage director with great variety in the location of appearances and disappearances, and the scene designer with great variety in the location of raised and sunken levels. Grouped together, trap elevators may provide the elevating and sinking of larger areas which are multiples of the single trap.

Fixed trap elevators operated by hydraulic plungers (C, 1) under the whole trap area constitute a complete and flexible arrangement for elevating and sinking the stage floor. Remote control of the fluid pressure variation and selective grouping makes possible the movement at different rates of speed or together, in one or both directions, of separate or various groups of traps simultaneously. Irregular-shaped raised levels can be produced by placing a section of beamed flooring of the necessary irregular shape upon one or more trap elevators and raising them to the desired height.

Fixed trap elevators with screw-jack operation (C, 1) supply the same variety and flexibility as the hydraulic plunger type, but without the possibility of speed variations, and without the expense of the elaborate hydraulic installation. Sinkage holes below the foundations of the stage must be made for either type.

Both the foregoing installations are extremely expensive. It is to be doubted whether any but the most elaborately equipped theatre should contain them. Other elevator installations to be described below are less expensive and produce almost the same effects.

Fixed trap elevators with hoist operation (C, 2) either electrically or hand powered, require the installation under the stage floor of a permanent structure of posts and beams from which the elevators are hung on cables. The presence of this structure precludes the possibility of lowering two or more traps combined in more than one dimension of the stage. If the beams run across stage, traps cannot be combined in

Fixed trap elevators, manual lift.

depth *; if the beams run the depth of the stage, traps cannot be combined in width.

Fixed trap elevators with manual lift operation (B, 3) (sometimes called opera traps) afford a system for creating raised levels, and very limited sunken levels, which can be installed under an existing stage provided there is sufficient height below stage. Each trap rests on two vertical frames set in vertical tracks. The frames for each trap may be raised together to produce a level platform or singly to slope the platform across the stage. The frames are held at desired heights by steel pins or ratchets engaging the tracks.

When at maximum height, the elevating frames must engage the vertical guides for about one-third their height to insure stability of the raised level. Therefore the height of the understage space must be 1½ times the height of the maximum raised level. Generally useful platform heights rarely exceed 10 feet.

The probable value of an installation of trap elevators may be estimated from the following: In 13 out of 49 productions which used raised levels, an average saving of 63 per cent could have been effected with trap elevators. The net saving would have been 16 per cent of all platforms used.

Portable trap elevators (B, 3) are assemblages of vertical guides, elevator, and necessary containing structure, mounted on casters to be freely moved about in the space below the stage for use under any stage trap. Two or more may be used in combination to raise, but not lower, combinations of stage traps. For general legitimate production, a set of portable trap elevators sufficient to elevate approximately 20 per cent of the trap area at one time is generally useful. Portable trap elevators may have either hoist operation or screw-jack operation, with hand or electric power in either case. Portable trap elevators presuppose the existence of a trap area, with the traps resting on floor beams. If the beams are adjustable, free selection of size, shape, and location of elevators is permitted.

Limits of Vertical Travel

The upward limit of travel of trap elevators relates to their scenic uses. There is potential value in being able to create a second-story scenic effect by means of elevators; this would call for a rise of 9 to 10 feet.

This downward limit may be set at the level at which an actor may step off a disappearance trap or staircase and clear the stage floor over his head; this calls for a sinkage of about 7 feet.

* In this chapter and in general stage practice, the terms deep and depth refer to horizontal dimensions from proscenium to back wall; wide, width, broad, and breadth refer to horizontal dimensions across the stage, and high and height to vertical dimensions above or below the stage.

Since the cost of installing a system of rising and sinking trap elevators is high, it is logical to recommend that these two upper and lower rise possibilities be accommodated.

Table Elevators

Fixed table elevators are designed to raise or sink strips of stage floor, each strip one trap (about 3 feet-6 inches or 4 feet) in depth, and two or more traps (15 feet and up) in width. They are mounted on plungers, or screw jacks, or set on steel trusses which are suspended on cables and run in vertical tracks at the ends. Because of the infrequent requirement for the elevation or sinking of a section of floor of one definite size in one definite location, their use is limited in theatrical and operatic production, although in stages of convention halls or concert halls, table elevators easily provide the desired stepped levels for speakers, choirs, or orchestras.

Portable table elevators (C, 2) are of two types according to the method used to move them horizontally below stage. The wagon type is mounted on casters and rolls backward and forward on tracks set on the floor of the basement. The crane type is mounted on end rollers which travel on tracks suspended below the stage floor.

The portable table elevator is moved horizontally in only one dimension and brought into position under a selected row of floor traps. The traps are removed and the elevator raised into their space. By setting

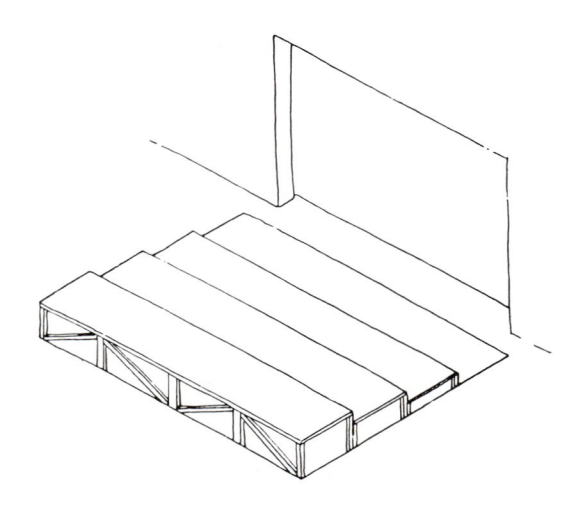

Fixed table elevators.

Driving mechanism for fixed table elevators.

the table elevator at a level lower than the stage and building platforms on it, a section of floor of any size, smaller than the table elevator, can be raised or lowered.

Sliding floor panels (C, 3): For many uses of trap elevators and table elevators, it is necessary that the stage floor be intact above the elevator until the elevator is used; e.g., a scene is played on a solid floor and at a certain instant an actor rises through the floor. For such mechanical effects, a section of floor must slide sidewise under the stage to allow the elevator to rise. If fixed elevators are installed, permanent guides and operating mechanism for the floor panels are also installed; if a system of flexible elevators is adopted, the mechanism for sliding the floor panels may also be demountable, portable, and adjustable. Portable trap elevators may contain the mechanism for sliding out a section of stage floor.

Plateau Elevators

Plateau elevators (C, 1) are designed to move large portions of the stage floor. Rare in American theatres, they exist in isolated instances. The Philadelphia Convention Hall and Radio City Music Hall are notable examples. They have three uses: to produce raised or sunken levels, to raise whole sets of scenery from below stage, and to produce spectacular production effects. Plateau elevators are permanently installed and have hydraulic plunger or screw-jack propulsion. Of infrequent use in drama or opera, their greatest usefulness is in elaborate musical productions or presentation.

The ultimate in the installation of floor elevators conceived by Friedrich Kranich is a scheme which envisons the sinking and elevating of the entire stage floor inside the cyclorama, the subdivision of the central portion into plateau elevators, and the further subdivision of these into table elevators, with a movable understage crane. The table elevators in turn are divided into trap elevators which may be operated singly or in groups. Kranich's system is designed for elaborate operatic production. Its greatest limitation is that the trusses running across stage between the table elevators restrict the depth (up- and downstage dimension) of both table and trap elevators, and prevent location of elevators in the space occupied by the trusses.

Some theatres have been projected in which the only means of shifting scenery is by sinking and elevating wagons, which are rolled off and on the elevators below stage. By this system, it is promised, complete changes of scene can be effected in 30 seconds. This, however, is three times as long as a full-stage change takes in a well-designed and well-equipped theatre.

Counterweights for Stage Elevators

Unless the operating mechanism can successfully sustain, overcome, and control the dead and live loads of the elevators, counterweight must be attached to balance at least the dead load. For hand-powered elevators, additional variable counterweight must be provided to balance at least a portion of the live load. Hydraulic, screw-jack, and motor windlass types of operation may generally be designed with sufficient lifting power and holding power in the mechanism to render the use of counterweights unnecessary.

General Precepts

1. Modern theatrical production (drama, opera, musical comedy) demands versatility of stage equipment. The usefulness of equipment is more than directly proportional to its flexibility.

2. As the size of stage elevators increases and their mobility decreases, their versatility decreases, and the number of times and variety of ways in which they can be used also decreases.

3. Raised platforms in a variety of shapes and sizes are much used in stage settings and appreciable savings in cost can be effected if stage elevators can be used.

4. Sinking the stage is infrequently required but the possibility of doing one particular production may sometimes depend on it.

Modular Systems

No system of traps or stage elevators will satisfy the infinite variety of dimensional demands that will be made upon it by scene designers.

The most that can be said for a system is that it will provide differences of level and of areas according to the size of the differential module which is applied to the vertical and horizontal dimensions. The vertical variation can be very small: ¼ inch or less if telemetering is applied to motor-driven movement, or 1 inch if manual setting is used. The horizontal variation within the system is gained by combining modules.

The shapes and levels obtainable by a system, however, can supply a large percentage of the total area, volume, and structure of all required raised levels, and the unique irregular shapes required by any specific setting can be achieved by the addition of specially built pieces.

Use of the Space below Stage

Entrances through the stage floor, by stairs or ladders, and the elevating and sinking of sections of the floor postulate that the space below the stage be assigned to these functions. The following precepts must prevail:

1. There must be as few permanent posts and beams or trusses as possible, and none within the space under the acting area.

2. The height of the understage space must provide for the maximum desired sinkage of traps or elevators, and must be at least 1½ times the desired maximum rise of elevators which are hoisted by cables, if such are used. The sinkage of elevators, used for actors only, need be just enough to clear the steepest balcony sight lines and to pro-

vide headroom under the stage floor. The sinkage of elevators for scenery must accommodate the highest scenery which will be set on the elevator.

3. Space at the sides for pulleys, drums, and counterweights must be allowed in the case of hoist elevators, and for pressure tanks, pipes, and valves for hydraulic elevators.

Machinery for hydraulic stage lifts.

4. The operating position for remote control elevators must be at the stage level where the operator can see the entire mobile area, preferably near the stage manager. Communication by telephone between the control station and the understage space is essential.

5. Access of actors from dressing rooms to understage stairs and elevators must be provided. This may be by a mezzanine gallery placed around the elevator pit, 8 or 10 feet below the stage floor. Automatic safety rails must protect this gallery except when the elevators are at the same level.

Two or more types of elevators may be combined in one installation. Plateau elevators on screw jacks may contain fixed table elevators, also on screw jacks. Plateau elevators may contain trap elevators on screw jacks or cable hoists, and plateau elevators may contain table elevators to work intact or subdivided to form trap elevators. Plateau elevators may contain revolving discs or wagons. All such elaborate combinations tend to multiply the amount of fixed apparatus and the amount of structure, thus reducing the adaptability of the equipment and limiting the ways in which it may be used.

Combinations

In planning an elevator installation, the first consideration may well be given to providing a trap elevator in any part of the trap area. Other elevator devices when added must not sacrifice this function.

Integration with Forestage and Open Stage Elevators

The trend toward performance outside the proscenium implies a demand for the same kind of mobility of the floor of the forestage and the open stage for the same reasons. It is therefore valid to plan a modular system of trap elevators which encompasses both the stage and the acting area beyond the proscenium.

If laws require that the portion of the stage directly under the fire curtain be of fixed fireproof construction, this portion of the floor should at least be given shape and dimensions consistent with the systemic trap elevators on both sides of it.

Electromechanical Control

As with the movement of rolling stages, the movement of stage elevators is now subject to precise electromechanical control from a remote point. Interconnection and grouping, presetting of travel distances and read-out of movements and positions of elevators and groups of elevators are now possible. See Chapter 11.

Evaluation of Stage Elevators

Stage elevators are expensive in comparison to other stage machinery on a basis of general usefulness. The theatre planner is well advised to consider carefully the possible uses of elevators before incorporating them in a theatre. Stage elevators have been but little used in American theatres generally, probably because of the cost. Some increased use, particularly of trap elevators, would improve the flexibility and efficiency of stages.

11: Stage machinery: in the flies

Equipment over the Stage

Equipment over the stage is used for the suspension and flying of scenery, lighting equipment, and other items which contribute to the performance. *Flying* is the operation of raising an object into the space above the stage. The nature of a flying system, its design, its physical properties, its quantitative character, and its spatial requirements depends upon the nature of the objects which must be *flown*. All large flat pieces of scenery can be easily cleared from the scenery space by flying. Without fly space the clearing and storage of such scenery as drops, ceilings, wide flat back walls, and cycloramas present a difficult technical problem. The full description of the great variety of scenic elements which can be shifted by *flying* is beyond the scope of this book.

Lighting instruments of many kinds (see Chapter 12) must be hung in the space above the stage, raised into position at various heights above the stage, and frequently lowered to the stage for repositioning, alterations, adjustments and repair.

People must be flown in such plays as THE CLOUDS, PETER PAN, HIGH TOR, and in many operas which specialize in gods descending.

The Flying Operation

The simplest example of *flying* is the suspending and raising of an object above the stage on a single line (the nautical name for a *rope in use* applies in the theatre).

Since the stagehand pulling the line to raise the object cannot be within the acting area, there must be two pulleys in the system allowing him to be offstage in a position outside the acting, scenery and storage areas. There must also be a device (belaying pin) to which he may fasten the line to keep the object in raised (flown) position.

Objects to be flown usually require at least two lines, which form a minimal *set*. Objects of large expanse which are hung and flown parallel to the proscenium require sets whose pulleys are so arranged, while objects which are hung and flown in nonlinear arrangement require that the lines be combinable into changeable sets with pulley locations variable.

The number of lines in any particular set, then, depends upon the

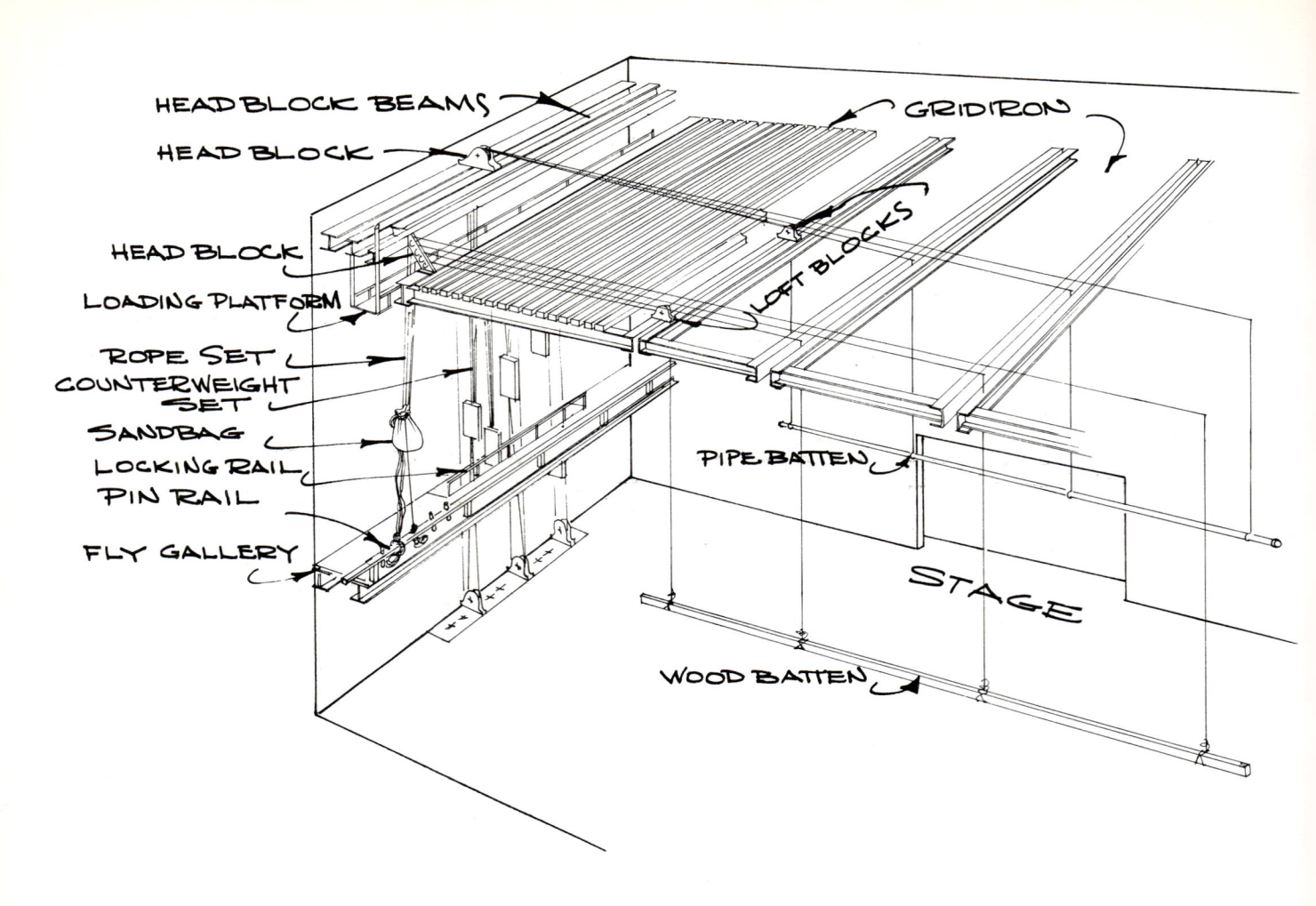

Stage block showing names and locations of flying equipment.

Stage of the John Fitzgerald Kennedy Theatre, University of Hawaii, shows pipe frame for cloth cyclorama, overhead cyc lights, fly gallery and pinrail, light bridge, counterweights, upstage and side-stage wagon docks.

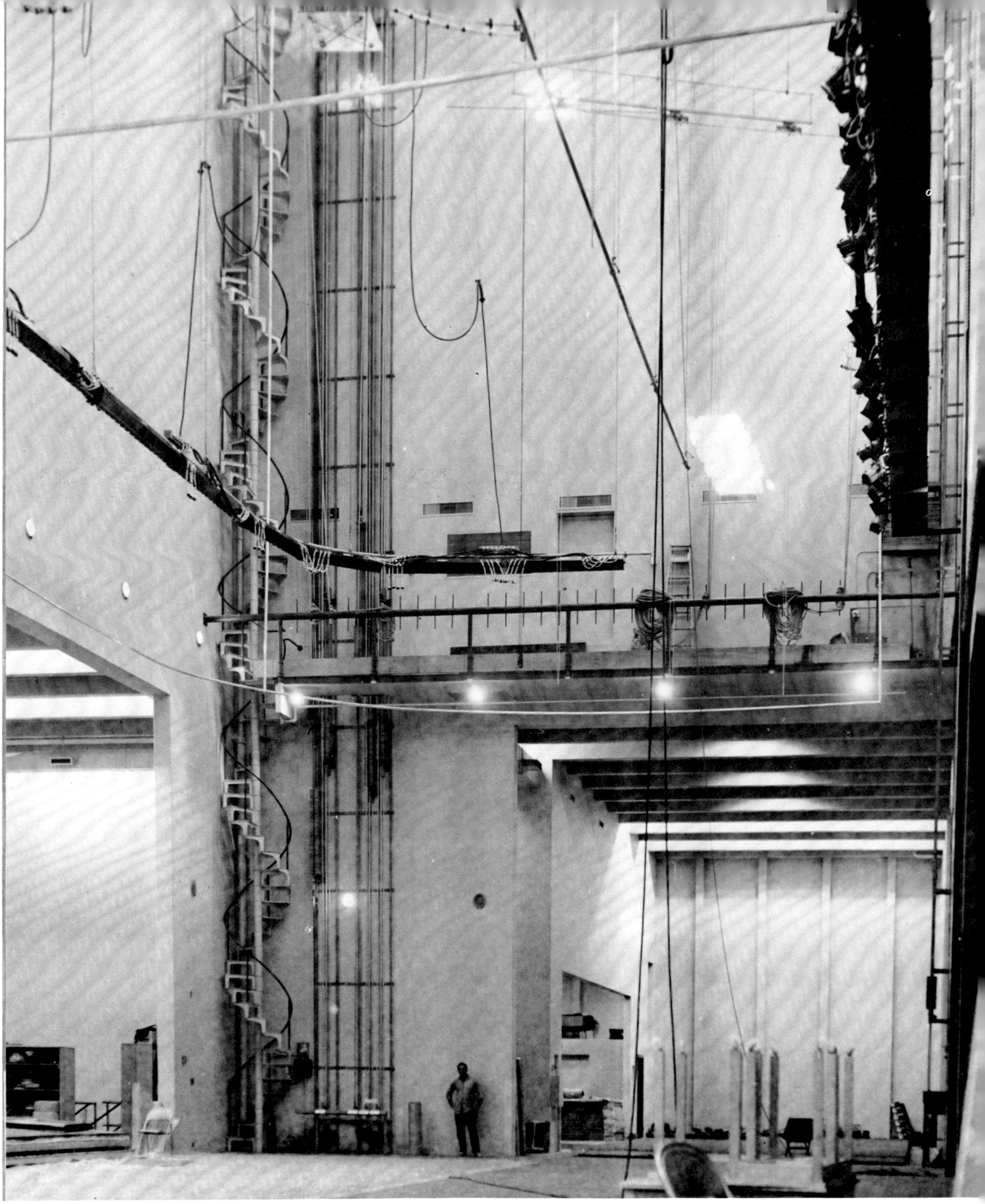

size and shape of the objects to be suspended and flown and the location of the points where lines may be attached to the scenery.

Structural Elements

The entire stage house is a structural system whose chief function, after protecting its occupants from the elements, is to provide proper accommodation and support for the flying equipment, effectively and efficiently transmitting to the foundations the imposed loads occasioned by the flying operation (together with dead loads and roof loads).

An efficiently designed stage house will do this with the greatest accommodation of structural design to the flying system and the least consumption of structural materials.

The gridiron, loading platform, head block beams, fly galleries, other working galleries, and pin rails are items of the overstage structure to which the flying system is attached. Because these items are installed before the more detailed items of the stage equipment and because the latter must be fastened to the structural parts, it is essential that the complete installation of overstage equipment be planned before the drawings and specifications for the masonry and steel are made. Too frequently, the steelwork has been ordered without careful consideration of the detailed stage equipment with the result that expensive alterations or special stage equipment are made necessary.

Stage equipment companies offer free advisory service regarding the detailed layout of overstage equipment, which is of some value to architects. The weakness of this service, however, is that certain standardized layouts are recommended for all stages. Insufficient regard for variation in the conditions of use results in the installation of elaborate rigging systems in stages where use would require a limited installation.

It must be stated emphatically that conditions of use must guide the planner in the selection of methods of handling scenery, the specification of stage equipment, the determination of the size, shape, and arrangement of the overstage space. A high-school stage will not require the same equipment as an opera house; a community theatre will not require the same equipment as a Broadway playhouse; nor the theatre in a women's college, the same as a metropolitan presentation house.

Gridiron looking toward the head blocks.

Gridiron

The gridiron is an openwork floor of steel located under the roof of the stage on which sheaves may be fastened either permanently or temporarily and through which ropes, either wire or hemp, may be dropped for the suspension of scenery, lighting equipment, actors, and anything else which the performance may require to be suspended. Examination of this definition will show the particular requirements which the gridiron must fulfill. The gridiron must support, with a generous safety factor, all loads which will be placed on it. Stage workers must be able to move about with safety and freedom; therefore the gridiron must allow at least a minimum of headroom under the roof structure: six feet under the lowest roof girders.

Blocks

Blocks must be fastened to the gridiron, both permanently and temporarily. It is sound practice to consider even those sheaves which are part of the initial installation, and to all intents permanent, as temporarily fastened. Stage loft blocks are manufactured with fastenings which render them easily movable. The use of blocks of this type and the design of the gridiron to receive them save many hours of labor in the initial installation and in the preparation of shows.

Ropes are dropped through the gridiron. For the greatest possible use, it is essential that ropes may be dropped in the maximum number of positions. Standard steel gridirons consist of 1½ inch x 3 inch channels laid web-up 3 inches apart, on 6- or 8-inch channels (web vertical), and afford slightly less than 50 per cent open space, allowing the location of spot lines (ropes through the gridiron) never more than 1½ inches from a desired position, a satisfactory solution.

Cable Slots

As will be made clear when flying systems are considered, most of the permanently installed ropes and blocks are arranged in rows perpendicular to the proscenium. The gridiron contains special steel to support the concentrated load created by this arrangement: pairs of channels set back to back, spaced by steel diaphragms, extend from the proscenium wall to the back wall and are suspended at intervals from the roof steel. The size of the channels is determined by the span and the safe load requirements of building codes. These cable slots are spaced according to the size of the flying system and this in turn is determined by the width of the scenery area.

Systems for Flying Scenery

The desired attribute of a system for flying scenery is that it facilitates the flying of any size, shape, or weight of scenery, lighting equipment, or other objects, set in any part of the scenery area in any position with relation to the proscenium and floor. Existing flying systems are designed on the premise that most scenery will be flown parallel to the proscenium.

There are two established systems for flying scenery, called in stage vernacular the rope (or *hemp*) system and the counterweight system. The counterweight system, though by no means new, is the later of the two systems to come into use. A few recent installations combine the two to make available the good features of both. A third system, the synchronous winch system developed by George C. Izenour, was introduced in 1959 with an initial installation at Hofstra College and has been installed in several college and university theatres.

Rope System

The *unit* of a rope system is a combination of three or more ropes (called lines) with their necessary loft blocks and head block, to form a *rope set*, or *line set*. The loft blocks are placed on the cable slots of the gridiron, 10 to 12 feet apart, in a row parallel to the proscenium. The head block is of the tandem type having separate sheaves for each rope arranged in an upward diagonal so that the longer lines are lifted higher above the gridiron. The head block is placed on *head block beams* at the side of the stage outside the scenery space, generally, though not always, close to the side wall. Each rope of a set extends from the stage floor, up through its own loft block, across the gridiron to and through the head block, and down to a pinrail on the fly gallery. In some existing theatres, the pinrail is placed on the stage floor. This is mentioned only to be deprecated: the numerous activities which take place on the stage floor demand that the pinrail and its attendant gear be located above the stage. The ropes of a set are used together to hang and fly wide flat pieces. They are used separately or selectively to fly smaller pieces, and selectively in combination with ropes from other sets to fly pieces which extend up and down stage.

Briefly stated, the practice is to place the piece of scenery on the floor, attach the ropes, adjust them for equal tension and level *trim*, pull the piece into the flies, and tie off ropes on the pinrail. Sandbags may be attached to the ropes above the pinrail partially to balance a heavy piece of scenery.

Battens

When it is necessary to hang a number of lighting instruments in a row over the stage or when the points of suspension of scenery do not coincide with the locations of the ropes of a set, a batten of 1½ or 2 inch i.d. standard steel pipe is used. Easily procurable, comparatively inexpensive, the pipe batten has become standard, and light mounting practices (see Chapter 12) have developed around it. However, pipe is a relatively flexible and weak shape under transverse loading. Experiments with Z-bar battens, truss battens, and hollow rectangular-sectioned battens are under way with the object of extending the span between supports and thereby reducing the number of lines required to fly any unit of flat scenery or row of lighting instruments. The use of light, but strong, aluminum alloys and of the stronger kinds of steel results in increased first costs but lighter equipment and more efficient use of the flying system.

Fly Gallery

A steel or reinforced concrete gallery is bracketed or cantilevered out from the wall on one or both sides of the stage for the operation of the flying systems. Its width ranges between 4 and 10 feet; its height ranges between 20 and 30 feet above the stage floor. Factors affecting the height are: (1) practical visibility into the flies for operation of hung scenery; (2) clearance under gallery to allow storing the highest generally used standing scenery beneath it.

Pinrail

A steel pipe of 3½ inch, or more, inside diameter is securely fastened to stanchions at the onstage edge of the fly gallery at a height of about 3 feet. Through holes in this pipe steel or hickory belaying pins are set vertically. Holes are oversized for easy fit. Rope sets are tied off on these pins. When many sets of lines are loaded and tied off, there is a great upward stress on the pinrail, requiring that the rail and its supports be designed to withstand an upward stress of at least 200 pounds per linear foot in commercial, community, and college theatres, and 500 pounds per linear foot in opera and presentation theatres. The floor load on fly galleries may be figured at the minimum for similar floors as given in the local codes.

Counterweight System

The counterweight system for flying scenery employs steel in all its parts with the single exception of a manila purchase line for hand operation. It is therefore more expensive per unit than the rope system, loses some flexibility which the rope system possesses, but gains appreciable advantages of long life, dependability, and safety over the rope system.

A counterweight unit or set consists of pipe batten, three or more wire ropes, loft blocks for each rope, head block, counterweight carriage, floor block or tension block, operating line, and rope lock. The pipe batten is hung horizontally on the wire ropes which are carried up to and over the loft blocks, across the gridiron, to and through the head block, and down to the top of the counterweight carriage where they are fastened by chains or turnbuckles which are adjustable for leveling (*trimming*) the batten. Because a batten will trim differently when loaded from the way it will when empty, due to the sag of ropes across the gridiron, the architect must specify that the theatre riggers trim all battens under a specimen distributed load about equal to an average load of scenery. The counterweight carriage runs up and down along the side wall a distance equal to the vertical run of the batten. It is guided by wire guides attached to the head block I-beams and the floor, or by T-section steel tracks which are fastened to angle steel crossbars on the

Flymen operating the T-track counterweight system on the fly gallery of the Radio City Music Hall.

Wire-guide counterweight installation with locking rail at the stage floor. Note: work-light strip, guardrails against which scenery may be stacked and free-standing wire-guide units. These are badly located and should be so installed only if they are for temporary use. The single floor block, center foreground, is particularly obstructive.

T-track counterweight installation with locking rail at the fly gallery. A pinrail for a rope system may be installed at the outer (near) side of the gallery. Counterweights run below the gallery to the floor.

Combination of T-track counterweight sets and rope sets. Kirby Theatre, Amherst College.

235

wall. A purchase line runs from the top of the carriage up to and over the head block, down through a rope lock, around a tension block at the floor, and up to tie to the bottom of the carriage. Counterweights are placed in the carriage at the loading platform.

Briefly stated, the operating procedure is to lower (*bring in*) the pipe batten to the floor thus raising (*taking out*) the carriage to the loading platform, affix the scenery to the pipe by snap chains or ropes, load counterweight into the carriage to balance the weight of the scenery, and fly the scenery by pulling down on the purchase line below the carriage. Many variations of this procedure are practiced by stagehands to handle diverse kinds of scenery.

Counterweight carriages are of three types, depending upon the kind of vertical guides used.

Wire Guides   The carriage runs up and down on two taut stranded cables stretched between head blocks and floor. This type is the least expensive, and is flexible in that sets may be moved up- and downstage. No fixed steel or wall anchors are necessary. The wire guides, however, allow certain horizontal sway in the carriages, requiring that the counterweights be spaced at least 12 inches apart to prevent fouling.

T-track Guides   The offstage side of the carriage is engaged to vertical steel tracks of T-section by means of sliders of H-section. Each carriage fits between two tracks and each track between two carriages, making the grouping of carriages desirable. Limits to this grouping are set by the allowable angle at which wire ropes may enter the head blocks. The T-tracks are fastened by steel U-clips to horizontal battens (L-section) which are in turn bracketed out from the stage wall. When the wall has setbacks to reduce its thickness toward the top, the brackets must become increasingly longer for each setback.

Lattice Track Guides   Both sides of the counterweight carriage engage vertical T-tracks. The webs of the Tees fit into slots in the top and bottom members (draw irons) of the carriage. Cross spreaders of steel, fastened between the tracks at intervals, form the lattice. This type of track is particularly useful for isolated counterweights, such as those for the fire curtain or the act curtain. The track may be set perpendicular to a wall or flat against a wall.

Extra Counterweight Carriages   Useful additions to a counterweight installation are two or more extra carriages with head blocks, purchase line, rope lock and tension block, but without wire ropes or pipe battens, strategically placed among the complete counterweight sets. These have four uses: (1) to be fastened to adjacent carriages and supply extra weight capacity

Detail: wire-guide counterweight sets.

Lattice track, left, and and wire-guide, right, counterweight sets parallel with the wall.

Detail: T-track counterweight sets.

237

when very heavy pieces are to be hung, (2) to carry weight which is applied intermittently to balance scenery which is detached from the batten at the floor (*carpet hoist*), (3) to counterweight special sets of lines which are installed in spot positions for individual shows, (4) to receive lines attached to side walls of box sets which are flown intact when the back wall is hung on an adjacent counterweight set.

TABLE 12. Table of Recommended Maximum Working Loads per Set of Counterweight Lines (This does not include loads of light bridges, fire curtains, act curtains, or motion picture screens and horns.)

Legitimate Theatre College Theatre Community Theatre Summer Theatre	700 pounds per set
Opera Presentation Spectacle	1000 pounds per set

TABLE 13. Recommended Optimum and Minimum Ratios of Sheave Diameter to Rope Diameter for Wire Rope

Construction of Rope	Optimum Ratio	Minimum Ratio
6 strands 7 wires each	72 to 1	42 to 1
6 " 19 " "	45 to 1	30 to 1
6 " 37 " "	27 to 1	18 to 1

Location of the Lock Rail

The generally accepted position for the lock rail in counterweight systems has been at the stage floor, so that stagehands might have ready access to the purchase lines while performing work on the floor. Under certain conditions it appears advisable to locate the lock rail on the fly gallery, namely, (1) when rope system and counterweight system are used in combination, (2) when operation of the flying equipment is delegated separately to certain stagehands (flymen) who do none of the work on the floor, (3) when it is planned to move scenery, whether on or off wagons, in the space ordinarily occupied by the lock rail on the floor, and especially when it is planned to move wagons through that space into storage docks. The numerous demands on the stage floor space make it generally desirable that all flying operations and as much of the flying equipment as possible be kept above and clear of the stage floor.

Loading Platform

Essential to a counterweight system and occasionally useful for a rope system, the loading platform is a steel gallery about 2½ feet wide hung between the gridiron and the head block I-beams below the level of the gridiron a distance which allows convenient loading of weights into carriages, i.e., level with the bottoms of the carriages when they are at the top of their run. The platform is open on the side toward the counterweights, and protected by a railing on the stage side. Access to the loading platform is by ladder, stair, or elevator from the stage floor or fly gallery; a ladder or stair leads from the loading platform to the gridiron.

Parallel I-beams are set 2 feet 6 inches or 3 feet above the level of the gridiron, near the side wall. The elevation above the gridiron lifts the wire ropes above the gridiron and prevents rubbing and wear. All ropes of the counterweight system change direction through about 90 degrees from approximately horizontal to vertical at this point. Hence there is great stress in both vertical and horizontal directions. Wide flange beams are used, and a channel is fastened to the onstage beam to resist horizontal stress. The horizontal stress may sometimes be transferred to the stage house structure by ties and to the gridiron structure by struts. Diaphragms tie the two head block beams together at intervals. Loading allowances for head block beams are specified in some building codes.

There is a great spread possible in the cost of flying systems. The theatre planner to be successful must design a flying system which is suited to uses of the particular theatre, neither insufficient to those uses nor too elaborate for them, and in any case within the building budget. It profits a theatre owner very little to be able to point with pride at the most elaborate flying system in America if the productions in his theatre never require the use of it.

Head Block Beams

Head blocks and head block I-beams. The planks on the gridiron are not a part of the installation. The contractors just forgot them.

Counterweight System for Stages with Wagon Docks Offstage at the Sides

When it is necessary to keep all side-wall parts of a counterweight system above the level of the fly gallery as when a wagon stage is to pass through an opening in the stage wall, a combination of pulleys having a mechanical advantage of two in favor of the scenery may be introduced above the counterweight carriage, whereby the vertical run of the counterweight is only half the vertical run of the scenery.

Comparison of Rope and Counterweight Systems

A rope system requires less structural steel, generally cheaper parts, and less installation labor than a counterweight system. Counterweight systems can be economically laid out to cost not much more than a rope system or can be very elaborate, requiring much steel work, expensive parts, and much installation labor. Neither rope system nor counterweight system alone are adequate to all problems of hanging and flying scenery. Each system possesses advantages which the other lacks. Counterweight sets are best for flying curtains, lighting equipment, light bridges, heavy framed pieces of scenery, and sets flown intact. Rope sets are best for hanging lightweight framed pieces, drops, borders, leg drops, and unframed pieces generally, for the special spotting and selecting of lines, and for the hanging of scenery perpendicular and oblique to the proscenium. Counterweight sets are fixed in position; rope sets may be moved about the gridiron with ease. Rope sets require greater manpower to operate than do counterweight sets. Rope system operation requires a higher degree of stagecraft than does counterweight operation.

The maximum use of a flying system is attained when the following vague condition is satisfied: any and all items of scenery, properties, lighting or sound equipment, and even actors, are flown and operated in the space over the stage to meet the demands of production. No specific criteria of adequacy can be derived from this. The most reliable source of criteria is the record of a number of productions. An examination of the flying problems in these productions shows that flown objects divide into two categories: those which occur with sufficient frequency and in sufficiently standard sizes that a suitable installation may be designed to handle them; and those which are so diverse in size and character and so infrequent in occurrence that each must be handled as a special problem by the stage technician, either by adapting standard equipment or by installing special equipment. The theatre planner can design equipment to fit the requirements of the former category, and he can supply some equipment whose flexibility will contribute to the solution of problems in the latter category.

Examination of some 200 sets of scenery for legitimate drama, musical shows, and opera discloses that elaborate musical productions make the greatest demands upon flying systems, both in sheer numbers of sets as well as in special effects.

Averaged, the different types of production require line sets per show as follows:

Elaborate Musical Production	30 or more sets
Ordinary Musical and Revue	10 to 20 sets
Opera	5 to 15 sets
Presentation	5 to 10 sets
Elaborate Drama	15 sets
Ordinary Drama	5 to 10 sets

Because of the variety of positions in which scenery is hung in different shows, a stage must be equipped with more sets than these figures indicate.

Although all kinds of scenery may occur in all types of productions, certain kinds of scenery occur with sufficiently greater frequency to warrant the design of flying equipment to handle more of those kinds. For dramatic production, which employs about 65 per cent box sets involving back walls and ceilings to be flown, the width of pieces to be flown is usually less than the full width of the proscenium. In musical production, opera, and presentation, all of which require side entrances and spectacular scenery, involving drops, borders, and curtains, the width of much flown scenery exceeds the proscenium width by 10 to 20 per cent.

Therefore on a stage intended for dramatic production wholly or to a large degree, the length of the pipe battens may be equal to or shorter than the proscenium width, whereas for the second group of productions, the battens may be 25 per cent longer than the proscenium is wide. The proscenium here is taken to mean the *working* proscenium, that is, the actual opening which is generally used; if it is planned to *close in* the structural opening with tormentors or curtains, the *net* opening is the working opening.

If the stage is intended for all types of production about equally, the shorter battens are recommended because temporary extensions can be added to short battens but long battens cannot be shortened without permanent alteration.

Motor-driven Counterweight Sets

Application of electric motive power to the operation of counterweight sets has various forms but relatively few existing installations. Expensive if applied to all sets, it is nonetheless effective and efficient if applied to the sets most frequently to be used, including the light bridge, the motion picture screen, and the cyclorama. Motors engaging the purchase lines of individual counterweight sets are located either below the stage or on the fly gallery.

Synchronous Winch System

The rope system and the counterweight system as so far described are based on the assumption that most flown scenery will be flat, broad and arranged parallel to the proscenium, as in an upside-down filing drawer. Whereas many scenic schemes, particularly traditional ones, have this arrangement, many other scenic schemes require a flying system which permits random variability in the positioning of flying lines and in the combination of lines into sets. This condition is approached, within certain limits, by the synchronous winch system.

Flying lines are individually positioned at infinitely variable increments up- and downstage and at 3- or 4-foot intervals across stage by virtue of the mobility of the loft blocks which are underhung from steel T-bars or Unistrut channels which are fastened under the stage roof structure. The across stage interval of 3 or 4 feet may be reduced by introducing special T-bar or Unistrut purlins between the main Tees or channels.

Each flying line running through a loft block is payed out or reeled in by a drum which is driven by a frequency-sensitive motor capable of variable speeds, under a load which is variable up to 250 pounds.

The winches are mounted in equal numbers on the front and back walls of the stage house above the gridiron. As many as six or eight of the motor-driven winches may be selectively grouped to be driven by one remotely positioned variable frequency generator. Two such generators facilitate running two groups of lines either up or down at the same time.

A console, located on the stage floor, and movable to afford the operator a view of the flies, contains the controls by which groups are selected; direction, distance and speed of movement are preset; movement is started by push button, and vertical travel is accurately displayed in feet, inches, and quarters of an inch.

Synchronous winches of SceneControl system designed by George C. Izenour, manufactured by J. R. Clancy, Inc.

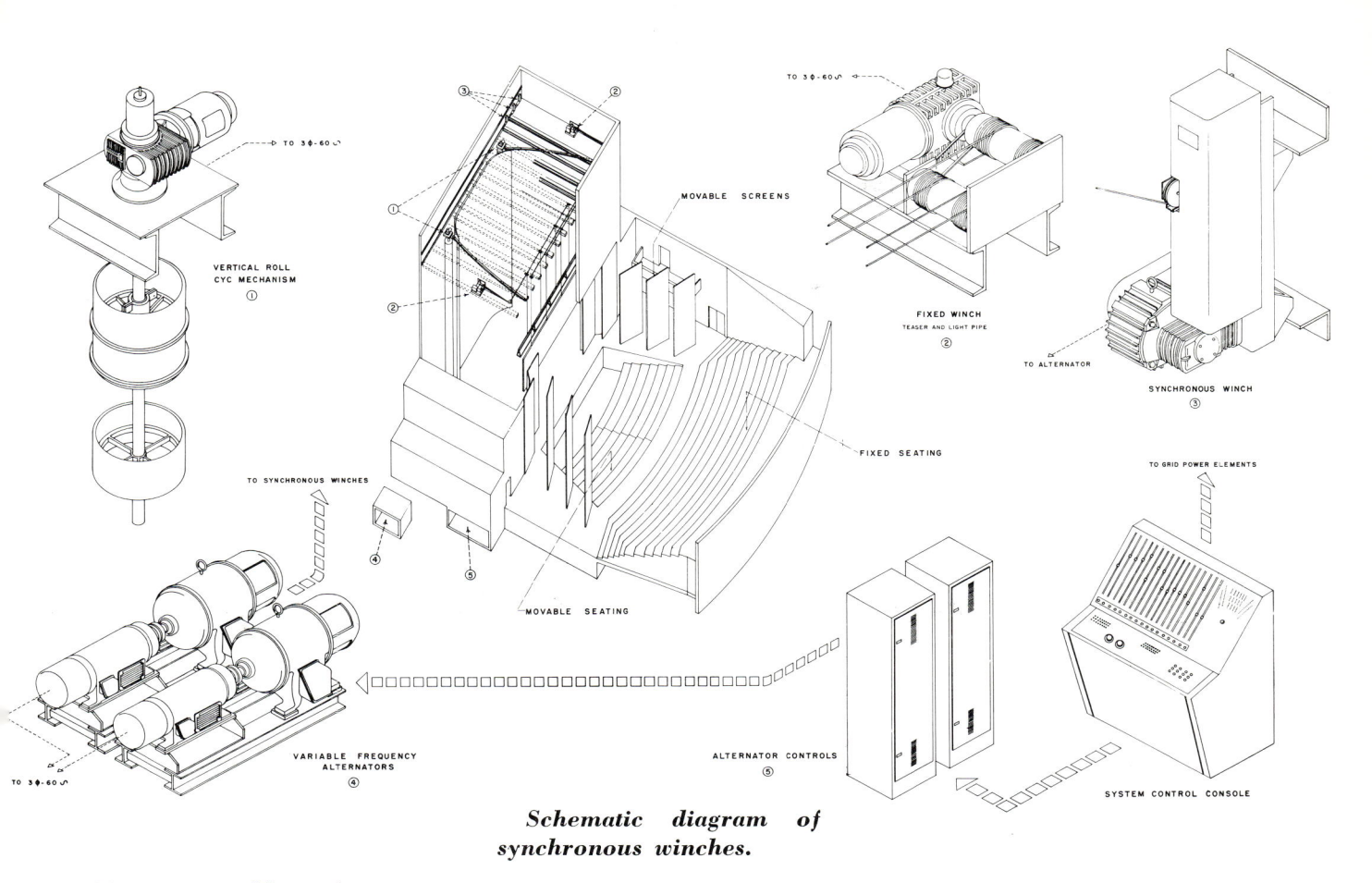

Schematic diagram of synchronous winches.

Hoisting cables from winch drums lead through swivel loft blocks which are adjustable in Unistrut channels. Chains, adjustable in channels, for dead-hanging scenery and lights.

Control console for synchronous winch system.

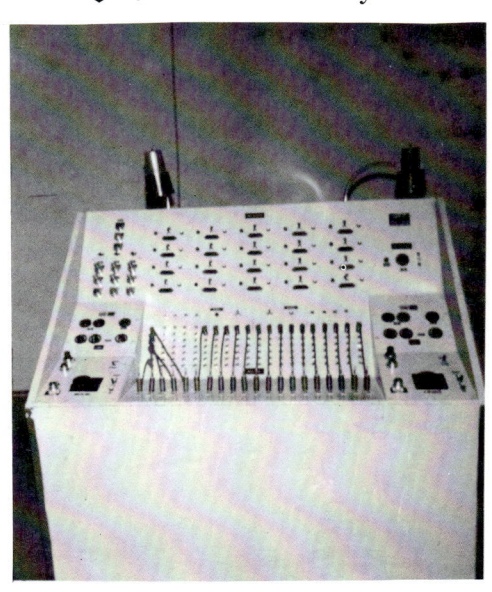

243

The advantages of the synchronous winch system are many:

1. Lifting lines may be selectively positioned anywhere over the stage according to the particular requirements of any production.

2. The load of flown scenery and other objects is imposed directly on the roof steel and not on the gridiron. The gridiron thus may be a lightly structured walkway with a very high ratio of open-to-closed area, unless it is decided to combine the synchronous winch system with rope or counterweight systems. There are justifications for considering such a combination.

3. The synchronous winch system operates, except for the drivers and the control devices, entirely above the gridiron, and thereby frees stage house walls of the encumbrances of tracked counterweights or of ropes and sandbags. The problem inherent in combining side stages for wagons and the counterweight system is eliminated.

4. Since no counterweights are involved, the arduous task of balancing scenery loads with iron counterweights or sandbags is eliminated.

5. Scenery is moved entirely by electricity, thus eliminating the manual effort of flying scenery.

6. Whereas the parallelism of the rope and counterweight systems is more congenial to flat scenery hung parallel to the proscenium, the synchronous winch system is equally congenial to scenery hung in any direction.

Combinations of Synchronous Winch System with Other Systems

As with several other innovations in theatre technology, this system is being adopted in theatres outside the commercial closed circle of New York and road-tour professional production. Since all theatres in this complex are equipped with either rope or counterweight systems, scenery is designed to fit those systems, and crews are trained and routined in its operation on them. If the production policy of a new theatre intends the presentation of shows designed for the older system and yet intends also to take advantage of modern technology for home-produced shows, a combination of systems is indicated.

Limitations in Synchronous Winch System

There are some limitations in any system. Present limitations in the synchronous winch system which may be overcome by future developments are: the limit of maximum speed (2 feet per minute) and the inability to start several pieces of scenery in motion in overlapping sequence. These two limitations are sufficient justification for combining a rope system with the synchronous winch system. A further justification, in a school situation, may be the desire to give students experience on the still widely used rope system.

Theatres of recent vintage which are now equipped with rope systems, counterweight systems or both may add or convert to the synchronous winch systems after making certain adjustments in their present systems and stage house structure.

Systems under Development

An alternate system for selectively positioning flying lines is the Robot-Grid in which winch units on wheels are moved about the gridiron to the positions required to fly scenery. To date no installation has been made, but a prototype has been contracted for a university theatre.

Heights

Heights backstage are determined from the probable maximum heights of scenery as follows: (1) the clear height of the stage house must accommodate the highest piece of hung scenery which will be used when it is flown to expose another piece of equal height; (2) clear height under galleries and through openings into storage spaces must accommodate the highest piece of standing scenery which will be used, plus the height of stage wagons if they are used. The highest standing scenery rarely exceeds 16 feet for legitimate drama and 30 feet for grand opera and musical comedy.

Flying Equipment over Storage Space

The use of the upper space in wagon docks to store scenery flown off wagons expands considerably the capacity of the storage space. Such storage is only necessary for handling the most elaborate scenic ensembles and must be considered marginal in planning and budgeting stage equipment.

This equipment may be used when any of the following methods of handling scenery are used: divided wagons, traverse wagons with straight path, traverse wagons with curved path.

Types of flying equipment over storage space:

1. Steel pipes hung under the ceiling to which blocks may be tied where and when needed. A short pipe for head blocks and a short pinrail at the floor or on a gallery.

2. Exposed I-beams to which underhang blocks may be clamped. Short I-beam over a short pinrail.

3. Unistrut or A-Frame channels to which blocks or eyebolts may be fastened.

4. Manual or electrical hoists rigged to travel on overhead tracks so that scenery may be lifted off wagons, moved laterally, and set down in the storage space.

5. Complete gridiron with rope sets or counterweight sets.

Optimum height of this space for flying is slightly more than twice the highest scenery which is set on the wagon.

Permanently Installed Equipment Which Is Hung

Certain items of the permanent equipment of a stage are hung either on regular units of the flying system or on special units employing similar equipment and principles. These are: the fire curtain, the act curtain, light bridges, teasers, traveling tormentors, light battens, cycloramas, and part or all of the inner proscenium. Only those items which require equipment different from that of the regular flying systems already discussed need be considered here.

Steel-framed asbestos curtain, seen from the stage side, before back asbestos fabric was applied. Purdue University Music Hall.

Hydraulic check for asbestos curtain.

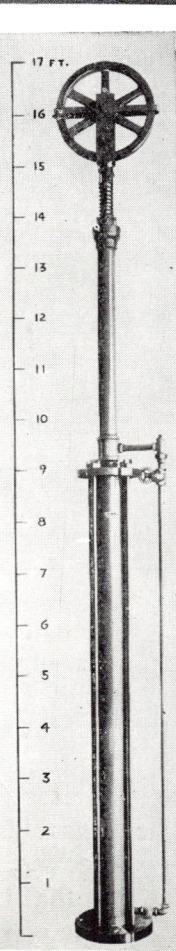

Asbestos curtain driving mechanism.

Codes

The building codes under which most theatres in the United States were built prescribed materials and devices so specifically that there was very little latitude left for the architect to produce anything but a conventional structure. This fact helps to account for the shortcomings of many theatres. As of this writing, the situation bids fair to improve. The New York City building code is in the process of being completely rewritten. For theatre buildings, a performance standard is projected. It is proposed that the architect may use any materials, form of building or equipment which will assure safety of the audience. And the safety standards as planned are based upon the psychological as well as physical factors which govern rate of audience flow. Supporting these salutary proposals is the contemplated requirement for rigid and continuing inspection and rigorous continuous training of theatre personnel in safety procedures.

Fire Curtain

Fire curtains may be of three types, the type selected for use depending upon the requirements of the National Board of Fire Insurance Underwriters and local building codes: flexible asbestos, asbestos cloth on rigid frame, and sheet steel curtain on rigid frame.

A flexible asbestos cloth curtain is made of wire-woven asbestos cloth of approved weight, tensile strength and fire-resistant rating, stretched between top and bottom steel pipe battens, hung on wire ropes—the number and spacing of which are specified by code—and permanently counterweighted with just less than enough weight to balance it.

Wire rope is regularly larger than that furnished in the counterweight system to give an added safety factor.

Loft blocks and head blocks are larger than those in the counterweight system and are mounted either on the gridiron (spaced as required by the spacing of the wire rope without regard for the regular cable slots) or on special channel brackets set into the proscenium wall. The head block is of the parallel type but with the groove for the operating line at the side of the wire rope grooves rather than in the center as in the counterweight system.

Counterweight carriage and track are of the lattice type and are located on the proscenium wall as close as convenient to the side of the opening. The track must be long enough to allow a run of the counterweight equal to the run of the bottom of the curtain (at least equal to the height of the proscenium opening).

Safety devices pertinent to the asbestos curtain are:

1. The release line, commonly called the cut line, which is the only device for securing the curtain in the high position. It is rigged in such a way that the curtain may be lowered by releasing or cutting it at either side of the stage or by the melting of fusible links placed in three

or more strategic positions along its length. Knives for cutting the release line are required standing equipment on each side of the proscenium.

2. Check chains which are attached to the gridiron and to the top batten of the curtain, of such length as to hold the top of the curtain above the proscenium opening. The check chains have the added effect of increasing the weight on the curtain side of the balance as the curtain is raised to overcompensate for the weight of the wire rope which passes to the counterweight side of the balance, and thus increase the tendency of the curtain to come down when released. As the curtain comes down, the weight of the chain is transferred to its fixed supports and the falling velocity of the curtain is reduced as it approaches the stage floor.

3. Hydraulic curtain check which reduces the downward speed of the curtain during the last few feet of its descent. This device is optional for lightweight curtains, whose downward velocity does not become destructive.

Guide wires are attached to the gridiron and the stage floor inside the smoke pockets to assure the straight running of the curtain.

Framed fire curtains are regularly too heavy to be operated manually. Electrically driven machines are installed on the gridiron. Regular operation is by electric switch located at the stage manager's station. Limit switches actuated by the counterweight stop the curtain at the top and bottom of its run, and a clutch release mechanism allows the curtain to descend when the release line (see above) is severed.

One type is connected by chain drive to the head block; another drives a shaft and drums upon which the wire ropes suspending respectively the counterweights and the curtain wind and unwind.

The fire curtain is purely a protective device and is maintained in perfect operating condition as such; its use for any other purpose in connection with performance is generally forbidden. In some states the legal requirement is that the fire curtain be raised within a short specified time before the beginning of the performance, and lowered immediately at the close of the performance. In such cases the assembling audience must look at the fire curtain for a considerable time; there is good reason that the fire curtain be designed and decorated in harmony with the auditorium. Paint used must be noncombustible.

Act Curtain

In all cases except those cited above, the act curtain is the device which separates the stage from the auditorium, before the performance, during intermissions, and after the performance. It is the largest single feature within the auditorium and it is directly in the line of audience vision. It is used to begin and end all performances, acts, and scenes, making the necessary transition into and out of the stage action. In operation and appearance, therefore, it must be sure, smooth, and pleasant.

Curtain actions: fly, draw or traverse, tableau, contour.

Detail: a draw curtain track.

Up-and-down Fly Action

The curtain is tied to a pipe batten and is operated like a unit of the counterweight system. Differences from a counterweight unit occur in the following parts: wire rope, loft blocks, head block and purchase line are larger to provide a greater safety factor and easier operation; counterweight and carriage are of the lattice type, fastened to the proscenium wall with the operating position near the stage manager's station.

Draw or Traverse Action

(The term traverse seems to be the basis for the stage vernacular corruption *traveler*.)

The curtain is divided at the center and is suspended at short intervals from carriers which slide or roll on a horizontal track located above the top of the proscenium opening. An endless operating line is rigged so that the curtain is parted in the middle and drawn to the sides of the opening, gathering in spaces allowed for it behind the proscenium on each side. Allowances must also be made for overlap of the two halves of the curtain behind the proscenium at both sides and at the top. Curtain tracks and carriers are designed to assure smooth and quiet operation. Devices (*rear-fold* and *back-pack*) are available which permit starting the whole curtain in motion simultaneously.

Tableau Action

The curtain is divided at the center and is suspended from a pipe batten. Two operating lines are run from the offstage top corners down through guide rings which are secured to the back of the curtain along carefully plotted diagonal curves to pickup points on the meeting edges. By pulling these lines, the curtain is caused to part at the center and rise diagonally to form a drapery.

Tableau curtains are spectacular and decorative but impractical as working act curtains. It is seldom possible to expose the entire acting area.

Contour (or Brail) Action

Several operating lines are run vertically, at regular intervals, down the back of the curtain through guide rings to pickup points along the bottom edge. By manual or motor operation of these lines, the curtain is caused to rise to selected heights. The shape, or contour, of the opening thus formed is variable. The limit to which one operating line may be raised above those next to it is determined by the amount of fullness made into the curtain.

Combination of Curtain Actions

It is possible to install an act curtain rigged so that a choice of actions is available to the users. It is desirable to install a combination rigging allowing the choice between fly and draw actions.

General Comment

Fly action requires fly space above the proscenium equal to the height of the opening. The other four actions may be installed in stages which lack fly space. The fly action is the most common in American theatres with the draw action a close second.

The act curtain is the most used single piece of apparatus in a theatre. It must be durable and dependable. It is an important decorative element in the house since the entire audience looks at it for a considerable time before the performance and during intermissions. The expenditure of money to procure attractive and durable fabrics, sturdy construction and dependable operation is warranted. Fabrics which are permanently flameproof or capable of being flameproofed without deterioration are essential.

Proscenium Framing Equipment

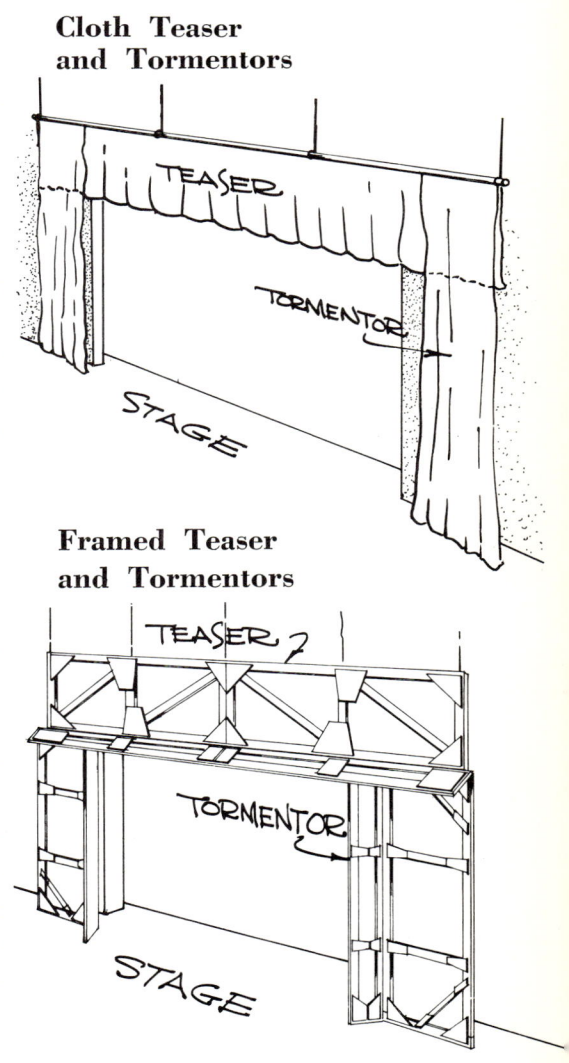

It is generally considered desirable to have some type of device directly upstage of the act curtain by which the height and width of the proscenium opening may be varied when the act curtain is closed. There are several suitable devices.

Cloth Teaser and Tormentors

These consist of a drapery (*teaser*) hung with fullness across the top of the opening, attached to a pipe batten and rigged to fly, and two tall, narrow draperies (*tormentors*) hung from short traverse tracks and rigged to draw at the sides of the proscenium. By raising or lowering the teaser and drawing the tormentors on- or offstage the height and width of the opening may be varied.

Cloth teaser and tormentors are decorative if made of the same fabric as the act curtain but they do not assure a definite limit to the opening because drafts may blow the curtains, and they may be displaced by various accidents. Furthermore, since the sight lines past their edges are very acute, it is necessary to place lighting instruments or other stage apparatus well above the bottom edge of the teaser and well offstage from the edges of the tormentors in order to conceal them.

Framed Teaser and Tormentors

These consist of a horizontal unit (teaser) across the top of the opening and two vertical units (tormentors) at the sides, each having a plane surface parallel to the proscenium wall and another (narrow) plane surface at the lower edge in the case of the teaser and at the onstage edges in the case of the tormentors, the second plane surface being set at an angle of from 90 to 135 degrees to the first. The result is a rigid frame surrounding the proscenium opening with a *reveal* or thickness receding upstage. The construction is of lightweight wood or metal covered with either fabric or rigid sheet material. The teaser is suspended from a flying unit. The tormentors are either set on the stage floor, mounted on small castered platforms or suspended on dead-hung tracks to allow movement on- and offstage. If hung from tracks the same tracks may support a *follower* curtain which will be drawn onstage

Contour curtain, Radio City Music Hall.

by the tormentor and maintain the side masking. The narrow reveal affords concealment for stage lighting instruments placed near to the acting area.

The framed teaser may be made an integral part of a flying light bridge (q.v.) and the tormentors may be developed into tormentor light towers, containing mounting positions for lighting instruments, platforms for operators, and access ladders.

The ultimate development of the proscenium framing device is a telescoping inner proscenium, constructed entirely of metal, motor-driven, and controlled from a remote position, incorporating the first flying light bridge and tormentor light towers.

Overhead Light Battens

The permanent stage equipment installation includes apparatus to provide mounting positions for lighting instruments and power supply for those instruments in space above the stage. Requirements of these positions are stated in Chapter 12. Certain battens of the counterweight system (q.v.) are selected as light battens, are equipped with counterweight carriages large enough to balance the heavy loads of lighting instruments, and are fitted with power outlets fed by multiconductor cable suspended from the gridiron.

Because there must be flexibility in the overhead light mounting positions, the cables must be installed so that they may be attached to any of several battens. There must be a take-up device to remove excess hanging cable from the fly space when light battens are raised high in the flies.

Flying Light Bridge

The most important overhead light mounting position is directly behind the teaser. Here are located spotlights for lighting acting areas, strip lights for blending and toning both the acting area and the settings, and special instruments for a number of particular uses. It is very desirable that operators be stationed in this position for manipulation of instruments during, as well as between, scenes of performances.

A flying light bridge constructed of metal, suspended from wire ropes, counterweighted and rigged to fly satisfies this requirement. The bridge may be lowered to the stage floor to facilitate the mounting of the many instruments which must be attached to it. Access to the bridge is afforded either by a rope ladder from the stage floor or by side galleries connecting with the fly galleries.

Stability can be imparted to the light bridge by brackets extending from its ends to vertical guide tracks mounted on the proscenium wall.

There have been some developments of combinations of double light battens and teaser to be operated together to comprise a light bridge, or separately if desired. Motor drives for bridge, light battens and framed teaser, capable of optional positioning and with ganging controls and limit switches, are desirable.

There are differences of opinion among authorities regarding the value of the flying light bridge in the first overhead light position. Those who favor it argue for its stability, its carrying capacity, its variety of light mounting positions, but above all for its capability of supporting operators in a position where they are frequently needed (1) to adjust instruments, (2) to operate follow spots, and especially (3) to operate projection apparatus. Those who do not favor the bridge minimize the need for human operators and argue in favor of double light battens. No one disputes the need to mount many diverse lighting instruments in this very important position.

Light bridge at the Adams Memorial Theatre, Williams College. The teaser is integral with the bridge. Note the swivel arms on the vertical stanchions of the bridge, the position of the border lights and the work lights for the stage.

View toward the proscenium, Adams Memorial Theatre, showing the light bridge and teaser, the tormentor, the lighting cables for the bridge, the fire curtain operating line, the stage manager's control panel, a lighting panel and the underside of the fly gallery.

The fly gallery projects outward to afford access to the light bridge. Below the gallery there is a perch with lighting positions. The tormentor flipper is divided into sections near the top to permit setting the teaser at various heights.

Very large stages, as for opera and presentation, may require additional flying bridges for the mounting and operation of lighting instruments in the fly space farther upstage. These take the place of upstage light battens.

Motion Picture Screen and Loud-speaker

Necessary to the production of motion pictures, the screen and loud-speakers must be cleared if the stage is to be used alternately for live shows. Most effective clearing is achieved by flying the screen with speaker in place on a motor-driven counterweight set.

Screens must be rigged upstage of framing curtains or panels, which adjust the screen width for the aspect ratios for various types of projection. With the normal 19 foot 6 inch height, widths vary from 36 feet for wide screen (aspect ratio 1.85 to 1) to 47 feet for Cinemascope (aspect ratio 2.35 to 1). Todd A-O is 2.2 to 1. Screens normally have a 3-inch black border.

Only in Cinerama, where it is permanently installed, is the curved projection screen essential. It has theoretical merit, but the small distortion caused by a flat screen is less than that which is apparent from seats close to the side of a curved screen. Also, a curved screen is difficult to rig and handle.

Fixed Winches

Electrically powered winches, controlled at either the stage manager's station or the synchronous winch system console, may be installed to operate the framed teaser, overhead light battens, light bridge and motion picture screen and speaker. They must have effective limit switches and infinitely variable positioning within the limits.

Concert Set

The concert set, requisite for music, must be massive if it is to be any good. Special rigging may be required to move it if it is not permanent. The ceiling can be flown backstage, in the overhead proscenium slot or even into the house over the orchestra pit. The sides can roll on dollies or swing and fly. So the concert set must be designed, and its storage and handling must be developed, before the stage machinery plan can be completed.

Control

The stage director and the scene designer are designers of spatial relationships, no matter what form of theatre they are using.

The stage director, with whom the choreographer may be combined for purposes of this statement, is concerned with the placement and movement of performers according to his plan for creating the maximum possible perceptual and responsive effect in the audience. Each director has his own body of principles for doing this, and each play calls for a unique selection and combination of these principles.

The scene designer, using his specialized knowledge of the visual effects of space, form, color and light, is committed to helping the stage director achieve the effects which he wants. Thus they become a working team which must use the stage, its parts, its equipment and the scenery designed for the particular play for the purposes stated.

The summation of many plays, directed by many directors working with many designers, postulates extreme, almost infinite, variability in the acting positions, paths of movement, scenic arrangement, and the nature of changes of these which must be made possible by the stage, its parts, and its equipment. The ideal specification of variability of size, shape, position, arrangement, and rate of change for these components can be easily stated in two words: *No limitations*. Two other words must be added to make the specification complete: *Absolutely reliable*.

The first part of the specification is an impossibility because there are finite limits to space in any building. The second is an imperative which all serious workers aspire to satisfy. It is pertinent to examine the amount and kinds of movement which theatrical production may require of the stage and its components and to evaluate the means of providing operation and control.

Within the limits of human strength, sight and reach, the human being himself is the most effective combination of prime mover and control device. The application of force and the control of the application is subject to a most delicate and rapid sensing system which is coupled with a judgement system capable, when trained, of adjusting to infinitely small changes in the influencing environment. The entire art of theatrical production is an aggregate of the functioning of a number of such human systems in response to an actively changing environment called a performance.

If the movement of components of the production involves the application of forces beyond the strength, sight, or reach of a human being or if the number of movements exceeds his capabilities, the possibility must be sought of extending his senses, multiplying his strength and multiplying his capabilities. This can be done in either of two ways: multiplying the number of human beings, or applying other sources of power and other sensing and control systems. The latter has been the method of electromechanical technology.

Electromechanical systems are capable of multiplying the force to be applied far beyond the capabilities of a single human being or even of a large group. They are capable of extending the effectiveness of a human being beyond a single location and thus encompass locations for power application, selectively or collectively. They are capable of sensing distances of movement and rates of movement and of sending back to the control position the necessary subtle information about both distance and rate of movement. Precautionary devices against overrun or overloading and against too abrupt stopping can be built into the control systems.

In most instances outside the theatre, the application and control of power has been toward the performance of reasonably limited tasks. The multiple variation required in the theatre has not been present nor has the subtlety of response dictated by rapidly changing environmental conditions been so exacting.

A planned performance is essential to the theatrical experience. All parts of the production are carefully studied, rehearsed and drilled in advance of showing to an audience. Yet it is axiomatic that no two performances are the same, for many reasons, and the efforts of all theatre workers from leading actress to stagehand are nevertheless bent toward adjusting to the difference in such a way that the total uniform effect upon the audience will be the maximum achievable by that particular performance. The fact that the performance is minutely planned seems to indicate the possibility of programming it for electronic control; the fact of intrinsic difference indicates that any such electronic control must be under the ultimate control of a human sense-and-respond system capable of exercising theatrical judgement. A movement may be preset but the human system must be able to start it, control its rate, and have the option of stopping it. If no differences are sensed by the human system the movement may be allowed to go as programmed; if some are, the human system must take control.

Components of the flying system should be capable of vertical movement, individually or in selective groupings, with limits set by the stage floor and the gridiron. Speed should be variable between 2 feet per minute and 5 feet per second. Load limits of 250 pounds on a single line and 1000 pounds on a group are sufficient. Sequential starting of at least three groups in the same direction with overlapping movement should be possible.

Curtains should be movable in either horizontal or vertical directions with variable rates up to 5 feet per second.

Light bridges should be capable of vertical movement at a fixed rate which may be slow (3 to 10 feet per minute). Light battens should follow the requirements for flying system components.

Proscenium framing devices (teasers and tormentors) may have a fixed, slow rate (about 10 feet per minute).

Wall panels, doors, etc., for side stages or for changing house shape, may have fixed low rate. Movement of these will not be part of a performance.

Forestage or open stage may have fixed, slow rate. The extent to which this component is subdivided into smaller units and the ramifications of individual and selectively grouped control of the movement of the units is a design decision. Minimal working positions for the forestage are orchestra pit level, house floor level and stage level. Variation of levels beyond these three contributes to design variety.

Seating area sections may be elevated, tilted or rotated and displaced horizontally in multiform theatres. Rate of movement may be slow and fixed.

Concert sets: side and back walls may be cleared from the acting area by movement horizontally, and ceiling sections by movement vertically with rotary movement about a horizontal axis to clear the fly loft for the operation of scenery. Movement may be slow and at a fixed rate.

Stage wagons, revolving stages and discs must be capable of movement at varying rates through varying distances with limits set by the stage walls.

The electromechanical systems to impart and control the movement of the afore-listed components may have digital controls which will discriminate movement by increments of one-quarter of an inch, but terminal positioning at the end of a movement must be precise within one thirty-second of an inch.

It is therefore theoretically possible, though it has not yet been realized, to bring control of all the above-listed components under one system making use of memory devices, such as cards, drums or tapes to record and preset a series of movements of selected components in a selected sequence, with variations of rate and distance within the capabilities of each component.

The control of intensity of stage lighting instruments is generally of an analogous nature and will be covered in Chapter 12; the control by electromechanical means of the height, azimuth, angular elevation, color and beam spread of spotlights has been developed in only rudimentary form and may yet be integrated with the digital system used for controlling stage components.

Whereas electromechanical control systems greatly extend the capabilities of the human being and are therefore desirable adjuncts of stage and theatre operation, they must nevertheless partake of the reliability of the human being both in terms of responding to ultimate human controls based on human sense, judgement and response and in terms of the essential reliability and fail-safe character of the responsible human being.

The area of decision for the theatre planner embraces:

1. The degree to which such systems will be installed. This involves a value judgement regarding the economies to be effected, the efficiency and effectiveness which may be realized, the initial investment and the disposition toward continuing maintenance which any intricate system requires.

2. The most effective control position. Visual surveillance of the moving components seems to dictate that the control position for onstage

components be backstage, and for out-front components, at the back of the house.

3. The expedient location of intermediate equipment such as amplifiers, alternators, etc. Since large quantities of current and voltages up to 600 volts are involved, it is desirable to place these components directly between the power entrance to the building and the points of power application, with resulting minimum runs of wire, Requirements of silence during performance dictate soundproof vaults. This equipment may be remote from the stage and should not be onstage in any case; it may be in low-value, unfinished basement space.

Lighting control, Tyrone Guthrie Theatre, Minneapolis.

12: Light

The use of light as a component of theatrical performance is highly developed artistically and technically. It is different from conventional uses of light to afford illumination for living or working, for specialized functions such as driving automobiles or landing aircraft, or for the artistic purposes of making buildings, rooms, sales displays or works of art appear attractive.

Stanley R. McCandless has analyzed the theatrical functions of light as being *visibility, naturalism, design and mood.* Fully treated and understood, these four terms do encompass the whole function of light in theatrical performance, but they must be understood in terms of the moving, changing, rising and falling, exciting, contrasting, emphatic, heightened, selected, sometimes distorted and stylized creation which a theatrical performance may be. The author, director, choreographer, scenic designer, costume designer and performers are all intent on producing in an audience a state of attention, interest, vicarious participation, emphatic response and emotional transport. This can only be achieved if the lighting is completely integrated with their efforts and, in addition, makes its own unique contribution in stimulation of the audience's senses by its properties of intensity, color, dimension and change.

Light has a dramatic function in that it is able to reveal and conceal people and things, show them in many modes, show many varying aspects of one sculptural form, simulate natural effects, create unnatural effects, please or displease, excite or soothe, disturb or mollify the audience.

For light to produce the enhancement of theatrical performance of which it is capable, the installation and operation of lighting equipment in a theatre must be carefully studied, thoroughly understood and adequately accommodated.

Lighting the Actor

An actor is seen by virtue of light reflected from his person toward the spectator. The spectator sees the portion of the actor's person which the light strikes. Thus the degree to which an actor is seen depends upon the direction of the light with relation to the spectator's line of vision. Light directed at the actor at right angles to the spectator's line of sight,

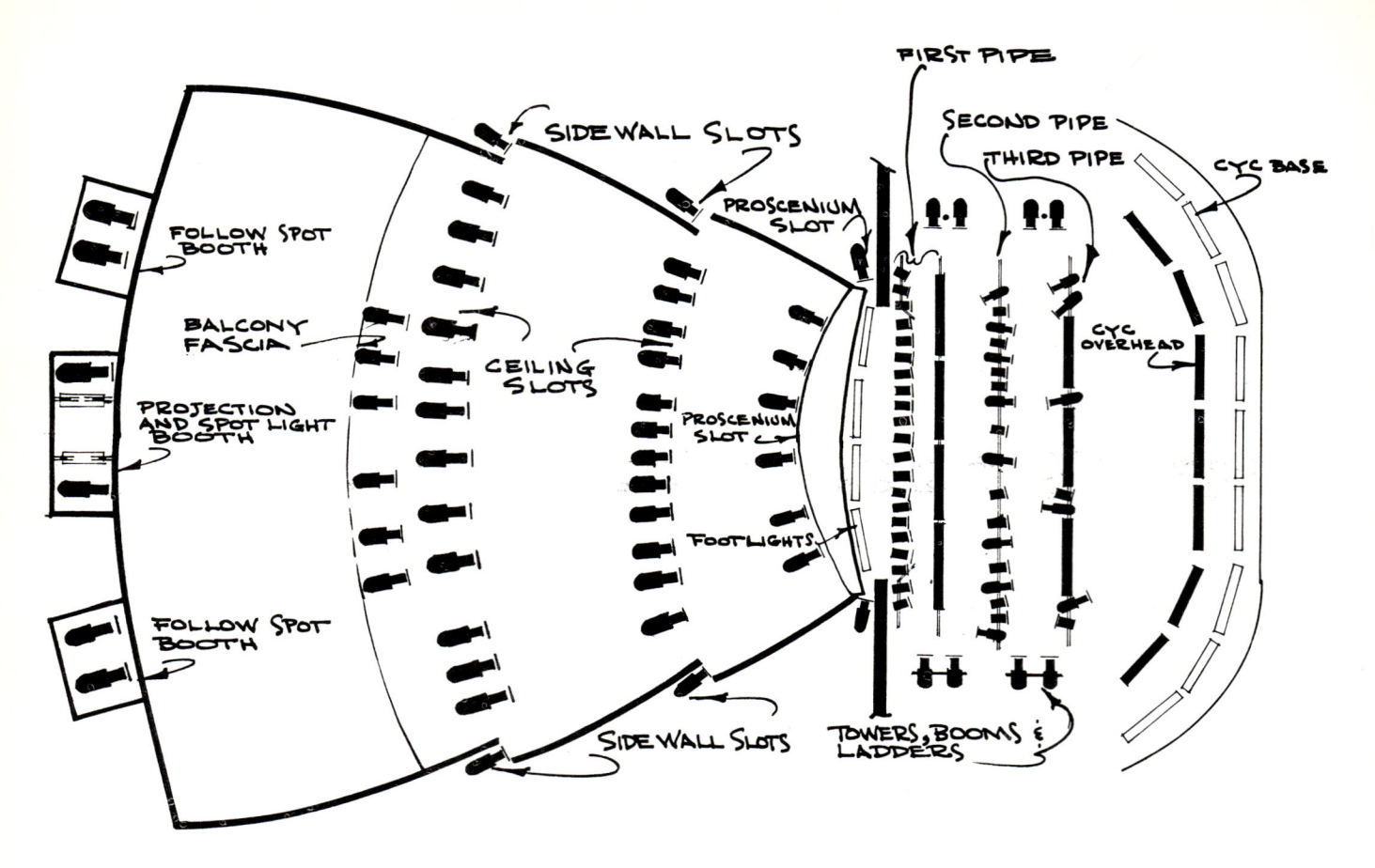

Light mounting positions for a proscenium theatre.

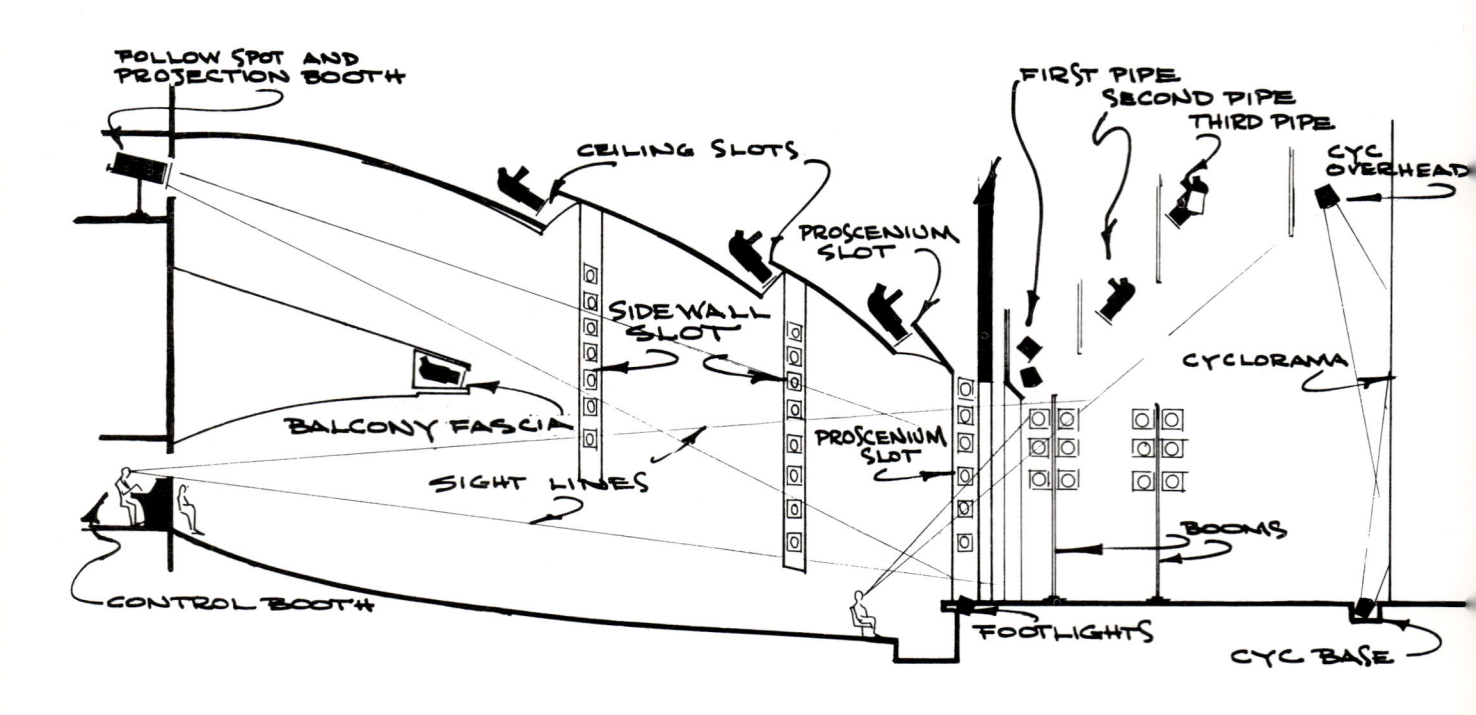

whether from above, below, or horizontally from the side, illuminates very little of the actor which the spectator can see. From above, for example, the top of the head, the ridge of the nose, the shoulders, and isolated outcrops are lighted; all else is not lighted and is therefore practically invisible. Similar results with respect to different parts of the figure obtain when the light is directed from below or from the sides. Such lighting is sometimes dramatically useful, to be sure, but not primarily as a means of seeing the actor. It accounts for the bizarre results when, as is too often done in schools, someone tries to light actors with footlights and border lights.

Pursuing this logic, it would seem that the best direction of light would be on the line of the spectator's vision, since thus the whole expanse of the actor as seen by the spectator would be illuminated. This is not the case. Light from a full front direction, as from lights mounted on the face of a first balcony, actually illuminates the actor too completely for good visibility. The actor is a mobile form and his face is a plastic medium of expression. It has three dimensions and surface modeling, the changing character and quality of which cannot be distinguished by a spectator without some play of light and shade. Light striking the actor from the front, diagonally above, achieves this, illuminates the figure to delineate form, and blends light and shade so that facial expression is emphasized and clarified. A balance of light from the opposite front-diagonal intensifies the modeling and provides illumination in the shadows. Light diagonally from above, furthermore, strikes the floor after passing the actor, projects the actor's shadow or shadows where they are least noticeable and least distracting, and keeps unwanted light off the scenery.

Although the front-diagonal direction is the most important for lighting actors, the full frontal direction, the low-side-diagonal directions and the straight-up and straight-down directions may each be uniquely valuable for the creation of certain visual effects. It can be logically stated that *any* direction in which light may be aimed at an actor in any part of the acting area will be needed at some time and that the degree to which a theatre satisfies this need is a measure of its adequacy. It therefore becomes a matter of providing as many light mounting positions as possible and, if limitations must be imposed, of discriminating between possible positions on the basis of most frequent use and relative ease or cost of installation.

Lighting the Scenery

Lighting the scenery fulfills first the function of naturalism. It renders the scenic investiture believable or acceptable to the viewer. It also is a major element in design and mood. It blends the visibility light and establishes the dominant color. Light directed at the scenery is usually diffuse and general. Since scenic surfaces are very large in comparison to actors' faces, they must have a much lower illumination, or they will take attention away from the actor.

No matter how important it is to have the scenery appear to be lighted from the source naturalism indicates—the fireplace, the window, the horizontal rays of the setting sun, the chandelier—the audience won't see much if those are the only sources. The most used devices for lighting the scenery are border lights, one row hung immediately upstage of the proscenium, one or more rows farther upstage as necessary.

Footlights are second in importance for this purpose and have the additional function of providing much illumination where it is most needed in some dance sequences. Footlights have the great limitation, if inexpertly used, of making everything on stage appear two-dimensional. Footlight designs must be complete before the design of the apron can be finished.

Many special effects which conventionally require footlights, among them the lighting of front curtains, can be achieved most efficiently by instruments either mounted on the balcony face or set into a hollow balcony parapet.

Light mounting positions for a three-proscenium theatre.

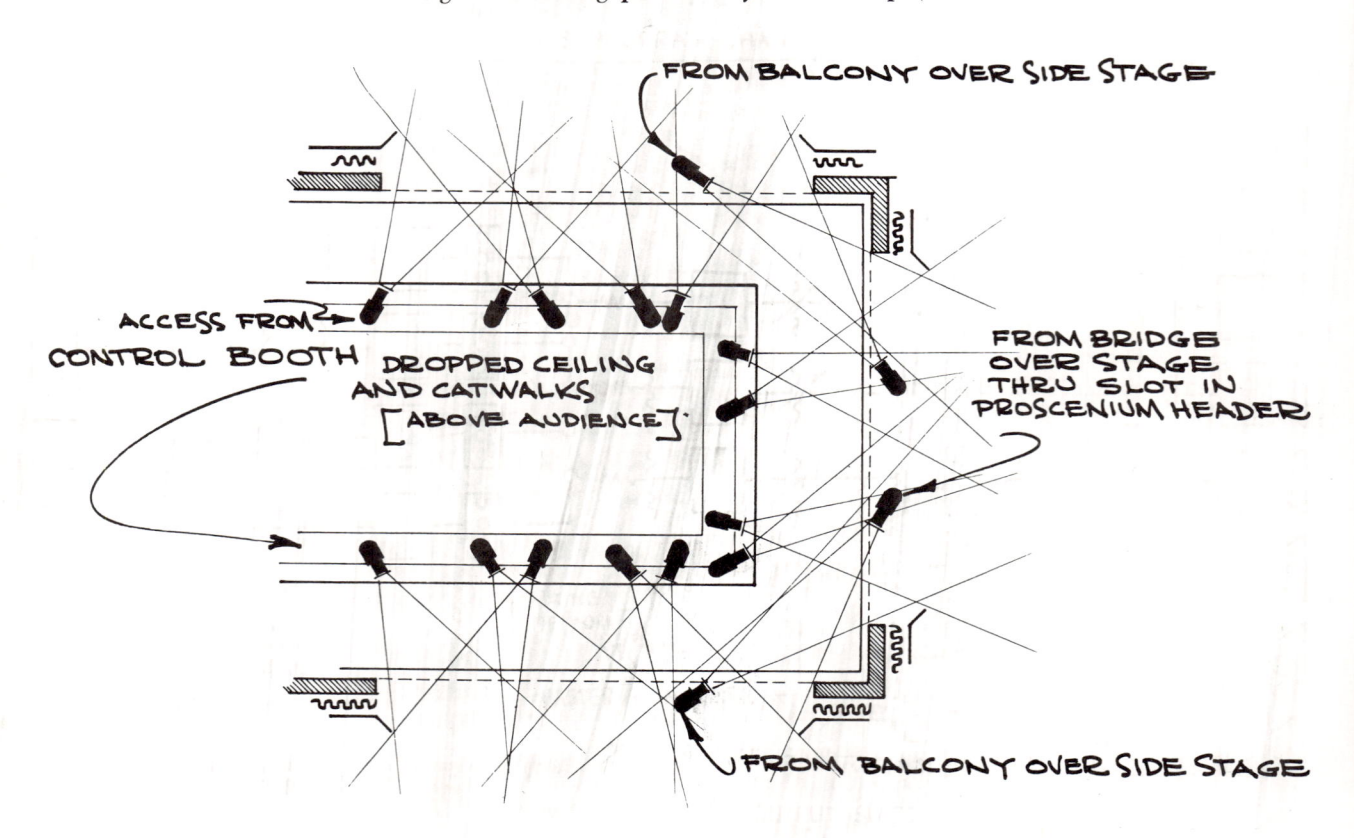

Backgrounds

The principal background surface is the cyclorama, or sky dome. There are two architectural requisites for cyclorama lighting:

1. Provision for flying a bridge, frame, or batten on which overhead cyclorama lights may be mounted;

2. Essential with a permanent cyclorama, usually desirable: a horizon lighting trough, to provide upward projection of light onto the cyclorama with minimum masking. The size and position of the cyclorama trough must be established by detailed planning of the cyclorama before the trapped area can be laid out or the stage floor structure designed.

In lighting scenery and background, the smaller the angle of light projection to the audience line of vision, the more even the distribution of light can be. When the cyclorama is lighted from a source close to it, it is difficult to keep it from being bright near the source and dark far from it. This situation accounts for the distances prescribed between ground rows in Chapter 11. Backings other than the cyclorama are lighted from overhead pipes, side towers or tormentors, or special instruments mounted on stands or on the scenery itself.

Special Effects

Motivating lights, the sunlight streaming through the window, the flickering light from the burning barn, are produced by instruments mounted in any mounting position which will accomplish the task.

Lights used for emphasis, to give one area more prominence than another, and for purposes of definition may often be mounted on balcony fascia, from which position the curtains and drops for scenes played in one may also be illuminated.

Other locations for specials include:

1. Extension of the optimum ceiling slot down the sides of the auditorium.

2. Ceiling and side proscenium slots for gauze and tormentor lighting, transformations, disappearances, fog and clouds.

3. Spotlight booths at the rear of the balcony at either side of the projection booth.

4. Pockets in the stage floor located at either side of and behind the acting area.

The long finger of light from the follow spot is a dramatic element in itself. It is used in spectacle, presentation, opera and musical shows. Follow spots require room. If they are used at all, it is often well to use many. The Radio City Music Hall uses eighteen. Follow spot operating positions require a substantial portion of the booth at the back of the balcony. Where scenery or motion pictures are projected from the rear, the stage must be deep enough to make possible beam spread sufficiently wide to cover the background area.

Projected Scenery

Described as scenery in Chapter 9, projection must also be considered in this chapter as a part of stage lighting. Lens projection from the rear requires distance behind the projection screen at least equal to the width of the screen. Multi-screen projection from the rear holds the distance requirement down by using several screens and projectors and limiting the screen width. Direct beam projection from the front requires a projection bridge or gallery occupying approximately 6 feet of fly space centered on the stage directly upstage of the act curtain.

Though stage lighting instruments change in size and power, the essential principles on which they are based, and the places where they are used, remain standard. There are four basic types: (1) spotlights, (2) strip lights, (3) floodlights, (4) projectors.

Specials include any type of instrument required for a particular function, designed and built for the job: fireplace glow, electrified oil lamps.

In designing ceiling and side-wall slots, and recesses in balcony fascia, the architect must provide space for all the types of instruments that may be used in all locations. He will not need to provide much tolerance since, as stage lighting instruments are improved, their size tends to decrease. He must provide:

1. Clear space for all necessary movement of the lighting instruments through a predetermined directional range.

2. Surface jogs, setbacks, beams or coffers to permit beams of light to pass from instruments to stage without spilling unwanted light on wall or ceiling surfaces. The breaks supplied by ceiling slots may facilitate adjusting the ceiling and wall sections to the optimum angles for sound distribution.

Light mounting equipment above an auditorium ceiling slot. Vertical and horizontal adjustment; clear space for instruments and clear space in front of instruments.

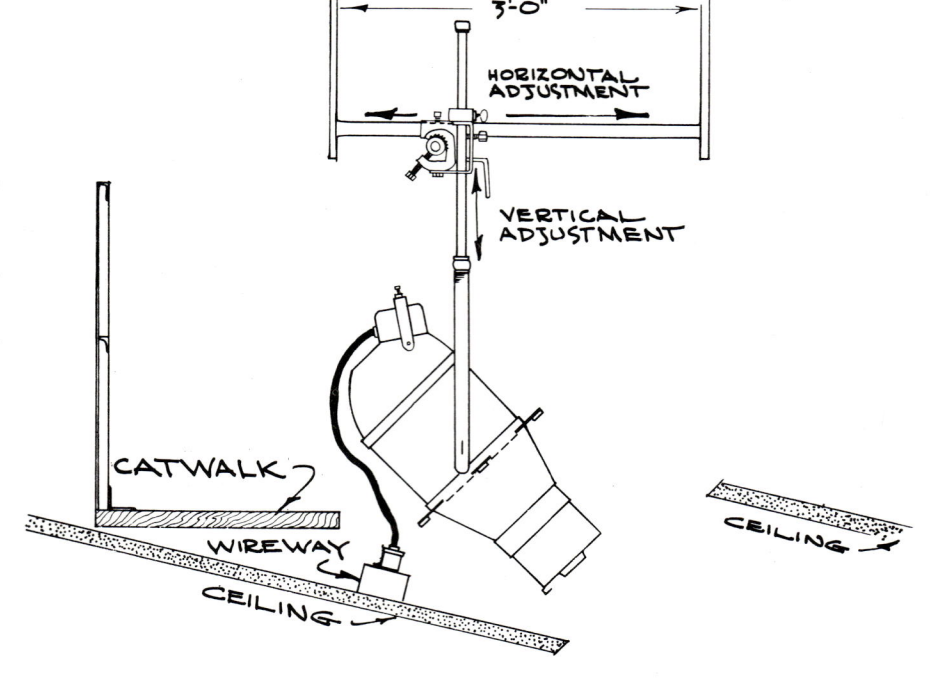

3. Access to all concealed lighting positions from backstage by direct and unobstructed routes apart from the routes of audience traffic.

4. Adequate working space for operators in each lighting position.

5. Mounting apparatus adjustable to allow the use of various types and sizes of instruments. Modern practice keeps all stage lighting instruments in a theatre interchangeable in location. This practice is essential in community theatres, most of which can afford only limited amounts of lighting equipment.

6. Electrical outlets equal to the maximum number of instruments which may be placed in any position. Connectors on all instruments standardized to fit all outlets.

Ceiling slots with ample space for operators to service and aim instruments in all desired directions. Catwalks for access. John Fitzgerald Kennedy Theatre, University of Hawaii.

A well-planned theatre must have provision for placing stage lighting instruments in all of the following positions:

Acting area spotlights, follow spotlights, front projections, special effects on curtains or front scrims.
  Essential for proper lighting of actors in frontal acting areas.
  Slots should extend from wall to wall.
  Requirements: Clear space for positioning and rotating instruments in plan and section, for maximal aiming. Clear working space for opera-

Instrument Mounting Positions

Ceiling Slots

265

tors. Instruments within reach of operators. Slots spaced not more than 15 feet apart measuring from the stage outward. Bridges, acoustical panels or catwalks may be substituted for slots if there is no hung ceiling.

Side-wall Slots   Acting area spotlights.

Essential for lighting the front corners of the onstage acting area and the front corners of forestage areas. Useful for low-angled side lighting. Slots should extend down from the ceiling to a level approximately 10 feet above stage level.

Side-wall slots can be vertical extensions of the ceiling slots.

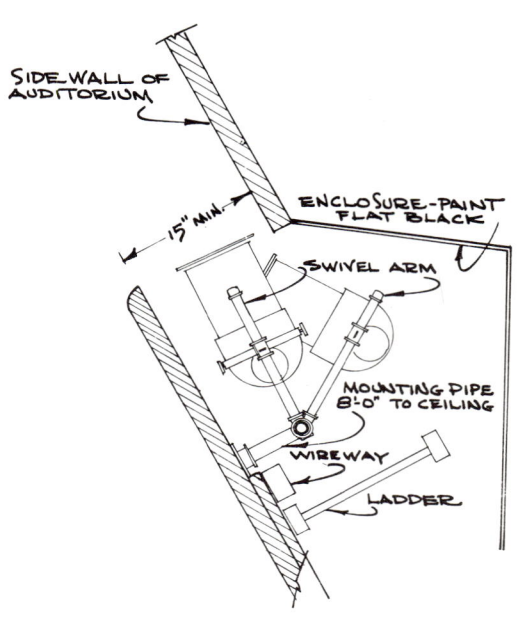

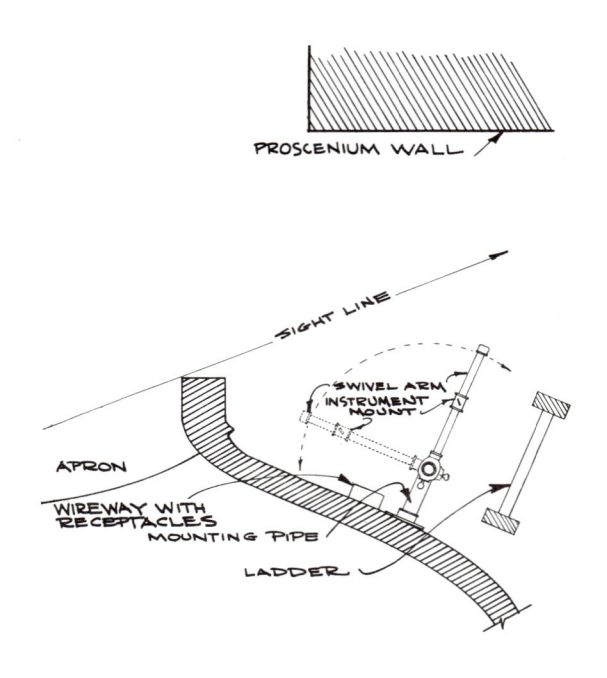

ABOVE: *Proscenium wall slot with entrance space.*

UPPER LEFT: *Side-wall light slot.*

LEFT: *A box boom; improvised position and concealment for lighting instruments which might better be in side-wall slots.*

266

Occasional acting area spotlights, especially when the full proscenium opening is used and when actors get close to the proscenium columns on the sides. More useful for special effects such as strong shafts of light directed sharply across the forestage or sharply downward for striking or grotesque effects, or for a wash of light on a scrim or curtain hung in the proscenium opening.

The ceiling proscenium slot may be used for a projection screen for slide shows or motion pictures with the house curtain closed to allow work backstage.

Proscenium Slots (sides and ceiling)

Spotting booth at the rear of the balcony. Automatic feed, 150 ampere, arc follow spots are equipped for the control of color and the shape of the beam. Radio City Music Hall.

Traditional in the theatre and still by no means outmoded is the strong lighting of principal performers by beams of light directed from the back of the house.

One spotlight booth, whose principal function is motion picture projection on the center line, is minimal; two located well toward the sides of the house are better. A ceiling slot near the back of the house may serve as the follow-spotting position if it is arranged to accommodate operators.

Spotlight Booth

The front of the balcony is a position used in commercial theatres for acting area spotlights. This is from necessity rather than choice because these theatres seldom have ceiling and side-wall slots. The balcony fascia is an appropriate position for supplemental, rather than primary, actor spotlighting and the proper position for instruments for frontal illumination of curtains, drops, etc., hung in the proscenium opening and for the projection of images on such surfaces.

Balcony Fascia

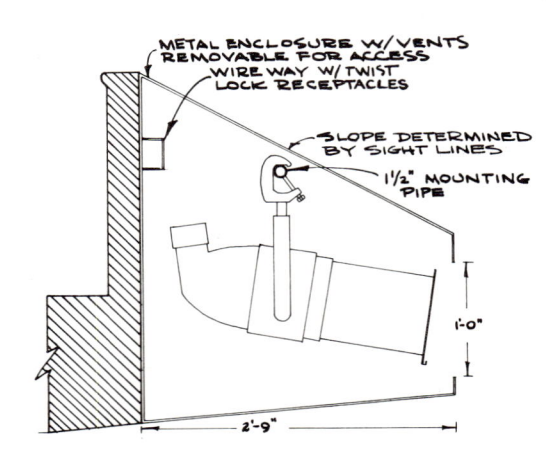

ABOVE: *Balcony front spotlights in a New York theatre. Absence of ceiling slots makes it necessary to use this position.*

LEFT: *Section of a balcony box which may be designed into a new theatre.*

Occasional special actor spotlights for such effects as campfire or fireplace light, and grotesque lighting. For this purpose a footlight trough is better than installed footlight units. Striplights in the footlight trough are sometimes used to produce a wash of toning light over the scenery or over front curtains, scrims, or drops. In combination with the proscenium slots, a scrim can be made opaque or given various degrees of transparency or can be tinted with a wash of colored light.

Conventionally called *first pipe, second pipe,* and so on, although recently developed techniques substitute other devices for the usual steel light-mounting pipes, those positions constitute narrow bands of space extending the full width of the acting area, from 7 to 10 feet apart up- and downstage, where all kinds of lighting instruments may be mounted for various purposes.

Each of the overhead pipes is potentially a location for acting area spotlights, strip lights for blending the acting areas, strips or floods for illuminating the scenery, projection machines for creating scenic images, or beam projectors for back-lighting the acting area.

Footlights

Overstage Positions

ABOVE: *Detail of light bridge framed entirely in Unistrut. Plywood floor is removable. Frames may be uncoupled to serve as separate light battens. Instruments may be attached to two or more faces of each piece of Unistrut.*

LEFT: *Light bridge constructed of pipe and structural steel. The teaser, right, is of wood and hardboard and is flown separately but may be attached to the bridge. Access to the bridge is from galleries on the proscenium wall. Sweet Briar College.*

Light bridge from stage. Border lights and spotlights are serviced from bridge floor. Also shown are the continuous proscenium light slot with the motion picture screen in the slot. Sweet Briar College.

Cables to bridge and light battens pass over bicycle wheel pulleys to idler counterweights and thence to junction boxes.

The first pipe position is by far the most used because it must carry the spotlights which cover most of the acting area, special area spots, the blending and toning lights for the acting area and the settings, image projectors and follow spots. Frequently operators must be in this position during the performance. Hence a flying light bridge may be hung here.

Second, third, fourth and subsequent pipes serve as positions for blending and toning strips for acting area and scenery and for beam projectors or spotlights to back-light or top-light actors.

The cyclorama pipe is frequently a complex battery of strip lights arrayed to furnish the principal illumination of the cyclorama. Careful positioning and aiming are necessary to produce even distribution of light over the cyclorama; three or four colors are used in combination with intensity variation to produce color changes. High wattages are necessary to facilitate the range of brightness required.

Variable Instrument Mounting Positions

Although the overstage positions are designated and thought of generally as fixed, to use them always in their fixed positions tends to reduce lighting design to a formula which is inimical to the postulate of variety as the essence of theatre art. It is therefore axiomatic that the overhead positions must be variable in height, location in horizontal plane, and instrumentation.

Side Stage Positions

Just as the side-wall slot positions in the house allow lighting the forestage and frontal acting areas at lower angles than do the ceiling slots, so the side stage positions facilitate directing beams of light sharply across the stage for strong side-lighting effects through openings in the scenery or through the openings created by the wings of a wing-and-drop setting.

Light mounting pipes behind the tormentors, galleries on the side walls of the stage house or pipes and metal frames, known respectively as booms and ladders, hung from the gridiron provide these side stage positions.

Stage Floor Positions

Footlights at the front edge of the stage, though no longer used in modern theatre styles to light actors, still have their uses. They light the scenery, and they are used to imitate archaic lighting of period productions.

An essential floor position is the base of the cyclorama. Here a continuous pit around the bottom of the cyclorama, equipped with sectional lids, contains the striplights which illuminate the bottom of the cyclorama.

Other stage floor positions are indeterminate: an individual setting and lighting design may require locating instruments at any position within the acting and scenery areas of the stage. Portable instruments are therefore placed where dictated by the design, exerting no specific demand on the plan of the stage. However, the location of instruments beneath the stage floor, directed upward, requires stage floor traps.

Arena Lighting

Lighting in the arena form is entirely a matter of lighting the actors and the acting area. There is no scenery to receive special lighting. Since the actors are seen by the audience seated all around them, the principles which govern lighting actors in the proscenium form apply fourfold and there must be instrument mounting positions for spotlighting each acting area from four sides as if each were a proscenium. The principle of front diagonal direction is still valid.

Arena lighting is *candid* in that, although it is desirable to keep lighting instruments outside the range of audience vision, doing this is so difficult that the arena lighting designer gives up and lets the audience see the instruments. The best that can be achieved in minimizing the distraction is to see that no bright light sources are inside the upward visual angle of 30 degrees. This is not always possible or always observed.

The desired condition is that no member of the audience will be disturbed or distracted by bright light sources within his zone of vision.

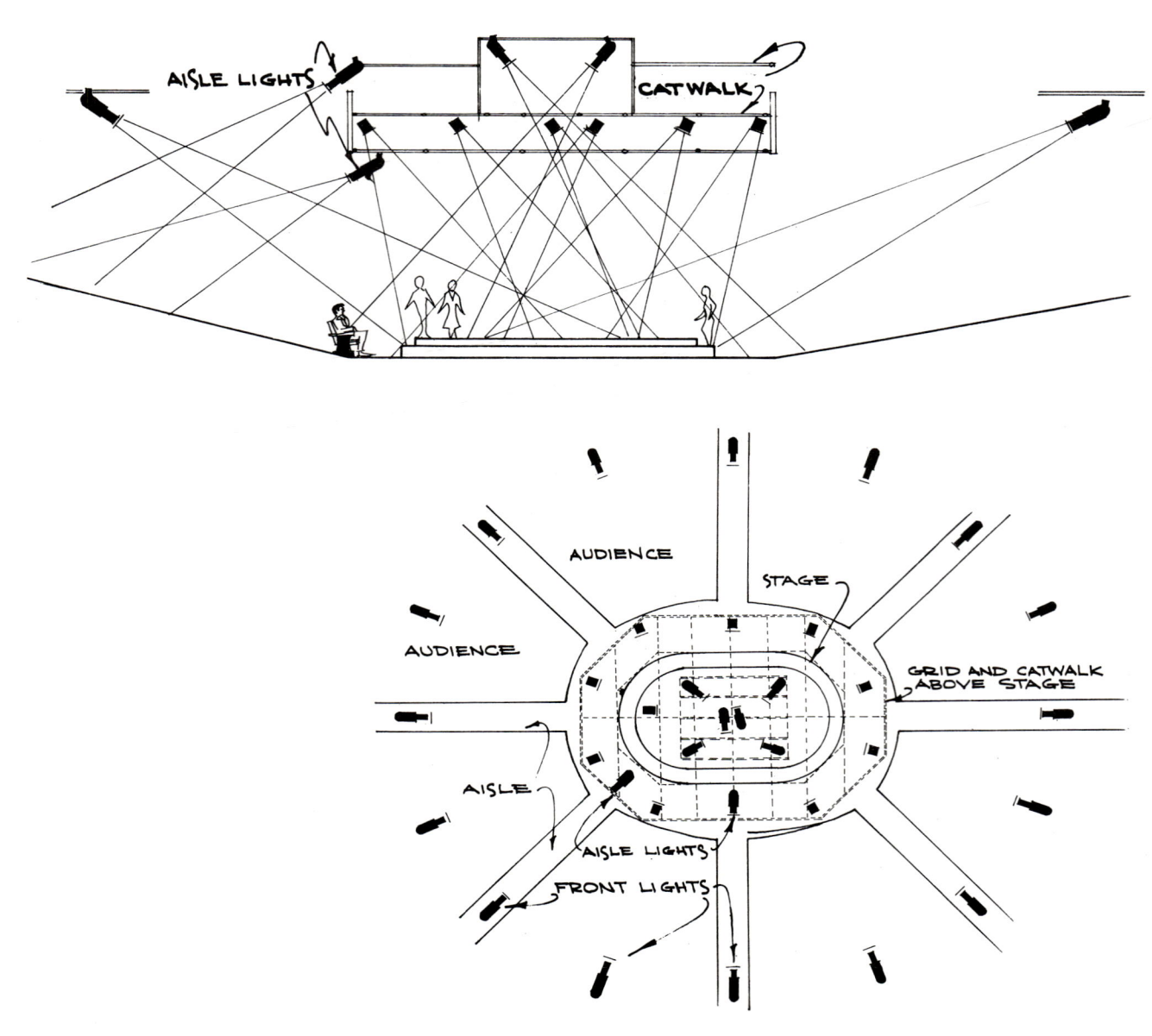

Lighting layout for arena theatre.

Open Stage Lighting

The condition of audience seeing lighting instruments applies in the open stage to the degree that the seating area extends around the acting area on one side and the light mounting positions extend around it on the other.

Control of Stage Lighting

The first three properties of light—intensity, color and dimension—are controlled for the purpose of accomplishing the previously stated theatrical functions of light. Control is implicit in the fourth property—change—just as change is implicit in the control of the other three properties. Even if the lighting of a performance is to have no internal change, the capability of change is required to bring the lighting to optimum conditions of visibility, naturalness and visual composition. But it is very seldom that the design of the lighting of a performance does not require some change in intensity, color or dimension during a show. For this change, control is necessary.

The theatre planner is concerned with the kinds of control systems, their relative cost, their effectiveness and the spaces required to accommodate them. Intensity control systems are divided into two principal categories: direct control systems in which the control is exerted on the service power to the lighting loads and indirect, or remote, control systems in which the control is first exerted on a signal current which in turn influences the service power to the instruments.

Direct Systems

Resistance dimmers are the conventional means of controlling light intensity. They vary from water barrels (the Alhambra in London still had some before the war) to plates engineered to compensate for the nonlinear output of the incandescent filament. Where only DC is available, resistance dimmers must be used; hence they are employed in portable equipment because DC is still encountered in numerous theatres, notably most of the legitimate houses in New York. The resistance dimmer wastes the power it does not pass to the lamp. It will not function with lights of lower wattage than the dimmer. It is cumbersome, heavy, and hot in operation.

Because the resistance dimmers are applied directly to the high wattage load circuits, because there is some hazard of electrical fires, and because the resistance dimmer board is the distribution center for load circuits, boards of this type are usually located backstage, either in an alcove in the proscenium wall, on a gallery above the stage near the proscenium wall, or in stage floor space which is in great demand for other uses. The operator in any of these positions cannot see the lighting effects which he is controlling and cannot take cues for light changes directly from the action.

The autotransformer is an excellent dimmer where AC is available. For school and community theatres it is particularly appropriate. Since it controls voltage, current not used at the lamp is not drawn from the mains. The resulting economy in power is important. The autotransformer will dim evenly to out any load up to its rated capacity. This makes it very flexible in that it can be switched from circuit to circuit irrespective of the circuit load. Autotransformers run cool, do not arc, and occupy no more space than resistance dimmers. Their only drawback for trouping is the fact that they must be limited to AC houses.

Certain makes of autotransformers have been designed into control consoles and placed in operating positions in front of the stage, allowing the operator to coordinate light changes with the performance and to correct errors which he himself can see when he makes them.

Direct dimming: resistance or auto-transformer dimmers permanently wired to stage lighting instruments. This system is inadequate for any presentation more elaborate than a lecture or a concert.

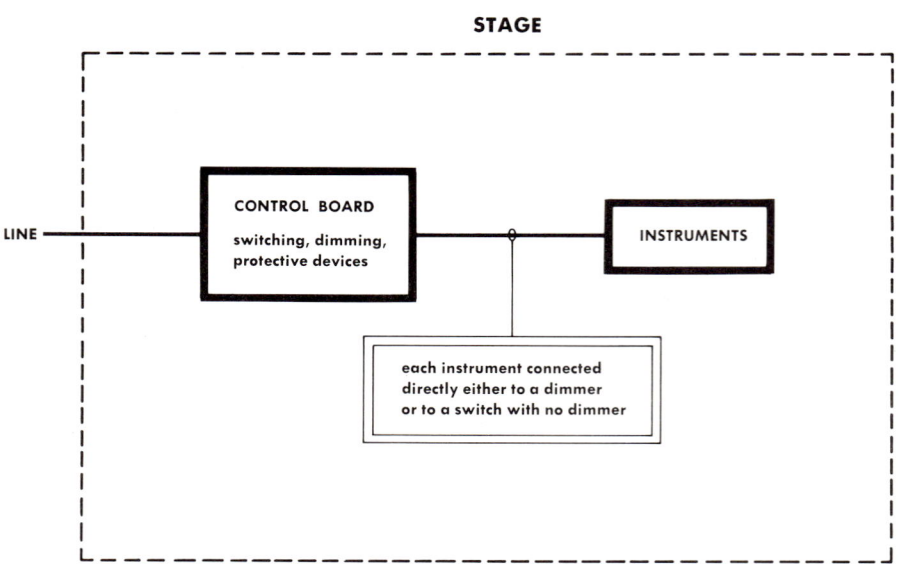

STAGE

LINE → CONTROL BOARD (switching, dimming, protective devices) → INSTRUMENTS

each instrument connected directly either to a dimmer or to a switch with no dimmer

In direct dimming, human control is exerted upon the lighting power loads by varying resistance or autoinductance in the load circuits. Autoinductance is not possible with direct current. In direct dimming the total lighting load must pass through the control board. This necessitates large switching and dimming components, dielectric barriers, large wire sizes and Code wiring practices. It is not practical, as to size, or economical, as to installation, to locate a direct dimming control board in the house. Direct dimming boards must be located backstage where the operator cannot take sight cues or see and correct his errors and where the control board and interconnect panel, if any, occupy space which is more valuable for other stage uses. Mastering, submastering and presetting are limited both by the size of the necessary parts and the primitive nature of the circuitry.

In indirect dimming, human control is exerted on low voltage circuits which control thyratron tubes, magnetic amplifiers or silicon-controlled rectifier-amplifiers, which in turn dim the lighting power loads. Therefore lighting power loads may go directly from the line through the dimmer bank, which may be in any convenient location (not at the stage or the control center), through the interconnect panel, which may be located conveniently either at the control center or onstage, to the lighting instrument outlets which are distributed about the theatre. The control center can be located where the operators can best see the stage.

In indirect control systems, low voltage signals permit miniaturization and close spacing of components which allows placing the control console out front where the operator can see the stage, while the actual dimmers which regulate the lighting loads in response to the low voltage signals may be located in low-value space and only the interconnecting panel where selected stage load circuits are connected to the dimmer circuits need be on or near the stage. In some recent installations, no part of the intensity control system has been placed on the stage, the interconnecting panel being located near the control console to be operated by console personnel.

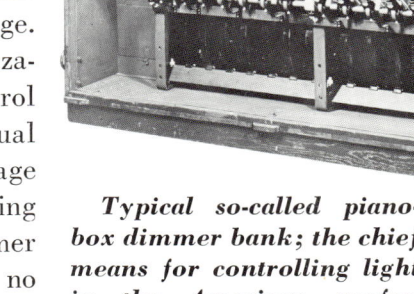

Typical so-called piano-box dimmer bank; the chief means for controlling light in the American professional theatre.

An installation of control boards for a New York production. Power to all stage lighting instruments is distributed through a maze of flexible cables. The installation is made anew for each production and when a production changes theatres.

Location of the dimmer bank may well depend on the location of the power entrance into the building since the power service to this component may range between 300 and 700 kva. There is some merit in establishing the shortest possible direct route between the power entrance, the dimmer bank, the interconnecting panel, and the majority of the lighting outlets for ease in wiring and saving in wire. There is also merit in running the load circuits through parts of the building which are not finished, such as above the auditorium ceiling and in the stage space.

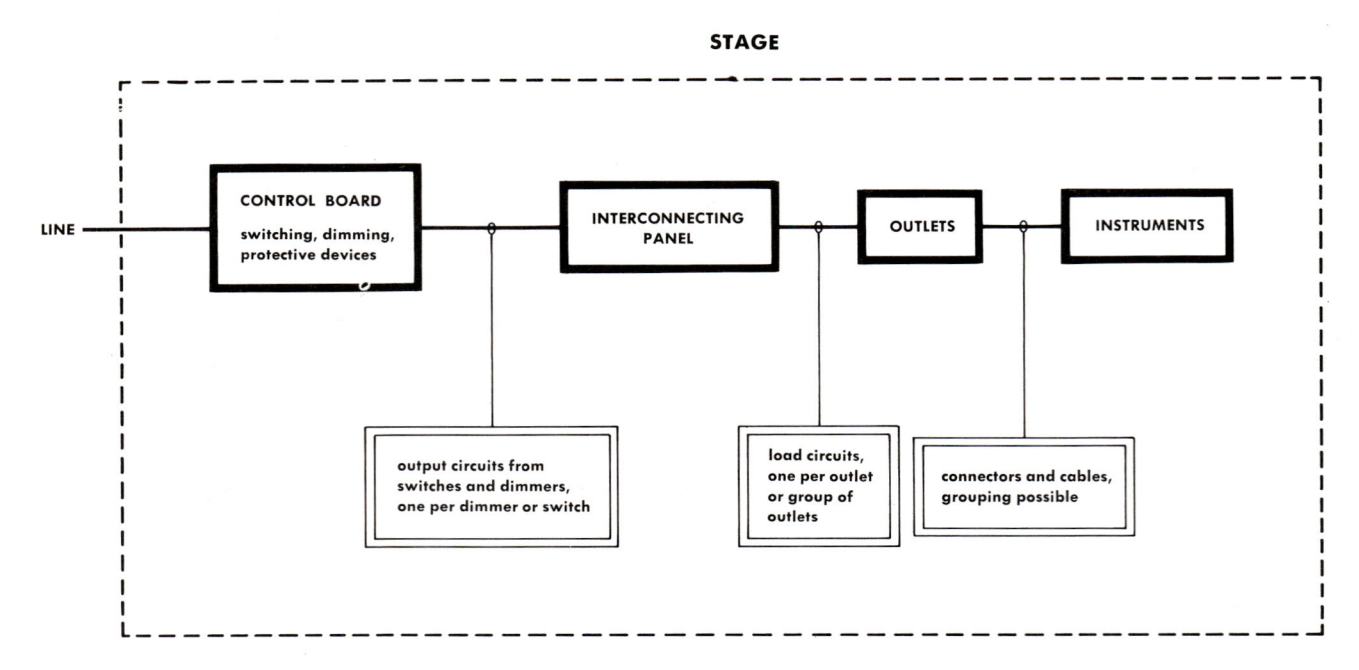

STAGE

LINE → CONTROL BOARD (switching, dimming, protective devices) → INTERCONNECTING PANEL → OUTLETS → INSTRUMENTS

- output circuits from switches and dimmers, one per dimmer or switch
- load circuits, one per outlet or group of outlets
- connectors and cables, grouping possible

Direct dimming: resistance or auto-transformer dimmers with selective connecting of load circuits to control circuits and of instruments to load circuits.

Auto-transformer dimmers with interconnecting panels and circuit breakers in a console over which an operator can see the stage.

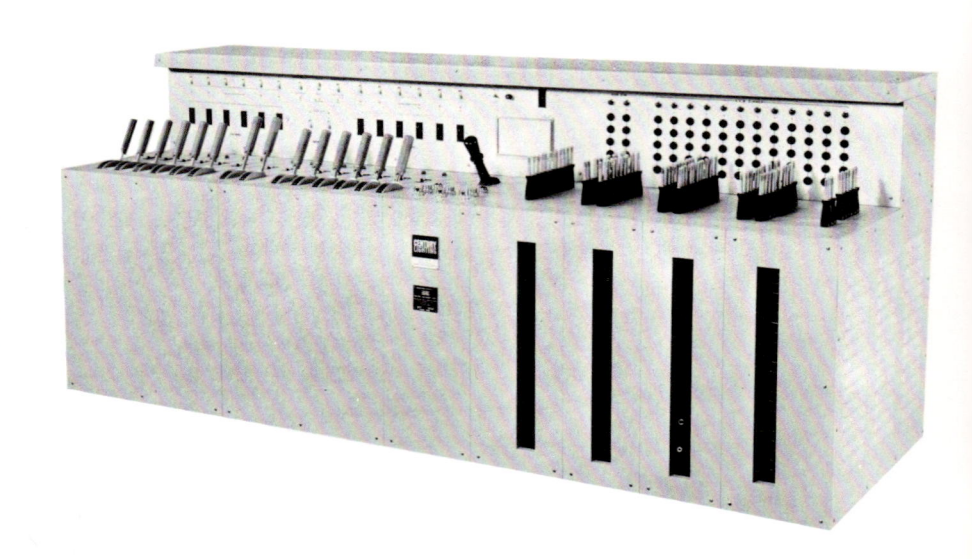

Indirect Dimming

There are three types of lighting dimmers currently in use which are capable of indirect control: thyratron tubes, magnetic-amplifiers, and semiconductors or silicon-controlled rectifier-amplifiers. All three require installation space for a bank of dimmers—one dimmer for each control circuit. The space may be away from the stage and away from the control room but it is advisable to locate it in line between the power entrance and the stage so that wire runs may be minimized. The silicon-controlled rectifier units are more compact than the other two types and require less auxiliary equipment; there is even the possibility that each load circuit may have its own control unit, thus eliminating the dimmer bank and the interconnecting panel and permitting power distribution directly from a distribution panel to the load outlets.

Indirect control systems are based on the assumption that there will be as many dimmers as there are control circuits, that there will be fewer dimmers, which are expensive components, than there are outlets, and that not all outlets will be used simultaneously. This is a valid assumption, though there is a tendency to underestimate the number of dimmers and control circuits required for high-quality lighting.

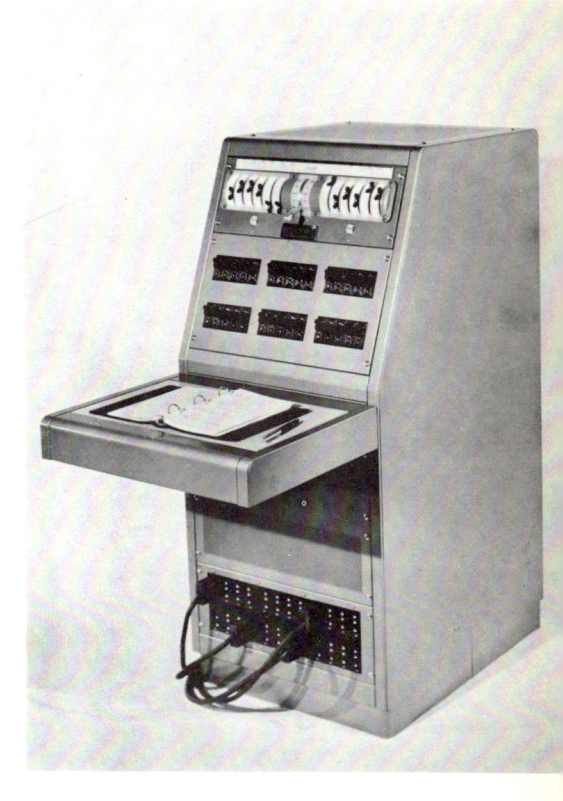

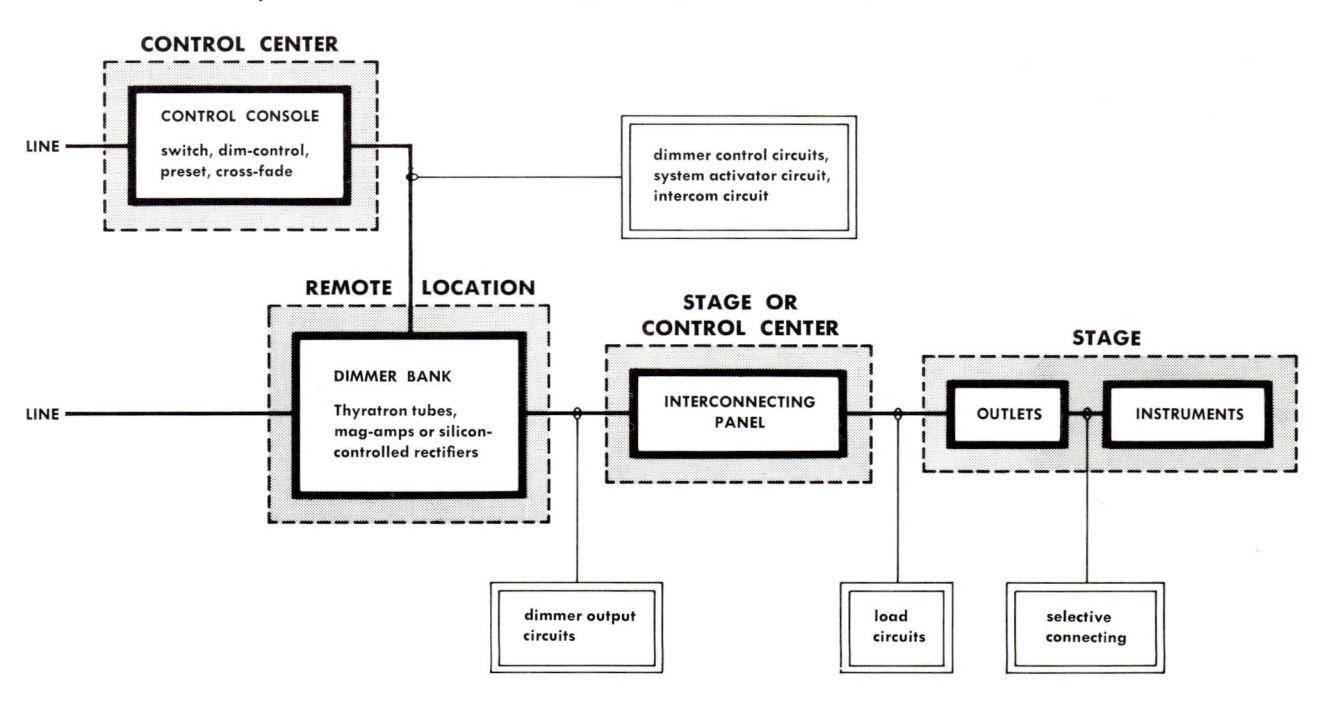

A package, console containing six silicon-controlled rectifier dimmers with two presets, fader and selective connecting of load circuits. Designed to be competitive with auto-transformer systems. ➤

Indirect dimming: thyraton tubes, magnetic amplifiers or silicon-controlled rectifiers with selective connecting of load circuits to dimmer circuits and of instruments to load circuits. ➤

277

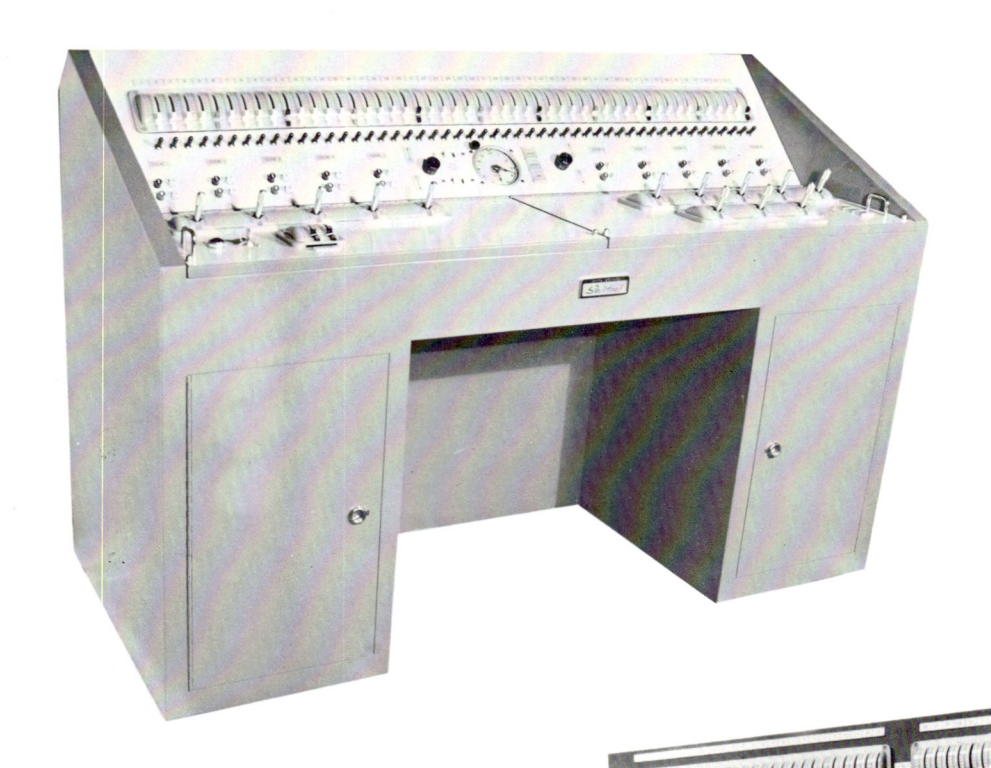

Control console and pre-set panel for silicon-controlled rectifier dimming system, Williams College. All potentiometer units are standardized in dimension for interchangeability. Scene submaster dimmers are featured in this system.

278

There are three places in the system where selection can determine which instruments will be lighted at any time: the control center where switches and dimmers may be on or off, the interconnect panel where load circuits are selectively connected to dimmer output circuits, and the outlets where instruments may be selectively connected to load circuits.

In one system, portable silicon-controlled rectifiers are used as dimmers and are selectively connected to control and power outlets at or near the light mounting positions, and the lighting instruments are plugged into them. The interconnect function is placed in the low-voltage circuitry at the control center, and the dimmer bank and load circuit interconnect panel are rendered unnecessary as separate components of the system. The power wiring to the instruments is less complicated and less costly. Clients may purchase a complete control system and complete power distribution system and acquire dimmers piecemeal as finances permit. A fault of this system is the bulk and the weight of the plug-battens and of the dimmers which must be plugged thereto and located within the stage space.

Control room. Left to right: sound control console, intercommunication systems, light control consoles, preset panel.

Control console for semi-automatic punched-card system. Two manual presets with fader. Card read-out at far left can be substituted for the presets. Cards are punched by hand. At right, corner of sound console.

Fully automatic control system. Light levels are set on console, center; on signal, levels are sensed and punched into cards by the unit at left; in unit at right cards are read to establish levels which the operator produces by fading from one scene to the next.

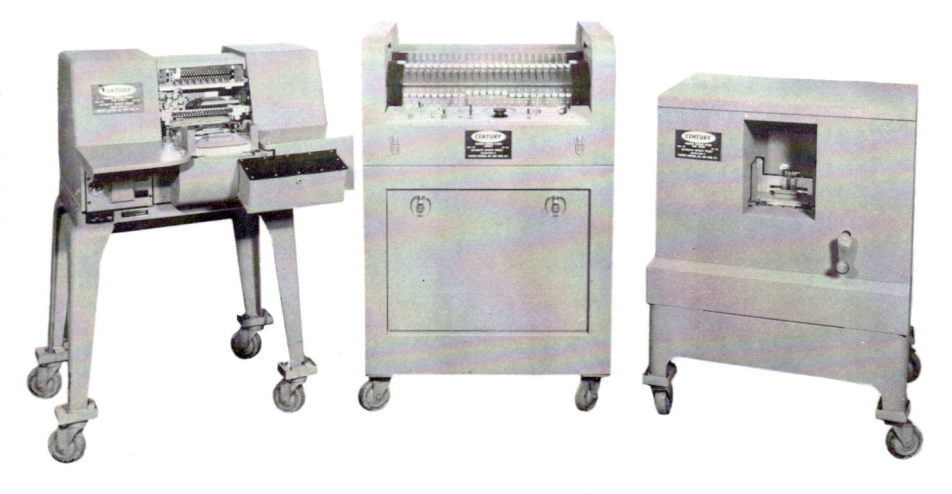

A system foreseen for the future will have the dimmers integrated with the lighting instruments, one dimmer per instrument, so that all selection of instruments-in-use will be done in the control center. Other previsioned features are programming systems for presetting, interconnecting and sequencing dimming operations subject to ultimate human control. Progress in the use of memory devices for storing preset information has been in the direction of punched cards and removable decks of potentiometers, each card or deck containing one preset.

280

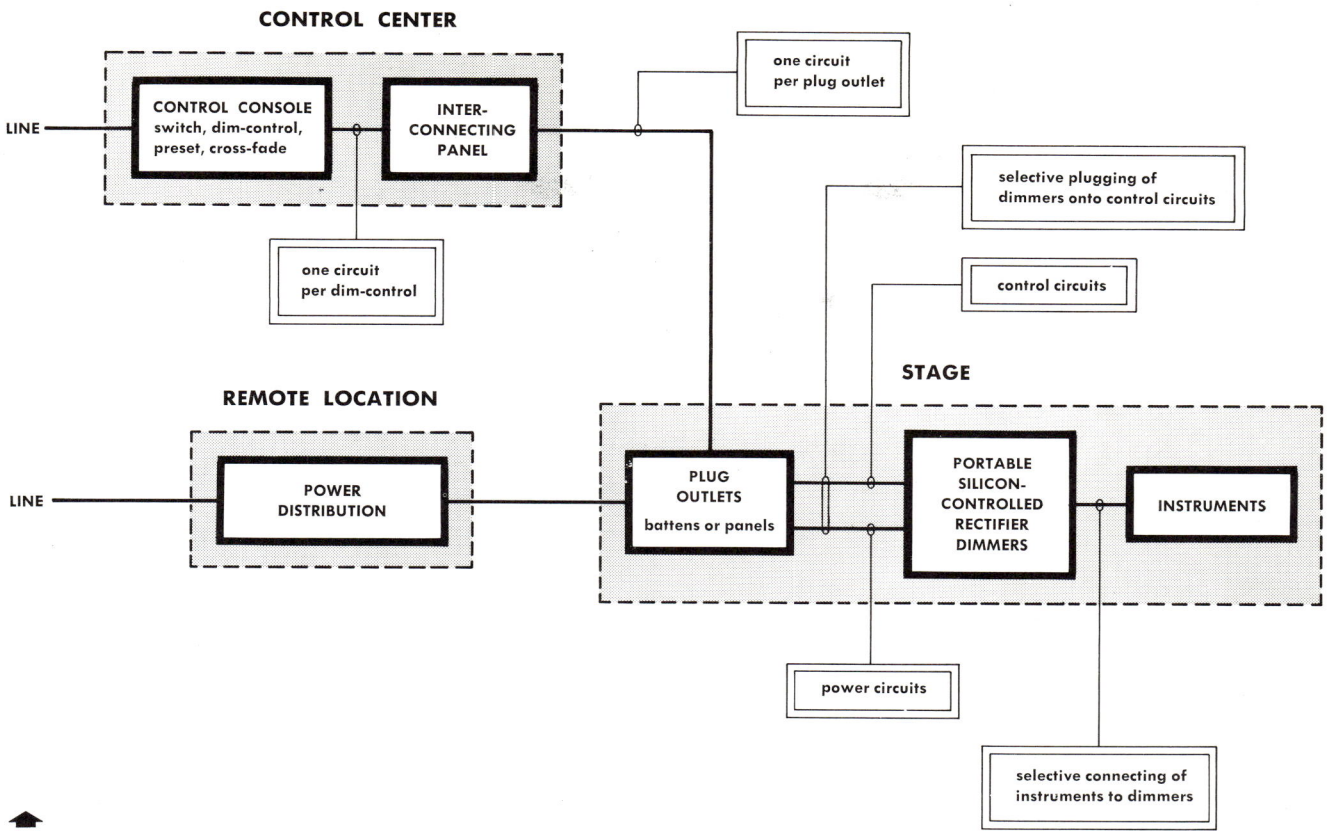

CONTROL CENTER

- **CONTROL CONSOLE** — switch, dim-control, preset, cross-fade
- **INTER-CONNECTING PANEL**

LINE →

one circuit per plug outlet

one circuit per dim-control

selective plugging of dimmers onto control circuits

control circuits

REMOTE LOCATION

- **POWER DISTRIBUTION**

LINE →

STAGE

- **PLUG OUTLETS** — battens or panels
- **PORTABLE SILICON-CONTROLLED RECTIFIER DIMMERS**
- **INSTRUMENTS**

power circuits

selective connecting of instruments to dimmers

⬆ *Indirect dimming: rectifier dimmers located at instrument mounting positions.*

Indirect dimming: dimmers integrated with lighting instruments; presets and sequences programmed. ⬇

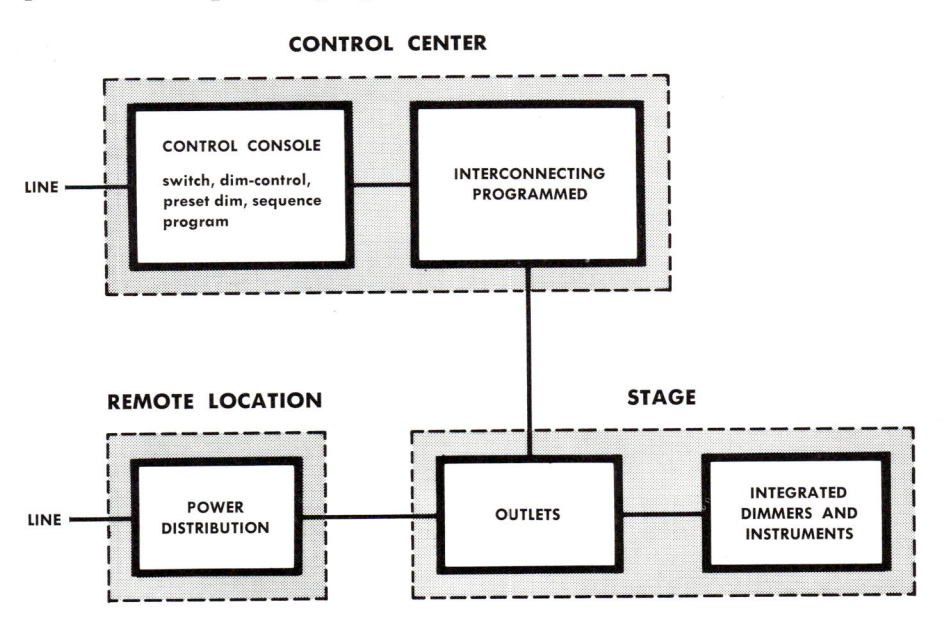

CONTROL CENTER

- **CONTROL CONSOLE** — switch, dim-control, preset dim, sequence program
- **INTERCONNECTING PROGRAMMED**

LINE →

REMOTE LOCATION

- **POWER DISTRIBUTION**

LINE →

STAGE

- **OUTLETS**
- **INTEGRATED DIMMERS AND INSTRUMENTS**

281

The bigger the audience and the theatre, the larger the acting areas and the longer the distance from lighting instruments to actors or areas lighted, the greater must be the power of the light sources.

TABLE 14. Electrical Requirements

Seating Capacity	Maximum Proscenium Width	Height	No. of Instruments (all types)	No. of Outlets	No. of Dimmers	Dimming Capacity (kilowatts)
200-400	24'	13'	30	50	12	50
400-600	34'	15'-18'	75	100	30	100
750-1000 (with cyc. for dramatic productions)	36'	20	180	190	60	225
1000-1500 (with stage curtains)	38'-48'	20'-25'	100	180	50	240
1600-2400 (for musicals, ballets, operas)	40'-50'	25'-30'	320	310	80	300

This table is developed from the typical stage lighting layouts shown in the Century Lighting, Inc., book *Century Theatre Lighting* (copyright 1960) to which reference may be made for detailed information regarding the layouts.

For arena stages or tents the number of circuits, instruments and wattages are proportional to the size of the acting area. Because it is not necessary to light the scenery, the lighting requirements in all categories are less than half of those for proscenium, open or extended stage.

These specifications are admittedly very rough, but most designers will be able to do satisfactory lighting with the indicated amounts of power listed. As in the case of space for lighting instruments, power requirements tend to decrease as equipment becomes more efficient.

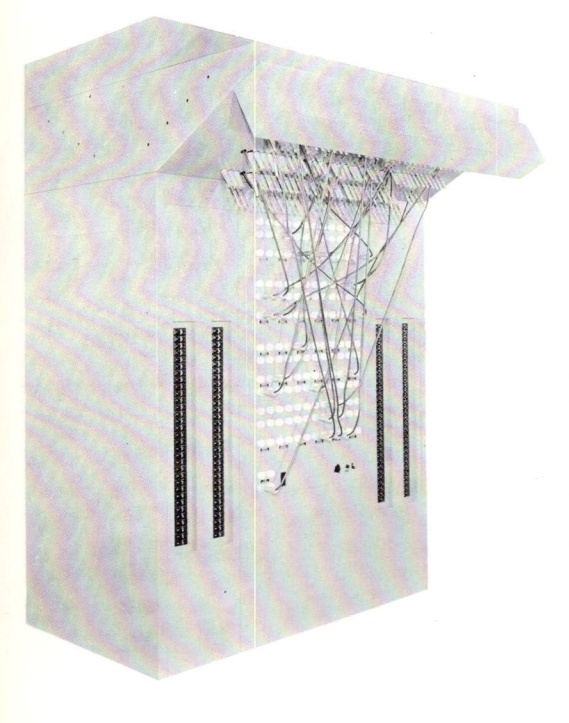

Two types of interconnecting panels.

Because not all load circuits are in use for lighting any one scene, it is feasible to have fewer dimmers than load circuits and to have a method of selectively connecting load circuits onto dimmer circuits, sometimes grouping two or more load circuits on one dimmer circuit. A panel to facilitate this is essential to any system which has maximum flexibility. It should be located for easy access and operation. Optional locations are on stage or in a proscenium splay, where it may be operated by stage electricians, or near the control console, where it may be operated by the console operator. In any case it should be located in the direct line of run between the dimmers and the lighting outlets to avoid running unnecessary lengths of conductor about the building.

Interconnecting (Load Selector) Panels

House lights are conventionally all dimmed together. Where colors are used as in Radio City Music Hall, it is standard practice to control all circuits of a color together. Balcony lights, under-balcony lights, chandelier may be controlled separately: progressive dimming from the back of the house toward the curtain coincident with bringing up of lights on the curtain sometimes serves to settle the audience and focus attention on the stage. There is no point in controlling

House Lights

House light control panel backstage. House lights, work lights, cleaning lights, lecture lighting and motion picture lighting may be controlled here to obviate disturbing the performance setup on the stage lighting control console.

circuits at the sides of the theatre separately. Louvered ceiling lights shining straight down to illuminate programs and aisles are separately controlled and dimmed out last, since they do not interfere with decorative lighting of walls and ceiling.

Power Runs

It is efficient to run lighting power lines as directly as possible from the point of entrance to the locations of the maximum number of light mounting positions with attention to the possibility of running them in unfinished space rather than embedding them behind finished walls and under floors. It is less costly at first, and it affords easier access for later alteration and repair. The large majority of light mounting positions are above the stage and the house; it is therefore most efficient to lift the power in the fewest and largest wires to a distribution point at or near that level, and thereby reduce the length of the numerous distributive circuits to the mounting positions. If this is not possible, the next most efficient procedure is to locate the dimmer bank near the power entrance and to arrange direct runs from the dimmer bank to the interconnect panel located either near the control center or in a convenient position backstage.

Motion Picture Projection Booth

To build any theatre without a motion picture projection booth is to limit its usefulness. Even legitimate shows require projection of motion-pictures from time to time: SPREAD EAGLE, PERSONAL APPEARANCE, I'D RATHER BE RIGHT. Moreover, it is economically unsound to build a booth which is not adequate for continuous run motion pictures. Even if film projection is limited to the use of 16-mm safety film, for which a projection booth is not legally necessary, the booth prevents the noise of the projector from disturbing the audience and permits operators to carry on necessary conversation.

No part of the theatre has been the subject of so much careful study and planning as the motion picture projection booth. Building codes treat of it extensively. Excellent recommended specifications may be obtained from the Society of Motion Picture and Television Engineers. It is shocking to note the number of booths containing code violations and built with no apparent reference to the recommended specifications, which are to be found particularly in school and community theatres where space is not always at a premium, and safety is certainly important. It is difficult to understand laxity in booth design when the legal requirements may be easily obtained.

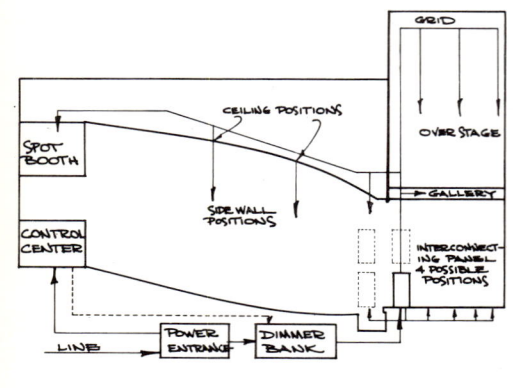

It is theoretically possible to run a motion picture show with two projectors. Despite the reliability of modern projection equipment, a third machine is an insurance against mechanical breakdown. In many large theatres the third machine is used for the news and shorts, leaving machines one and two for the feature picture. Todd A-O, Cinerama and

Power distribution for indirect dimming with dimmer bank in basement and interconnecting panel backstage.

284

some front effect projections employ 70-mm projectors, which require no more floor space than the standard 35-mm machines. On the basis of these requisites, even if it is planned to equip the theatre with only two projectors, the booths should be adequate for four. It is much easier to change production policy than it is to change a building.

Another requisite which must be stressed is the importance of having space enough for machines. It is also important to have space for its own sake. The operators spend a long time in the booth, the work is highly responsible and often trying. The psychological factors accompanying unwarranted cramped quarters are not to be lightly dismissed. Moreover, it is easier to make a big booth a safe booth. Reels of film not in the vault can be physically so widely separated that combustion of one will not set off another. Moreover, with a big booth, it is less likely that one operator will get in another's way if it becomes necessary to leave the booth in an emergency. For inspection of film and making up the show, the operators should have a separate room which is in itself a film vault ventilated to the open air, located behind the projection booth. This need not be large. The splicing table can be located against the wall into which is built the closed rack containing individual reels. This room should contain one or more motor-driven rewind machines. Adjacent to the projection booth itself there should be an office for the chief projectionist. In motion picture houses there is a certain amount of paper work for the projectionist. It is also desirable to have a place to use an outside telephone during the show as distinct from the intercommunication system used in operating the show which has its station in the booth itself. The functions of office and light maintenance shop are sometimes combined so that the same room contains the desk and rack for carbons, parts, oil, and small accessories. Finally, the projectionists need a lavatory.

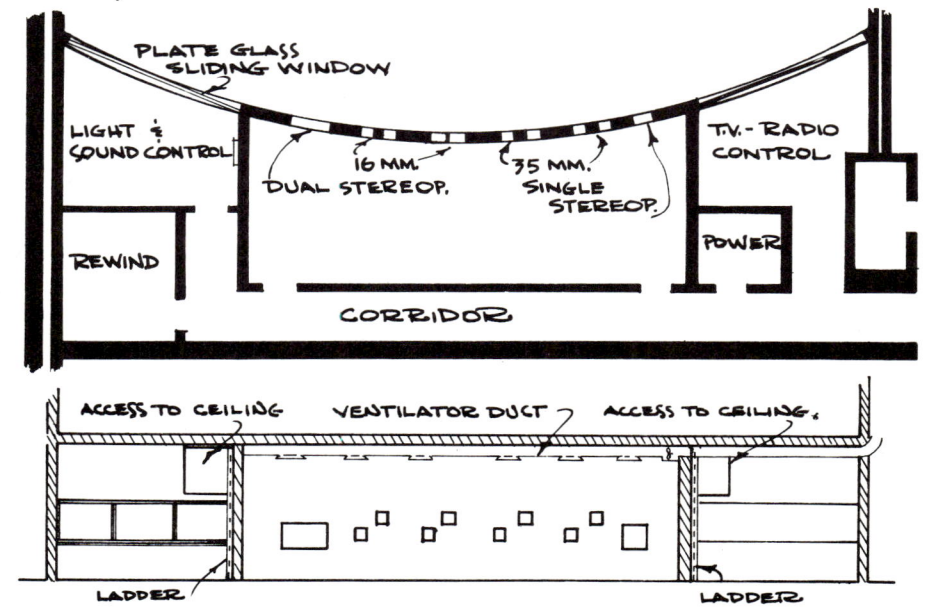

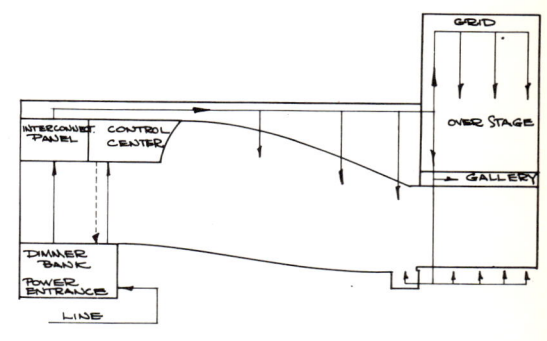

Power distribution with dimmer bank under lobby and interconnecting panel near control center.

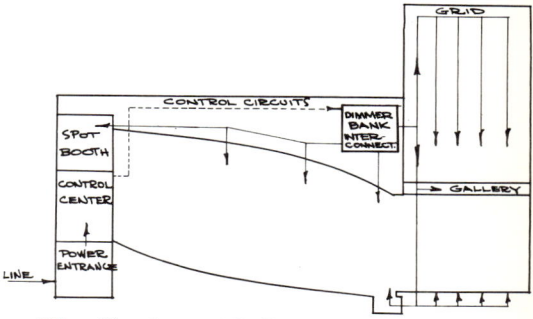

Distribution with dimmer bank and interconnecting panel over house.

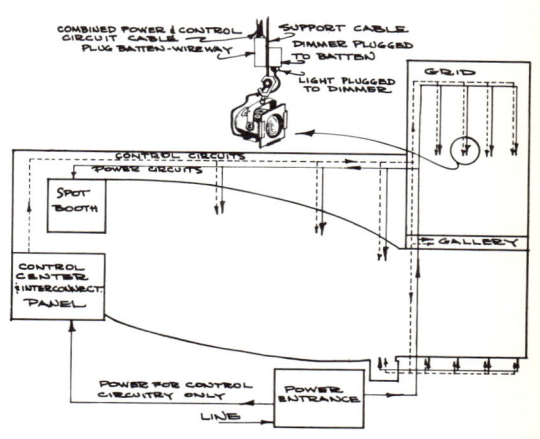

▲ *Distribution with interconnecting function at the control center and dimmers at the lighting instruments.*

◀ *Plan and elevation control rooms, the projection room equipped for teaching with slides and films.*

Projection machines, however quiet, emit a certain amount of high-frequency noise which probably contributes to the fatigue of those exposed to it day after day. A sound-absorbent ceiling and sound-absorbent material on the walls are therefore requisite. Also, it is necessary to cool the booth even in the winter time. Despite the safety requirement that all lamp houses be ventilated directly to the outside, the lamp house picks up and reradiates enough heat to make the booth an exceedingly uncomfortable place. With the tightening of the building codes, tuberculosis has ceased to be the projectionists' occupational disease. However, it is asserted by some operators, and not without confirming evidence, that certain booths will "turn you into an old man in three years."

One of the best ways to insure a good performance is to do all that is possible for the safety and comfort of the operators. It is not pleasant to earn one's living under conditions which are trying because of the theatre planner's negligence or ignorance. Fortunately there are numerous booths which can be cited as models, notably Radio City Music Hall and the Brooklyn Paramount Theatre.

Requirements for follow spots and projection booths, if generously met, will provide operating facilities across most of the back of the balcony. When this section of the theatre is being laid out, the facilities for sound control (Chapter 13) will also be located in this area, thus necessitating the use of the whole back of the house as operating area.

To serve his client properly, the architect will make architectural provision for the most elaborate and advanced means of stage and house lighting, even if the lights and apparatus are not available at the moment. By this means, the theatre can be progressively improved without architectural alteration. Moreover, the building cost where such provision is made is seldom appreciably more than that of a theatre in which architectural features render improvement impossible.

Motion picture projection booth, Radio City Music Hall.

13: Sound and intercommunication

Chapter 4 outlined the means by which audibility of the show could be assured within the limits of what can be achieved architecturally. Even with the best acoustical planning, however, there is a limit (about 2500 seats) to the size of a theatre in which unamplified speech can be satisfactorily projected to all listeners. Larger houses may be satisfactory for opera or orchestral music, but speech loses some intelligibility.

Even in the small theatre where the actor can easily be heard by the whole audience, the play often demands projection of sound in ways which cannot be satisfactorily achieved by mechanical means. Ariel, invisible, flies about above the audience, playing his tabor and pipe. The ectoplasmic figure of Hamlet's father must speak in a voice acceptable as that of a ghost. The laughter of Lazarus must fill the house. The voice of Mephisto must interpose itself between Marguerita and the entrances from which she successively tries to escape from the church. Church scenes to be artistically credible must sound highly reverberant.

For purposes of the show, the audience must be able to hear any sound, at any intensity, from any apparent source or sources, moving source, or no source, and the sound must have any predetermined frequency spectrum and any desired reverberant quality or echo. All this must be possible for not only a single sound but a group of unrelated sounds simultaneously employed.

A large proportion of legitimate productions use electronic sound control equipment * for one or more of the purposes outlined above. Many theatres have architectural shortcomings which make them unusable without electronic reinforcement.

However, the development of completely flexible apparatus for control of sound has been slow. The first equipment answering this description was developed at Stevens Institute of Technology and was first publicly employed by the Metropolitan Opera on November 24th, 1940. As showmen and technicians learn the technique of controlling sound electronically, many values traditionally assigned to light, scenery, and business are undertaken by auditory means. The first notable example of this is THE LIVING NEWSPAPER. Time, locale, at-

* For detailed treatment of the use of electronic sound control equipment in the theatre see Burris-Meyer, H., and Mallory, V., *Sound in the Theatre*, Theatre Arts Books, 1959.

287

mosphere, and mood may be created by auditory means, and arbitrarily designed sounds may be used as direct emotional stimuli. Up to the time of this writing, though most new theatres and concert halls have electronic sound reinforcing systems, very few have ever been planned to provide complete control of the auditory component of the performance.

In legitimate production, equipment is usually trouped with the show and suffers from varying limitations imposed by house structure and acoustics, in the same manner as stage lighting is sometimes rendered inefficient because of architectural restriction of equipment and instrument placement. As has been pointed out previously, architectural restriction on any phase of production limits the use of the theatre and raises production cost. Therefore, *provision for electronic sound control installation must be incorporated in the original design.*

BASIC OBJECTIVES
(1) Reinforcement

Sound reinforcement consists of achieving intelligibility for speech and acceptable intensity for music or other sounds, the actual source of which is in sight of the audience. This involves recreating at the auditor's position the intensity level and frequency spectrum which is characteristic of the source, less a small amount of intensity at certain frequencies which would be absorbed in free air at the desired aesthetic distance. In the case of music, the desired reverberant characteristic must be added. In practice, these objectives can be accomplished only by control of frequency spectrum and reverberation, as well as intensity.

The intelligibility of speech depends upon the projection to the hearer of the high frequencies which give consonants their character. Reinforcement often may be limited to reinstating in the sound the high frequencies absorbed by the house to the extent to which they are absorbed. Reinforcing the whole speech spectrum often results only in noise with little or no increase in intelligibility.

(2) Motion Picture Sound

Motion picture sound reproducing equipment is powerful and, to a limited extent, capable of being adjusted in frequency response to compensate for acoustical limitations of the house. The knowledge of those facts too often made the builder of the motion picture theatre neglect acoustical planning and use too much sound-absorbent surface material. The result is that sound distribution is uneven, and the current reigning film siren pants like a 200-ton steam locomotive if heard in the first row, while she is just comfortably audible in the last. When a theatre is designed for good sound distribution from the stage without benefit of reinforcement, the motion picture sound will not have to be unconvincing in some locations to be heard in others.

(3) Legitimate Productions and Opera

In live shows, the sound is limited in point of origin, direction of movement and essential characteristics only by the imagination of the playwright. Problems vary from simple reinforcement to creation and projection of synthetic voices in auditory perspective. Where the human voice is used in speech or song, it must be reproduced with such fidelity that the audience will not suspect that electronic control equipment is being employed. If this condition cannot be met, it is better to abandon electronic sound control. After all, there are many productions and theatres that do not require it.

Sound comes to the audience from the stage, the orchestra pit, the side stages, the auditorium walls, the auditorium ceiling, from above the proscenium, from the back of the house, and from the floor. The architect must, therefore, provide loud-speaker mounting positions which will enable sound to come directly or by reflection from all these locations.

Man's directional perception of sound is notably weak in the vertical plane, owing to the fact that his ears are at the same level. This fact enormously simplifies the problem of public address (PA). The loud-speaker can be located above the source, and project its signal to the audience just as the unamplified first reflection of the voice is reflected from the ceiling. The audience, watching the source, and possibly hearing a little sound directly from it, need not suspect that most of the sound comes from above the source. This is well exemplified in the Radio City Music Hall where almost every sound except from the motion picture is projected to the audience from loud-speakers above the proscenium.

Man's directional sense is so good in the horizontal plane that he will instantly identify the reproduced sound when, as is too often the case, loud-speakers are placed at either side of the source or proscenium. Unless he is on the center line of the house, he is lucky if he can understand speech, and music will sound fuzzy due to the sound from the two sources not being in phase when it reaches him. This misuse of the sound system condemns many open-air concerts, pageants and operas to artistic mediocrity. Except where highly directional loud-speakers are necessary to project sound under badly designed balconies and cannot reach their segment of the audience from above the source, no loud-speaker should be used for reinforcement except above the source or proscenium. Unless a multichannel system is used, loud-speakers *must* be located on the center line of the house.

The motion picture screen is within the sight lines, so sound projected through it can reach every part of the house directly. Sound projected from above a solid screen will appear to come from the picture.

When music from an orchestra or an opera or speech from a play is picked up from a number of places on a line perpendicular to the center

Loud-speaker Mounting Positions

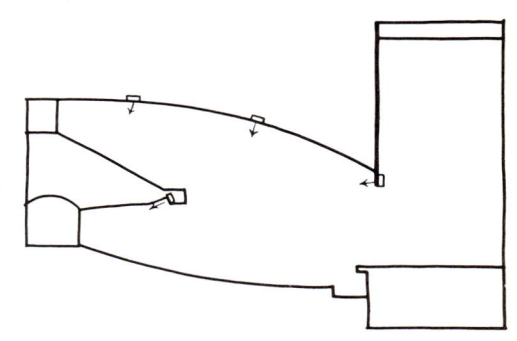

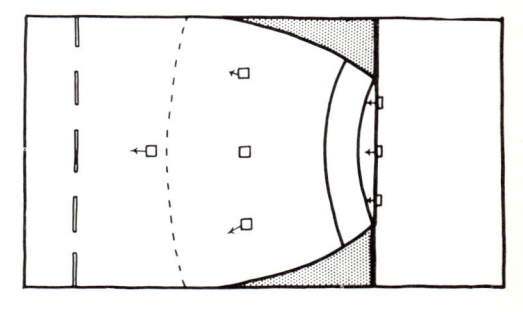

Loud-speaker mounting positions necessary for auditory perspective about the house. Permanent proscenium loud-speakers or false proscenium loud-speakers for stereophonic reinforcement.

Stereophonic Projection

289

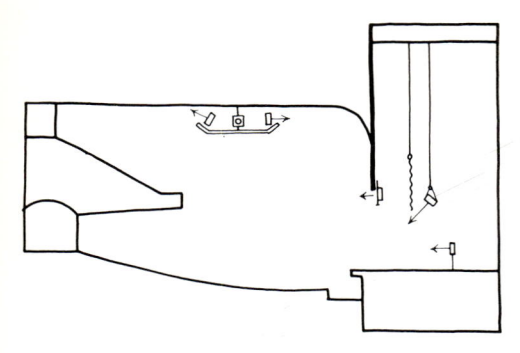

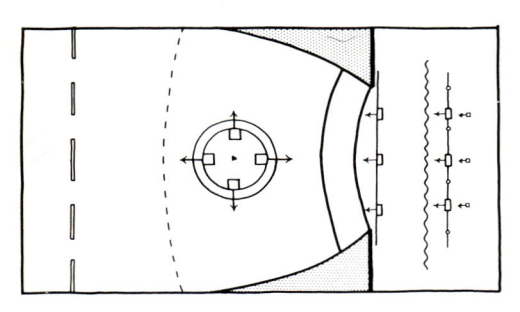

Temporary loud-speaker mounting positions: four loud-speakers in the chandelier reflecting from ceiling and walls, three in a false proscenium, others hung behind a masking border and set on stands upstage for dubbing.

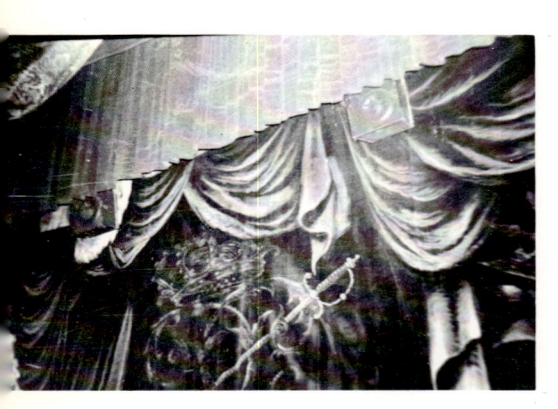

Stevens Sound Control System, Mark I. Loud-speakers flown upstage of the teaser to project sound through the proscenium arch. Metropolitan Opera production of ORFEO.

line of the house, and each section is separately reproduced from a loud-speaker above the pickup position, the resultant stereophonic reinforcement can give the performance a definition and dynamic range beyond that which is possible with the unamplified performance. First demonstrated by Leopold Stokowski and the Bell Telephone Laboratories, this system supersedes others wherever the requisite musical taste, knowledge and funds are available.

Movement of sound is achieved by varying the signal intensity progressively between adjacent loud-speakers. The installation of loud-speaker mounting positions must be so planned as to make possible the apparent movement of sound source in any direction—about, above, around or below the house or stage—without interruption or apparently jumping from point to point. This means that the points of origin or reflection of sound cannot be more than approximately 30 degrees apart. The closer they are to the audience, the closer they must be together: the smaller the point of origin, the closer it must be to the adjacent points. For example, when the sound source is a loud-speaker with a diameter of a silver dollar and it is used not more than 20 feet from the first row, it must be not more than 12 feet from the next unit if the sound source is to appear to pass smoothly along the path between the two units. If the point of apparent sound origin is a wall area of 100 square feet, the edge of that area may be 15 feet from the next similar wall area, provided, of course, that the audience is not close. Sound appearing to originate from the ceiling of the theatre may appear to come from any point between two units placed as much as 50 feet apart, provided the sound comes by reflection.

For maximum usefulness, there must be as much flexibility in mounting position and in direction in which the loud-speaker is pointed as there is for a lighting unit. Moreover, all loud-speaker mounting positions must be concealed. It is often unwise to point loud-speakers directly at the audience, if the nature of the source of sound is not to be disclosed.

Loud-speaker mounting positions may be determined by calculating distances between sound sources and from reflection angles as indicated. These must be numerous and of sufficient size to permit flexibility in pointing the loud-speaker. The architect's ingenuity in determining mounting positions is called into play to provide means of concealment. Loud-speakers in the chandelier can cover almost all the ceiling and wall areas. Speakers mounted behind grilles, for ventilation and house lighting, can be very useful though the areas they cover are often restricted. Ceiling slots or false beams, used for front mounting of stage lights or similar to them, can often be effectively employed. Concealment for loud-speakers mounted on the back wall of the house and pointed toward the ceiling must usually be provided by special architectural devices. The most useful area for loud-speaker location is, as previously noted, above and about the proscenium. If much of this area is grilled to conceal organ pipes, etc., loud-speaker mounting position becomes very flexible and will be varied according to the demands of the individual production.

As in the case of architectural provision for the mounting of stage lights, mounting positions for loud-speakers must be equipped with permanent loud-speaker outlets.

Backstage Outlets

When speech or other sound is made to appear to come from an actor or a location on stage which is not the actual source of the sound, loud-speakers must be located upstage of the apparent sound source. This condition requires the largest number of loud-speaker outlets onstage, i.e., one at each side of the acting area, one over the proscenium for each 15 feet of proscenium width, one below stage, one upstage center in a floor pocket and one in the flies. In practice, the maximum demand seldom exceeds one below stage, three outlets onstage, and three outlets in the flies.

Pickup

Provision for picking up the sound to be controlled is no less important than loud-speaker placement. For sound reinforcement, microphones must be located wherever the performer is to appear. This requirement calls for a larger number of microphones than any other condition. The original installation in Radio City Music Hall provided for 55 microphones for stage and orchestra pit.

Distance between microphones and their position with respect to the performer must be planned with reference to the characteristics of the microphone. The smallest stage will need at least three hung in front and an equal number in the orchestra pit, and provision for three more in the footlights or in props for local pickup.

Offstage Pickups

Offstage microphone connections will be necessary for all sounds which originate on the stage but not in the acting area. The most arduous operatic demands have not to date required more than three on either side.

The best pickup position is above and in front of the performer. The small hanging microphone can be concealed behind the teaser. Even if visible, it is less distracting than the conventional footlight microphone.

For recorded sound (and tape is the only type of record worth considering for use in the theatre), the reproducer must be handled by the sound technican who also operates the distribution equipment. The tape reproducer must, therefore, be located in the sound control booth.

Motion Picture Sound

While it is possible to use the theatre sound control system for motion pictures, this is unwise. The projectors should be connected to their own independent system adjusted to the characteristics of the projectors, controlled from the motion picture projection booth and used only for motion pictures.

Sound Control Booth and Equipment

The sound control console must be located so that the operator can see and hear the show. The best installations are in a booth with open front at the back of the balcony. The booth must have a hard ceiling and live back wall so that the operator can hear as well as the audience. For easy communication there should be direct access to the motion picture projection and spotting booths from the sound control booth.

The control system consists of two parts: the input mixing panel and the output mixing panel with appropriate provision for input and loudspeaker switching on either side. All electronic equipment is located at this point except where very long microphone lines are necessary, in which case the necessary voltage amplifiers must be located close to the microphone position (on a shelf in the proscenium splay or on the stage wall), and the control circuit carried to the console. This procedure involves only a change of location of certain items but no change in circuit or operation.

Open sound control booth above top balcony. Radio City Music Hall.

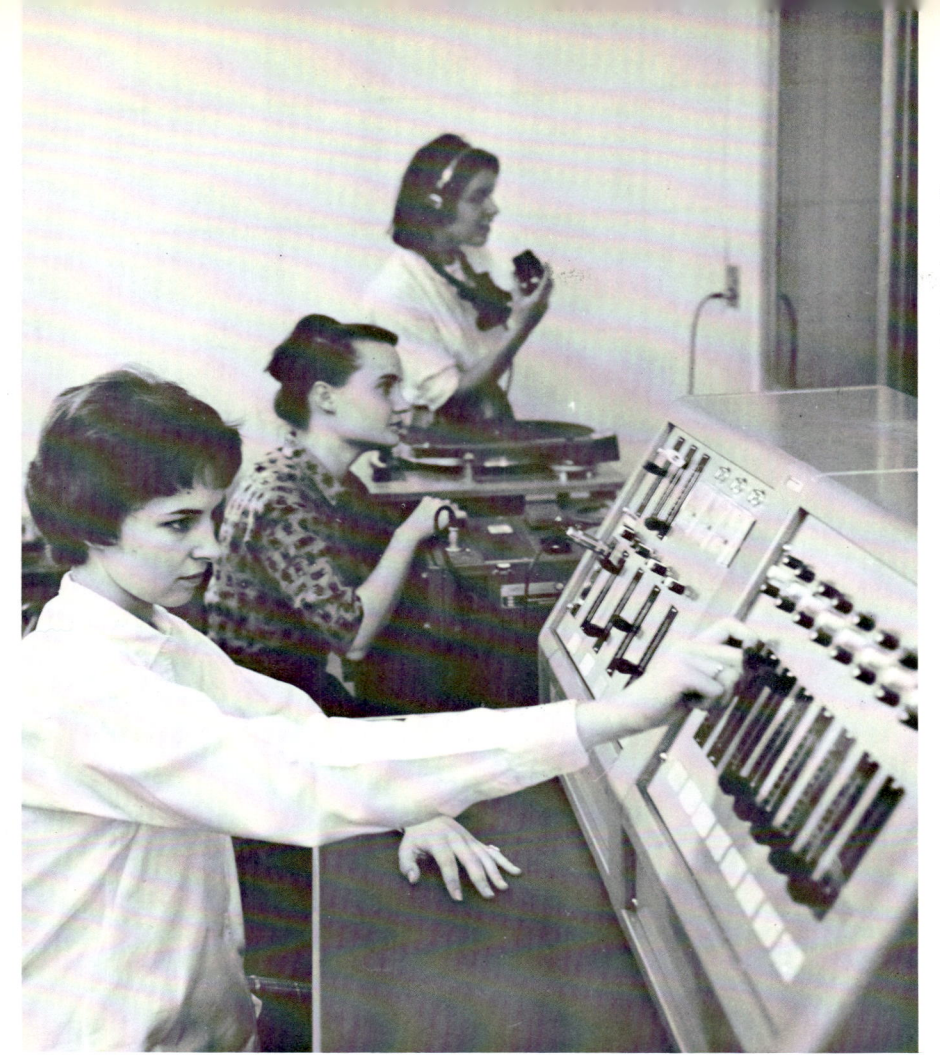

The sound control equipment in the Control Room of the theatre at Sweet Briar College includes microphone input, tape input and custom-built console. Disc turntable is portable and used for dubbing.

Wiring

Standard radio wiring practice is satisfactory for theatrical sound installations. The following precepts embrace strictly theatrical procedure:

1. It is good practice to assure isolation of microphone lines from loud-speaker lines by carrying microphone lines on one side of the house and loud-speaker lines on the other. As noted in Chapter 6, microphone lines must be kept as far as possible from electric motors, power lines, power transformers, motor generators.

2. Microphone cable to connect microphone to outlet should not be made up in lengths of more than 25 feet since repeated coiling of long lengths will result in breaking of shield. For flexibility all input lines should be made identical and be equipped with identical connectors.

3. Loud-speaker outlets should be equipped with female twist lock connectors.

4. There must be a single ground for all electronic sound equipment.

Sound Control System

The Stevens Sound Control System, Mark 1, designed by Vincent Mallory, provides facilities for complete control of the auditory component of the show.

Electronic sound control equipment varies so greatly in quality and performance that it seems important to note a few basic, essential characteristics here. Inferior equipment will wreck any show. The best is, in the last analysis, the cheapest. The specification which follows is derived from the Stevens Sound Control System, as used in the Metropolitan Opera and installed wholly or in part in numerous new theatres. Equipment which has the characteristics specified is good enough for any theatre. Any further restriction of response characteristic or power will serve not only to limit the unit concerned but to restrict the use of the whole system and limit the manner and degree in which it may be increased in size and flexibility. The Block Schematic Diagram contains enough units to handle adequately any play or opera by any production means so far envisioned in any theatre up to a 1,000,000-cubic foot capacity.

Detailed and excellent specifications for stage lighting, mechanical equipment, control devices, and communications systems are published by the equipment manufacturers. No manufacturer produces a complete sound control system for theatre use. For that reason the sound control system specification is here set forth in some detail.

BLOCK DIAGRAM OF COMPLETE SYSTEM

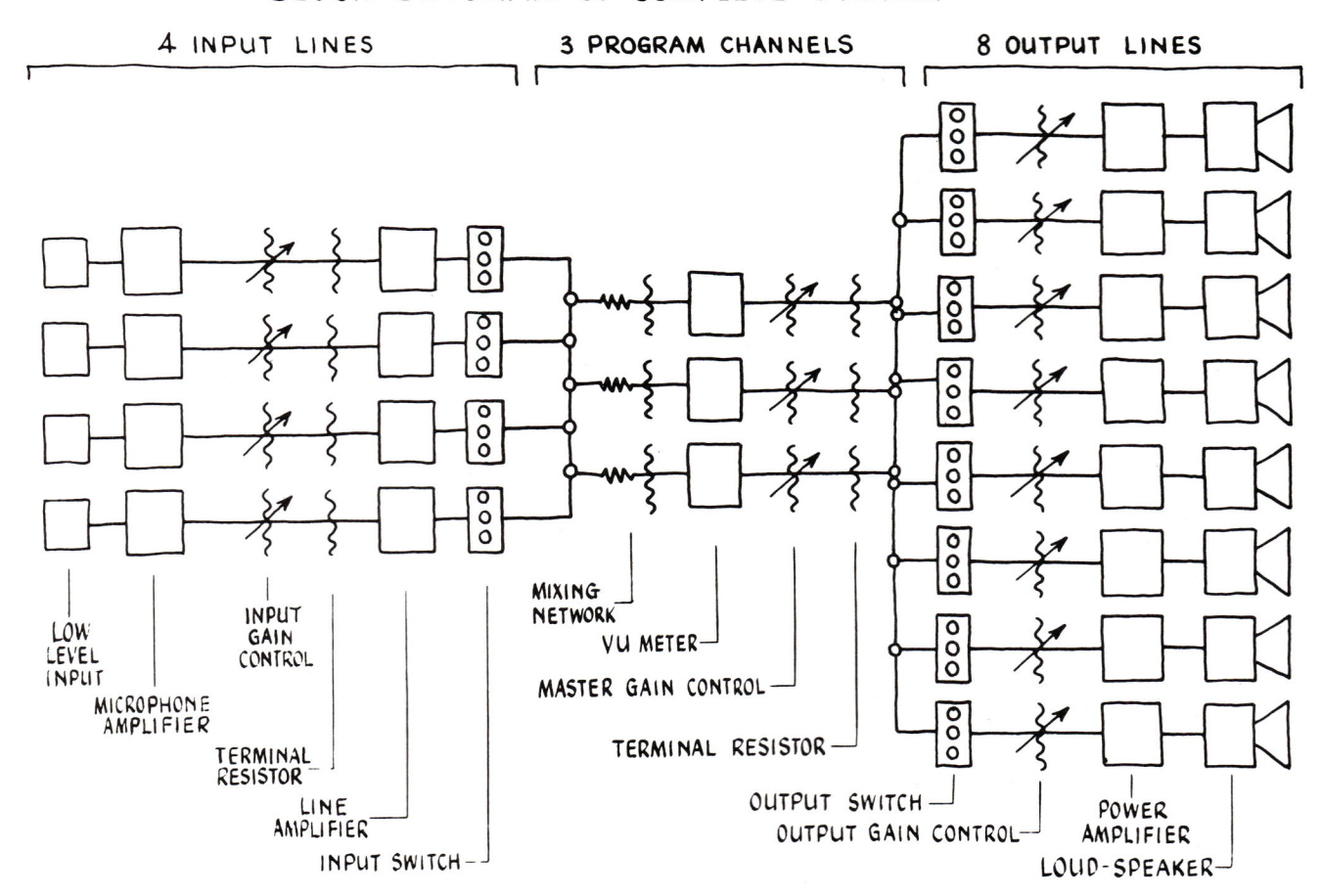

4 INPUT LINES — 3 PROGRAM CHANNELS — 8 OUTPUT LINES

LOW LEVEL INPUT
MICROPHONE AMPLIFIER
INPUT GAIN CONTROL
TERMINAL RESISTOR
LINE AMPLIFIER
INPUT SWITCH
MIXING NETWORK
VU METER
MASTER GAIN CONTROL
TERMINAL RESISTOR
OUTPUT SWITCH
OUTPUT GAIN CONTROL
POWER AMPLIFIER
LOUD-SPEAKER

I. MICROPHONES, CABLE AND CONNECTORS

1.1 Microphones to have either a low-level or a high-level output, as specified, and to have a flat frequency characteristic from 50 to 15,000 cycles.

1.2 Low-level type to be capable of unidirectional pickup.

High-level type to have an adjustable directional characteristic.

1.3 Frequency response must be substantially unchanged when used for distant pickup or for close talking.

1.4 Impedance into which the microphone works to be low—30 or 150 ohms, so that it may be operated at a distance from its amplifier.

1.5 All microphones to be in the same output level and impedance range so that they can be readily interchanged without adjustment at the amplifier input.

1.6 Vendor of microphones to furnish such plugs as necessary to connect microphone to cable, and couplings to permit microphone to be suspended.

1.7 The shield of microphone cable shall in no case be used as a signal conductor.

1.8 Microphone cable to have at least two conductors, color-coded, enclosed in a woven metal shield and then covered with a layer of good quality rubber.

1.9 Over-all diameter is to be not less than .25 inch.

1.10 Connectors to be metal-enclosed, locking type.

1.11 Provision shall be made in the connectors to connect metal shell to cable sheath.

II. TURNTABLES AND REPRODUCERS

2.1 Turntable to be driven by an hysteresis synchronous motor; to operate on 105 to 120 volts, 60-cycle alternating current.

2.2 Switching to be provided to operate turntable at 33⅓ rpm for microgroove discs and 78 rpm for sound effect discs.

2.3 Turntable and reproducer arm to take 16-inch diameter discs.

2.4 One monophonic reproducer cartridge, plug-in type, to be furnished, equipped with 1-mil diamond stylus and with one spare 2.7-mil diamond stylus.

2.5 Reproducer arm to be viscous damped.

2.6 Turntable and reproducer arm, assembled on flat panel.

2.7 Equalizing transformer to provide 50 ohm output and RIAA equalization to be located on panel.

Note:

Turntable reproducer not to be connected into the system, but to be used for dubbing from disc to magnetic tape.

2.8 The magnetic tape recorder-reproducer shall be professional equipment, having the following characteristics:

2.9 To be enclosed in a rugged carrying case and to weigh not more than 30 pounds.

2.10 To operate on standard 60-cycle commercial electric mains.

2.11 To have an over-all record-reproduce frequency response within ± 2 db (decibels) from 30 to 15,000 cycles per second with less than 4-db loss at 15,000 cycles.

2.12 To have a fixed NARTB equalization for record and for reproduce.

2.13 To have a single tape speed of 7.5 inches per second.

2.14 To provide full-width, single-track recording to permit editing and to provide a signal to noise ratio of at least 55 db.

2.15 Reliable adjustment of head orientation shall be provided.

2.16 To provide VU indication during recording and reproducing as well as monitoring from the tape during recording.

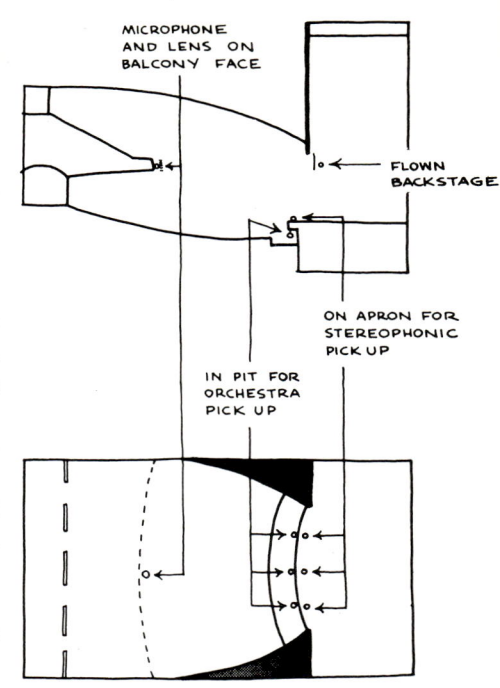

PRINCIPAL MICROPHONE POSITIONS

2.17 To provide a normal recording level (0 on VU meter) at least 12 db below the 3% distortion level.

2.18 To provide a transformer isolated output of 0 VU (+ 4 dbm) (1.228 volts) into 600-ohm line.

2.19 To provide a 0 VU 600-ohm line bridging input, plus a 50/150-ohm microphone input with separate gain controls for each.

III. RACK AND DESK ASSEMBLIES

3.1 Rack to be standard "rear door only" rack, constructed of $\frac{1}{16}''$ thick cold-rolled steel, and drilled to mount 19'' panels.

3.2 Available panel space to be 70'' x 19''.

3.3 Depth to be 18''.

3.4 Slate gray finish.

3.5 Panel mounting holes to be accurately drilled and tapped for #10-32 machine screws on $1\frac{1}{4}'' - \frac{1}{2}''$ centers.

3.6 Panel mounting screws and finishing washers to be supplied by the vendor.

3.7 Desk assembly, to contain input and output control panels, microphone and line amplifiers and the associated power supplies, to be a double unit assembly, comprising:

3.8 A double unit desk panel cabinet $9\frac{1}{8}''$ high x 42'' long x 16'' deep, constructed from $\frac{1}{16}''$ steel and welded into an integral unit. It shall contain two upper panels, each $17\frac{1}{4}''$ x 19'' mounted at an angle of 22 degrees from the horizontal. Mounting holes shall be at standard rack panel spacing.

3.9 A double unit extension table top constructed of $\frac{1}{16}''$ thick formica bonded to $\frac{3}{4}''$ thick plywood suitably braced underneath. It shall be 30'' wide, 55'' long and $2\frac{1}{2}''$ deep.

3.10 Pedestal unit constructed from $\frac{1}{16}''$ thick furniture steel with reinforced base and rigidly welded into one integral unit. For three sides, standard steel panels shall be furnished. For the front a ventilated door shall be furnished.

3.11 To support the 55'' table top of paragraph 3.9, a matching end pedestal and floor brace shall be furnished. The end pedestal shall be 6'' wide and 24'' deep. The floor brace shall be $25\frac{1}{2}''$ long.

Portable sound control consoles. Channel selector switches are color-coded lock-out push buttons. The operator is producing a thunder effect with a brush on mesh screen attached to a phonograph pickup.

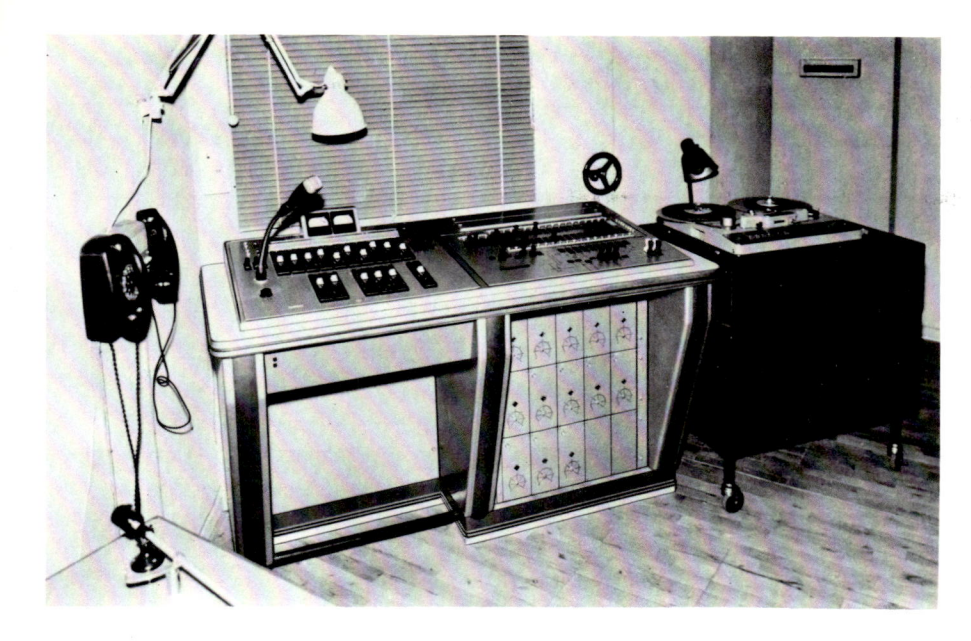

Telefunken sound control console and audio-tape console on casters.

IV. MICROPHONE AND LINE AMPLIFIERS

4.1   Each amplifier to be a plug-in type self-contained except for power supply, and to contain input and output isolating transformers.

4.2   Gain at 1,000 cycles to be not less than 40 db. With a frequency response at within ± 1 db from 30 cycles to 15 kilocycles.

4.3   Output of the line amplifier to be not less than + 18 dbm with a noise amplifier to be not less than + 4 dbm, with a noise output not greater than −72 dbm.

4.4   The output circuit of each type of amplifier to operate into a 600-ohm load impedance.

4.5   The input circuit of the line amplifier to operate from a 600-ohm load. The single input circuit of the microphone amplifier shall be adjustable to either 150- or 600-ohm input impedance.

4.6   Both types of amplifiers to mount with manufacturer designated power supplies and appropriate to amplifiers, in matching rack trays.

V. INPUT CONTROL PANEL

5.1   Input controls to be mounted on a ⅛″ steel panel, slate gray finish, 19″ x 12¼″.

5.2   To contain the circuit which transfers the output of any or all of the voltage amplifiers to any of three channels, namely, red channel, white channel, and green channel.

5.3   Channels to be so color-coded.

5.4   Each panel to contain four gain controls, each connected to the input of one of the four line amplifiers. These controls to be "T" attenuators with vertical rather than rotary movement, 600 ohms to 600 ohms.

5.5   Four triple push-button switches.

5.6   These switches connect line amplifiers to various channels.

5.7   In each channel a master control "T" attenuator, 600 ohms to 600 ohms.

5.8   In each channel, one 4″ x 4¼″ VU Meter. Written guarantee of ballistic characteristic meeting standard ASA CT6-5-1954, will be required.

5.9   Each channel to be terminated at this point by a noninductive 600-ohm resistor.

5.10   Each panel enclosure to include outlet connectors to three sets of cables to be externally connected to the output control panel.

5.11   Pilot light circuit showing the color of the channel into which each line amplifier is connected, to be included in this panel.

VI. SPECTRUM CONTROL

6.1   The frequency spectrum control shall comprise a constant impedance "T" Program Equalizer.

6.2   Input and output impedances to be 600 ohms.

6.3   Program equalizer to permit increase or decrease of the low frequencies, decrease of the high frequencies and increase of the high frequencies with emphasis at 3,000, 5,000 or 10,000 cycles as selected by operator.

6.4   At least 12 db of increase and 16 of decrease shall be available.

6.5   A key shall be provided for switching the program equalizer in or out of the circuit. This switching shall not introduce noise into the program and shall be accomplished without apparent change in the signal level.

6.6   Insertion loss of the program equalizer shall be not greater than 14 db.

6.7   It shall be designed for insertion between the microphone amplifier and the line amplifier.

VII. OUTPUT CONTROL PANEL

7.1   Output controls to be mounted on a ⅛″ steel panel having an angle of 22 degrees, slate gray finish, 19″ x 12¼″. The controls are:

7.2   Triple push-button switches to connect the inputs of the power amplifiers into the selected channel.

7.3   In the input line to each power amplifier, a 25,000-ohm potentiometer designed for attenuation in 20 steps of 2 db each.

Portable sound control console. At a station in the audience an operator may control inputs to balance direct and reproduced sound.

7.4 Eight sets of switches and controls shall be mounted on the output control panel.

7.5 Pilot light circuit showing the color of the channel into which each power amplifier is connected, to be included in this control panel.

7.6 Panel enclosure to include input connectors for three sets of cables from input control panel, as well as output connectors to power amplifiers.

VIII. POWER AMPLIFIER

8.1 Each power amplifier to be rack mounting, self-contained, with its own voltage supply, to operate from the 120-volt commercial alternating-current mains.

8.2 Input circuit to be isolated by an input transformer having a primary impedance of at least 25,000 ohms.

8.3 Amplifier, when used in a bridging connection across a 600-ohm line, to have a gain of at least 45 db.

8.4 Output power to be at least 40 watts with less than 2 per cent total harmonic distortion at full output from 30 to 20,000 cps and with less than 1 per cent harmonic distortion at half power output.

8.5 Unweighted output noise level to be 80 db or better, below rated output.

8.6 Output to operate into 4, 8, 16 ohms and 70 volt line.

8.7 Frequency characteristic to be within ± 1 db from 30 to 15,000 cycles.

8.8 Chassis containing this power amplifier to be drilled for vertical mounting on a standard relay rack.

8.9 Amplifier to occupy not more than $12\frac{1}{4}''$ of panel space, to be covered by a 16-gauge steel panel, gray enamel finish.

IX. LOUD-SPEAKERS, CABLE AND CONNECTORS

9.1 Loud-speakers to be capable of handling continuously full rated power of associated power amplifier, without damage or severe distortion.

9.2 Loud-speakers to be permanent magnet field.

9.3 Useful frequency range 35 to 15,000 cycles.

9.4 To be housed in a nonresonating structure having sufficient volume to preclude over-damping of the loud-speaker mechanism. An enclosure designed and furnished by the loud-speaker manufacturer is preferred.

9.5 70-volt line matching transformer to be included within enclosure. 32 watts with less than 0.5-db insertion loss.

9.6 Cable: Two-conductor, #12-gauge stage cable.

9.7 Connectors: Shall be locking, armored, two-conductor connectors.

All equipment is to be assembled and connected in conformity with practices covering such installations established by I.A.T.S.E.

It will be noted that the specifications provide that each unit shall have a flat response characteristic or be compensated to a flat characteristic in itself, with the single exception that the adjustable compensation specified in the voltage amplifier may be used to flatten the ends of the microphone response. The necessity for interchangeability and for increasing the number of units in the system does not allow variations from flat characteristic in one unit to compensate for opposite variations in another unit.

While in small systems it may be argued that single amplifier units, instead of separate voltage and power amplifiers will do, a single unit arrangement defeats flexibility and therefore has no place except in a motion picture sound system or simple public address system.

Intercommunication

For the purpose of coordinating the activities of a theatre, it is necessary that there be instantaneous communication between many parts of the plant. Cues must be transmitted to various parts of the stage, the trap room, the projection booth, etc.; dressing room calls must be made; department heads must exchange information; and the audience has to be called back into the house at the end of the intermission. All of these requirements vary in their special demands, and the satisfying of all of them by a single simple system is no small task. Nevertheless such a system must be installed unless the preparation of a show is to be difficult and wasteful, and its operation inefficient and unreliable.

Four types of activity in the theatre require intercommunication: rehearsal and performance, plant maintenance, rigging, and light rehearsal; the most complex requirement is the first, and it is for performance that the fixed permanent and most elaborate system is installed. The requirements for such a system are here set forth. It must be noted, however, that at dress rehearsal, independent communication channels from the house are required, from lighting designer to lighting control, from sound designer to sound control. These channels may be single special telephones, or one channel may be a pair of walkie-talkie radios which, because they can be moved easily, are also useful for rigging.

Intercommunication system for a medium-sized well-equipped community theatre.

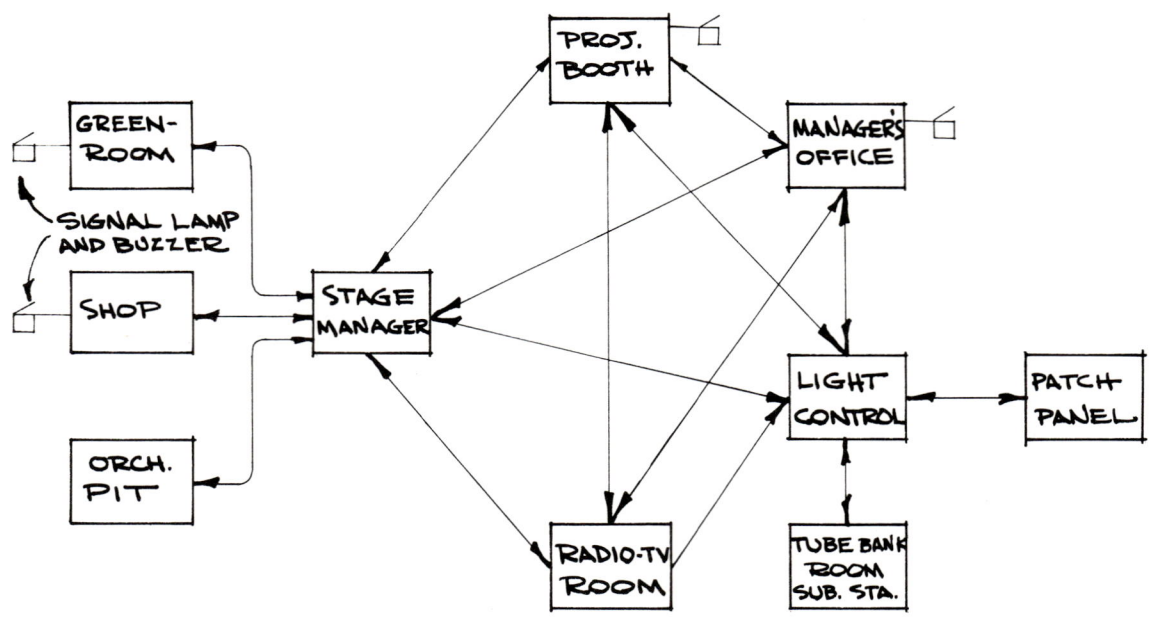

The requirements will be here set forth by a progressive listing of the requirements of the various types of stations. First, the control for performance and rehearsal must be at the stage manager's station, for that is the point from which most cues originate and to which most information must be conveyed. The stage manager must be able to communicate by voice or cue with (1) the opposite side of the stage, (2) the fly gallery, (3) the trap room, (4) the switchboard, (5) the orchestra, (6) the spotting booth, (7) the motion picture projection booth, (8) the sound control station. He must be able to communicate by voice with (9) the dressing rooms, (10) the green room, (11) the box office, (12) the shops, (13) the offices, (14) outside telephone switchboard.

He must have voice (PA), chime, or buzzer communication with foyer, lobby, and lounge, to recall the audience at the end of intermissions. He must be able to communicate with a number of stations simultaneously. Communication between stations listed must be possible without turning the stage manager into a telephone switchboard operator.

When the theatre is large and active enough to make an intercommunicating dial phone system economically justifiable, such a system is satisfactory for communication between stage manager's station and all stations not directly connected with the operation of the show. If such a system is not justified, however, it must be possible to shift the control of all telephones in the system from stage manager's station to that of the house PBX, so that the system can still function at times when the stage is not occupied.

Dialing or calling numbers, however, takes too long to be satisfactory as a means of instantaneous communication. Therefore all stations involved in the operation of the show, and that excludes only the offices and sometimes the shop, must be called by a single movement connection, simultaneously if necessary. Where stations are isolated from the stage, the talk-back loud-speaking telephone can be used to speed up communication further by making it unnecessary for the wrong person to pick up the phone, call for the person to whom the message is directed, and pass over the handset.

Stage Telephones

The talk-back loud-speaking telephone may be used on stage and at stations where it can be heard from the stage, during assembly, lighting, and rehearsal. On such occasions, a microphone may be used on an extension in the house for giving directions, and all stations ganged together, so that all directions go to all stations. This rehearsal and assembly technique has an added advantage in expediting the work in hand in that no station can talk back to the person giving directions, and much time often spent in discussion is thereby saved.

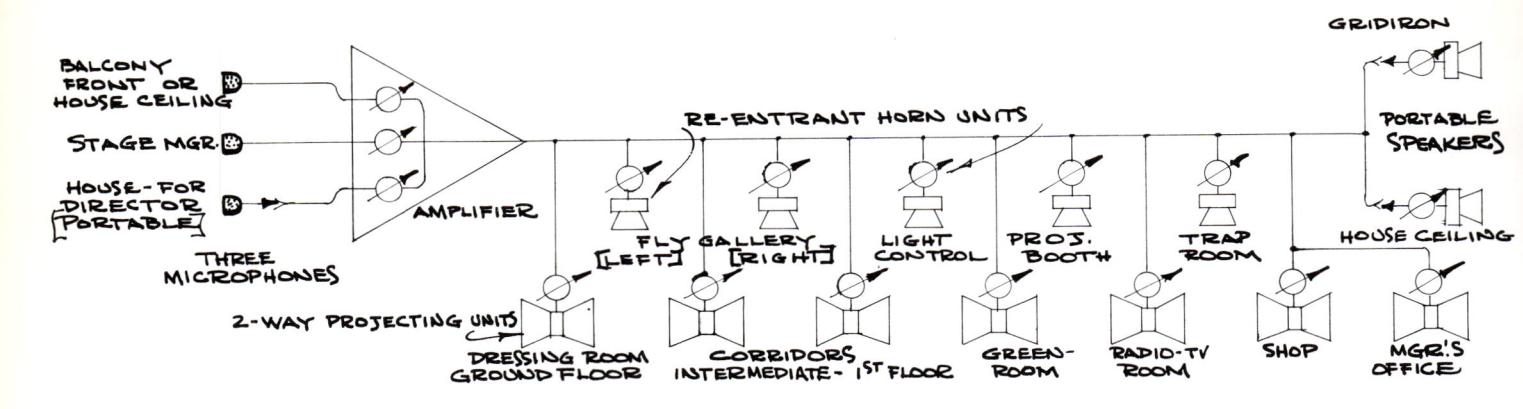

System for monitoring the performance.

The stage manager's station is a castered console which may be rolled to a controlling position. At the right is the panel for controlling work lights, cleaning lights and lecture lights. This obviates activating the stage lighting controls except for rehearsals and performances. Above is a lighting perch and gallery containing the interconnecting panel.

302

The fewer the cues which emanate from the stage manager, the more smoothly the show will run, since each cue passing from person to person suffers from the doubling of the human element hazard. It is therefore wise to run on dead cues as much as possible, and such operation is facilitated if all departments and persons who have to respond to cues hear the whole show, no matter where they are situated. The loud-speaking telephone system may be hooked up to stage microphones during performance as a means to this end. Whenever the stage manager wishes to, he can cut in with whatever other communication may be necessary. Whenever loud-speaking telephones are not so located as to be inaudible from the house, they can be equipped with automatic volume controls which vary the output level inversely as the signal. Whispers will come through such a system, while a loud signal will reduce itself to the same level as the whisper which cannot be heard in the house. The telephone with the loud-speaking features listed and with provision for plugging in head and chest sets where quiet operation is required is the most useful theatre intercommunication system and is an important part of a permanent installation.

Cueing Systems

Cueing must be simple, silent, positive, and must work in both directions. It must provide for difference between warn and dead cues so that the receiver will not mistake one for the other, and fail to initiate his operation, or get it early. Of the multitude of systems so far devised, only two seem worth considering. The first, particularly useful in elaborate productions, involves a box at the stage manager's station equipped with three or more numbered keys, and a pilot light for each station. All cues in the script are numbered. The stage manager sets up the number of the cue next in order and presses a master key which causes the cue number to light up at all stations simultaneously. The lighting of the cue number constitutes the warn, and the stations which it affects acknowledge the warn by pressing a button which lights the pilot light opposite their station numbers at the stage manager's station. The dead cue is shot by opening the master switch, at which all stations black out.

A more conventional cue system consists merely of lights at various stations controlled by push buttons, switches, or keys at the stage manager's station, and in the best installations a return cue is provided. Cue keys are best pilot lighted and color-coded. A system such as this is satisfactory for all but very elaborate productions, and for them it is perhaps better practice to run the show on dead cues which each person who normally receives cues takes directly from seeing the show or hearing it or both. Monitoring the show, a PA system to all stations effectively eliminates the necessity for most cueing.

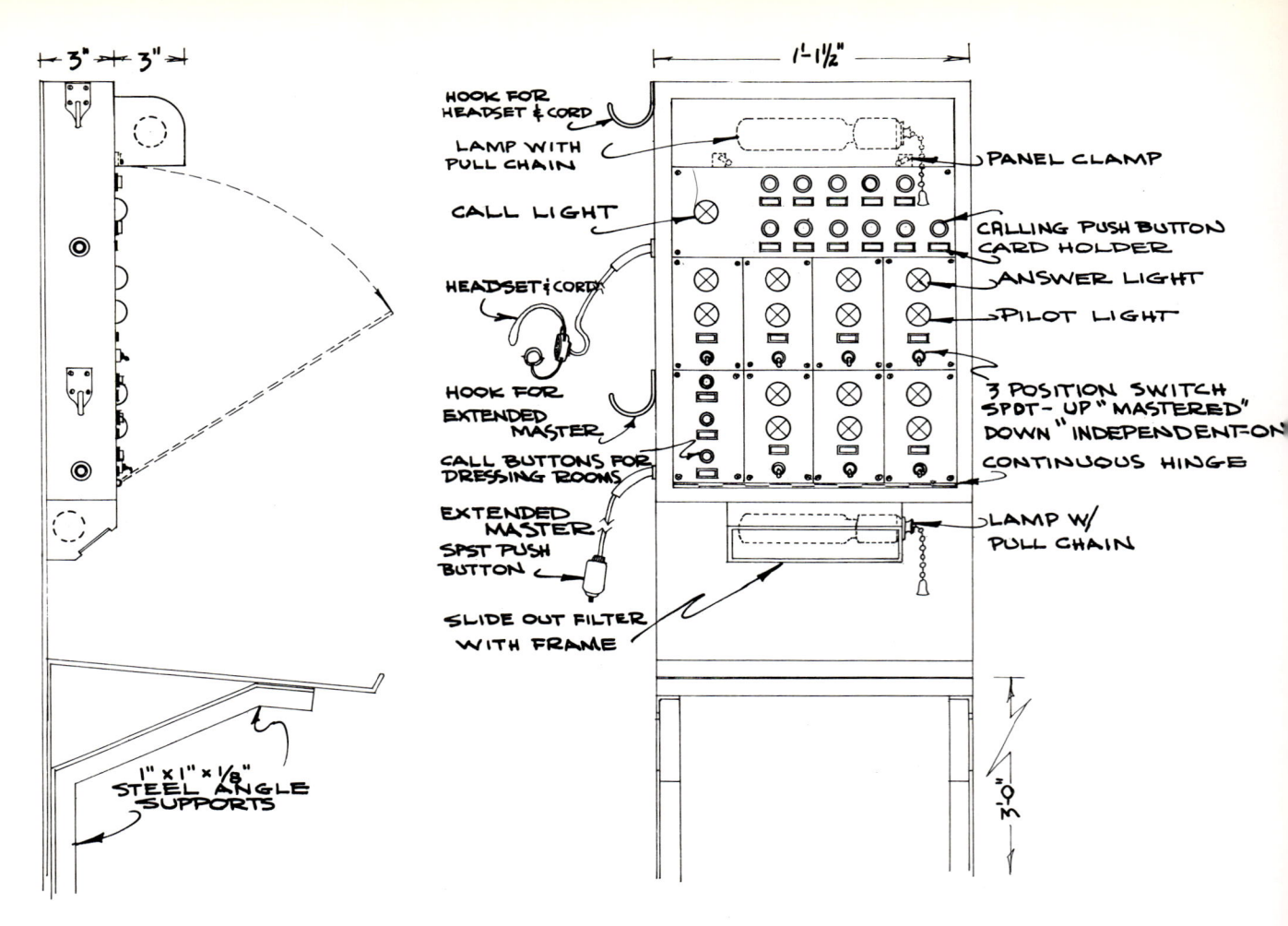

Extension cords on headset and master push button switch allow the stage manager to give cues from position with a view of the stage. The instrument panel hinges down for access.

Station Specifications

Opposite prompt side of the stage: Telephone call light, cue light (or cue number box), cue acknowledgment key. If the stage is large, loud-speaker for assembly and rehearsal.

Fly gallery: Same as opposite prompt (OP).

Trap room: Same as OP plus a click signal on the cue light and telephone call. Loud-speaker included irrespective of the stage size. The click signal, a device similar to a buzzer, save that the magnet holds the clapper as long as it is energized, so that only a click rather than a buzz is heard, calls attention to the cue or telephone call light, and is useful at all stations where the operator has duties which move him about so that the lights are not constantly in his line of vision. The audience seldom notices a click but can hear a buzzer in the next block.

Switchboard: Same as OP.

Orchestra (conductor's stand): Same as OP.

Spotting booth (and every position where house spots are operated): Same as trap room.

Motion picture projection booth: Same as trap room, plus outside telephone.

Sound control station: Same as trap room.

Dressing rooms: Talk-back loud-speaking telephone, preferably one built into the wall between every pair of dressing rooms. Talk-back button in each room.

It should be noted here that the Actors Equity Association recommended specification calls for two separate intercommunication systems to all dressing rooms: the monitor system from the stage manager and the telephone from the stage. The system here suggested amply satisfies the functional, if not the installation, requirement. In several new theatres, the stage monitor system is a wired television network.

Greenroom: Talk-back loud-speaking telephone. Outside pay telephone in booth, more than one if casts are large.

Box office; other offices: Telephone with buzzer call.

Shops: If the shops are used as part of the stage, communication to them is the same as to the trap room. If they are not, the same system is used as for the dressing rooms.

Outside telephones form the theatre's intercommunication system not associated with the running of the show. The average legitimate house in New York uses so few extensions that it doesn't need a switchboard. The Music Hall, despite the fact that the process of production is far from complete within the theatre, has a large PBX. The decision about how many extensions to put in, and where to put them, depends upon whether they can earn their keep. It is safe to assume that they will in all departments housed in separate rooms where the departments work all day throughout a considerable part of the season.

Talk-back telephones must be pilot lighted at the stage manager's station. Lights must be associated with keys and the keys must return to the open position when they are released. It must be possible for the stage manager to cut out his microphone and loud-speaker and substitute a telephone handset during performance. There must be provision for ganging all stations and feeding the system from a microphone in the house, during rehearsal, or on stage during the show. Amplifiers must be simple, rugged, and accessible. Class B will do.

All switches and keys must be silent. Mercury switches will handle voltages too high for telephone keys.

There must be provision for substituting head and breast sets and loud-speaking telephones for all telephone handsets used at operating positions and button extensions for cue keys at all stations where cues may originate.

The stage manager's cue and telephone keys may well consist of one double throw key per station, which will stay closed in the telephone position and return from cue position.

Obviously, the intercommunication system must be designed for the specific theatre, and its characteristics will depend largely upon the uses to which the theatre is to be put. No satisfactory system has ever been designed by a person outside the theatre. Some elaborate and costly installations have proved so cumbersome and so unreliable that they gather dust while the stage manager shoots his cues by means of a muffled buzzer hooked to a couple of dry cells or by waving a handkerchief.

The most effective cueing is, of course, that supplied by the band at the circus. On signal from the ringmaster, it establishes the timing of the performance, and people and animals take their warn, entrance, and act cues from the music. The opera also operates on music cues, as can many other shows in which music is played more or less continuously.

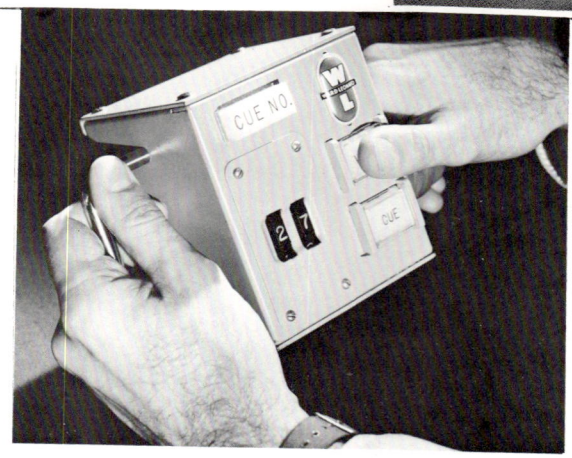

When the stage manager presses the warn *button the cue number adds one at his station and at all remote stations and the* warn *signal is lighted. When he pushes the* cue *button the cue signal is lighted at all remote stations. When he releases the* cue *button all signals go off.*

14: Production services

Up to this point the functions of the theatre involved in performance have been treated. This chapter is concerned with the preparation of the production that must precede performance and the architectural requisites arising therefrom.

Six major steps in the theatrical process before performance are:
1. Script is written
2. An organization is formed
3. The production is designed and planned
4. The production is prepared and manufactured
5. The production is assembled
6. The production is rehearsed.

Steps (5) and (6) have been treated in Chapter 8. The first four steps must receive consideration, because they are integral functions of the total theatre plant, whether they take place under the same roof as the performance or in a separate building or buildings remote from the theatre. Where the process of production is carried through by one organization the former situation is advantageous.

Organization

There are two basic types of the theatre organization: (1) the organization within which the process of production is complete and often within the single building; (2) the organization in which all technical elements of the production are prepared by independent contractors. The first form is standard for most theatres in Europe, and for community, university and college, high school, stock (including summer stock) and repertory (including opera) theatres in America. Most theatres in these categories are organized to plan and execute the entire work of theatrical production, including, in the case of professional and graduate theatre schools and music conservatories, writing and composing the plays and operas which are produced.

The second type of organization in which the functions of theatrical production are divided among many entrepreneurs is the American system of professional play production centered in New York, called the combination system. In it, scenery, lights, costumes are prepared by individual contractors and assembled with the other elements of production only when completed.

Some organizations employ elements of both systems. Many factors influence the type of organization which will function in any theatre at any time. In the interests of efficiency, represented, if in no other field, by the saving of transportation costs, the theatre should be designed to be as self-sufficient as possible.

The theatrical organization has two principal functions: production and business. Production includes all of the activity of preparing and presenting the theatrical production: casting, rehearsing actors, music, dances, designing the production, and manufacture and assembly of the scenic elements. Business includes providing plant and procuring the facilities for the producing personnel, promoting an audience, receiving income and making expenditures, observing laws, and keeping accounts and records.

Theatrical organizations are extremely diverse; often functions and subfunctions are vested in the same person. Any categorical division stated here is schematic for purposes of exposition and must be subjected to modification in consideration of the factors in a particular situation.

The policies of any theatrical organization are in the hands of a managerial body which requires offices. From a single managing director or general manager, this managerial body may expand to comprise producer, production manager, stage manager, dance director, art director, technical director, and numerous assistants, and in schools, acting and speech coaches.

An example of a completely expanded organization is Radio City Music Hall and of a completely contracted one is the combination producer who may maintain a small office and a secretary between productions, but engages a complete producing organization by contract only when he has a play to produce and only for the production of that one play.

The demand for working facilities for a theatrical organization ranges then from a single office to numerous specialized offices and studios for the staff of a resident, continuing, repertory or stock company.

The Play Is Written

The preparation of scripts, musical scores, libretti and choreography is seldom done in the theatre. During the preparation of a production, however, rewriting of script, rescoring of music and redesigning of dances are often necessary. The complete theatre plant must contain, then, studios for playwright, composer, and choreographer with appropriate equipment. Civic and college art centers, of which there is a growing number, often fill these requirements.

Opera houses will contain music libraries.

The professional theatre school will have seminar rooms for play writing courses.

Casting	**Waiting room:** Comfortable furniture.	**THE PLAY IS PRODUCED**
	Casting director's office: Standard office equipment	**Talent**
Tryouts or Auditions	**Audition room:** Minimum 15′ x 20′	
	Platform at one end, several chairs.	
	Acoustics good for voice. Piano, if for musical auditions.	

Ballet rehearsal room. Mirror wall, wall bar, acting area marked on floor.

Audition room necessary only if theatre or rehearsal room are not available for tryouts and auditions.

Rehearsals

Rehearsal room:

Minimum size: acting area of same size and shape as that of the theatre for which show is being prepared, *plus* narrow strip of offstage space for actors, *plus* generous space for director, stage manager, and author on one long side.

Washable floor without carpet, glareless general illumination minimum about 15 fc at floor level. Acoustics good for voice.

Equipment: 24 sturdy chairs. Three small sturdy tables, an assortment of strong standard household furniture (no upholstered pieces and no special pieces). Levels, ramps and platforms as they are to be in performance.

Use of the stage by other production departments often necessitates rehearsals elsewhere. Hence the rehearsal room is necessary to continued activity under good conditions. A lounge may serve as a rehearsal room, but it must meet the space and light requirements to do so adequately. The regular lounge furniture must not be used for rehearsals; it will be damaged.

Rehearsal room may double as broadcast studio, in which case it should first conform

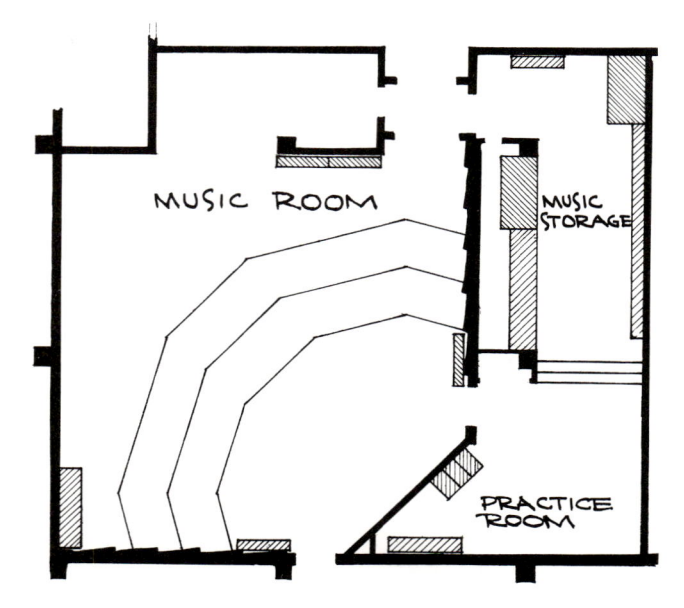

Orchestra rehearsal room with asymmetrical shape and sound barrier walls. Richard Montgomery High School, Rockville, Maryland. Burket and Tilghman, architects.

to studio requirements in shape, size and acoustical characteristics.

Professional theatre school or repertory theatre often has several productions in process simultaneously, hence needs several rehearsal rooms.

For rehearsal in the theatre: easy passage between auditorium and stage. A ramp from the aisle to the stage, better than stairs which are dangerous in a darkened theatre.

Rehearsal lights. A setup of lights independent of stage lighting control board to illuminate the acting area but not to shine into the eyes of the director, minimum 15 fc at floor level.

Rehearsal of singers requires:
1. Piano, light.
Rehearsal piano onstage. Performance piano in pit should *not* be used.
2. If not in the theatre, then a rehearsal room, preferably designed for broadcast pickup. Because of acoustic differences, a number of singing rehearsals must be held in the theatre.

Rehearsal of dancers requires:
Rehearsal room as above. Piano. Dance floor.

Rehearsal of musicians requires:
Orchestra pit, or rehearsal studio large enough to permit arrangement of instruments as in pit. Preferably designed for radio pickup. Lighting similar to rehearsal room above.

Some music rehearsals must be held in the theatre for acoustic reasons.

During the rehearsal period, the physical production (scenery, properties, costumes, lights, and sound) is being prepared on drawing boards, in shops and in studios, and usually makes no demands upon the stage or its equipment. Rehearsals of any kind of production are best conducted in the theatre in which the performance is to be given. Other uses of the theatre often make this impossible, in which case rehearsal spaces as specified above are required.

Dance Drill and Practice

Dance practice room (studio):
Rehearsal room as above, *plus* one mirror wall, wall bars on other walls, hardwood floor, piano.

311

Comment: Dance requires rehearsal and practice space separate from the stage and in addition to the cast rehearsal room.

Showers and dressing rooms convenient to the dance practice room.

Music Practice
(Schools, Conservatories, and some repertory companies.)

Practice rooms for musicians and singers:
Minimum 100 sq ft each. Piano in each. Music stands. Acoustically isolated from the house and from each other.

Orchestra practice room
(See Rehearsal room)

Instrument storage and locker room:
Minimum 200 sq ft. Shape optional. Located near practice rooms but with good access to orchestra pit and outside, for loading and unloading instruments.

Rest Periods

Recreation room, or lounge:
The theatre greenroom, (Chapter 8) if near rehearsal and practice rooms.

Snack bar:
Vending machines for light food and drinks. Lunchroom cooking and serving equipment optional.

Comment: Affords sustenance through long rehearsals.

Costumes

A theatrical costume department must be equipped to fabricate any imaginable costume. The process is more involved than tailoring or dressmaking because theatrical production knows no limitation of style, material or color. Actor's shapes must sometimes be changed to conform to requirements of design or to make up for natural deficiencies.

Actors measured for costumes and wigs

Fitting room
(See below)

Materials purchased and stored

Supply room:
Materials consist largely of cloth in bolts, sewing materials, small supplies, pattern paper in rolls. Deep shelves for bulk materials. Shallow shelves for sewing materials. Some mothproof storage space for woolens, felts and furs.

Patterns drafted from measurements

Costume shop:
Pattern drafting table. Minimum 3′ x 6′ with

	working space all around it. Hard surface. Clean area.
Muslin garment made up from pattern and fitted	**Costume shop and fitting room** (See below)
Cloth is dyed	**Dye shop:** Storage for dyestuffs. Closed cabinet with shelves. Space for demijohns of acid. Small chemist's table with balance and weights.

MATERIALS

COSTUMES

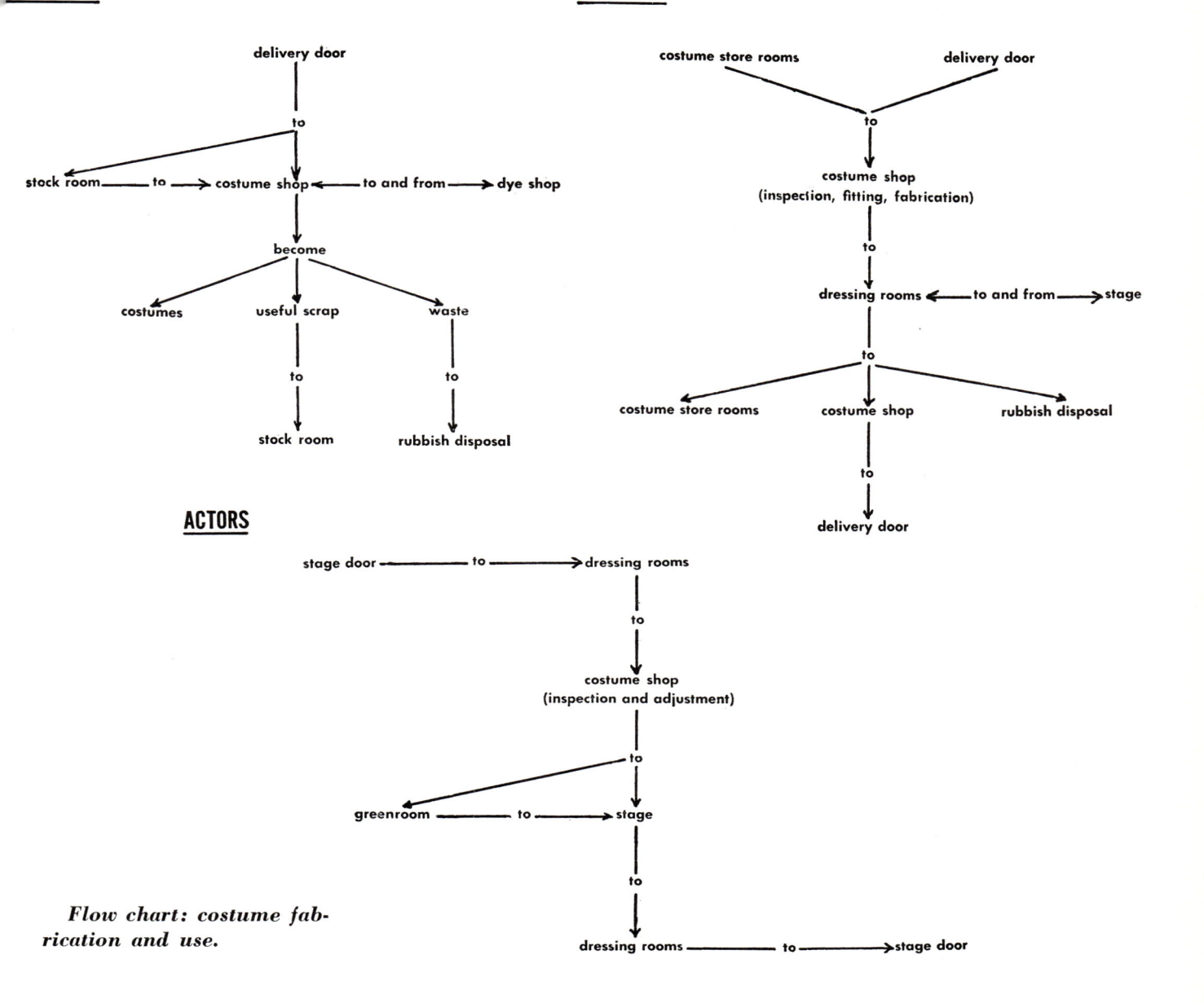

ACTORS

Flow chart: costume fabrication and use.

313

Dye vats, water supply, gas or electric heat, drying racks, (preferably in separate room). Air circulation supplying warm dry air to speed the drying of cloth, and separate from the system for the rest of building to isolate the odors associated with the dye process.

With the increased use of synthetic materials which cannot be dyed, and the wide range of colors available in most fabrics, the dye shop as a separate facility is not always justified. If there is no dye shop, the paint shop may be used.

Cloth is painted

Large table:
Surface must be proof against paint, water and acid. Clear working space around table.

Cloth is pressed

Costume shop:
Hand ironing boards, electric ironers, steam presser.

Cloth is cut

Cutting tables:
Minimum 3′ x 6′ with clear space all around. Preferably arranged so that two tables may be put together for big jobs (trains, capes, etc.).

Cloth is sewn into actual garments

Power sewing machines:
Allow 5′ x 8′ floor space for each, including operator.

Hand sewing tables:
Allow 4′ x 6′ floor space for each, including worker.

Garments are fitted

Fitting room:
Minimum 100 sq ft.
Podium, 3′ x 3′ x 1′ high.
Full-length mirror.
Small cabinet for fitting supplies.

Garments are finished and trimmed

Hand sewing tables
(See above)

Costume accessories are made and procured

Accessories shop:
Minimum 10′ x 15′.

Small wood- and metal-working benches with tools.

Accessories constitute hats and shoes, plus all decorative and useful implements which may pertain to costumes, from spectacles to broadswords. The craftsman in costume accessories is generally able to make use of wood- and metalworking tools and machines in the scenery or property shops. If such shops are not available, he must be equipped to work in wood, leather, sheet metal, wire, cardboard, and plaster of paris. In planning a theatre, it is advisable to supply the shop space with cabinets. It would be either uneconomical or impossible, perhaps both, to attempt to furnish all the equipment which might be necessary for some unspecified future job.

Fitting in costume shop. Radio City Music Hall.

Costumes are shipped	Shipping room, if the costume department is separate from the theatre. Minimum 10′ x 20′. Assembly counters, space for hampers and trunks. Access to street via wide corridors or elevators.
Costume shop administration	Office. Minimum 100 sq ft.

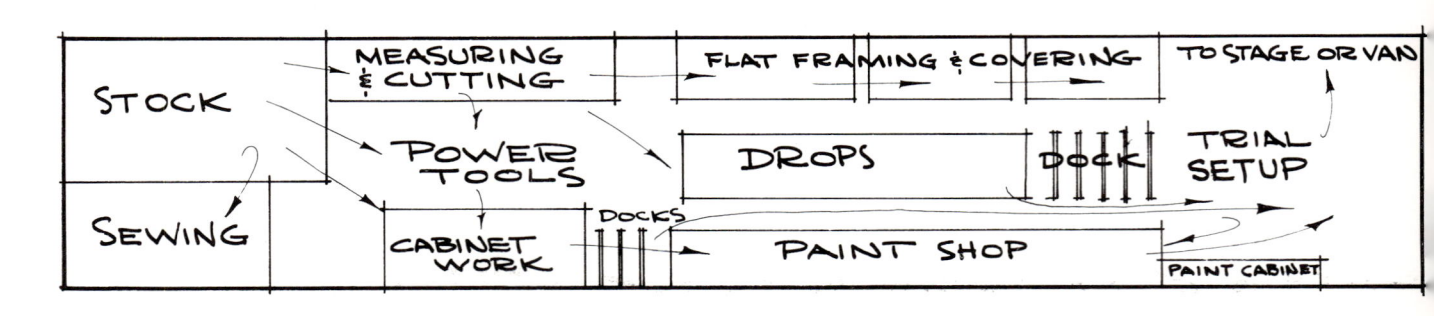

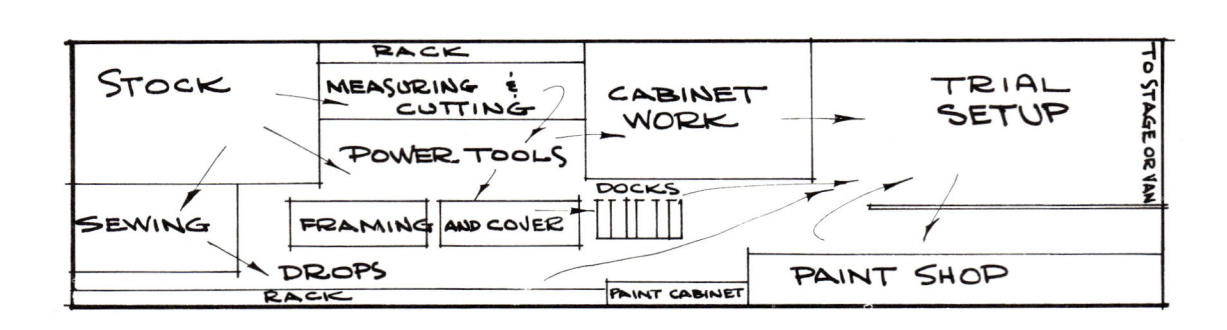

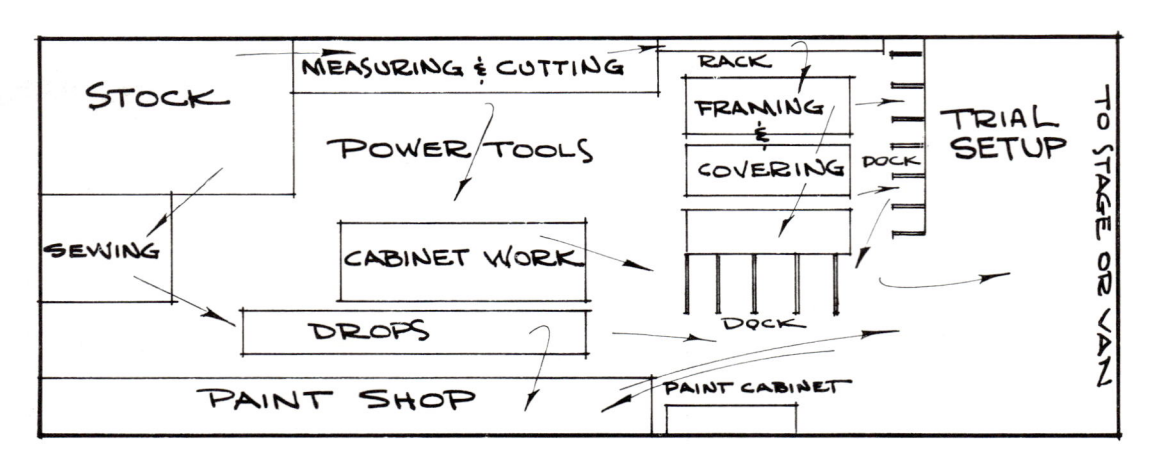

Schematic diagrams of scene shop layouts. Areas are proportional but not to scale. Sizes depend upon the size of scenery to be built. Adaptable to other floor plans.

Scenery is designed

Design studio:
Drafting tables, model building bench and equipment, reference files and bookshelves, cabinets for filing sketches and drawings. Cabinets for storage of drawing materials.

For professional schools and conservatories, collection of source material, design library, models. Museum.

Scenery is planned

Technician's office:
Desk, chair, and filing cabinet, bookshelves, drafting table, cabinet for drawings and materials.

Production drafting room:
Drafting tables, model making bench and

Scenery

Scene shop. A traverse stage wagon carrying a complete setting and properties may be rolled into the shop from the stage. Paint shop is out of the picture, left.

317

A framing bench for scenery. Note the preset right angle corner and the hardware trays. Precut lumber is stored below.

Scenery is manufactured

equipment, files for technical data, cabinets for material samples, wallboard for moulding samples, wall covered with tack boards.

Scene shop:
Supply room for storage of bulky materials, especially lumber, building board, and rolls of cloth and chicken wire. Cabinets for small supplies. Tool racks.

Measure and mark, cut, work-up:
Power woodworking tools: pullover saw, table saw, saber saw, mortiser, jointer, drill press and router.

Join into frame, flameproof, cover:
Woodworking benches, assembly benches, covering benches. Each 6' x 16' minimum with 3' of working space all around. Storage racks for finished and partially completed scenery.

Drops, ceilings and trial assembly:
Trial assembly area big enough to receive sets of scenery assembled as if on stage.

Rigging equipment overhead.

(Scene shops, except for a few in New York City, are often too small for their uses. For shops planned with the minimum space for efficient work under the conditions stated, see the illustrations.)

318

Metal working shop:

Lathe, break, drill press, saw, sheet metal shears, electric welding equipment, hand tools. Facilities for performance of the simpler processes of fabrication in sheet metals and steel (worked cold) are desirable. There is little demand for hot shaping of iron and steel; the small amount which is required may be most economically done at a smithy. The metalworking shop may, in all but the largest repertory theatres, be combined with the lighting shop.

Location:

Noise is produced in both scene shop and metalworking shop. Sound isolation from noise-sensitive areas is essential.

Scenery is painted

Paint shop:

There are two principal methods of painting scenery, on a paint frame or on a paint floor, neither of which is an adequate substitute for the other, because the effects produced differ.

Paint frame:

Minimum 1½ times acting area width, full proscenium height, hung on counterweighted rigging which may be motor-driven against a blank wall so as to sink past the working floor to bring the top within easy working reach of a person standing on the floor. Sinkage equals height minus 6′. Access to bottom of sinkage well for cleanout and to retrieve dropped tools. Bottom of sinkage well troughed and pitched to high-capacity drain. Automatic ejector or sump pump in well if bottom is below sewer main. Easily accessible cleanout trap in drainage line. No sharp turns in drainage line. Working floor at paint frame pitched to drain, to allow washing. Slight curb at edge for safety.

Paint floor:

(Minimum area somewhat greater than paint frame.) In some instances the stage floor or scene shop floor may be used as a paint floor, but more often other uses of the stage and shop make this impossible.

Painting in the scene shop or on stage produces objectionable dampness, dirt and dust in these spaces.

Painting tools and supplies:

Bins for dry colors. Fireproof locker for flam-

Two paint frames back to back, one with scenery attached. Painters stand on the floor and scenery is raised through a trap as they paint it.

mable paints and ingredients. Ventilated cabinets with flat shelves made of bronze wire mesh for storing brushes. Space for barrels of glue, whiting, and flameproofing. Power outlets for air compressor motor.

Ventilating and heating of paint shop:
The ideal situation comprises high-capacity circulation of warm dry air, separate from the system for the rest of the building, to produce rapid drying of painted scenery.

Sink with hot and cold water. Three-burner gas or electric stove. Double boiler tank to take three 12 qt pails, with automatic heat and water controls.

Lighting of paint shop:
Evenly distributed, about 25 fc minimum, white or daylight fluorescent or cold cathode lighting. Auxiliary circuit to supply evenly distributed incandescent light from stage-type floodlights, allowing test of the painting under stage colors. Projection space. Ideally there should be space in front of the paint frame to allow projection of an image from a slide for enlargement onto scenery. A pyramid of clear space with its altitude horizontal and its apex ½ the width of the frame in front of the frame. Projection may be from a movable tower or stepladder at apex.

Access to the paint shop:
Scenery is brought to the paint shop in large units. Frequently one dimension equals the width of the frame, and sometimes framed scenery equals the width and height of the frame. Therefore access to the frame should be in a straight line, preferably parallel to the frame. It should not be necessary to swing or turn scenery through spaces where other work is in progress.

Surface finishes in paint shop. Many ingredients of scene paint induce corrosion of metals. Much water is used both in scene painting and in cleaning the paint shop. Therefore surfaces must be either of wood which is replaceable if it rots, or of concrete, tile, or noncorroding metals or enamels.

Scenery is stored

A continuing theatre organization may effect considerable saving of time, labor, and materials by the storage and re-use of scenery. The apparent saving in labor and materials may be cancelled by the costs of land and building. This is true in New York City where rental of storage space is too high to make the storage of scenery economical. The apparent saving may also be cancelled by transportation costs if the storage space is not near the scene shop and stage. The saving in time is real in any case. In places where land costs are lower than in New York City, there is the likelihood that a triple saving will be achieved by efficient storage and re-use of scenery.

A policy of storing only standard pieces of scenery which are most likely to be used again, guarantees against filling the storage space with useless items.

For efficient storage, scenery must be categorized according to its space-filling characteristics. There are four main categories: rolled scenery, flat scenery, architectural trim, and three-dimensional pieces. Each of these categories requires specially shaped storage space. The total space must be subdivided according to the expected quantities of scenery in each category to be stored. The entire space, furthermore, must be easily accessible from the stage and the scene shop.

Storage of scenery under the stage in fireproof vaults is permitted in the current New York building code. Though its use may be restricted this space will be needed at times and should not be omitted.

Scenery is shipped out

Loading doors, covered loading space, platform level with floor of motor trucks: Changes of grade necessary to effect this made outside the building. Straight paths of movement from shop to trucks. (See Chapter 8.)

If scenery goes directly from paint shop to stage in the same building, paint shop and stage on same level: clear, wide, straight paths of movement, as short as possible.

Scenery is washed

High-pressure hose connectable to mixing hot- and cold-water supply in paint shop. Force control valve in nozzle. Scrub brushes, long- and short-handled. Drains at bottom of well and in working floor as described above.

Stage Lighting

Lighting is designed

Guided by the stage designer's concept of the visual aspect desired, the lighting required by the playwright's script, and the director's projected stage action as it expresses demands upon the lighting, lighting is designed by the stage designer himself or by the lighting designer. If by the stage designer, it is done in his office or studio. If by a lighting designer, a studio-office is necessary.

Equipment: standard office furniture, file cabinets, shelves for reference books, drafting table, racks or cabinets for the storing of blueprints.

Lighting is planned

Lighting office or studio:
The plan for the lighting graphically implements the design. It consists of a *lighting layout* in the form of mechanical drawings showing the location of all lighting instruments on plans, sections and elevations of the set or sets, *instrument schedule* stating all particulars about each instrument and identifying each instrument by an index number for reference to the layout, and *cue sheet*, giving in sequence of performance all operations of lighting instruments with adequate cues taken from the script or the stage action.

Lighting apparatus is procured

Three sources: owned by the organization, purchased, rented.

It is most economical for a continuing theatrical organization to own the bulk of its lighting apparatus. This implies a large initial investment but ease of procurement, coupled with the savings effected by re-use, warrants it. Progressive purchase over a period of years allows a growing organization to acquire in time all necessary apparatus.

Instrument storage:
Adequate storage for a full complement of lighting instruments, accessible to the stage and to the lighting shop, and planned for efficient use of three-dimensional space, is a necessary part of the theatre plan, whether the apparatus is all procured initially or over a period of time.

Lamp and accessory storage:
Many small devices are necessary for the mounting and operation of stage lighting instruments. Stage cables are necessary to connect

instruments to stage outlets. Used directly in connection with assembly of lighting instruments on stage, these objects should be stored close to the stage.

Fabrication, maintenance, repair, and experimentation:
The modification of instruments to perform special functions, the construction of new instruments and parts of instruments, repair, and maintenance require a small workshop equipped with machines and tools for the fabrication of sheet metal, steel (worked cold), and wire. There must be equipment for bending, cutting and threading iron pipe and conduit.

Rapid change of show in repertory and stock productions demands that a standard layout of lighting instruments be kept mounted in performance positions. A plan for lighting, similar to that first enunciated by Stanley McCandless is made the basis of lighting all productions, and special instruments, held to the irreducible minimum, are installed to meet nonstandard requirements of each particular production.

Properties are designed	The design of properties is a duty of the stage designer and is done in his studio. (See above.)	**Properties**
Properties are procured	Properties are either bought, rented, or made. As with lighting instruments, the ownership of properties by a continuing theatre organization is warranted by the ease of procurement and the financial savings effected thereby. The more productions an organization presents the greater are the savings of time and money.	

Property shop:
Inasmuch as the category of properties embraces all conceivable objects, it is patently impossible to purchase and own all those which may be required. Hence there must be provision for the fabrication of properties in wood, metal, plastic substances, fabrics and other materials. Examples of made properties are a maguey plant native to Mexico but needed for a play produced in New England, a replica of an iron safe, made light enough for a quick scene shift, and leg shackles to make no noise because they are worn by the ghostly chain gang in the *Emperor Jones*.

323

Property storeroom:
Adjustable shelves for small objects. Ample open space for large objects. Access to stage and property shop direct and wide. Largest object a grand piano. Planned for maximum use of three-dimensional space. Items hung from overhead wherever possible.

Sound: Electronics	Sound control is planned	**Technical director's office**
	Equipment assembled	**Shop:** If equipment is not permanently installed in the theatre.
	Equipment tested and maintained	**Shop** (above): Equipment: Work bench, storage cabinets and shelves. Vacuum Tube Volt-ohm Milliammeter Tube Tester, Audio Oscillator, C-R-Oscilloscope, 5″ preferable, usual electronics shop hand tools.

With the increased use of electronic control

Portable tape recorder suitable for theatre use. Can be used to record, edit, dub and reproduce.

	for stage lighting and machinery, electronic maintenance becomes increasingly important and may require more shop space than the electrical shop.
Recording	Permanent studio for conservatories of music. Other theatres: portable equipment kept in sound shop, used in studios, or rehearsal rooms for making up show records, voice training, performance records.

The theatre school or conservatory may start its training with the basic elements of the arts of the theatre. The plant will, in such cases, need standard school facilities for such a curriculum: classrooms, demonstration amphitheatre, seminar rooms, drafting rooms, and numerous rehearsal rooms.	**School**
Management	**Administration and Business**

In presentation, opera, repertory, and the motion picture palace, the operation is large enough to require a large executive staff and an appropriate suite of offices. Even the smallest motion picture house has a manager's office which serves as the treasurer's office, necessary wherever ticket cages or counters are used.

Equipment: Standard office equipment for receipt and expenditure of money and keeping records: desks, chairs, files, accounting machines, safe.

Promotion of Audience

The public relations person of a theatrical organization is called a theatrical press agent, but his duties encompass the exploitation of all means of public relations for the promotion of audiences.

Equipment: Standard office equipment, plus large table for laying out publicity material. Large shelves for the temporary storage of same. Standard files for pictures and typescript.

Ticket Sale

The member of a theatrical organization who is charged with the sale of tickets and held accountable for the money received therefrom is called the treasurer. The treasurer's office is in essence an accounting office and is so staffed and equipped. In a small theatre the treasurer's office is connected with the box office or is combined with it. When connected, it sometimes also serves as the manager's office. (See Box Office, Chapter 5.)

Secretarial Functions

General stenography and typing, and filing, are often augmented by the typing and duplicating of scripts under pressure of time limitations.

Equipment: for regular use, typewriter desks, chairs, files, and supply cabinets according to the needs of the organization. Reserve typing facilities for pressure periods. High-speed duplicating equipment.

Theatre in the Georgian style. Music and art wings left and right, Sweet Briar College.

15: Over-all considerations

This chapter treats those elements and factors of theatre planning which pertain to the theatre as a whole, to more than one part of the theatre or aspect of the theatrical function, and to the interrelationship of the various parts of the whole theatre insofar as the relationship is not implicit in the parts themselves.

Just as each part of the theatre must serve discrete functions, so the complete theatre plant must:

1. Accommodate an audience
2. Accommodate a performance
3. Bring audience and performance together in the most effective relationship.

These functions are universal and interdependent and combine to make possible the *total uniform effect* which is the requirement of the audience and the purpose of the showman.

Functional requisites are identical irrespective of the origin of the theatre building project. The *origin* of a plan for a theatre is sometimes confused with function. The theatre planner must not be tempted to compromise basic function with the objectives of making money, affording a focal point for social activity, establishing or maintaining social prestige. The theatre which fulfills its basic functions adequately will titillate the sensibilities of the dilettante and make money for the impresario. It will not accomplish these ends to the satisfaction of anyone if any essential part of the theatre is sacrificed and the *total uniform effect* thereby compromised, to make possible a diamond horseshoe, an imposing façade or a tricky stage.

Failure to recognize the interdependence of theatrical functions has resulted in theatres in which each separate part fulfilled its own particular function but the theatre as a whole did not. For example, there has been a tendency to build, usually on college campuses, theatres which have stages adequate for legitimate or even musical production, but house capacities of intimate or newsreel motion picture theatres.

Universality

Interdependence

327

The tiny audience cannot contribute the kind or amount of response which is its part in a live performance. Despite an adequate production, the show suffers and the audience doesn't get its money's worth of pleasure in participation. The fact that the theatre may not have been built as a commercial venture and does not have to support the cost of the plant does not excuse it from paying its own production and operating costs.

Optimum audience-performance relationship, made possible by the correct size, shape, and arrangement of the house and the acting area as dictated by the type of production being presented, may be vitiated by an unpleasant experience of difficult access to the theatre, too closely spaced seats, or poor ventilation. Undue concession to local social *mores* in the arrangement of the house may vitiate the basic audience-performance relationship. Concentration on the accommodation of the audience to the

Aerial view of Murphy Hall, Music and Dramatic Arts Building, University of Kansas. Kansas State Architect and Brinkman and Hagan, architects.

neglect of the performance may produce theatres in which the performance cannot possibly have an advantageous orientation toward the audience. Conversely, though of rarer instance, concentration on accommodation of the performance to the neglect of the audience predisposes the audience unsympathetically toward the efforts of the performers.

Theatre Function vs Other Functions

Theatre function is also perhaps more often violated as a result of the client's demand that the theatre be used for many activities: commencement requiring 6000 seats and no stage; the glee club with 1000 seats and a concert set; a symphony orchestra, 3000 seats and a concert set, exhibitions, cafeteria, or basketball court on a flat floor. Obviously few of these functions can be combined in one room without one or more of them suffering. Using the stage house as an example, although other parts of a theatre are often subject to such unenlightened decisions, it must be emphasized that *theatrical functions must be the primary deter-*

Aerial view of the Hopkins Center for the Arts, Dartmouth College.

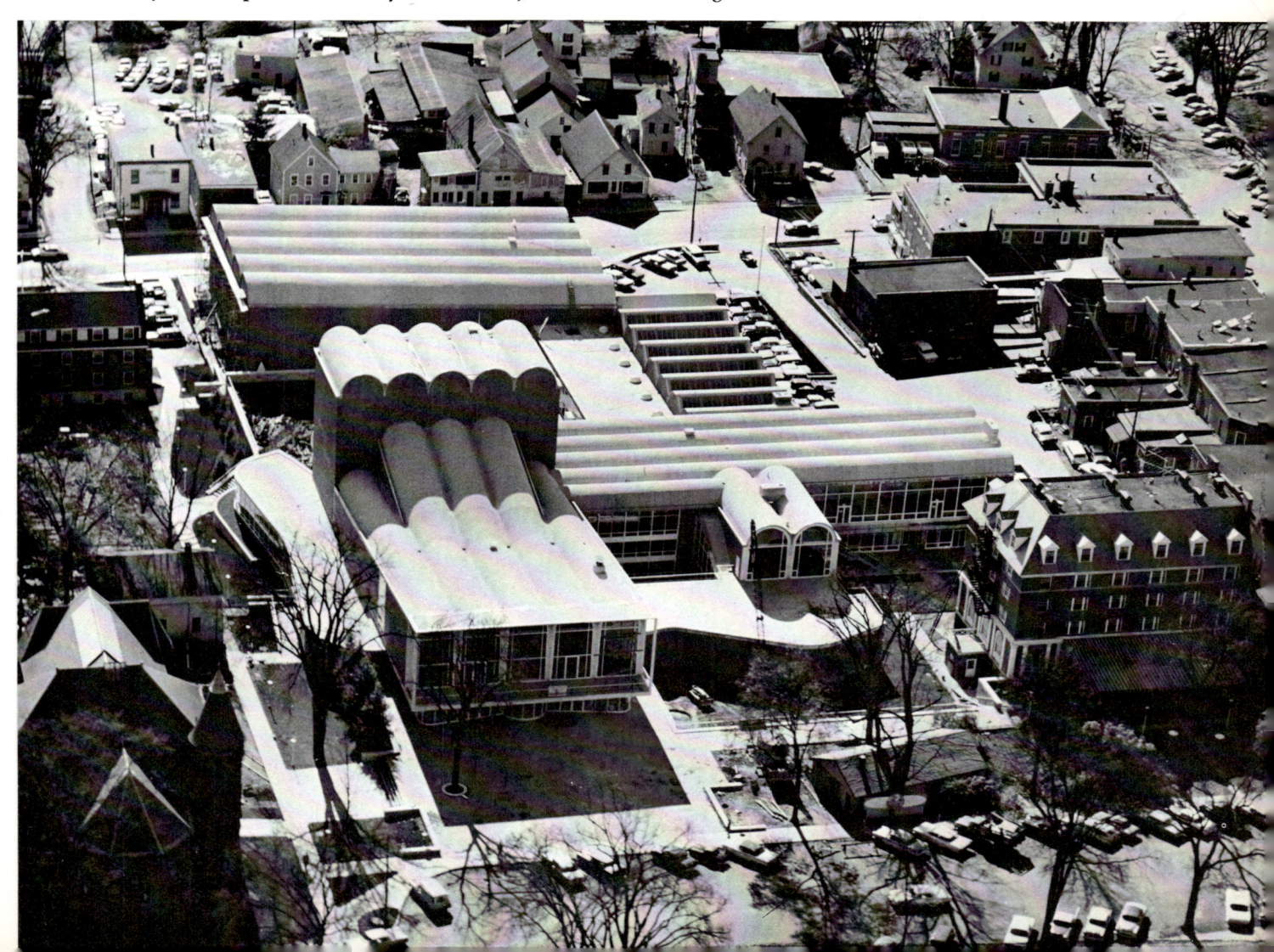

Intimate theatre with alley serving both it and large theatre at left. Stages are joined and served by common shops. Ira Aldridge Theatre, Howard University.

minants of the size, shape, and arrangement of the parts of the theatre building and that in no other kind of building is suitability of form to function more precisely demanded.

Theatre Function and Architectural Style

Many bad theatres have been built because ill-considered demands of the client forced the adoption of an architectural style ill-suited to the theatre, or prescribed the omission of an essential part such as a fly loft. A theatre can be built in almost any architectural style if the designer is resourceful.

Functionally good theatres have been designed to comply with conservative architectural styles such as Gothic or Georgian, and on the other hand, careful consideration of theatrical functions within the contemporary style, or styles, has also produced some distinguished architectural design in theatres. The theatre worker is justified in holding to the principle, which may amount to heresy among some architectural aestheticians, that whatever the architectural style and exterior form may be, the building *must function well as a theatre.*

Despite much disparagement, the American commercial theatre is the heart of the American theatre because it produces the new plays which, when no longer new, furnish the principal dramatic nourishment for all other kinds of theatre organizations in the country. Yet the system of production in American commercial theatre makes very little economic sense to anyone except the investor who is content with tax-deductible losses, the owner of a theatre housing a solid hit and the producer of, and investors and participants in, such a hit. Its entire economy, from the choice of play to the last few cut-rate weeks of a two-year run, is based on the expectation of a hit. Money is sought by the producer and furnished by the backers in the hope of fabulous return. Money is spent on production preparation in determined and sometimes frantic efforts, often futile, to make the presentation a smash hit in order to earn that return. If the show flops, the investor loses all that went into scenery, costumes, lights, wages, salaries, royalties and rent. If it is a hit, all the anticipation and expenditure was valid.

The Professional Theatre Organized for Profit

Theatre on a spacious site in a benign climate. Compare this picture with the one on page 60.

Present commercial theatre buildings are sometimes money makers only because they were built in an earlier time at much lower building costs than prevail today. Meanwhile, as is ever true, Manhattan real estate values have increased, and the intrinsic value of the theatres, because of the value for other uses of the land they occupy, competes effectively with their earning power as theatres.

It is doubtful if new commercial theatres will be built in the likeness of existing ones because of their sheer inability to earn enough to support the costs of production, operation, maintenance and investment in land and building.

The American commercial theatre is restricted to the preservation of the existing order of obsolescence by various factors of which the most forceful is the single fact of interchangeability: every theatre must be able to accommodate every production and every production must be able to fit into every theatre. Thus a standard of theatre form, equipment and procedures which was created in the twenties has prevailed and no significant changes in any of these can be made unless they are made in all theatres in the commercial group, both inside and outside New York. Furthermore when new theatres are built, if they are to house productions which fit into the existing theatres, they must agree in form, equipment and procedures with this standard, thus perpetuating an archaic status quo.

These commercial theatre standards were established, moreover, when the living theatre was the principal form of mass entertainment and when production and operating costs were, conservatively estimated, one tenth of present costs and admission prices were one-fourth today's, a much more favorable ratio than now obtains. Then theatres were such attractive real estate investments that they proliferated; now the economics of urban real estate discourages investment in a single occupancy structure which makes no use of the valuable space above it, and which produces income only one-seventh of the time when it is tenanted, and even that tenancy is erratic.

The construction of new theatres for commercial production will depend on the adoption of new concepts in planning, building, and operating theatres which may make investment in new buildings attractive. Such concepts must be based, in part at least, upon an examination of the present economic structure of the commercial theatre and the elimination therefrom of the causes of economic absurdity.

The opinion is justified that unless commercial theatres can be incorporated in buildings which include other occupancies which share the fixed and variable charges of capital, taxes and operations there will be no new theatres built with a profit motive.

There have been new theatres built to house professional production in the late fifties and early sixties but they have all had philanthropic or governmental support, or combinations of both. The O'Keefe Center in Toronto, and the Fisher Theatre in Detroit are examples. These theatres, planned to house both touring attractions and home-produced shows, may signal a breakthrough of a kind in the improvement of design and equipment of theatres for commercial use, because they have incorporated some new features of form and equipment while retaining the standard of interchangeability required to house touring companies. In such instances the touring companies, prepared to go into the old theatres, have not been able to take advantage of the more modern equipment but have disregarded it in favor of the standard items. The local companies,

Theatre in an arts center: communication above, music right. Experimental theatre back of main stage. Temple University. Nolen and Swinburne, architects.

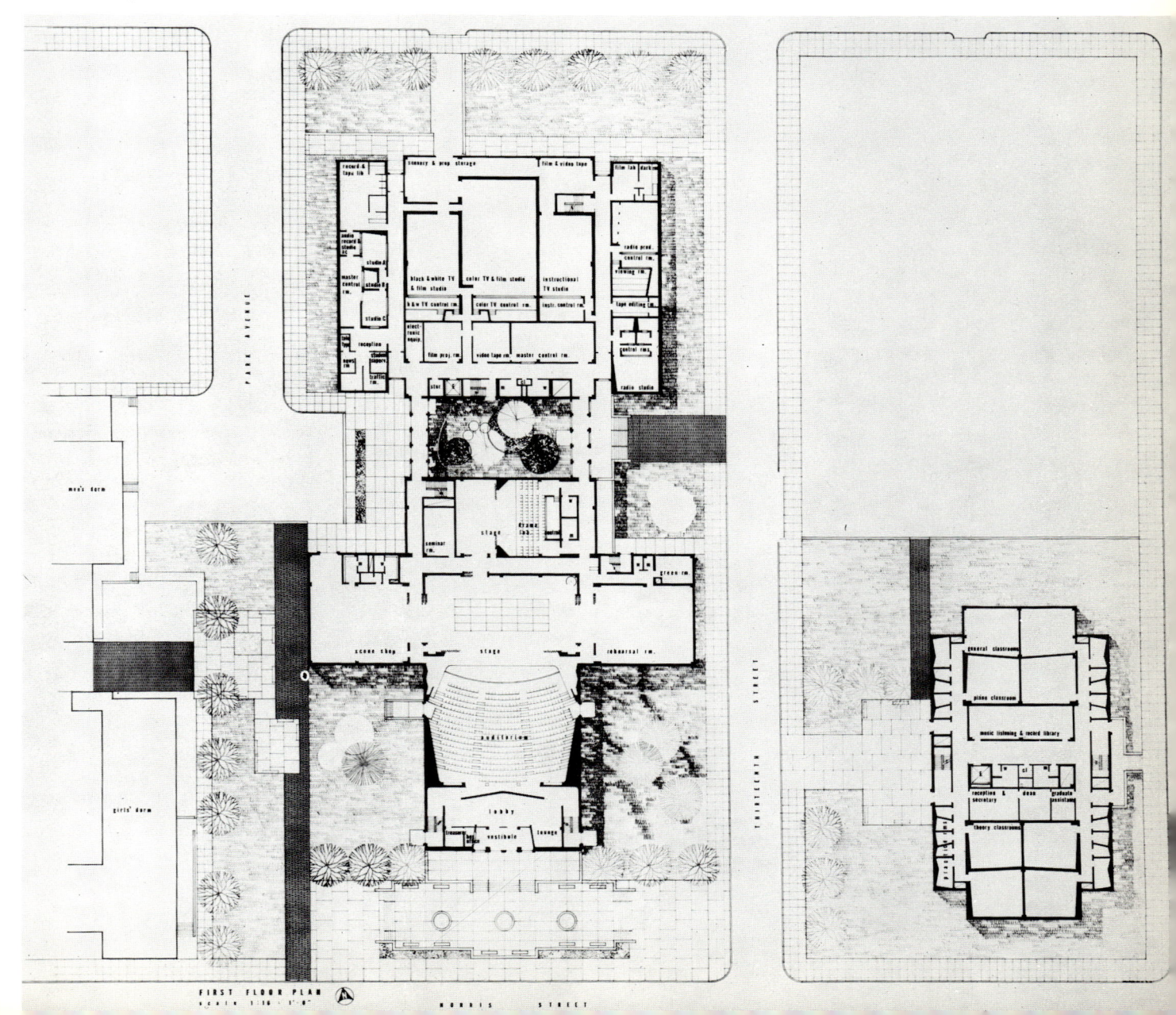

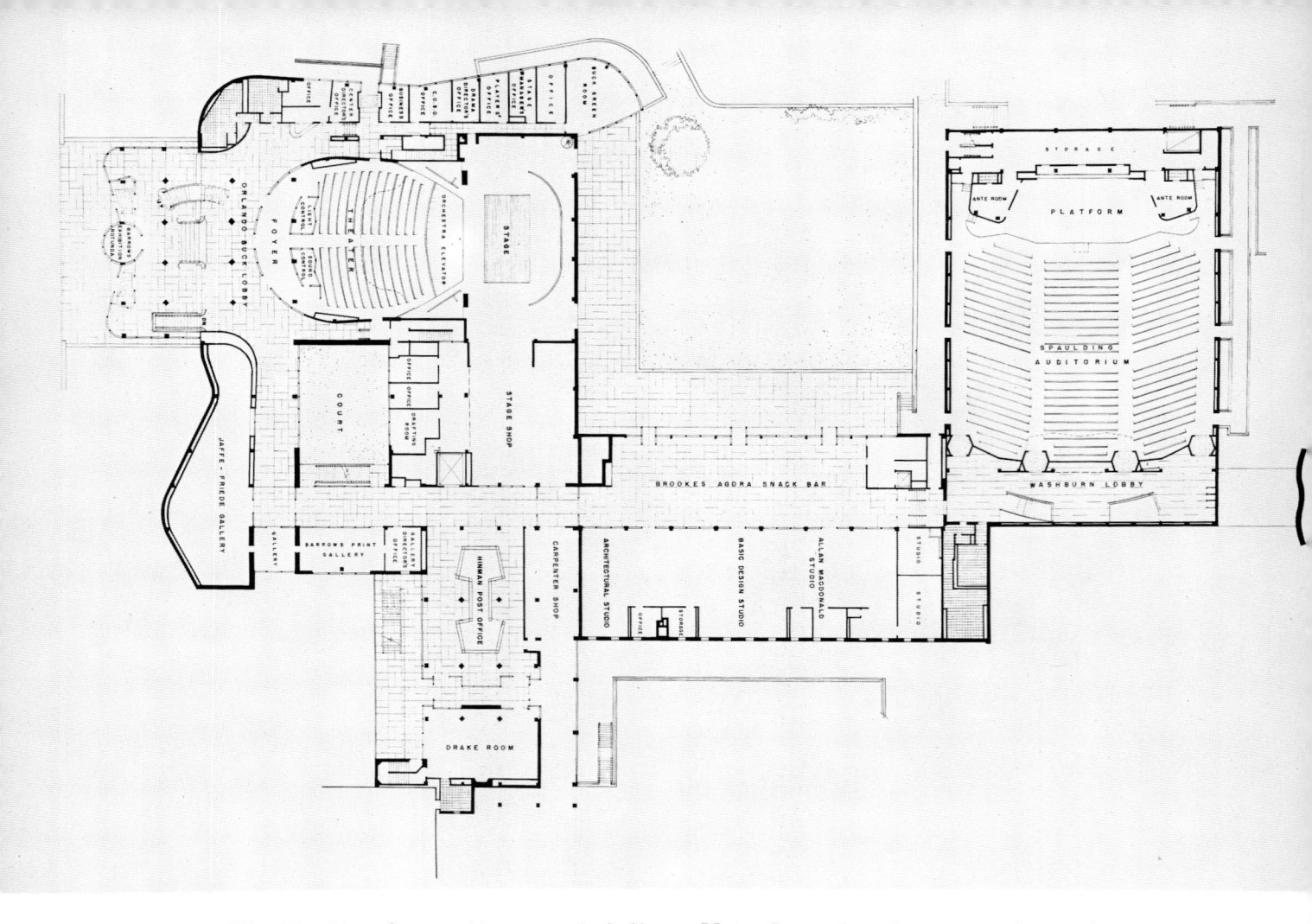

The Hopkins Center, Dartmouth College: Main floor plan, basement plan and section.

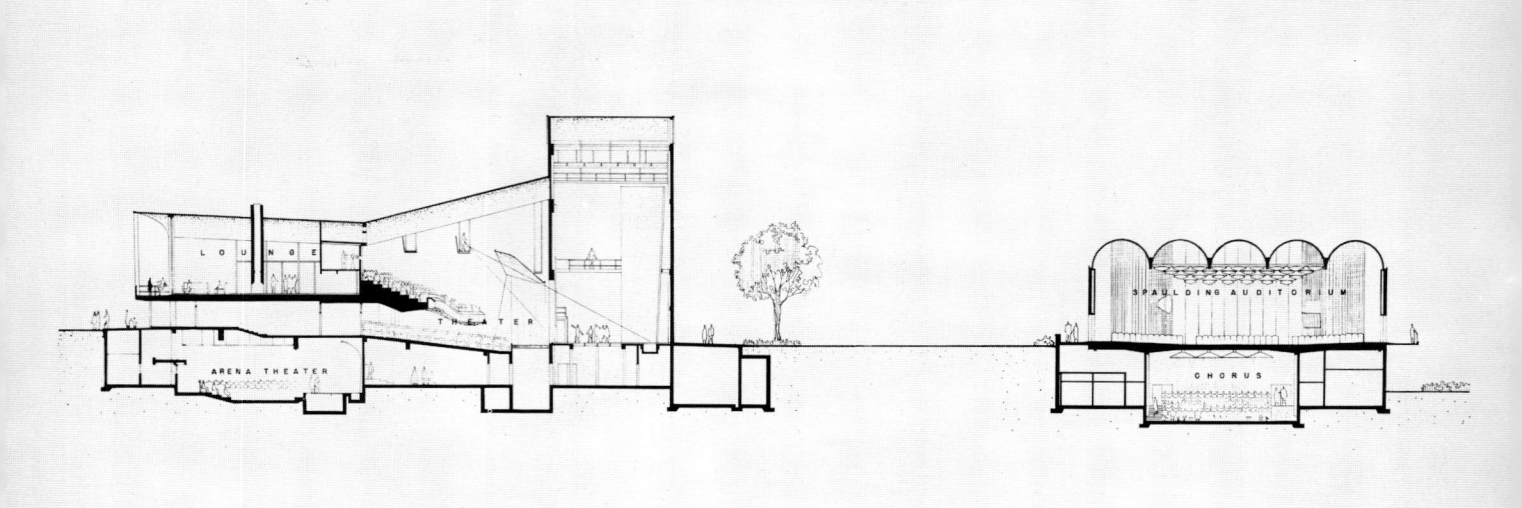

334

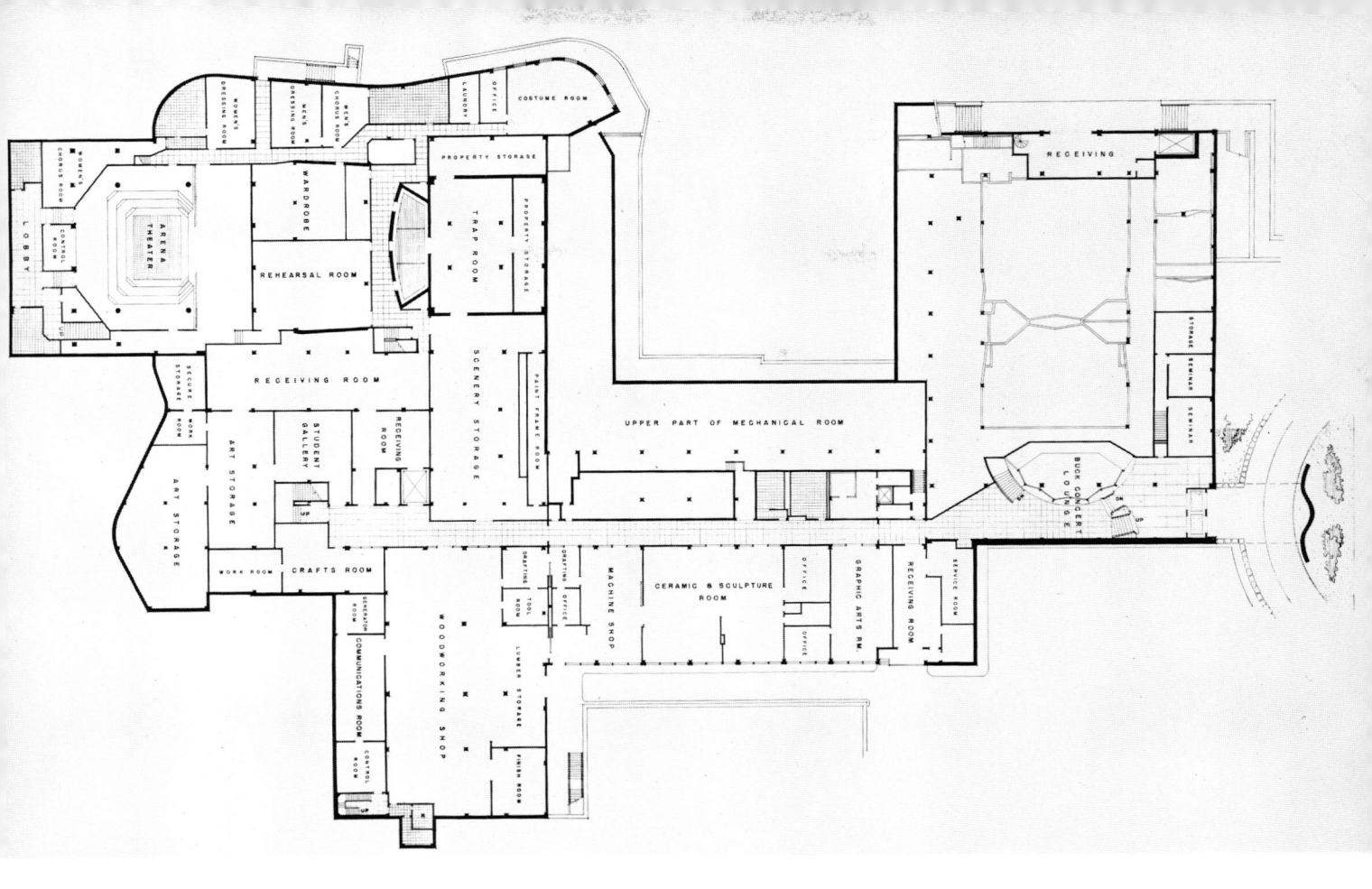

on the other hand, not restricted by the requirements of touring into older theatres have the productional advantages afforded by the newer features of plan and equipment: variable forestages, side stages and proscenium entrances, electronic lighting control with out-front control center, and motorized stage equipment.

The developing trend in American professional theatre appears to be toward the nonprofit professional organization, each organization resident in one theatre and in one city. The outstanding summer Shakespeare festival theatres, the theatres in Lincoln Center, the new theatre that Seattle inherited from its World's Fair, and the several incipient and striving resident companies scattered around the country are of this type. Not all of them have new theatres, but all have the possibility of taking advantage of modern technology without regard for the requirements of touring companies that are restricted to a fifty-year-old standard. And all of them have the opportunity to choose a theatre of unique form, equipment and operating procedures or one in which the form, equipment and procedures are compatible with those of other theatres for purposes of exchange of companies and touring, with resulting enrichment of the theatrical product. The dilemma is challenging. Uniqueness: no

Nonprofit Professional Theatres

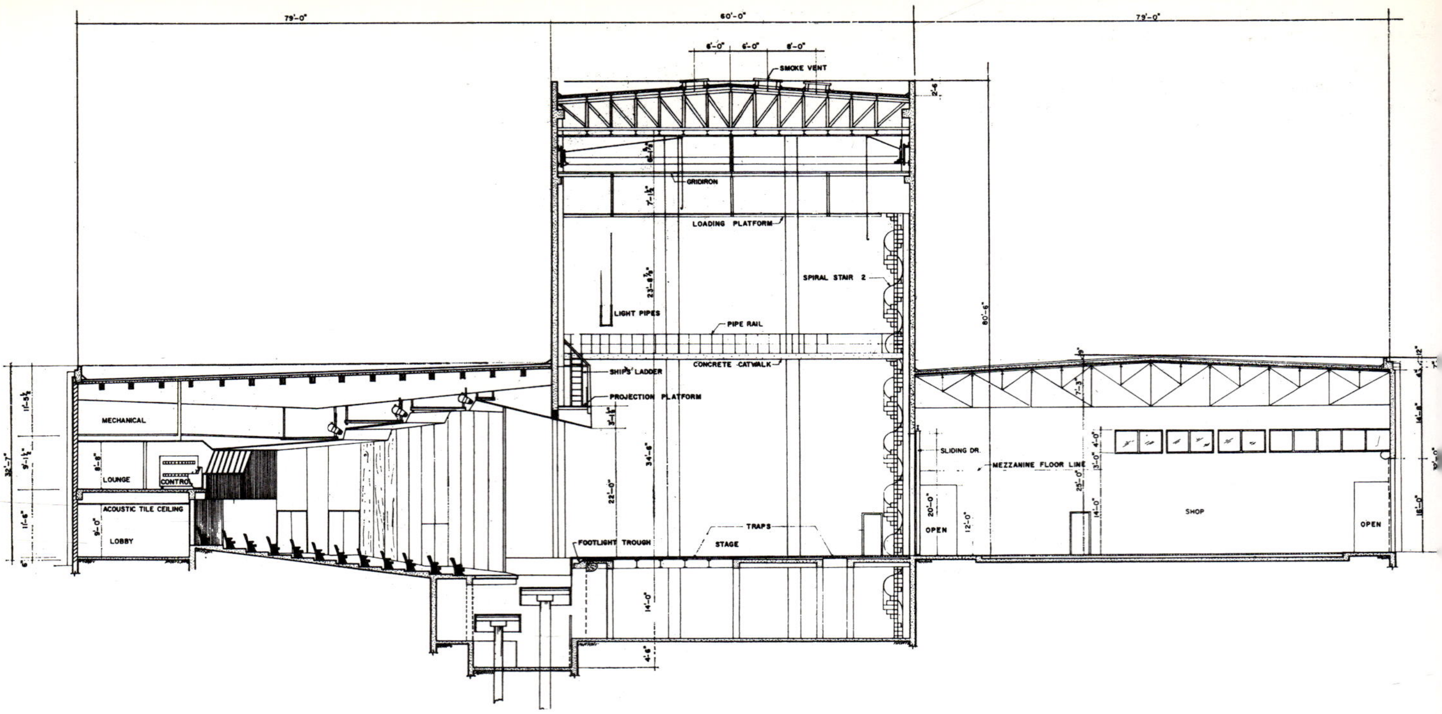
SMOKE VENT
GRIDIRON
LOADING PLATFORM
SPIRAL STAIR 2
LIGHT PIPES
PIPE RAIL
CONCRETE CATWALK
SHIPS' LADDER
PROJECTION PLATFORM
MECHANICAL
LOUNGE
CONTROL
ACOUSTIC TILE CEILING
LOBBY
FOOTLIGHT TROUGH
TRAPS
STAGE
SLIDING DR.
MEZZANINE FLOOR LINE
OPEN
SHOP
OPEN

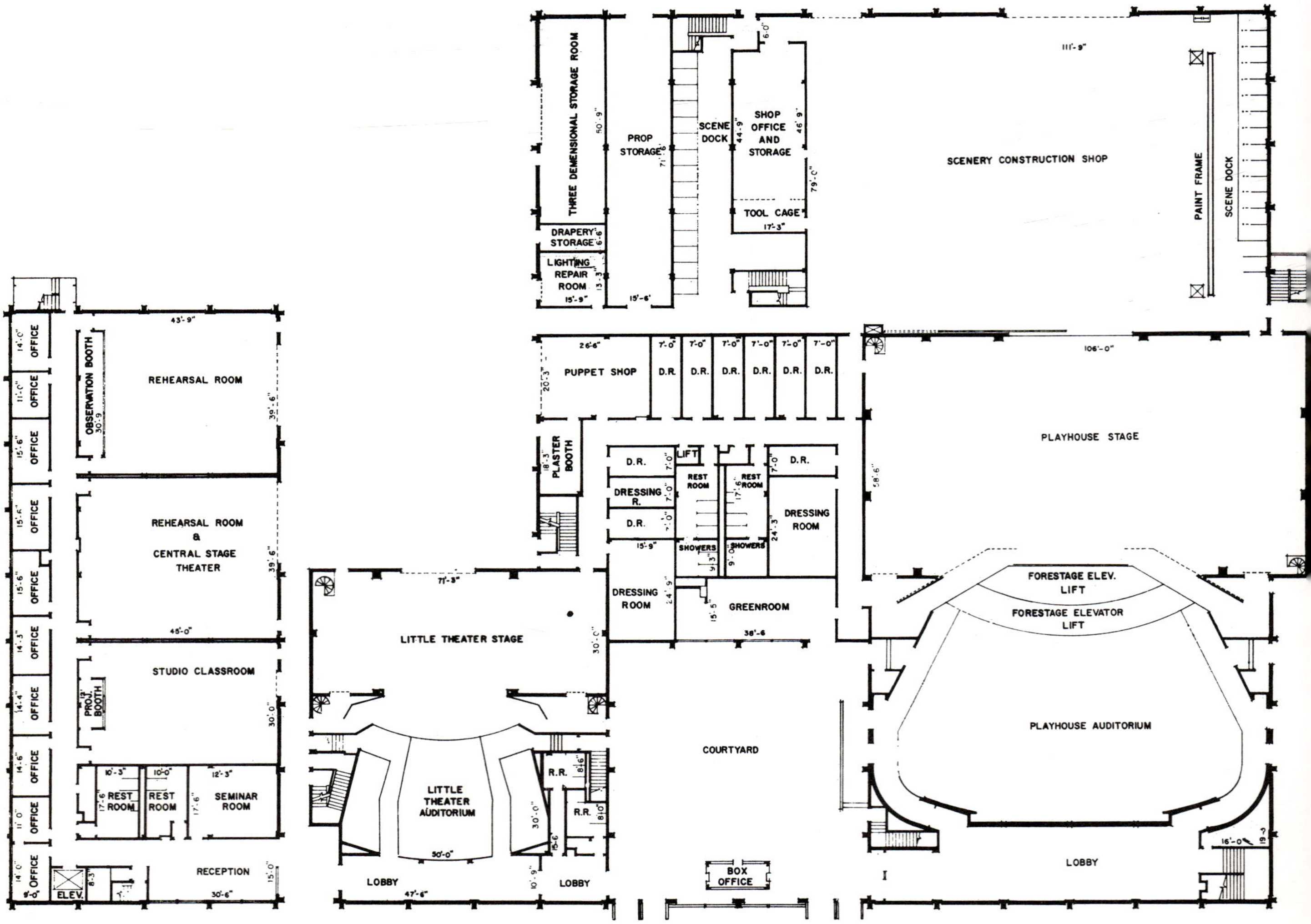
THREE DEMENSIONAL STORAGE ROOM
DRAPERY STORAGE
LIGHTING REPAIR ROOM
PROP STORAGE
SCENE DOCK
SHOP OFFICE AND STORAGE
TOOL CAGE
SCENERY CONSTRUCTION SHOP
PAINT FRAME
SCENE DOCK
PUPPET SHOP
D.R.
PLASTER BOOTH
LIFT
REST ROOM
DRESSING R.
DRESSING ROOM
SHOWERS
GREENROOM
PLAYHOUSE STAGE
FORESTAGE ELEV. LIFT
FORESTAGE ELEVATOR LIFT
PLAYHOUSE AUDITORIUM
LOBBY
COURTYARD
BOX OFFICE
LITTLE THEATER STAGE
LITTLE THEATER AUDITORIUM
R.R.
LOBBY
OFFICE
ELEV.
OBSERVATION BOOTH
REHEARSAL ROOM
REHEARSAL ROOM & CENTRAL STAGE THEATER
STUDIO CLASSROOM
PROJ. BOOTH
REST ROOM
SEMINAR ROOM
RECEPTION

The Department of Theatre Arts, University of California, Los Angeles. LEFT: *Section through Playhouse.* RIGHT: *Section through Little Theatre.* LOWER LEFT: *Ground floor plan.*

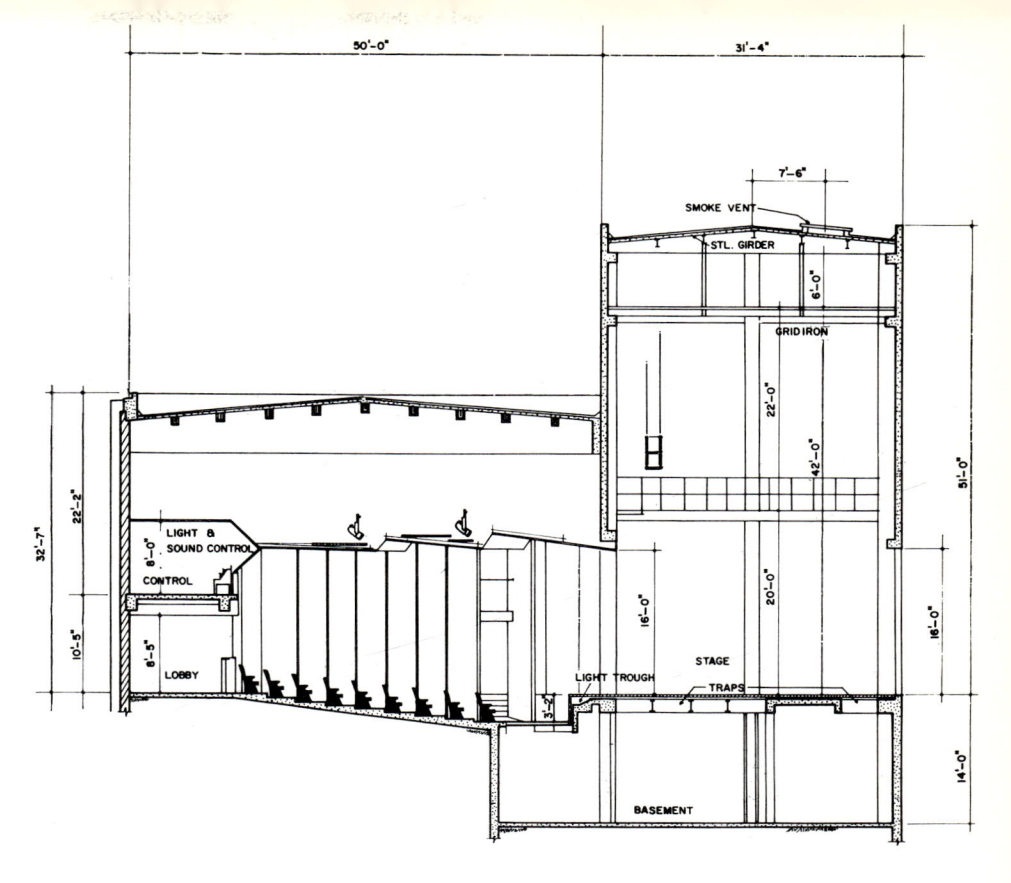

exchange. Standardization: exchange with the danger of establishing a new status quo. The solution may lie in incorporating in several theatres modern standards mutually adopted by the theatre organizations brought together in such an association as ANTA. The solution certainly lies in the acceptance of certain basic tenets of effective theatrical presentation aided by modern technology and not based on a 1920 model.

Educational Theatre

The achievement of a successful school or college theatre depends heavily upon the definition of its program of use. School purposes for a theatre are diverse including general assembly, public address, the democratic process, social functions like dances and dinners, general teaching functions, music practice, music teaching, musical performances, theatre teaching, theatre practice and performance. In many of these functions, with theatre taken as an example, there are levels, or degrees, of complexity or completeness which may determine the properties of the theatre. Theatre teaching and practice may progress from simplicity toward complexity, according to students' capabilities along somewhat the following sequence: actors in pantomime, actors improvising dialogue with pantomime, actors with a prepared script, actors with a prepared script in costume and make-up, actors with prepared script in costume and make-up with suggested scenery, the same with lighting for dramatic effect, and finally all the elements of a production combined to make a complete theatrical experience. School theatres may be planned to accommodate only certain levels in this progression, recognizing that the later levels may be too time-consuming or complex. The educational process, from primary grades through university, however, must provide for the highest degree of achievement within the capabilities of the most advanced students at each level, terminating with theatre art of the highest order of excellence.

Community Functions of Educational Theatre

The theatre in the educational institution is often the only legitimate theatre in the community. To serve the community best it should accommodate all local activities in the performing arts: the orchestra, the drama group, ballet, chorus, the traveling commercial production, the touring violinist and the Easter pageant. Many of these activities would originate, improve and proliferate if there were a good place to perform. Local individuals and organizations concerned with the performing arts can be counted on to support the building of a good theatre suitable to their needs in the local high school or college. The planning of an educational theatre should not be undertaken until all the local needs in the performing arts have been surveyed and support has been mobilized for the best possible theatre.

Nontheatrical Considerations

Nontheatrical factors inevitably demand consideration in the planning of a school theatre. The position of the study and practice of theatre in the total school program must be established. The degree of emphasis given to theatre in the curriculum or as an activity must determine in some measure the extent of the theatre plant, its equipment and its use.

Architectural design may attempt to govern the form of the theatre though recently architects have been more disposed toward achieving a structural and design solution which provides adequately for the functional requirements.

Building economics may be a prime determining factor; the building must be built with the available money or it will not be built. It is wrong, however, to think that no more money will ever be available and to accept inadequate or inappropriate facilities as final. In one instance a theatre director was advised to withdraw entirely from a program because the building being planned would be totally unsuited to play production though appropriate for other required functions. His firm stand brought forth an additional appropriation and the addition of a usable theatre. In another instance a planned theatre was built to the extent permitted by available funds and left looking obviously incomplete until new funds were brought forth by the stratagem. The inclination to shrink sizes below acceptable minima, to amputate functions permanently, to telescope uses and thus seriously compromise the effectiveness of all uses of the building must be suppressed by the planners who wish to achieve an attractive workable theatre.

HOPKINS CENTER JULY-AUGUST 1963 CALENDAR

Sun	Mon	Tue	Wed	Thu	Fri	Sat
7 Piano recital LONNY EPSTEIN Spaulding 8:30	**8** Film: TRIO Studio Theater 8:00 Chamber Music	**9**	**10** Chamber Music ESTIVAL QUARTET Spaulding 8:30	**11**	**12** Play: MUCH ADO ABOUT NOTHING Center Theater 8:30	**13** Play: MUCH ADO ABOUT NOTHING Center Theater 8:30
14 Orchestra Concert, Spaulding 8:30	**15** Film: FACE TO FACE, Studio Theater 8:00	**16**	**17** Chamber Music ESTIVAL QUARTET Spaulding 8:30	**18** Play: MUCH ADO ABOUT NOTHING Center Theater 8:30	**19** Play: MUCH ADO ABOUT NOTHING Center Theater 8:30	**20** Play: MUCH ADO ABOUT NOTHING Center Theater 8:30
21 Orchestra Concert, Spaulding 8:30	**22** Film: THE LADY VANISHES Studio Theater 8:00	**23**	**24** Chamber Music ESTIVAL QUARTET Spaulding 8:30	**25** Play: THE COUNTRY WIFE Center Theater 8:30	**26** Play: MUCH ADO ABOUT NOTHING Center Theater 8:30	**27** Play: THE COUNTRY WIFE Center Theater 8:30
28 Orchestra Concert, Spaulding 8:30	**29** Film: NOTHING SACRED, Studio Theater 8:00	**30**	**31** Chamber Music ESTIVAL QUARTET Spaulding 8:30	**1** Play: MUCH ADO ABOUT NOTHING Center Theater 8:30	**2** Play: THE COUNTRY WIFE Center Theater 8:30	**3** Play: THE COUNTRY WIFE Center Theater 8:30
4 Orchestra Concert, Spaulding 8:30	**5**	**6**	**7** Chamber Music ESTIVAL QUARTET Spaulding 8:30	**8** Play: MAN AND SUPERMAN Center Theater 8:30	**9** Play: THE COUNTRY WIFE Center Theater 8:30	**10** Play: MAN AND SUPERMAN, Center Theater 8:30
11 Orchestra Concert Spaulding 8:30	**12** Film: SEVEN DAYS TO NOON Studio Theater 8:00	**13** Play: MUCH ADO ABOUT NOTHING Center Theater 8:30	**14** Chamber Music Guest Soloists Spaulding 8:30	**15** Play: MAN AND SUPERMAN Center Theater 8:30	**16** Play: THE COUNTRY WIFE Center Theater 8:30	**17** "Pops" Concert Spaulding 11:00 Play: MUCH ADO ABOUT NOTHING Center Theater 2:30 Orchestra-Choral Concert Spaulding 8:30
18 Play: MAN AND SUPERMAN Center Theater 8:30	**19**	**20**	**21**	**22** Play: THE COUNTRY WIFE Center Theater 8:30	**23** Play: MAN AND SUPERMAN Center Theater 8:30	**24** Play: MAN AND SUPERMAN Center Theater 8:30

Schedule, typical of the demands placed upon a center for the performing arts by the college and the community. Hopkins Center, Dartmouth College.

339

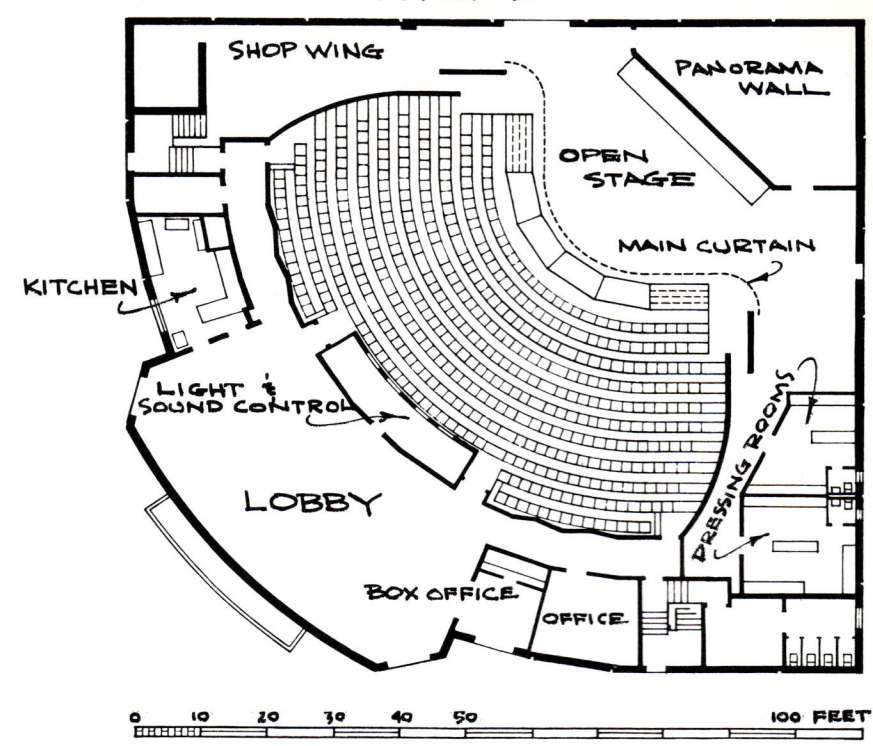

Plan, section and artist's sketch of the theatre at Western Springs, Ohio. James Hull Miller, designer. Fugard, Burt, Wilkinson and Orth, architects.

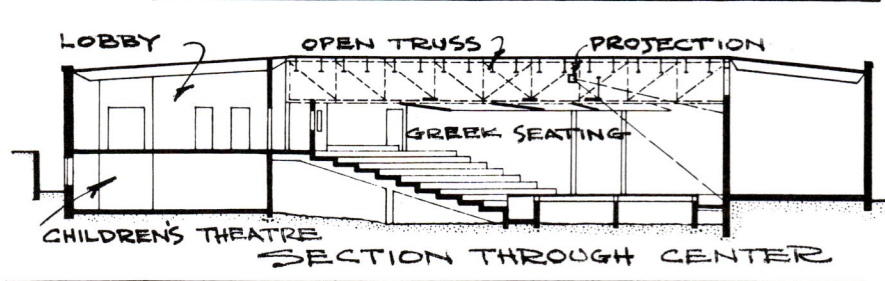

340

All Purpose Is No Purpose

A danger in school theatre planning is to suppose that the theatrical functions can be satisfied in an all-purpose space. Theatre art is specialized as to sizes, shapes, arrangement and equipment of space. Specialization is compromised by the all-purpose space, and theatrical functions are negated.

Limited Purposes

The school theatres planned for open stage performance, projected scenery, and no flying capability appear to satisfy requirements of a performance facility with limited provisions for simplified and restricted scenic investiture. If producers are content to work within the imposed limitations, an effective kind of simplified theatrical experience can be achieved. Such plants provide performance facilities so much better than those in many existing schools that they merit consideration. It should not be assumed, however, that such plans afford facilities for *complete* theatrical production.

The educational objective has two aspects: to teach theatre and to teach other material *by* theatre. To teach theatre requires the existence of an exemplary theatre plant just as to teach surgery requires an exemplary operating room.

Teaching *by* theatre is the use of theatre, its plant and its techniques, as a direct or indirect medium for imparting other subjects. Directly, drama may be presented in a liberal arts program as the epitome or representation of past cultures, ancillary to studies in languages, literatures, history, anthropology and sociology. Directly also, dramatization of situations may be a teaching method for numerous departments of instruction. Indirectly, participation in theatrical productions fosters creative imagination and expression, development of desirable character traits, understanding of human nature, and the discipline of cooperation. Even where theatre facilities must be incorporated in a building primarily for other than theatrical uses, theatre function must be borne in mind, and the basic theatrical requisites must be supplied, or it cannot as a theatre contribute to the attainment of nontheatrical educational objectives.

Even the teaching of theatre arts is a function separate from the basic functions of theatrical production and exerts requirements which must not be allowed to encroach upon them: the use of the house as classroom at times when it is needed for production activity; seating capacity established by teaching requirements rather than by theatrical considerations.

Site

The theatre site must be big enough to hold the theatre and to provide access and outside audience handling facilities. This statement stands opposed to the idea that the building may be made to fit the land by adjustment and rearrangement of its interior spaces without regard for their optimum functional arrangement. Urban real estate is conveniently divided into predominantly rectangular parcels. The result is that urban theatres have been arranged to fit onto predominantly rectangular plans. High costs of urban land have prompted the building of theatres on sites so much too small that the functioning of the theatres, as analyzed in this book, has been impaired and the financial and artistic success and continuance of the theatres have been jeopardized. Prior to 1938, when no other occupancy was allowed in a building containing a theatre, there was some justification for the niggardly use of land. Since 1938, however, the New York building ordinance has been liberalized to permit other income-producing occupancies in a theatre building.

The project of combining two or more theatres on one plot of ground so that a large building might be raised over their combined lobbies and auditoriums has been advanced with some prospects of adoption.

Theatres in schools and colleges have been frequently subjected to restraints imposed by preconceived master plans, in which either a site has been allocated to a theatre before determining adequately the theatre's space requirements, or considerations of campus design have imposed restrictions upon the physical size and shape of, and access to, the theatre building.

This book can only urge that consideration be given to the requisite functional shape and size of, and access to, the theatre building before a site is selected. The problem is as simple in its essence, though not in its execution, as buying a hat: no matter how handsome the hat is, it must fit or one does not buy it. No one cuts off an ear or slashes the hatband to make a hat fit. Yet a hat lasts one season, a theatre, fifty years.

Fortunately architectural design theory has veered away from the concept that all buildings must be rectangular in plan and have imposing, balanced façades, toward the concept of allowing the exterior and plan of the building to develop logically from the optimum arrangement of its interior spaces, and its siting to evolve from traffic requirements. This concept favors the production of workable theatres.

Growth   Many theatres have been planned merely to satisfy demands for a plant to house adequately an existing production program only to find that growth of the activity very soon rendered the new plant inadequate. Anticipation of growth as a result of increase in the cultural interest of the population, attractiveness of the new plant, increase in participation in the arts, increase in the number of college and university students,

Drama Teaching Station scheme for secondary schools developed by Horace Robinson. Provides wide variation in form, simply achieved.

PROSCENIUM ARRANGEMENT 0 ―――― 8FT.

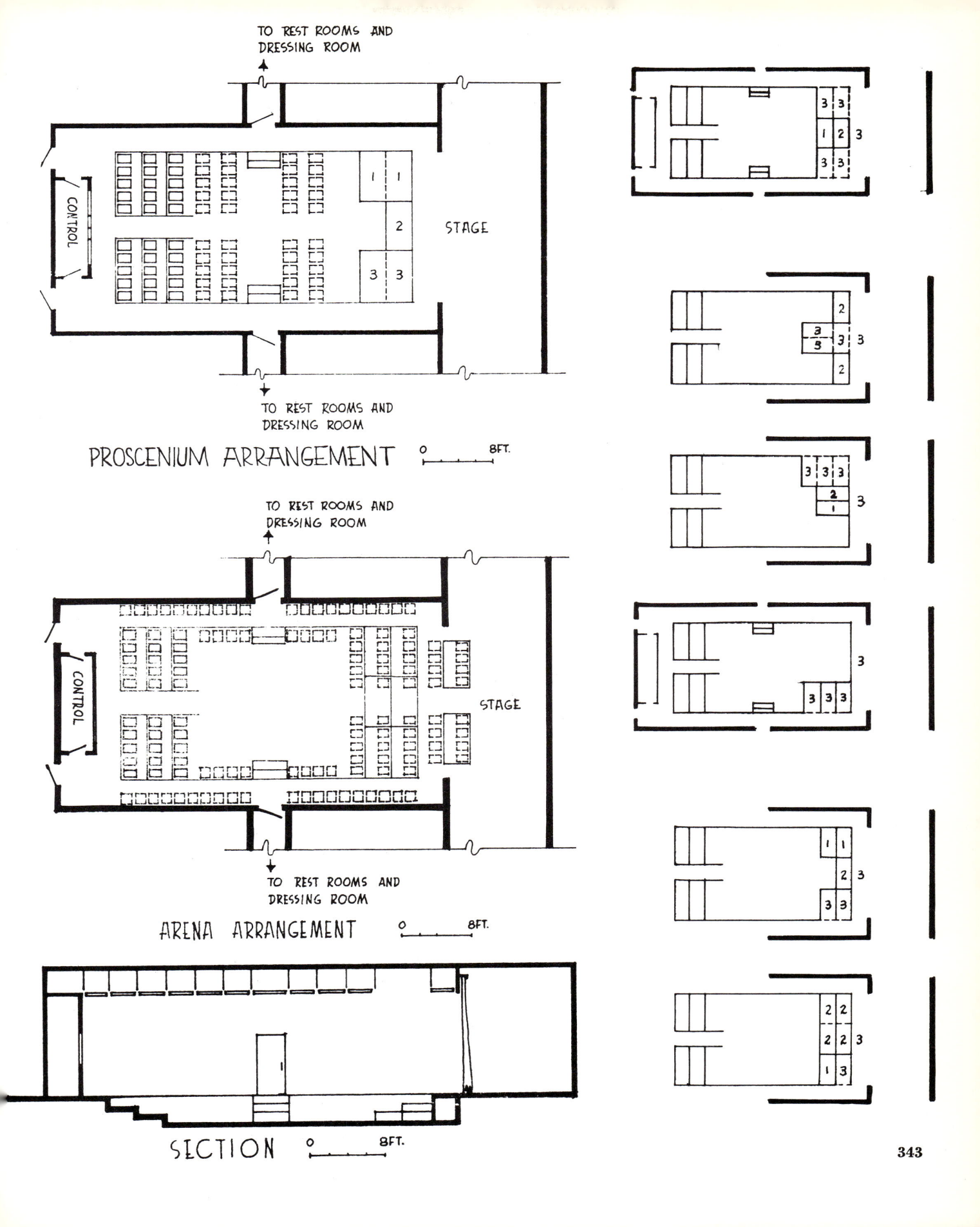

ARENA ARRANGEMENT 0 ―――― 8FT.

SECTION 0 ―――― 8FT.

343

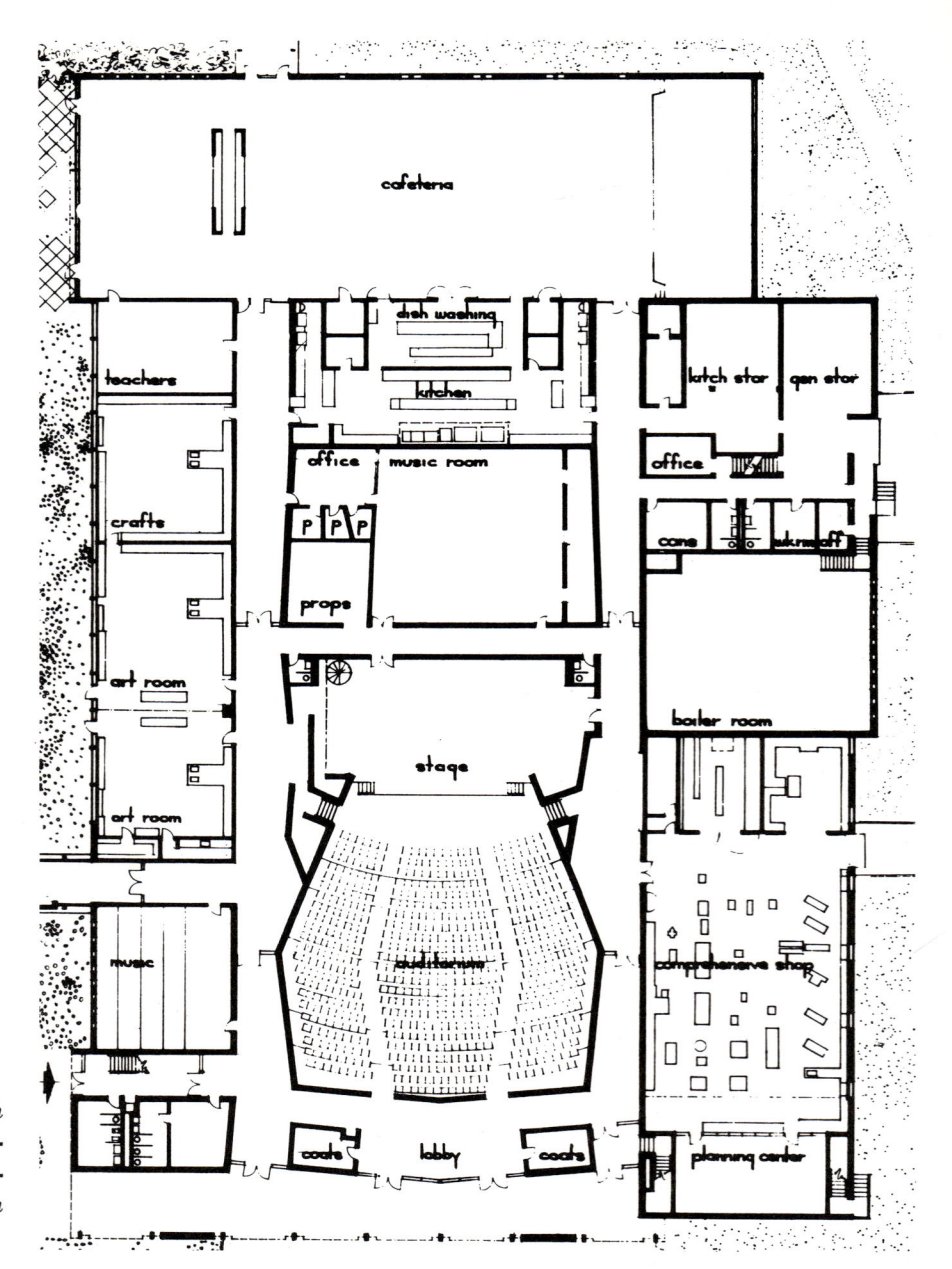

Ground floor plan, South Senior High School auditorium, Newton, Massachusetts. Korslund, LeNorman and Quann, architects.

increase in avocational participation in theatre is an essential part of wise theatre planning.

Development of the Plan

The client must decide: production type or types, production form or forms, capacity or capacities, production services required, other compatible uses of the building. The client *should know or be told* the inevitable effects of compromise or adjustment of theatre functions to other requirements. The client should then prepare statements of type, form, capacity, services and other uses in as much detail as possible. The preferred form of statement has two parts: (1) a program for the building which lists in functional groups all spaces required, describes uses of the spaces, and states desired dimensions with attention to essential heights and the equipment and special environmental requirements (light, heat, air conditioning, ventilation) of each space; (2) drawings to illustrate relationships as rough as they have to be but as carefully made as they can be. Though probably not skilled as a draftsman, the client can nonetheless develop his own ideas graphically to supplement his verbal statements.

If the client presents the architect with a well-thought-out set of requirements, the architect has a good chance to come up with a satisfactory, workable scheme *the first time*. But the client seldom provides such guidance. It is unfair to the architect to give him only the non-theatrical considerations. He may well come up with a good theatre, but one not suited to the client's needs. Sometimes he doesn't even get a good theatre. One famous badly designed theatre was planned by an architect who, according to the publicity, "had never designed a theatre before, but had some very interesting ideas." They were, and the people who try to produce plays there wish he hadn't.

The system of programming spaces which can be useful in many kinds of construction can produce a very bad theatre unless it is used as *a guide rather than a specification*. In one theatre, the projection booth was programmed at so many square feet. As the plan developed, it appeared that the booth could be made larger than programmed and thereby save some expensive structural complications, but the programmer would have none of it, though he proposed to reduce the gridiron height and eliminate the lounge to save money. Moreover, the fact that spaces are fixed at certain areas can (and has) made awkward the spatial relations between them, and access from one part of the theatre to another. Certainly the required area and height of each part of the theatre must be established in the form of minima as a guide to the architect, but the architect must be able to approach the problem from the basic theatrical necessity rather than juggling a lot of spaces. Functional relationships of spaces are as important as optimal sizes and shapes. Sizes and shapes should be stated in desired optima and acceptable minima which have been carefully determined with the proviso that increases to accommodate structural design will be tolerated but that reductions will not.

The production type and the theatre form determine the *performance-audience relationship*. In concrete terms this means: (1) the size and shape of the acting area, open or forestage, side stages, and orchestra pit; (2) optimum audience; (3) the shape and size of structural proscenium opening and provisions for adjusting it. These shapes and di-

Sketches for the McAlister College Theatre showing the arrangements for proscenium form and open-stage form of production. G. C. Izenour, designer.

mensions constitute the starting point from which design expands and evolves in consideration of both performance and audience. The two main divisions, as has been implied in the topical arrangement of this book, are (1) the house and its related spaces, and (2) the stage and its related spaces. The first constitutes the accommodation of the audience in terms of reception, traffic, seeing, hearing, comfort and safety; the second constitutes accommodation of the performance in terms of preparation, reception, assembly, rehearsal, performance, removal and possibly storage. Either division taken by itself may be planned by a straightforward process of adapting the form to the stated requirement. But *neither division can be planned by itself* until the fundamental relationship which exists between them has been established.

It is important to note, in this connection, that the term multipurpose is not synonymous with multiform. Recent usage defines *purpose* as applying to different kinds of planned presentations: lectures, commencements, motion pictures, opera, symphony concert; *form* is defined as applying to the size, shape and arrangement of the theatre, and *multiform* as applying to the possibility of two or more sizes, shapes and arrangements of the theatre, to accommodate different purposes or variation in performance-audience relationship within one purpose. Many purposes may be well served by a single form. The same play, the same

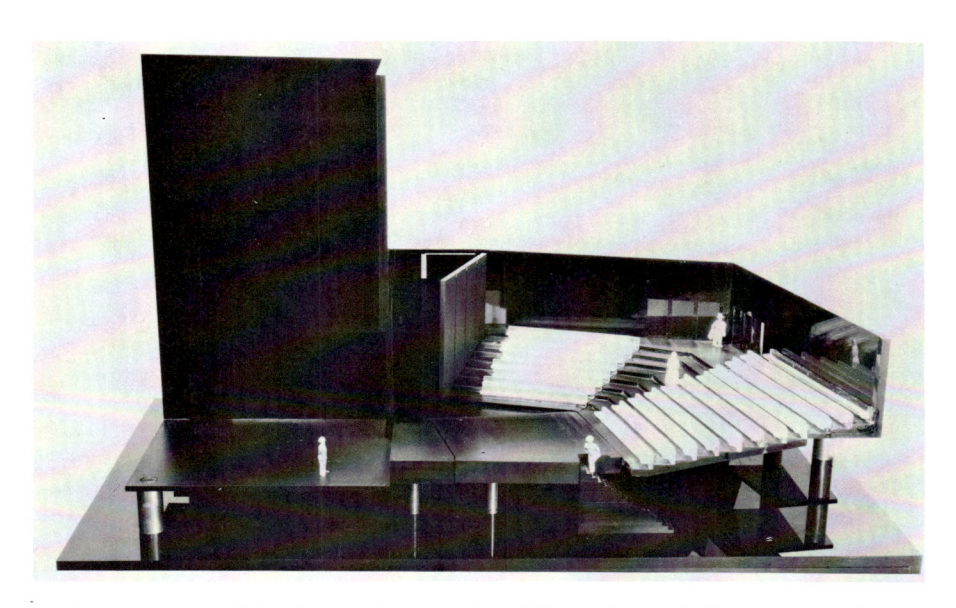

Cut-away model of the theatre for Wittenberg College. TOP: **Open-stage arrangement.** BOTTOM: **Proscenium arrangement.** *G. C. Izenour, designer.*

purpose, may be accomplished in many forms. It is questionable whether a theatre which can vary the form of performance-audience relationship to any considerable extent by changing the position of seats, or shape or location of the stage, is justified on economic or operational grounds except where the purpose is frankly and principally to experiment with various dramatic forms and technical devices.

However the need is apparent in many instances for an auditorium which can be altered in form to render it optimal in acoustics, capacity and performance-audience relationship for two or more purposes.

In the context of this chapter the alterable portions of the theatre are those which are normally thought of as structure: walls, floors and ceilings. Alterable equipment, that which is applied to or set inside the structure, has been treated previously.

Altering Performance-Audience Relationship

The four theatre forms which provide different performance-audience relationships have been discussed in Chapter 7. Attempts have been made to realize all four forms in one theatre by moving parts of the seating area, both horizontally and vertically, by elevating portions of the theatre floor thus cleared of seats and by moving wall panels. Notable are the Loeb Drama Center at Harvard University and the projected theatres for the University of New Mexico, Carnegie Institute of Technology and Charlottetown, Prince Edward Island.

Altering Seating Capacity

The economics of performance differ between different kinds of attractions. Shows which have high performance costs, like symphony concerts, operas and musical shows, require larger seating capacities. Plays and chamber music concerts, on the other hand, may be shown to smaller audiences. Hence, if only one audience facility can be built and it must accommodate the various performing arts, including the one requiring the greatest capacity, there is reason to attempt an alteration of the form to make it congenial to both the larger audiences for concerts and the smaller audiences for plays.

Acoustical Adjustment

There is an optimum reverberation time for concert which is consistent with the house of larger capacity and volume and a shorter optimum for spoken drama which can only be obtained by reducing the volume. Hence it is desirable to close off seating areas and balconies at the back of the house and to lower the ceiling so that, in effect, a house of smaller seating capacity with appearance, sight lines and acoustical properties appropriate to that capacity is created within the structural shell of the larger theatre.

When the same theatre must be used alternately for stage performances and concerts the sound reflecting enclosure (*concert set*) which is needed to mix and reflect musical sounds must be cleared from the

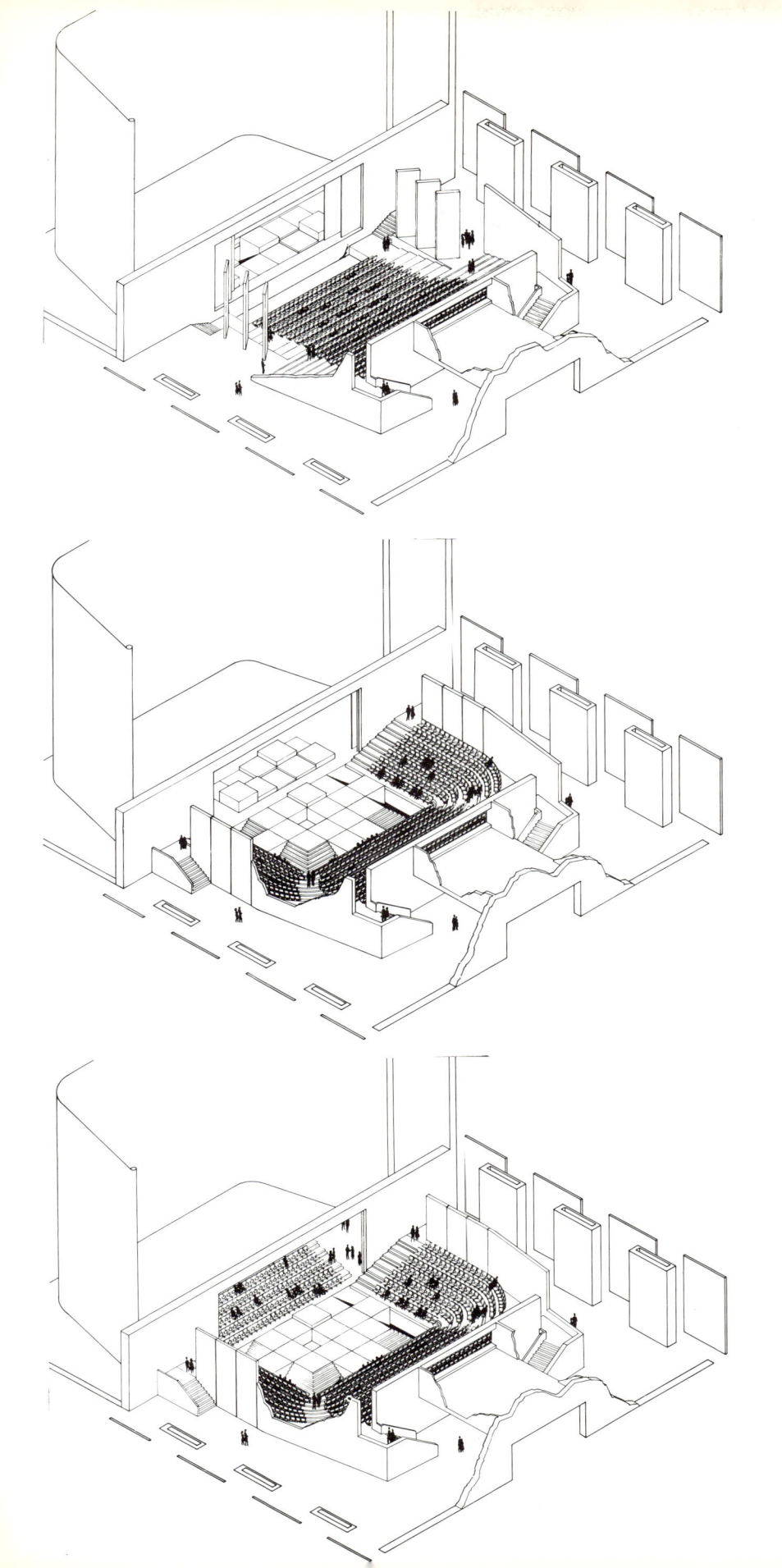

The theatre for Carnegie Institute of Technology. Three arrangements: TOP, *proscenium;* MIDDLE, *open stage;* BOTTOM, *arena. Paul Schweikher, architect. G. C. Izenour, designer.*

stage at will—quickly, efficiently and safely. Since acoustically effective concert sets must be massive, the setting and clearing of this set approaches the magnitude of structural alteration.

Adjustment of the Stage Opening

The table of proscenium widths in Chapter 3 states a range from 26 to 80 feet between the minimum for drama and maximum for opera. The multipurpose theatre should be capable of an amount of proscenium adjustment perhaps not so extreme in range. Partially closing a traverse curtain produces intolerable sight lines from side seats. Leaving these seats unoccupied gives an impression of improvisation. Structural alteration is required whereby the side seats are eliminated and the opening is reduced in both width and height. Side-wall panels may be moved to cut out the side sections of seats and to create a narrower proscenium opening. Or panels may be drawn out of the fixed proscenium, moving diagonally away from the audience so that the width of the opening is reduced without impairing the sight lines from the side seats.

Multipurpose Structures

When building budgets are limited, ideas of multipurpose theatres or auditoriums arise. The genesis of such ideas is often valid: to give a community or a school or college the most building utility for its money. The danger in such proposals is that they may compromise the requirements not only of theatre but also of any of the other proposed uses, so as to render some or all of the uses impractical and therefore valueless to the owner.

Effective multi-use depends first upon scheduling. If two or more uses demand the building at the same time, the dual use is not possible.

Essential functional requirements of each use must be honored. The combination of theatre with cafeteria to make a so-called *cafetorium* for a high school must render the acoustics of the cafeteria suitable for theatrical uses. The use of a gymnasium for theatrical purposes (*gymnatorium*) overlooks the fact that setting chairs and having large numbers of people walk on the gymnasium floor in outdoor shoes mutilates the floor which should be kept in perfect condition for athletic activity.

Effective multi-use depends on the recognition of similarities in the uses to be combined. Musical presentation of different kinds (excepting operetta, chamber opera, and musical plays) are alike in that seeing is of less importance than hearing. Thus capacities are not restricted to the requirements of seeing small detail of facial expression as they are in the presentation of plays. Furthermore, musical presentations are usually single performances rather than runs. A symphony orchestra plays a particular program only once in a city; an opera is performed only in repertory with others; a musician gives a single concert. Thus, in each of these cases there is reason to plan for large capacity; the problems of size and shape become those of optimum capacity, optimum acoustics and optimum arrangement for the various kinds of musical performance to audiences of 1500 to 3000 or more.

Plays, operettas, chamber operas and musical shows, on the other hand, depend for their effectiveness upon the audience seeing, as well as hearing, the performance and are customarily performed several times in a so-called run. Capacity may and should therefore be limited by the requirements of good seeing and by the inevitable financial requirements of successful operation.

To be practical economically, changes of capacity and shape, intended to produce optimum conditions for each kind of presentation, must be efficient in terms of time and labor, or the initial objective of the multi-use design is vitiated. The installation of a concert set on a stage for a symphony orchestra and its removal for the subsequent setup, dress rehearsal and performance of an opera should be capable of accomplishment to permit performances on successive evenings. The amount of mechanization to achieve this change is a matter of local economics and local orientation to the modern technology of electro-mechanical power applications. The initial costs of electromechanical installations may appear to be high but the savings in time and labor required to effect numerous change-overs in a long period of operation may warrant the initial outlay.

A common demand upon college theatres is that they serve also as classrooms, lecture halls, and motion picture theatres. The reasonable attempt is to get maximum use from a high-capacity assembly hall. The person scheduling the use of the hall must understand the demands of stage preparation, assembly and rehearsal which are essential ingredients of the performance process and not allow nontheatrical uses to interfere with this preparatory process. The planner can facilitate this kind of multi-use by providing completely adequate equipment for uses of the house with the curtain down so that quiet work may be done on the stage while the house is being used and so that no rearrangement of the stage area will be required for these other uses: the movie screen flown in a slot in the ceiling ahead of the proscenium; a variable forestage to provide space for lectern, speakers and seminar table; forestage and house acoustics planned so that musical presentations may be made mostly in the forestage area with little or no invasion of the stage; lighting controls designed to afford illumination for the other uses without interfering with instruments, connections or control board settings for the current theatrical production.

Experimental Theatres

The designation *experimental theatre* is sometimes adopted by organizations which lack the patience or skill to learn or employ established production forms, or the facilities for adequate production, and undertake to hide their shortcomings under a respected banner. They merit no consideration here.

There are, however, a few specific theatre situations which admit the construction of experimental theatres. A theatre school which already has one or more theatres of conventional form and which uses them to the full extent of their potentialities can use, and even needs, experimental facilities. It is only by experiment that new forms and techniques may be tested, and the theatre school is the logical place for the tests to be made. The theatre school, of all producing organizations, is under the greatest pressure to create performance opportunities for the greatest number of people and the most diversity of staging in a given season. For this reason also, an experimental theatre is desirable. Maximum variation in theatre form with the minimum expenditure of time and human energy is the *desideratum*.

An experimental theatre must be a flexible theatre in which many production schemes may be put to test. It is *not* a theatre capable of only a single production type. To provide an untried form of theatre for an organization which has no other theatre worthy of the name is to ask that organization to turn its back on the whole body of accumulated theatre practice, both artistic and technical, and to undertake production in a milieu for which there is little precedent and less knowledge. The theatre planner must make sure that the people for whom he provides an experimental form of theatre are able and willing to experiment.

Divisible Theatres

A very real problem faces school administrators when there is apparent need for a large theatre for school and community uses and a restricted building budget. The cost of the large theatre can be better justified if there is an effective and simple way to subdivide it into three or more rooms which might be used for large classes. Such subdivision must meet rigid conditions of sound isolation if the rooms are to be used freely; the separation must be done by moving walls, rather than by drawing curtains or folding partitions.

In all the changes of form which have been discussed the task is one of moving large and weighty sections of the building. This can only be done by machines, and both structures and machines must be designed as systems capable of rapid change by easily understood and easily operated control devices.

Dual or Multiple Uses of Other Spaces

Aside from multipurpose and multiform of performance there are multiple uses of other spaces which may be planned when budgetary limitations dictate:

The side stages in the Ace Morgan Theatre at Denison University serve as classrooms when the curtains are closed.

The trap room in the Pickard Theatre at Bowdoin serves as a classroom and, by a clever conversion of chalk-boards into make-up mirrors and tables, as a dressing room. Classrooms may easily be used as dressing rooms but there should be proper provision of costume racks, make-up tables, mirrors and lights, and adequate curtaining of windows. Washbowls and showers should be nearby.

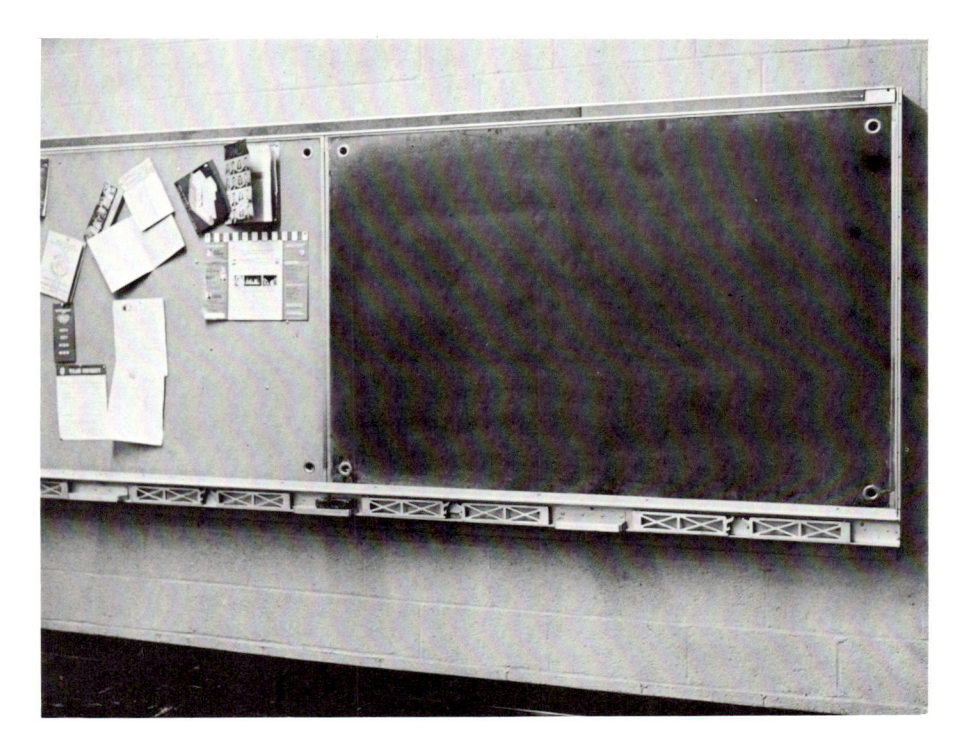

Classroom to dressing room conversion. Blackboards and pinboards open to become make-up tables, with mirrors and lights in place. Pickard Theatre, Bowdoin College, McKim, Mead and White, architects.

By raising a wall panel to expose a counter and extending some fold-away clothes racks, a seminar room in the Wright Memorial Theatre at Middlebury College is converted into a coat-checking facility.

Arts and crafts shops of various kinds may serve as shops for the preparation of scenery, properties and costumes.

Wagon docks at the sides or back of stages may be used as scene shops or as rehearsal spaces but only if there is adequate noise attenuation between them and the stage.

Lounges and lobbies may serve as meeting rooms, libraries, rehearsal rooms and exhibition galleries. Corollary requirements such as kitchen facilities, display panels, portable tables and chairs and their storage, additional janitorial care, and security measures must be considered.

The lobbies of a theatre may serve as general lounge space for non-theatregoers provided that admission controls are set up between the lounge and the house. The second floor lobby of the Hopkins Center at Dartmouth College merges with a general lounge area which is used by students who are not attending the performance. This lounge is also used for social gatherings during nonperformance hours. The lobbies of Las Vegas hotels have unique and interesting dual uses while obviating the necessity for lobbies specific to their connecting theatres.

All instances of multiple use are subject to careful scrutiny and control as to scheduling. The theatre worker may reasonably be jealous of other uses which infringe his rightful claim to all spaces of primarily theatrical function, as instructors or administrators may be of theatrical invasion of nontheatrical spaces.

One scheme for dual use or shared use which should be mentioned only to be deprecated is that of relating two houses of different seating capacities to one stage with prosceniums in both walls of the stage. The presumed reason for this arrangement is to save the cost of a second stage and its equipment. The complication of the stage equipment, proscenium equipment, lighting controls, etc., is an evil which compounds the greater evil of one of the houses with its attendant public and front service rooms rendered useless when the other is in use, effectively cutting the use of, and income from, both houses in half.

Built-in Deterrents

The planner must be made aware of limitations which are inherent in certain forms of theatre. He should know what he is getting and what he is not getting. This book has presented most, if not all, of the components of a complete theatre. The omission of any of these components renders the theatre to some degree incomplete. The absence of some of the components can be compensated for by improvisation but never with full effectiveness. A missing box office can be replaced by a table in the lobby but security, an orderly working space, communications and admission control at the exterior door are lacking. The absence of a flyloft can be compensated for by overhead masking, rolling drops, traversing curtains. But overhead masking is arbitrary, the effects of rolled drops are archaic, and traversing curtains vitiate the use of offstage space for storage of scenery. Other components if absent cannot be replaced by substitutes: absence of stage traps prevents entrances through the stage floor; absence of front lighting positions prevents adequate lighting of actors in the frontal stage areas; inadequate public spaces offer no recourse from congestion during intermissions other than the sidewalk. There are some recurrent results of bad planning which deserve emphasis as especially to be avoided. These faults may be considered to be built-in deterrents to effective use of a theatre.

Actors are human beings. Their movements may be minute or heroic. They must have space in which to move. They frequently move on and about furniture which has its own specific scalar relationships to human beings. Side stages, projecting forestages, even proscenium acting areas must therefore be planned not in terms of minima but rather in terms of the heroic scale of movement associated with Shakespearian or tragic Greek acting.

Stage Areas Too Small for Action

A larger acting area on one side of the center line than on the other inevitably attracts most of the important stage action, favors the seats near it and, because it is off-center, increases the number of relatively poorer seats. In addition it tends to induce a monotony of directorial pattern and monotony has no place in the theatre.

Eccentricity of Stage Shape

A stage must have sufficient depth to accommodate acting areas, scenery space and crossover space. Chapter 9 makes the requirements abundantly clear.

Insufficient Stage Depth

The inability to create openings of random size at random locations in the stage floor will force departure from the playwright's intention and require directorial improvisation in an estimated 20 per cent of plays produced and will hamper both design and directorial creativeness.

Absence of Traps in the Stage

A few spotlights permanently fixed in a small slot in the ceiling of the house do not permit effective lighting of actors in the frontal areas of the stage or on a forestage. See Chapter 12.

Inadequate Front Lighting Positions

The stage, the scene shop and the scenery storage rooms are not large open spaces especially provided for the run of air-conditioning ducts; in fact air-conditioning ducts run through these spaces can effectively destroy the intended function of these rooms. The planner must specify and jealously guard the required *clear* heights of these spaces.

Mechanical Encroachments on Theatre Functions

Absence of the Fly Loft

This eliminates the whole system of hanging and storing scenery by raising it into the space above the stage. It prevents production in historic and traditional styles which depend upon flown scenery.

Fixed Forestage

This interposes space between performers and audience if performers are working in a set behind the proscenium.

If performers are working on the forestage, bad conditions of seeing are created in both sides of the house. The performer cannot orient himself toward all parts of the audience at the same time and the audience on the two sides cannot possibly get similar effects of a performance.

Omission of Provisions for Scenery

Schemes for the elimination of scenery and scenery-handling devices apparently arise from the valid realization that scenery requires both effort and expense, that scenery-handling devices and the space they require constitute a large portion of the total theatre plant, rationalized into the supposition that since the play and the actors are, admittedly, the major conveyors of the illusion to the audience, scenery is unnecessary.

There has been ample opportunity in the course of the theatre's twenty-five hundred years for scenery to be eliminated. If it has not been, it is probably important to the theatre.

The Psychology of Minima

Building costs being what they are, the American bargaining temperament being what it is and the cold facts of financing being what they are, the psychology of *minima* is hard to avoid. In the new theatre, the client wishes to achieve all the available improvements in theatre technology but he has only limited financial resources. Two thought processes frequently invade the planning sessions: (1) What are the smallest possible dimensions? and (2) Who will supply and install for the lowest price?

And, miraculously, when the building is completed and dedicated the psychology of *maxima* dominates, and it is the biggest, finest, most modern, best and most completely equipped theatre ever built.

The two psychologies are inconsistent, of course.

Caveat

Theatre planners appear to have been guilty of three erroneous practices in developing their basic plans:

1. Subservience to custom. There are numerous examples of duplication in existing theatre forms which appear to indicate the acceptance without question of existing forms as good.

2. Misplaced emphasis in the drawing up of programs, generally to the neglect of theatrical requirements.

3. Adoption of partly thought-out schemes involving changing the shape of the theatre. Often such schemes have the merit of well-founded

dissatisfaction with existing forms but lack sufficient consideration of the practical aspects of realization. A simplified statement of the theatrical functions sometimes is accepted without expanding those functions to include their practical ramifications.

The Mystique of the Single Architectural Enclosure

Architectural theorists appear to be entranced by the idea of unifying the performance and the audience in one room. Actually there is not and cannot be a unity of audience and performance. There is a basic duality in the theatre experience. The performance acts; the audience reacts. Both the performance and the audience need the recognition of this duality for the achievement of total uniform theatrical effect. A member of the audience, when called upon to participate in a performance, becomes aware of his existence as an individual and loses his wished-for submersion in the reacting, responding audience-as-a-whole. Similarly, when performers approach close to the audience or mingle with it, the assumed identity of the dramatic character falls away, the theatrical illusion is destroyed and the theatre experience is vitiated.

Attractiveness

The size of the house does not guarantee the size of the audience, even where there is a large potential audience and a good show. The house must be well appointed and this item must be figured into the building costs. Moreover, good appointments often pay for themselves more rapidly than almost any other feature in theatre construction. Attending the Shakespeare Festival Theatres at both Stratfords (Ontario and Connecticut) is a pleasant experience even if the show may not be superior, because of the conveniences, the beauty of the locations, the spacious lobbies and the comfortable and well-decorated houses. A luxurious community theatre within commuting distance of Times Square enjoys steady patronage despite distinctly grade B performances. This is largely because the house is one of the most attractive and comfortable in the country.

Structure

Since this is not a book on architectural engineering, structural considerations in the planning of theatres must be limited to those which affect the functioning of the building. Certain trends in the architectural structure militate against theatrical effectiveness: the elimination of mass from structure may at the same time eliminate needed acoustical isolation; glass walls may require special provisions for lightproofing the theatre; concrete vaults in the roof of the stage house may arbitrarily determine the points of suspension of the gridiron whereas the functional design of the gridiron might better determine the structure of the roof of the stage.

The stage with its apparatus, which is of the essence changeable, the proscenium, forestage, house side walls and ceiling, all of which may also be movable, must be recognized as systematic machinery rather than as enclosed spaces into which equipment will be fitted. The closer the design of the theatre as a building approaches the design of an integrated, operable mechanism, the better is the result likely to be.

Nothing in the canon of theatre planning precludes the use of new structural systems, new materials, new techniques of construction, except failure of these novelties to produce a workable theatre. It is likely, on the other hand, that intelligent and resourceful planning of new theatres may call for innovations in structure which may startle conventional structural engineers.

Economics

This book is written at a time when it is particularly important to study the economic aspects of any theatrical enterprise before undertaking a building to house it. There is increasing competition for the entertainment dollar and the leisure hour, notably in the fields of spectator sports and television. To compete, the theatre, any type of theatre, has to furnish a good show. Building costs are high; every part of a projected theatre must withstand careful examination and merit inclusion in the building on the basis of effectiveness.

The conditions limiting commercial theatre building, especially in a metropolis, have been cited. The current burgeoning art centers, cultural centers, centers for the performing arts built by foundation, state or

Plan of the Los Angeles Music Center. See page 45 for the section.

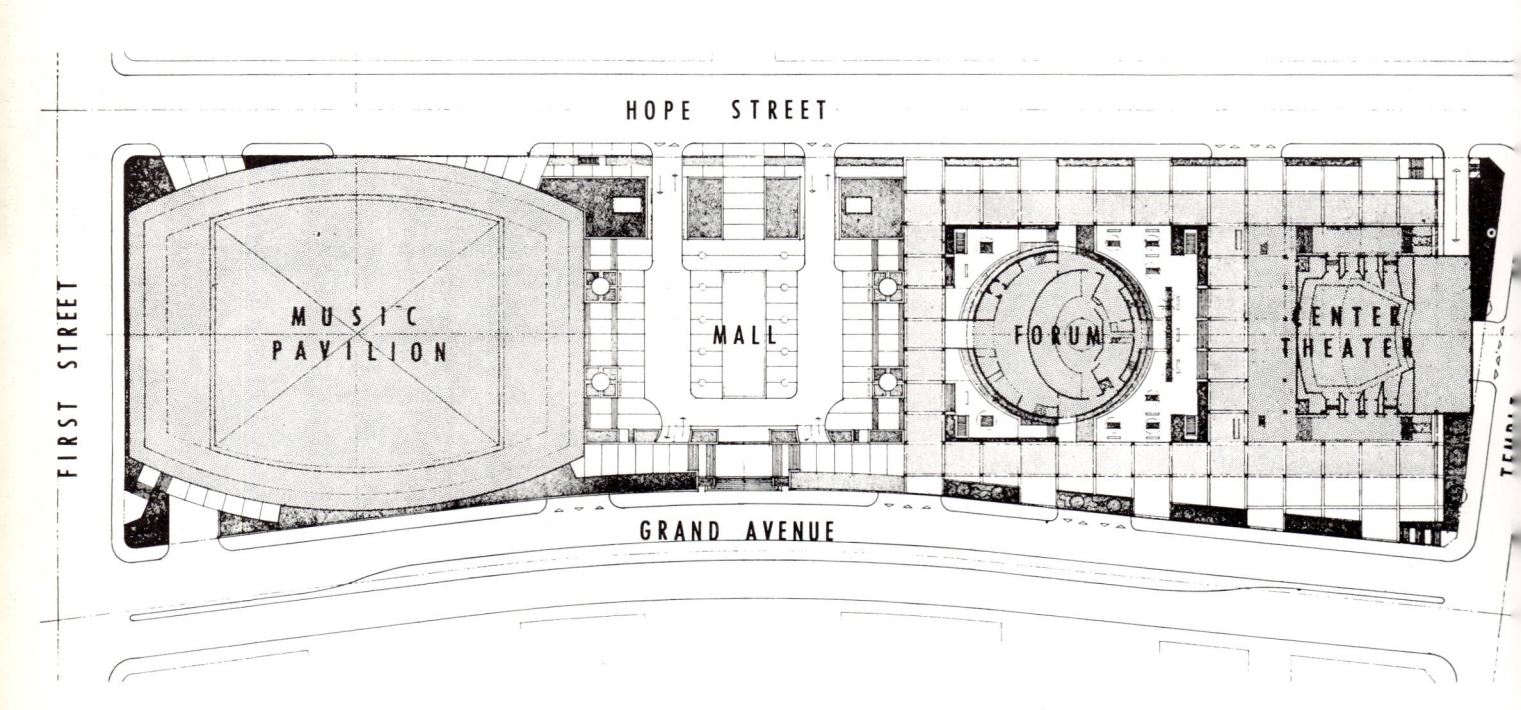

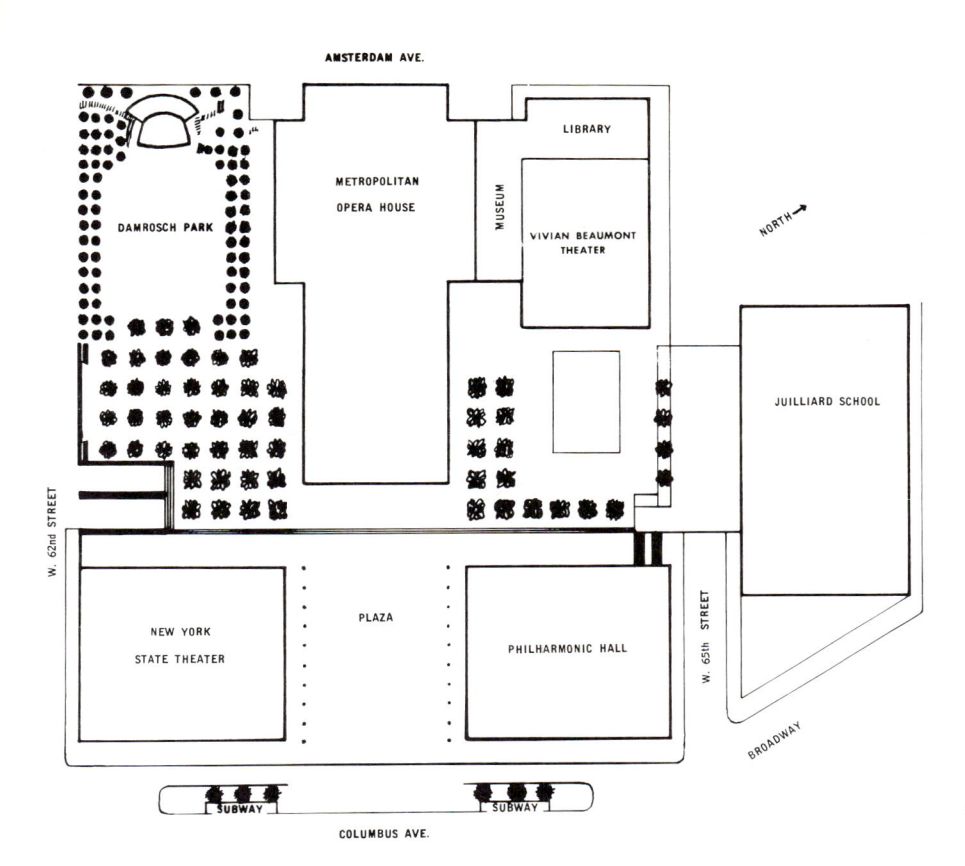

Lincoln Center for the Performing Arts plan and model.

organization funds or public subscription relieve the producer of paying off the mortgage. But if the *production* cannot support itself, it will require an angel, and the day may well come when there is no subsidy and the show degenerates to what the box office can afford. The subsidized theatre is the controlled theatre. Artistic freedom and artistic integrity may be difficult to maintain under such circumstances.

The repeatedly threatened cancellation of the Metropolitan Opera season illustrates the plight of theatres whose production facilities are obsolete, and whose operation is inefficient. To build a theatre building which cannot pay its own way is almost certain to limit the number and scope of theatrical performances for which there is an audience.

The success of any theatre may be measured in dollars or in terms of artistic achievement. The same conditions make for success however measured, and there are almost no valid exceptions. In theatre, financial and artistic success are basically interdependent. The opera often has to limit rehearsals for financial reasons to the point where it cannot achieve a finished performance. The commercial production of a play may cost so much to polish that it will flop unless it is a sell-out. And the tragic result of this unquestioning acceptance of a basically unsound situation is that the Lincoln Center Opera House is too small to support a grade A production out of box office receipts alone, and the opera house planned for the National Cultural Center must similarly lose money or put on inferior shows. There is no valid technical or artistic reason that this situation should exist.

The importance of the economic criterion in commercial production need only be acknowledged. Less obvious is the necessity for an economically sound school, college or community theatre. To attempt to teach the theatre in a plant incapable of high standards of production or capable of production quality only at such cost in labor as to make a commercial production impossible is very bad pedagogy. The inefficient school theatre must perforce put on a low-grade performance, or expend an unjustified amount of effort and money to get a passable show. Neither alternative is educationally warranted.

Operating Economy

The rapidity with which money can be lost in the theatre is proverbial. Not even a hit playing to full houses is sure to be profitable. A famous Broadway producer was often one show behind his bills, despite his spectacular string of highly successful shows. The Winthrop Ames' Gilbert and Sullivan revivals, conceded to be the finest productions those operettas had ever had, played to large houses for several seasons, yet are reported to have been something less than a financial success. David Belasco's production of Molnar's MIMA cost so much to produce and so much to operate that it was mathematically impossible at prevailing prices for it ever to pay out. At least one prominent community theatre can operate only because its angel underwrites the annual deficit. The high production and operating costs of plays, more than any other single factor, account for the reduction in the number of legitimate houses in New York and the virtual disappearance of the road. Nothing any theatre planner can design or build into a theatre can stop a producer from putting on a show with a basically unsound budget. The most the planner can do is to make the theatre efficient in its operation. This in itself will help to reduce the red figure.

While operating costs do not vary from production to production in the house presenting motion pictures only, the total operating cost is the largest single expense item. In the case of the motion picture theatre, more than any other performance type, the audience patronizes the comfortable, well-appointed, well-maintained house, and will often choose such a house rather than seek a preferred picture.

Audience

The one and only irreplaceable element in the theatre is the audience, which wants entertainment and will pay for it. The actor-audience relationship to be most effective demands a certain scale. A small house invites a patronizing attitude and is by that fact defeatist. It also fails to take in enough money to put on a good show. For a theatre to be architecturally and economically sound, the dimensions of the house must be established by the limits of seeing and hearing required for the largest type of production for which the house is planned.

A concomitant of this principle is that the income-producing capacity of the house limits the size of the production it should be designed to accommodate. For example, a house which can gross no more than $30,000 a week need not have a stage capable of mounting THE ETERNAL ROAD. Conversely, a stage on which grand opera can be produced demands a house which can gross $75,000 a week (in 1964 dollars).

It follows then that any theatre must be planned so as to be able to pay its way whether or not that is requisite in the type of operation immediately envisioned. To pay its way, the commercial theatre must amortize building cost, must amortize potential decline in ground value or must pay ground rent. It must pay taxes, production costs, and operating expenses. To be successful it must earn a profit on capital invested. In noncommercial operation, the theatre is usually relieved of one or more of the cost items. It sometimes needs to provide only for building maintenance and replacement. It is usually built on tax-exempt land, the cost of which is seldom charged to the theatre as such. A noncommercial theatre often has to pay its own operation cost. Gifts and popular subscription of capital funds may pay for land and building. In an educational institution, maintenance and some operating costs may be charged against the teaching function which has income from tuitions and possibly endowment. Profits, if any, may usually be allocated to the improvement of the plant, contingent reserve or an eleemosynary use.

An interesting fable concerning audience choice is the story of a theatre which was owned by a large motion picture exhibiting organization, as were also a large number of neighborhood houses in the area. This theatre always made money, but when it was operating, the neighborhood houses of the same chain had very poor audiences. It was discovered that the chain made more money with the theatre closed than with it open. This situation was in part attributable to high costs of operation as contrasted with the neighborhood houses.

Just as there is an upper limit to capacity (about 2,000) beyond which operating costs increase very rapidly, so there is a lower limit below which operating costs do not drop appreciably. It takes the same number of people backstage (house crew) and only a few more ushers to staff the Shubert Theatre (capacity about 1,400) as the Little Theatre (capacity 299). The implications as to economical size are obvious.

Stage

Much has already been made of the relation of the production facilities to audience size. There are economic limits to stage size also. An inadequate stage makes productions so poor that you can't give seats away, or so costly that you can't sell them. Conversely a production requiring an extraordinarily large and highly mechanized stage cannot be operated or amortized in a house whose potential gross is low. *The economic limit for stage size is the stage which will accommodate as elaborate a show as the house capacity can support.*

It may appear that the economies of having production complete within the plant, freedom from certain costs and taxes, and the availability of cheap or free labor, favor noncommercial operation. This notion has led to the feeling that lower operating costs could compensate for structural deficiencies. However, this is not the case. Under commercial operation, working capital is at least adequate or there is no operation. The commercial theatre must, by its nature, appeal to as large an audience as possible. The best available personnel for planning, publicizing, preparing, operating and performing in a theatre are available to commercial productions because high rates of pay are possible, and the result is that the commercial standard of performance is substantially above that which the noncommercial theatre can achieve except at rare intervals. Low operating costs do not offset this combination of advantages. The theatre which expects to attract an audience, whether it be a summer theatre, a theatre in the high school, or an opera house in the metropolis, must be planned to the specifications adequate for successful commercial operation if it is to fulfill its purpose.

Labor Costs

Where operation of the theatre is simple, easy, and efficient, precision of operation is assured and there is economy of both time and effort. One man with a winch can get counterweights up to the loading gallery better and faster than five men with block and tackle. One man at a switch can shift a full stage setting mounted on a motor-driven stage wagon.

As has been previously indicated, inefficiency which will break a commercial production can stultify the same production in a school or community theatre. Despite this apparently obvious situation, many high school theatres, built at costs sufficient for theatres in which practically anything could be presented, contain stages unsuited for mounting the simplest of plays. One college has a theatre which has some architectural virtues, but it is on the top floor of a building. Scenery can be gotten to the stage only by being carried on the roof of an elevator to the floor below the theatre, thence up a flight of stairs and thence through the house to the stage. Some theatres into which it may be easy to take the show impose difficulties on the process of setting up the show, including the erection of temporary flying systems inside a permanent plaster dome or rebuilding all scenic units to stand vertical on a sloped floor.

Theatres without stage crossovers, with remote dressing rooms, with inadequate lavatories and showers, without traps, without intercommunication systems, render operation difficult. The sum of these disadvantages is to make a theatre which nobody wants. Although somebody may have to put up with it, it will be abandoned as soon as anything better is available. It cannot compete with a theatre which does not cost so much to operate either in dollars or in volunteer man hours.

To make a theatre economically sound, it is necessary to spend enough on the plant to insure minimum production and operation costs. This principle, although it seems obvious, is sometimes very difficult to demonstrate to people who build theatres for others to operate. The theatre is probably the only place where the folly of inefficiency is not only condoned, but vigorously defended.

Storage

Perhaps only less fortunate than the show which is too expensive and elaborate for the theatre is the show which, playing in repertory, has to be taken out and stored between performances. This is one of the major operating expenses of opera where shows are frequently hauled back and forth between the warehouse and the theatre. Even where ground space is at a premium, this situation can be somewhat mitigated where building codes provide, as does the current New York code, for the storage of scenery below stage in fireproof vaults to which access can be had by stage elevator. In the college or community theatre where sets are stored to be re-used, if only as material in new sets, the cost of productions, labor excluded, can often be 30 to 50 per cent less than the cost of the same productions identically designed and built for commercial production. The storage function is requisite if the theatre is ever to do repertory economically, and the theatre in which storage facilities permit parts of one show to be re-used for another will always have an economic advantage over the theatre in which the production is destroyed at the end of the run.

Other Sources of Income

Chapter 5 sets up the requisites for multiple uses for the lounge. The bar in the Metropolitan Opera House and the ballroom in the Philadelphia Academy of Music may well have other uses than those connected immediately with the performance. The Free Synagogue uses Carnegie Hall. Town Hall was used for motion pictures during its first years of operation for the months between concert sessions. It is often feasible to originate radio and television programs in theatres. It is axiomatic that the more continuous the operation of a theatre, the more money it can take in; the more types of activity it can house or types of production it can mount, the more certain it is that its operation will be financially successful.

Costs

Cost often determines whether or not a theatre is to be built. The first rough estimate for theatres in which any type of production can be mounted may be derived from:

1. Local building costs per cubic foot for construction using similar materials to those planned for the theatre.

2. Audience size. A minimum house capacity which may be expected to be reasonably safe for commercial legitimate operation is in the neighborhood of 1,000. Minimum cubage for 1,000 seats is approximately 250,000.

3. The stage for economical legitimate operation will have at least the cubage of the house.

If the theatre builder has not sufficient funds to build for the cubage thus derived, he had better not build at all but look for a structure with walls and a roof which may be rebuilt for theatrical purposes.

Priorities

Theatre buildings often cost more than those responsible for their construction at first envision. When a limited budget will not provide all that is desired, compromises are sought. The nature of these compromises often determines the immediate usefulness and ultimate fate of the theatre. It is therefore necessary to plan at the outset what will be built as a minimum, and the order in which compromises will be made, if necessary.

It is obvious that the first requisite is a building which can be operated efficiently. Therefore shape and size of house and stage cannot be limited below what was planned as an optimum. A shop connected with, and opening onto, the stage may be left for future construction, but the principal stage area cannot be cut down, because increasing such area after the theatre is once built is much more expensive than building correctly in the first place. It is probably better to build another theatre than to try to improve one which is basically wrong. Public rooms, offices, etc., at

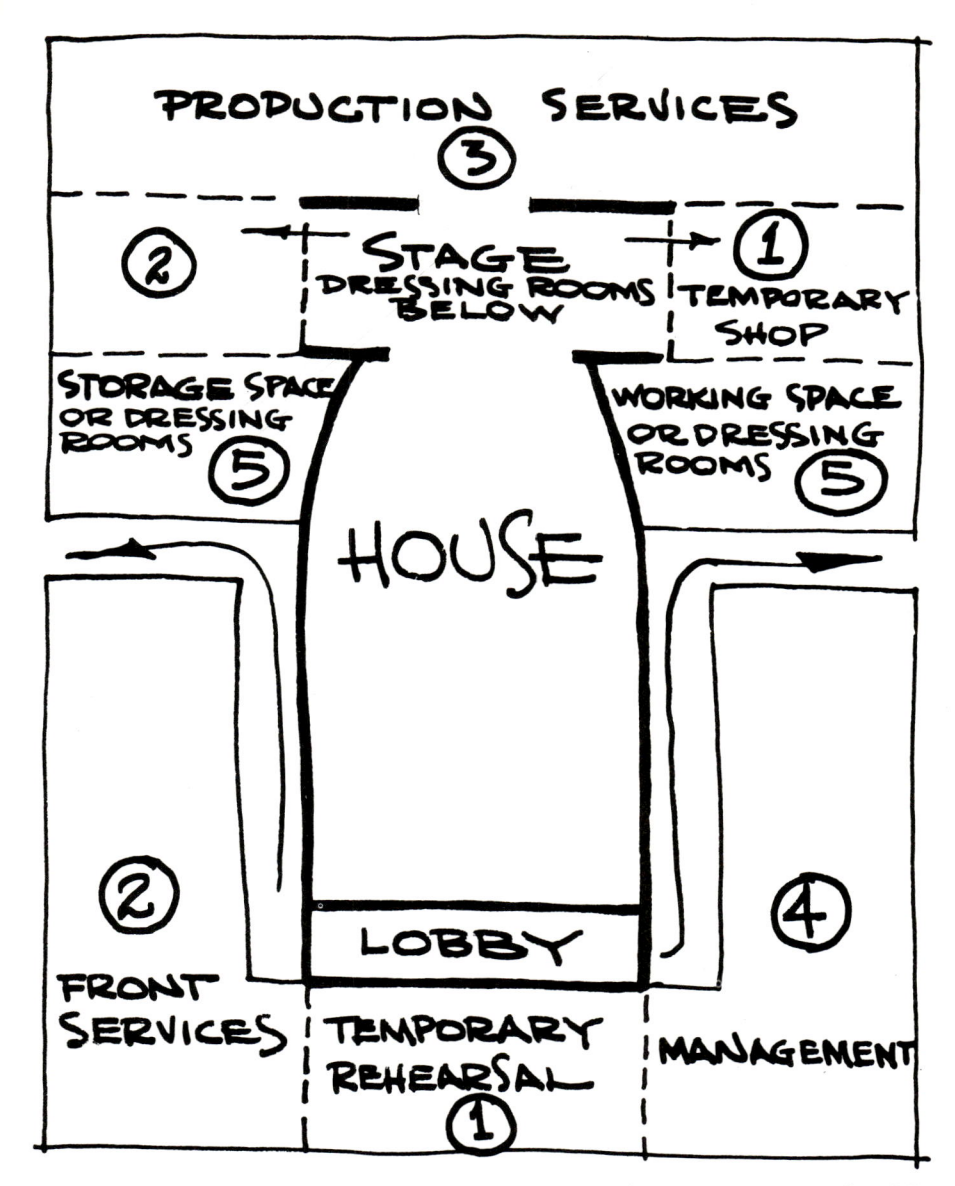

Numerical order, based on importance of function, in which additions to the basic theatre block may be made.

the back of the house (the foyer and lobby) can be added after the building has been in operation for some seasons. Theatre builders do not generally like to change the portion of the building containing the public rooms, since it is the section usually first seen from the outside and presents the theatre's façade. However, if a temporary lobby is used for functions of lobby, lounge, and foyer, the audience will be no worse off than it is in the average commercial legitimate house now. Adequate facilities can be built when funds become available. Deferment of construction of portions of the front of the house as here indicated will in no way interfere with the efficiency of production, but will interfere with the comfort of the audience until the audience is in the house.

365

Much stage equipment is portable and may be acquired as funds are available provided the essential structural provisions are made in the original construction. If an adequate trap room is built in the original instance, elevators can be installed at any time. If an adequate gridiron is constructed, counterweight and line sets can be added as necessary. If an adequate lighting control system is planned and conduit and control room for it are installed, lighting instruments, accessories and control units can be added as acquired. In fact, with the exception of the gridiron, the ventilation system and the seats, almost all items of theatre equipment can be added after the theatre is built. If a good theatre is to be achieved and funds do not permit its completion, it is a waste of the money to restrict the shape or size of house or stage. If these cannot be built to specifications which will make possible efficient operation and audience comfort, a theatre building project should not be undertaken.

Sources of Information

This book has presented the essential elements of good theatre planning, and has defended those elements on various grounds. Other sources are noted in the bibliography. Theatre consultants are listed with the U.S. Institute of Theatre Technology, ANTA's National Theatre Service, the American Institute of Architects and the American Educational Theatre Association.

The consultant may confine himself to a particular element of the theatre; there are some who can adduce many years of experience in all phases of theatre operation.

The consultant should:

1. Review the purpose and indicate modifications of the concept, the program and economics. This purpose will in many cases need to be validated by a survey of the projected needs of all persons or organizations involved in the performing arts who might be served by the theatre.

2. Draw or review the program given the architect.

3. Review plans as they develop and accomplish the reconciliation of the many disparate and often conflicting elements.

4. Study and assume responsibility for approval of the final architect's drawings and specifications.

5. Study and advise on acceptance or rejection of bids, or proposed substitutions of items of equipment by suppliers of equipment.

6. Counsel the client as questions arise during construction.

7. Plan and supervise acceptance tests on all elements of the theatre and equipment which require such test.

Though only retained for a few of these functions, the consultant must have cognizance of, and familiarity with, them all, to be sure that his proposals are sound with relation to the total project.

The one indispensable element in theatre—the audience. Place des Arts, Montreal. Affleck, Desbarats, Dimakopoulos, Lebensold and Sise, architects.

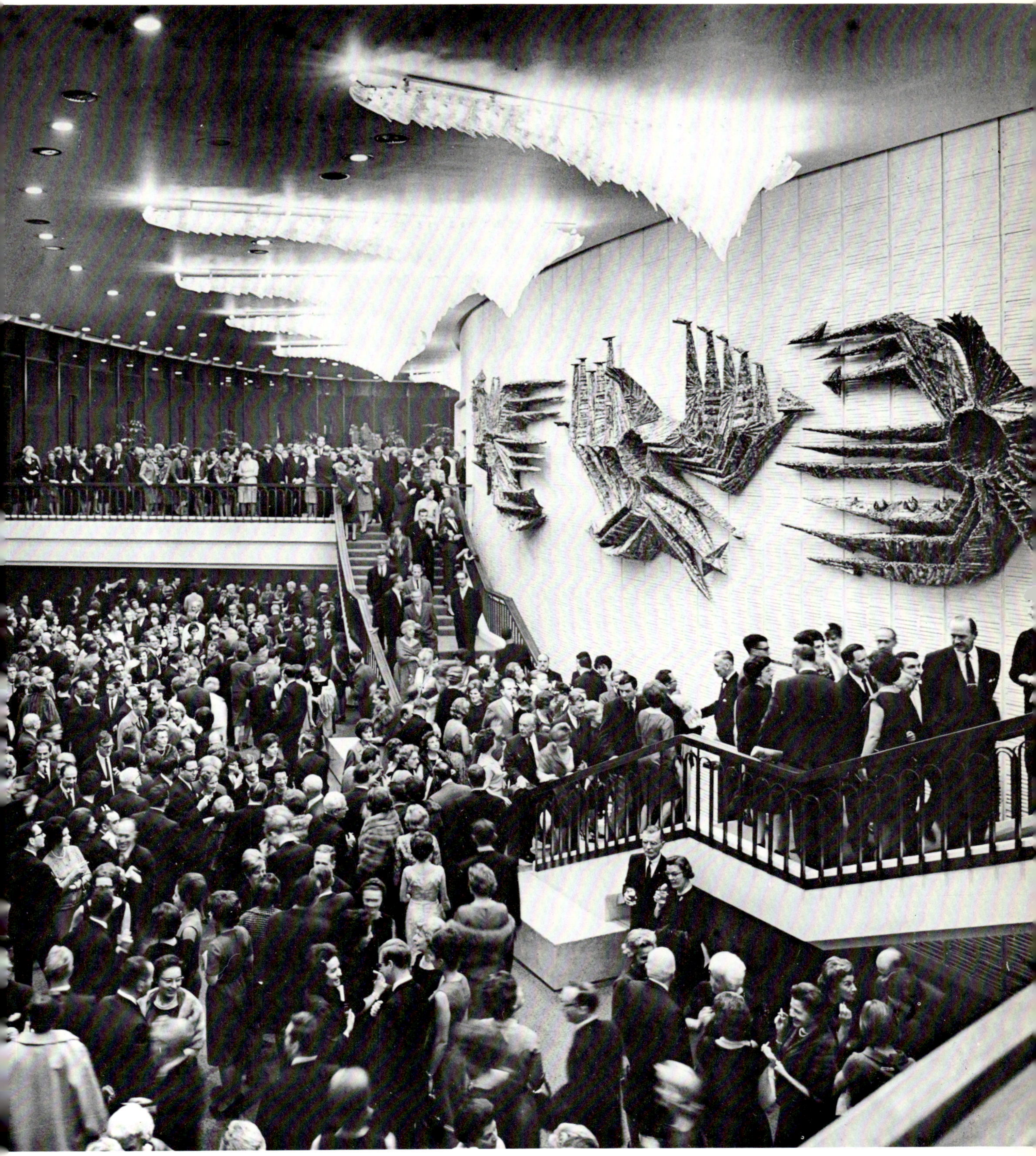

16: Theatres 1964 to 1975

The reprinting of THEATRES AND AUDITORIUMS offers an opportunity for a critical appraisal of theatres built or building since publication of this edition in 1964. Much has happened. Many theatres have been built, more are planned, and the theatre planner and architect have more precept and experience to refer to than ever before.

EXPERIMENTS The decade '64–'74 has been one of experimentation in theatre forms. The extreme experiment was gutting a conventional Broadway theatre, constructing a free-form theatre inside it for one show which lasted two weeks, restoring the theatre to its status quo ante, per contract, and doing the same thing, but with a different free form, in the same theatre about a year later. A more reasonable experiment was the carefully thought-out scheme for a theatre at California Institute of the Arts which can achieve any free-form that anyone can dream up, but requiring much time and labor to effect changes of form. A third is the seemingly timeless construction of the Sydney, Australia, Opera House which certainly announces to all who view it from the air that "the trumpets shall sound" but internally squeezes the stage into the apex of the cone of the trumpet.

Massive mechanical installations have been made to change the interior shape and size of the theatre, some of which have been effective; new machinery has been installed, some of which has failed before its first use. The reports of such expensive failures have inspired caution. The newest installations are still to be time tested.

There has been planning of theatres and parts of theatres based on speculation, sometimes on experiment, occasionally on research. Computer techniques have been applied to development of house floor contours, new and flexible lighting positions have been adopted, some acoustical consultants have learned enough about theatre production and audiences to produce satisfactory theatres and avoid the classic errors which have resulted from scientific virtuosity coupled with artistic ignorance. Functional effectiveness and economies appear to be motivating specifications where, previously, slavish imitation and whim had been the determinants.

Experimentation in theatrical presentation and developments in theatre architecture have been stimulated by other entertainment media, as well as other forces.

AESTHETIC INFLUENCES

The tendency to follow the scene sequence pattern and freedom that characterize film and television and Shakespeare prevails among playwrights, whose scripts often call for many changes of locale. If plays of this structure are to be produced in scenery which has any semblance of contributive significance, the stages must be versatile as to size, shape and location of playing areas, and must have equipment capable of achieving literally instantaneous changes of scene. The audience which is also conditioned to the kaleidoscopic changes of film and the tube will not be satisfied with less.

And yet—the three-act form, in one, two or three sets, persists. Plays by Pinter and Storey, as contemporary writers, and O'Neill, Shaw and Ibsen, whose plays are regularly revived, are examples of the persistence of the form. Realistic scenery hangs on, as evidenced by occasional ecstatic praise by first-line critics.

There has, however, been a departure from realism and illusion in scenery with a countering emphasis on abstract or symbolic designs. The reasons are multiple: disdain for anything that has been done before, desire to be inventive either for one's own sake or for the sake of the production, desire to experiment with new materials or new lighting devices, and an artistic (i.e. a creative) urge. This trend, in all its manifest variations, does not gainsay the fundamental special requirements of scenery, of whatever kind it may be.

In arena theatre or on a thrust stage there has been a reduction of emphasis upon concealment and masking. Scenery, if indeed there is any, and props must, perforce, be changed in full view of the audience. A modicum of revelation is preserved by having actors find their places during a blackout and bringing up the scene lighting to show them in character.

There has been considerable departure from the concept that scenery, and costumes, and properties, and lighting, and sound have the primary raison d'etre of assisting the actors.

SOCIOLOGICAL INFLUENCES

Two trends, happening more or less simultaneously, have greatly influenced developments in theatres in the last decade. The first is long-term gradual decline of the legitimate theatre in New York. There have been many contributing causes that can only be listed here: the presistence in the use of theatres more than fifty years old; the increase in the cost-benefit ratio of all but a few smash hits in any season; reduction in the number of road theatres in the country and the increase in the costs of road travel; the counter-attraction of films and television, not only for audiences but also for theatrical talents of all kinds; the social degradation of the New York theatre district and the increase in street crime rates in the city; the cost of theatre tickets and the ancillary costs and inconveniences of getting to the theatres from the suburbs and even from the outer reaches of the city itself.

The second trend is decentralization of the theatre. Many urban centers outside New York City have developed cultural identities of their own and have pushed effectively for home-grown cultural events. The growth of performing arts, both in and outside the curricula in higher education, has increased the widely distributed alumni who are theatre-oriented and capable of either participating in or supporting performing arts. Theatre education has penetrated downward through secondary school to primary grades, thus assuring the continuation of this growth. There already exist four excellent theatres built expressly for productions by and for children in U.S. cities. The study ARTS AND THE PEOPLE, made and published by the American Council for the Arts in Education, with the support of the New York State Council for the Arts, shows clearly that the people in New York State are further ahead in desire for the arts than the communities of the state are equipped to respond.

There have been strong community demands for performance facilities perhaps because upward mobility leads to increased participation in the arts and upward mobility has been the dominant socio-economic condition of the '64–'74 decade.

A third influence on the development of widespread interest in the theatrical arts has been television. Whereas music has been the popular art of the century because of radio, the theatrical arts, dance and acting, having the visual stimulus of movement as a principal component, appear to be catching up.

ECONOMIC FACTORS

Building costs are higher than they were in 1964 and are expected to go higher; investments have proven not to have the same behavior as building costs; an empty brick or stone building with sound structure and roof, abandoned either by trade or the clergy, looks more and more like a potential theatre; unfinished concrete block walls are less expensive than mosaic-tiled or even smooth-plastered walls, and grade-B-and-better white pine that cost $92.00 per thousand board feet in 1930 in not available today at any price and grade C select costs $750.00 per thousand if it can be purchased at all. Everything costs more and everybody wants more of everything; upward mobility, generally distributed, has affected all wages and salaries.

While stock market prices soared until the bull market peaked in January 1973 money was generally available for projects of all kinds. In the first nine years of the decade with which we are concerned, Lockheed and Lincoln Center both went handsomely over budget and the deficits were met, colleges and universities increased alumni fund goals annually and exceeded them as regularly. Government budgets at all levels increased and government tax-exempts were subscribed as fast as issued. Donors contributed generously for performing arts centers.

Since January 1973 evidence from many sources generates the suspicion that the boom is over. Money is lent at record interest rates (for the U.S. at least). Charitable gifts are not keeping step with the inflation.

Belt tightening seems to be in order. Inflation pervades worldwide and, by definition, inflation means that more money buys less. For such reasons, conversions, restorations, making-do with less-then-ideal buildings and parts of buildings, insisting on proven equipment which does not hide future repair and replacement costs, in sum, getting the most for the money, now seems to be the guiding principle.

Economical means of play production follow this principle: thrust and arena stages, with their obvious savings in equipment and scenic costs; abstract scenery that lets audience imagination fill the gaps; unit sets; uniform costumes with character-signifying accessories; neutral backgrounds instead of gorgeous sunsets, projections and other cost-minimizing and labor-saving stratagems are used.

The theatre planner must give careful thought to such economic factors.

EDUCATIONAL INFLUENCES

There has been a general incipient increase in arts education at all levels. The Federal Government and several foundations have supported pilot programs, notably those engendered by the Elementary and Secondary Schools Act and those of the JDR 3rd Fund which embraced the motto: All the Arts for All Children. The boards of education of three states have taken the position that in public education the arts shall have equal curricular status with the sciences.

Consequently space is being made in, or added to, existing schools, and new or newly-planned schools include spaces and equipment for the arts.

The Democratic Imperative

Very large universities have large and varied performing arts programs, purposes and basic commitments that as many students as possible shall be exposed to the arts by participation or at least by seeing performances. Vocational and technical colleges and secondary schools, are instituting at least minimal opportunities for participation or spectatorship.

In the large universities, when possible, facilities of optimum size for each kind of performance are being created; when not possible, one maximum-sized facility capable of reduction in capacity is considered. A version of Gresham's Law tends to operate in this instance: a plant capable of seating a large number and with maintenance and operating costs commensurate with the largest capacity will not willingly be reduced in capacity to satisfy a poorly understood aesthetic principle that prescribes the optimum performance—audience relationship. Though a municipal coliseum capable of housing Ringling Brothers-Barnum and Bailey Circus is hardly suitable for the performance of a solo guitarist, it has happened.

The problems of competition between departments for the use of the single performance facility are discussed later.

Publications

A most significant happening after the publication of THEATRES AND AUDITORIUMS, Second Edition, in 1964, was the beginning of publication, in May 1965, of THEATRE DESIGN AND TECHNOLOGY under the aegis of United States Institute for Theatre Technology and the editorship of Ned A. Bowman. The editors, Bowman and later Thomas S. Watson, have selected outstanding examples of new theatres and obtained informed, descriptive and critical articles for inclusion with regular frequency. The entire set belongs in the theatre planner's working library. The same may be said of TABS, the house publication of Rank, Strand Electric, Ltd., which includes the lively writing of Frederick Bentham, with the reservation that British and Continental conditions of theatre do not precisely parallel those in the United States. THEATRE CRAFTS devotes an occasional issue to, and prints articles on, theatres. BÜHNENTECHNISCHE RUNDSCHAU, official organ of the Deutchen Theater-technischer Gesselschaft and the German section of the Organisation Internationale des Scenographes et Techniciens de Theatre, covers theatre building and equipment throughout the world in exemplary breadth and detail.

A significant conference, sponsored by the U.S. Office of Education, assembled a small group of experts representing all specializations related to secondary school theatre to evolve architectural recommendations for secondary, and tertiary, school theatre space and equipment, which were embodied in a final report, Project no. 5-8290, Contract No. OE-6-10-025, and contributed considerably to a book by the project director, Horace W. Robinson, entitled ARCHITECTURE FOR THE EDUCATIONAL THEATRE (University of Oregon Books, 1969). These two documents are dependable guides in the planning of high school theatres.

The THEATRE ORIENTATION PACKAGE, prepared by the U.S. Institute of Theatre Technology Commission on Theatre Architecture, consists of a catalogue of American theatres built since 1960 and 255 slides in two carousels. Theatres are categorized by form, purpose (including multi-), capacity, and stage type. Basic facts include owner, construction data, capacity, architect and consultants. A bibliography lists works on the history of theatre forms and techniques, programming and planning, and books and articles undertaking to place theatre in social and economic context. The slides were chosen for innovation (not necessarily useful as models), function, and architectural distinction, including some which are distinctive but disastrous as theatres. Despite the lack of critical comment, the package is a most comprehensive overview of the contemporary American Theatre.

Codes and Zoning Regulations

With the revision of the New York City Building Code in 1968 the blight on theatre building in New York was lifted. Theatres can be built below, on, or above grade, inside other buildings and, with a water deluge fire curtain, dispense with the proscenium, the steel and asbestos fire curtain and the firewall between stage and house. It does, however, require new and effective preventive and protective procedures and systems. Further, a new New York City zoning regulation allows builders of new buildings to include about 20 per cent increase in rental space if a theatre is included in the structure. These legal changes have generated the building of four new legitimate theatres and a motion picture theatre, and others are projected, which correct many of the faults and inconveniences of the old-code theatres. These two regulations have served not only the commercial theatre in New York, but as the basis for variances from code limitations in other places.

CATEGORIES

Despite the fact that a good theatre is a good theatre whether it be on Broadway or a college campus, several distinct types are evolving. They may differ in purpose and operating patterns but not in the fundamental requisites for establishing that performance-audience relationship which is the basic theatre experience.

Generally they fall into five categories:

The commercial theatre—built and operated for profit.
The community civic art center theatre—a cultural facility.
The performing arts center.
The non-profit regional resident professional theatre.
The educational theatre—built as a laboratory for instruction in the performing arts.

The categories sometimes overlap. Resident professional theatres perform play series for children, tour to schools, and have apprentice programs, and are thus at least para-educational. Several universities now support resident professional companies combining theatre culture for their communities with live exemplification of dramatic expertise for their students.

Commercial

The New York Building Code of 1968 has been of particular help to the commercial theatre in that the theatre may now share the taxes and many overhead costs with other tenants of the same building. It opens

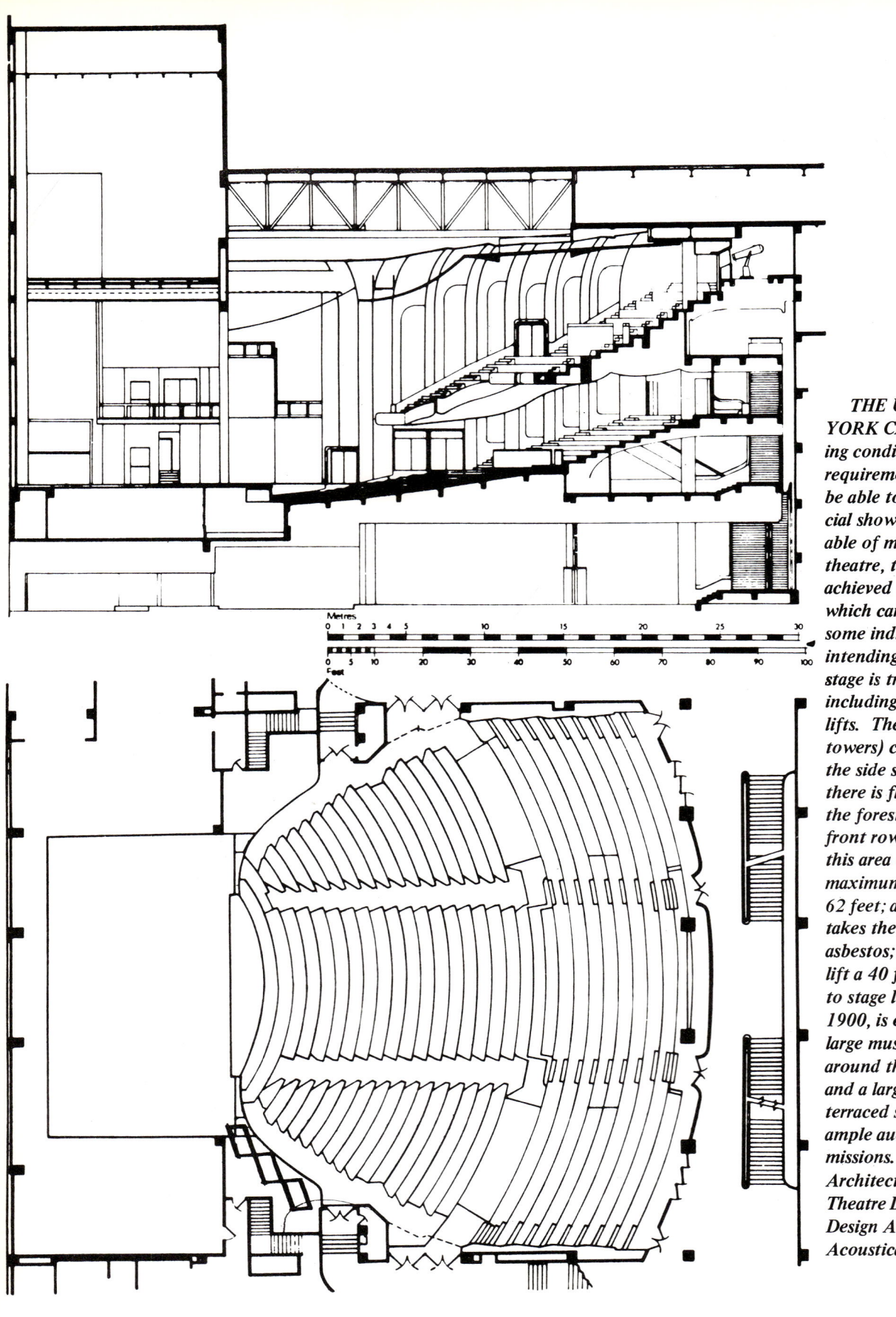

THE URIS THEATRE, NEW YORK CITY. Within the limiting conditions established by the requirement that theatres must be able to accomodate commercial shows which must be capable of moving from theatre to theatre, the Uris Theatre has achieved considerable flexibility which can be used by venturesome individual productions not intending to tour: the entire stage is trapped through to and including the two orchestra pit lifts. The box booms (light towers) can be stored to make the side stages into acting areas; there is flying equipment over the forestage, orchestra pit and front rows, and the ceiling over this area can be flown out; the maximum proscenium width is 62 feet; a deluge water curtain takes the place of the old-style asbestos; a loading elevator can lift a 40 foot trailer from street to stage level. The capacity, 1900, is economically sound for large musical shows. Promenade around the house at both levels and a large lounge under the terraced seating area afford ample audience space for intermissions.
Architects: Emory Roth and Son
Theatre Designer: Ralph Alswang
Design Associate: William Cruse
Acoustical Consultant: C.P. Boner

the sidewalk level for spacious vestibules and lobbies and for at-grade commercial enterprises such as restaurants and boutiques.

In addition to these benefits, the facilities for performance are enhanced. Performance-audience configurations can depart from the rigid formality of the proscenium theatre of the nineteenth and early-twentieth century and take any of the variety of forms which have developed experimentally since the twenties. Furthermore, the Code provides amply for audience safety when these freer forms are used.

The dinner theatre is descended from the night club. Eating-and-drinking while watching a show has persisted from ancient Rome. The newcomer is the legitimate play or modest musical performed at first in a hotel dining room and more recently in buildings remodeled or expressly designed as dinner theatres.

Often the form is arena or thrust stage, the play usually requires

**Dinner Theatre
(also commercial)**

LA COMEDIA DINNER THEATRE is located close enough to both Dayton and Cincinnati, Ohio, to draw patronage from both. It is an exellent example of the dinner theatre designed and built specifically for the purpose. Two years in the planning, it grew out of a study of over fifty operating dinner theatres. The stage can be used in either proscenium or thrust form and has scenery handling capabilities far beyond those of most dinner theatres. Theatrical and dining functions are well separated. With a capacity of 450, it has a greater profit potential than many theatres of the type.
Designer: Joseph Bok Mitchell
Architect: Harry E. Misel, Jr.
Consultants:
  Theatre: Larry Riddle
  Acoustics: Harold Burris-Meyer

VINCENT SARDI'S DINNER THEATRE at Franklin Square, Long Island, planned to be first of a chain of dinner theatres under the Sardi banner, is a complete renovation of a famous nightclub, the Casa Seville. It has a capacity of 700 seated at tables on six levels. With an ample proscenium stage, a thrust apron and an orchestra pit, various modes of performance are possible. Plan is copyright © All rights reserved.
Theatre design: Michael Hotopp, Paul de Pass

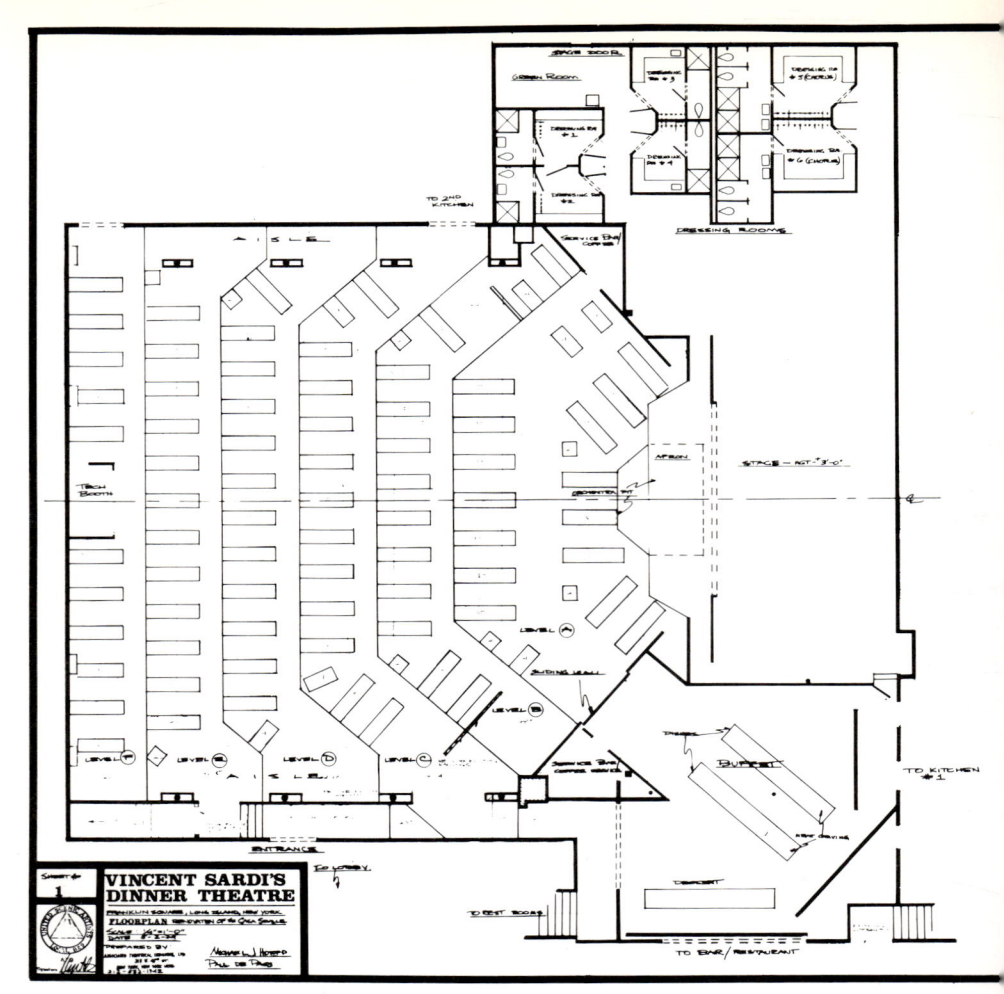

only one simple set with minimal effects, and the music, if any, is by a piano or a small combo. Even with these restrictions the category has proven financially successful and is growing rapidly, spreading into suburbs and exurbs throughout the country, currently numbering nearly 200 establishments, employing more actors than Broadway and tripling Broadway's annual gross income.

The dinner theatre has advantages for the patron. Having reserved for dinner and performance on a single ticket, he drives only a few miles from his home to the theatre and parks his car only once. The dinner is usually buffet, sometimes with roll-away buffet tables on the stage. Drinks are served during intermissions. Neil Simon is the favorite playwright, but heavier fare succeeds when done with distinction.

The combination of bar, restaurant kitchen, buffet tables, dining tables with visibility from all seats to the stage; with scene changing capability, stage lighting, entrances for actors, and a pit or platform for orchestra or piano, presents a new and interesting problem to the architect.

Civic Arts/Cultural Center

The decade 1964–1974 has seen a proliferation of civic arts centers, many as a part of urban renewal programs. And since they depend upon

(to page 379)

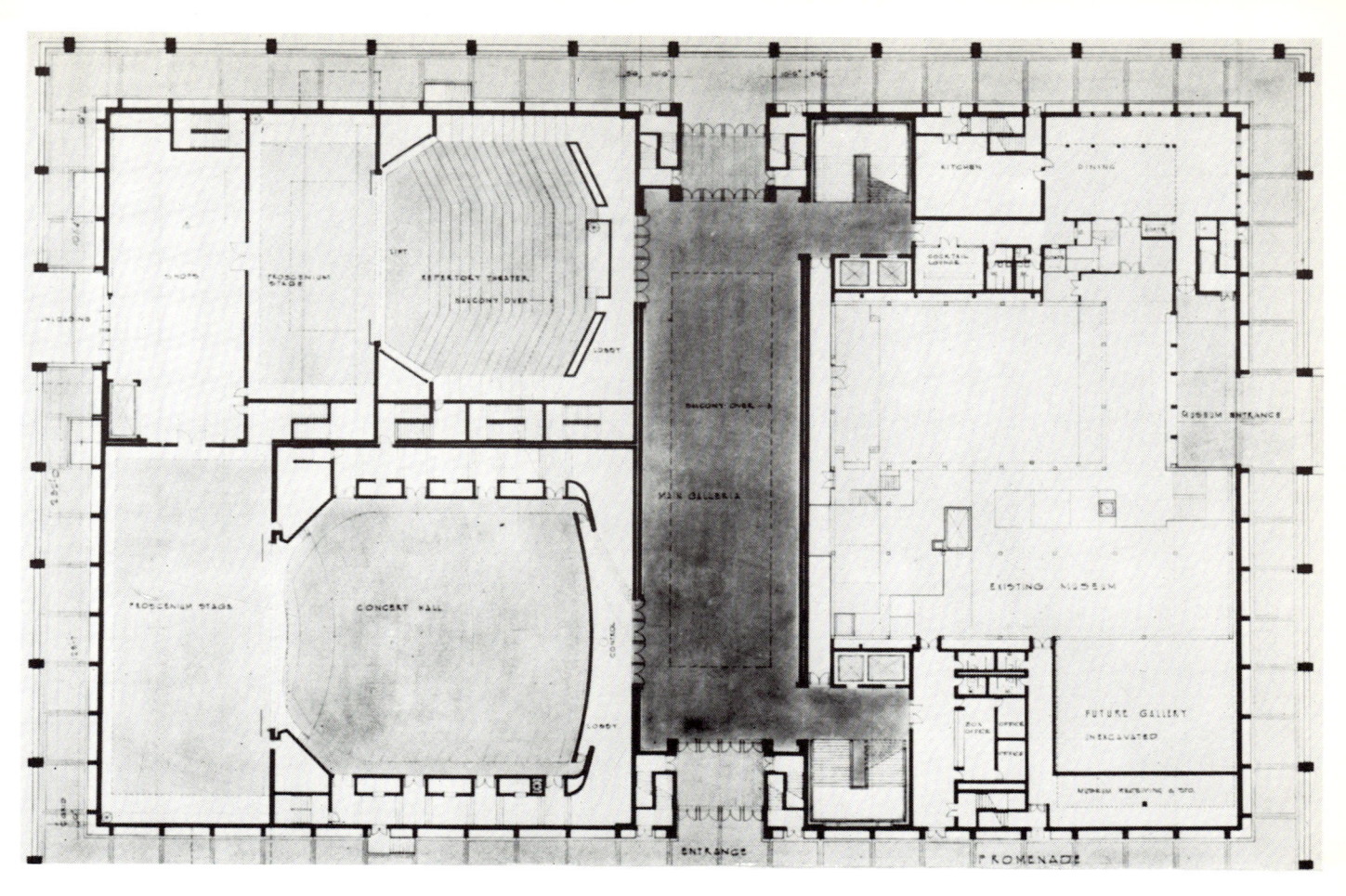

THE ATLANTA MEMORIAL CULTURAL CENTER. This building is a memorial to Atlanta's leaders in the arts and patrons of the center who perished at Orly, France, while the center was still unfinished. The structure, with two theatres, embraces an already existing art museum, a mutually advantageous arrangement. Theatres and museum share the generously proportioned galleria. Structurally and functionally, the theatres are good examples of time-proven forms. The concert hall is the home of the local symphony and books touring attractions. With a plywood band shell demountable in minutes, it serves equally well for opera and large musicals. The small theatre houses Theatre Alliance, an active resident company. It has adequate seating capacity.

Architect: Toombs, Amisano and Wells

Consultants: General: Harld Burris-Meyer
              Edward C. Cole
              Acoustical: Vern O. Knudsen
              Lighting: Stanley R. McCandless

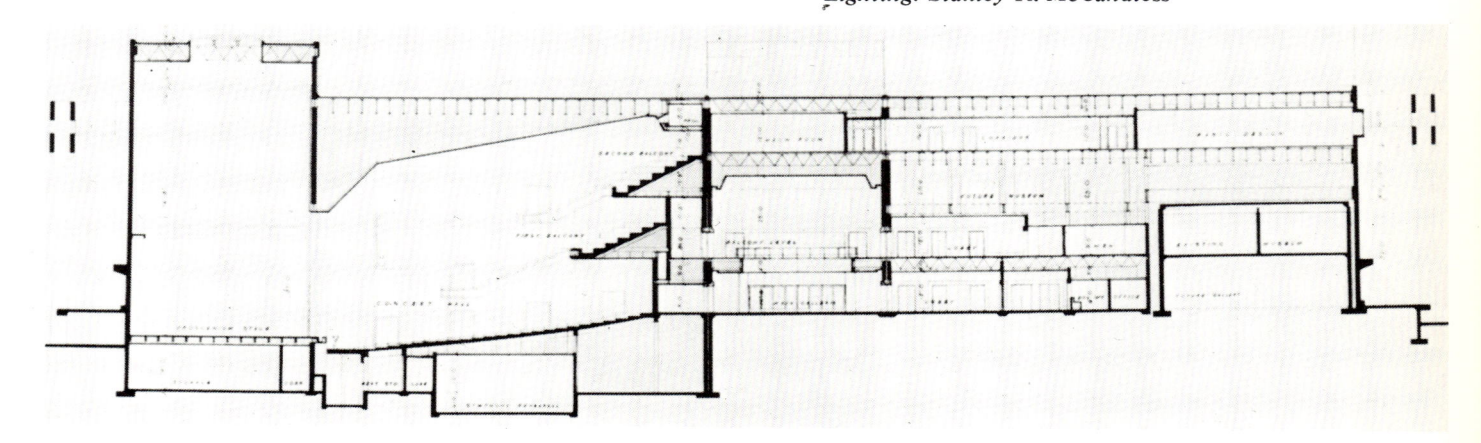

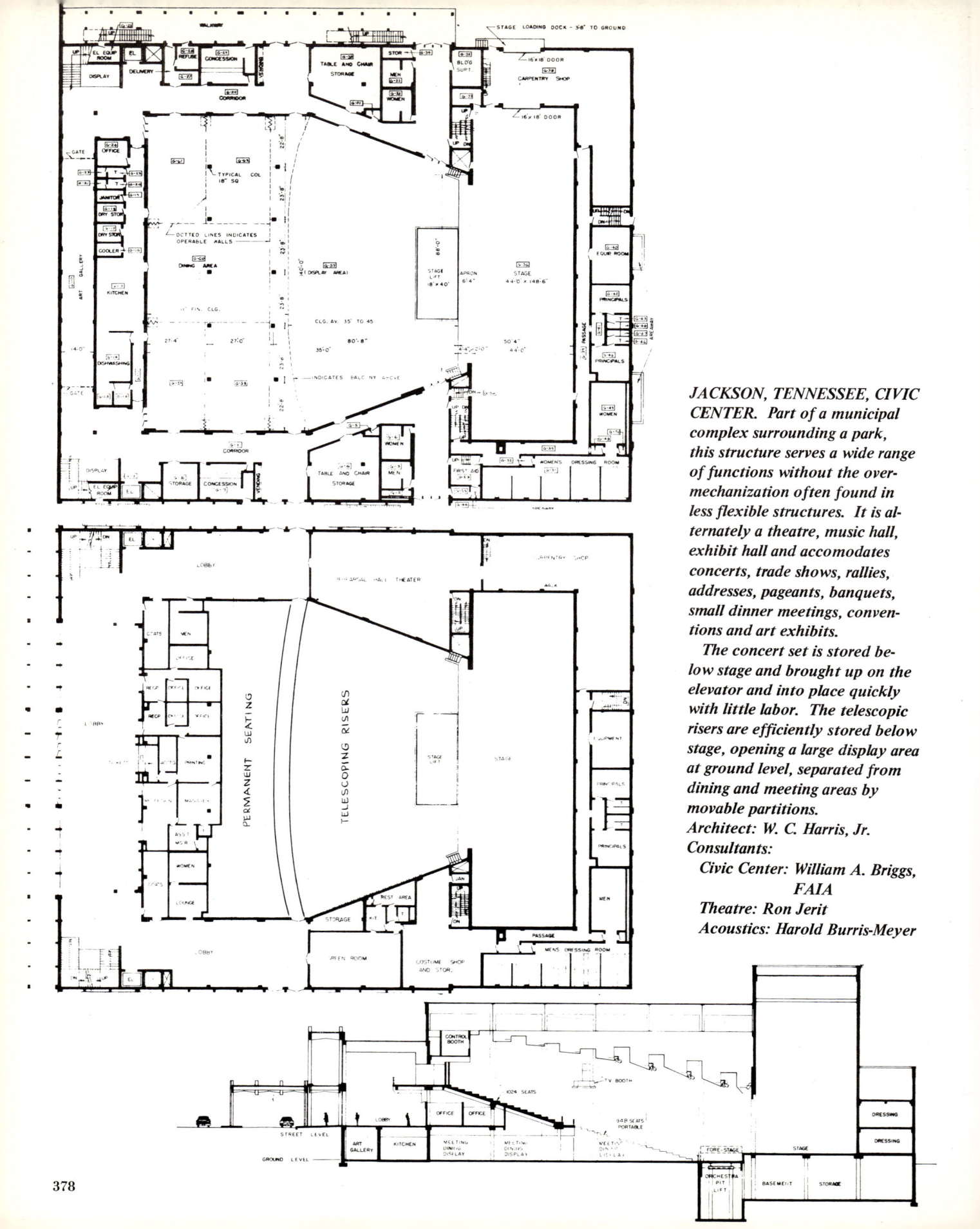

JACKSON, TENNESSEE, CIVIC CENTER. *Part of a municipal complex surrounding a park, this structure serves a wide range of functions without the over-mechanization often found in less flexible structures. It is alternately a theatre, music hall, exhibit hall and accomodates concerts, trade shows, rallies, addresses, pageants, banquets, small dinner meetings, conventions and art exhibits.*

The concert set is stored below stage and brought up on the elevator and into place quickly with little labor. The telescopic risers are efficiently stored below stage, opening a large display area at ground level, separated from dining and meeting areas by movable partitions.
Architect: *W. C. Harris, Jr.*
Consultants:
  Civic Center: *William A. Briggs, FAIA*
  Theatre: *Ron Jerit*
  Acoustics: *Harold Burris-Meyer*

municipal, state and federal support, they undertake to accomodate as many arts activities as they can. In a typical situation there are 26 member organizations in the civic art center. Two require no physical facilities and five will use the center only as a meeting place.

Planning such a center requires developing physical requirements and a calendar of activities for each organization. Then multi-use facilities can be planned. It is hard to plan a complex that will satisfy most of the users. Nevertheless a number of notable art center structures have been built or are a-building.

Basic requirements of most centers are: a legitimate theatre, a theatre for musicals, opera, symphony orchestra with support facilities, an art gallery, art studios, instrument and orchestra rehearsal rooms. In addition, an arena for hockey, basketball and boxing, and an open-air theatre are often included. Where one of these facilities exists, it can often be incorporated in the new plan.

The organization of a civic arts center varies with the source of support. The City Council is the responsible authority at High Point, N.C. An existing independent Civic Arts Council is the planning and operating agency in Tampa. In Alabama, the State Legislature established a public corporation, the Birmingham-Jefferson (County) Civic Center Authority, authorized to "construct, maintain, control, operate and manage a civic center." The Legislature then levied a special tax, payable to the Authority, to be used by it to finance the design and construction of the theatre.

A civic center theatre may be used by a college. Such a joint use is planned for Marshall University and the Huntington (W. Va.) Community Players. Florida International University has planned to use a theatre projected for the Interama (Inter America Center Authority) Cultural Area.

The Art Center in New Haven, Connecticut, embraces a music school, a school of visual and craft arts, a regional high school for the performing arts; these three are realized to date. A repertory theatre, an art-film theatre, rental shops, offices and apartments, and a parking garage are either under construction, projected or under consideration. The completed project will fill both sides of a short downtown street which will become a pedestrian plaza. A concert hall/opera house has been proposed for a nearby site where a superannuated arena for hockey, boxing, basketball, ice, dog, antique and boat shows will be demolished.

(to page 383)

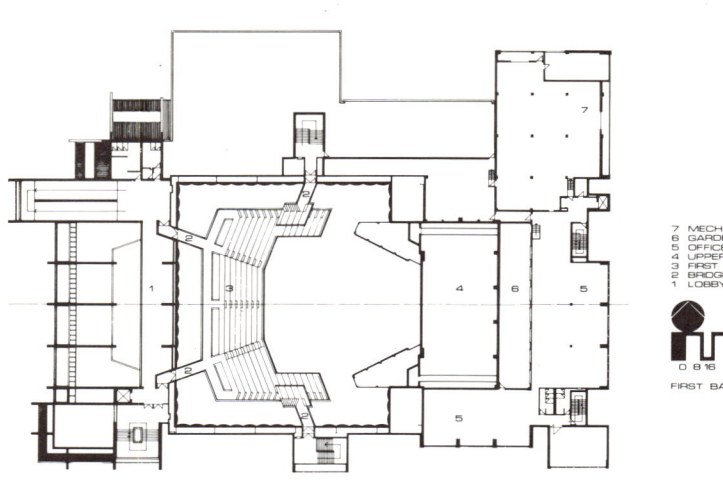

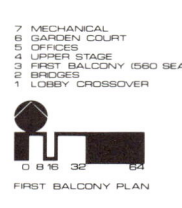

7 MECHANICAL
6 GARDEN COURT
5 OFFICES
4 UPPER STAGE
3 FIRST BALCONY (560 SEATS)
2 BRIDGES
1 LOBBY CROSSOVER

FIRST BALCONY PLAN

HAMILTON PLACE, HAMILTON, ONTARIO. *This building is perhaps the most exemplary civic performing arts center. It was financed entirely by popular subscription, not grants. It is integrated with other civic and cultural buildings in the Civic Square, at a center of public transportation, and on a pedestrian plaza. It is called affectionately "the people place."*

Functionally, acoustic characteristics are changed from concert mode to stage performance mode by five simple mechanisms: a proscenium curtain, more realistically a "flying wall," eight and a half tons, surfaced with British Columbia cedar three to four inches thick which isolates the stage from the hall acoustically and is the reflecting wall behind the musicians; two forestage lifts, which, when chairs are removed into chair storage under the hall, are brought to stage level to contain a full symphony and 100 voice chorus, the musicians in the same room with the audience; twelve bays of pivoting cedar panels in each proscenium splay which are rotatable for directed reflection, total absorption or entrances to the forestage; cedar-faced and acoustically shaped canopy, part of which can be lowered for better reflection of sounds from performers on stage; panels of absorbent fabric which hang like colored medieval banners when in the stage mode reduce reverberation time and are brailed (under computer control) to produce selectively more reverberation in the concert mode.

Architect: *Trevor P. Garwood-Jones*
Consultants:
  Theatre: *Vincent Piacentini of Bolt, Beranek and Newman*
  Acoustics: *Russell Johnson*

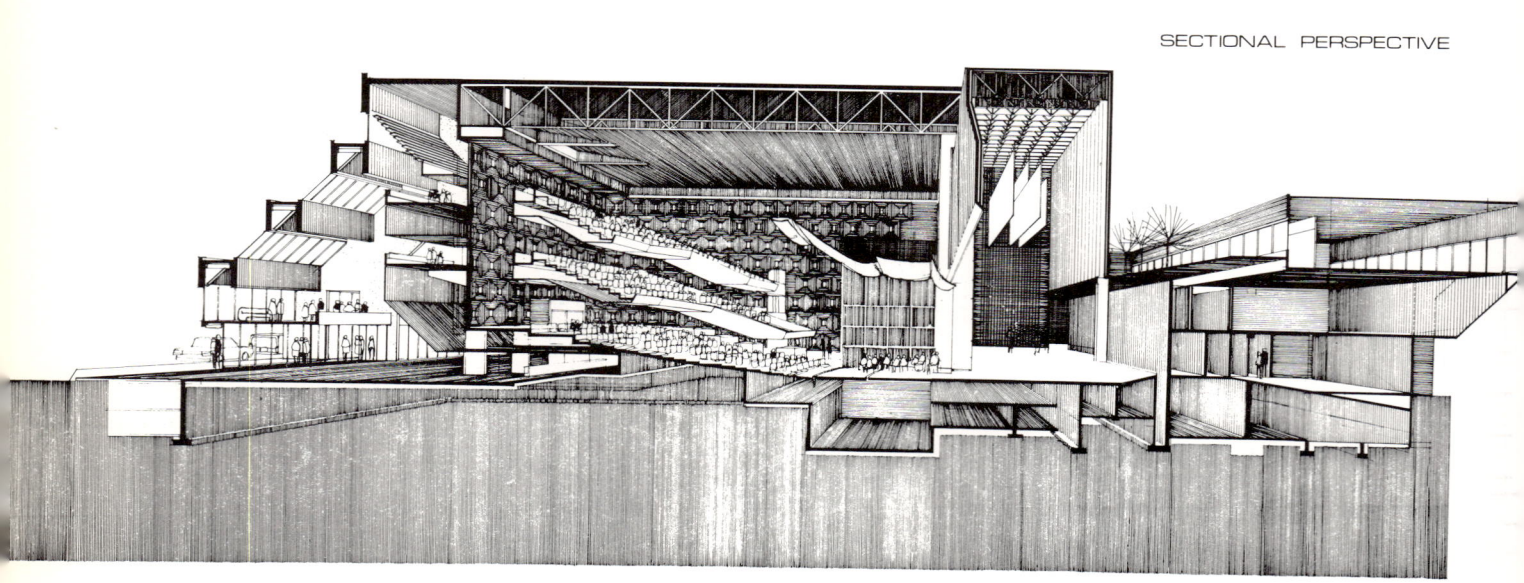

SECTIONAL PERSPECTIVE

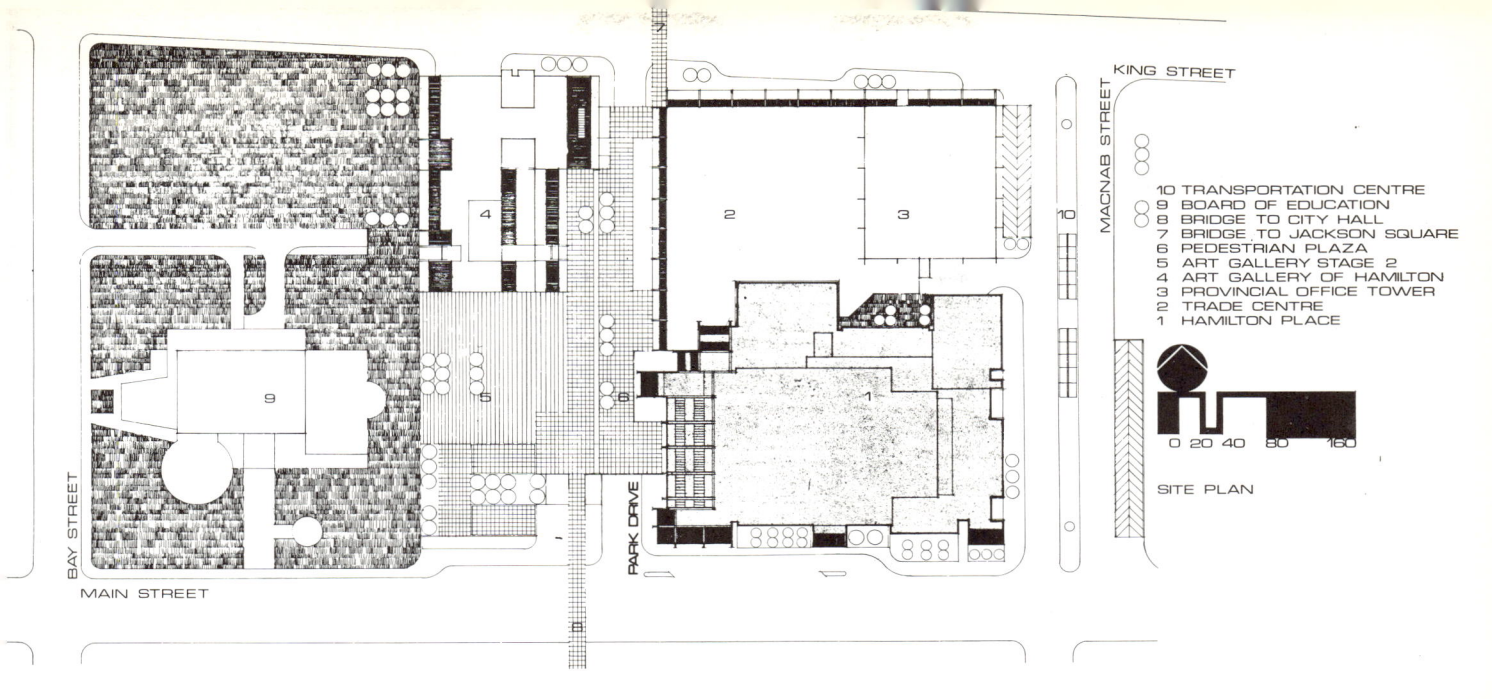

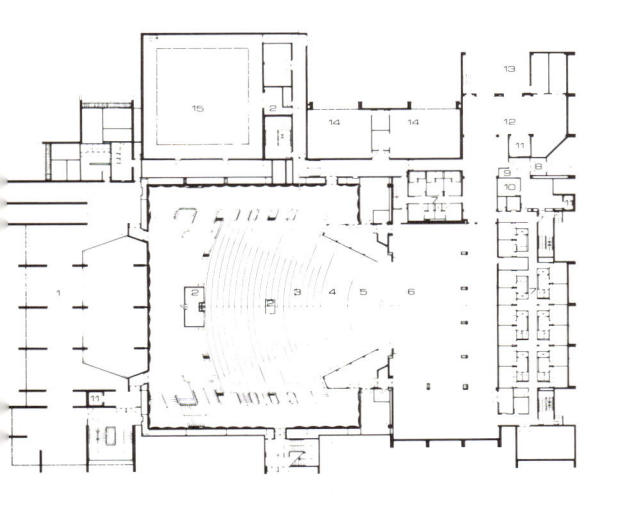

10	TRANSPORTATION CENTRE
9	BOARD OF EDUCATION
8	BRIDGE TO CITY HALL
7	BRIDGE TO JACKSON SQUARE
6	PEDESTRIAN PLAZA
5	ART GALLERY STAGE 2
4	ART GALLERY OF HAMILTON
3	PROVINCIAL OFFICE TOWER
2	TRADE CENTRE
1	HAMILTON PLACE

SITE PLAN

15	UPPER STUDIO THEATRE
14	MEETING ROOMS
13	TRUCKING
12	LOADING & UNLOADING
11	ELEVATORS
10	STAGE MANAGER
9	GUARD
8	STAGE DOOR
7	DRESSING ROOMS
6	STAGE
5	LIFT 1 (80 SEATS)
4	LIFT 2 (134 SEATS)
3	ORCHESTRA (971 SEATS)
2	CONTROLS
1	PIANO NOBILE

ORCHESTRA FLOOR PLAN

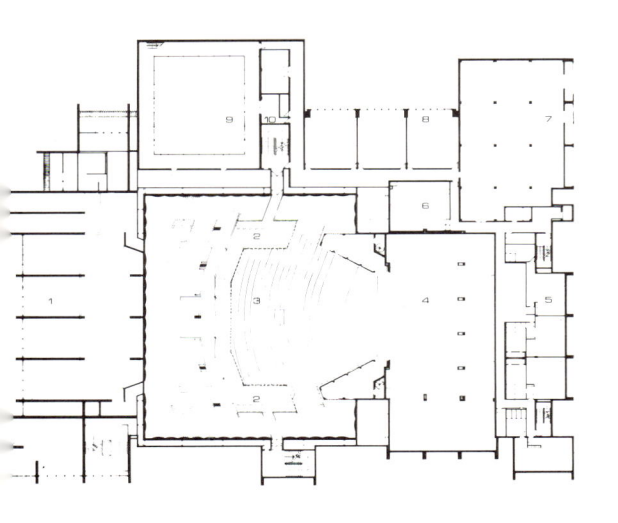

10	CONTROL
9	UPPER STUDIO THEATRE
8	MEETING ROOMS
7	MECHANICAL
6	PROPS & WORKSHOP
5	CHORUS ROOMS
4	UPPER STAGE
3	UPPER ORCHESTRA
2	FIRST BALCONY
1	UPPER PIANO NOBILE

MEZZANINE FLOOR PLAN

381

UNIVERSITY OF AKRON, EDWIN J. THOMAS PERFORMING ARTS HALL (1973). *This is an outstanding example of university-community cooperation to get a performance facility which both badly needed. Initiated by the President of the University and organized to embrace the whole city and surrounding area, a campaign raised over $7.8 million from 400 businessmen and corporations, over 4000 individuals, 100 clubs and organizations, and 43 foundations toward a total cost of $13.9 million to build an elegant multi-purpose hall. Capacity is varied from 3000 to 2400, to 900 by lowering a catenary-form ceiling and acoustics are varied to match by computer-controlled rolling absorption blankets hung behind transsondent metal-screen side walls. The hall can book any touring or local attraction with audience potential of from 800 to 3000. Its announced first season includes among others: the opera TOSCA, the EMMET KELLY JR. CIRCUS, a jazz quartet, the PDQ BACH, the National Players in three plays, and a puppet theatre. The souvenir opening program does not indicate any uses of the hall by the University, nor is the hall equipped, beyond the existence of a scene shop and a rehearsal room, for teaching or production preparation. Ada Louise Huxtable's description and enthusiastic appraisal are in the NEW YORK TIMES of Sunday, October 21, 1973.*

Architects: *Caudill, Rowlett and Scott, Houston; Dalton, van Dijk, Johnson and Partners, Cleveland*

Consultants: *Theatre: George C. Izenour   Acoustics: Vern O. Knudsen*

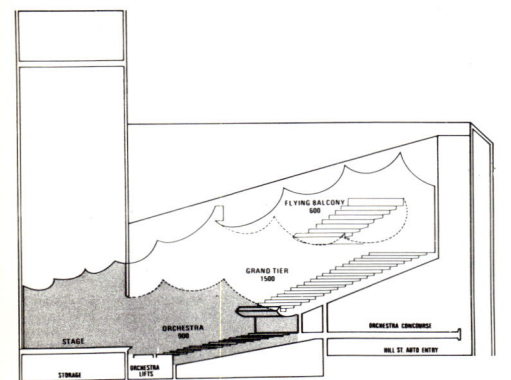

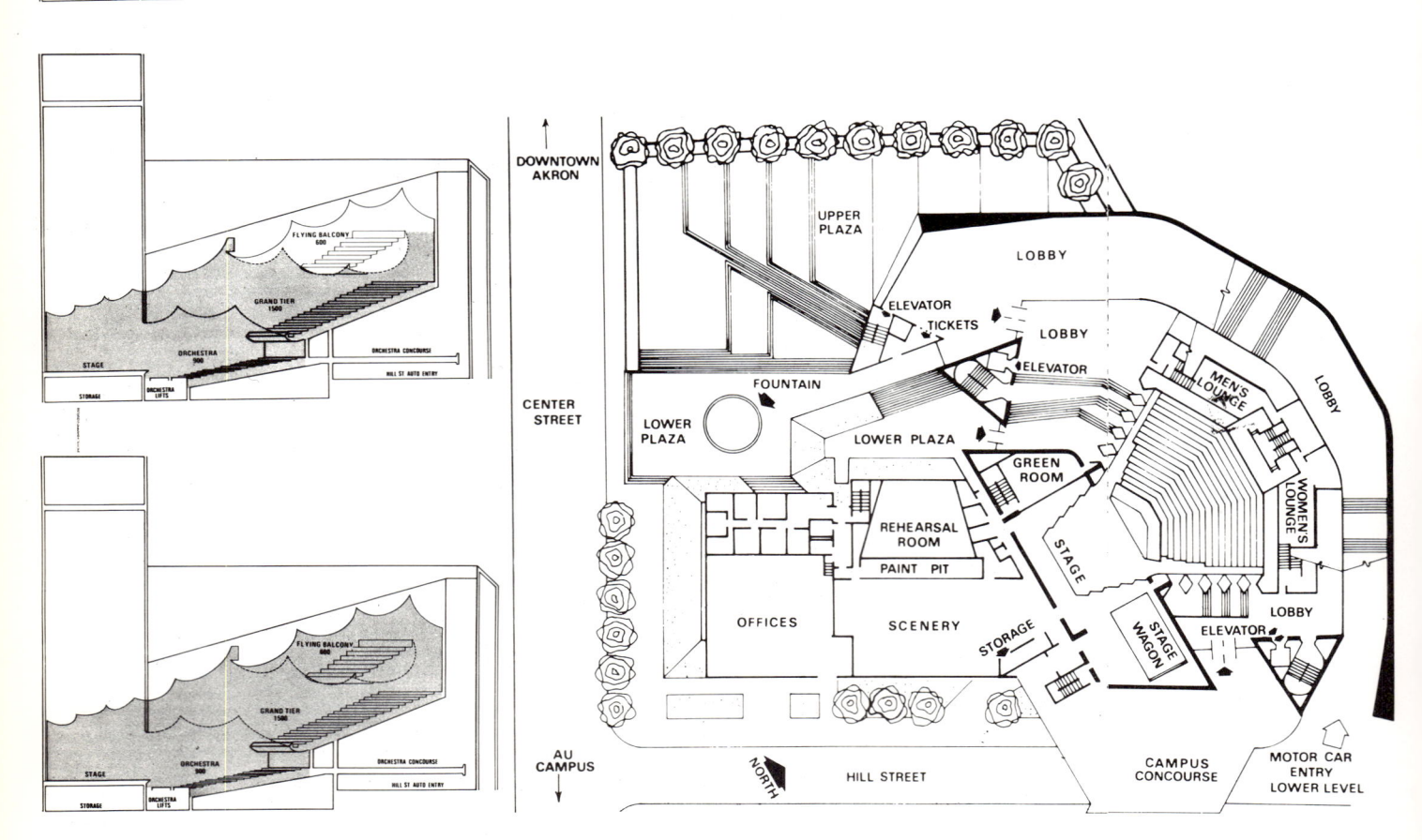

382

These have flowered in the past decade. They have been in either of two kinds: several performance facilities grouped, separated or under one roof, each designed for a specific type of performance, or a single multi-use facility, flexible as to audience size, volume, acoustic char-

Performing Arts Center

J P STEVENS TOWER

1 OFFICES
2 LOBBY
3 GRID
4 THEATRE
5 STAGE
6 REHEARSAL

46TH STREET
SECTION

Non-Profit Residential Professional Theatre

acteristics, and stage equipment, and therefore adaptable to different types of performance.

Several Facilities. The first kind has occurred in very large urban centers with nearby population numbering into several millions, and often with attractiveness for tourists and other sound reasons for assembling great numbers of people from distant parts of the country and even from distant lands: New York City, Washington, D.C., and Los Angeles.

The valid reason for performing arts centers of this category is the presence of sufficient potential audience to warrant simultaneous performances in various arts on a continuous schedule.

A sub-set of this kind is the large university campus and community where performing arts departments use the performance spaces as laboratories at times when they are not used for performances, where locally prepared performances are likely to be grouped in time to accord with the academic (and athletic) calendar, and where touring performances of all kinds may be booked for the cultural enrichment of the community in the open dates: the Krannert Center, University of Illinois.

Variable Single Facility. The second category is found in smaller communities and campuses where, for reasons both demographic and economic, only one building is warranted. George Izenour has achieved a design which provides excellent accomodations for four types of performance—symphony, opera, musical show and drama—and is capable of housing satisfactorily many other events which involve the assembly of 800 or more persons. His works are numerous and have been treated in several architectural and theatrical journals.

Resident professional theatres have proliferated in communities and in universities that have community orientation and commitment. This is a salubrious expansion of professional theatre when the traditional professional theatre, Broadway and the road, has contracted alarmingly.

Too frequently these organizations have been forced by lack of capital to settle for theatres with limited facilities, both backstage and out-front, much below standards either for effective play production or adequate hospitality toward audiences. Most, if not all, of these theatres depend upon financial support beyond receipts from ticket sales. Frequently there are too few seats so that when success has led to subscription of the entire house there are no seats left to sell to the great transient audience which may be attracted by favorable reviews. The equivalent of continuing subsidy to meet running costs might well be spent as interest on sufficient borrowed capital to build a theatre with capacity to bring in at the box office the operating costs and money to retire the loan. Certain non-profit professional theatres have been so artistically successful that they have become accepted com-

(to page 386)

THE AMERICAN PLACE THEATRE, NEW YORK. This theatre was built under the special zoning regulation and the updated Building Code of the City of New York (see page 373). Housing, on a thirty-year lease, the highly experimental company, which has gained fame for its work in a church in the New York theatre district and is dedicated to the search for new authors and to producing in many styles, this theatre satisfies, except for some cutbacks during the later planning stages, all the carefully developed requirements of the company. It has a thrust stage which can be divided into modular, interlocking sections, ample conventional stage space, terraced seating areas which can be converted into acting areas, seats which fold down to permit platforms over them, galleries on both sidewalls of the house which can be used by actors, numerous entrances for performers, permitting them to mingle with the audience, and flying rigging and light-mounting positions easily accessible for operators over the entire space.

Unlike most New York theatres, American Place contains shops for the preparation of scenery, properties and costumes, and rehearsal rooms which make the company self-sufficient in the one building, though the shops were reduced in size and convenience from those which were originally planned.

Theatre Architect: Richard H. Kaplan
Consultants:
  Technical: Kert Lundell
  Lighting, Sound Communications: Roger Morgan
  Acoustics: Goodfriend and Ostergaard

ponents of their communities' culture, yet cannot possibly seat the eager citizens who want to see their shows, and are consequently in the situation of acquiring, or planning, theatres better suited to their popularity. Others appear to have opted for "intimate" theatres, meaning theatres seating audiences of 400 or less, and the attendant posture of perpetual paupership, preferring to risk all on the generosity of individuals, governments, foundations and the prevailing vagaries of financial markets.

Regulations within show business which punish resident professional theatres for having seating capacities above the poverty level and inhibit managements that abhor this paupership, must be corrected if benefits of increased popularity (i.e. appreciation and support by the populace expressed in paid attendance) are to be equitably shared. Paradoxically, sadness attaches to the SRO sign for two reasons: irretrievable loss of potential income, and inability of eager people to see a good show. This dolor has no relief when a tight season's schedule, sold out to subscribers, precludes additional performances.

Education Theatre

In terms of number of theatres built, the educational community is where the greatest action has been in the past decade. The distribution maps and lists published in THEATRE DESIGN AND TECHNOLOGY are evidence of this fact. The authors have attempted to gather significant examples from a variety of situations and theatre forms, and have, of course, been limited to the courteous responses to their invitations for their opportunities to select. It is significant that the examples contain fewer single theatres than multiple theatres and theatres in combination with other arts under one roof or in a complex of buildings. There is one complete college, on a newly planned campus, where the buildings for the performing and visual arts predominate, with, almost incidentally, buildings for the natural sciences, social sciences, humanities and a library.

EXAMPLES OF EDUCATIONAL THEATRES

SAN DIEGO STATE UNIVERSITY THEATRE. California contains many good theatres in colleges and universities. To select one is not to downgrade the others but to let the one illustrate the general situation.

Not shown, for lack of space, are many details that prove the thorough thinking that preceded design and construction. A list may be helpful to other planners: compressed air system for pneumatic tools with air cables reeled at the shop ceiling; a castered platform below stage for entrances and exits through traps; a floated shop floor for sound absorption; a digital read-out cueing system; a panel-board saw; laundromat equipment in the dye shop; industrial adjustable steel shelving in prop storerooms; a self-charging battery-powered extension platform for working at heights up to 25 feet; rolling rack with removable trays for nails and screws; steel drawer racks for small hardware; rust-proof, acid-proof paint storage bins; three-color strip lights at the paint frame; framed canvas laundry carts, castered, for handling and storing curtains; an explosive-proof and toxic-proof spray room for work with flammables and plastics; a drafting room for design and technical students, with blueprint machine; a time clock system; a sound system with two tape transports, two studio turntables, four precue cartridge units, and a 15 channel patch; a scissors-type lift for the orchestra pit which cost $5,000 installed versus an estimated $50,000 for a hydraulic system; and all steel supporting the stage traps removable to create any opening up to 32 feet by 16 feet.

SDSU would do theatre planners a service by publishing a booklet of the superb photographs of the theatre and its equipment.

Architects:
   Design: Al Dennis, Office of Architects and Construction, State of California
   State Supervising: Carl C. McElvey
Consultants: Theatre: Hunton D. Sellman, Don W. Powell
               Acoustics: Donald T. Loye

View of theatre complex taken from University's outdoor bowl. The 63,000 square foot building includes a 500 seat adaptable theatre and a 190 seat rearrangement experimental theatre.

387

the 1st floor

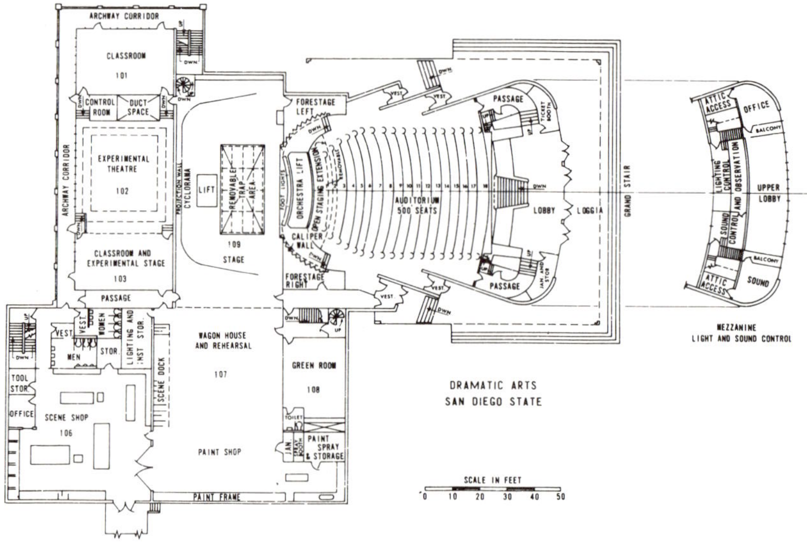

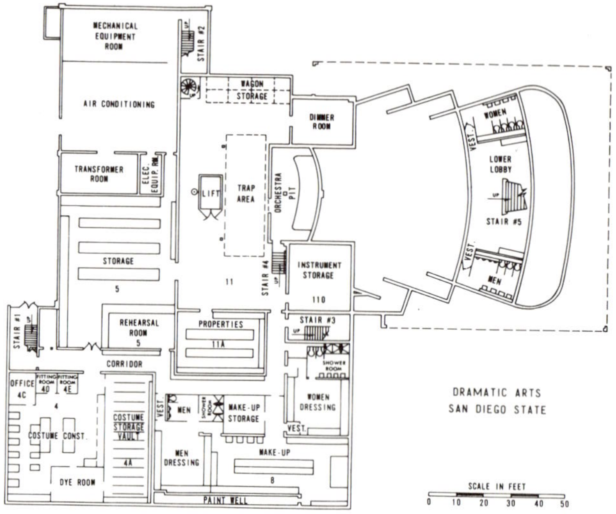

the 2nd floor

the basement

DRAMATIC ARTS
SAN DIEGO STATE

388

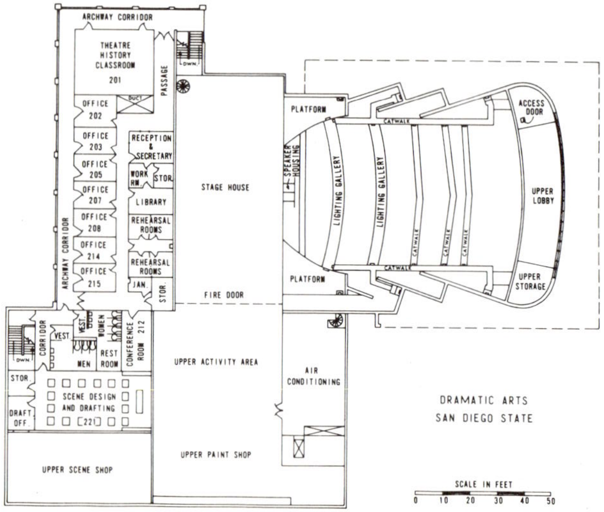

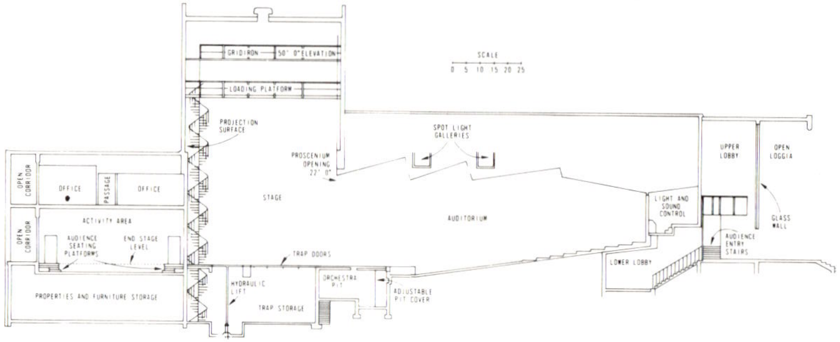

UNIVERSITY OF MICHIGAN, POWER CENTER FOR THE PERFORMING ARTS. As the drawings show, this building is purely a theatre. There are no teaching spaces. Its function is, simply, to receive and present productions which have been prepared elsewhere. It has a mixture of good and bad features: excellent vertical sightlines and very bad horizontal sightlines from side seats. There is good but circuitous access to the ceiling lighting slots from backstage, but no access to the lighting ladders except through the balcony, but no indoor passages for workers or others from the lobbies to backstage at ground level, though there is a tunnel which comes up into the control room at the back of the main floor. The capacity, maximum 1412, minimum 1295, is adequate to support elaborate productions. Balcony capacity is 455. No seat is more than 75 feet from the stage. The stage can accommodate large and elaborate production in both depth and height. Frontal entrances onto the thrust are through tunnels which can be seated-over when not in use.

The appearance of the building is a delight.
Architects: Kevin Roche, John Dinkeloo Associates
Lighting and Stage Co-designer: Jo Mielziner
Acoustical Consultants: Bolt, Beranek and Newman

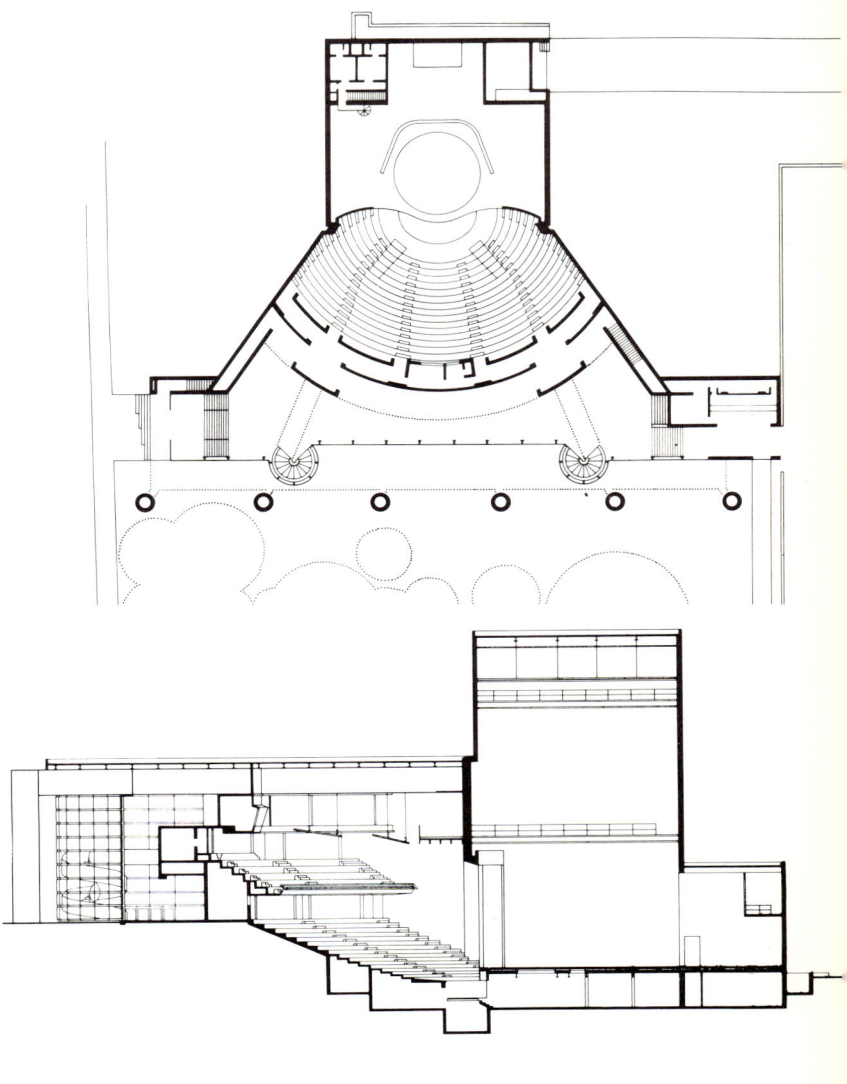

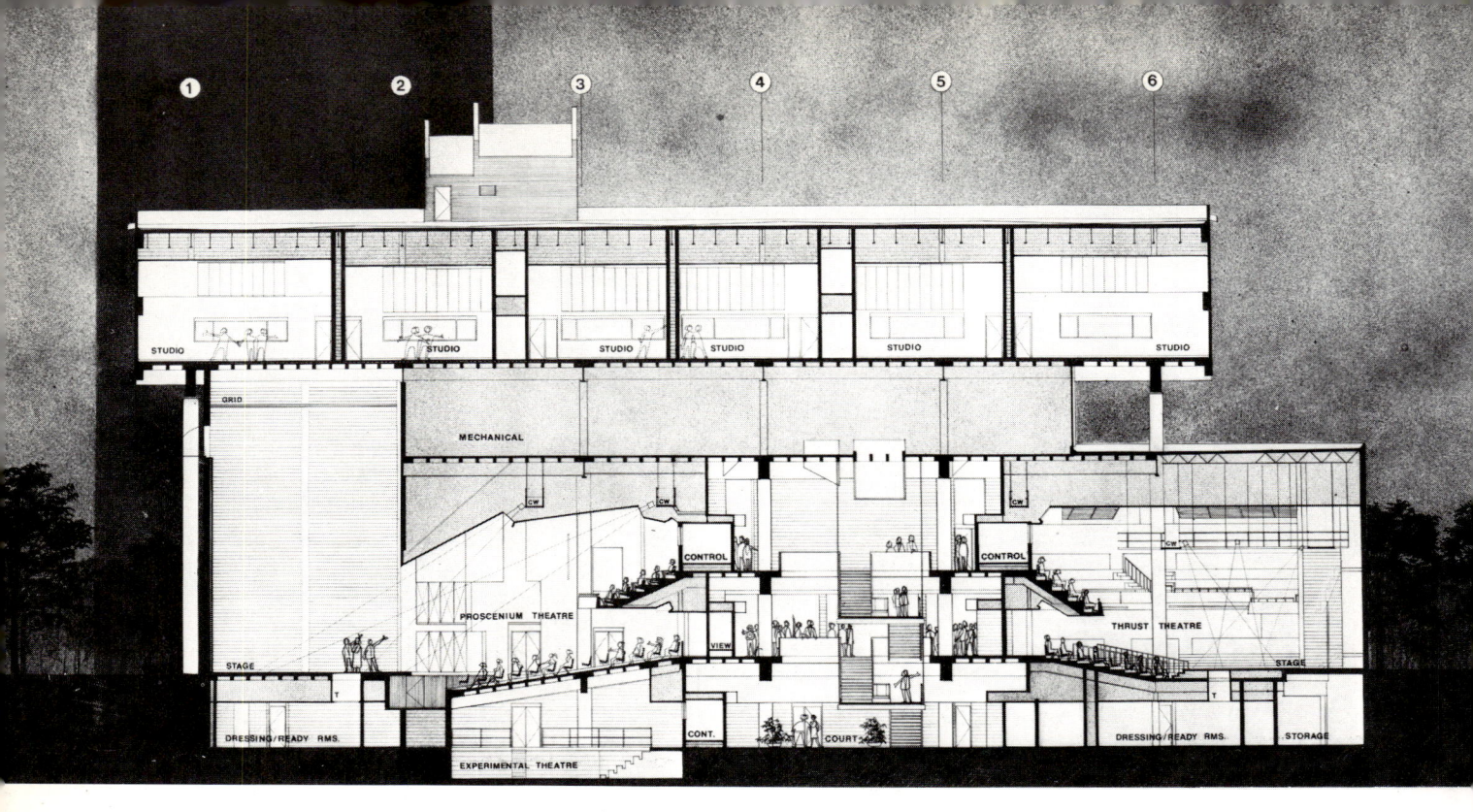

RARIG CENTER. UNIVERSITY OF MINNESOTA, MINNE-APOLIS. Assuming that faculty offices, classrooms, design and technical drafting rooms, light and sound laboratories and scenery, properties and costume storage are in another building, this is a noteworthy complex of theatres for performances and experimentation. The building itself must be regarded as an experiment; it has novel features which must be tested and evaluated by use.

Many of the recommended features of good theatres are present: all seats in all theatres within the limits of stereoscopic vision to the stages; good floor slopes, comfortable seats well spaced; ample and impressive public spaces; elevating orchestra pit; spacious, well located control rooms; separation of sound-sensitive areas; and adequate working circulation.

One wonders, however, what the rationale is regarding the break-up of the sidewalls of the proscenium theatre and if these sidewalls might have better light-mounting slots than the break-up provides; if a single under-audience entrance with no entrances at all from the house at audience-left is adequate for actors' entrances to the thrust stage; why there are no flying facilities over thrust and inner stages; why the inner stage is so shallow; if the single shop is adequate to produce scenery and props for four theatres; why there are so few traps in the thrust and proscenium stages; and if there are enough restroom facilities on the second floor for the balcony audiences of two theatres and the entire audience of a third.

Architect: Ralph Rapson and Associates, Inc.
Theatre Consultant: Theodore Fuchs

391

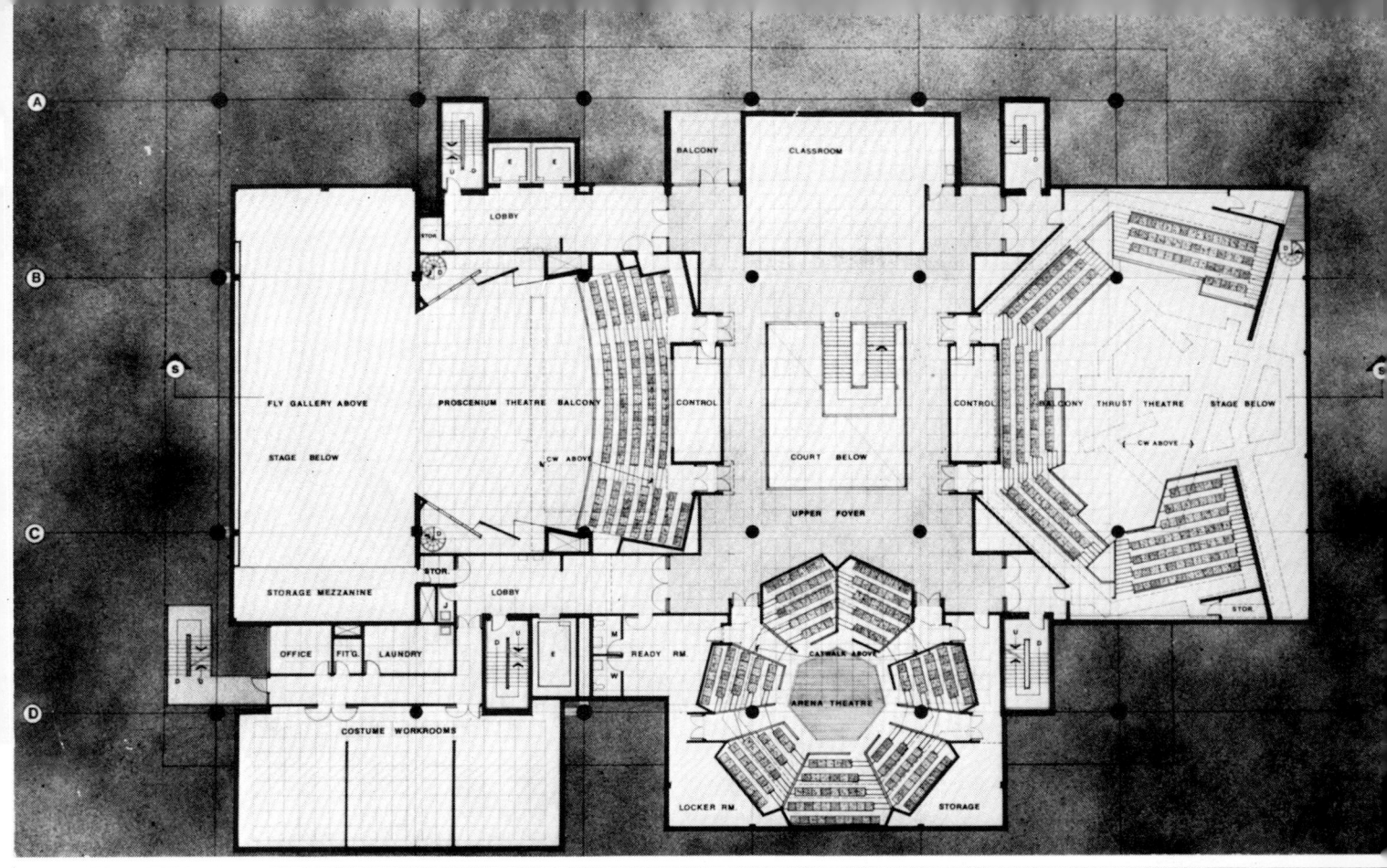

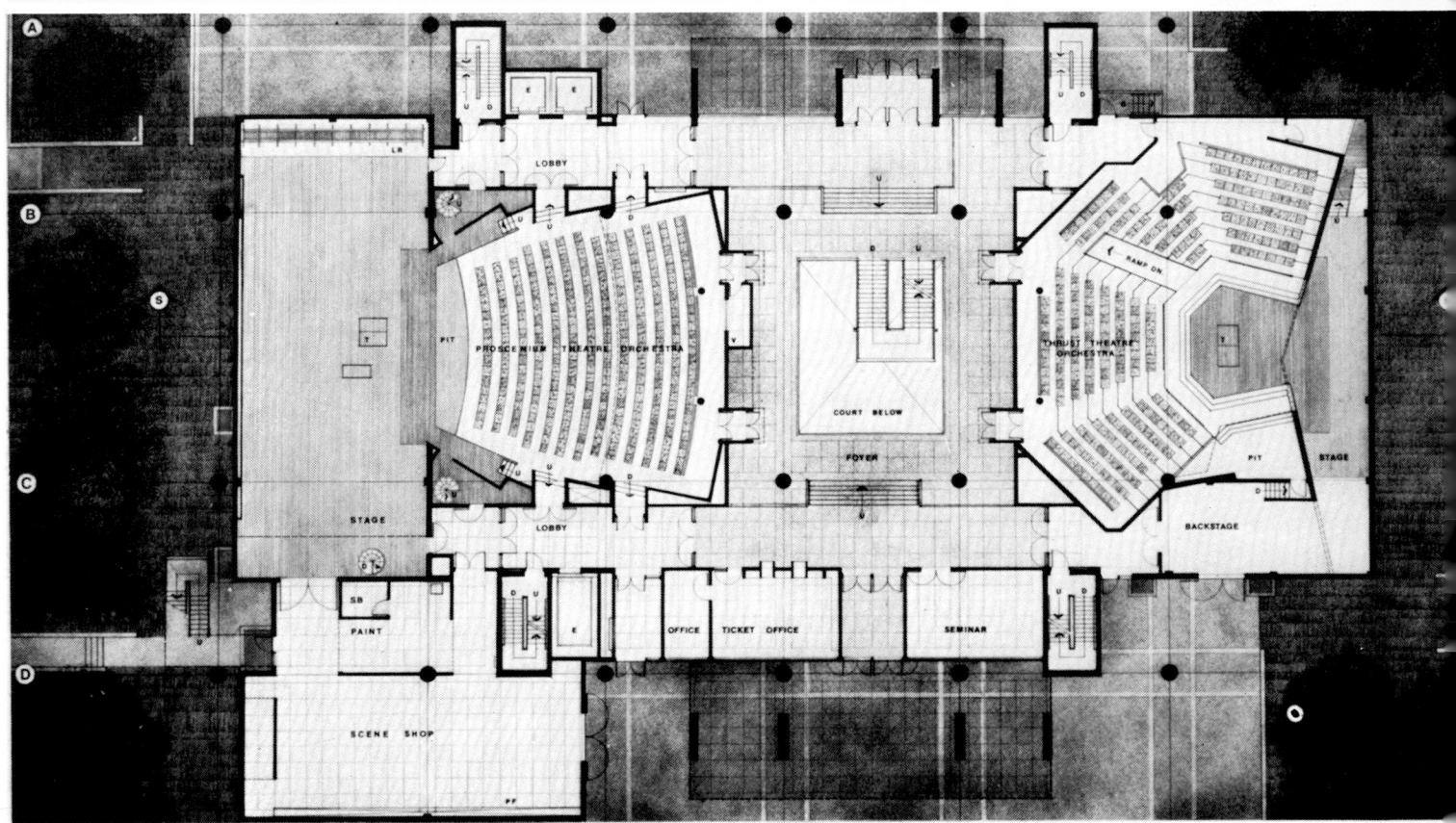

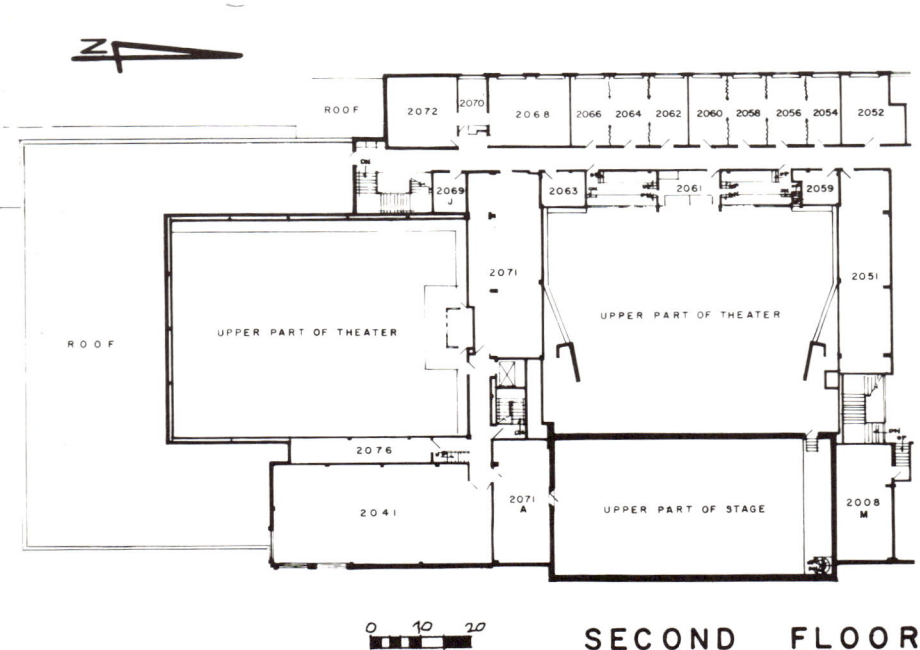

OHIO STATE UNIVERSITY, DRAKE UNION THEATRES (1972). The James Thurber theatre seats 622, is sound isolated by a separate foundation and double walls filled with rigid foam. It is proscenium form with ample sidestages with movable panels, wagon storage offstage both sides, forestage-orchestra lift, cubicles for outer garments on the sidewalls of the house, but limited trapping capability onstage. The Stadium II Theatre is free-form with plywood panels hung on some walls to put back reverberation taken out by sound-absorbent concrete blocks, pierced and filled with fiberglass. The careful programming that went into this plant failed in a few instances: a large inventory of costumes has usurped a planned drafting room, and the paint frame is on the wrong side of the shop; drops and other large painted pieces must be turned through 180 degrees to show their proper sides to the audience. Loading into the lower workshop requires a 90 degree change of direction onto the elevator. An unique arrangement is the makeup tables in a long corridor outside the dressing rooms. The audience is well served as to traffic, comforts and conveniences and the production services are well arranged and spacious.

Architects: Tibbles, Crumbly and Musson
Consultants:
   Theatre: Russell Hastings
   Sound: Erwin Steward
   Lighting: David Locklin

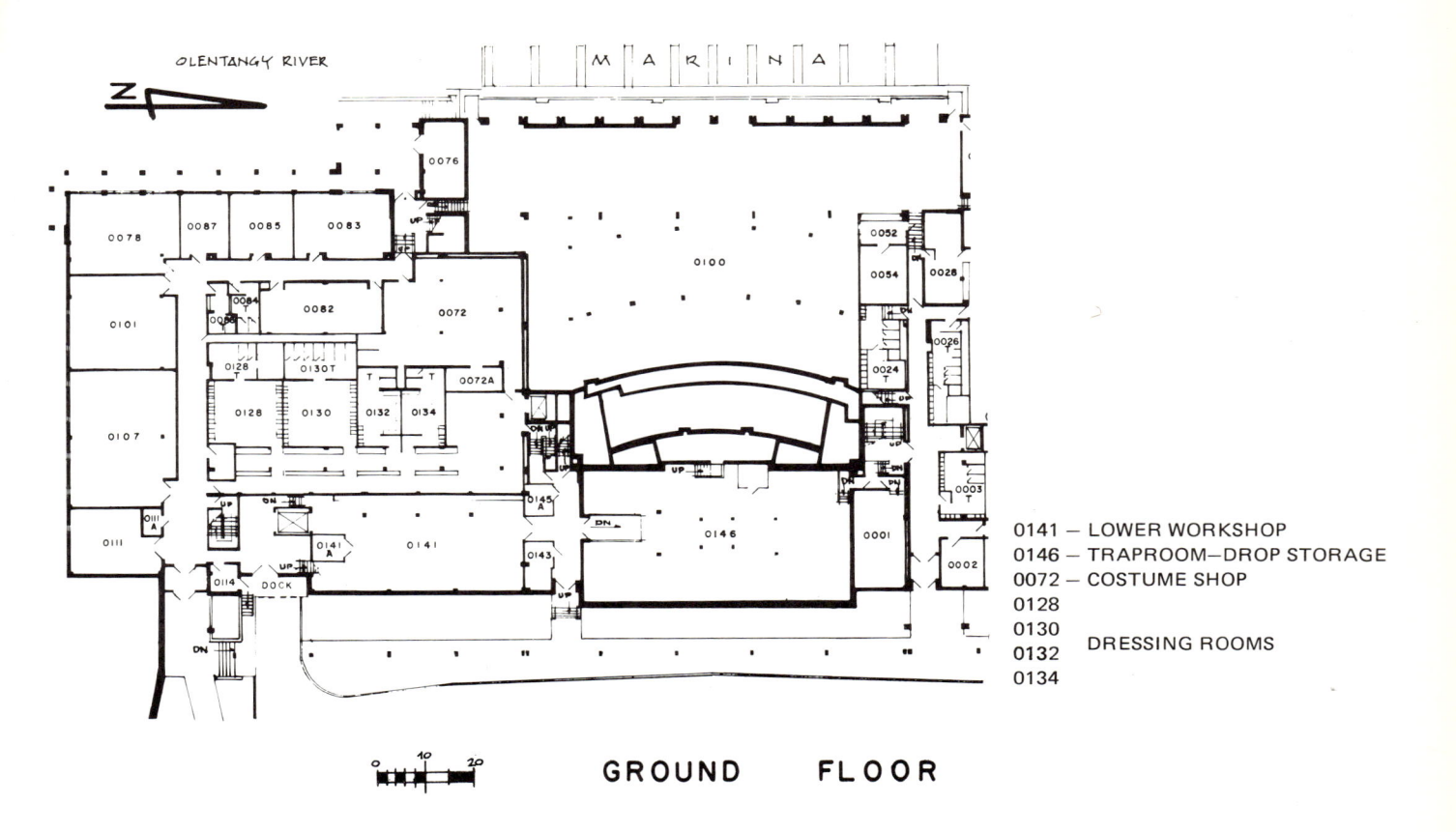

OLENTANGY RIVER
MARINA

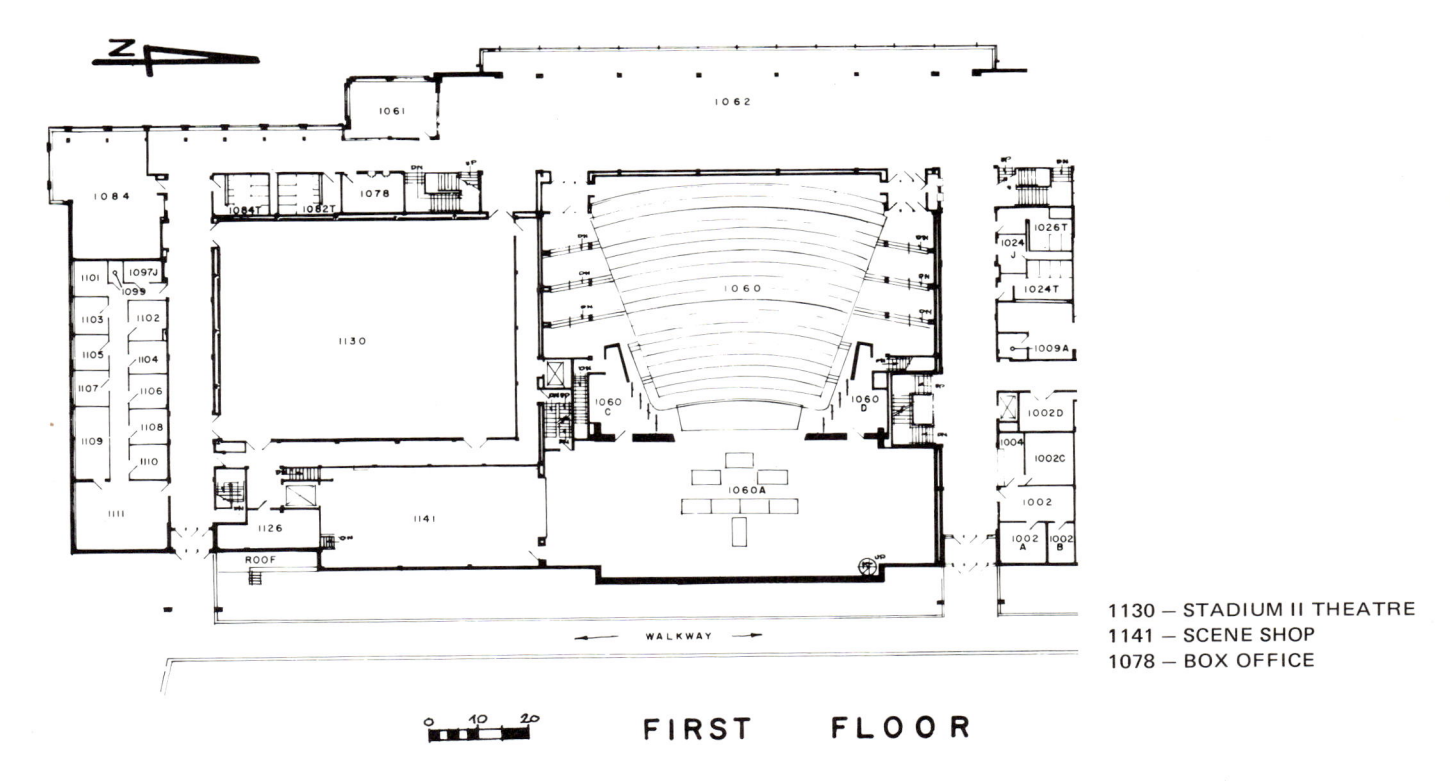

0141 — LOWER WORKSHOP
0146 — TRAPROOM—DROP STORAGE
0072 — COSTUME SHOP
0128
0130   DRESSING ROOMS
0132
0134

GROUND FLOOR

1130 — STADIUM II THEATRE
1141 — SCENE SHOP
1078 — BOX OFFICE

FIRST FLOOR

393

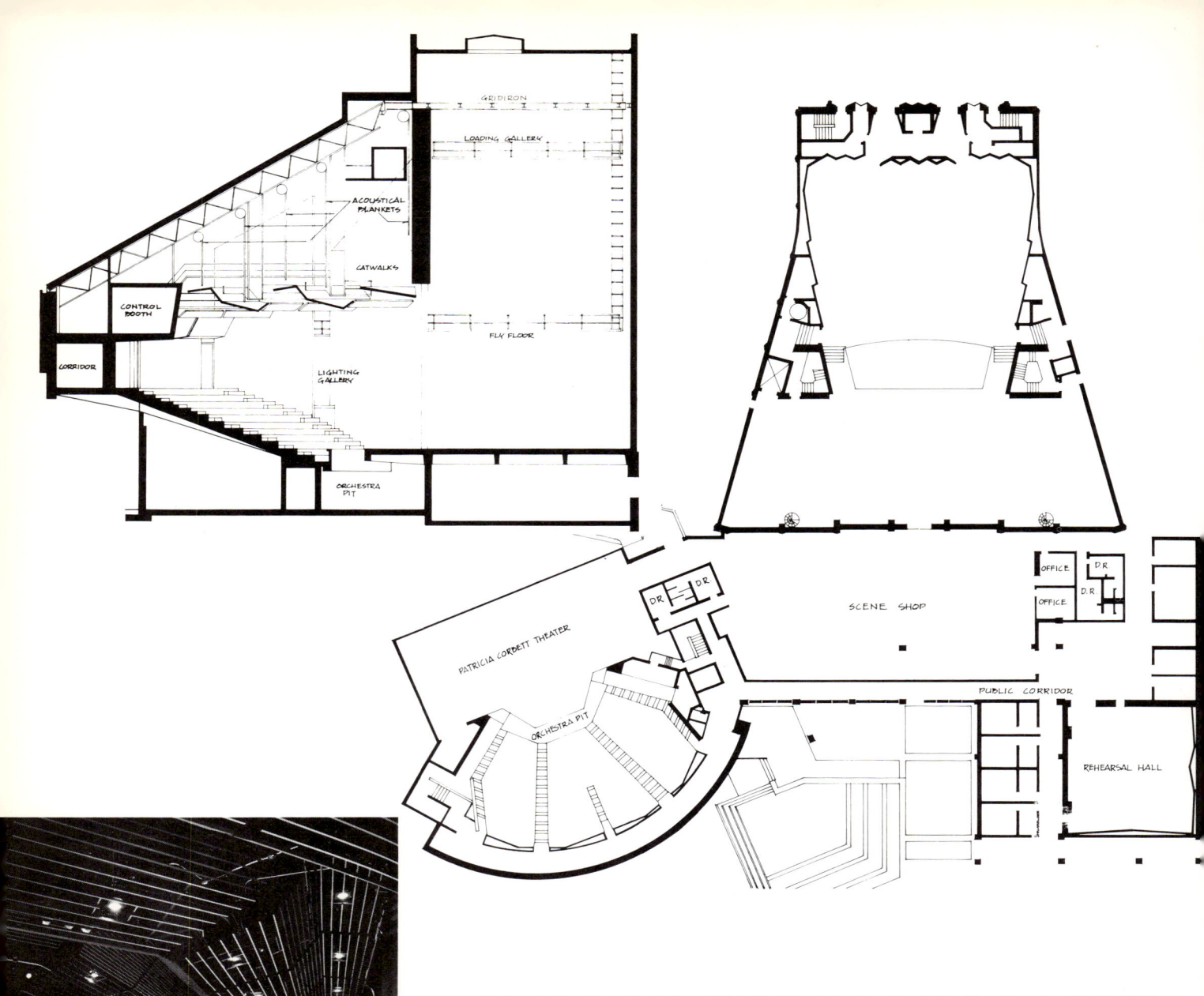

UNIVERSITY OF CINCINNATI COLLEGE–CONSERVATORY OF MUSIC, PATRICIA CORBETT THEATRE (1971). The highly ornamental side walls and the bright metal organ pipes can distract audience attention from the performance on stage. The ceiling tube panels do not conceal operators on the overhead catwalks. The stage has no traps. There is inadequate storage space and too few dressing rooms for an active musical theatre.

However, the theatre has a good form and sightlines; the modified thrust stage lends itself to musical presentation. An orchestra lift would permit a variety of configurations. The stage is of good size and proportion and there is a scene shop large enough to accomodate scene building and painting, not only for this theatre but for the adjoining Corbett Auditorium which is used for larger productions.

Architects: Architekton, Inc., Cincinnati
    William J. Brown, Project Director
    Gordon Simmons, Project Architect

Consultants:
    Theatre: Ming Cho Lee
    Lighting: Hans Sondheimer
    Acoustics: Daniel Martin

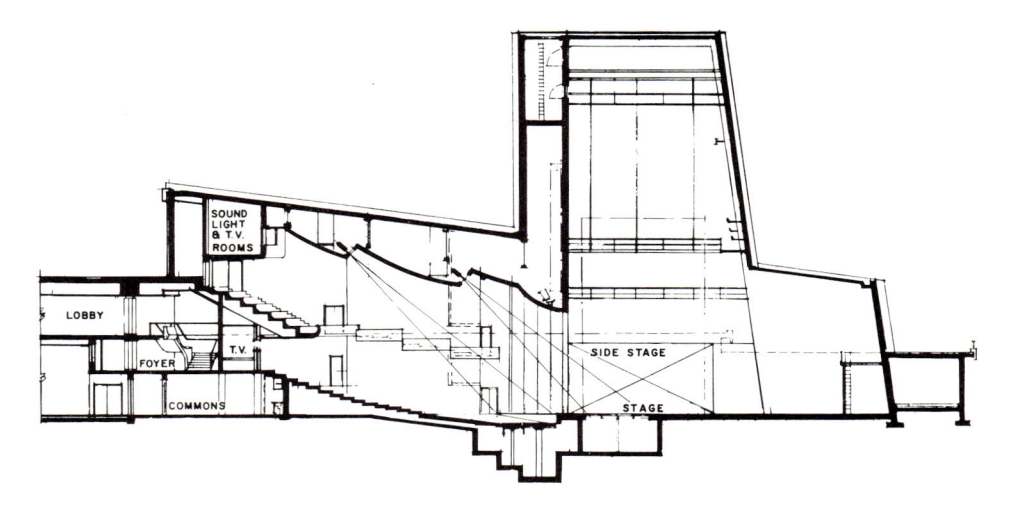

SECTION THROUGH THE FESTIVAL THEATRE

UNIVERSITY OF ILLINOIS AT URBANA–CHAMPAIGN, THE KRANNERT CENTER FOR THE PERFORMING ARTS. *This is one of the best facilities for teaching, practice and presentation of the performing arts to be found anywhere. Built on two city blocks with two levels of underground parking and with spacious lobby common to five theatres, it also has offices, classrooms, studios, rehearsal rooms and shops on three floors around and between the theatres and, with one exception, the performance support facilities adjacent to the appropriate theatres.*

Praise and admiration outweigh adverse criticism, offered in full recognition of the difficulties of correcting what are seen as faults, and engendered only by the awareness of practical operational values: it is regrettable that the routes for transporting scenery and properties from the shop to all but one of the stages are long, circuitous and restrictive as to dimensions. The choice between a central common lobby with its strong communal values and a central production service facility with its practical values in time–and labor–saving, is a basic, and difficult, design decision, with ongoing consequences.

Architect: Max Abramovitz, of Harrison and Abramovitz, Architects
Consultants:
  Theatre Design: Jo Mielziner
  Theatre Equipment: George C. Izenour
  Acoustics: Cyril M. Harris

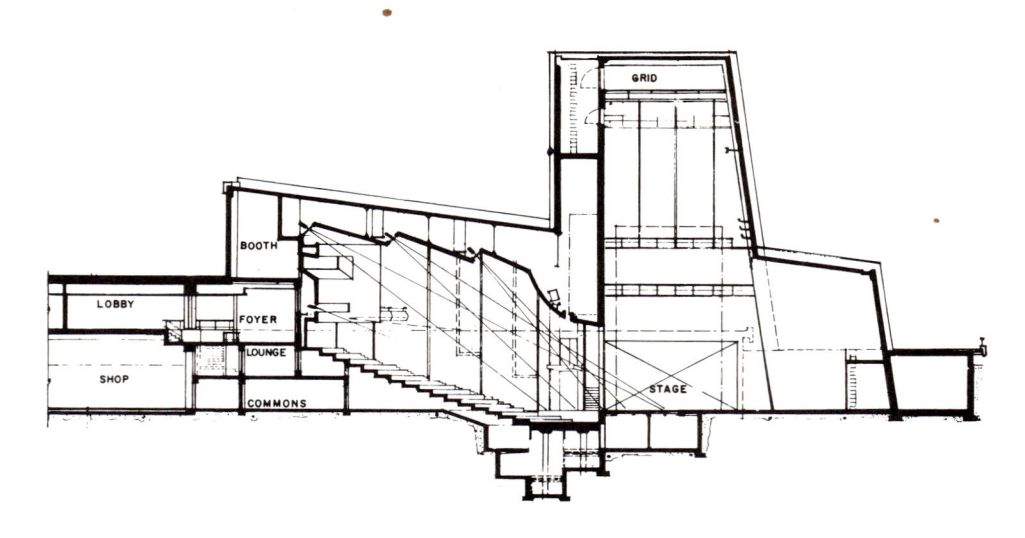

SECTION THROUGH THE PLAYHOUSE

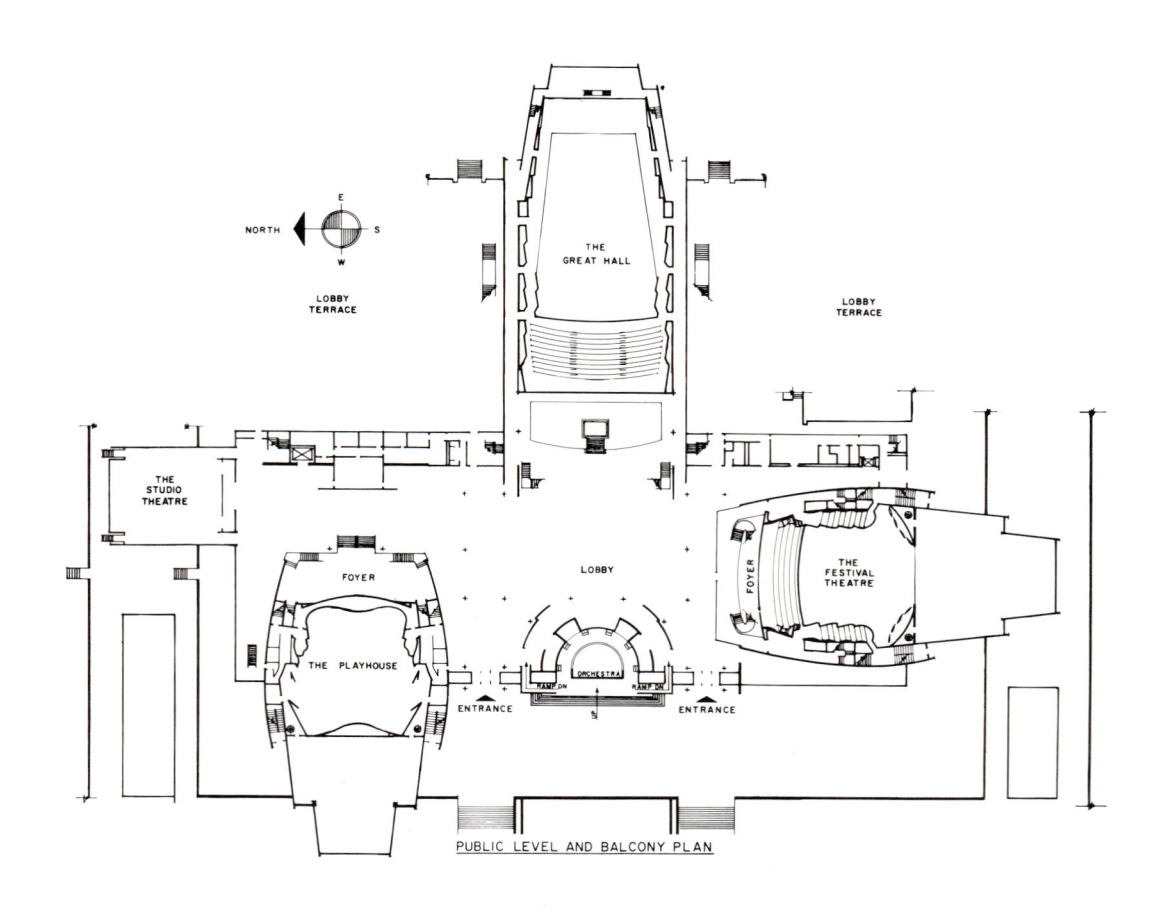

PUBLIC LEVEL AND BALCONY PLAN

STAGE LEVEL PLAN

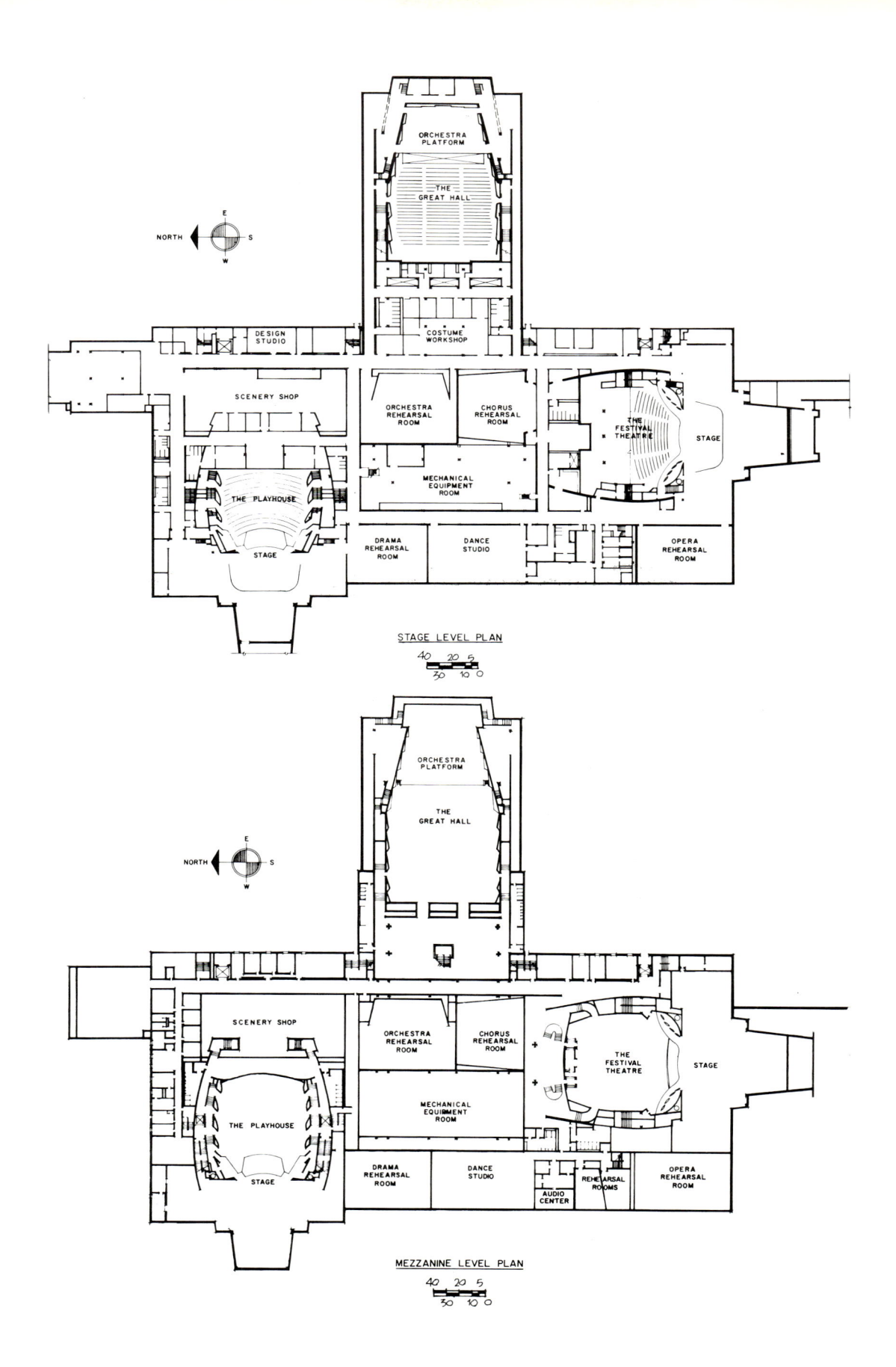

MEZZANINE LEVEL PLAN

TRINITY UNIVERSITY, THE RUTH TAYLOR THEATRE. Paul Baker, Chairman of the Department of Drama at Trinity, and also Director of the Dallas Theatre Center, has been a pioneer in the design and use of multi-form theatres. This theatre is his latest achievement, a versatile theatre capable of several conformations with little mechanical assistance and moderate human effort.

The principal theatre, Theatre One, is supplemented by two smaller theatres: Cafe Theatre under the foyer for cabaret and other after-theatre entertainments, and Attic Two Theatre for small productions and student work. Productions can be prepared simultaneously in all three theatres, though it is doubtful if sound isolation is adequate for simultaneous performances. The variations in form of Theatre One are obvious in the plans. The acting gallery is unique and offers the director opportunities for startling performance effects. The spread of the side-stage permits a cinerama effect: the audience's lateral vision entirely filled by the performance.

Two weaknesses are apparent: the dimensions of scenery which may be moved from shop to stage are permanently established by the right angle turn which must be made and the width and height of the passageway, and the lighting control operator has a poor view of effects created on scenery set or hung upstage.

Architects: O'Neil Ford and Associates and Bartlett Cocke and Associates
Project Architect: Arthur J. Rogers

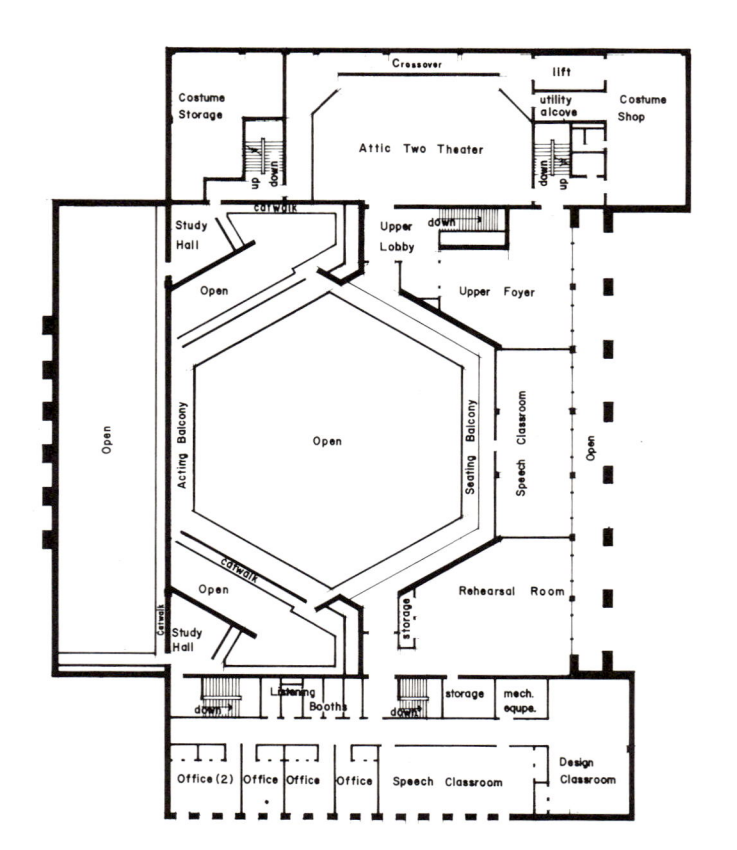

LEVEL FOUR

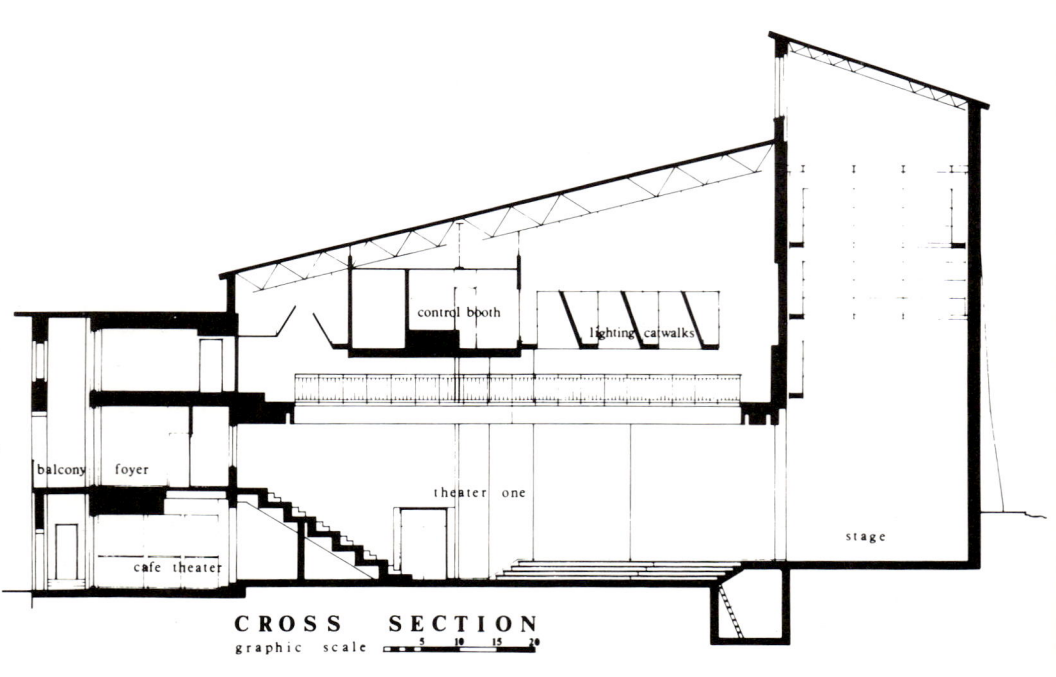

CROSS SECTION

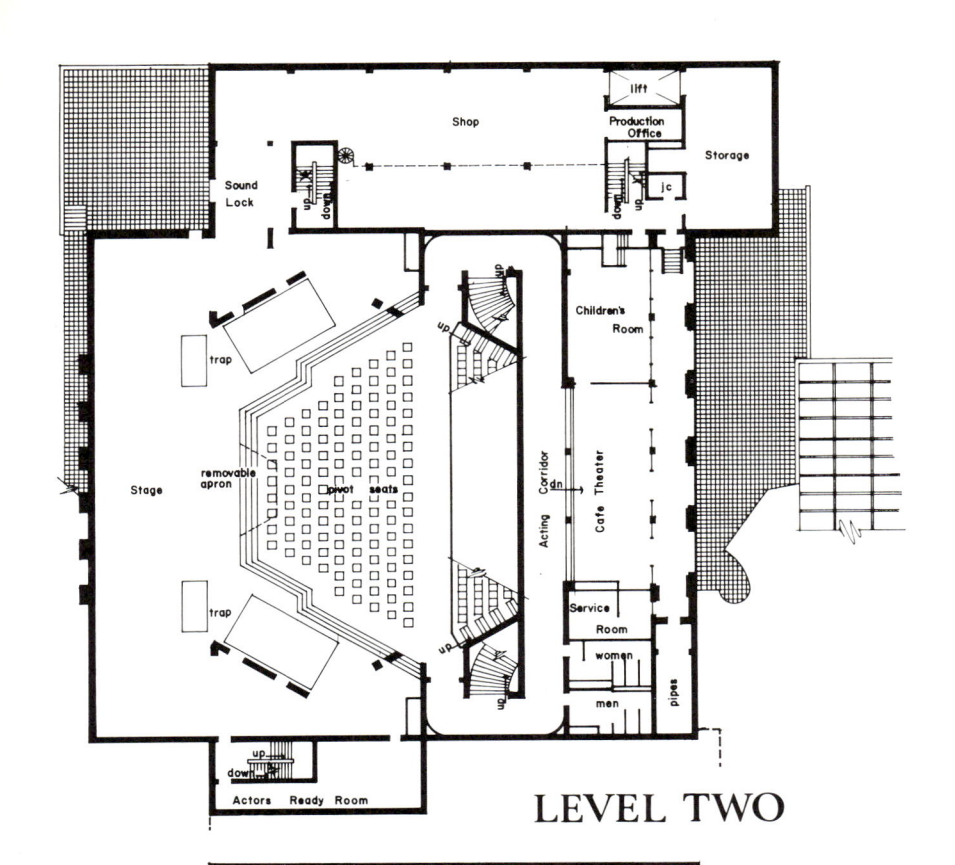

Trinity University, The Ruth Taylor Theatre

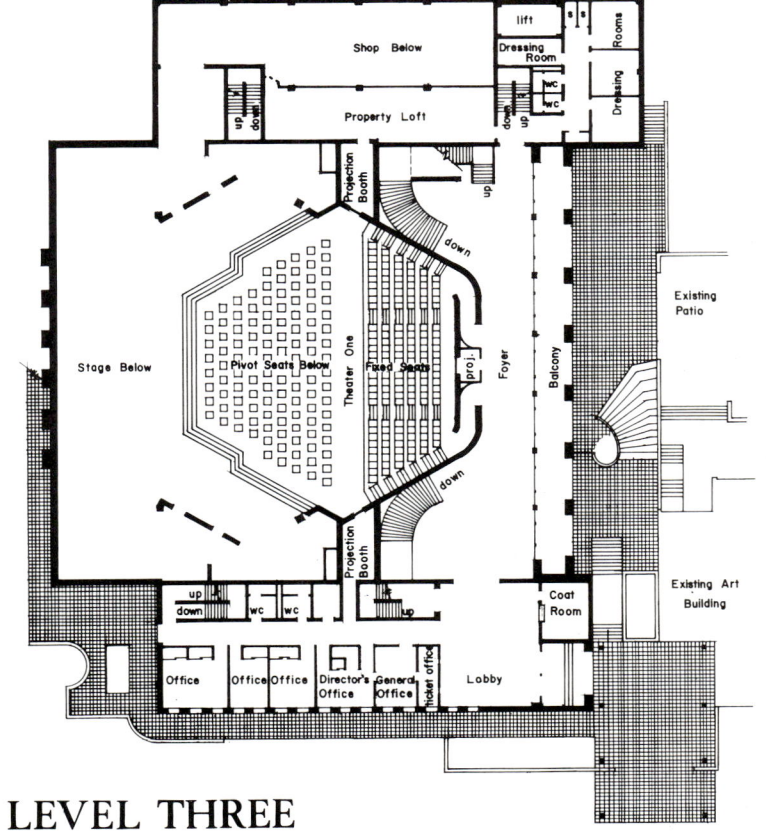

LEVEL TWO

LEVEL THREE

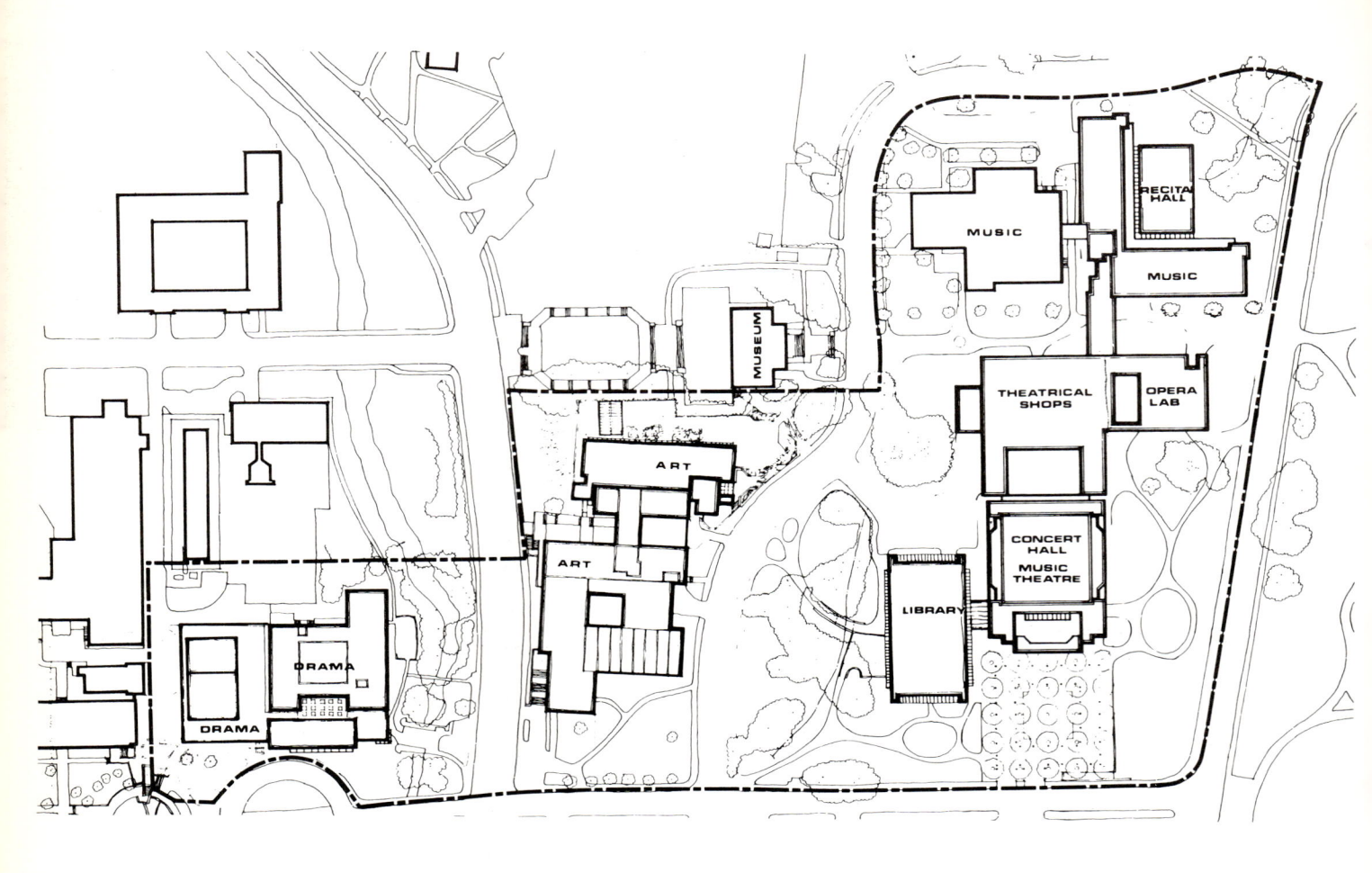

UNIVERSITY OF TEXAS AT AUSTIN: COLLEGE OF FINE ARTS AND PERFORMING ARTS CENTER. Meeting in September and December 1973, the Board of Regents of the University of Texas System approved preliminary plans for five new buildings, alterations and additions to two existing buildings and site development plans for the College of Fine Arts and Performing Arts Center, to include:

* Music, which will have a 3000 seat concert hall, a 700 seat recital hall, a 400 seat opera-laboratory theatre, classrooms, studios, and offices;
* Drama, which will have added to its present Drama Building, with its free-form Theatre Room, workshops and classrooms, a new 500 seat proscenium theatre, enlarged production services, class and rehearsal rooms, offices and spaces for the new Department of Dance;
* Arts, which will have a three-story addition and alterations to its present building to accomodate the multiplying sub-disiplines in the arts, and an enlarged museum;
* Fine Arts library/administration building.

The new facilities are planned to meet increasing demands in all the arts and accomodate developing new programs at graduate and undergraduate levels as well as to serve the cultural needs of the University and its surrounding community. Obviously the object of much careful thought and thorough programming, this complex can be among the best in the country.

Architects: Fisher and Spillman, Incorporated.
Consultants:
 Theatre: Jean Rosenthal Associates
 Acoustics: C. P. Boner and Associates

ADDITION TO DRAMA BUILDING SECTION

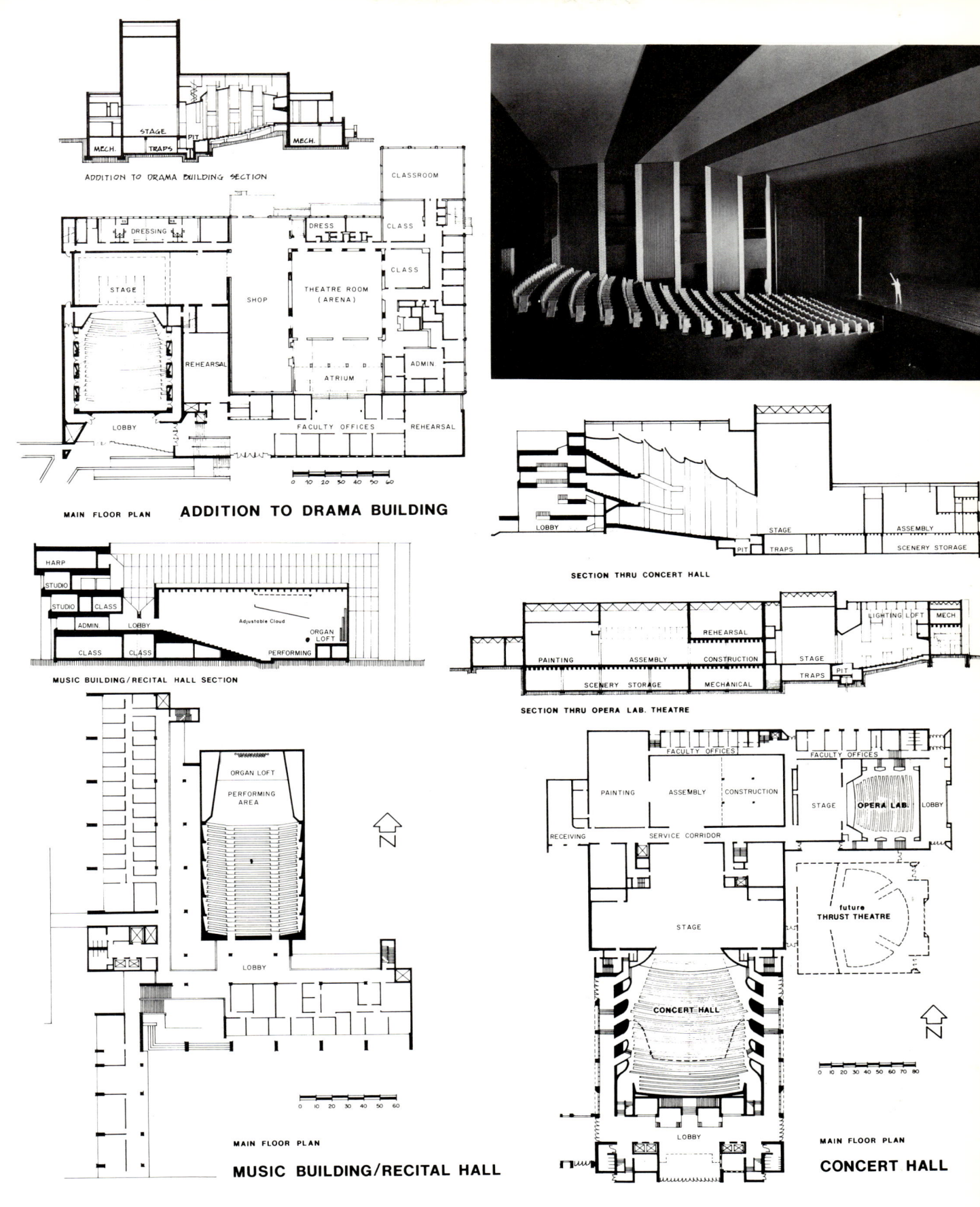

MAIN FLOOR PLAN — ADDITION TO DRAMA BUILDING

MUSIC BUILDING/RECITAL HALL SECTION

MAIN FLOOR PLAN — MUSIC BUILDING/RECITAL HALL

SECTION THRU CONCERT HALL

SECTION THRU OPERA LAB. THEATRE

MAIN FLOOR PLAN — CONCERT HALL

401

FLORIDA ATLANTIC UNIVERSITY, HUMANITIES BUILDING, LABORATORY FOR THE ARTS: THEATRE, MUSIC, DANCE, VISUAL ARTS (1966). Built on a limited budget further reduced during planning, this building retains essential elements despite severe economic restrictions, necessitating ingenious planning in structure and use. Music and art studios form a V enclosing the theatre. This arrangement eliminates external walls. A high ground water table necessitated building the theatre a level above grade and made a large area below the house available for services: dressing rooms which accommodate a company of 80 plus 8 principals, a large costume studio and costume storage with 130 feet of racks, generous design studio, property storage, a full stage rehearsal room, ballet and dance studios and the studio theatre. The walled-in trap room extends the orchestra pit so it can accommodate any orchestra larger than the pit elevator capacity of 35.

RECITAL

THE CHERRY ORCHARD

The theatre was planned to mount any production which can be got onto any stage in America. Individually-controlled aluminum panels which serve as a curtain make possible one or more openings of any size or shape extending almost halfway around the audience. With wagons coming in from the shop, ample rigging and a mobile trap elevator, which can lift several traps, scenery can be moved by any method. Several productions can be kept live in repertory without rehanging when shows change. The stage can work as an extended stage, an open stage, or a proscenium stage without structural limitations. There is provision for projection of 16mm, 35mm and 70mm film and wide-screen television. A demountable concert set encloses a large orchestra. Small ensembles and soloists perform on the pit elevator at stage height with the aluminum curtain down.

A patio serves as a theatre lounge, a covered outdoor art gallery and, with the Green Room open, a large reception area. The building cost less per square foot than a dormitory built at the same time.

Concessions made to budget limitations resulted in omission of a planned balcony which reduced capacity from 800 to 548 (no seat is more than 65 feet from the stage). The loading door is at stage right, making for a long carry to the shops. The paint frame on the end wall of the shop necessitates sweeping the shop area when taking a large piece from the frame to the stage, and adequate dead storage for scenery must wait for an adjacent structure projected in future campus development.
Architect: Clinton Gamble, FAIA
General and Acoustical Consultant: Harold Burris-Meyer

GROUND FLOOR PLAN

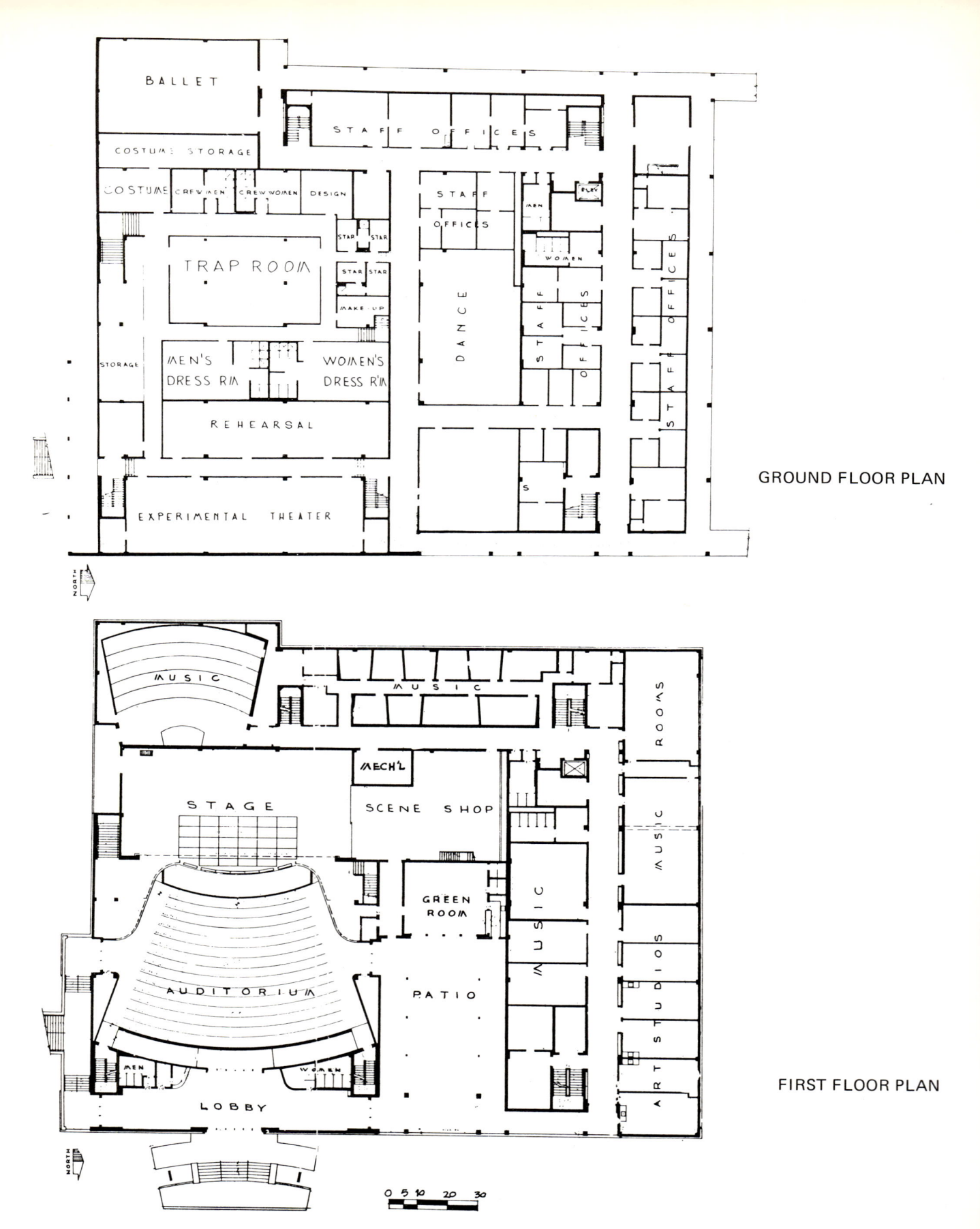

FIRST FLOOR PLAN

SECOND FLOOR PLAN

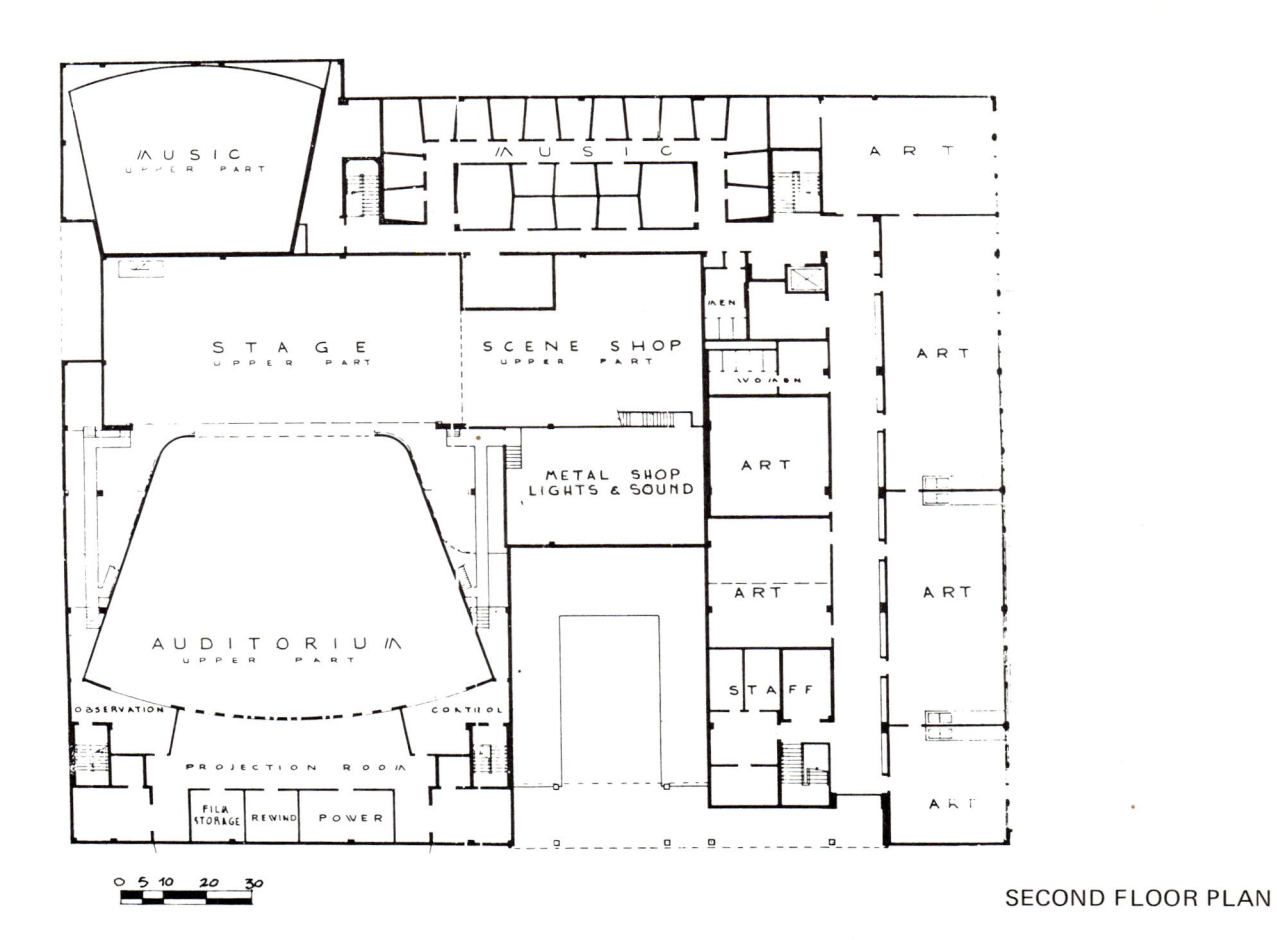

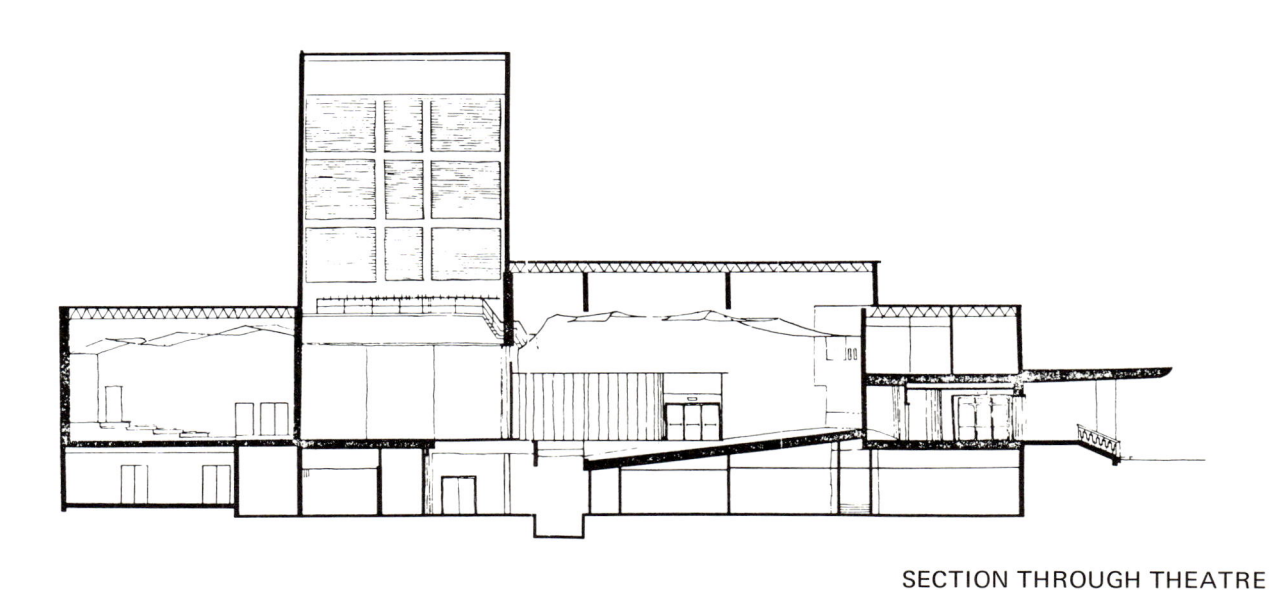

SECTION THROUGH THEATRE

UNIVERSITY OF NEW MEXICO, THE FINE ARTS CENTER: Art Museum (1963), Music Building (1964), Popejoy Hall (1966), New Rodey Theatre (1973). In twelve years of phased construction, this has become one of the most complete facilities for showing and teaching the arts in the United States. Horizontal dimensions may be related to the Popejoy Hall structural proscenium width of 63 feet.

The complex contains the buildings listed above and a free-form experimental theatre, and numerous class, practice and rehearsal rooms, studios, and production services, all clustered around a main lobby which is, in effect, a pedestrian plaza, serving all the performance spaces and emphasizing the community not only of the arts but also of the University. Each hall has its own functional lobby which serves as additional sound-isolation from the plaza.

Such a complex can hardly be without faults, some of which show in the plans: loading into and out of the Popejoy stage involves a 90 degree turn; it might better have been through the stage sidewall in the southwest corner of the stage; transport of scenic and other materials from the shop to the experimental theatre is circuitous and involves a change of floors; the scene shop will probably prove too small to serve the spacious stages of the Rodey and the Popejoy.

POPEJOY HALL: this hall presents 150 programs a year, averaging just under five per week. Two completely different programs in one day are not unusual. About one-third of the programs are University generated; the balance divide between bookings by the Popejoy management and the efforts of eight community music or theatre groups that call Popejoy their home. The University subsidizes the hall to the extent that rental fees do not cover operating expenses. Between 1966 and February 1974 attendance has been 1.2 million in the 2000 seat house.

With this kind of schedule the ability to change the hall from concert mode to theatre mode or the reverse in 90 minutes with four men, using the Izenour-designed orchestra shell is a great advantage.

Architects: Edward Holien and William R. Buckley
Consultants:
   Theatre: George C. Izenour
   Acoustics: Bolt, Beranek and Newman
   Purcell and Noppe

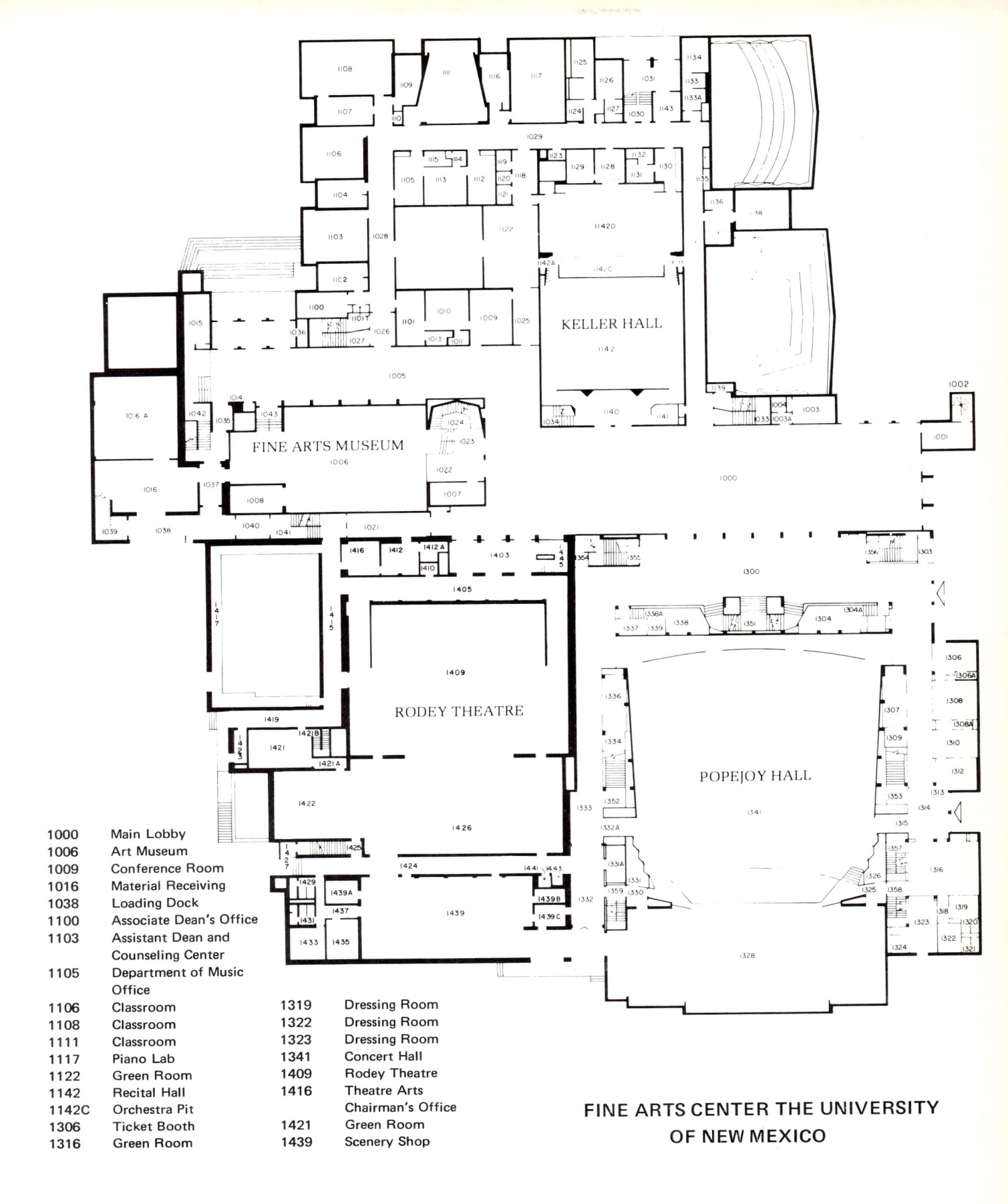

1000	Main Lobby		
1006	Art Museum		
1009	Conference Room		
1016	Material Receiving		
1038	Loading Dock		
1100	Associate Dean's Office		
1103	Assistant Dean and Counseling Center		
1105	Department of Music Office		
1106	Classroom	1319	Dressing Room
1108	Classroom	1322	Dressing Room
1111	Classroom	1323	Dressing Room
1117	Piano Lab	1341	Concert Hall
1122	Green Room	1409	Rodey Theatre
1142	Recital Hall	1416	Theatre Arts Chairman's Office
1142C	Orchestra Pit		
1306	Ticket Booth	1421	Green Room
1316	Green Room	1439	Scenery Shop

FINE ARTS CENTER THE UNIVERSITY OF NEW MEXICO

UNIVERSITY OF CALIFORNIA SANTA CRUZ, PERFORMING ARTS CENTER. This complex has facilities for theatre, music, dance and the visual arts. An open plan gives all arts their own courts for outdoor activity. Music practice rooms are sound isolated at the outer perimeter. The theatre follows the form of the Tyrone Guthrie Theatre in Minneapolis but with better backstage space and a flying system. Given fair weather the theatre service court has area enough for a scene shop but it would need equipment and should have at least canvas protection against the occasionl rain, morning fog, and the hot afternoon sun which does weird things to scene paint. The photograph shows the stage set with chairs for a University ceremony.

Architects: Ralph Rapson and Associates, Inc., Minneapolis
Theatre Consultants: Jules Fisher Associates

BALDWIN–WALLACE COLLEGE, ART AND DRAMA CENTER (1972), BEREA OHIO. With only slight deviations from the optimal arrangements for audience and for production preparation functions, the architects and planners have achieved a complete and well-thought-out plant for the curricula in theatre, speech and the visual arts, within a rather rigid, formalized ground plan. There is evidence of thorough analysis of the requirements. Commendable are: large side stages, optimal location of sound and light control stations, good relationships among the functional spaces, attention to sound isolation by double walls and a good working traffic pattern.

Inconvenience may arise in: admitting the entire audience from only one side into very long seat rows: lack of cross-over at the rear of the house; getting pianos, harps and other large instruments into the orchestra pit; a permanent forestage with the first row of seats 20 feet from the curtain line; keeping the painting area of the stage clean; ticket buyers cluttering one of the entrances to the house; transporting scenery supplies from the loading dock to the stagecrafts classroom (shop); and access from the light and sound booths to the catwalks and thence backstage.

The permanent, trapped, forestage/orchestra pit might better have been an orchestra lift, affording the options of forestage, orchestra pit, or added seating space.

A special problem which received a unique solution was the position of the College under the principal flight path from Cleveland Hopkins International Airport. 16,000 square feet of sheet lead-antimony alloy were laid on the roof of the building as a sound barrier.

Architects: Heine, Grider and Williamson, Berea, Ohio
Acoustical consultants: Bolt, Beranek and Newman

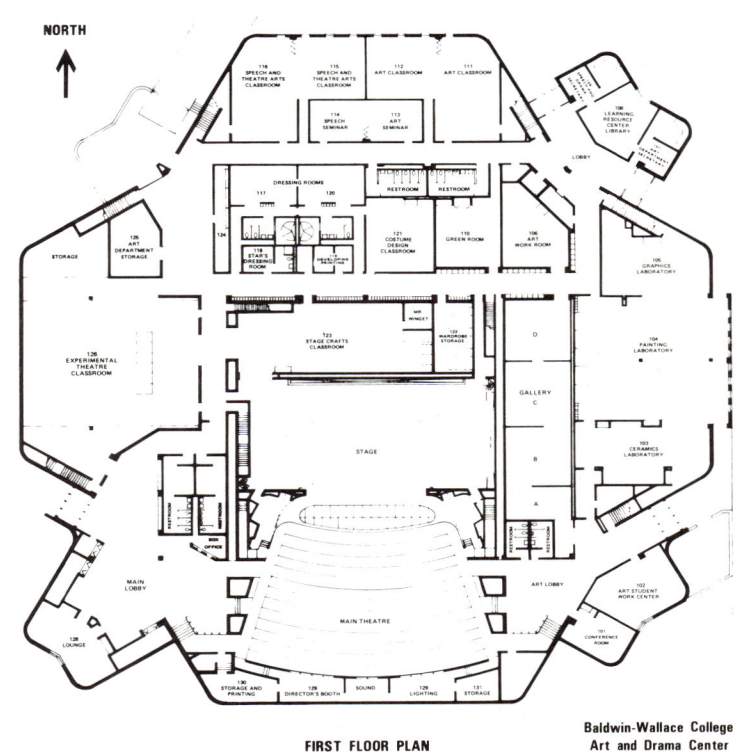

FIRST FLOOR PLAN

Baldwin-Wallace College
Art and Drama Center

GROUND FLOOR

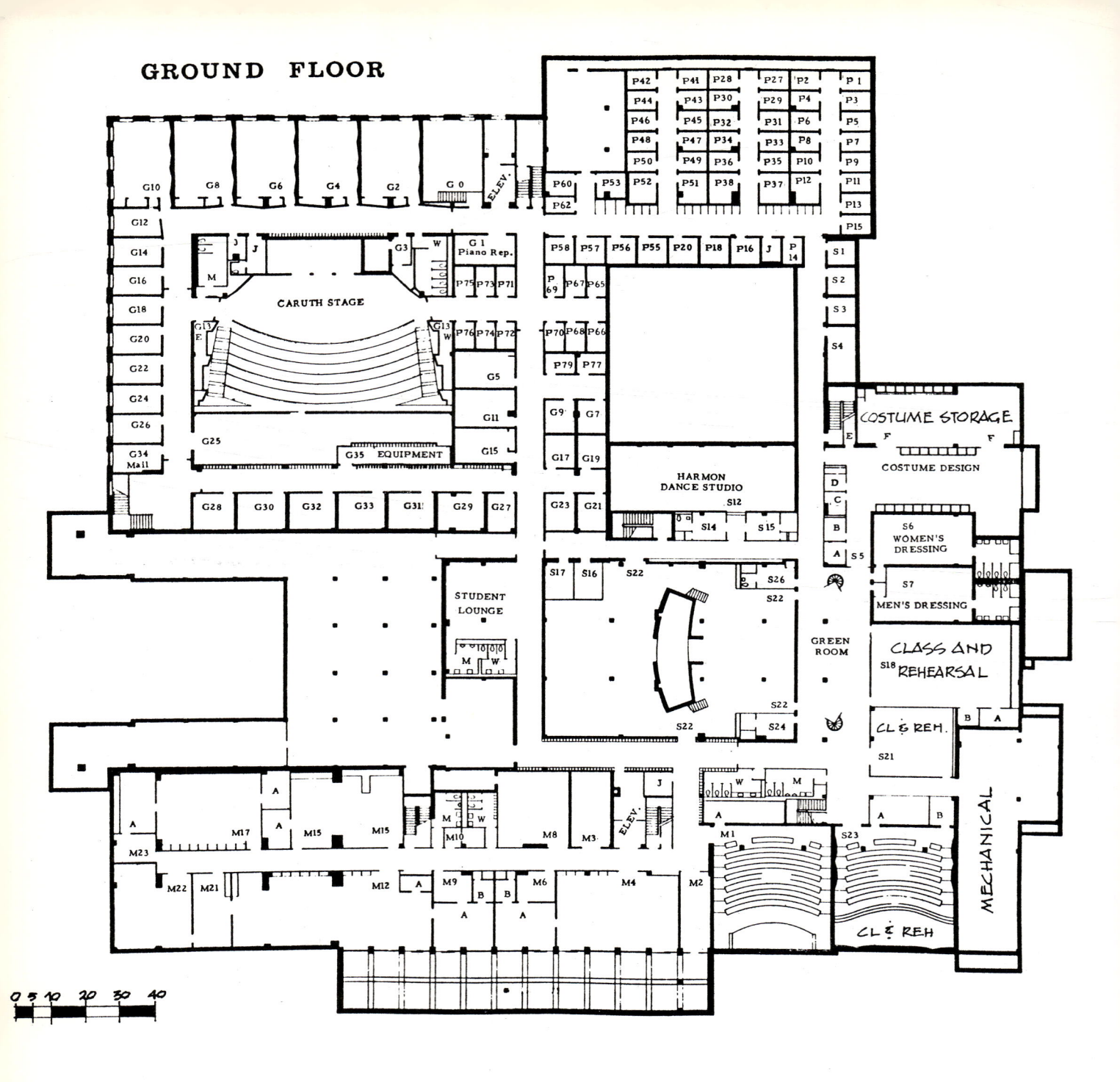

SOUTHERN METHODIST UNIVERSITY: OWENS ARTS CENTER, MEADOWS SCHOOL OF THE ARTS; RUTH COLLINS SHARP DRAMA BUILDING; THE BOB HOPE THEATRE; THE MARGO JONES EXPERIMENTAL THEATRE: *This large complex houses theatres, music, dance, visual arts and a tele-cine workshop. Two floors are shown; an additional upper floor contains the upper parts of all theatres, workshops, rehearsal halls and galleries, with additional teaching spaces*

FIRST FLOOR

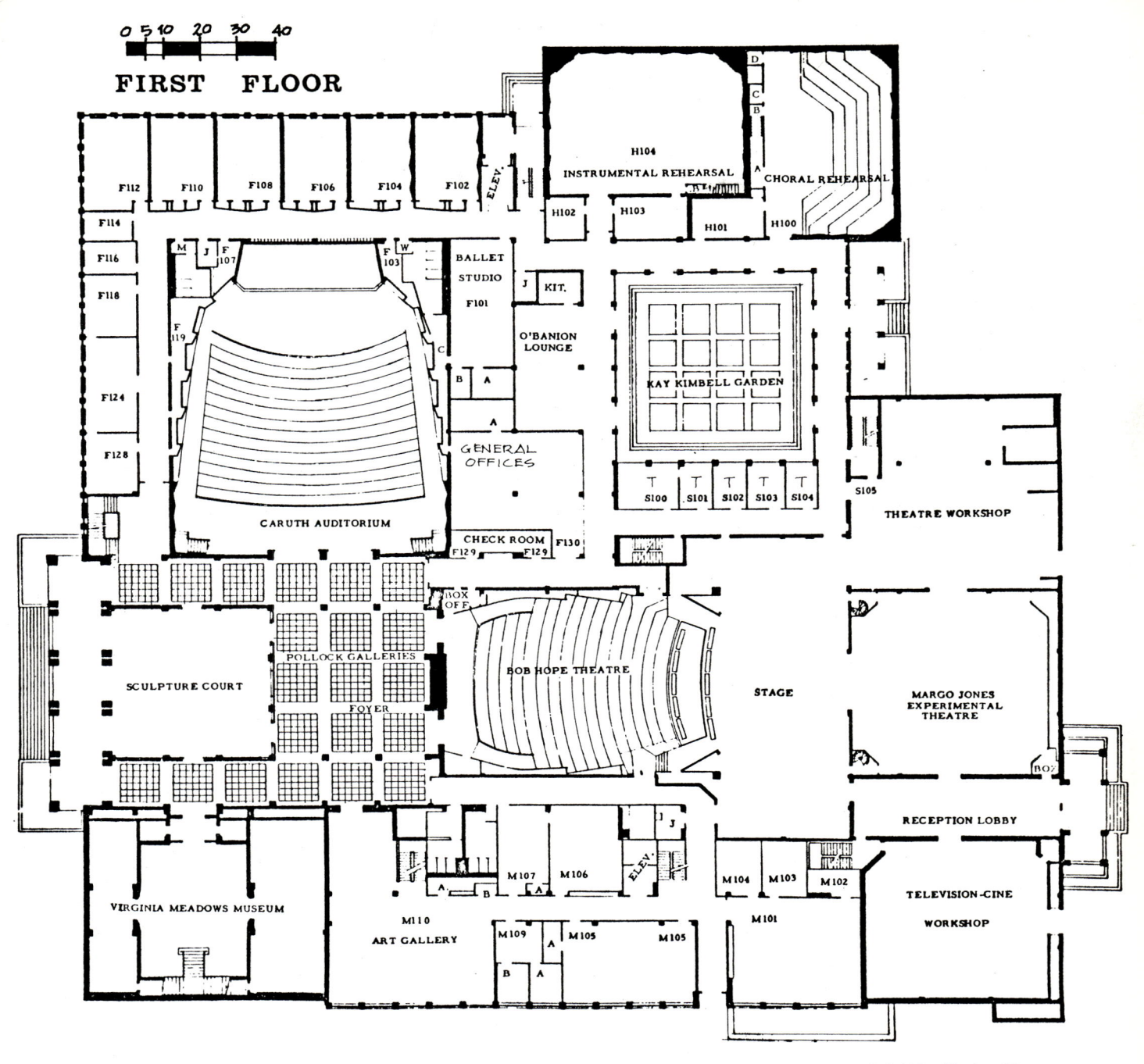

F, G, H, P: Music offices, class, practice
S: Theatre or Speech offices, class, rehearse
M: Art offices, galleries, studios, class

between and around. Copious as it is, there appear to be some shortcomings: circuitous routes or spiral stairs from dressing rooms to the Bob Hope Theatre stage; few restrooms for three audiences; probable sound interference between workshop, Margo Jones Theatre and Bob Hope Theatre; little storage space for scenery or properties; no paint frame.
Architects: George Dahl and Associates.
Consultants:
  Theatre: Peter Wolf
  Acoustics: C. P. Boner and Associates

SMITH COLLEGE CENTER FOR THE PERFORMING ARTS (1968). Another superb facility for teaching and presenting theatre arts. The plan is self-explanatory except for a ramp at the left (stage right) side of the building to admit wheel-chair patrons to the first rows where some chairs are removable, and the staircase in the student's lounge was changed to a freestanding poured-in-place concrete staircase. This is another example of careful analysis and thorough programming. Among many commendable features of structure or equipment are those shown: three sets of light slots in sidewall of THEATRE 14; a ramp direct from director's seat to stage, short-cutting the long way around caused by continental seating; a portable derrick for the operation illustrated and many other chores involving lifting and moving.

Architects: Helge Westermann, Richard Miller and Associates
Consultants: Theatre: Joel Rubin   Acoustics: Wilhelm Jordan

412

STAGE LEVEL FLOOR PLAN

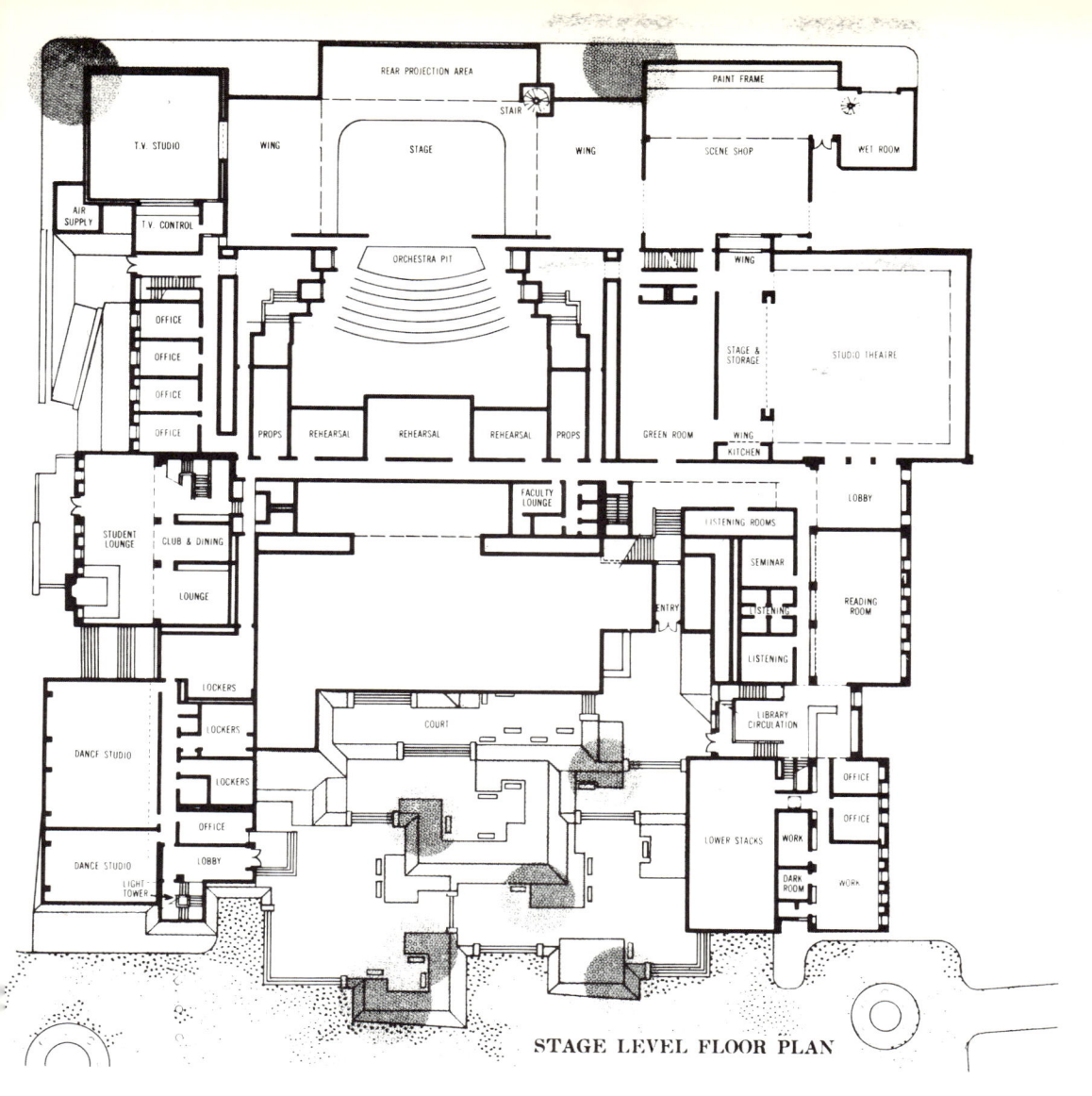

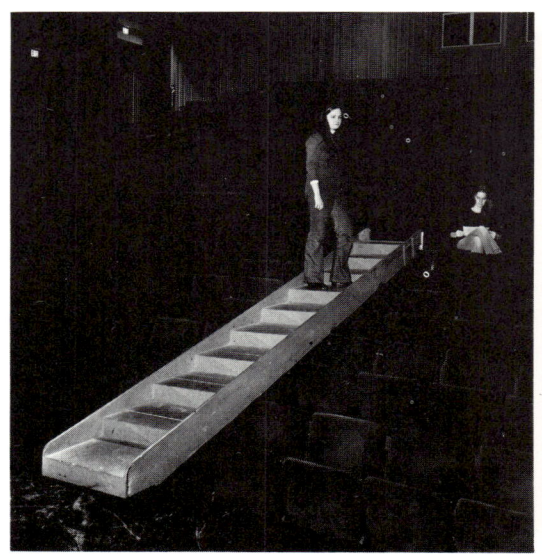

Key to plan and section:

A	Arcade
AG	Animation Graphics
B	Balcony
C	Class
CD	Costume Design
D	Dressing
F	Freight
Lo	Lobby
M	Mechanical
MT	Mobile Television Unit
R	Rehearsal
S	Service Tunnel
St	Storage
StC	Student Commons
TF	Television and Film Arts
TFU	Television and Film Arts (Upper Part)
To	Toilet
TW	Theatre Workshop
TWU	Theatre Workshop (Upper Part)

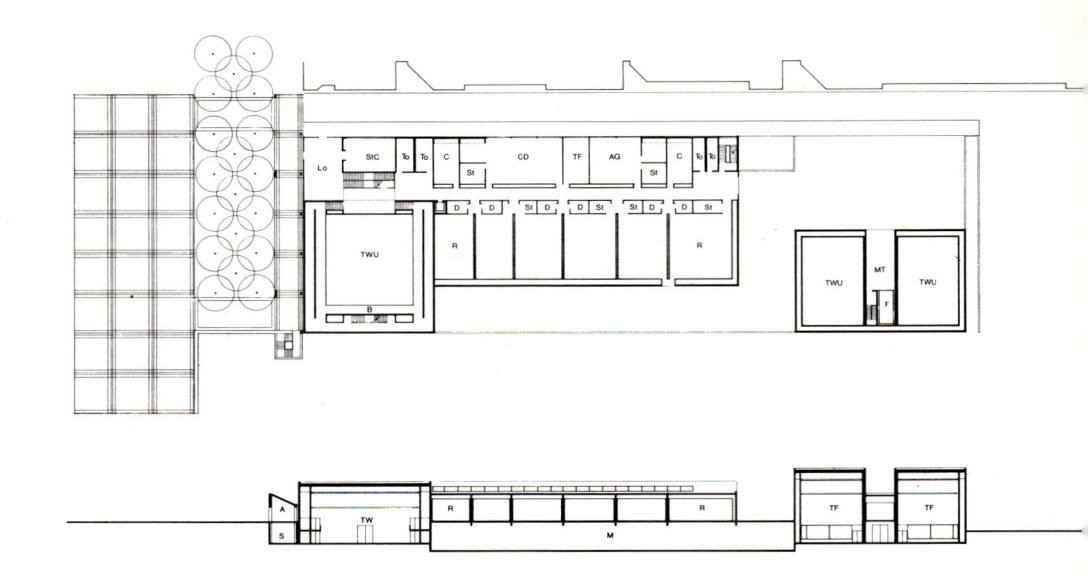

STATE UNIVERSITY OF NEW YORK, COLLEGE OF THE ARTS, PURCHASE, N.Y. *An entire college campus devoted to major studies in the arts is the ultimate in facilities for students of the arts. Theatre, dance and music have specifically designed theatres; music, dance and theatre arts have separate instructional buildings, and film and television are embraced by theatre, but with their own studios.*

"*The focus....will be the performing arts....to be used by the college, community and visiting professionals....all theatres must be multi-purpose. Theatre A–1400 Seat Opera House....visiting symphony orchestras, repertory companies as well as student shows....*

Theatre B–750 Seat Hanamachi (wrap-around) Theatre....possibility of action surrounding the audience....small scenes, antiphonal responses, entrances from all sides and a variety of other effects....

Theatre C–600 Seat Theatre of Music and Dance....small chamber concerts, classical ballet and drama....deeply pitched seating....score desks in boxes for music scholars, elevating orchestra pit....

Theatre D–100 to 500 Seat Experimental Theatre....variety of audience-stage relationships....'total environment' theatre....large lift drops to floor below, where props and seats are stored....a wide range of scenic effects and mixed media...."

(Excerpts from ARCHITECTURE FOR THE ARTS: THE STATE UNIVERSITY OF NEW YORK COLLEGE AT PURCHASE. See Bibliography.)

A thoroughly detailed analysis of the physical requirements for teaching in all the arts was made before designing and drawing began (see Bibiography).

Architect for the master plan, the Performing Arts Center and the instructional buildings for Music and Theatre: Edward Larrabee Barnes, FAIA

Consultants:
For Theatre Arts: Norris Houghton
Theatres: Ming Cho Lee
Acoustics: Bolt, Beranek and Newman

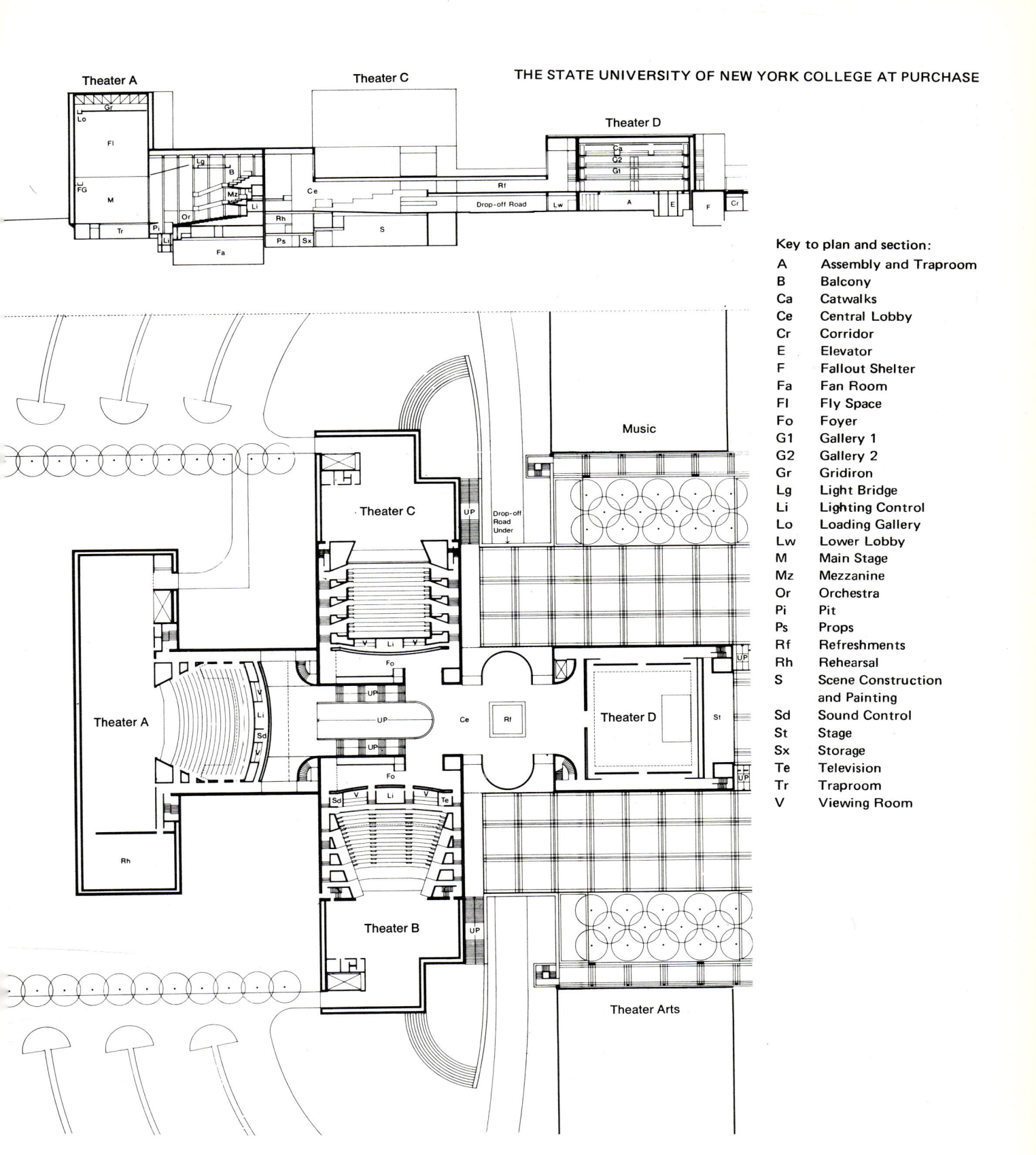

THE STATE UNIVERSITY OF NEW YORK COLLEGE AT PURCHASE

Key to plan and section:

A	Assembly and Traproom
B	Balcony
Ca	Catwalks
Ce	Central Lobby
Cr	Corridor
E	Elevator
F	Fallout Shelter
Fa	Fan Room
Fl	Fly Space
Fo	Foyer
G1	Gallery 1
G2	Gallery 2
Gr	Gridiron
Lg	Light Bridge
Li	Lighting Control
Lo	Loading Gallery
Lw	Lower Lobby
M	Main Stage
Mz	Mezzanine
Or	Orchestra
Pi	Pit
Ps	Props
Rf	Refreshments
Rh	Rehearsal
S	Scene Construction and Painting
Sd	Sound Control
St	Stage
Sx	Storage
Te	Television
Tr	Traproom
V	Viewing Room

415

Theatre A

Theatre B

Theatre C

Theatre D

CHILDREN'S THEATRE COMPANY OF THE MINNEAPOLIS SOCIETY OF FINE ARTS. This theatre can serve as a model of thorough advanced analysis, detailed programming and innovative architectural solution. The plans and section with accompanying room keys tell the story.
Architect: Kenzo Tange and Urtec, Tokyo; associated with Parker Klein Associates, Minneapolis
Consultants: John C. Donahue, Director; Karlis Ozols, Production Coordinator, and staff of Children's Theatre Company

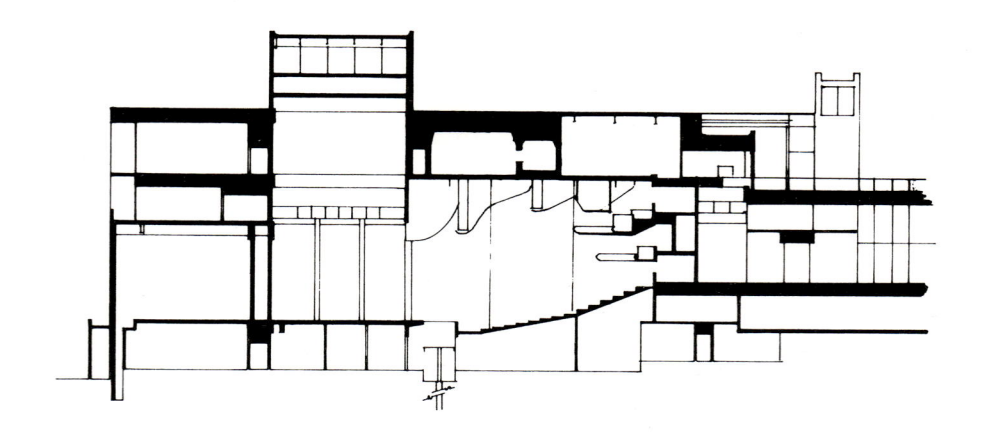

BASEMENT

1. Principals' dressing rooms and toilets
2. Costume storage (two locations)
3. Special effects room, sound isolated, tunnel to under-stage
4. Group dressing rooms, M and W, 16 each, showers and toilets
5. Paint frame well
6. Office
7. Musicians' green room, sound isolated, warmup, music classroom
8. Trap room. 3 feet X 6 feet traps, overall area 36 X 36 feet
9. Actors' green room with kitchenette
10. Live scenery storage for repertory. Orchestra lift to stage
11. Props storage
12. General storage
13. Elevators for audience, restaurant, shop freight, handicapped
14. Kitchen preparations, freezer, cooler
15. Electrical
16. Mechanical
17. Stage Manager

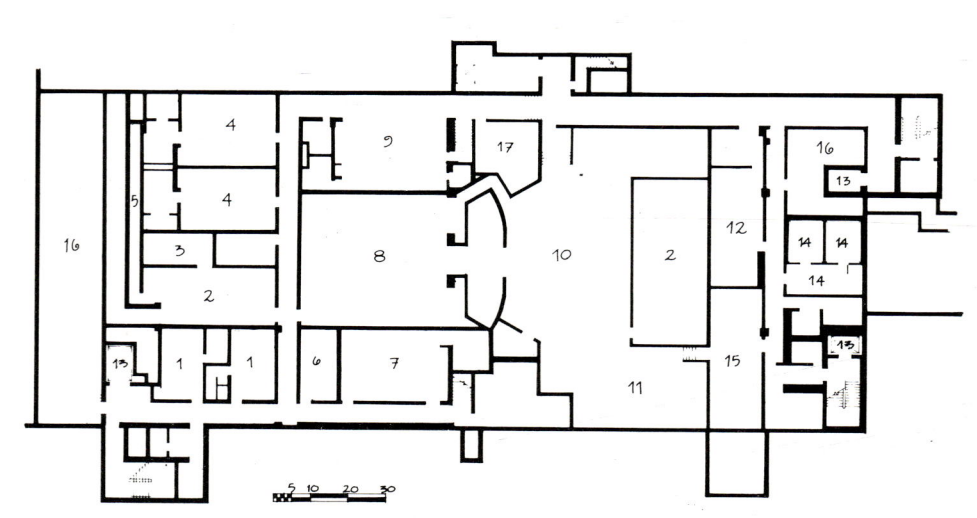

418

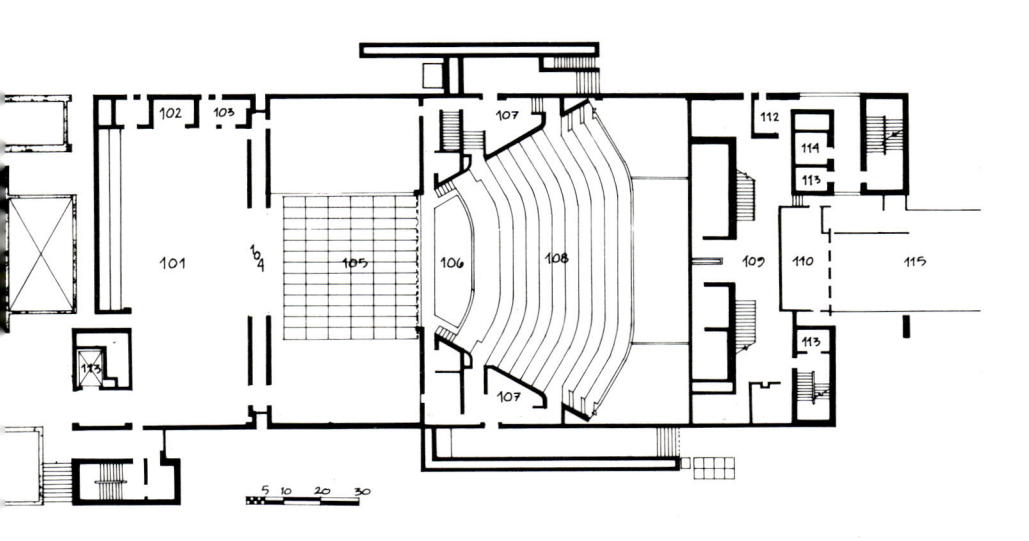

GROUND FLOOR (street level)
- 101 Scene shop
- 102 Walk-in spray booth
- 103 Technical director's office
- 104 Structural separation: sound isolation from theatre
- 105 Stage. 40 feet deep, 90 feet wide, 90 feet to grid. Proscenium 36 feet wide, 24 feet high
- 106 Orchestra pit lift
- 107 Vestibules
- 108 Main floor of house. 548 seats in 15 rows
- 109 Lower lobby
- 110 Ticket office (4 windows), cloak room displays
- 111 Ushers
- 112 Ticket manager
- 113 Elevators
- 114 Kiosk preparation

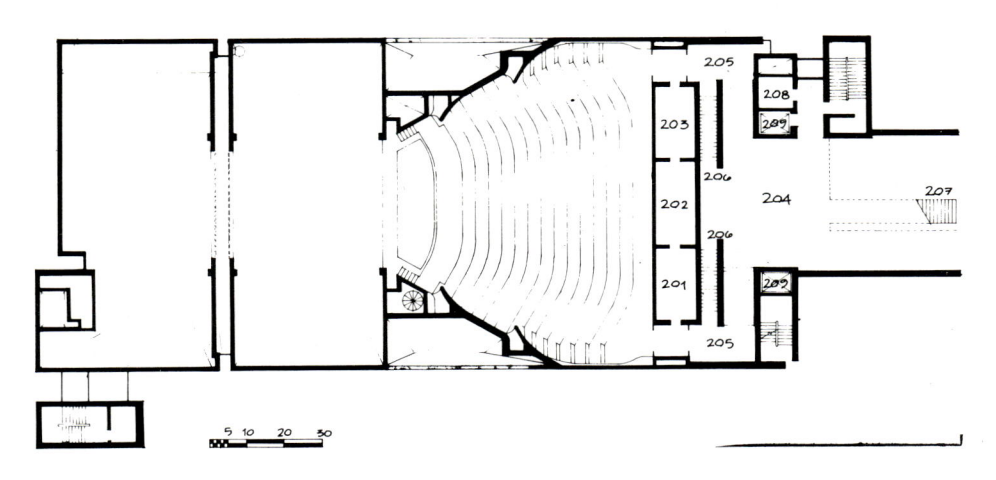

MAIN FLOOR
- 201 Late audience viewing room; loudspeakers, sound-isolated
- 202 Light controls: 8 foot window can be opened
- 203 Sound Control; window can be opened
- 204 Main lobby
- 205 Entrances to main house floor
- 206 Stairs to balconies
- 207 Stairs to restaurant
- 208 Restroom for handicapped. Others elsewhere in building
- 209 Elevators

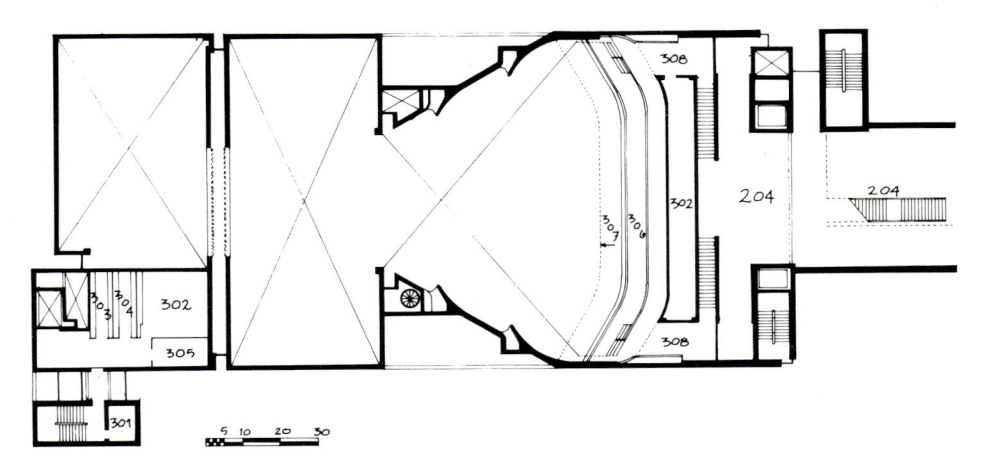

LOWER BALCONY
- 301 Showers and lockers for technical staff
- 302 General storage
- 303 Shoes storage
- 304 Hats storage
- 305 Valuables storage
- 306 Lower balcony
- 307 Edge of upper balcony
- 204 Main lobby (below)

419

UPPER BALCONY
- 401 Props shop
- 402 Walk-in spray room with vent
- 403 Costume shop
- 404 Roof terrace
- 405 Laundry and dye room
- 406 Live costume storage
- 407 Dressing room
- 408 Wigmaker
- 409 U-shaped catwalk around stage, 30 feet above stage, and access to ceiling-slot catwalks
- 410 Catwalks (four) ceiling light slots
- 411 Traps in ceiling removable for loudspeakers, air-conditioning outlets, and rigging over the forestage
- 412 Sound-isolated spotlight booth
- 413 Access to sidewall light slots
- 414 Theatre director's office with view of stage
- 415 Secretary's office
- 416 Kitchette
- 416 Kitchenette
- 417 Upper balcony
- 418 Bridge
- 419 Elevators
- 420 Restaurant kitchen

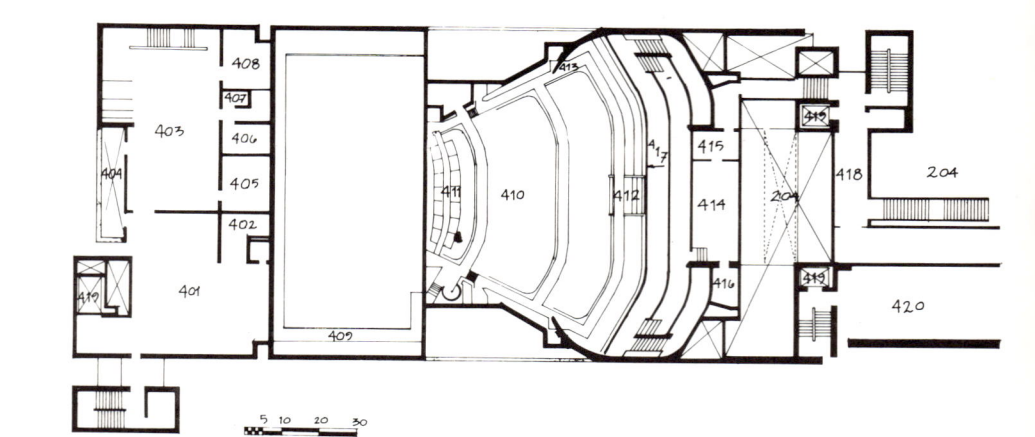

TOP FLOOR
- 501 Dance studio, 30 feet × 60 feet. Mirrors, barres. Rehearsal room for plays
- 502 Lockers and showers for 120 Childrens' Theatre Company students
- 503 Office suite
- 504 General Manager
- 505 Audio-visual library
- 506 Darkroom
- 507 Recording studio
- 508 Control room
- 509 Voice booth
- 510 Studio theatre
- 511 Library, lounge
- 512 School principal's office
- 513 Stage design studio
- 514 Stage design office
- 515 Open
- 516 Elevators
- 517 Restaurant kitchen
- 518 Restaurant
- 519 Future terrace restaurant

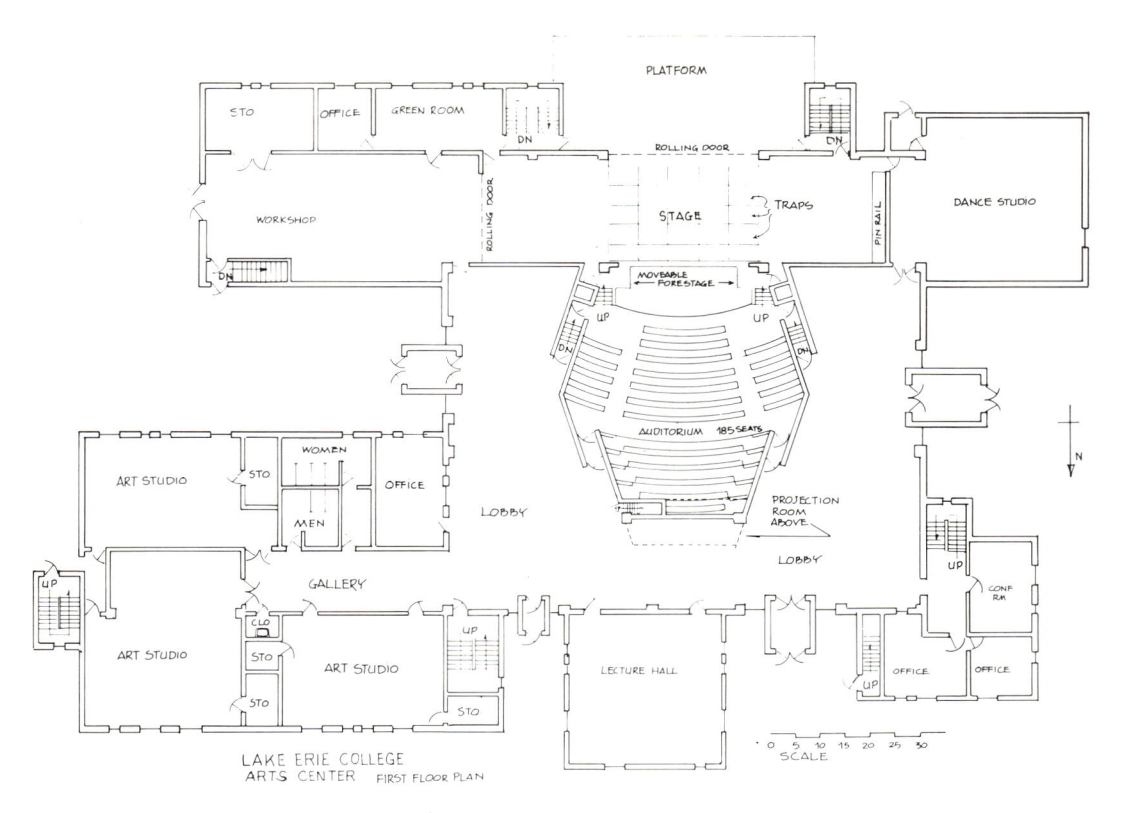

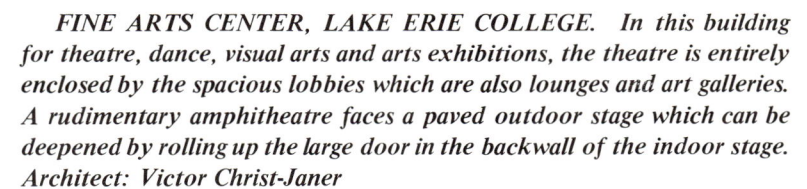

FINE ARTS CENTER, LAKE ERIE COLLEGE. In this building for theatre, dance, visual arts and arts exhibitions, the theatre is entirely enclosed by the spacious lobbies which are also lounges and art galleries. A rudimentary amphitheatre faces a paved outdoor stage which can be deepened by rolling up the large door in the backwall of the indoor stage.
Architect: Victor Christ-Janer
Theatre Consultant: Clyde Blakeley

Festivals

The oldest form of organized theatre is staging a comeback. From ancient Greece to city and state parks, college campuses and national capitals, the form has shown renewed vigor.

Limited Programs. Joseph Papp's Theatre in the Park playing Shakespeare, pre-1964 to be sure, was the leader in demonstrating the effectiveness of festivals. The three Stratfords also were in the vanguard. There are now many others, some with exemplary theatres, indoors, outdoors or a combination of both. Usually playing in limited repertory, several have opted for the thrust or open stage forms as a means of reducing the scenic burden.

A unique theatre, the Saratoga Performing Arts Center was built in 1966 by the New York State Park and Recreation Commission, specifically for summer festivals of music, opera and dance. With seating for a large audience inside on an amply sloped ramp, its open sides afford good vision and hearing for an additional large audience seated on a grassed natural amphitheatre outside.

A sequel under the same auspices and management is a similar theatre in a large arts complex entitled ART PARK, beside the Niagara River in Lewiston, New York, which opened in 1974.

Multi-Play Festivals. Lasting a week or more, with ten or more plays and daily, twice or thrice daily changes of plays, multi-play festivals have come strongly into the national and international theatre scene since 1964: international festivals at Edinborough, Monaco and elsewhere; state, regional, and national festivals of community theatre, high school theatre, and college theatre in the United States. These festivals are logistic problems of the first magnitude requiring the maximum efficiency in theatre operation with ample space for receipt and storage of incoming and outgoing scenery, properties, and costume trunks of several companies, many dressing rooms and versatile stage equipment. The best of the academic theatres with at least two performance spaces are the best suited for multi-play festivals.

The Streets

The street theatre, a trailer or several trailers which mount a stage, lights and a PA system, has found a place in New York and Los Angeles. It is credited, in addition to cultural and entertainment value, with helping to keep down the crime rate. The medieval strolling players are here again!

TEATRO RODANTE. Theatres for street performances vary from planks on barrels to multi-truck outfits costing into six figures. The choice for exhibition herein departs from the last-decade time limit and from continental United States. The TEATRO RODANTE UNIVERSITARIO, designed by Rafael Cruz-Emeric at the University of Puerto Rico in 1947, toured the towns and villages all over the island for many years with such classics as SANCHO PANZA, and plays by Moliere and Lope da Vega, directed by Leo Lavandero. Musicians atop the bus announced the arrival of the three-vehicle caravan (the bus with the company, the theatre, and a generator/utility truck), continued to play while the audience watched the ten-minute set-up, and the play began.

423

GOODSPEED OPERA HOUSE, EAST HADDAM, CONNECTICUT (1877 -- restored 1963). Occupying the two top floors of what must have been, to East Haddam, a huge, magnificent, building Goodspeed's Opera House presented performers who came from New York by boat, debarked and unloaded their costume trunks on the landing, and had them loaded into a rudimentary hand-operated lift for hauling up to stage level. In disrepair for many years, condemned at one time, the building has been handsomely restored by the Goodspeed Opera House Foundation. There are three fireproof escape stairs and a modern elevator, ample for the modest seating capacity. The summer schedule contains revived or new musical shows, and a variety of other attractions fills out the year. MAN OF LA MANCHA was first produced at Goodspeed.

Architect for the restoration : Sage Goodwin
Architectural Designer: Frederic Palmer
Theatre Consultant: Donald Oenslager

GUSMAN PHILHARMONIC HALL, MIAMI, FLORIDA. The transformation of the plush Olympia movie palace into the justly acclaimed Gusman Philharmonic Hall involved no basic structural change and no loss of the gingerbread decor. The pipe organ remains. The additions consist of a demountable plywood concert set, reflective panels, and the necessary operating controls.
Architect: Morris Lapidus, Associates
Consultant: George Gill

RESTORATIONS RENOVATIONS and CONVERSIONS

Restorations

To the satisfaction of theatre historians, antiquarians, conservationists and others who see value, both financial and non-material, in preservation, several theatres and "opera houses" have followed the lead of the Central City (Colorado) Opera House, restored and renovated in 1932, and been brought back into useful life since 1964. The Goodspeed Opera House, East Haddam, Connecticut, reopened in 1963 before the publication of the second edition. The Auditorium Theatre in Chicago was restored and reactivated in 1967 and Ford's Theatre in Washington in 1968. A few others, deserving of new careers as active theatres, have been restored to some degree but are operated as museums or simply as tourist attractions.

In most cases the theatres have been restored to period style in the house and public rooms, but have been modernized in house lighting (electric lamps in gas fixtures), plumbing, stage equipment, lighting, lighting control and sound systems, with the structure, seating and exit facilities made to conform to building codes or at least rendered adequate for the granting of code variances.

Fine old movie palaces can make fine new concert halls and opera houses. A significant breakthrough and a masterpiece of restoration and renovation is the *new* St. Louis Powell Symphony Hall which was the *old* St. Louis Theatre, a motion-picture-presentation palace (1925). It opened to the praise of both music and architectural critics January 24, 1974. The renovation cost about $2,000,000 whereas a new hall of comparable accomodations could cost between $15,000,000 and $20,000,000. Other sponsors will be well advised to act before all the motion picture palaces are demolished.

Renovations

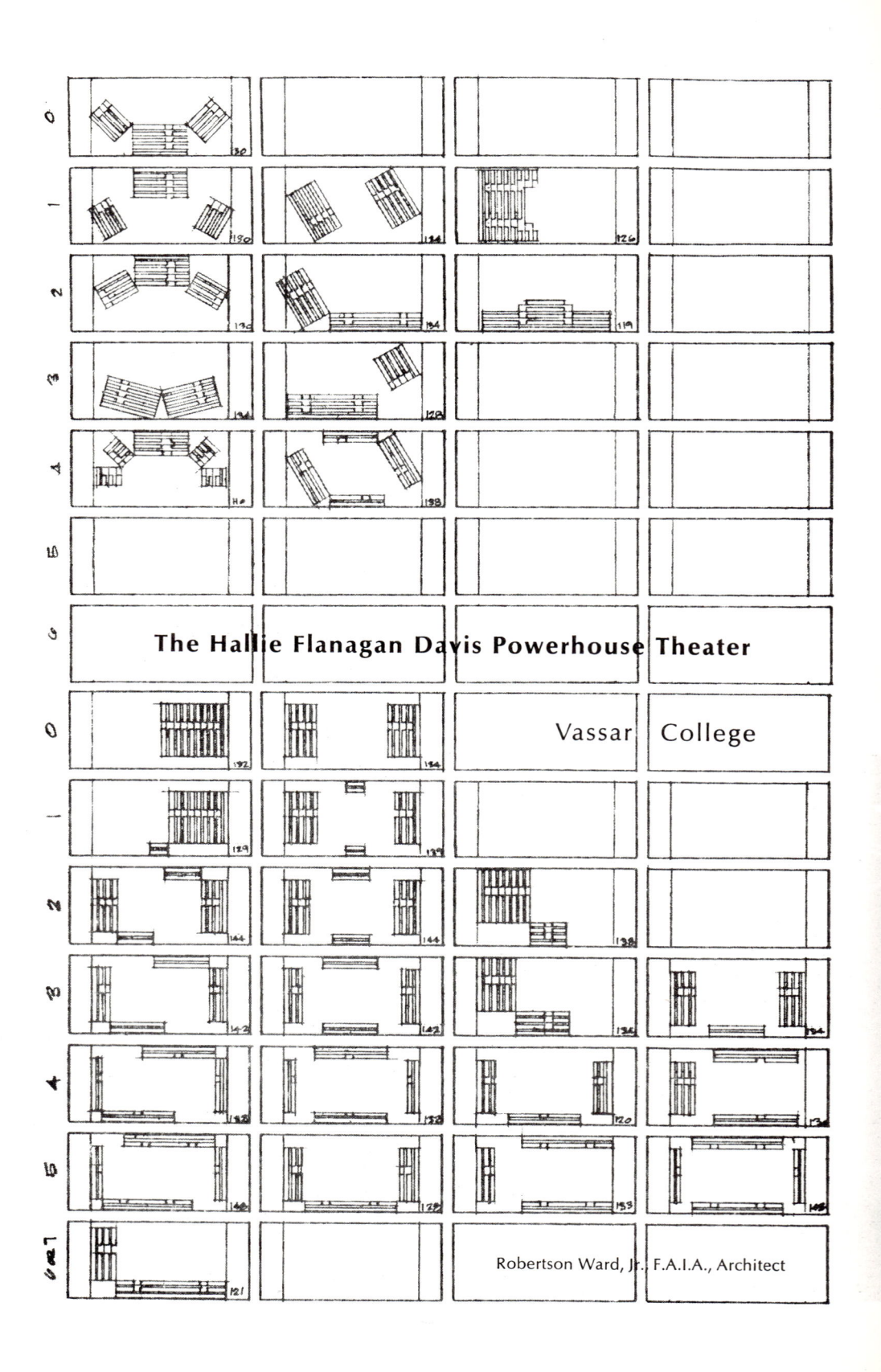

The Hallie Flanagan Davis Powerhouse Theater

Vassar College

Robertson Ward, Jr., F.A.I.A., Architect

VASSAR COLLEGE, HALLIE FLANAGAN DAVIS POWERHOUSE THEATRE. The abandoned electric powerhouse, a sturdy masonry building 35 feet by 80 feet with clear inside height of 30 feet, by thorough and ingenious planning and designing, utilization of existing features (gantry crane and a tunnel), and addition of a one-story-and-basement block, 25 feet by 80 feet, along one side, has been made into a versatile free-form studio theatre, capable of many configurations, eminently suited to the creative efforts of students in a small liberal arts college.

Consultant: Thaddeus Gesek

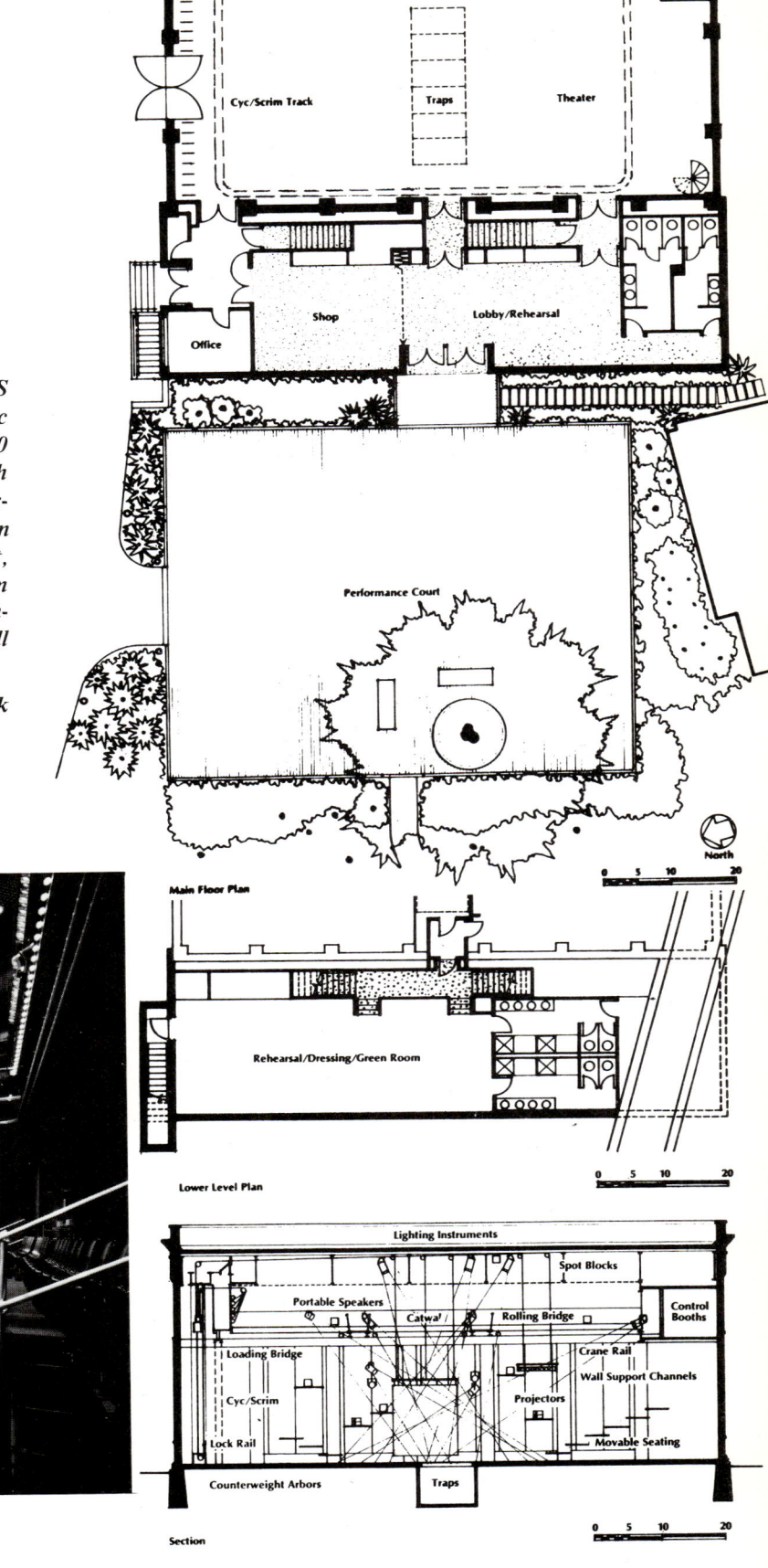

Main Floor Plan

Lower Level Plan

Section

Conversions

Two successful conversions of non-theatrical spaces into free-form theatres are the Hallie Flanagan Davis Powerhouse Theatre at Vassar College and the Margaret Jonsson Theatre at the University of Dallas.

Patrick Kelly, Director of the University Theatre, University of Dallas, and his wife, Judy, in a report for PLANNING FOR HIGHER EDUCATION, February 1974, have ably stated the philosophy behind the use of admittedly limited, but carefully thought out and economically achieved play production facilities.

The growth of interest in all performing arts at collegiate level has inevitably produced competition and conflict over the use of the performance facility, where only one such exists in a college. Music, dance, drama and film departments need presentation facilities of their own. Restriction to a shared facility seriously impedes the full development of performances as exemplary teaching devices in all the performing arts, limits time for experiment, preparation and rehearsal, wastes time in changeovers, diffuses responsibility for the plant and its equipment, and induces personal animosities.

THEATRE FORMS

The statements on pages 125–145 need only be amplified by statements and examples of the forms which have found favor since 1964.

Proscenium (page 127)

This is still the dominant form in all commercial theatres and performing arts centers, whether civic or educational. Variations within this form have become popular: the forestage lift with level changes to create an orchestra pit or additional seats at floor level; the lift sometimes subdivided for more varied arrangements; sidestages, either open, enclosed by flying panels or traverse curtains, or as openings in the proscenium's sidewalls, closed by panels or curtains (pages 130, 140–143).

An unusual variation in the proscenium form is the floor trap system at the Uris Theatre, New York. It is designed primarily for sinkage, the traps having a vertical range of from two feet above stage level to eight feet below it. The trapped area is 64 feet wide and 36 feet deep onstage and meets matching sections of the apron and forestage so that the whole floor from the first row of seats to the back of the acting area can be given configurations in 4′ × 3′ modules within the stated vertical limits. Each trap is supported by four many-sectioned telescoping posts. A single scissors-type movable lift is centered under one trap to raise or lower it, and it is held at a desired height by bolts put through holes in the post sections. Comment from users is that considerable labor time is required to set the traps in a new configuration.

Open Stage (pages 128, 340)

This form has found favor in community theatres where economies of money and time have priority, in secondary schools where limited

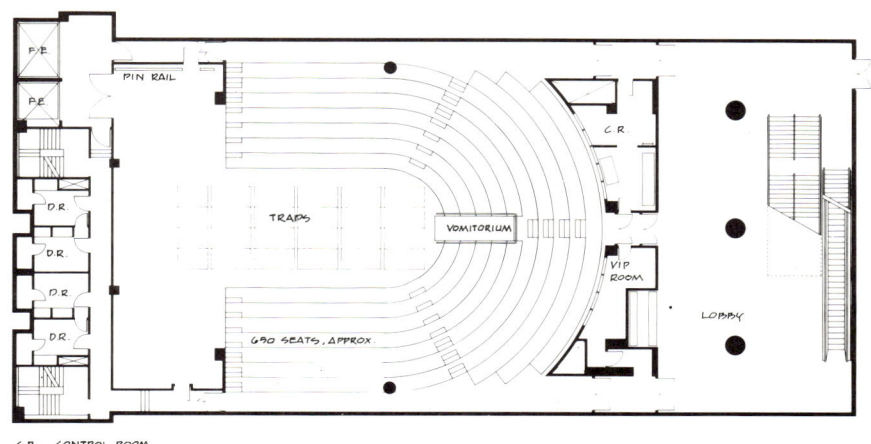

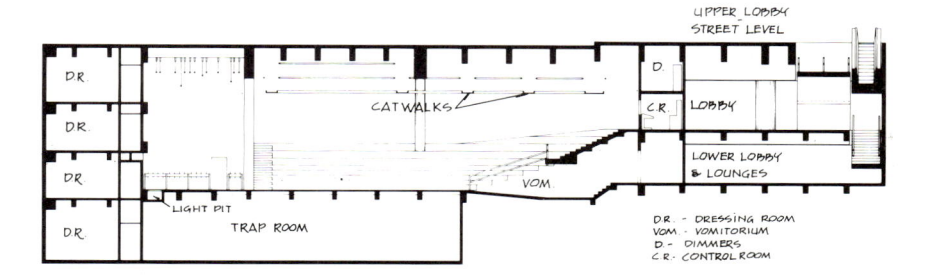

THE JOSEPH E. LEVINE THEATRE/CIRCLE IN THE SQUARE. From a celebrated twenty-year record as the pioneer off-Broadway theatre, Circle in the Square has come into a modern ultra-thrust theatre with ample seating capacity and staging facilities which include a completely trapped stage floor, lighting catwalks, side galleries for audience access or for acting areas and entrances, and a useful, conventional stage and a flying system. U-shaped stadium seating recalls the Teatro Farnese at Parma, Italy (1618–1619) and offers a uniquely different configuration of curtained proscenium and deep thrust stage which may challenge some directors.
Building architects: Emory Roth and Sons
Theatre architect: Alan Sayles
Theatre and Lighting
  Consultant: Jules Fisher

funds have been coupled with limited educational objectives, and in a few small colleges. Not all open stage theatres have proven theatrically or practically effective. A well-designed theatre with conventional seating may have an open stage or a proscenium stage or an extended stage with minimal special equipment and a few minutes changeover time.

Thrust Stage

This term, not differentiated from *open stage* in the 1964 edition (page 128), has emerged as the name for the stage which projects forwards so that the acting area is surrounded by a semi-circle, or more, of audience.

The form, which appeared first on this continent in Stratford, Ontario, and was repeated in Minneapolis with embellishments, has grown in popularity, though it has not shed any of the characteristics described on pages 128–129.

Many of the non-profit resident professional theatres, regional or academic, have opted for the thrust stage form because of its economies of space and productional requirements. The form has also been preferred by a few colleges and included in one university complex as a supplementary theatre.

Recent examples of thrust and open stage theatres have incorporated the space and equipment for changing scenic backgrounds, and have backstage space adequate to receive and store movable units of scenery.

(to page 432)

THE UNIVERSITY OF NORTH CAROLINA, CHAPEL HILL. *A revolving seating bank will orient the audience not only toward a conventional (spacious and well equipped) proscenium stage, but toward any number of scenes set on a continuous stage which extends 150° around the turntable on each side and on a balcony around the east side which extends over the vestibule, as an upper acting area. An appraisal of this plant in 1986 by someone who has experienced it for ten years will be a valued contribution to the literature on theatre planning.*
Architects: Odell Associates, Inc.
Consultants:
  General: R. Keith Michael
  Technical: Gordon W. Pearlman
          Jean Rosenthal Associates, Inc.

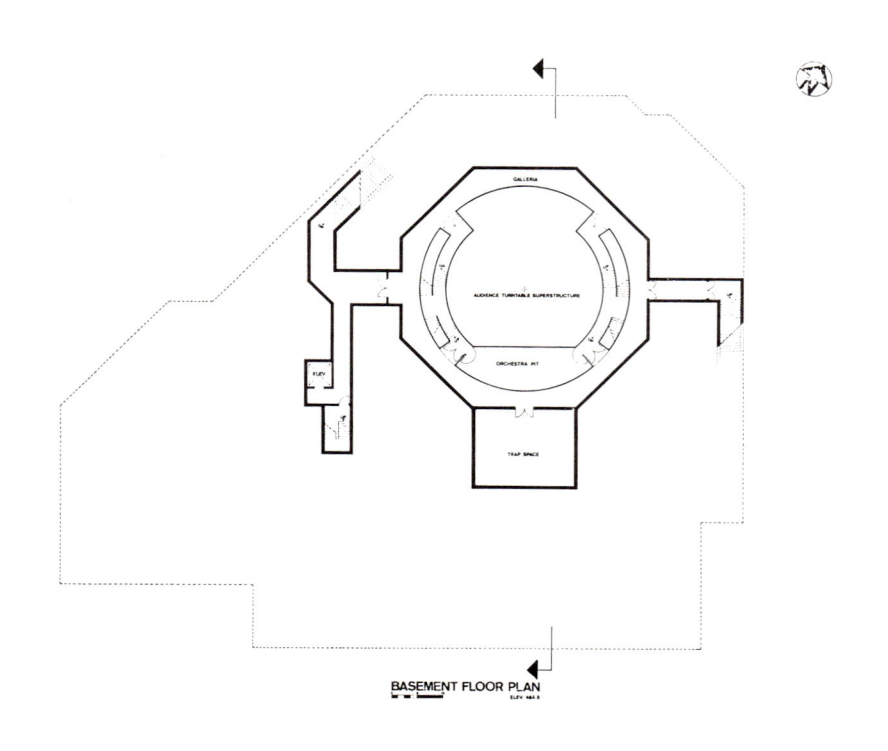

BASEMENT FLOOR PLAN

FIRST FLOOR PLAN

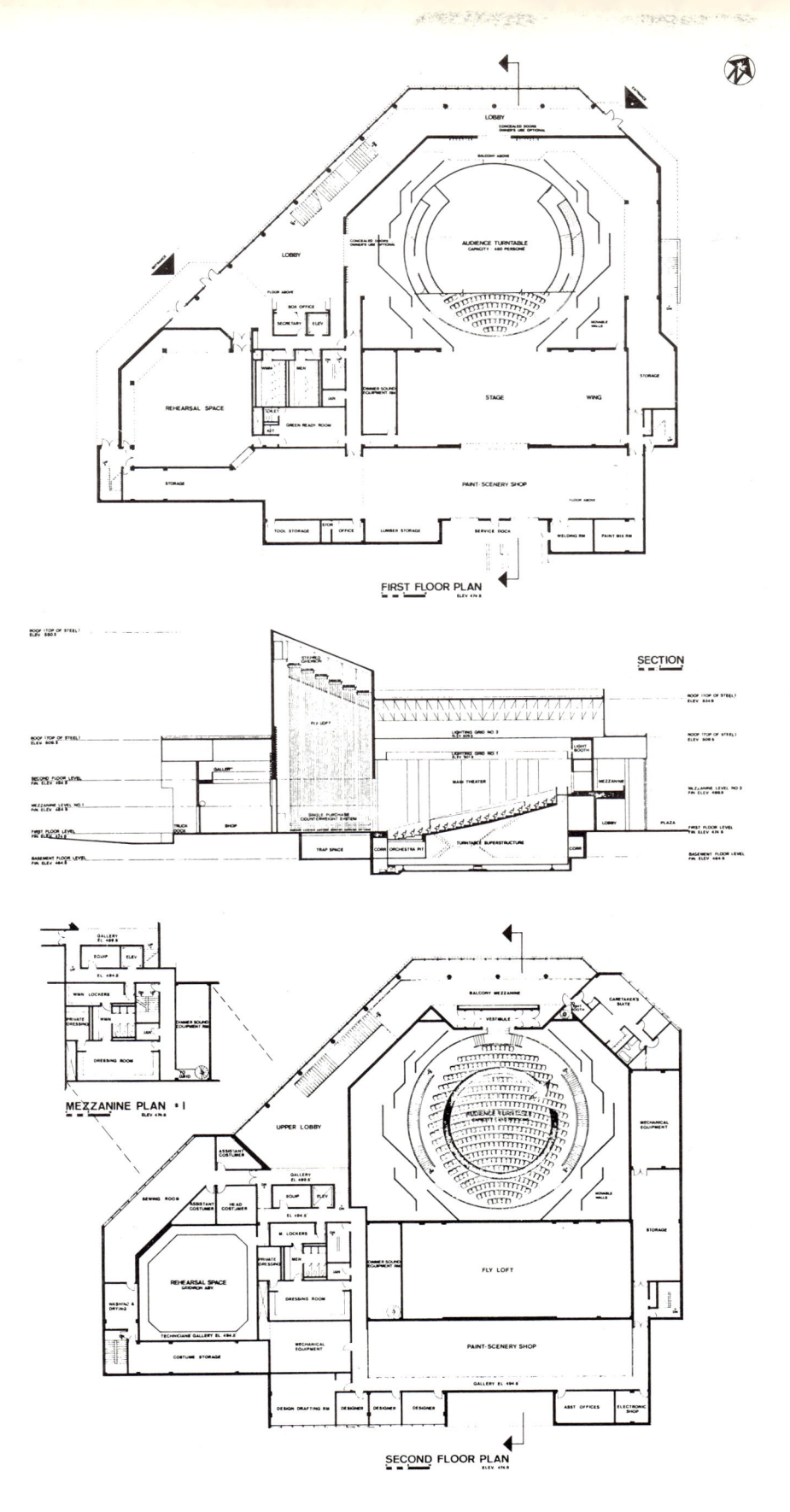

SECTION

MEZZANINE PLAN #1

SECOND FLOOR PLAN

Arena or Central Staging (page 129)

Despite the success of Arena Stage in Washington, this form has subsided among newly-built theatres. It appears as one of four theatres in Rarig Center at the University of Minnesota and continues as an option in any free-form theatre.

Multi- Stage

With stages on three or four sides of the seating area, this form was unique at Baylor University under Paul Baker, was imitated with the addition of balconies over the side stages at Denison University, and was reiterated by Baker in the Ruth Taylor Theatre at Trinity University, San Antonio.

New forms of theatres, some of which have been merely ideas for some time and others which have existed as unique examples are:

Surround Stage

See University of North Carolina, pp. 430-31.

Revolving Ring Stage

The audience is in a fixed seating bank and a ring stage moves, passing under the seat bank, and exposes scenes in sequence to the audience. There is no prototype of this form in the United States.

Multiform (pages 131–134)

In the Loeb Drama Center at Harvard University (1962), George Izenour applied electro-mechanization to change of form to produce, in a single space, four acceptable forms of theatre: proscenium, thrust stage, arena, and extended stage. The proscenium form is nearly conventional, the departures being two seating banks on hydraulic lifts in front of a cross aisle, and movable wall panels in place of what are, conventionally, splayed walls beside the proscenium. To make a thrust stage form, the lifts are brought to stage level which is also the floor level inside the wall panels, the panels are rolled back on overhead tracks, the seating banks are rotated 90 degrees and rolled into the spaces left by the panels. The tops of the lifts make the thrust stage. To make the arena form, the seating banks are rotated another 90 degrees and rolled onto the stage and portable seats are placed in the side spaces. The extended stage form is made with seating banks in proscenium-form position, the panels are rolled back and the side stages, thus opened, are used as acting areas.

A report on eleven years use of the Loeb Drama Center states that three-fourths of the productions are done in proscenium form, one-fourth in thrust stage form, and two or three in arena form, with no mention of use of the extended stage form.

The system, modified to omit the arena form and to make the structure simpler and the movements more efficient, has been designed into theatres at McAlister College, the University of New Mexico, and others.

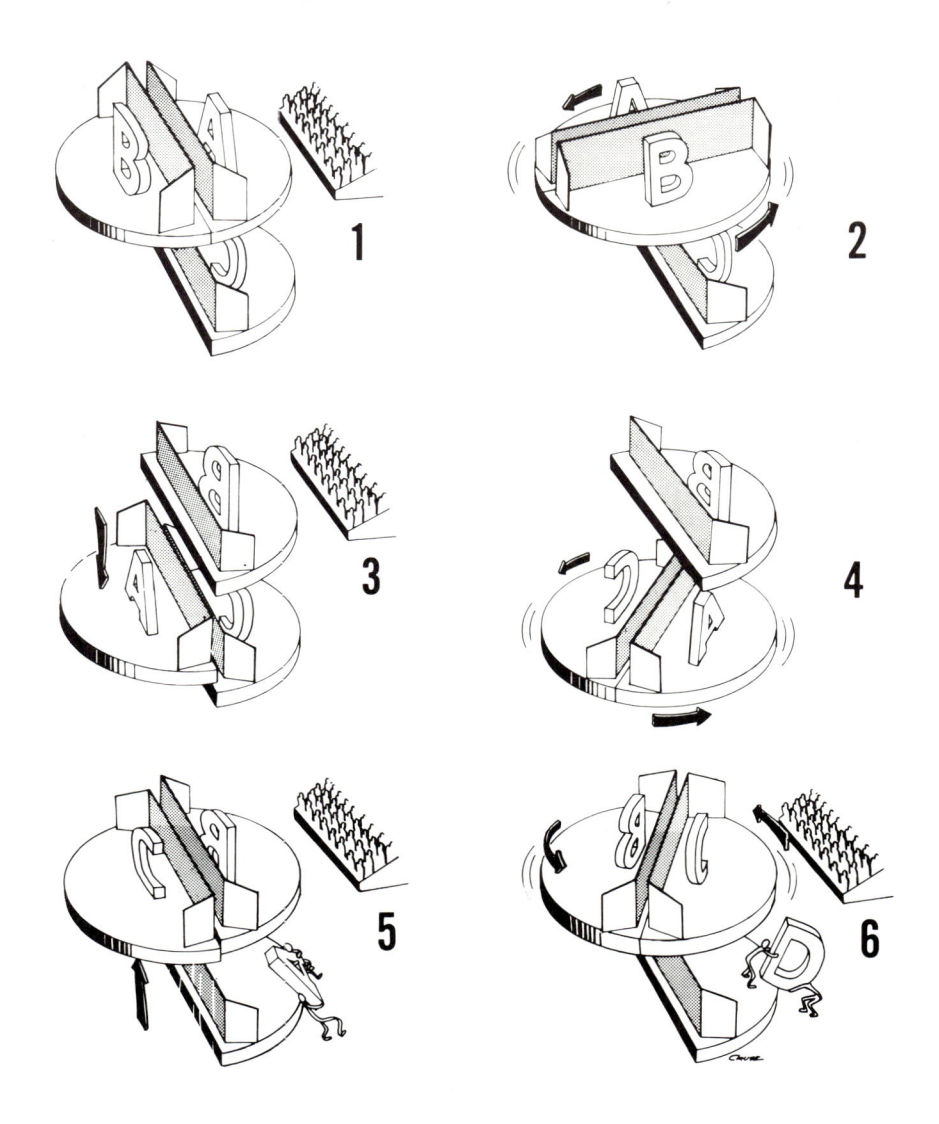

BIRMINGHAM–SOUTHERN COLLEGE THEATRE (1968). This theatre is certainly the most mechanized, probably the most illustrated, and one of the most discussed college theatres in the country, and the most thoroughly thought-out and unique system of changing scenes sequentially. Professor Arnold Powell, originator of the scheme, and chief user, has written a five-year retrospective appraisal of it in THEATRE DESIGN AND TECHNOLOGY, February 1974, in which he candidly states its chief fault, the slowness of both the elevator and the turntable, extolls its performance otherwise, and admits insufficient experimentation with the various performance-audience relationships that may be achieved by moving the forward seating banks onto the side stages. Though Professor Powell claims versatility in the system as adequate substitute for the absent flying system, it is to be noted that since the discs cannot carry scenery which must be hung and flown an essential part of stage technique is missing.

Revolving Stage-Discs, Lifts, and Movable Seating Sections

UNIVERSITY OF NEW MEXICO, NEW RODEY THEATRE. *This theatre has provision for change of form, ranging from proscenium with or without orchestra pit, to proscenium with side stages, to thrust stage with facility of flying over the thrust.*
Architect: William R. Buckley
Consultants: See Popejoy Hall

Free Form Theatres

Free form is defined as the capability to achieve a large variety of performance-audience relationships employing mechanical, electro-mechanical, or manned methods of altering the shapes and positions of the acting and seating areas. The ultimate of free-form is the division of the entire floor into modular sections each capable of being raised, and sometimes lowered; the overhead structure designed and equipped to facilitate lighting all areas and flying scenery, actors, and properties in conformity with whatever configuration is selected; and actors, and audience, entrances planned in similar conformity, usually embracing entrances at, or from above or below, the main-floor level.

Free-form theatres, simplified, have increased in number as teaching aids in secondary schools and, more fully developed, as experimental laboratories in colleges and universities. In a few instances the principal theatre of professional companies: the American Place Theatre in New York and the Lederer Theatre of the Trinity Square Players in Providence, R.I., are free-form theatres. Progress has been made in the mechanization and integrated systemization of the variation of floor form and seating, overhead grids for lighting and the flying of scenery and actors, and entrances of audiences and performers to the variable seating banks and acting areas.

A few theatres in the United States have embraced a form in which the entire floor of the theatre space (no proscenium) is divided into modular lifts.

The Theatre Room at the University of Texas has one electrical jack on a dolly, in the basement, which is used under one 10′ × 10′ floor section at a time and rolled from one to the next. Square-sectioned posts at the corners of each platform telescope into fixed hollow stanchions. Platform heights are variable in small increments and maintained simply by steel pins through holes in the posts at the tops of the stanchions.

The floor of the theatre at California Institute of the Arts is divided into 4′ × 4′ sections, each on a pneumatic-lift column. The hose of a single portable air compressor is manually connected to the air cylinder below the column and a manual valve is opened to send compressed air into the cylinder to raise the floor section. Positive positioning is achieved by the same pin-in-hole method as at the University of Texas. Vertical increments are 6 inches.

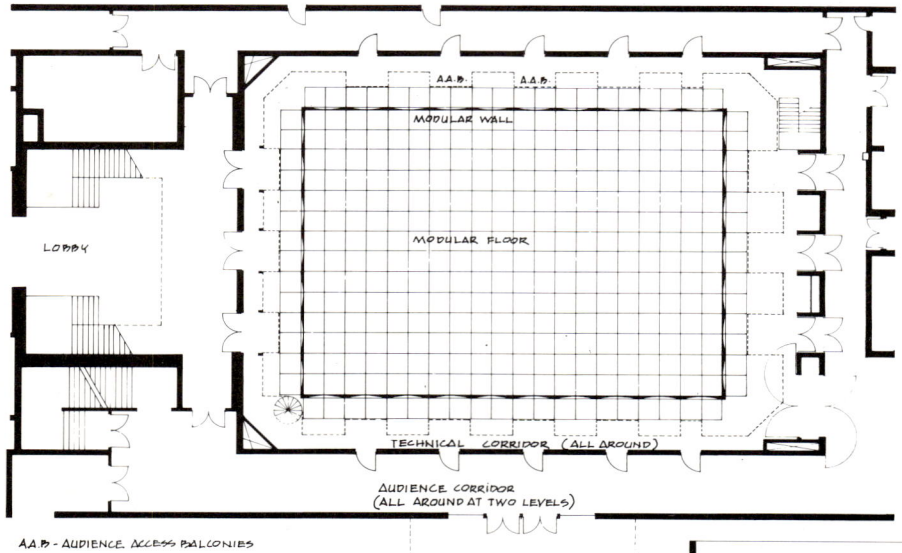

California Institute
of the Arts
Modular Theatre

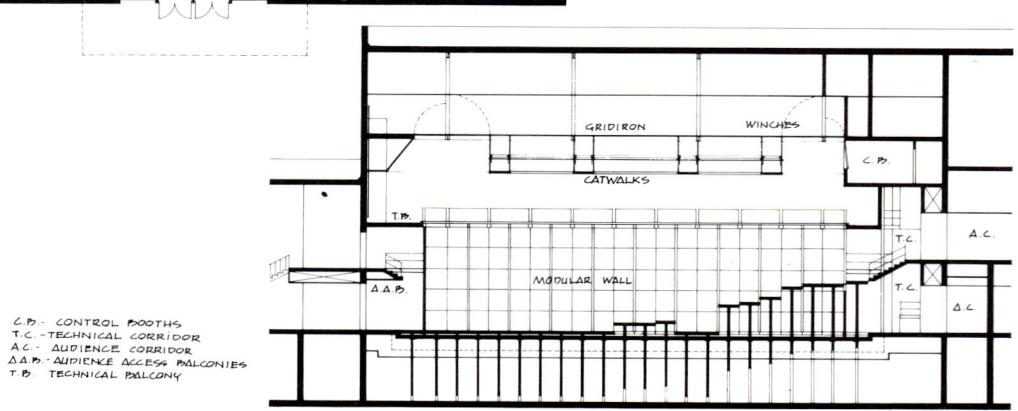

C.B. - CONTROL BOOTHS
T.C. - TECHNICAL CORRIDOR
A.C. - AUDIENCE CORRIDOR
A.A.B. - AUDIENCE ACCESS BALCONIES
T.B. - TECHNICAL BALCONY

CALIFORNIA INSTITUTE OF THE ARTS, MODULAR THEATRE. This theatre is the most thoroughly integrated free-form teaching theatre of all those studied. Its floor system relates to its wall-panel system and both relate to its audience traffic and working circulation. Its overhead systems for flying and lighting are adjustable to any performance-audience configuration that can be given to the floor and wall systems.

The modules are four-foot squares, into which both floor and walls are entirely divided. The floor lift system is described hereafter. The wall panels may be opened anywhere, vertically in combinations of the modules, and horizontally limited only by the hinging position. Thus actors may enter onto platforms at various levels and the audience may enter through openings made at floor or balcony levels according to the specially designed seating for a particular production.

The flying system uses Paul Birkle Sigma-pac portable winch units (see Technology: Flying Systems). Two concentric rectangular catwalks hung from the grid and the balcony surrounding the theatre afford multiple light-mounting positions capable of lighting acting areas anywhere in the theatre from a variety of directions.

An explicit, illustrated, description of this theatre is published in ARCHITECTURAL FORUM, April 1972.

Building Architects: Ladd and Kelsey
Theatre Designer: Jules Fisher, with Herbert Blau
Consulting Engineer for theatre systems: Olaf Sööt

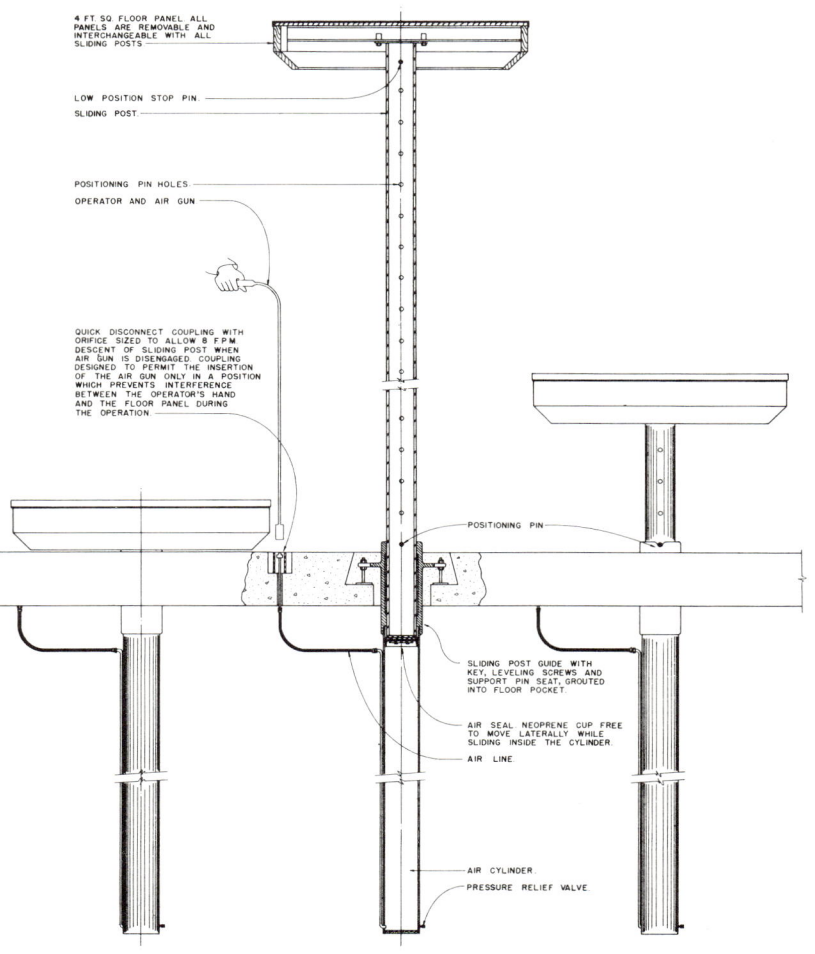

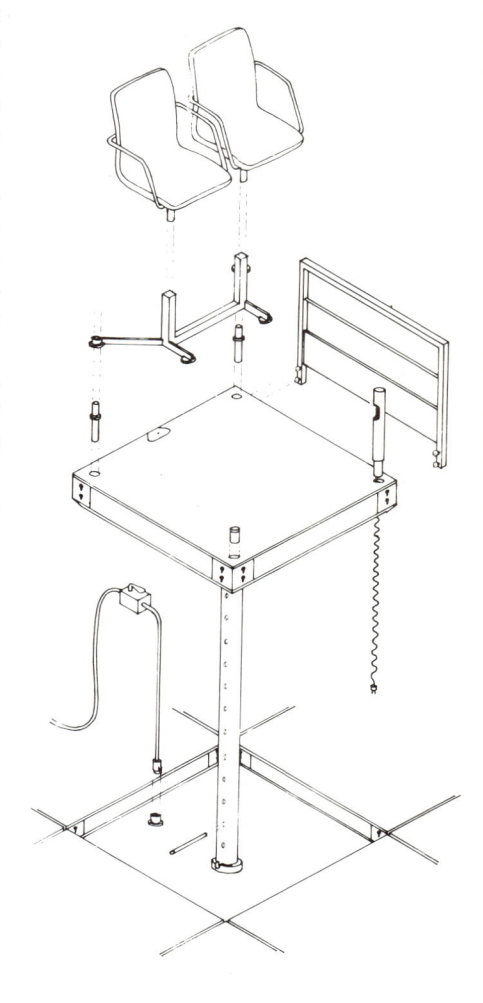

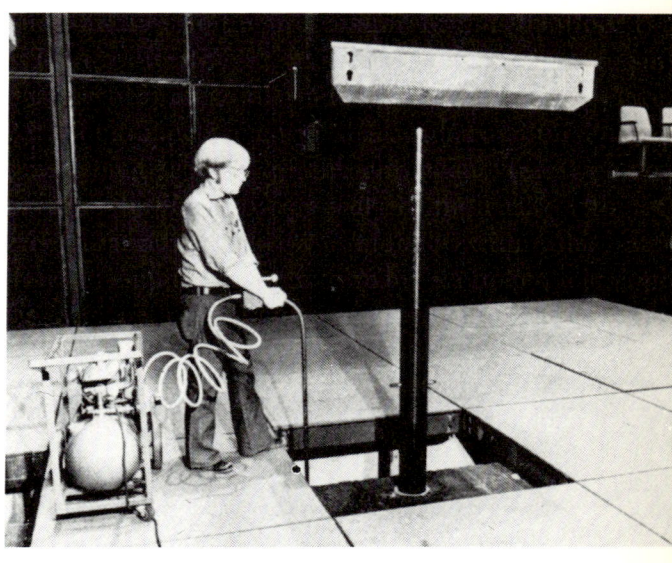

TECHNOLOGY

Flying Systems: Proscenium

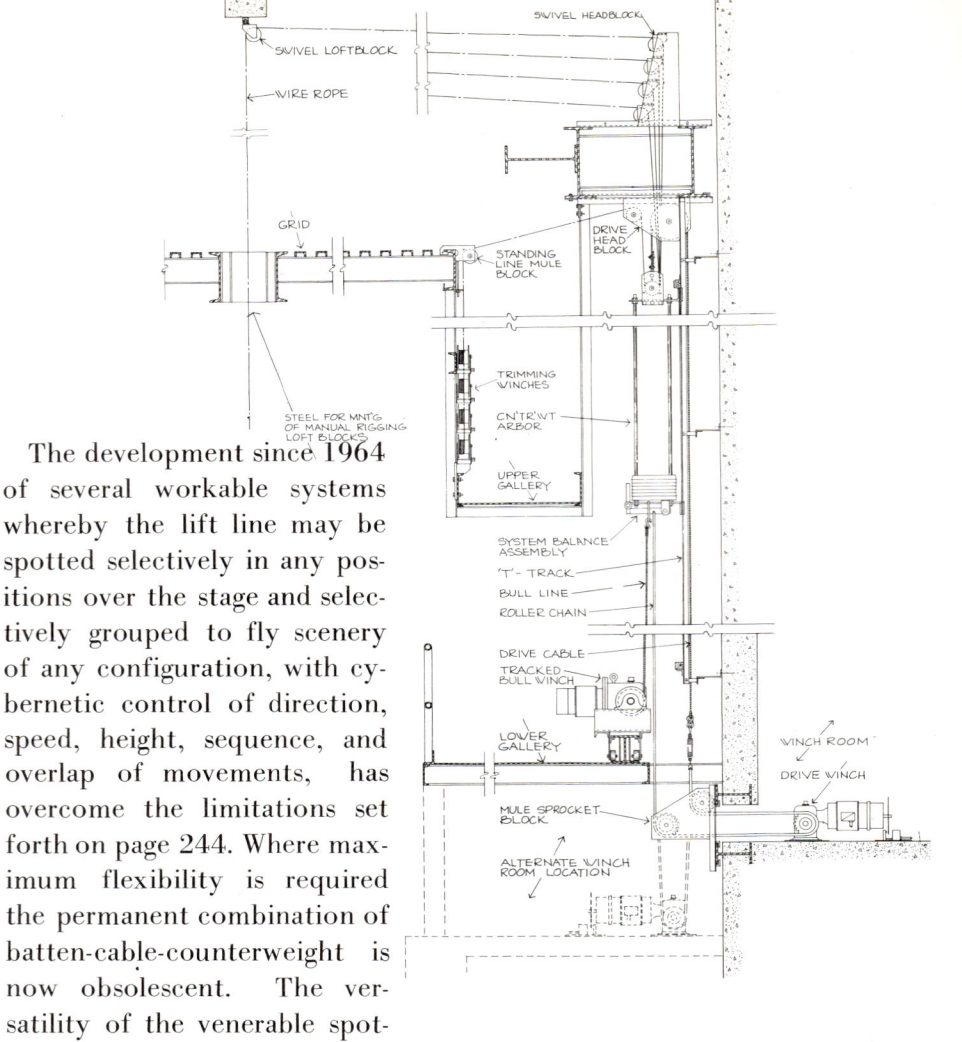

The development since 1964 of several workable systems whereby the lift line may be spotted selectively in any positions over the stage and selectively grouped to fly scenery of any configuration, with cybernetic control of direction, speed, height, sequence, and overlap of movements, has overcome the limitations set forth on page 244. Where maximum flexibility is required the permanent combination of batten-cable-counterweight is now obsolescent. The versatility of the venerable spotline system is achieved without the labor, unpredictability, and the hazard of hemp lines and sandbags.

George Izenour and his associates have developed and made several installations of a system whereby lift lines may be selectively spotted and individually trimmed though they are in groups permanently related to specific counterweight arbors. The arbors are motor-driven and the movement is telemetered to a control console. The scenery is thus balanced on one set of lines by a counterweight and the drive motor needs only enough power to move the balanced set; it will lock, immobile, if the set is not balanced.

Paul Birkle has developed, and the Peter Albrecht Corporation has made installations of, the Sigma-Pac system in which modular motor-winch units, each with no more than two lift lines, may be located anywhere on the grid, grouped for control by a patch panel, the lines attached to scenery of any configuration and trimmed, and the flying operation controlled as to speed, height and sequence at a remote console.

439

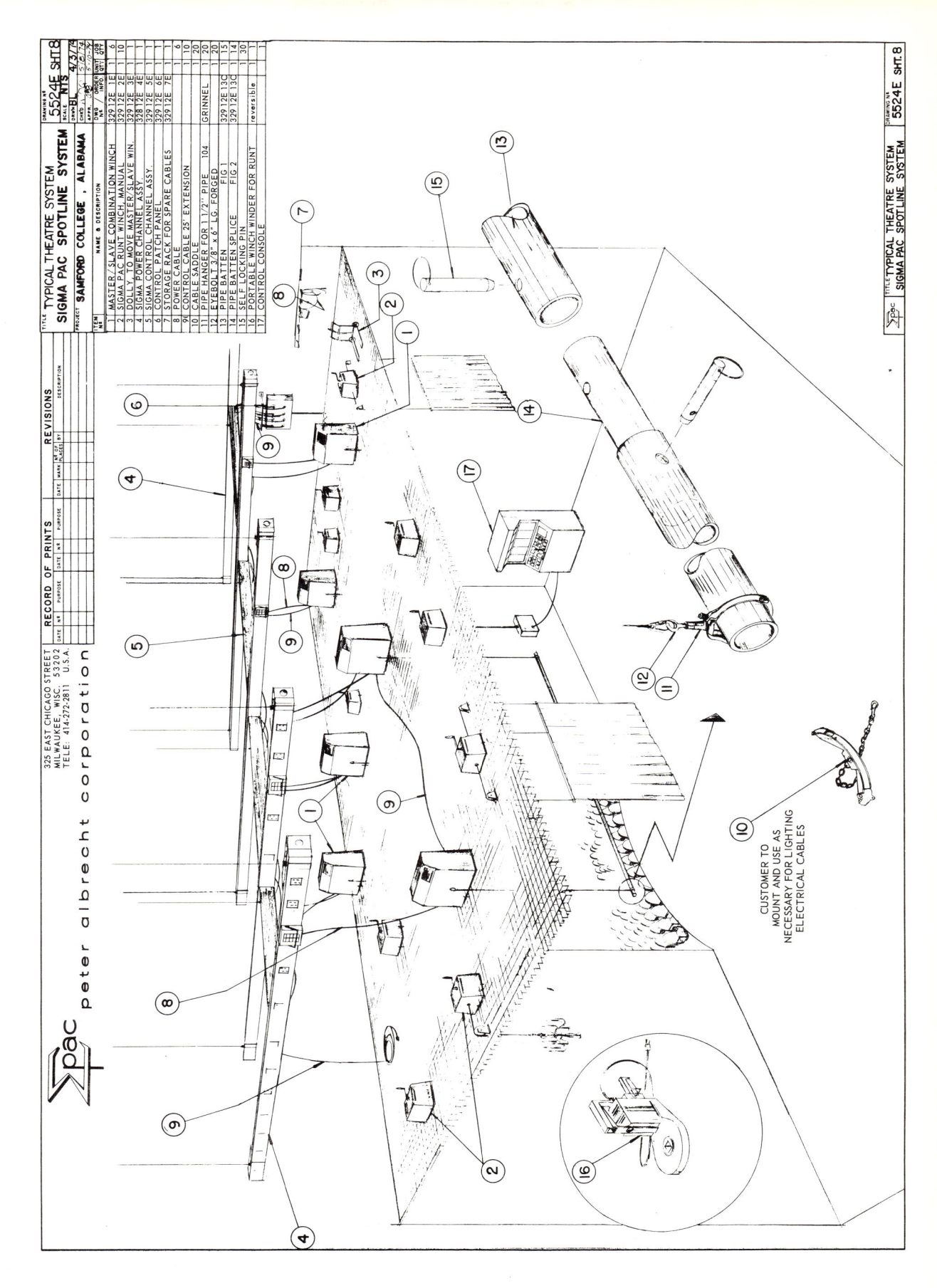

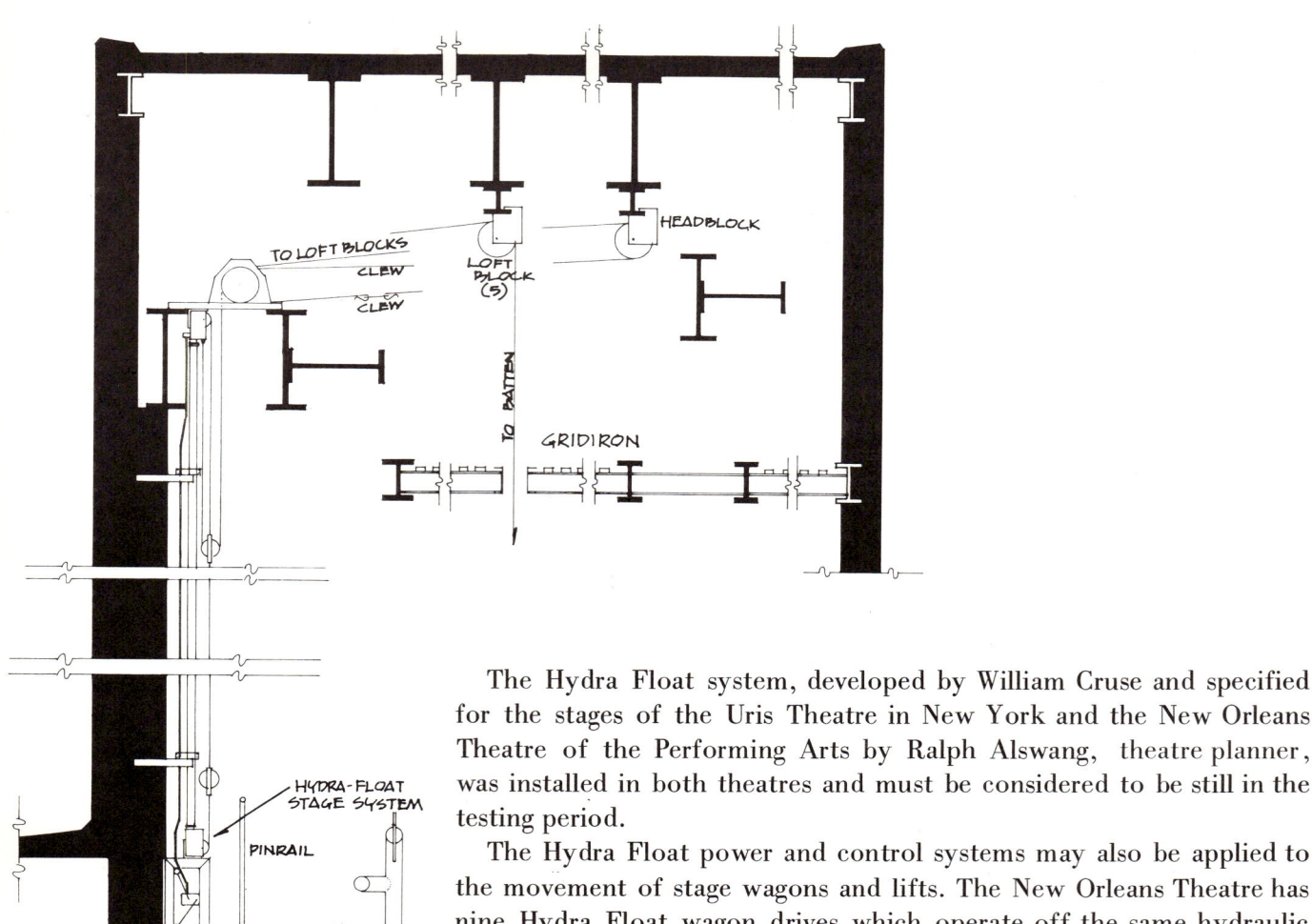

The Hydra Float system, developed by William Cruse and specified for the stages of the Uris Theatre in New York and the New Orleans Theatre of the Performing Arts by Ralph Alswang, theatre planner, was installed in both theatres and must be considered to be still in the testing period.

The Hydra Float power and control systems may also be applied to the movement of stage wagons and lifts. The New Orleans Theatre has nine Hydra Float wagon drives which operate off the same hydraulic power unit and six sections of orchestra lift draw their power from the same source. Thus motors for movement of scenery, stage wagons, orchestra lifts and, if desired, stage floor lifts are replaced by a single power source, and control of all the movement systems can be brought into one console.*

Flying Systems: Thrust, Arena, Free-Form

In proscenium theatres the entire overstage space has been developed into a complete mechanism to aid in the presentation of any kind of show. To date the spaces above the various forms of open stages have been restricted almost entirely to the placement of, access to, and operation of, lighting instruments. There is seldom adequate height for flying scenery without blocking the beams of spotlights, and there has been little attention to the theatrical values inherent in the flying of performers or objects during the progress of the show. Yet the significance and effectiveness of the great staircase in MAN OF LA MANCHA in the thrust-stage ANTA-Washington Square Theatre depended upon the possibility of installing special rigging over the thrust stage.

*THEATRE CRAFTS, March/April, 1970

In free-form theatres the presumption is that, since the acting and seating areas can be given any of a multitude of locations and configurations, it is necessary to be able to locate lighting instruments to light any location at sundry elevations throughout the whole space. It must also be assumed that actors, or pieces of scenery or furniture, might be lifted into the overhead space, an easily satisfied expectation on a proscenium stage. It is not so easily achieved when the locations of audience and performers are in no way limited. The only solutions are completely adjustable systems of stage lighting and flying equipment, accessible to working personnel. The desiderata are: random spotting of lift lines, random selective grouping of lines, adequate hoisting systems, height sufficient for the flown objects to clear spotlight beams, working access, and take-off and landing positions for Peter Pan or the Rhine maidens.

Movement of Scenery on Stage Floor: Air Casters

The compressed air system by which objects are lifted off the floor is new. The system bids fair to tranquilize all the betes noires that harrass the movement of scenery, platforms, and stage wagons about the stage floor on roller or ball- casters. The system has been used successfully at the University of California, Los Angeles.*

Projection

The carousel type of slide projector, used sometimes in its standard model and at other times modified as to lenses and controls, has become a useful instrument for front or rear projection of realistic or abstract effects onto stage screens. The super-8 and 16mm motion picture cameras and projectors put cinema techniques into the hands of live theatre artists; playwrights are writing film sequences, flashbacks, shock effects, any action they can make relevant, into play scripts with the expectation that the effects can be produced and introduced on cue.

Sophistication of projection control equipment makes possible rapid changes of multiple projections, either by programmed electronic memories or by manually-operated controls, so that projections may be synchronized with a varying performance tempo.

Josef Svoboda has become the virtually undisputed leader in the combination of advanced projection techniques and architectonic scenery, with surfaces to receive projection in many planes from front, back or sides, combining slides and film, even showing the projected moving image of an actor who will appear alternately on film and live on stage, in continuing action.

A production of I AND ALBERT at the Picadilly Theatre in London used 36 Kodak Carousels projecting from the rear onto eight screens.** I AND ALBERT was designed by Luciana Arrighi and executed by Theatre Projects.

The Delius opera, A VILLAGE ROMEO AND JULIET, was presented

---

* THEATRE DESIGN AND TECHNOLOGY, May 1970, 28-29.
** TABS, June 1973, 58-60.

at the Kennedy Center Opera House by the Washington Opera Society with still and moving projections. No better statement of the effectiveness of this kind of scenery can be made than that on the jacket of the Capitol album of the opera, from which the following excerpts are taken:

"The spell of the Delius music was heightened to an extra ordinary degree by the warm, glowing colors in the changing imagery of the projections. . . . Gone were the canvas trees, one-dimensional forests, painted skies, flat vistas, tons of lumber and hardware. In their place we were shown a production that could be transported altogether in a space about one five hundredth of that needed for conventional productions. . . ."

"This ten-minute interlude is the most well-known passage from the score and is performed in symphony programs under the title, 'The Walk to the Paradise Garden.' In opera performances it is intended to be played with a darkened stage and lowered curtain, but in Washington we saw the walk to the Paradise Garden. . . . We saw them as shadowy figures walking through a sylvan landscape of trees, flowers, streams, and wooded paths. Sometimes they would be lost to view and sometimes we saw them embrace, always surrounded with nature's magnificence. During the last two minutes of the interlude, the stage brightened again, and the real singers themselves were revealed approaching the Paradise Garden, the final scene of the tragic opera. This 'walk' was photographed in the parklands of Marin County, in northern California, and the filmed Sali and Vreli were, of course, models in the same Aldredge costumes worn by the singers."

Staging Associates, Ltd., of New York, made the slides and films and furnished the projection equipment. They have also done Delius' KONGA with the Washington group and the rock opera TOMMY with the Seattle Opera Association.

Modern theatres, in any form, may need spaces and placements for rear projection behind any position where a screen might be placed and for front projection from a number of positions in front of the scenery, as well as the conventional standard projection booth.

Acoustics: Sound

Audiences have learned to accept lighting units hung almost anywhere to assure visibility for the performer or anything else the director may want seen, and by and large the show is usually satisfactorily visible. Not so with sound, The days when performers could use both hands instead of holding one in front of the face to support a microphone are gone. Loudspeakers on both sides of the proscenium which guarantee the unintelligibility of speech while deafening the audiences are standard equipment in theatres where performers a generation ago made themselves clearly understood without electronic distortion.

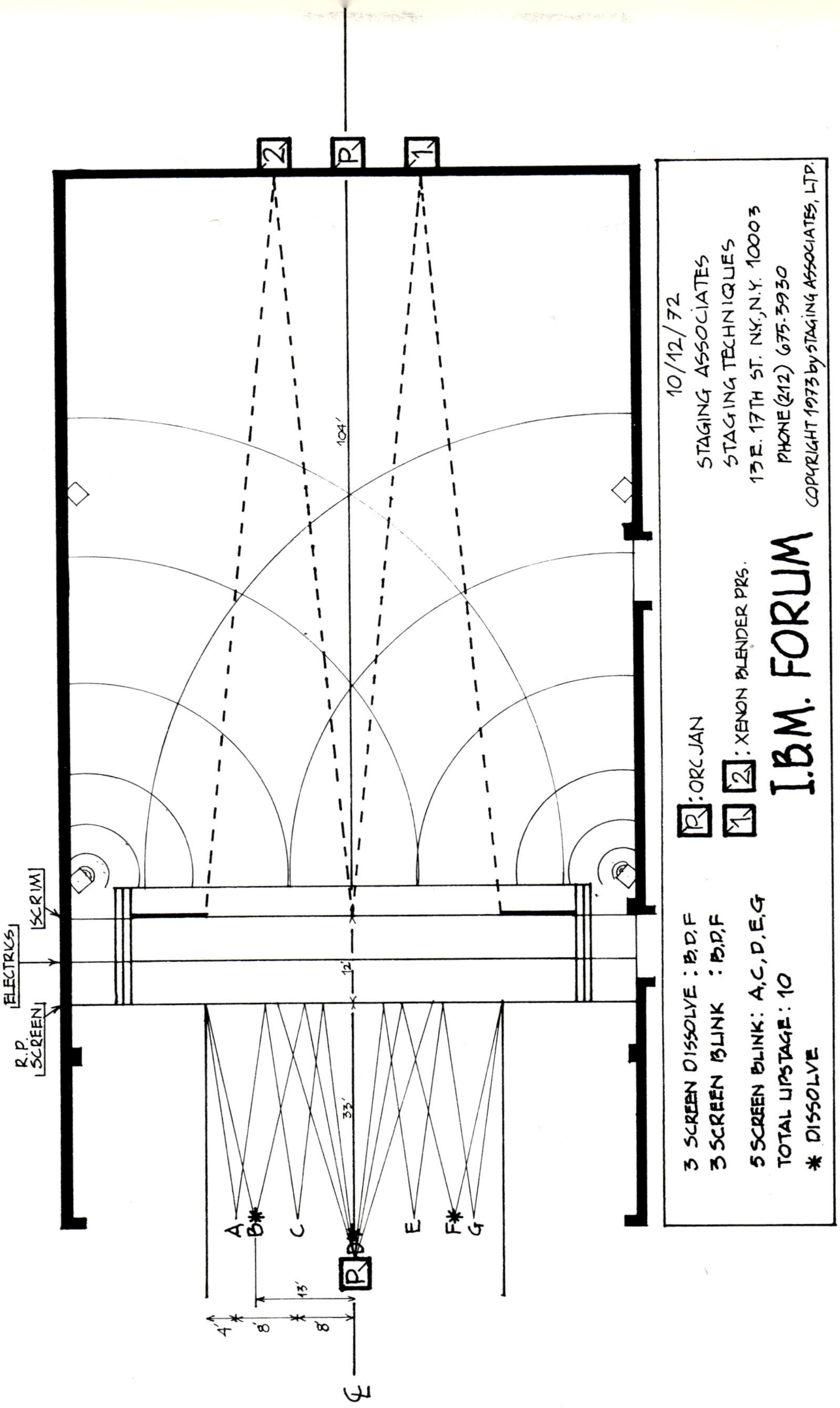

I.B.M. FORUM
P : ORC JAN
1 2 : XENON BLENDER PRS.
10/12/72
STAGING ASSOCIATES
STAGING TECHNIQUES
13 E. 17TH ST. NY., N.Y. 10003
PHONE (212) 675-3930
COPYRIGHT 1973 by STAGING ASSOCIATES, LTD.
3 SCREEN DISSOLVE : B,D,F
3 SCREEN BLINK : B,D,F
5 SCREEN BLINK : A,C,D,E,G
TOTAL LIPSTAGE : 10
✱ DISSOLVE
R.P. SCREEN
ELECTRICS
SCRIM
104'
12'
33'
13'
4'
8'
8'
A
B
C
D
E
F
G
P
1
2

With multiple forms for the theatre acoustical problems lurk in many places. A ceiling with many and/or wide, cuts for lights may act with the house as a pair of coupled spaces and lead to acoustical feedback. Parallel walls often engender standing waves. The actor on a thrust, or arena stage, cannot talk through the back of his head.

Every theatre of every type requires acoustical planning, as an integral part of architectural planning. To avoid acoustical disaster, the acoustical planner must know the theatre. He must plan the electronic reinforcement and sound control along with the architectural acoustical planning or trouble may result. David Klepper has published* a list of maximum sizes for theatres in which unamplified speech can be clearly understood if the architectural planning has been well done, viz:

unidirection	1800 seats maximum
thrust stage	1200 seats maximum
arena stage	450 seats maximum

These figures presuppose a more-than-ordinarily good speaking voice.

Audience partly or totally surrounding performance creates acoustical problems in that reflection of performance sound from the audience is much less than if it were reflected off rigid sidewalls or backwalls, because the audience is more sound-absorbent than walls. Thrust stage and arena seating banks are usually on about a 5/12 slope for sight line purposes and almost completely eliminate walls as reflectors of sound. The only available reflective surface in a thrust stage or arena theatre is the ceiling which must be broken for lighting and, at best, intercepts a very small portion of the sound wave, which it must then reflect in all directions over the spreadout seating area. The result is a very small, generally ineffective, reinforcement of the performance-created sound. In any case, the less conventional the form of the theatre, the more difficult becomes the acoustical problem. But it can be solved.

Control and Communication

Control systems and communication systems have multiplied and become more sophisticated than they were in 1964. The backstage control station (see illustration) of the Gusman Philharmonic Hall, a renovated film palace in Miami, Florida, contains one intercommunications system connecting all spaces in the building, another connecting to all technical operations locations: a lighting control board with cross-connect panel, controls for lifts and acoustic panels, a public address system, a smoke and fire detection alarm, a microphone jack panel, and closed circuit television camera connections and monitor, with the dimmer bank nearby (at the right rear of the picture). Compare this with 1964 examples illustrated on pages 154, 155, 302 and 304.

*THEATRE DESIGN AND TECHNOLOGY, Report of USITT Committee on Sound and Acoustics.

Safety

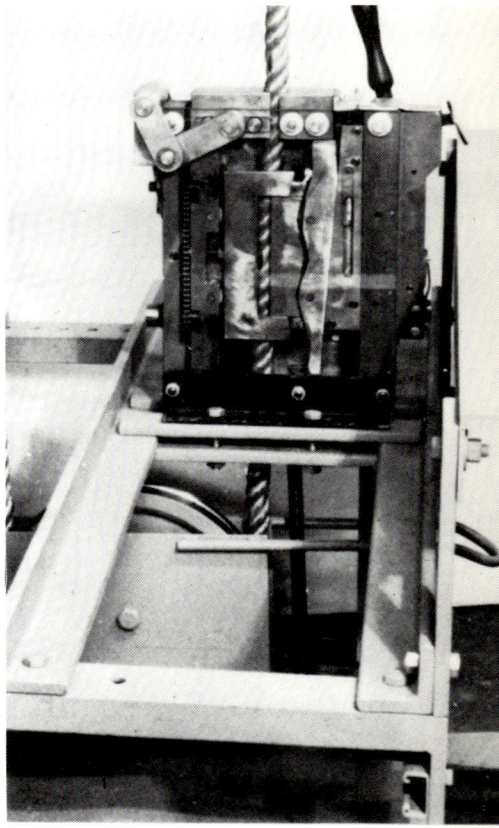

NIOSH. The U.S. Department of Health Education and Welfare has concerned itself with occupational safety and health by establishing the National Institute for Occupational Safety and Health (NIOSH). Its publications treat of industrial hazards. Stage machinery and scene construction in new materials, notably plastics, are the subjects of recommended safety procedures. The theatres should keep abreast of NIOSH's current publications.

Fail-Safe Rope Lock. Runaway counterweight sets which cause damage to equipment or scenery, injury to persons, and an occasional fatality may now be prevented by a fail-safe rope lock manufactured by Tiffin Scenic Studios. The rope lock will not release if the imbalance in the set is greater than the operator's pulling power and *unless* the operator has one foot on a treadle.

Production Services

Though there has been some progress in providing adequate spaces and equipment for the work of preparing productions and relating these to each other along the logical lines of flow from entrance door or delivery dock to the stage, these functions often appear to have been the last, or the least, considered in planning, and rendered subservient to other requirements as the first victims of budget cuts.

Scene Shops. A thorough study of shop operations and spaces required for them was made in 1970 and published in SCENERY FOR THE THEATRE, Second Edition, 1971. The Model A scene shop developed in this study measured 220 feet long and 76 feet wide. Professional shops, capable of processing the scenery for several New York productions simultaneously, require floor area equal to that of a football field, 300 × 100 feet. The total area of the shops of the new Slovak National Theatre in Bratislava, a repertory organization, is 365 × 92 feet.*

The developed application of many new techniques to scene and costume production has necessitated speciality shops for work in metal, fiberglass, thermoplastics, and foam-produced plastics, with equipment, ventilation and space adequate to each specialty, all logically related to the overall assembly process.

CAVEATS

Accompanying the elaboration and use of electronic and electro-mechanical, pneumatic and hydraulic devices in the theatre there is a dual and basic obligation upon the user: inspection and maintenance. This is seldom mentioned, or even hinted, during the planning and design conferences prior to contract and construction, nor in promotional literature. Caveat emptor is a cogent principle in this situation. Guarantees and warrantees have limitations as to both responsibilities and time. The acceptance test of a building and equipment is made when both are in conformity with the contract documents. The client must demand, incisively, a statement of the recommended interval between inspections or replacements of parts, and probable costs of maintenance. If, after obtaining this information, the client does not foresee the sure capability of meeting these costs on a regular budgeted basis he should beware of acquiring equipment requiring such care.

He should, furthermore, realize that effective operation of much of the recently developed, sophisticated apparatus can only be done by trained, possibly scarce, and probably high-salaried personnel. He should establish a firm policy of absolute prohibition against well-meaning but ignorant tinkering.

Theatre being labor-intensive even when a production is prepared, installed, and presented in a theatre with a rigid single form, any change of form in a multi-form or free-form theatre adds labor in proportion to the complexity of the changes. If mechanization is added to reduce

*THEATRE DESIGN AND TECHNOLOGY, No. 20, February 1970

labor it must be reliable over a long period of time. Breakdowns which cancel or interrupt performances are anathema to both management and audience.

Fascination with mechanical aids may dull the perception that though a motor company can call back thousands, even millions, of cars to correct a fault, faults in the design, structure, and heavy equipment of a building cannot be so readily rectified.

This is in no sense a diatribe against technological sophistication in the theatre; it has been too long coming. If complex equipment is properly designed and installed, operated and maintained only by qualified personnel and utilized to something approaching its maximum capabilities, at least sometimes, by the designers, directors, playwrights and other conceptualizers, it merits acquisition.

The manufacturer-dealer-installer should supply operation and maintenance manuals, written in understandable language with technical terms translated into dictionary English and with adequate diagrams.

IN SUMMARY

The preceding text has attempted to state some of the accomplishments in theatre building since 1964, following the outline and referring to pages of the 1964 edition.

It is perhaps appropriate to end with a resume of the salient accomplishments and failures of the decade.

Many architects and some professional engineers have shown increased understanding of the demands which the total theatre phenomenon exerts upon the design of the theatre building. There is a growing number of capable theatre consultants who base counsel to both clients and architects on sound knowledge of functional requirements, of technological advances, of economics of theatre operation, and on a firm dedication to the purpose of producing good theatres. There are fewer evidences of wrong thinking, fadism, or subservience to irrelevant design factors, such as an abstract-geometric ground-plan, fashionable rooflines, or a monumentally impressive exterior into which functional spaces are squeezed in procrustean fashion. This latter observation is a matter of gratification to the authors who are delighted that though Procrustes still has some influence he seems only to be alive and well and living in Sydney, Australia. Theatres illustrating this fault have been intentionally omitted. With limited space the decision was made to show only examples with a predominance of good features.

There is evidence of careful and thorough programming of theatre plants, starting with statements of intended use, feasibility studies and detailed analysis of theatrical desiderata; recognition of these as the prime determinants; schematic graphing of functional and spacial relationships, and finally, planning from the inside out.

Features which have been increasingly evident are adequate provision for audiences in lobbies, lounges, easily accessible and comfortable seats, and good sightlines; light slots in ceilings and sidewalls with easy access thereto; lighting and sound control rooms out-front and in favored viewing and hearing positions; forestage/orchestra pit elevators subdivided for flexible arrangement and variety of use, including a semblance of thrust stage; adequate stage space, frequently with provision for full-stage wagon storage at the sides; thrust stages with provisions for setting and changing scenery and storing it backstage.

Weaknesses noted with sufficient frequency to warrant mention and regret are: theatres with inadequate seating capacity, inadequate sizes and illogical arrangement of production service spaces, in relation to each other and to the stage, often resulting from site limitations but sometimes from overemphasis on public spaces versus working spaces; lack of adequate working circulation to all work-spaces separate from audience areas; lack of flexibility in stage floor arrangements, i.e. traps and/or lifts; lack of provisions for flying scenery, objects or actors over the forestage, thrust, or arena stages; lack of side-stages (extended stage) in proscenium theatres, or if they exist, inadequacies as to area, lighting and scenery handling capabilities, and limited access for actors.

On balance, the achievements appear to exceed the misdeeds by a large measure.

AFTER THOUGHTS

The Metropolitan Opera House, where it is referred to in the 1964 text, is the "old Met" which was located on Broadway south of Times Square and is no more. The Metropolitan Opera Company is in its new home, the focal building of Lincoln Center (p. 159) with modern and effective accomodations for all aspects of preparing and presenting grand opera.

The Theatre for Carnegie Institute of Technology (p. 349) was not built. The project of new facilities for the School of Fine Arts of the, now, Carnegie-Mellon University is undergoing further study.

Reference materials and credits

In the considerable literature on the theatre, the following publications are perhaps the most authoritative and useful in theatre planning.

Bowman, Ned, and Engel, Glorianne, compilers. *Recent Publications on Theatre Architecture.* Theatre Architecture Project of the American Educational Theatre Association, Department of Speech and Theatre Arts, University of Pittsburgh. A continuing bibliography, uncritical but extensive, which lists all periodical articles on theatre architecture as well as newly published books.

Burris-Meyer, Harold, and Cole, Edward C. *Scenery for the Theatre.* Boston: Little, Brown and Co., 1938, 2nd Edition 1971

Burris-Meyer, Harold, and Goodfriend, Lewis S. *Acoustics for the Architect.* New York: Reinhold Publishing Corp., 1957.

Burris-Meyer, Harold, and Mallory, Vincent. *Sound in the Theatre.* Mineola, N.Y.: Radio Magazines, Inc., 1959.

Gillette, Arnold S. *Stage Scenery: Its Construction and Rigging.* New York: Harper and Brothers, 1959.

Gruver, Bert. *The Stage Manager's Handbook.* New York: Drama Books, 1962.

Knudsen, Vern O., and Harris, Cyril M. *Acoustical Designing in Architecture.* New York: John Wiley and Sons, 1950.

Kranich, Friedrich. *Bühnentechnik der Gegenwart.* Munich and Berlin: Verlag von R. Oldenbourg, 1933.

McCandless, Stanley R. *A Method of Lighting the Stage,* 4th ed. New York: Theatre Arts Books, 1958.

Parker, W. Oren, and Smith, Harvey K. *Scene Design and Stage Lighting.* New York: Holt, Rinehart and Winston, Inc., 1963, 3rd Edition 1974

Rubin, Joel E., and Watson, Leland H. *Theatrical Lighting Practice.* New York: Theatre Arts Books, 1954.

Sabine, Hale J. *Less Noise—Better Hearing.* Chicago: The Celotex Corp., 1941.

Theil, Hans Wolfram. *Saalbau.* Munich: Verlag Georg D. W. Callwey, 1959.

CATALOGS:

Clancy catalog, *Stage Equipment Catalog,* J. R. Clancy, Inc., Syracuse, N.Y.

Century catalog, *Century Theatre Lighting,* Century Lighting, Inc., New York, N.Y.

Kleigl catalog, *Theatrical Lighting,* Kleigl Bros., New York, N.Y.

Vasconcellos catalog, *Stage Equipment Catalog,* Joseph Vasconcellos, Inc., West Babylon, N.Y.

SUPPLEMENTARY POST-1964 BIBLIOGRAPHY FOR CHAPTER 16

Baumel, William J. and Bowen, William G., *Performing Arts: The Economic Dilemma.* New York: Twentieth Century Fund, 1966.

Burris-Meyer, Harold, and Cole, Edward C. *Scenery for the Theatre* 2nd ed., revised. Boston and Toronto: Little, Brown and Company, 1971.

Drexler, Arthur, (Ed.) *Architecture for the Arts: The State University of New York College at Purchase.* New York, The Museum of Modern Art, 1971.

Gard, Robert, Balch, Marston, and Tompkin, Pauline B. *Theatre in America.* Madison, Wisconsin: Dembar Educational Research Services, 1968.

Gatton, James B. and Deering, Francis R. *The People Place: A Study of Civic and Convention Centers.* Houston: Caudill, Rowlett and Scott, 1970.

Illinois, University of, Foundation and Inland Container Corporation: *The Krannert Center for the Performing Arts.* Hannibal, Missouri: Western Publishing Co. (n.d.)

Mielziner, Jo. *The Shapes of our Theatre.* New York: Clarkson H. Potter, 1970.

The New York City Record. *Building Code of the City of New York.* City Record Office, Municipal Building, New York. December 6, 1968.

New York State Education Department and Educational Facilities Laboratories. *Facilities for the Performing Arts: Proceedings of Fifth Annual Conference on College Facilities.* Office of Administration Services in Higher Education, Albany, 1967.

Nicoll, Allardyce. *The Development of the Theatre* 5th ed. revised. London, Harrap, 1966.

OISTT Commission of Architects. *Social, Cultural Facilities, Multi-purpose Halls, Flexible Theatres (especially Master plan; pre-architectural study for convention/performing arts/ parking* at Denver, Colorado, 1972). Avignon, 1973.

Parker, W. Oren, and Smith, Harvey K. *Scene Design and Stage Lighting* 3rd ed. revised. New York: Holt, Reinhart and Winston, 1974.

Robertson, Horace W. *Architecture for the Educational Theatre.* Eugene; University of Oregon Books, 1969.

Rockefeller Brothers Fund Panel. . *The Performing Arts: Problems and Prospects.* New York: McGraw-Hill, 1965.

Rosenthal, Jean, and Wertenbaker, Lael. *The Magic of Light.* Boston and Toronto: Little, Brown and Co., in association with Theatre Arts Books, 1972.

Silverman, Maxwell. *Contemporary Theatre Architecture: An Illustrated Survey.* New York. New York Public Library, 1965.

State University of New York, College at Purchase, Office of Facilities Director: *Facility Program for Performing Arts Center, 1968.* (Unpublished)

U.S. Office of Education Bureau of Research. *Recommendations for Secondary and Tertiary School Theatre Space and Equipment.* Project No. 5-8290, Contract No. OE-6-10-025. Washington, 1966.

Multi-media

The Theatre Orientation Package. United States Institute of Theatre Technology. Commission on Theatre Architecture. New York, 1973.

Periodicals

Architectural Record, McGraw-Hill, Inc., New York

Bühnentechnische Rundschau. Verlag: Klasing and Co. Berlin, 1907 — .

Planning for Higher Education. Society for College and University Planning, in association with Education Facilities Laboratories. New York, 1972 — Campus Theatre in Found Space (in Vol. 3, No. 1)

Progressive Architecture. New York, 1947 — .

TABS. Rank Strand Electric Ltd. London. 1957 — .

Theatre Crafts. Emmaus, PA. Rodale Press, Inc., 1967 — .

Theatre Design and Technology. Journal of the United States Institute of Theatre Technology, New York, 1965 — .

CREDITS

(Credits for pictures on one page are in sequence from top to bottom separated by commas and from left to right separated by hyphens.)

8, 13, Graphic Industries, Ltd.
14, 15, 16, Wide World Photos, Inc.
19, Adrian Bouchard
20, Thomas L. Williams
24, William E. Davis
25, Larry Obsitnik
26, Cosmo-Sileo
27, George E. Joseph
29, Florence J. Beckers
32, Korab
38, Andrew Smith of Panda
39, Friedman-Abeles
40, Federal Aviation Agency
49, drawing by Robert E. Costello, Jr.
54, Bob Serating
55, James Y. Young
57, Korab
58, Adrian Bouchard
60, 62, Wide World Photos, Inc.
78, 81, from LESS NOISE—BETTER HEARING by Hale J. Sabine, published by the Celotex Corporation.
80, Judy Cohen
82, University of Connecticut Photographic Laboratory
84, Feature Four, Ltd.
86, Mike Myers
88, Ann Evry
90, Bob Serating
91, Adrian Bouchard
92, Panda Photography
93, Ann Evry
95, 96, Adrian Bouchard
97, Harold Burris-Meyer, Roderick MacArthur
98, Andrew Smith of Panda, Joseph Mazza
99, Ann Evry, James Y. Young
101, Will Weisberg
102, Korab
103, Panda
104, Bob Serating
105, Panda, Adrian Bouchard, Ann Evry
106, Adrian Bouchard
131, Daniel Frasnay
133, Roland Thompson (3)
138, Korab
140, Duff Johnston

144, 150, James Y. Young
151, Robert J. Graham
152, Cosmo-Sileo
154, Edward C. Cole
155, South Florida University Public Relations Office
159, Cosmo-Sileo
160, Ann Evry
169, South Florida University Public Relations Office
170, Robert J. Graham
180, 182, 184, A. Burton Street
189, Wallace Dace
195, Elemer Nagy (2)
196, Korab
225, South Florida University Public Relations Office
229, Robert J. Graham
234, McManus
242, 243, Edward C. Cole
252, Cosmo-Sileo
258, Duff Johnston
265, James Y. Young
269, Edward C. Cole, Gene Campbell
270, Gene Campbell, Edward C. Cole
277, 278, Frank H. Bauer
279, James Y. Young
280, Vincent A. Finnegan
282, Bud Leske—Vincent A. Finnegan
283, Edward C. Cole
290, Harold Burris-Meyer
293, Gene Campbell
298, Vedel's Reklame-Foto
304, Edward C. Cole
306, Frank H. Bauer
309, 315, Impact Photos, Inc.
318, Harold Burris-Meyer
324, Lewis S. Goodfriend
326, Gene Campbell
329, Adrian Bouchard
330, Ann Evry
331, Stan Rivera
340, drawing by Richard Leacroft
346, drawings by Robert Stewart; photos: Stevens Izenour
347, Stevens Izenour
353, Bowdoin College Photographer
367, Panda Associates

452

SUPPLEMENTARY PHOTO CREDITS FOR CHAPTER 16

379, Moore's Studio, Inc.
380, 381, Studio Two
383, Akron University News Service
385, Martha Holmes
387, San Diego State University Audio-Visual Services
389, Bob Kalmbach
390, University of Minnesota Photo Laboratories, Jay Harlem Studio
392, Ohio State University Photo Services
394, Walt Burton
399, Jeremiah O. Bragstad
401, Frank Armstrong, News and Information Service, University of Texas, Austin
402, 403, Bill Watkins, Florida Atlantic Photographic Laboratory
406, John Whiteside (top three), John Shunny
408, Rapson
409, Hastings, Willinger and Associates
412, 413, Gordon Daniels
416, 417, Louis Checkman
421, Clyde W. Blakeley
423, Jose Toro
424, Wilson H. Brownell
425, 445, Rachline Studio
427, Arax-Serjian Studios
434, Bob Dauner
435, Mears
436, Jules Fisher
437, Tom Brosterman
445, (Rope lock) Brühl Studio

ACKNOWLEDGMENTS

For assistance in procurement of illustrations (by pages):

8, 13, 44, 367, Fred Lebensold
14, 15, 16, 62, 98, City Investing Company, Robert Dowling and Alfred Ilch
18, 344, Educational Facilities Laboratories, Ford Foundation
19, 58, 91, 95, 96, 105, 106, 140, 154, 242, 243, 269, 270, 283, 304, 329, 334-35, 339, Dartmouth College, Hopkins Center for the Arts, Warner Bentley, John Scotford, Robert Donnelly and Jerome Hanley, and Dartmouth College Photographic Services.
20, 21, William and Mary College, James P. James, Jr., and Roger Sherman.
22, Carl Duval Cress, Jr.
23, Irving Bowman
24, Joseph H. Carner
25, *Arkansas Gazette* and Joseph H. Carner
23, 139, 152, 159, 252, 286, 292, 309, 315, Radio City Music Hall and Edward Serlin
27, New York Shakespeare Festival and Hilmar Salles
29, Don Sundquist
32, 33, 57, 102, 138, 196, Arena Stage, Zelda Fichandler, and Lawrence Bahler
36, The Stardust Inn
38, 84, 92, 98, 103, 105, 109, The O'Keefe Centre for the Performing Arts and Hugh P. Walker
39, American Shakespeare Festival Theatre and Academy
40, Federal Aviation Agency
43, W. L. Pereira
45, 358, Welton Becket and Associates and John C. Knight
46, 54, 90, 104, 110, 359, Wallace Harrison, Max Abramovitz, and Walter Colvin
47, 56, Howard and Thorn and Edwin L. Howard
50, 134, Holien and Buckley and Edward O. Holien
55, 99, 144, 150, 151, 170, 229, 265, 279, 331, University of Hawaii, John Fitzgerald Kennedy Theatre of the East-West Center, Joel Trapido.
66, Björn Hedvall
82, University of Connecticut Public Relations Office
86, 135, 155, 167, 225, 243, 346, 347, 349, George C. Izenour
88, 93, 99, 105, 160, 330, Howard University and Hilyard Robinson
97, Cinema 2
97, American National Theatre and Academy
101, The Waldorf-Astoria and Edward M. Seay
119, Demuth Development Corporation and N. L. Demuth
122, 235, 317, Amherst College, Kirby Memorial Theatre
131, The Lido, Paris, and Robert Rouzard
133, Denison University and Edward Wright
140, 258, 267, Kliegl Brothers, Inc. and Joel Rubin
141, 285, Virginia Museum of Fine Arts Theatre
141, University of Oregon and Horace Robinson
142, 145, Middlebury University, Eric Volkert and Chandler A. Potter

453

143, James M. Hunter
180, 182, 184, Yale University School of Drama
183, Garson Kanin and David Pardoll
189, Wallace Dace
195, Elemer Nagy
222, 237, Joseph Vasconcellos, Inc.
230, 239, 246, 249, J. R. Clancy, Inc.
234, Plymouth Cordage Company
253, Williams College, Adams Memorial Theatre
266, 268, 275, 276, 280, 282, Century Lighting, Inc., Edward F. Kook and Charles Levy
269, 270, 293, 326, Sweet Briar College, Peter Daniel, and Wallace Dace
277, 278, 282, 306, Ward Leonard Electric Company, Stephen Skirpan, and Richard Thompson
289, 290, from SOUND IN THE THEATRE by Burris-Meyer and Mallory published by Radio Magazines, Inc.
298, Telefunken Aktiengesellschaft and Jüncke Oberdieck

324, Lewis S. Goodfriend and Associates
328, University of Kansas and Lewin Goff
333, Temple University and Paul Randall
336-337, University of California, Los Angeles, Jack Morrison, and *Educational Theatre News*
340, James Hull Miller and Albert M. Koga
343, Horace Robinson
344, Leonard Quann
353, Bowdoin College and William H. Moody

For giving information and for being generally helpful:

Alex Alden, Leo Delsasso, Fred Fuelling, E. Lawrence Goodman, Jack L. Hartman, Philip King, Robert Ludlum, Richard G. Preeble, and Lyle Yerges.

SUPPLEMENTARY ACKNOWLEDGEMENTS FOR CHAPTER 16

374, 440, Ralph Alswang
375, Larry Riddle, Joseph Bok Mitchell, J. Bok Enterprises, Inc.
376, Vincent Sardi, Jr., Michael Hotopp, Paul de Pass
377, Toombs, Amisano, and Wells, Architects, Little, Brown and Co.
378, 379, William C. Harris, A.I.A.
380, 381, Trevor P. Garwood-Jones, Architect, Russell Johnson, B. Harry Lennard, Vincent Piacentini, Jr.
382, 383, Clinton E. Norton, Managing Director, Edwin J. Thomas Performing Arts Hall, University of Akron
384, 385, Wynn Handman, Kert F. Lundell (drawings)
387, 388, Don W. Powell, William Hertner
389, University of Michigan Information Service, R. Craig Wolf, Ralph P. Beebe; P. Kinsella of Kevin Roche, John Dinkeloo and Associates
390, 391, Kenneth Graham, Wendell Josal, Kay M. Lockhart, Ralph Rapson, FAIA, and Associates
392, 393, John A. Walker, W. Alan Kirk
394, University of Cincinnati Information Office, and College-Conservatory of Music, Steven Waxler
395-397, University of Illinois Foundation; The Krannert Center for The Performing Arts, Michael Brotman, Director, Bill Nash, Building Superintendent; Peter Franklin-White
398, 399, Paul Baker
400, 401, E.D. Walker, Deputy Chancellor; Peter Garvie, Dean of Fine Arts; David Nancarrow, Associate Dean of Fine Arts, University of Texas, Austin
402-405, Division of University Relations, Florida Atlantic University

406, 407, University of New Mexico; William J. Martin, Director of Popejoy Hall
408, Kay M. Lockhart, Ralph Rapson, FAIA
409, Mrs. Edith Green, Office of College Relations, Baldwin-Wallace College
410, 411, Burnet Hobgood, William Eckart
412, 413, Smith College, Thomas Mendenhall, William Hatch, Diane Fetter, THEATRE AT SMITH (a booklet)
414-417, Museum of Modern Art, Department of Publications, Frances Keech, Permissions Editor; Arthur Drexler, Director Department of Architecture and Design; Edward Larrabee Barnes, FAIA; State University of New York College at Purchase; Norris Houghton, Dean of Theatre Arts, Norman D. Taylor, Director of Facilities
418-420, Children's Theatre Company of The Minneapolis Society of Fine Arts: John Clark Donahue, Artistic Director, George Muschamp, Publicity Director
421, Clyde W. Blakeley, Victor Christjaner, Eldon Winkler
423, The University of Puerto Rico, Leo S. Lavendero, Rafael Cruz-Emeric (drawings)
424, Goodspeed Opera House Foundation, Michael Price
425, 445, Morris Lapidus, George Gill
426, 427, Vassar College, Thaddeus J. Gesek, Robertson Ward, Jr., FAIA
429, Jules Fisher Associates, Robert Davis, Ken Vineberg (drawings)
430, 431, A.G. Odell, FAIA; Arthur L. Housman

433, Arnold F. Powell
434, Clayton Karkosh, Robert Hartung
435, Loren Winship, University of Texas; Little, Brown and Co.
436-437, Olaf Sööt, Jules Fisher, Robert Davis (drawings)
438, G.C. Izenour, Little, Brown and Company, C.J. Senie, (drawing)
439, Peter Albrecht Corporation, Paul Birkle.
440, William Cruse
442, (for permission to quote) Capitol Records, Inc., and John Coveney
443, Staging Associates, Ltd., G. Randall Will, President
445, (rope lock) Tiffin Scenic Studios, James F. Kuebler.

Index

Page numbers in italic type indicate illustrations.

Accessories shop, 314-15
Accidents, treatment, 163
Ace Morgan Theatre, Denison University, *132, 133*
Act curtain, 248-50
Acting area, 126, 136-37, 146, 148
Actor's Equity Association, 305
Actors, requirement, 1
  entrances and exits, 137
Acoustical measurements, 76
Acoustical planning, 78, 287
Acoustics, 75-88. *See also* Audibility *and* Sound
  adjustment of, 348-50
  architectural, 125
  building materials, 76
  reverberation time, 82-87, 348-50
Adams Memorial Theatre, Williams College, *253*
Administration, 325-26
Admission control, 56
Air-conditioning, 111, 116-17
  air intake, 116-17
  circulation, 120
  control, 121
  cooling, 118
  cycle, 116-17
  dehumidifying, 119
  dressing rooms, 121
  ducts, 120
  dust removal, 117
  fan, 119-20
  foyer, 94
  heating, 117-18, 121-22
  humidifying, 118
  outside sources, 121-22
  production shops, 121
  public rooms, 120-21
  sterilization, 119
  system, 116-17, *117*
Air intake, 116-17
Aisles, 57-58, 66-67
  center, 110
  lights, 73
  straight radial, *66*
  traffic in, 57-58
Alternators, 113
American Shakespeare Festival Theatre, *39, 47, 56*
Ames, Winthrop, 360
Amplifiers: microphone, 297
  power, sound control, 299
Anderson, Maxwell, *High Tor,* 171
Angle of polychromatic vision, *63*
Animals, production element, 167
ANTA Theatre, New York, *97*
Aprons, between stage and audience, 6
Arena performance, 6
Arena stage, 72, *72*
  lighting, 271-72
  performance-audience relationships, 129-30
  scenery, 194
Arena Stage, Washington, D.C., *32, 57, 102, 138, 196*
Arena theatre, *11, 272*
Aristophanes, *The Clouds,* 171

Arkansas Art Center, Little Rock, *24, 25*
Arts center, 7, 23
Asbestos curtain. *246. 247-48*
Assembly time, audience, 37
Atlas, Leopold, L., 131
Audibility, 75-88, 287. *See also* Acoustics *and* Sound
  action of sound, 78
  acoustical planning, 78, 287
  distribution, 79-81
  noise elimination, procedure, 76
  noise level, 75
  requirements, 75
  reverberation time, 82-87, 348-50
  sound transmission, 75-76
Audience: circulation of, 166
  comfort and safety of, 8, 89-110
  economic operation, 361-62
  inside theatre, 48-61, 107-10
    aisles, 57-58
    box office, 95-98
    checking facilities, 51-53, 101
    crossovers, 55-57
    exits, 60-61, 62, 110
    foyer, 49-50, 53, 92-95
    at intermission, 60-61
    lavatories, 106
    lobby, 51, 53, 99-101
    lounge, 61, 101-4
    seating, 58-59
    vestibule, 48, 94-95
  kinds of, 3, 5
    cabaret, 5
    concert, 5
    drama, 5
    grand opera, 3
    motion picture, 5
    musical comedy, 3
    night club, 5
    operetta, 3
    pageant, 3
    presentation, 5
    revue, 3
    vaudeville, 3
  outside theatre, 38-48, 89-92
    curb loading, 40-41, 48, 62
    exterior lighting for, 89-91
    motor transportation, 38-40, 42-43, 89-92
    parking, 42-43, 48, 62
  and performance, relationship, 126-35, 328-29, 346-48
  promotion of, 325
  requirements of, 1
  traffic, 37-62
    aisles, 57-58
    assembly time, 37
    continental seating, 58-59
    crossovers, 55, 57
    exit, 60-61
    final curtain, 62
    foyer, 50-53
    intermission, 60-61
    intermission routine, 59
    loading facilities, 40-41, *42,* 48
    lobby, 51
    lounge, 61

marquee to seat, 48
   motor transportation, 38-40
   parking, 42, 43, *44, 45, 46, 47*, 48
   seating, 59
   transit time, 37
   visual requirements of, 63-65
Audience flow chart, *52*
Audition room, 309-10
Auditorium, 107, 110
   comfort in, 107
   exits, 110
   lights, 283
   section and plan, 65-68, *78*
Auditory components: drama, legitimate, 4
   grand opera, 2
   motion pictures, 4
   musical comedy, 2
   operetta, 2
   pageant, 2
   presentation, 5
   revue, 2
   vaudeville, 2
Automobile call, illuminated, 89
Auto-transformer dimmers, *276*

Backgrounds, lighting, 263
Backstage: areas, *125, 126*
   operation, 153-70
   service board, 113, 115
Balcony, 69-70, *178*
   fascia, 267
   floors, 70
   front spotlights, *268*
   lobby, 101
   outdoor, *99*
   sight lines, 69-70
Balcony box, *268*
Ballet rehearsal room, *309*
Bar, in lounge, 61, 103, *104*
Battens, 232-33, 252
Belasco, David, 360
Bell Telephone Laboratories, 290
Bethesda, Md., West Bethesda High School, *18*
Beyer, Rolf, *180*
Black Hills Playhouse, Black Hills, South Dakota, *29*
Block Schematic Diagram, 294
Blocks, 231
Blowers, 124
   for organ, 145
Booth Theatre, 122
Booths: doorman's, 157, 161, 162
   motion picture projection, 284
   sound control, 292
Bowdoin College, Pickard Theatre, 353
Box boom, *266*
Box office, 57, 95, 97-98
   traffic to, 50, *50, 51*
Brail action curtain, 250
Broadhurst Theatre, 122
Brooklyn Paramount Theatre, 286
Building codes, 34, 51, 247
Buildings, theatre: architect's problem, 34
   architectural style and function, 330
   attractiveness, 357
   and audience, 361-62
   changing demands on, 6-7
   client's problem, 34-36
   college, 20, 337-38
   commercial legitimate, 12, 15, 17, 331-35

   community, 22
   costs, 364
   definition, 1
   development of plan, 344-48
   economics, 358-61
   facilities in, primarily for other uses, 30-31
   festival, 30
   high school, 17-20, 337-38
   interdependence of functions, 327-29
   intimate motion picture, 27
   motion picture palace, 26
   neighborhood motion picture, 27
   opera house, 7-8, 12
   precautions, 356-57
   presentation, 26
   priorities, 364-66
   production type, 344-46
   in shopping centers, 30
   site, 48, 341-42
   structure, 357-58
   summer, 28
   universality, 327
Burlesque theatre: audience transit time, 37
   basic requirements, 4
Business administration, 325-26

Cabaret, basic requirements, 4-5
Cable slots, 231
Cables, to bridge and battens, *270*
California, University of, Los Angeles, Department of Theatre Arts, *336, 337*
Capacity of house, visibility, 67
Carnegie Hall, 364
Carnegie Institute of Technology, 348, *349*
Carpet, 100-101
   fluorescent lines in, 100
Castered pieces, individual, 200-201
Ceiling slots, *265*
Ceilings: distribution of sound, 81
   foyer, 94
   lobby, 100
   lounge, 101
Center Theatre, The, 26
Central staging, 129-30
Change dispensers, automatic, 95
Check room, 101
   facilities, 51, 53, 101, *101*
   location, 101
   racks, 101
   self-service, 101
   size, 101
Chicago Civic Opera House, 107
Cinema 2, New York, *97*
Cinerama, 254
Circuits, stage lighting, 282, 283
Circulation: air, 120-21
   audience, 166
   working, 166, 168
Civic Center, Charleston, West Va., *23*
Classroom to dressing room conversion, *353*
Coatroom, location, 51
Codes, building, 34, 247
College theatre, 20
   box office, 98
   lobby area per seat, 51
   lounge area per seat, 61
   parking, 48
Colorado State College, *143*
Comfort, of audience, 89-110

457

Commercial legitimate theatre, 12, 15, 17
  lobby area per seat, 51
  lounge area per seat, 61
Communication, 225, 300-306
Community theatre, 22
  educational, 338
  lobby area per seat, 51
  lounge area per seat, 61
Company switch, 114
Composers, requirements, 1
Concealed lights, 74
Concert set, *86*, 254
Concert theatre: audience transit time, 37
  basic requirements, 4-5
  intermission routine, 59
  marquee to seat traffic, 48
Continental seating, 58-59, *59*, 66, *66*
Contour (or Brail) action curtain, 250, *252*
Control:
  board, 114, *275*
  console, *276, 280*
  devices, 121
  by director and designer, 254-58
  room, *279, 285*
  sound booth, 292
  stage lighting, 273
    centers, 280
    systems, 274-75, 277-79, *280*
Cooling: air-conditioning, 118-19
  coil, 124
  foyer, 94
  stage, 121
Costumes, 154
  production element, 167
  production services, 312-16
  shop, 312-13, 314, *315*
Counterweight: extra, 236
  sets, motor driven, 241
  stage elevators, 223-24
  system, 233-36, 240-41
Coverings, stage floor, 218
Crampton Auditorium, Howard University, *88, 93, 99, 105, 160, 297*
Crossovers, traffic in, 55, 57, *175*
Cueing system, 300-306
Curb-loading facilities, 48, 62
Current, electric, 113
Curtains: act, 248-50
  actions, *249*
  asbestos, 247-48
  Brail action, 250
  combination of actions, 250
  contour action, 250
  draw, 250
  fire, 247-48
  tableau action, 250
  traverse action, 250
  up-and-down, fly action, 250
Curved-path traverse wagon, 206-7
Cyclorama, the, 81, 183-93, *186, 188, 189, 229*
  functions, 183-85
  lighting, 263, 270-71
  movement, 189-90
  projected, 191-93
  size and shape, 189
  types, 173-74, 185-87

Dance theatre: acting area, 146
  audience transit time, 37
  basic requirements, 4

  orchestra, 147
  practice room, 311-12
  proscenium, 147
Darling, Robert, *182*
Dartmouth College, Hopkins Center, *19*, 23, *58, 91, 95, 96, 105, 106*, 135, *140, 154, 329, 334, 339, 354*
Dead spots, sound, 80
Decorative lighting, 73-74
Dehumidifying, 119
  paint shop, 121
Denison University, Ace Morgan Theatre, 135, 353
Depth of house, 67-68
Design studio, 317
Designers: production element, 164
  requirements, basic, 1
Directors: production element, 164
  requirements, basic, 1
Dimming: direct, 274, *274, 276*
  of house lights, 114
  indirect, 274-75, 277-79, *277, 281*
Discs: multiple, 208-12
  reciprocating segment, 209
  revolving, 208-9
  storage for, 211
Distractions, lighting, 74
Distribution: panel, main, 113-14
  power, 113-14
  sound, 79-81
Divided wagons, 201-3, *202*
Doorman's booth, 157, 161, 162
Doors: exit lights, 73
  exterior, *92*
  foyer, 92
  loading, 164, 165, 166, 167
  lobby, 99
  open out, 92
Drains, onstage, 123-24
Drama, legitimate theatre: acting area, 148
  audience transit time, 37
  basic requirements, 4-5
  intermission routine, 59
  marquee to seat traffic, 48
  orchestra, 149
  proscenium, 71, 149
  sound, 288-89
Drama Teaching Station, *343*
Draperies, 174
Draw curtain, 250
Draw curtain track, *249*
Dress parade, 154
Dress rehearsal, 155
Dressing room, 157, *159*, 161
  air-conditioning, 121
  quick change, 160
  wash basins in, 123
Drops, 173-74
Ducts, air-conditioning, 120
Dust removal, from air, 117
Dye shop, 313-14

Echoes, 80
Economics, theatre, 358-60
Educational theatre, 337-41
Electric current, 113
Electrical equipment: company switch, 114
  current, 113
  lighting *See* Lighting
  location, 113
  main distribution panel, 113-14
  outside lights, 116

458

permanent stage lighting control board, 114-15
   sub-panels, 115-16
   variations, 115-16
Electromechanical systems, 255-58
Electronics, 324-25
Elevators, 219-21, *219, 220,* 223-26
   combinations, 225-26
   counterweights for stage, 223-24
   evaluation of stage, 226
   fixed table, 222
   fixed trap, 220-21
   operation methods, 220
   plateau, 219, 223, 225
   portable table, 222-23
   portable trap, 221
   raised and sunken acting levels, 218-19
   remote control, 225
   sectional, 145
   sliding floor panels, 223
   stage, 224, 226
   table, 219
   trap, 219, 220-22, 224, 225
Encino Theatre, Los Angeles, *43*
Entertainment, theatrical, variedness, 1
Entrance door, traffic, 51
Entrances, actors', 137
   through stage floor, 224
Equipment: adjustment of permanent, 153
   electrical. *See* Electrical equipment
   flying, over storage space, 245
   installation of new, 153
   lighting, installation, 154
   over stage, 227
   for stage machinery, 200-209 *passim*
   permanently installed, 245
   proscenium framing, 251-52
   sound control, 154, 292, 294-300
   stage, for scenery, 164
Exits: auditorium, 110
   lights, 73
   lounge, 104
   traffic, 60-61
Experimental theatres, *132,* 351-52
Extended stage, *11, 65,* 72, *140, 141, 143*
   performance-audience relationship, 130
Exterior: lighting, 89-91
   sets, 179

Fan, air-conditioning, 119-20
Fiberglas panel, *195*
Fiberglas screen, *195*
Filters, air, 117
Final curtain, traffic, 62
Fire curtain, 247-48
Fire hose, 123
Fire regulations, 73
Fire wall, 143
First aid room, 163
Fisher Theater, Detroit, 333
Fitting room, 312, 314
Flat framed scenery, 175-76
Floodlights, 264
Floor dish, 70
Floor slope, 68-69, *69, 70*
Floors: foyer, 94
   lobby, 99
   lounge, 101
   stage, 212-18
     coverings, 218
     loads, 213-14

   panels, sliding, 223
   soft wood, 213-14
   tracks and guides, 210-11
   traps, 212, 214-16
Flow chart: for actors, *156*
   for costumes, *313*
   for scenery, *165*
   for stage hands, *161*
Fly action curtain, 250
Fly gallery, 233, *253*
Fly space, *188*
Flying, 227-30
   defined, 227
   equipment over stage, 227, *228*
   equipment over storage space, 245
   light bridge, 252-54
   scenery systems, 231-32
   structural elements, 230
   systems, 231-33
Folk opera: acting area, 148
   basic requirements, 2-3
   orchestra, 149
   proscenium, 149
Follow spots, 263, 265
Footlights, 262, 269, 271
Forestage, sinking, 145
Foyer, 49-50, *50,* 53, 94-95, *109*
   air-conditioning, 94
   area per seat, 50
   arrangement, 50
   audience traffic, 50-53
   ceiling, 94
   cooling, 94
   decoration, 95
   doors, 92
   floor, 94
   heating, 94
   lighting, 94
   rails, 95
   ticker taker's box, 94-95
   ticket windows, 50
   wall surfaces, 94
Foyer-lobby combinations, 53
Free form theatre, 134
Front service rooms, *53,* 89-110, 114
   air-conditioning, 120-21
   box office, 95-98
   checkroom, 101
   foyer, 94-95
   lavatories, 106
   lobby, 99-101
   lounge, 101-4
   multiple uses, 106-7
Functional relationship, ideagraph, *9*
Furniture: lobby, 100
   lounge, 61, 102

Generating equipment, location, 113
Glycol vapor, 119, *119*
Golden Theatre, 122
Grand Opera. *See* Opera house
Greek theatres, 71
Greenroom, 158, *160,* 161, 305
Gridiron, *188, 230,* 231
Guide lines, luminous, 73
Guides: floor, 21
   lattice track, 236-37
   T-track, 236
   wire, 236
Gymnasium with stage, *18*

Hartford, University of, Millard Auditorium, *195*

Harvard University, Loeb Drama Center, 348
Head blocks, *230*, 239, *239*
Heating, 111, 117-22
  air-conditioning, 117-18
  box office, 98
  foyer, 94
  paint shop, 320
  stage, 121, 122
Hedgerow Theatre, 107
Heights, backstage, 245
Helen Hayes Theatre, *14*
High school theatre, 17-20, 325
  box office, 98
  lighting, 90-91
  lobby area per seat, 51
  lounge area per seat, 61
Hofstra College, 232
Hopkins Center, Dartmouth College, *19, 23, 58, 91, 95, 96, 105, 106,* 135, *140, 154, 329, 334, 339, 354*
Hose lines, 123
House. *See* Auditorium
House lights, 283
  control panel, *283*
Howard University, Ira Aldridge Theatre, *330*
Humidifying, 118
Humidistat, air-conditioning control, 118, 121
Humidity control, 94
Hydraulic stage lifts, *225*

Illumination. *See* Lighting
Input control, sound, 297-98
Installation, of equipment, 153, 154
Instruments, lighting, 264-65
  mounting positions, 265-71
Intercommunication, *300*, 300-306
  cueing system, 303
  stage telephone, 301-3
  station specifications, 304-6
Interconnecting panels, 282
Interior, theatre, *24*
Interiors, *174, 175, 176, 177, 178*
Intermission: routine, 59
  traffic, 60-61
Intimate motion picture theatre, 27
Intimate theatre, *330*
Ira Aldridge Theatre, Howard University, *330*
Izenour, George C., *86, 134, 135,* 232, *242, 346, 347, 349*

Jackknife wagons, *203,* 204-5
John Fitzgerald Kennedy Theatre, University of Hawaii, *55, 99, 144, 151, 170,* 229, *265*
Jorgensen Auditorium, University of Connecticut, *80, 82*

Kabuki Theatre, 151
Kansas, University of, Murphy Hall, *328*
Kirby Theatre, Amherst College, *235*
Kranich, Friedrich, 198, 210, 223

Labor costs, 362-63
Lattice track guides, 236-37
  counterweight set, *237*
Lavatories: for actors, 158
  facilities, 106, 123-24
  location, 61, 101-2, 106
  for musicians, 162

Lens projected scenery, 191
Lido, Paris, *131*
Light bridge, *253, 269, 270*
Lighting, 72-74, 259-86
  of the actor, 259-61
  aisle, 73
  for arena stage, 271-72
  box office, 98
  color control, 74
  control, *258,* 273-80
  control board, permanent stage, 113-15
  of cyclorama, 263, 271
  decorative, 73-74
  dimmers for house, 114
  distractions, 74
  effects, rehearsal, 154
  elements preventing good, 74
  equipment, installation of, 154
  exit doors, 73
  exteriors, 90-91
  flying light bridge, 252-54
  foyer, 94
  functions, basic, 72, 259
  layout, *272*
  lobby, 100
  lounge, 103
  McCandless method, 72
  mood, 74
  music stand, 74
  for open stage, 273
  outside, 116
  overhead light battens, 252
  paint shop, 320
  power lines, 284
  production element, 166
  projection, 264-71
    balcony fascia, 267
    ceiling slots, 265-66
    footlights, 269
    proscenium slots, 267
    side-wall slots, 266
    spotlight booth, 267
  stage, 259-86, 322-23
    backgrounds, 263
    circuits, 282, 283
    control, 113-15, 273-80
    follow spots, 263, 265
    instruments, 264, 265-69, 271
    motion picture projection booth, 284-86
    office or studio, 322
    power, 284
    production services, 322-23
  of the scenery, 261-62
  special effects, 263
  visibility, 73
Light mounting equipment, *264*
Light mounting positions, *260, 262,* 265-69, 271
Lights: aisle, 73
  border, 262
  ceiling, 284
  footlights, 262, 269, 271
  house, 283-84
  motivating, 263
  outside, 116
  spot, 252, 264, 265-67
  strip, 252, 264
Lincoln Center, 23, *46, 54, 90, 104, 110,* 122, *359, 360*
Loading: door, 164, 166, 167
  facilities, 40-41, *40, 41, 42,* 48
  off-street, *42*
  platform, 164, 238-39

"Loading-in the show," operations involved in, 153-55
Lobby, 25, 51, *54, 57, 58, 60, 95, 98, 99,* 99-101
   area per seat, 51
   arrangement, 53
   audience traffic, 51
   carpet, 49, 100-101
   ceiling, 100
   design, 51-53
   doors, 51, 99
   floor, 99
   furnishings, 100
   lighting, 100
   outdoor, *55*
   signs, illuminated, 100
   sound in, 99
   stairs to balconies, 100-101
   ticket taker in, 51
   traffic in, *51*
Lobby-lounge, *102*
Lock rail location, 238
Locker room, 163
Los Angeles Music Center, *45, 358*
Loudspeakers, 299
   motion picture, 254
   mounting positions, 289, *289, 290, 297*
Lounge, *60, 61, 98,* 101-4, *103, 105, 109*
   area per seat, 61
   bar, 61, 103
   ceiling, 101
   exits, 104
   floor, 101
   furniture, 61, 102
   lavatories, 61, 101, 102
   lighting, 103
   location, 101
   outdoor, 104
   telephone, 61
   traffic, 61
   walls, 101
Lunt-Fontanne Theatre, *14, 98*
Lynchburg, Va., Art Center, *22, 42*

Machinery, stage, 197-258
   in the flies, 227-58
     act curtain, 248-51
     cable slots, 231
     concert set, 254
     counterweight system, 232, 233-36, 238-39, 240-41
     equipment over stage, 227
     equipment over storage space, 245
     fire curtain, 247-48
     fly action curtain, 250
     fly gallery, 230, 233
     flying light bridge, 252-54
     flying scenery systems, 227, 230, 231-32, 233, 245
     guides, 236
     head block beams, 230, 232, 239
     lattice track guides, 236
     lighting instruments, 227, 232
     loading platform, 230, 238
     lock rail location, 238
     motion picture screen and loudspeaker, 254
     overhead light battens, 252
     pinrail, 230, 233
     proscenium framing equipment, 251-52
     rope systems, 232, 238-39, 240-41
     structural elements, 230
     synchronous winch system, 242-44
     T-track guides, 236
     teasers and tormentors, 251-52
     winches, 254
     wire guides, 236
   on stage floor, 197-226
     guides, 210
     requirements, basic, 197-99
     rolling, 200-210
     running, 199-200
     stage floor, 212-18, 223
     tracks, 210-11
     traps, 212, 214-18
     understage, 218-26
Mackay, Steele, 135
Madison Square Theatre, 135
Main distribution panel, 113
Majestic Theatre, 122
Make-up room, 158
Mallory, Vincent, *294*
Malmö Municipal Theatre, *59*
Management, 325
Marquee, *16, 92*
   and audience traffic, 48
   draining, 90
   lighting, 89-91
McAlister College Theatre, *346*
McCandless, Stanley R., 259
McCandless method of lighting, 72
Metal working shop, 319
Metropolitan Opera, 12, 287, 294, 360, 364
Microphone amplifiers, 297
Microphone connectors, 295
Middlebury College, 135
   Wright Memorial Theatre, *142, 354*
Millard Auditorium, Fuller Music Center, University of Hartford, *195*
Miller, James Hull, *340*
Minnesota, University of, Northrop Auditorium, *86*
Mirrors, lobby, 100
Monitoring system, *302*
Mood, lighting for, 74
Motion picture: angle of projection, 65
   loudspeaker, 254
   projection booth, 284-86, *286*
   projection panel, 114
   screen, 254
   sound, 288-89, 291-92
Motion picture theatre: audience transit time, 37
   balcony, 69-70
   basic requirements, 4-5
   box office, 98
   drive-in, 70
   floor slope, 69-70
   intimate motion picture theatre, 27
   lobby area per seat, 51
   lounge area per seat, 61
   marquee to seat traffic, 48
   neighborhood motion picture theatre, 27
   palace, the, 26
Motor generators, location, 113
Motor transportation, audience, 38-40, 43
Multiple discs, 208-12
Multiscreen system, *195*
Multi-set shows, 12
Murphy Hall, Music and Dramatic Arts Building, University of Kansas, *328*
Music stand lights, 74

461

Musical comedy theatre: acting area, 148
  audience transit time, 37
  basic requirements, 2-3
  intermission routine, 59
  marquee to seat traffic, 48
  orchestra, 149
  proscenium, 71, 149
Musical drama, 148, 149
Musicians: production element, 162
  requirements, basic, 1
  room for, 162, 312

Nagy, Elemer, 192, *195*
National Board of Fire Underwriters, 110, 213, 247
National Building Code, 213
National Cultural Center, 360
New Mexico, University of, 23, 348
  Fine Arts Center, *50*
  School of Fine Arts, *134*
New York City Building Code, 34, 213, 247
New York Shakespeare Festival, 27
Newton, Mass., South Senior High School auditorium, *344*
Night club, basic requirements, 4-5
Noise, transmission and elimination of, 75-76
Noise level, 75
Northrop Auditorium, University of Minnesota, *86*

Oberammergau Festival, 30
Odor removal, 117
Office, stage manager's, 163
O'Keefe Centre, Toronto, *38, 84, 92, 98, 103, 105, 109, 333*
Open stage, *10*, 72
  performance-audience relationship, 128-29
  scenery, 194
Opera house, 7-8, 12
  acting area, 146
  audience transit time, 37
  basic requirements, 2-3
  intermission routine, 59
  lobby area per seat, 51
  lounge area per seat, 61
  marquee to seat traffic, 48
  orchestra, 147
  proscenium, 71, 147
  Renaissance opera houses, 71
  sound, 288-89
Operating economy, 360-61
Operetta: acting area, 148
  basic requirements, 2-3
  orchestra, 149
  proscenium, 71, 149
Orchestra: lift, 74, *144*
  pit, 74, 143-44, *144*, 147, 149, 162
  practice room, *310*, 312
  shell, 81, *195*
Oregon, University of, theatre, *141*
Organ, 145
Organization, production services, 307-8
Outdoor balcony, *99*
Outdoor lobby, *55*
Outdoor theatre, 27
Output control panel, 298-99
Outside: lights, 116
  panel, 115

Package console, *277*
Pageant: acting area, 146
  audience transit time, 37
  basic requirements, 2-3
  orchestra, 147
  proscenium, 147
Paint floor, 319
Paint frame, 319, *319*
Paint shop, 319, 320
  dehumidification, 121
Panels: main distribution, 113-14
  sliding floor, 223
  sub-panels, 113, 115, 116
Papp, Joseph, 27
Park Theatre, Stockholm, *66*
Parker, W. Oren, *184*
Parking facilities, 42-43, *43, 44, 45, 46, 47,* 48, 62
Passages, 158, 162, 163, 167
People, production element, 156, 157-64
Performance: economics of, 348
  planned, 256-58
Performance-audience arrangements:
  arena staging, 129-30
  central staging, 129-30
  extended stage, 130
  free form, 134-35
  interpenetrating audience, 130-31
  multiform, 131-32
  open stage, 128-29
  proscenium, 127-28
Performance-audience relationship, 126, 345-48
Performing arts, centers for, 7
Phi Beta Kappa Hall, College of William and Mary, *20, 21*
Philadelphia Academy of Music, 364
Philadelphia Convention Hall, 223
Philharmonic Hall, Lincoln Center, *54, 90, 104, 110*
Piano-box dimmer bank, *275*
Pickard Theatre, Bowdoin College, *353*
Pickup of sound, 291
Pinrail, 233
Pipe frames, 200
Piping, 122-24
Pit elevator, *152*
Place des Arts, Montreal, *367*
Plateau elevators, 223
Platform, loading, 164, 238-39
Play is written, the, 308
Playwrights, basic requirements, 1
Plumbing, 111, 122-24
Plymouth Theatre, 122
Polychromatic vision, angle of, *63*
Powder room, 106
Power, 111-16
  alternators, 113
  amplifier, sound control, 289
  auxiliary supply, 111-13
  company switch, 114
  distribution panels, 113-14, 115, *284, 285*
  house board, 114
  lighting control boards, 114-15
  lines, 284
  location, 113
  plant, 111
  requirements, 111
  for stage machinery, 199-209 *passim*
Power amplifier, 299
Power lines, lighting, 284
Practice rooms, 312
Presentation theatre, 26-27

audience transit time, 37
basic requirements, 5
marquee to seat traffic, 48
proscenium width, 71
Prince Edward Island, Charlottetown, 348
Producer, requirements, 1
Production elements: 156-67
  animals, 167
  costumes, 167
  designers, 164
  directors, 164
  lighting equipment, 166-67
  musicians, 162
  people, 156, 157-64
  pianos, 167
  properties, 165-66
  scenery, 164
  sound apparatus, 167
  stage hands, 163
  stage managers, 163
  talent, 157-61
  things, 156, 164-67
Production services, 307-26
  administration and business, 325
  costumes, 312-16
  drafting room, 317-18
  organization, 307-8
  play is written, 308
  press agent, 325
  properties, 323-24
  scenery, 317-21
  school or conservatory, 325
  secretarial functions, 326
  sound control, 324-25
  stage lighting, 322-23
  talent, 309-12
  ticket sale, 325
Production shops, air-conditioning, 121
Projected scenery, 191-93
Projection: lighting, 264
  motion picture, 284-86
  screen, motion picture, 254
  stereophonic, 289-91
Projectors, 264, 269
Promotion of audience, 325
Properties: fitted to sets, 154
  production element, 165-66
  production services, 323-24
Property shop, 323
Propulsion, rolling stages, 211-12
Proscenium, 137-39, *142*, *144*, *253*
  arch, liberation from, 6
  design, 137
  entrance, *141*
  flexibility, 139
  form, 137
  framing equipment, 251-52
  light slot, *141*
  lighting, 267
  performance-audience relationship, 127-28
  sizes, 147, 149
  typical, 137-39
  wall slot, *266*
  widths, 71, 350
Proscenium theatre, *9*, *10*, *260*, *262*
Provincetown Theatre, 107
Public rooms. *See* Front service rooms
Puppet show, basic requirements, 5
Purdue University Music Hall, *246*

Queen Elizabeth Theatre, Vancouver, *8*, *13*; 44

Quick change dressing room, 160

Rack and desk assemblies, 296
Racks, 165
Radio City Music Hall, *26*, 68, 74, *139*, *152*, *159*, 223, *234*, 263, *267*, 283, 286, *286*, 289, 291, *292*, 308, *315*
Rails in foyer, 95
Raised acting level, 218-23
Ramps: between stage and audience, 6
  exterior, 91
Realism in scenery, *36*
Receiving space, 164, 165, 166
Reception room, 161
Reciprocating segment, *208*, 209
Recreation room, 312
Rectifiers, location, 113
Rehearsal, 310-11
  dress, 155
  lighting effects, 154
  production parts, 154
  room, 310-11
  scenic effects, 154
  sound effects, 154
Removable beams, stage floor traps, *214*
Removable framing, *217*
Repair shop, 164
Reproducers, sound, 295-96
Requirements, theatre, basic, 1, 4-5
Resident companies, 7
Restaurant, *104*
Reverberation of sound, 82, 85, 87
  optimum time, *83*
Revolving disc, portable, *207*
Revolving stage, *207*
Revue theatre: acting area, 146
  basic requirements, 2-3
  orchestra, 147
  proscenium, 71, 147
Ripple tank, *79*
Robinson, Hilyard, *88*
Robinson, Horace, *343*
Robot-Grid, 245
Rockville, Md., Richard Montgomery High School, *310*
Rolling machinery, 200-10, 211-12
  castered pieces, 200-201
  curved-path traverse wagons, 206-7
  divided wagons, 201-3
  jackknife wagons, 204-5
  multiple discs, 209-12
  propulsion of, 211-12
  reciprocating segment, 209
  revolving stage or disc, 207-9
  straight-path traverse wagons, 205-6
  upstage wagons, 203-4
Rolling multiple discs, 209-10
Rope systems, 232
  and counterweight system, 240-42
Routine: cabaret, 5
  concert, 5
  drama, legitimate, 5
  folk opera, 3
  grand opera, 3
  motion picture, 5
  musical comedy, 3
  night club, 5
  operetta, 3
  pageant, 3
  presentation, 5
  revue, 3
  vaudeville, 3
Roxy Theatre, The, 26

Royal Theatre, 122
Running machinery, 199-200

Safety, of audience, 89-110
Salzburg Festival, 30
San Francisco Opera Co., 12
Scene designer, 254-55
Scene shop, *316, 317,* 318
Scenery, 171-96, *173*
   abstractionism in, 6
   for arena stage, 194-95
   brought to theatre, 164
   crossover passage, 176-78
   cyclorama, 183-90, 193
   dismantled, 164
   equipment, installation of, 154
   exterior sets, 179-80
   flat framed, 174-76
   flow chart for, *165*
   flying systems, 231-32
   framing bench for, *318*
   functions, 172
   history, 171-72
   interiors, 176-79
   lighting, 178, 261-62
   multiplication of, 6
   multi-scene schemes, 180-83
   for open stage, 194-95
   production element, 164
   production services, 317-21
   projected, 191-94, 264-65
   repaired, 164
   shifts, 197-98, 200-209 *passim*
   space, 126, 176, 178-79, *199*
   stage equipment for, 164
   for stage machinery, 200-209 *passim*
   storage, 164, 190-91, 320-21
   structure, 172-73
   types, 173-74
   variety in, 194
   wing and drop settings, 190
   working space, 190-91
Schedule of an arts center, *339*
Schlanger, Ben, 70
School theatre. *See* High school theatre
Screen. *See* Projection screen
Seating, 59, 66, *69,* 106, *133*
   capacity, altering, 348
   comfort, 59, 107, 110
   continental, 58-59, *59, 66*
   curvature, 66, *67*
   spacing, 59, 107, 110
   stagger, 66, *66*
Secretarial functions, 326
Section, auditorium, 68-70
Sets: exterior, 179
   properties fitted to, 154
Shadow projected scenery, 191
Shakespeare Festival Theatre:
   Stratford, Conn., 357
   Stratford, Ont., 30, 357
Shakespeare in the Park, 27
Shelves, 165
Shifts, speed of: curved-path traverse wagons, 206
   divided wagons, 202
   individual castered pieces, 201
   jackknife wagons, 204
   reciprocating segment, 209
   revolving stage or disc, 208
   running pieces, 200
   straight-path traverse wagon, 205
   upstage wagon, 203
Shop panel, 115

Showers, 123-24
Shubert Alley, 122
Shubert Theatre, 122
Side stage, *140, 142*
Side-wall light slot, *266*
Sight line angle, *68, 69*
Sight lines, 64-65, *70, 72,* 144
   balcony, 70
   basic, *185*
Signs: automobile call, illuminated, 89
   illuminated, in lobby, 100
   outside lights, 116
Sinking forestage, 145
Site, theatre, *38, 39, 47,* 341-42
   and audience traffic, 48
   plan, *28*
Sliding floor panels, 223
Slop sinks, 123
Smoking room, 106
Society of Motion Picture and Television Engineers, 284
Sound, 75-88, 287-306
   absorption, 85, 87
   action of, *76, 78*
   airborne noises, 75-76, 77
   amplifiers, 297
   apparatus, production element, 167
   assemblies, rack and desk, 296
   and ceiling under balcony, 81
   control. *See* Sound control
   dead spots, 80
   distribution, 79-81
   drama, legitimate, 288
   echoes, 80
   effects, rehearsal, 154
   elimination, of noise, 76
   equipment, installation of, 154
   in foyer-lobby, 53
   input control, 297-98
   lobby, 99
   loudspeakers, 254, 289, 290-91, 299
   microphones, 295
   motion picture, 288, 291-92
   objectives, basic, 288-89
   opera, 288
   outlets, backstage, 291
   output control, 298-99
   pickup, 291
   power amplifier, 299
   production services, 324-25
   reflected, *81*
   reinforcement, 288
   reproducers, 295-96
   reverberation, 81, 82, 85-86
   solid-borne noises, 75-76, 77
   spark photographs, 80, 81
   specifications dealing with, 76
   spectrum control, 298
   stereophonic projection, 289-91
   sources, 76, 81
   transmission, 75-76
   turntables, 295-96
   wiring for, 293
Sound control: booth, 291, *292, 292*
   console, portable, *296,* 298
   electronic, 144, 154, 287, 288, 289
   equipment, 292, *293,* 294-300
   system, 294-300
South Florida University, Tampa, *155, 167*
Spark photographs, 80, 81
Spectacle, audience transit time, 37
Spectrum control, 298
Speed of shifts. *See* Shifts

Spotlights, 264, 265-67
Spotting booth, 267
Sprinkler system, 123
Stage: air-conditioning, 121
  definition, 125
  economic operation, 362
  elevators, 219-26
  equipment, 199. See also Machinery, stage
  floor, 212-18
  functional divisions, 125-26
  heating, 121, 122
  lighting. See Lighting, stage
  machinery. See Machinery, stage
  opening, adjustment of, 350
  propulsion of rolling, 211-12
  revolving, 208-9
  space, 124-26, *199*, *202*, 354-55
  space below, use of, 224-25
  sprinkler system, 123
  telephones, 301-3
  waiting space on, 158
Stage anteroom, 158, 160, 161
Stage director, 254
Stage entrance, 161, 162
Stage equipment companies, 230
Stage floor, 212-18, 223
  acting area, 218
  coverings, 218
  loads, 213
  panels, sliding, 223
  soft wood, 213-14
  traps, 214-18
Stage hands, production element, 163
Stage machinery: in the flies, 227-58
  on the stage floor, 197-226
Stage managers, production element, 163
Stage manager's console, *154*, *155*
Stage manager's station, *302*, *304*, *306*
Stagehouse, 25
Staggering of seats, 66
Stairs: between stage and audience, 6
  carpet, 100-101
  exterior, 91
Standpipes, 123
Stardust Inn, Las Vegas, *36*
Station specifications, intercommunication system, 304-6
Stereophonic projection, 289-91
Sterilization of air, 119
Stevens Institute of Technology, 287
Stevens Sound Control System, Mark I, *290*, *294*, *294*
Stokowski, Leopold, 290
Storage space, 126, 190-91
  discs, portable, 211
  economic operation, 363-64
  instrument: lighting, 322
    musical, 312
  property, 324
  scenery, 190-91, 320-21
  for stage machinery, 200-209 *passim*
  wagons, portable, 211
Straight-path traverse wagon, 205-6
Strip lights, 264
Structure, scenery, 172-73
Structures, multipurpose, 350
Subject matter: burlesque, 4
  cabaret, 4
  concert, 4
  dance, 4
  drama, legitimate, 4
  grand opera, 2
  motion picture, 4
  musical comedy, 2
  operetta, 2
  pageant, 2
  presentation, 5
  puppets, 5
  revue, 2
  vaudeville, 2
Sub-panels, 115
Summer theatre, 28, *29*
  lobby area per seat, 51
  lounge area per seat, 61
Sump pump, 124
Sunken acting level, 218-23
Supply room, 312
Sweet Briar College, *269*, *270*, *293*, *326*
Switch, company, 114
Switchboards, portable, 114
Symphonic drama, 146, 147
Synchronous winch system, 242-44
Synchronous winches, *242*, *243*

Table elevators, 222-23, *222*
Tableau action curtain, 250
Talent: production element, 157-62
  production services, 309-12
Tape recorder, portable, *324*
Teaching, by theatre, 341
Teasers, 251-52
Technician's office, 317
Telephones, stage, 301-5
Television, 70, 144
Temple University Theatre, *333*
Theatre: architectural style, 330
  buildings. See Buildings, theatre
  college, 20, 342, 351
  commercial legitimate, 12-17
  community, 22
  definition, 1
  economics, 338, 358-60
  educational, 337-41
  experimental, 351-52
  festival, 30
  flexible, *135*
  free form, 134
  function, 329-30
  growth, 342-44
  high school, 17-20
  income sources, other, 364
  labor costs, 362-63
  motion picture, 26, 27
  multiform, 131-32
  multipurpose, 6, 350-51
  operating economy, 360-61
  organized for profit, 331-35
  precautions, 356-57
  presentation, 26-27
  in shopping centers, 30
  summer, 28
  uses of, multiple, 6
Theatre school, 325
Theatre-in-the-round, 129
Theatrical functions, interdependence of, 328
Thermostat, air-conditioning control, 121
Things, production element, 164-67
Ticket bar, 97
Ticket counter, *96*, *97*
Ticket desk, *97*
Ticket sale, 325
Ticket taker, 51
Ticket window. See Box office
Toilets, 158, 162
Tormentors, 251-52

465

Total uniform effect, 127
Town Hall, 364
Tracks, 210-11
Traffic, audience, 37-62
   aisles, 57-58
   assembly time, 37
   continental seating, 58-59
   crossovers, 55, 57
   exit, 60-61
   final curtain, 62
   foyer, 50-53, 94
   intermission, 60-61
   intermission routine, 59
   loading facilities, 40-41, *42*, 48
   lobby, 51, *51*
   lounge, 61
   marquee to seat, 48
   motor transportation, 38-40
   parking, 42, 43, *44, 45, 46, 47*, 48
   seating, 59
   transit time, 37
Transformers, location, 113
Transit time, audience, 37
Transportation, of audience, 38-39
Trap room, 218
   drain in, 123-24
   size, 218
   sprinkler system, 123
Traps, stage floor, 213, 214-18, *217*. *See also* Elevators
   integration of wagons with, 212
   size and location, 214, 216-18
Traverse action curtain, 250
Traverse wagons: curved path, *206*
   motor-driven, *170*
   straight path, *204*
T-track counterweight set, *234, 235, 237*
T-track guides, 236
Turnstile box office, 95, 98
Turntables, 295-96
Tyrone Guthrie Theatre, Minneapolis, *140, 258*

Understage machinery. *See* Machinery, understage
Understage panel, 114-15
Uniform effect, total, 127
Unistrut channels, *145, 243, 269*
University theatre. *See* College theatre
Upstage wagon, 203-4
Urban, Joseph, 65

Vacuum cleaning piping, 124
Vaudeville theatre, 146-47
   acting area, 146
   audience transit time, 37
   basic requirements, 2-3
   orchestra, 147
   proscenium, 71, 147
Ventilation, 116-17. *See also* Air-conditioning
   box office, 98
   paint shop, 320
   stage, 121
Vestibule, 48-50, *93*, 94-95, 157, 161, 162
Virginia Museum of Fine Arts Theatre, *141*
Visibility, 66, 72, 73. *See also* Lighting
   stage lighting, 259-61
Vision, 63-74
   aisles, 66-67
   angle of, *63*

   auditorium plan, 65-68
   decorative lighting, 73-74
   depth of house, 67-68
   distractions, 74
   floor dish, 70
   floor slope, 69-70
   light, 72-74
   proscenium widths, 71
   seating, 66
   section, 68-70
   sight lines, 64-65
   stagger, 66
   visibility, 73
Visual acuity, 34
Visual components: cabaret, 4
   concert, 4
   drama, legitimate, 4
   folk opera, 2
   grand opera, 2
   motion pictures, 4
   musical comedy, 2
   night club, 4
   operetta, 2
   pageant, 2
   revue, 2
   vaudeville, 2
Voltage, standard, 113

Wagon stage frequency, 210
Wagons: curved-path traverse, 206-7
   divided, 201-3
   equipment, 202, 203, 205, 206, 209
   integration with stage floor traps, 212
   jackknife, 204-5
   power, 202, 203, 204, 205, 206, 209
   propulsion, 211-12
   reciprocating segment, 209
   speed of shifts, 202, 203, 204, 205, 206, 209
   storage for, 202, 203, 204, 205, 206, 209, 211
   straight-path traverse, 205-6
   upstage, 203-4
   wheels, location on, 212
Waldorf-Astoria Hotel, New York, *101*
Wall radiators, *122*
Walls, 94, 99, 101
Wardrobe room, 167
Wash basins, 123, 124
Washington National Airport, *40*
Water curtain, 123
Water tank, 123
Western Springs, Ohio, theatre, *340*
Wilder, Thornton, *The Skin of Our Teeth*, 131
William and Mary, College of, Phi Beta Kappa Hall, *20, 21*
Williams College, *278*
Winch system, synchronous, 242-44
Winches, fixed, 254
Wing and drop setting, *179*, 190
Wire guides, *234*, 236, *237*
Wiring, sound, 293
Wittenberg College theatre, *347*
Working circulation, *167*, 168
Working loads, maximum, 238
Working space, 126
   scenery, 190-91
Wright Memorial Theatre, Middlebury College, *142*

Yale University Theatre, 131, 135, *180, 182, 184,* 192

SUPPLEMENTARY
INDEX
FOR
CHAPTER 16

Abramovitz, Max, Architect, 395
Acoustics in difficult theatre forms, 444
Acoustics: sound, 442
Air casters, 441
Akron, University of, 382
Alswang, Ralph, 374, 440
American Place Theatre, *384, 385*, 435
ANTA Washington Square Theatre, 440
Architekton, Inc., 394
Architecture for The Educational Theatre, 372
Arrighi, Luciana, 441
ART PARK, Lewiston, New York, 442
Atlanta Memorial Cultural Center, 377
A VILLAGE ROMEO AND JULIET, use of projections, 441, 442

Backstage control station, 444, *445*
Baker, Paul, 398
Baldwin-Wallace College Art and Drama Center, 409, *409*
Barnes, Edward Larrabee, FAIA, 414
Bartlett Cocke and Associates, 398
Bentham, Fredrick, 372
Birkle, Paul, 438
Birmingham-Jefferson (County) Civic Center Authority, 379
Birmingham-Southern College Theatre, *433, 433*
Blakeley, Clyde, 421
Blau, Herbert, 437
Bob Hope Theatre, Southern Methodist University, 410, *411*
Bolt, Beranek and Newman, 380, 389, 406, 409, 414
Boner, C.P. and Associates, 374, 400, 411
Bowman, Ned A., 372
Briggs, William A., FAIA, 378
Brown, William J., 394
Buckley, William R., Architect, 406
Building Code, City of New York 1968, 373
  effects of, 373, *374*, 375
Bühnentechnische Rundschau, 372
Burris-Meyer, Harold, 375, 377, 378, 403

California Institute of The Arts, 368
  Modular Theatre, 435, 436, 437, *437*
California, University of, Santa Cruz, Performing Arts Center, 408, *408*
Carousels, use of, in projection, 441
Categories of Theatres, 373
Caudill, Rowlett and Scott, 382
CAVEATS, 446-449
Center for The Performing Arts, Smith College, 412, *412, 413*
Cincinnati, University of, College-Conservatory of Music, *394, 394*

Civic Arts/Cultural Center, 376
Civic art center, organization of, 379
Children's Theatre Company of the Minneapolis Society of Fine Arts, 418, *418-420*
Christ-Janer, Victor, 421
College of Fine Arts, University of Texas, 400, *400, 401*
Commercial Theatre, 373
Commission on Theatre Architecture, U.S. Institute of Theatre Technology, 372
Computer techniques applied the planning, 368
Control and Communication, 444, *445*
Conversions, *425, 427, 427, 428*
Cruse, William, 374, 440
Cruz-Emeric, Rafael, 423

Dalton, van Dijk, Johnson and Partners, 382
Democratic imperative, 371
Dennis, Al, 387
de Pass, Paul, 376
Derrick, portable, *413*
Deutchen Theatre technischer Gesselschaft, 372
Dinner theatre, 375, 376, *376*
Director's ramp, *413*
Donahue, John C., 418
Drake Union Theatres, Ohio State University, *392, 393*

Edwin J. Thomas Performing Arts Hall,
  design of, *382, 383*
  financing of, 382
  program of, 382
  appraisal of, 382
Educational theatre, 386
Emory Roth and Sons, 429
Experiments, 368

Fail-safe rope lock, 445, *445*
Festivals, 422
  limited, 422
  multi-play, 422
Fine Arts Center, Lake Erie College, 421, *421*
Fine Arts Center, University of New Mexico, 406, *406, 407*
Fisher, Jules, 429, 437
Fisher and Spillman, Incorporated, 400
Florida Atlantic University Humanities Building, 402, *402-405*
Florida International University, 379
Flying systems, 438-441
Free-form theatres,
  systems, versatility required, 440, 441
Fuchs, Theodore, 390

Gamble, Clinton, FAIA, 403
Garwood-Jones, Trevor P., 380
George Dahl and Associates, 411
Gesek, Thaddeus, 427
Gill, George, 425

467

Goodfriend and Ostergaard, 385
Goodspeed Opera House, 424, *424*, 425
   Foundation, 424
Goodwin, Sage, 424

Hallie Flanagan Powerhouse Theatre, 426
   427, *427*, 428
Hamilton Place, Hamilton, Ontario, 380,
   380, 381
Harris, Cyril M., 395
Harris, W.C. Jr., 378
Harrison and Abramovitz, Architects,
   395
Harvard University, Loeb Drama Center
   evaluation, 432
Hastings, Russell, 392
Heine, Grider and Williamson, Architects,
   409
High Point, N.C. City Council, 379
Holien, Edward, Architect, 406
Hotopp, Michael, 376
Houghton, Norris, 414
Humanities Building, Florida Atlantic
   University, 402, 403, *402-405*
Huntington (West Virginia) Community
   Players, 379
Huxtable, Ada Louise, 382
Hydra float flying system, 440, *440*

I AND ALBERT, use of projections, 441
Illinois, University of, Urbana-Champaign,
   395, *395-399*
Influences, 369
   aesthetic, 369
   sociological, 369
   economic factors, 370
   educational, 371
Integrated systemization, 435
Innovations, 425, 426, 427, *427*
Interama Cultural Area, 379
Izenour, George C., 382, 395, 406, 432,
   438, *438*

Jackson, Tennessee, Cultural Center,
   378, 379
James Thurber Theatre, 392, *392, 393*
Jean Rosenthal Associates, Inc., 400,
   430
Jerit, Ron, 378
J.F. Kennedy Center Opera House, 442
Johnson, Russell, 380
Jordan, Wilhelm, 412
Joseph E. Levine Theatre, Circle in the
   Square, 429, *429*
Jules Fisher and Associates, 408

Keller Hall, University of New Mexico,
   406, *407*
Kenzo Tange and Urtec, Architects, 418
Kevin Roche, John Dinkeloo Associates,
   389
Knudsen, Vern O., 377, 382
Krannert Center for The Performing
   Arts, University of Illinois, 395,
   395-397

Laboratory for The Arts, Florida Atlantic
   University, 402, *402*, 403, *403-405*
La Comedia Dinner Theatre, *375*
Ladd and Kelsey, Architects, 437
Lake Erie College Fine Arts Center, 421
   421

Lavandero, Leo S., 423
Lederer Theatre, Trinity Square Players,
   435
Light mounting positions, *412*
Locklin, David, 392
Loeb Drama Center, Harvard University,
   evaluation, 432
Lope da Vega, 423
Loye, Donald T., 387
Lundell, Kert, 385

MAN OF LA MANCHA, 424, 440
Margo Jones Experimental Theatre
   Southern Methodist University,
   410, *411*
Marshall University, 379
Martin, Daniel, 394
Massive mechanical installations, 368
McAlister College, 432
McCandless, Stanley R., 377
McElvey, Carl C., 387
Meadows School of The Arts Southern
   Methodist University, 410, *410*,
   411
Michael, R. Keith, 430
Mielziner, Jo, 389, 395
Ming Cho Lee, 394, 414
Minneapolis Society of Fine Arts Child-
   ren's Theatre Company, 418,
   418-420
Minnesota, University of, 390, 391
Misel, Harry E. Jr., 375
Mitchell, Joseph Bok, 375
Modular lift floor sections, 435
Modular Theatre, model of, 436
   plan and section, 436
Moliere, 423
Morgan, Roger, 385
Morris Lapidus Associates, 425
Motion pictures used with live actors,
   441

New Haven, Connecticut, Art Center of,
   components of, 379
New Mexico, University of, The Fine
   Arts Center, 406, *406, 407*, 432
   434, *434*
New York City Building Code 1968, 373
New York State Park and Recreational
   Commission, 422
NIOSH, 445
Non-Profit Resident Professional Theatre,
   384, *384*, 385
North Carolina, University of, Chapel Hill,
   430, *430, 431*

Odell Associates, Inc., 430
Ohio State University, 392, *392, 393*
O'Neil Ford and Associates, 398
Oenslager, Donald, 424
Orchestra shell, *406*
Opera House, Sydney, Australia, 368
Organisation Internationale des Sceno-
   graphes et Techniciens de Theatre,
   372
Owens Arts Center, Southern Methodist
   University, 410, *410, 411*
Ozols, Karlis, 418

Palmer, Frederic, Architectural designer,
   424
Papp, Joseph, 422
Parker Klein Associates, 418

Patricia Corbett Theatre (1971), 394, *394*
Pearlman, Gordon W., 430
Performing Arts Center, Smith College, 412, *412*, *413*
Performing Arts Center, 383
 several facilities, 384
 variable single facility, 384
Performing Arts Center, University of California, Santa Cruz, 408, *408*
Performing Arts Center, University of Texas, 400, *400*, *401*
Peter Albrecht Corporation, 438-439
Piacentini, Vincent, 380
Picadilly Theatre, London, production of I AND ALBERT, 441
Pneumatic lift for floor sections, California Institute of the Arts Modular Theatre, 435, *437*
Popejoy Hall, University of New Mexico, 406, *407*
Powell, Arnold, 433
Powell, Don H., 387
Power Center for the Performing Arts, University of Michigan, 389, *389*
Production Services, 446
Projection, 441, 442
Projection, a layout for, *443*
Publications, 372
Purcell and Noppe, 406

Ralph Rapson and Associates, Inc., 390, 408
Rank, Strand Electric, Ltd, 372
Rarig Center, University of Minnesota, 390, *390*, *391*
Realistic scenery, persistence of, 369
Renovations:
 Lowell Symphony Hall, St. Louis, 425
 Gusman Symphony Hall, Miami, 425, *425*
Restorations, 424, 425
 Central City Opera House, 425
 Auditorium Theatre, Chicago, 425
 Ford's Theatre, Washington, 425
Richard Miller and Associates, 412
Riddle, Larry, 375
Robinson, Horace W., 372
Rodey Theatre, University of New Mexico Mexico, 406, *407*, 434, *434*
Rogers, Arthur J., 398
Rubin, Joel, 412
Ruth Collins Sharp Drama Building Southern Methodist University, 410, *410*, *411*
Ruth Taylor Theatre, Trinity University, 398

Safety, 445
SANCHO PANZA, 423
San Diego State University Theatre, 386, *386*, *387*, *388*
Santa Cruz Campus, University of California, Performing Arts Center, 422 *408*
Saratoga Performing Arts Center, 422
Sayles, Alan, 429
Seating capacities, unamplified speech, 444
Seattle Opera Association, production rock opera TOMMY, 442
Scenery movement on stage floor: air casters, 441
Sellman, Hunton D., 381
Shop sizes, 446

Sigma-Pac flying system, 438, *439*
Simmons, Gordon, 394
Simon, Neil, 376
Smith College Center for The Performing Arts, 412, *412*, *413*
Sondheimer, Hans, 394
Sööt, Olaf, 437
Staging Techniques, Inc., 442
State University of New York College of The Arts, 414, *414-417*
 Theatre Arts Building, 414, *415*
 Theatre A, *415*, *416*
 Theatre B, *415*, *416*
 Theatre C, *415*, *417*
 Theatre D, *415*, *417*
Steward, Erwin, 392
Street theatre, 422
Summary, 447-448
SUNY College at Purchase, 414, *414-417*
Svoboda, Joseph, 441
Sydney, Australia, Opera House, 368

TABS, 372
Tampa Civic Arts Council, 379
Teatro Rodante, Teatro Rodante Universitario, Puerto Rico, 423, *423*
Technology, 438-445
Texas, University of, Austin, College of Fine Arts and Performing Arts Center, 400, *400*, *401*
THEATRES AND AUDITORIUMS, 372
Theatre Arts Building, SUNY, Purchase, *414*, *415*
Theatres, categories of, 373
THEATRE CRAFTS, 372
THEATRE DESIGN AND TECHNOLOGY, 372
Theatre forms, 428
 proscenium, 428
 open stage, 428, *429*
 thrust stage, 429, *429*
 arena or central staging, 432
 multi-stage, 398, *398*, *399*, 432, 433
 surround stage, 430, *430*, *431*
 revolving ring stage, 432
 free-form, 427, *427*, 434, *434*, 435, *435*
Theatre in the Park, 422
Theatre not built, 448
Theatre Orientation Package, 372
Theatre Projects, 441
Theatre Room, University of Texas, Austin, modular lift floor sections, 435
The "old Met", 448
Tibbles, Crumley, and Musson, Architects, 392
Toombs, Amisano and Wells, 377
Traps, stage floor, 428
Trinity Square Players, 435
Trinity University, Ruth Taylor Theatre, 398, *398*, *399*

University of California, Los Angeles: use of air casters, 441
University of Michigan, 389
University of Puerto Rico, 423
University Theatre, Florida Atlantic University, 402, *402*, *403*, *403-405*
Uris Theatre, 374, *374*, 428
U.S. Office of Education, 372

Vassar College, 426, 427
Vincent Sardi's Dinner Theatre, 376

Ward, Robertson, Jr., FAIA, Architect, 426
Washington Opera Society production of A VILLAGE ROMEO AND JULIET by Delius, production of KONGA, by Delius, 441, 442
Watson, Thomas S., 372
Westermann, Helge, 412